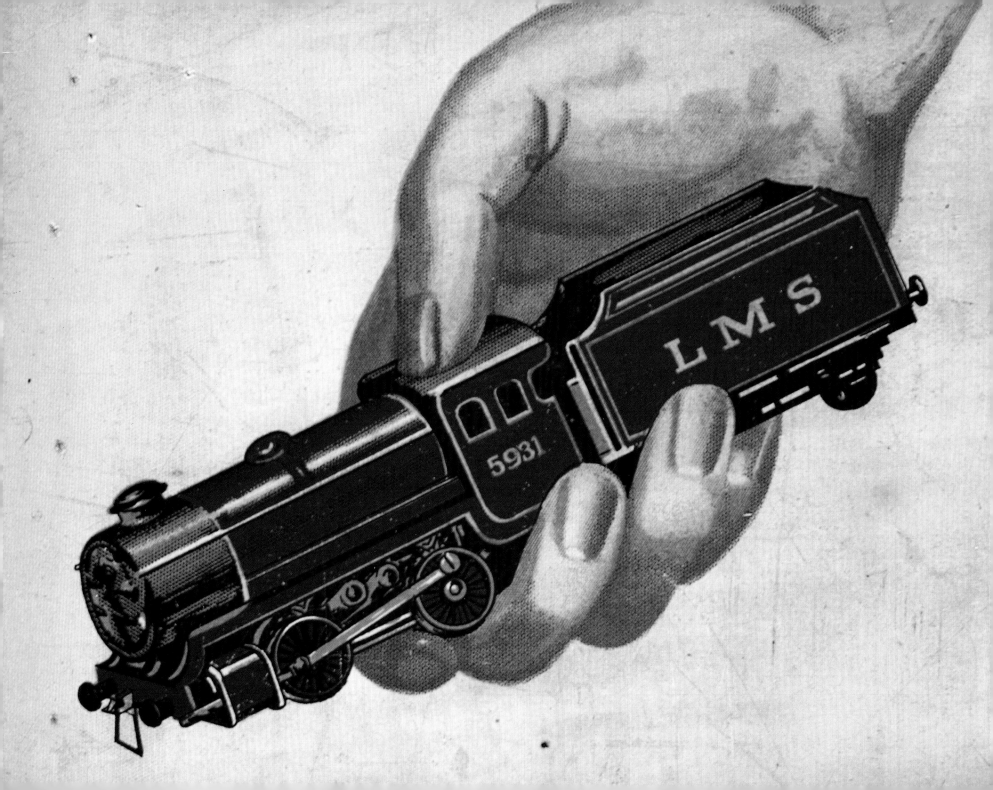

The History of
TRIX HO/OO MODEL RAILWAYS IN BRITAIN

Tony Matthewman

NEW CAVENDISH BOOKS

Dedicated to my wife Mavis and our children
Julie, Ruth and Mark for all their patience
and understanding.

**First edition published in Great Britain
by New Cavendish Books - 1994**

Specification;
424 pages, over 400 full colour illustrations
and 171 b&w illustrations

Design and Typesetting - John B Cooper
Editorial and Production Consultant - Allen Levy
Editor - Narisa Chakra

Printed and bound in Thailand
by Amarin Printing Group, Bangkok

ISBN 0 904568 76 8

New Cavendish Books,
3 Denbigh Road, London W11 2SJ

CONTENTS

ACKNOWLEDGEMENTS

The enormous amount of help and cooperation given in the preparation of this book has come from many quarters as the list below will show. One of the pleasures has been the high degree of assistance from fellow collectors from around the world who gladly loaned their treasured material for research or photography. Companies who were previously involved in sub-contract work on Trix products have freely given of their valuable time to provide essential information. In addition, I would like to thank the photographer, Marcus Lyon, whose patience and dedication to his craft are self evident in this publication, and Dr. Ross Couper of the University of Northumbria for his expertise regarding corrosion in Zinc Alloys.

Personnel

Günther Albrecht (formerly of TRIX Mangold GmbH)
John Atkin
Stuart Bean
Duncan Bell
Bill Best (former Service Manager of Trix Ltd)
Lilli Sommer (owner/partner of Trix Ltd)
Jeff Carpenter
Michael Catalani (formerly of Trix Ltd)
Tony Clack*
Barbara R. Dickerson*
H.G. Dörfler (TRIX Mangold GmbH.)
Werner Fehnert (Translator)
Michael Foster
Frank Gratton*(former Works Manager)
Peter Grant
Pat Hammond
E.F.G. Hanebeck (formerly of Trix Products Ltd)
Louis Hertz (America)
John Hills-Harrop
Allan Hinchliffe
John Hopkinson
Pete Hislop
Emil Jakob (Germany)
Dave Johnson.
W.E.H. Jones
Mrs Milton C. Heaney (Canada)
Mike Joyce (Australia)
Arthur Katz (formerly of Mettoy Ltd)
Günther Krauss (Germany)
Dave Norville
Franz Nowack (Germany)
David O'Brien
Jeremy O'Keefe
Trevor Phillips
Nathan Polk (Polk's Model Craft Hobbies of New York)
Ron Pordage (formerly of British Trix Ltd)
S.C.Pritchard (Pritchard Patent Product Co Ltd)
Mrs O.W. Randall*
K. R. Reddy*
John Ridley
Wolfgang Repenn (Germany)
Ernest Rozsa (Liliput Model Railways (UK)Ltd)
Terry Rozsa (Liliput Model Railways(UK) Ltd)
P. Sansom (formerly of Trix Ltd)
Reinhold Schuele (Canada)
Vic Taylor*
Doris Thompson*
Reg Thompson*
'Nan' Twisteton*
Dixon Upcott
Dick Walters*
Paul Werner (formerly of Counting Instruments Ltd)
Herr Wiesnet (TRIX Mangold GmbH)

* (Former employees of Precision Models Ltd)

Companies

Bonar Instruments Ltd
Britains Ltd
Ebonestos Industries Ltd
Fry's Diecastings Ltd
Hertfordshire BTR Ltd
Hunt International Co (USA)
IDRA Ltd (Ex British Diecasting & Engineering Co Ltd)
Liliput Model Railways (UK) Ltd
Metal Castings (Worcester) Ltd
New Zealand Railways (Publicity & Advertising Branch)
Northampton Chronicle & Echo
Pritchard Patent Product Co Ltd
Selman & Son Ltd
Silcoms Ltd
Tresco Plastics Ltd
G.&R. Wrenn Ltd

Finally to Jürgen Schlegel who on behalf of his company, TRIX-Mangold GmbH has had the courtesy to allow the reproduction of any TRIX literature, catalogues, trademarks, photographs and like subjects.

TRIX Express, TRIX International, Minitrix, TRIX EMS are all registered trade marks of TRIX-Mangold GmbH Nuremberg, Germany.

Many of the captions include a key letter at the end of the caption, for example (A). This is to denote that the item photographed comes from a collection other than the authors.
(A) David O'Brien. (B) Stuart Bean.
(C) Franz Nowack. (D) Trevor Phillips.
(E) John Atkin. (F) Duncan Bell.
(G) Jeff Carpenter. (H) Michael Foster.
(I) Pete Hislop. (J) Günther Krauss.
(K) Dave Johnson. (L) Mike Joyce.
(M) Dave Norville.

PREFACE

My interest in Trix model railways started in the Christmas of 1947 when I received my first Trix Twin Railway set from my parents. I was nine years old at the time and vividly remember fitting the track together on the carpet floor in my bedroom on that Christmas morning, before excitedly asking my father to wire it up to the controller and transformer. Then came the moment of anticipation as the lever and knob on the controller were operated to enable the locomotive and its train of wagons to pull smoothly away and go round the track in the correct manner. How wrong I was! Firstly the locomotive jerked backwards, derailing the wagons, and then, after frantic movements of the controller lever and knob, the locomotive sped forward at what seemed to be about 200 mph only to come to rest on the carpet after a spectacular roll off the first bend of the track. My father was not amused and accused me of trying to break the locomotive.

After a short time I managed to master the controls and played for many hours on the carpeted floor, my favourite position being with my head at the exit of an old Hornby O gauge tunnel watching the Trix train rattle through. It was not long before I was given a second 0-4-0 engine and tender, plus a variety of secondhand coaches and wagons. My only misgivings were that at school my Trix Twin model railway was, in my eyes, unjustly ridiculed by my so-called friends as they poked fun at me for not getting the Hornby Dublo range, which was at the time more realistic. However, they had not seen what I had seen, and that was the wonderful pre-war 'Coronation' locomotive with its matching coaches that I often watched running on a permanent layout at a friend's house. This locomotive confirmed my affection for Trix, and thus, when the BR 'Scotsman' came available in the early 1950s I was determined to buy one so that I could show my doubting school friends how realistic a Trix locomotive could be in looks and operation. The only snag was that at £10 it was far too expensive for my father to buy, or for me to save up for from my 6d. a week pocket money. But after a year of collecting and selling old newspapers to the local Huddersfield scrap paper merchant, and doing simple repairs on Trix locomotives for the model shop that was keeping a 'Scotsman' for me, the day eventually arrived when I proudly took it home. Today this locomotive still holds pride of place in my collection.

The author.

7

Other interests took their toll on the Trix Twin Railway during my teenage years and it was relegated to a suitcase in the sooty loft of my parents' home. It was only many years later, after the birth of our son, that he, my wife and myself, together with our two daughters took a boat journey from our home in the Isle-of-Man to my parents home in Huddersfield, and, remembering the Trix Twin Railway in the loft, rescued it from under a deep layer of soot.

My interest was rekindled, and the quest for more Trix items began, with the excuse that it was for our son. The collection gained momentum very rapidly as nobody was interested in the Trix range at that time, (1972), and model shops were only too happy to get rid of stock at a give-away price. What a different story now! Through a happy coincidence, I was put in touch with a fellow enthusiast in Huddersfield during 1974 with whom for many years I shared a common enthusiasm for the Trix model railway. This was Allan Hinchliffe who, with Stuart Bean, founded on 26 April 1975 the TTR Collectors' Association of which I am proud to be one of the 12 founder members. The TTRCA enjoys a healthy membership across the world, being devoted to the collecting and running of all Trix HO/OO gauge trains.

I was asked to write one or two articles for the society publication, the *TTRCA Gazette*, and it became obvious that there was a need for much further study on the subject. My research snow-balled and it became obvious that the end product should be a book. In the beginning it certainly seemed a daunting task. An early contact was Ernest Rozsa of Liliput Model Railways (UK) Ltd and the designer/draughts-man Michael Catalani also helped me on my way. Many long and very pleasant hours were spent chatting to both these gentlemen about the technical aspects of the DC range and the politics of the various British 'Trix' companies. Eventually with the kindness of Ernest Rozsa I was able to consult a large quantity of post-war (and a few pre-war) drawings which answered most of my technical queries and also gave an insight into many interesting modifications and proposed new products.

It was John Atkin who led the way regarding research into the early company history in Britain, and without his contacts and skills in finding the right people and extracting the information required, many of the facts recorded in this book would never have come to light. The company history section of this book owes John Atkin a great deal, and his continued help, guidance and gentle but persuasive corrections are greatly appreciated. His contacts with the very helpful ex-employees of Precision Models Ltd in Northampton were very valuable, and I must thank these good people of Northampton for entering into the spirit of the task. John Atkin also contacted many of the subcontract companies who readily gave their support and help, supplying large amounts of very useful information that had remained in their files.

On the German side, Franz Nowack opened many doors enabling me to gain important historical and technical documents crucial to the successful completion of the Trix story. His highly skilled powers of technical observation and deduction have contributed greatly.

This book has been a difficult challenge with many twists and turns caused by the very chequered history of the Trix HO/OO Model Railway in Britain, but it is hoped that it will appeal to the historian and collector alike. Every endeavour has been made to ensure that the historical and technical details are correct, and where possible official documents, both German and British, were consulted. However, despite this, it is quite possible for a hitherto unknown variation to exist and come to light after the book has gone to press. This, however, is part of the joy of collecting – a hobby that cuts across all barriers of class or creed.

Tony Matthewman
1994

POSTSCRIPT.
Since finishing the book I have learnt that in 1988 Dapol Model Railways in Cheshire bought the tooling for part of the ex-British Trix/Liliput range. In 1990 Herpa-Fritz Wagener purchased the complete Liliput continental range plus tooling which included much of the British range. After only two years, in 1992, Herpa-Fritz Wagener sold this stock to Bachmann Industries Europe Ltd, owned by Kadar Industries of Hong Kong. Perhaps this really is the end of the line as only the shell retains something of 'Trix'. Maybe now the ghost of British Trix should be allowed to rest.

I have lived all my life with toys and particularly with trains. The family connection started with the birth of my grandfather Ignatz 150 years ago and the development of the Bing Werke in Germany. My father first manufactured Trix Trains over 50 years ago.

As the last surviving member of this branch of the Bing family, it gives me great satisfaction that the History of Trix Trains in Britain has been written (and published) and I should like to offer my congratulations to Mr. Matthewman and Mr. Atkin, including their associates, on such a great achievement.

Letter from Mrs Sommer-Bing.

The *Bing Post* dated April 1918 announcing the death of Ignaz Bing during the previous month.

Stephan Bing.

COMPANY HISTORY

THE BEGINNING

From the year 1919 Stephan Bing was the managing director of the world famous company Bing-Werke AG that was founded by his father Ignatz Bing and his uncle, Adolf Bing. However, he was a man of high principles and due to business and financial disagreements resigned from the board of directors in 1927.

Stephan Bing was not a man to sit still, and during the latter part of October 1928 purchased Vereinigte Spielwarenfabriken Andreas Förtner & J Haffner's Nachfolger KG of Nuremberg. This company, situated on Bärenschanze Strasse, was founded in 1925 by the amalgamation of the manufacturing businesses of Andreas Förtner and the late Johann Haffner, the latter taken over by his son. Förtner was a manufacturer of a large range of metal toys and Haffner an established manufacturer of lead figures.

The company was changed from a limited partnership to a limited liability and thus became Vereinigte Spielwarenfabriken Andreas Förtner & J Haffner's Nachf. GmbH.,(The United Toy Factory Andreas Förtner, late J. Haffner Ltd), The company under the new ownership had a registered capital of RM 100,000, (approximately £5,000), and retained the services of a former executive Max Erlanger as sales manager thus ensuring a continuity with existing sales outlets. Stephan Bing was fortunate in being able to persuade certain trusted employees of Bing-Werke AG to join him in his venture, including Siegfried Kahn who had held the position of technical manager with Bing-Werke AG, and it was in this role as technical manager, later to become general manager, that he took control of design and development of the new company.

During 1929 the company acquired larger leasehold premises at Kobergerstrasse 15, Nuremberg into which the manufacturing facilities were transferred, enabling the first major new product of the company to be produced. This was the Trix Metallbaukasten system which was put onto the market in late 1930 or early 1931. The Metallbaukasten was a new concept in metal construction systems as the holes in the parts were arranged in such a way as to be more versatile than other metal construction systems such as Meccano.

It was the brainchild of Siegfried Kahn and was patented in his name, becoming quickly successful and selling in multiple stores in Germany, such as EHP and Woolworths. 90 pfennig bought a basic unit which consisted of 23 metal parts, along with nuts and bolts, enabling simple models to be made. By purchasing further units very impressive models could be made. The system was further developed in later years with the introduction of different parts and, at the time of writing in (1993), is still in production in Nuremberg.

The metal construction system was the first product to use the trade mark 'TRIX', and a lot of thought was given to the choice of a name for the products of the new company with 'TRIX' being chosen for its easily pronounced name. The derivation of the name 'TRIX' has been lost in obscurity. One possible speculation is that it may have been derived from the following two sources; the basic pattern of holes in the flat strips of the Metallbaukasten were arranged in three rows, and the Latin prefix for three is 'TRI', while the initial name of the rival Meccano-construction system was 'Mechanics Made Easy' from which one could extract the phonetic sound of 'ics' as in 'X'. It is interesting to note

that in 1932 Meccano Ltd introduced their 'X' Series outfits, which also had strips with three rows of holes, to compete with the Trix system. However, the Meccano holes were set in a different pattern to those on the Trix parts. The Meccano 'X' system was not produced after 1936.

The trade mark 'ANFOE' used on tinplate toys originally manufactured by the former company, was still applied to certain tinplate toys manufactured by the new company and,although these toys were quickly phased out, the facilities and skilled staff were retained. More specialised toys were developed including clockwork and electric boats, cannons, money boxes, Morse equipment and experimental sets but these were produced mostly with the 'TRIX' trademark, although as with the Trix Metallbaukasten both the 'TRIX' and 'ANFOE' trademarks were displayed on some of the packaging.

The metal construction system played a very important role in Britain as it was instrumental in the formation of Trix Ltd. Due to the success of the Trix Metallbaukasten it was decided to expand the business to Britain and France granting manufacturing licences in those countries. (Knöbel & Sammer of Wallern in

Austria, and Leopold of Barcelona in Spain were also licence agents). The Bing toy empire had enjoyed many successes in Britain, mainly due to commercial ties with Bassett-Lowke Ltd, but also attributed to the fact that a lifelong friendship had begun between Stephan Bing and Wenman Joseph Bassett-Lowke, the founder and a director of Bassett-Lowke Ltd, when the former in his younger days had spent a few years in England.

Thus on 17 February 1932 Trix Ltd was formed with a capital of £100, (divided into 100 £1 shares), to act as agents for the German company. The registered office was situated at 4, Golden Lane, London EC1. The first directors were W.J. Bassett-Lowke and Leo Gross, the latter a merchant of Austrian birth who had earlier acted as an agent for Bing-Werke AG in Britain. The majority of the shares were held by a solicitor with Herbert Oppenheimer Nathan & Vandyke who acted for Trix Ltd. A watchful eye was kept on the new company on behalf of Vereinigte Spielwarenfabriken Andreas Förtner & J. Haffner's Nachf. GmbH. by Julius Stein, a German who had lived in England since 1914 and was an old friend of Stephan Bing. Mr Stein later became company secretary of Trix Ltd in 1935, a post which he was to retain until the

Trix Passenger Boat circa 1937.
Powered by Trix Construction electric motor.(J)

1933 Trix boat, Cat.No.2000, powered by a Trix Electric Motor 2050.

takeover in 1957 by Ewart Holdings Ltd.

Vereinigte Spielwarenfabriken Andreas Förtner & J. Haffner's Nachf. GmbH. granted a licence to the newly-formed Trix Ltd to enable the Trix Construction system, (Trix Metallbaukasten), to be manufactured in Britain. Manufacture took place at Winteringham Ltd, whose factory was situated at Stimpson Avenue, Northampton. Winteringham was a satellite manufacturing company for Bassett-Lowke Ltd with W.J. Bassett-Lowke as one of the directors, together with the long-serving and skilled engineer James Mackenzie, a Highland Scot who was the managing director. He was ably assisted by Robert Bindon Blood, a flamboyant character who joined Winteringham Ltd when they moved to Stimpson Avenue in 1931 as a trained production engineer and a very enthusiastic model railway man. He took the position of assistant works manager and in the following years designed and put into production many excellent O gauge models, eventually filling the vacant position of managing director when J. Mackenzie left the company in 1937.

The tooling for the Trix Construction parts was sent over from Nuremberg in either late 1931 or very early 1932 and at the same time large presses and guillotines were installed in the press room. Production quickly commenced, but was resented by many of the workforce as the standards were well below that for which they were renowned. The first advertisements for the Trix Construction system appeared in the magazine *Hobbies and Practical Wireless* on 12 March 1932.

This magazine advertised itself as the 'Official Trix Organ' in which articles on new models, general information, Trix Club news and advertisements appeared on a weekly basis with only a few breaks until 1934. The small Trix Construction sets were based exactly on the contents and box design of their Nuremberg counterparts and were sold in Woolworth stores, at the famous Woolworth price of 6d. each, and at all Hobbies Ltd depots, Curry's and other leading toy shops.

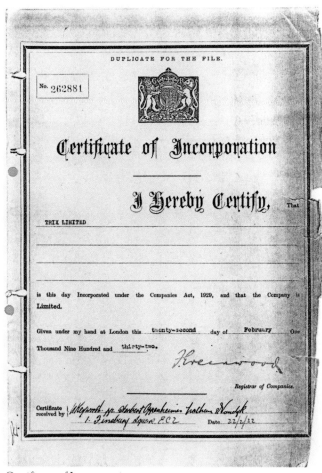

Certificate of Incorporation of Trix Limited dated 22 February 1932.

A letterhead of Trix Ltd dated 9 July 1932.

12 March 1932 edition of the magazine *Hobbies and Practical Wireless*.

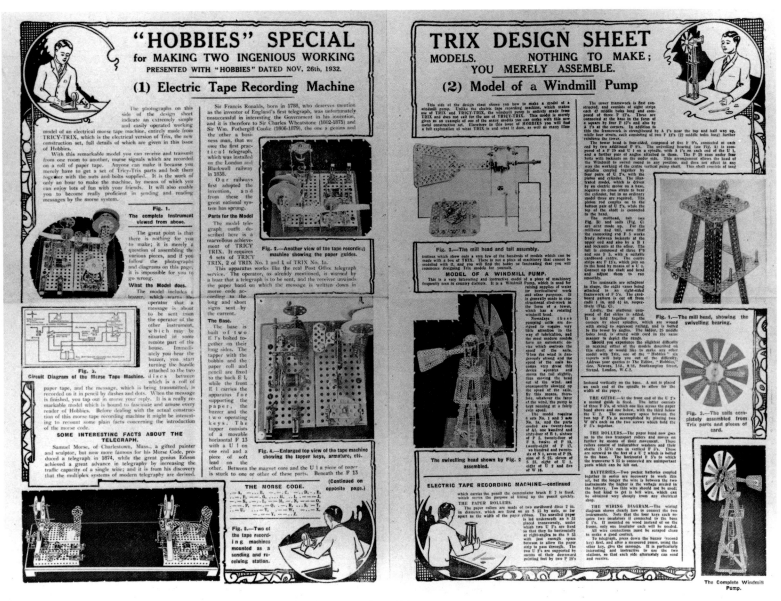

A special Trix Design Sheet presented with *Hobbies* magazine dated 26 November 1932.

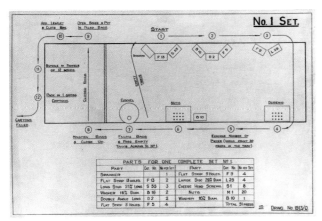

A drawing dated 3 March 1932 for the packing arrangement for a Trix Construction No.1 set.

A 'report' appeared in *Hobbies and Practical Wireless* in May 1932 describing a visit to the Trix factory which makes interesting reading and is reproduced below:

'Have you ever wondered, as you proudly handle the neatly-finished shining parts of your Trix sets how they are made ? A few days ago we had the pleasure of visiting the Northampton Trix factory and seeing for ourselves the astonishing processes which go to produce these inexpensive little sets that can build all the realistic models we have been publishing during the past weeks.

'First we inspected the raw material, Siemens Martin steel, which is packed in coils of various widths, according to the different lengths of the parts. The steel is electro-zinced to prevent rusting. The coils are then mounted upon the machines, which press out the parts. At the time of our visit F17s were being made, and each one is formed in several operations, all these opera-

Part of a late 1933 Trix Constructional catalogue showing how the system had expanded to include motors, gears and electrical parts.

tions being performed at one time by the special machines used. The parts drop into a box at the base, whilst the waste material comes out through the other end of the machine. With such parts as U1s, U2s, and A1s, which as you know, are bent, there are more stages before the part is formed, the punching, the blanking and other operations. Some dies produce more parts than others; for instance, a machine will turn out 9,000 F17s an hour, against 21,600 F5s and 7,000 washers and discs. The shorter strips are made six and eight at a time.

15

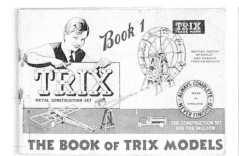

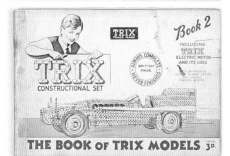

Early 1930s Trix Construction instruction books.

A 1938 No.2 Trix Constructional Set.

Pre-war Trix Construction Sets.
Above left: French Electro E.
Above right: 1933 British No.2.
Bottom: German 1c. Note the trade mark ANFOE.

'The box of rough parts then comes to the barrelling machine, where its contents are emptied into a drum, which acts as a sieve, cleaning the parts and removing all the small punchings and pieces of scrap. The parts are then placed in a second drum, in which they are polished by a special patented process. The finished parts are packed in containers, specially made to facilitate packing, and they are conveyed down a chute into a room below, where the packing is in full progress.

'The cardboard Trix boxes, which arrive in crates of 5,000, are stored in this room, as well as the wooden parts boxes.

'It is most interesting to watch the assembling tables where the packing goes on at an amazing speed. 10,000 boxes of Trix a day are turned out by the girl packers who have special parts with which to deal. The nuts and bolts are counted on special machines. The cardboard Trix boxes go round the table collecting the parts and are packed in dozens by the last girl in the team. These intriguing little boxes go out in gross cartons to be delivered to the wholesalers, retailers, and finally, to be bought by you.'

The sets sold quite well but not on the same scale as Meccano and production ceased in Britain in the 1960s.

R. Bindon Blood.

During 1932 Franz Bing, the son of Stephan Bing, emigrated to England where he organised the sales side of the new Trix business from the London office, while Siegfried Kahn commuted between Nuremberg and Northampton looking after the technical side of the products. Siegfried Kahn was well liked by the Northampton workforce and was reported to be extremely pleasant and very grateful for anything done for him, although also demanding the highest standards.

The early 1930s saw many changes in the day-to-day running in the factory of Winteringham Ltd and it was in February 1934 that Mettoy Ltd took a hand in the events. This new company occupied the basement and ground floor and entered into an agreement whereby Winteringham Ltd would produce toys for them

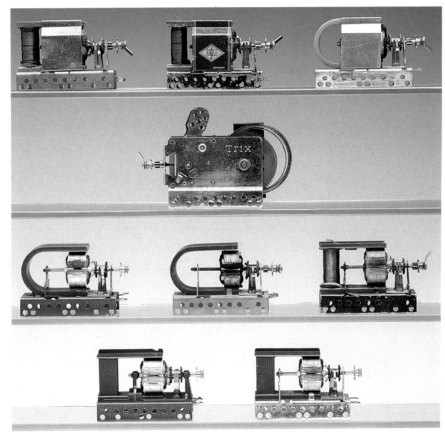

A range of Trix Construction motors ranging from the early 1930's to the 1980's.

at an agreed price.

Mettoy undertook the development of stamped, lithographed toys and was responsible for the provision of presstools for these toys and their clockwork mechanisms. Within a couple of years business had grown to such an extent that Winteringham found it difficult to finance the growing turnover and it was mutually agreed that Mettoy would take over the day-to-day running of the factory. This situation was put in the hands of Arthur Katz and his partner Philip Ullmann, a German who was the founder of Mettoy Ltd. However, as Arthur Katz has made quite clear, it should be noted that at no time was Mettoy involved with any design, development or manufacture of items for Trix Ltd. In 1938 Mettoy moved out of the factory in Stimpson Avenue to a building already used by them for storage which was in Harlestone Road, Northampton. This move was brought about by the large amount of space required at the Stimpson Avenue factory due to the heavy demand for the new model railway system called Trix Twin Railways introduced earlier which was to radically change the concept of table-top model railways.

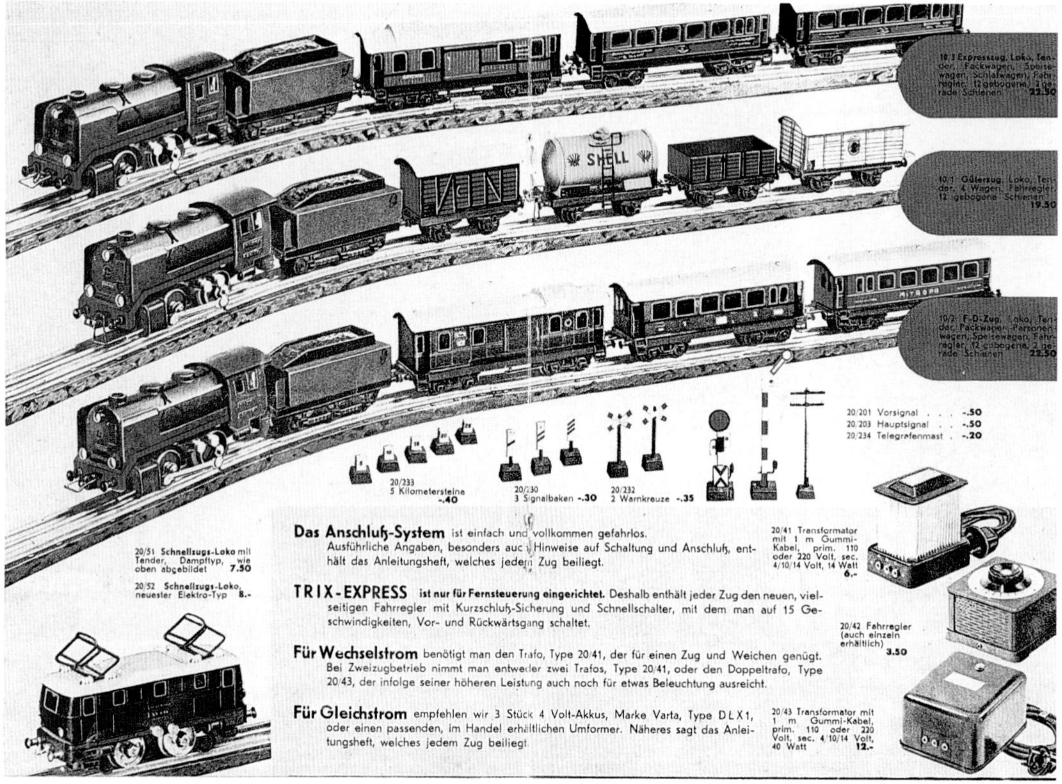

The centre spread of the 1935 Trix Express catalogue.

THE PRE-WAR YEARS.

Maybe it was the need to develop new and exciting products, or maybe the gentle persuasion of W. J. Bassett-Lowke, that prompted the design and development of the Trix model railway system – no one can be sure. However the design and development was undertaken at the factory of Vereinigte Spielwarenfabriken Andreas Förtner & J. Haffner's Nachf. GmbH in Nuremberg, by a team which included Ernst Beyer and Oswald Fischer, led and inspired by Siegfried Kahn. It was a triumph of skill and ingenuity which was the hallmark of German toymakers in Nuremberg.

The Bing Table-Top Model Railway system, inspired and introduced to Britain by W.J. Bassett-Lowke and his friend Henry Greenly in the 1920s, depicted the locomotives and rolling stock in a rather crude toy-like manner with the almost exclusive use of tinplate in the construction of the items. Oswald Fischer was the ingenious engineer behind the design of this early table-top model railway, and once again it was mainly his ideas and inventions which were applied to the new model railway system based on a scale of loosely 3.5mm to the foot. Many 'modern' materials and new manufacturing methods were used in its construction, including a cast metal alloy locomotive body shell and a bakelite-based track. Various new refinements, including the ability to run two locomotives on the same track under totally independent control, all helped to make the new table-top railway much closer to the concept of a 'model railway' than anything that had preceded it. It was the ability to run two trains independently that was to be one of the main attractions and was instrumental in the adoption of the trade name of Trix Twin Railway which was, surprisingly, only used by the British manufacturers. It is understood that an agreement was reached with Gebr. Märklin & Cie. GmbH. regarding the Patent appertaining to the two-train running system.

After hectic activity during 1933 and 1934 the Trix Express model railway was launched on

Circular advertising the coloured 1935 catalogue.

April 1936 Bassett-Lowke Twin Train Catalogue.

English translation of early 1935 Trix-Express trade leaflet.

Early 1935 Trix Express trade leaflet. (J)

Trix-Express is well tested!

Our experimental train has just finished a 200 kilometre run, and after weeks of continuous testing no visible wear is noticeable. All the gears and bearings are still in good order. No diminishing of the pulling power of this busy little engine was observed as it pulled 15 four-wheeled wagons, some loaded with small nails. During this test the direction of the engine was constantly changed, the reversing mechanism working entirely satisfactorily.

Trix-Express is ready for the market!

Not only does the Trix-Express train work all the mechanical details, but furthermore, like all Trix items, the design and development is finished including the mechanics, the elegant outline, the level of prices, the construction of the details, the way of selling, plus the packaging and advertising material available for a well devised system.

On our travellings we will show you the prototype designs as you couldn't observe exactly which was shown by our staff at the (Leipzig) fair as it was too busy. However, you will find all the important features about Trix-Express, in short, at the rear of this leaflet.

Trix-Express, the item for dealers!

You need only find a place and it 'goes' by itself. We help you by our proved Trix promotional and advertising literature. The railway takes up little room on the shelves of the shop as a small niche allows easy storage, and it is very easy to build up and demonstrate.

With Trix-Express only can you run two trains at the same time on one rail. Because of this every boy will want the second train and further accessories.

Only Trix-Express brings the inevitable additional deals!

What the Trix-Express can do.

This miniature electric train with its elegant and true to life outline, runs similar to a full size electric train taking its current source from a transformer, converter, batteries or accumulator for every level of forward and backward motion. The practical and inexpensive way of connection to the current source is by way of a special regulating resistance with current breaker. This regulator, which is delivered with every train, has a clever and easy to handle combination of a knob for speed control with a fast working switch which allows a speedy and easy control of the train.

Two trains on one rail.

An exceptional special novelty, is that two trains can operate on one track with different speeds or direction, this brings a quantity of new facilities into play. Suitable signals and electromagnetic points are available. Points and crossings cannot be faulted, and the design of the rails and their way of connection is something entirely new. The rails cannot be bent but the connections are flexible and quickly made, so that one can even build them up on an uneven surface.

A whole layout on one table!

The playing boy does not require large facilities for a layout, as even the smallest room in a home can accommodate a comprehensive system. As there is only one size of train available this also means that for extra sales, you the dealer, can always have enough items in stock without taking up too much storage space and without costing too much money.

FROM A SMALL STORAGE SPACE, LARGE DEALS.

3 March 1935 at the Leipzig Spring Fair. Two sets were available initially, a goods set and a passenger set plus a varied selection of wagons, coaches and lineside accessories – all in the style of the Deutsche Reichsbahn. The locomotive used was a simple 0-4-0 tender locomotive whose AC/DC mechanism was to be the corner stone for all future Trix locomotives up to the change over to Direct Current drive in the 1950s. To cope with the ever-increasing demands for the company's products, additional premises were acquired at Schillerstrasse 10 in Nuremberg during 1935.

The Trix Express model railway was not available in Britain until the Christmas of 1935 when it was distributed and sold by Bassett-Lowke Ltd under the advertised name of Bassett-Lowke Twin-Train Table Railway. Although most of the packaging and literature used the trade name of Trix Express, some of the boxes had Bassett-Lowke inspired labels pasted over the original Trix Express labels, a practice which continued only for a short period. However, the locomotive and coaches in the goods and passenger sets were of different livery to those sold in Germany being finished in green similar to that of the Southern Railway livery. The new model railway system was a resounding success, and Trix Ltd having anticipated this fact had set the wheels in motion for expansion and the financing of the production in Britain.

On 18 February 1936 additional directors were appointed to the board of Trix Ltd, namely Stephan Bing, Siegfried Kahn, Hermann Oppenheim and Jack Davis Somper, and the registered office was moved during May to more suitable premises at 45/47 Clerkenwell Road, London EC1. H. Oppenheim was a banker from Frankfurt who had joined S. Bing as a partner at the beginning of 1936 taking 26% of the shares in Vereinigte Spielwarenfabriken Andreas Förtner & J. Haffner's Nachf. GmbH., leaving S. Bing with 74%.

J. D. Somper, who was a friend of W.J. Bassett-Lowke and the Chairman of D. Smith & Sons Ltd of Lea Bridge Road, London, a company of toy manufacturers, was persuaded to arrange for his company to help with the finance and manufacturing facilities needed for expanding Trix production. A manufacturing licence was granted by the

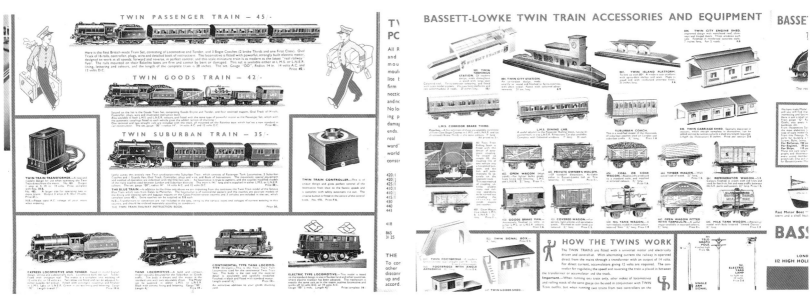

Extracts from the November 1936 Bassett-Lowke Twin Train catalogue. (H)

One of the first general advertisements in December 1935 showing the 'Bassett-Lowke Twin Train Table Railway'.

A February 1936 advertisement which mentions the Twin Train Coaches (Trix Express) in SR colours.

A November 1936 advertisement inviting people to 'Meet The English Twins'.

German company, although the actual manufacture of the Trix items was still carried out at the Winteringham factory in Northampton, the main help being in the form of financial backing provided by D. Smith & Sons Ltd.

The first British outline locomotives were 0-4-0 tank and tender engines in LMS and LNER livery with a matching compliment of coaches and wagons, plus accessories to a British pattern. All were ready in the shops by November 1936 in readiness for the Christmas trade. Sales exceeded all expectations and it was obvious that a new financial structure was required to satisfy the demands of the public and the inevitable future development costs. The work force at Winteringham Ltd had by this time been increased to approximately 200 to cope with the work. This finance was obtained by Trix Ltd in July 1937 from a Debenture provided by Barclays Bank Ltd with D. Smith & Sons Ltd acting as guarantors.

1937 was a very exciting period in the development of Trix Express and the Trix Twin Railway system, both being expanded greatly with many new items available to the public. It was initially envisaged that Trix Twin would appeal exclusively to the juvenile sector, but it soon became apparent that its appeal spread across all age groups and more realistic models were needed.

News of new models and current progress was conveyed to Trix model railway enthusiasts by *The TTR Gazette* which was sent to the owners free of charge when they registered their ownership with Trix Ltd. No.1 was dated November-December 1937. German enthusiasts had been fortunate to have their version *Trix Express Dienst* over one year earlier in March 1936. Both versions were edited by Siegfried Kahn.

The very first scale model was a Southern Railway Suburban Electric Train, which was available as a set comprising a motor coach and two matching coaches, plus other sundry items.

1936 Shop counter display card.

November 1936 Trix Twin Railway price list.(I)

1936 Trix Twin Railway catalogue.

This set was made available to the public in February 1937 nearly five months before the prototype actually ran on the newly electrified Southern Railway line between London and Portsmouth, and this modelling feat was achieved with the cooperation of C. Grasemann who was Publicity Officer of the Southern Railway. Working Trix Twin Railway (TTR) layouts using this new model were used by Southern Railway on Waterloo station and in the booking hall of Charing Cross Underground as a publicity exercise, the Waterloo layout being operated by a very young Michael J. Catalani,

(who later was to remain with Trix Ltd as one of the design team for many years), together with Bill Best and others not known.

1937 also saw the introduction of the Trix Express Pacific locomotive whose chassis, with slight modifications, was used for the British outline Pacifics the following year. Also introduced was the 'Diesel Flyer' two-coach unit developed from the Southern Electric motor unit. Thus, from a basic toy locomotive, progress was quickly achieved, a progress which was watched with great interest by rival manufacturers.

The same year also saw some joint ventures, although the words 'joint venture' seem rather irrelevant as up to the middle of 1938 both the German and British companies were more or less owned and operated by the same personnel. In France, diversification from the production of Trix Construction Sets, manufactured under licence since 1932 by Maison Gobin-Daudé of Rue Beranger in Paris, was planned. This firm was a long-established company mainly specialising in the manufacture of nuts and bolts including eyelets for use on boots and shoes. The owners of the company, Monsieur Gaston Gobin-Daudé and Monsieur Nouvelet, who were already acting as agents for Trix Express and TTR items, showed considerable interest in setting up production in Paris of a French outline Trix locomotive and matching coaches.

This joint cooperation led to a locomotive and matching coaches being launched on to the market. The locomotive, which was a representation of the NORD Chapelon Pacific with a reduced 4-4-0 wheel arrangement, used a Trix Express chassis, TTR coach bogies for the tender, while the cast bodies of the engine and tender were of French manufacture. The matching coaches used bodies cast in France and were fitted to standard TTR bogie coach chassis with the words MADE IN FRANCE stamped on the underside. A few of the railway accessories were also made in France under licence, including the track and some of the electrical equipment. A bureau and showroom were opened during 1938 at 29 Boulevard Saint-Martin in Paris to promote the Trix Express 'F' products, but sales were poor, even though the NORD set was made available on the British market. The political events of 1938 and 1939 quickly overtook any hope of this French manufacturing venture becoming successful. However, business ties between Maison Gobin Daudé and Trix Ltd continued for many years after the war.

The other joint venture was the promotion of Trix Express and TTR in America helped by a large display in the premises of their agents F.A.O. Schwarz of New York, and the production of joint catalogues during 1937 and 1938. The 1938/1939 edition included the celebrated 'American Pacific' with a complement of matching goods wagons and station acces-sories, including the Many-Ways system of station buildings introduced in 1937. Bearing in mind the problems that were to beset the partners during 1938, it is interesting to note that the 1937/1938 catalogue was printed in Germany, while the 1938/1939 version was printed in Britain.

These problems took their toll on the finances of Vereinigte Spielwarenfabriken Andreas Förtner & J. Haffner's Nachf. GmbH. and especially Trix Ltd, who in the past had been assisted in its endeavours by the parent company. Unfortunately, the financial worries were by this time compounded by the power of the Nazi regime, and it was becoming increasingly difficult during 1937 for companies with Jewish owner-ship to conduct their business. Thus Vereinigte Spielwarenfabriken Andreas Förtner & J. Haffner's Nachf. GmbH. were doomed. It was impossible to transfer money from Germany to Britain and a devastating blow to Trix Ltd was the withdrawal of the financial and manufac-turing backing of D. Smith & Sons Ltd in February 1938.

At this point James Daniel Kiley came to the rescue. He was the managing director of Whyte Risdale Ltd, a large toy wholesaler, and from September 1937 the chairman of Machinery (Smith's Patents) Ltd, a company of Iron-founders and Engineers of Lea Bridge Road, London, certain of whose directors were affiliated to D. Smith & Sons Ltd. Kiley was a friend of J. Stein, the company secretary of Trix Ltd, and his company was approached with a view to helping with the financing and production of Trix products.

Machinery (Smith's Patents) Ltd agreed to assist, but instead of participating in the actual manufacture of Trix railway items, the company helped with production by using the facilities of its draughtsman to draw the designs provided by Trix Ltd and also to order the Trix model railway items from sub-contractors to their requirements. To put it simply, Machinery (Smith's Patents) Ltd acted as a go-between which lessened the immediate financial burden of continued development. They were granted a manufac-turing licence at the beginning of 1938. Earlier, probably in late 1937, Machinery (Smith's Patents) Ltd made an advance of £12,000 to Trix

A Trix display in the downstairs showroom of the Bassett-Lowke London shop circa 1936. Note the mixture of German and early British wooden buildings plus the large 'Central Station' on the left constructed by Twining Models Ltd for Bassett-Lowke Ltd.

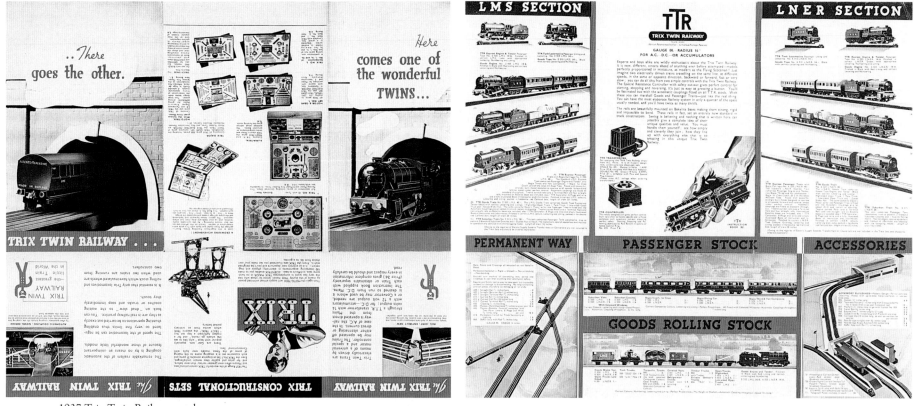

1937 Trix Twin Railway catalogue.

Ltd to further help their cause.

For his rewards in masterminding the above arrangements for the benefit of Trix Ltd, Kiley was invited on to the board of directors of Trix Ltd in February 1938 and took up the post of chairman in 1941, a post which he held until his death in 1953. The manufacturing relationship probably ceased with the advent of Precision Models Ltd in 1941, but the company still maintained a controlling hold on the financial affairs of Trix Ltd as article 75 of the the new Articles of Association of Trix Ltd, drawn up in the same year, stated: 'So long as the company shall owe to Machinery (Smith's Patent) Ltd a sum of not less than £5,000 or so long as the said Machinery (Smith's Patents) Ltd shall be the registered proprietors or the beneficial owners of the share capital in the Company to an extent of not less than £5,000...Machinery (Smith's Patents) Ltd shall have the right...to appoint one Director of the Company...' In addition, Article 81(a) stated '...whilst the Company shall owe Machinery (Smith's Patents) Ltd any part of a loan of £12,000 now outstanding, the Company shall not without the previous consent in writing from Machinery (Smith's Patents) Ltd create any Mortgage or charge upon its business...' It is not certain when this loan was repaid but Machinery (Smith's Patents) Ltd ceased to be shareholders in 1947 and went into Voluntary Liquidation in October of the same year.

During the latter part of 1937 it became increasingly difficult for people of Jewish origin to lead a normal life in Germany and personal safety became a problem. Eventually in 1938 under Anti-Semitic laws, members of the Jewish community were not allowed to own or partly own a business. As a condition of being allowed to emigrate, an 'enforced' agreement of sale of Vereinigte Spielwarenfabriken Andreas Förtner & J. Haffner's Nachf. GmbH. was entered into between the Partners and Ernst Voelk, who as a

former business associate and a person who fulfilled the qualifications required by the Nazi regime to run a company, had been approached by the Partners earlier. Ernst Voelk was the President of the Chamber of Trade in Nuremberg and the owner of Johann Distler K.G., an old-established toy manufacturing company, also in Nuremberg, which he had taken over in similar circumstances. The purchase agreement, which was signed on 27 April 1938 and sanctioned by the Foreign Exchange Bank in Germany on 10 May 1938, was very severe in the commitments it imposed on the partners S. Bing and H. Oppenheim, including the general manager S. Kahn, and their manufacturing bases and sales

The first editions of the *Trix Express Dienst* and *The TTR Gazette*.

An advertisement leaflet for the Three-Coach Southern Electric Train.

A 1938 publicity photograph for use with a Bassett-Lowke Twin Train advertisement.

x The Model Railway News December, 1936

Meet The English Twins!

PASSENGER LOCOMOTIVE AND TENDER.
In L.N.E.R. or L.M.S. pattern and colours with diecast body, smartly and substantially built. Two shoes are fitted and can be adjusted for either outside rail pick-up, according to method of operation. Tender fitted with automatic couplings. Price complete **14/6**

NORTHAMPTON MADE THIS YEAR.

Gauge "OO" 14 in. radius. Electrically controlled. 12 volts d.c. or 14 volts a.c.

For months past our customers have been asking "When shall we have the famous 'Twin Trains' in British design and colours?" We are now able to announce they are READY IN STOCK and are ON SALE at our branches at London and Manchester, and at our Head Office, Northampton.

This year there are three new Sets, Passenger, Goods and Suburban, available in L.M.S. or L.N.E.R. colours. Supporting these is a complete new range of rolling stock, both Passenger and Goods. The powerful electric driving unit is of the same design, with slight improvements, working off 14 volts a.c. or 12 volts d.c.

L.M.S. DINING CAR. Price 3/-.
Passenger Rolling Stock on the Twin Train Railway has improved in both quantity and quality this year. There are 1st class Coaches, Dining and Restaurant Cars, Bogie Brake Thirds and Suburban Coaches and Vans, in correct lettering, lining and colours of either L.M.S. or L.N.E.R. All vehicles have automatic couplings and are fitted with realistic Celastoid windows. Suburban coaches and vans **1/6**. All other Passenger Rolling Stock **3/6**.

L.M.S. OPEN WAGON. Price 1/-.
The Twin Train Railway is amply stocked with smart goods wagons, in correct English colours. Each vehicle is fitted with special automatic couplings, making the hobby more fascinating, as "real railway" operations, such as goods yard shunting, can be carried out. Covered and Timber wagons **1/3**. U.D. Milk and "Esso" Oil wagons **1/9**. Goods Brake Vans and Coal wagons **1/6**, and so forth.

RAIL, straight (as illustrated) or curved, **9d.** per length. Twin Train Track is mounted on a smart black bakelite base giving perfect insulation and smooth running. All the rails, points and crossovers have neat snap joints, making a firm foundation for the layout. This idea sets a new standard in model track construction. Points. Hand-operated **10/6**. Electrically operated, complete with levers, plug and wire, **16/6** per pair.

Send for the
TWIN TRAIN BOOKLET,
T.T. 43,
giving full description of the T.T. range. Free and post free. *Or* call at Holborn, where a complete outfit is being demonstrated.

Here is the **GOODS SET**, comprising Engine and Tender, 3 assorted wagons, 1 Goods Brake Van, Oval of 14 rails, Controller and Connections. Price **42/-**

The other sets are:—
PASSENGER TRAIN SET, consisting of Passenger Engine and Tender, 2 Bogie Third Class Coaches, 1 1st Class Coach, Oval Track of 16 rails, Controller and Connections. Price **45/-**; and
SUBURBAN SET, made up of Passenger Tank Locomotive, 2 Suburban Coaches, Guard's Van, Oval Track, Controller and Connections. Price **35/-**   Each set complete with illustrated book of instructions.

BASSETT-LOWKE LTD.
NORTHAMPTON.
LONDON: 112, High Holborn, W.C.I.
MANCHESTER: 28, Corporation Street.

A December 1936 advertisement announcing the appearance of the 'Twin Trains' in British outline and colour.

Special Catalog 1937/38

for the famous

TRIX EXPRESS

also called **TRIX Twin Railway** (T.T.R.) the high class miniature electric Table Trains, the best little Train in the world.

Distant Control System.

Many new features, entirely new in Model Train history.

A new Thrill to Model Train Amateurs!
Two trains running on the **same** track, at the **same** time, at **different** speeds, in the same or opposite direction, backward or forward, fast, slow or very slow, one train to stop whilst the other is still running, to reverse one train or both simultaneously or one after the other, and a lot of other interesting and thrilling Railway operations,

All this done at your bidding, by distant control!
A complete Layout within the limited space of a table!

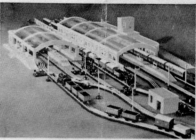

A complete show at:

F. A. O. SCHWARZ
745 Fifth Ave., at 58 th. St.
NEW-YORK
BRANCH STORES AT 40 NEWBURY ST. **BOSTON** MASS. — **ARDMORE** PENN.

Special 1937/38 Trix Express/TTR export catalogue. (C)

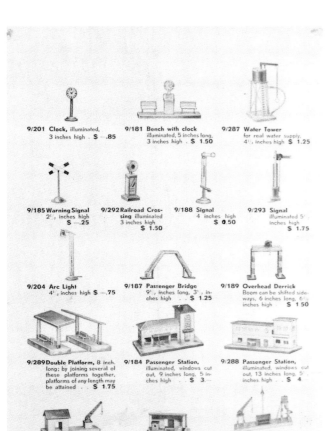

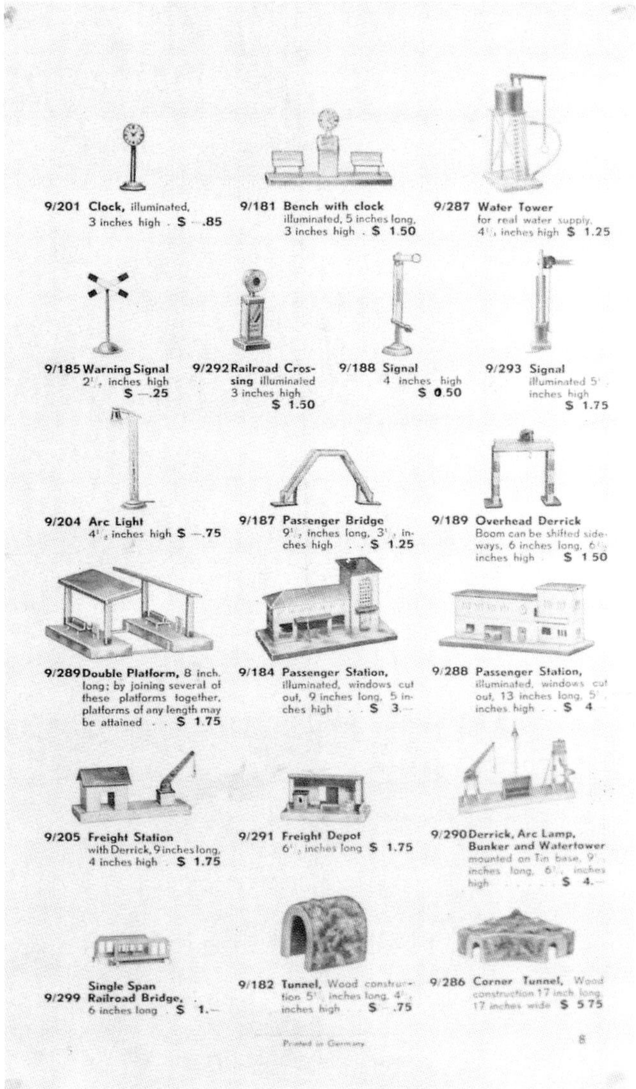

9/201 **Clock**, illuminated,
3 inches high . $ —.85

9/181 **Bench with clock**
illuminated, 5 inches long,
3 inches high . $ 1.50

9/287 **Water Tower**
for real water supply,
4½ inches high $ 1.25

9/185 **Warning Signal**
2½ inches high
$ —.25

9/292 **Railroad Cros-**
sing illuminated
3 inches high
$ 1.50

9/188 **Signal**
4 inches high
$ 0.50

9/293 **Signal**
illuminated 5½
inches high
$ 1.75

9/204 **Arc Light**
4½ inches high $ —.75

9/187 **Passenger Bridge**
9½ inches long, 3½ in-
ches high . . $ 1.25

9/189 **Overhead Derrick**
Boom can be shifted side-
ways, 6 inches long, 6½
inches high . $ 1.50

9/289 **Double Platform**, 8 inch.
long; by joining several of
these platforms together,
platforms of any length may
be attained . $ 1.75

9/184 **Passenger Station,**
illuminated, windows cut
out, 9 inches long, 5 in-
ches high . . $ 3.—

9/288 **Passenger Station,**
illuminated, windows cut
out, 13 inches long, 5½
inches high . $ 4

9/205 **Freight Station**
with Derrick, 9 inches long,
4 inches high . $ 1.75

9/291 **Freight Depot**
6½ inches long $ 1.75

9/290 **Derrick, Arc Lamp,**
Bunker and Watertower
mounted on Tin base, 9½
inches long, 6½ inches
high . . . . $ 4.—

9/299 **Single Span**
Railroad Bridge,
6 inches long . $ 1.—

9/182 **Tunnel**, Wood construction 5½ inches long, 4½
inches high . $ —.75

9/286 **Corner Tunnel**, Wood
construction 17 inch long,
17 inches wide $ .75

Printed in Germany

8

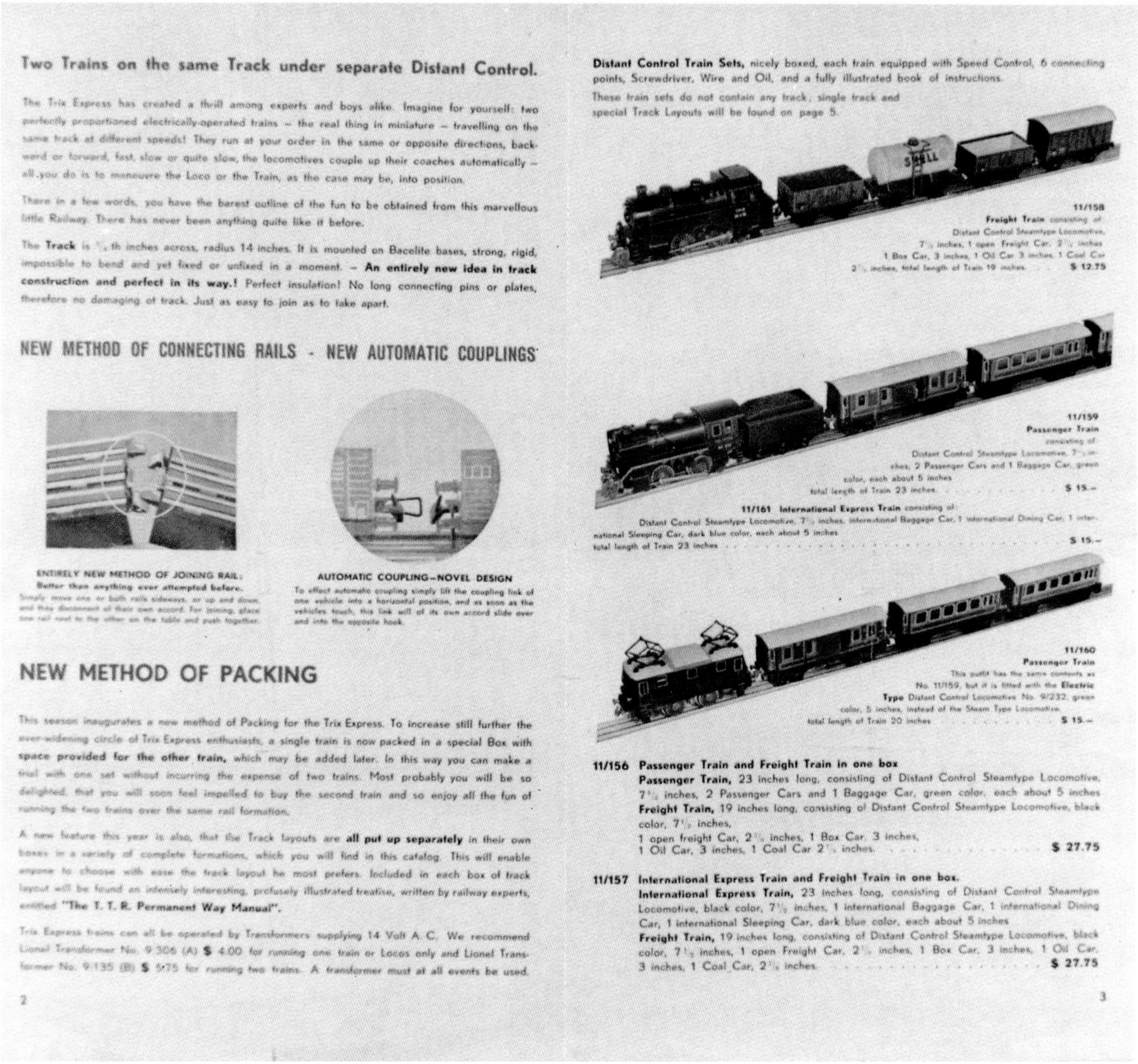

Two Trains on the same Track under separate Distant Control.

The Trix Express has created a thrill among experts and boys alike. Imagine for yourself: two perfectly proportioned electrically-operated trains – the real thing in miniature – travelling on the same track at different speeds! They run at your order in the same or opposite directions, backward or forward, fast, slow or quite slow, the locomotives couple up their coaches automatically – all you do is to manœuvre the Loco or the Train, as the case may be, into position.

There in a few words, you have the barest outline of the fun to be obtained from this marvellous little Railway. There has never been anything quite like it before.

The **Track** is ⅝th inches across, radius 14 inches. It is mounted on Bacelite bases, strong, rigid, impossible to bend and yet fixed or unfixed in a moment. – **An entirely new idea in track construction and perfect in its way.!** Perfect insulation! No long connecting pins or plates, therefore no damaging of track. Just as easy to join as to take apart.

NEW METHOD OF CONNECTING RAILS - NEW AUTOMATIC COUPLINGS

ENTIRELY NEW METHOD OF JOINING RAIL.
Better than anything ever attempted before.
Simply move one or both rails sideways, or up and down, and they disconnect of their own accord. For joining, place one rail next to the other on the table and push together.

AUTOMATIC COUPLING—NOVEL DESIGN
To effect automatic coupling simply lift the coupling link of one vehicle into a horizontal position, and as soon as the vehicles touch, this link will of its own accord slide over and into the opposite hook.

NEW METHOD OF PACKING

This season inaugurates a new method of Packing for the Trix Express. To increase still further the ever-widening circle of Trix Express enthusiasts, a single train is now packed in a special Box with **space provided for the other train,** which may be added later. In this way you can make a trial with one set without incurring the expense of two trains. Most probably you will be so delighted, that you will soon feel impelled to buy the second train and so enjoy all the fun of running the two trains over the same rail formation.

A new feature this year is also, that the Track layouts are **all put up separately** in their own boxes in a variety of complete formations, which you will find in this catalog. This will enable anyone to choose with ease the track layout he most prefers. Included in each box of track layout will be found an intensely interesting, profusely illustrated treatise, written by railway experts, entitled **"The T. T. R. Permanent Way Manual".**

Trix Express trains can all be operated by Transformers supplying 14 Volt A. C. We recommend Lionel Transformer No. 9/306 (A) $ 4.00 for running one train or Locos only and Lionel Trans-former No. 9/135 (B) $ 5.75 for running two trains. A transformer must at all events be used.

2

Distant Control Train Sets, nicely boxed, each train equipped with Speed Control, 6 connecting points, Screwdriver, Wire and Oil, and a fully illustrated book of instructions.
These train sets do not contain any track, single track and special Track Layouts will be found on page 5.

11/158
Freight Train consisting of
Distant Control Steamtype Locomotive,
7½ inches, 1 open Freight Car, 2½ inches,
1 Box Car, 3 inches, 1 Oil Car 3 inches, 1 Coal Car
2½ inches, total length of Train 19 inches
$ 12.75

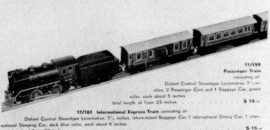

11/159
Passenger Train
consisting of
Distant Control Steamtype Locomotive, 7½ inches, 2 Passenger Cars and 1 Baggage Car, green
color, each about 5 inches
total length of Train 23 inches
$ 15.—

11/161 **International Express Train** consisting of
Distant Control Steamtype Locomotive, 7½ inches, international Baggage Car, 1 International Dining Car, 1 international Sleeping Car, dark blue color, each about 5 inches
total length of Train 23 inches
$ 15.—

11/160
Passenger Train
This outfit has the same contents as
No. 11/159, but it is fitted with the **Electric**
Type Distant Control Locomotive No. 9/232, green
color, 5 inches, instead of the Steam Type Locomotive,
total length of Train 20 inches
$ 15.—

11/156 **Passenger Train and Freight Train in one box.**
Passenger Train, 23 inches long, consisting of Distant Control Steamtype Locomotive,
7½ inches, 2 Passenger Cars and 1 Baggage Car, green color, each about 5 inches
Freight Train, 19 inches long, consisting of Distant Control Steamtype Locomotive, black
color, 7½ inches,
1 open freight Car, 2½ inches, 1 Box Car, 3 inches,
1 Oil Car, 3 inches, 1 Coal Car 2½ inches. . . . . $ 27.75

11/157 **International Express Train and Freight Train in one box.**
International Express Train, 23 inches long, consisting of Distant Control Steamtype
Locomotive, black color, 7½ inches, 1 international Baggage Car, 1 international Dining
Car, 1 international Sleeping Car, dark blue color, each about 5 inches
Freight Train, 19 inches long, consisting of Distant Control Steamtype Locomotive, black
color, 7½ inches, 1 open Freight Car, 2½ inches, 1 Box Car, 3 inches, 1 Oil Car,
3 inches, 1 Coal Car, 2½ inches. . . . . $ 27.75

3

The latest Addition

9/253 4–6–2 Pacific Type Express Locomotive and Bogie Tender. Scale length 10½ inches. A perfect Sacle Model with working Walschaerts valve – motion, electric light, Distant Control, Twin train working Automatic coupling front and rear. Runs perfectly on standard Trix curves. **$ 24.–**

9/254 Speed Control A speed Control is needed for every locomotive; the train sets comprise one for every locomotive, included in the price for the set. This neatly designed unit gives perfect control from very slow to fastest speeds. Complete with **Automatic Cut-out,** ensuring perfect safety. Starting, stopping and reversing operated by red button in centre of speed control ring **$ 3.25**

Fitted with white headlight and red rear light. When the train is reversed the lights are also reversed automatically.

9/232 Distant Control Electric Type Locomotive, green color, handpainted 5 inches **$ 6.75**

11/162 Distant Control Diesel-Type Train-2 Coach Unit. Scale Model. Special bogie motor units, giving extra adhesion at high speeds and on curves. Scale length 17 inches. Runs perfectly on standard Trix curves. **$ 20.–** Rails and Fittings extra

9/252 Distant Control Steam type Locomotive with tender, black color, handpainted, 7½ inches **$ 6.75**

9/231 Distant Control Tender Locomotive, black color, handpainted 4½ inches **$ 6.75**

9/278 Distant **Signal,** distant controlled 3 inches high **$ 3.50**

9/220 Home **Signal,** distant controlled 4 inches high **$ 3.50**

9/238 Automatic Crossing Gate, distant controlled 3 inches by 4½ inches per unit **$ 6.50**

9/279 Connecting points per set of 6 **$ –.50**

9/280 Connecting cable, **$ –.35**

4

Track Layouts and single Track Units

Track Layouts as per diagrams, packed in strong cardboard boxes, containing a manual, called **"The T. T. R. Permanent Way Manual",** with many interesting hints as to constructing, developing and operating a system of Layouts, written by Railway experts.

Track for TRIX Express. Construction is a revolution in itself. You will find an important description of the new features on page 2 of this catalog.

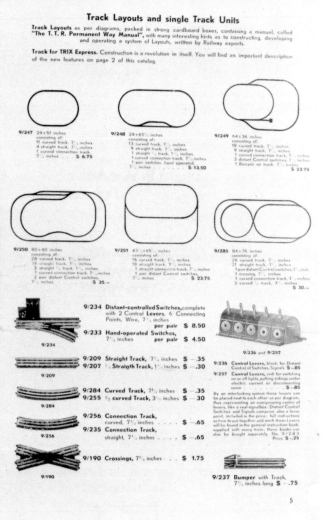

9/247 29 x 51 inches consisting of: 11 curved track, 7½ inches; 4 straight track, 7½ inches; 1 curved connection track, 7½ inches **$ 6.75**

9/248 29 x 65½ inches consisting of: 13 curved track, 7½ inches; 9 straight track, 7½ inches; 1 straight ½ track, 1½ inches; 1 curved connection track, 7½ inches; 1 pair switches, hand operated, 7½ inches **$ 13.50**

9/249 64 x 36 inches consisting of: 18 curved track, 7½ inches; 9 straight track, 7½ inches; 1 curved connection track, 7½ inches; 3 distant Control switches, 7½ inches; 1 Bumper on track, 7½ inches **$ 23.75**

9/250 80 x 40 inches consisting of: 28 curved track, 7½ inches; 19 straight track, 7½ inches; 2 straight ½ track, 1½ inches; 1 curved connection track, 7½ inches; 2 pair distant Control switches, 7½ inches **$ 35.–**

9/251 43½ x 65½ inches consisting of: 16 curved track, 7½ inches; 18 straight track, 7½ inches; 1 straight connection track, 7½ inches; 1 pair distant Conrol switches, 7½ inches **$ 23.75**

9/285 84 x 36 inches consisting of: 26 curved track, 7½ inches; 21 straight track, 7½ inches; 1 pair distant Control switches, 7½ inch; 1 crossing, 7½ inches; 1 curved connection track, 7½ inches; 2 curved ½ track, 3½ inches **$ 30.–**

9/234 Distant-controlled Switches, complete with 2 Control **Levers,** 6 Connecting Points, Wire, 7½ inches per pair **$ 8.50**

9/233 Hand-operated Switches, 7½ inches per pair **$ 4.50**

9/209 Straight Track, 7½ inches **$ –.35**

9/207 ½ Straigth Track, 1½ inches **$ –.30**

9/284 Curved Track, 7½ inches **$ –.35**

9/255 ½ curved Track, 3½ inches **$ –.30**

9/256 Connection Track, curved, 7½ inches **$ –.65**

9/235 Connection Track, straight, 7½ inches **$ –.65**

9/190 Crossings, 7½ inches **$ 1.75**

9/234 — 9/209 — 9/284 — 9/256 — 9/190

9/236 and 9/257

9/236 Control Levers, black, for Distant Control of Switches, Signals **$ -.85**

9/257 Control Levers, red, for switching on or off lights, putting sidings under electric current or disconnecting same **$ -.85**

By an interlocking system these levers can be placed neat to each other as per diagram, thus representing an evergrowing centre of levers, like a real signalbox. Distant Control Switches and Signals comprise also a lever point, included in the price; full instructions as how to put together and work these Levers will be found in the general instruction book, supplied with every train; these books can also be bought separately, No. 9/283 Price **$ -.25**

9/237 Bumper with Track, 7½ inches long **$ –.75**

5

Rolling Stock for Trix Express (T.T.R.) Miniature electric Table Railw

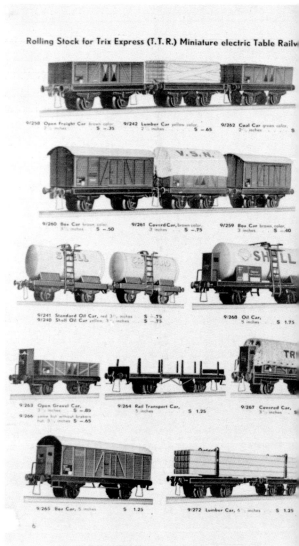

9/258 Open Freight Car brown color, 2½ inches **$ –.35**

9/242 Lumber Car yellow color, 2½ inches **$ –.65**

9/262 Coal Car green color, 2½ inches **$**

9/260 Box Car brown color, 3½ inches **$ –.50**

9/261 Coverd Car, brown color, 3 inches **$ –.75**

9/259 Box Car brown color, 3 inches **$ –.40**

9/241 Standard Oil Car, red 3½ inches **$ –.75**

9/240 Shell Oil Car yellow, 3½ inches **$ –.75**

9/268 Oil Car, 5 inches **$ 1.75**

9/263 Open Gravel Car, 3½ inches **$ –.85**

9/266 same but without brakers hut, 3½ inches **$ –.65**

9/264 Rail Transport Car, 5 inches **$ 1.25**

9/267 Covered Car, 3½ inches **$**

9/265 Box Car, 5 inches **$ 1.25**

9/272 Lumber Car, 6½ inches **$ 1.25**

6

Wagon Lits Series, dark blue color:

9/269	Baggage Car, 5½ inches	$ 1.25
9/270	Dining Car, 5½ inches	$ 1.25
9/271	Sleeping Car, 5½ inches	$ 1.25
9/275*	Baggage Car, 8½ inches	$ 3.75
9/276*	Dining Car, 8½ inches	$ 3.25
9/277*	Sleeping Car, 8½ inches	$ 3.25

Mitropa Series, red color:

9/273*	Dining Car, 8½ inches	$ 3.25
9/274*	Sleeping Car, 8½ inches	$ 3.25
	*) ready to insert lighting outfit 9/281	

9/281	Lighting Sets to fit Cars, marked with asterisks	per Set	$ 1.25
9/282	Railroad Figures of metal, 15 in a Box	per Box	$ .85
9/283	Instruction Books		$ .25

Miniature Accessories
scaled for Trix Express (T. T. R.) Electric Table Trains.

| 9/295 | 9/294 | 9/296 | 9/208 |
| Automatic Drop Gate, 4½ inches long . $ 2. | Overhead Passenger Bridge with automatic light, 7½ inches long, 5 inches high $ 2.75 | Twin Drop Gate with house, 8 inches long $ 4.75 | Signal Bridge, illuminated, 9 inches $ 3.25 |

9/295 · 9/294 · 9/296 are fitted with a special device, by means of which the mechanism is set to work automatically whenever a train passes; barriers go down and red or green lamps are set alight.

| 9/183 | 9/180 | 9/202 | 9/186 |
| Guardhouse, 3½ inches long $ .75 | Signal Tower, illuminated, 4 inches long . $ 1.50 | Railroad Crossing, illuminated, 2 barriers 5 inches long $ 1.75 | Railroad Gate, illuminated, 5 inches long $ 1.25 |

7

outlets in Britain and France.

The total selling price for the business was fixed at just over RM 537,000, (approximately £26,850), which included all the machinery, tooling, stock etc. plus the rights to Patents and Trademarks. This was later shown to be far below the true value of the business. The partners and S. Kahn were not allowed to participate or help in the manufacture or distribution of Trix Construction Sets and model railway items in any country, although they could cooperate with the licence holders in Britain and France and also Trix Ltd, as long as these companies complied with the terms of the agreement. With the loss of rights to most of the Patents and Trademarks, Trix Ltd even had to pay royalties to the German company if they wished to continue with the production of the British Trix items.

These terms of sale also stated, that although Machinery (Smith's Patents) Ltd and S.A. Gobin-Daudé were allowed to retain the licence to manufacture and trade in Trix Construction Sets, TTR and Trix Express model railways and their accessories, apart from the home markets, their sales territory was restricted to the British and French Colonies and Dependencies, which would be exclusive to them. It was also agreed that the original partners should select a company in the USA which could act as agents for both German and British products, again providing that sales were restricted to that country. The combined Trix Express and TTR 1938/39 Special Catalogue intended for the American market was the result of this part of the agreement, and as mentioned earlier, was

printed in England.

It was also stipulated that the licence agents in Britain and France had to continue to purchase, up to the year 1942, exclusively from the new owners, Trix locomotives and accessories, including remote and hand-operated track points, to the value of RM 800,000, (£40,000), inclusive of orders already received. This clause thus answers the question as to why no points or locomotive chassis, including certain other accessories, were manufactured in Britain before September 1939.

A new company under the chairmanship of Ernst Voelk was formed as a limited partnership taking the name of the former company Vereinigte Spielwarenfabriken Andreas Förtner & J. Haffner's Nachfolger, (dropping the letters GmbH.), on 10 May 1938. This new company was owned by seven shareholders giving a share capital of RM 300,000, (£15,000). The trade name of 'Trix' was added to the beginning of the company name and was used in catalogues and advertising literature but was not used in an official capacity, for example, on Patent specifications and the submission of company procedures to the authorities. All the workers under contract to the former owners were reinstated, except for the Jewish employees who received compensation from their past employers. The removal of this group of workers resulted in serious delays in the introduction of new models.

The former company, Vereinigte Spielwarenfabriken Andreas Förtner & J.Haffner's Nachf. GmbH. was obliged under the terms of the agreement to change its name taking the title of

Other Bassett-Lowke Activities.

As a TABLE RAILWAY ENTHUSIAST you are no doubt interested in ALL MODELS. So when you are in London call and see our Fine Display at High Holborn, or, if you are in the North of England, Manchester. Our staff will welcome your enquiries. We also have a Showroom at Northampton, where our direct Mail Order business is situated, and if you cannot call you will be certain of **Satisfaction through the post.**

The Full Range of our Productions is given in the Illustrated Catalogues named below :

A 98—"MODEL RAILWAYS AND THEIR EQUIPMENT." From Gauge "O.O." to Passenger-carrying Railway.
B 98—"STATIONARY ENGINES, BOILERS, CASTINGS AND FITTINGS." For the Model Maker.
S 98—"SHIPS AND SHIP FITTINGS." For Model Maker and Model Owner.
Each Section 6d. Post Free.
FB 98—FREE BOOKLET of popular "O" GAUGE TRAINS.

The THREE-COACH "SOUTHERN ELECTRIC" TRAIN.

A Model in "OO" Gauge that will appeal to the Scale Model Enthusiast.

Officially approved by the Southern Railway, the set consists of a model Third-class Motor Coach, working off 14 volts A.C. and 12 volts D.C.; two Bogie Coaches, 1st class Corridor and Brake 3rd Corridor, fitted automatic couplings; Oval Track 28-in. by 42½-in.; Controller for regulating the train, with automatic cut-out; Plugs, Connections, and Oil.

55/-

Bassett-Lowke Ltd. Northampton

LONDON BRANCH : 112, HIGH HOLBORN, W.C.1

MANCHESTER BRANCH : 28, CORPORATION STREET

NORTHAMPTON CALLING

MARVELLOUS BARGAINS in TWIN TRAIN SETS and ACCESSORIES
A STOCK-TAKING CLEARANCE of TWIN TRAINS
(1936 pattern)
IN ABSOLUTELY NEW CONDITION.

PASSENGER SETS. consisting of Locomotive and Tender, two Bogie Coaches, one Bogie Guards Van, oval Track and Controller finished in Southern colours, ... Sale Price **35s.**

MITROPA EXPRESS TRAIN SETS. Locomotive, Tender and three Bogie Vehicles, oval Track and Controller ... Sale Price **40s.**

Locomotive and Tender (as illus.) **11 6**

ROLLING STOCK.	s.	d.
Bogie Coaches in Southern colours, 5¼-ins. long	1	4
Bogie Brake Vans	1	4
Suburban Coaches	0	6
Covered Goods Wagons	0	7
Large Covered Wagons	0	8
Tarpaulin Wagons	1	0
Timber Wagons	0	9
Mitropa Diners or Sleepers	1	2

ATTRACTIVE STATIONS and RAILWAY BUILDINGS in WOOD.

	s.	d.
Engine Sheds in wood	2	6
Goods Shed	2	0
Footbridges	1	6
Engine Sheds, large size	4	0
Carriage Sheds	2	0
Island Platforms, with shelter and seats	4	0
Twin City Stations	6	0

All the above are Standard Trix productions (foreign made, 1936 pattern) and should appeal to all those who wish to increase their Trix lay-out at Bargain Prices.
N.B.—Please note that none of the current range of Twin Trains are reduced in price.

TANK LOCOMOTIVE
Continental Type. (Foreign).

This is the Twin Train Tank Locomotive used for the Continental Twin Train Sets. The body is die cast and the external detail is accurately and carefully modelled. Finished in black and fitted with standard motor. Length overall 4½".
Price 15/-
An attractive addition to your goods shunting yard.

Spring 1938 Bassett-Lowke leaflet offering a stock-taking clearance of early Twin Train items plus the availability of the exciting new 'Continental' range.

The TWIN TRAIN Scale Models from the CONTINENT.

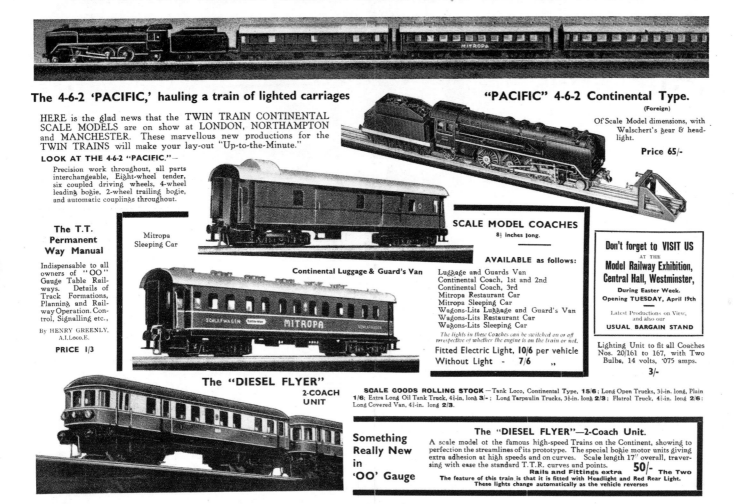

The 4-6-2 'PACIFIC,' hauling a train of lighted carriages

HERE is the glad news that the TWIN TRAIN CONTINENTAL SCALE MODELS are on show at LONDON, NORTHAMPTON and MANCHESTER. These marvellous new productions for the TWIN TRAINS will make your lay-out "Up-to-the-Minute."

LOOK AT THE 4-6-2 "PACIFIC."—

Precision work throughout, all parts interchangeable, Eight-wheel tender, six coupled driving wheels, 4-wheel leading bogie, 2-wheel trailing bogie, and automatic couplings throughout.

"PACIFIC" 4-6-2 Continental Type.

(Foreign)

Of Scale Model dimensions, with Walschert's gear & headlight.

Price 65/-

The T.T. Permanent Way Manual

Indispensable to all owners of "OO" Gauge Table Railways. Details of Track Formations, Planning and Railway Operation. Control, Signalling etc.,

By HENRY GREENLY, A.I.Loco.E.

PRICE 1/3

Mitropa Sleeping Car

Continental Luggage & Guard's Van

SCALE MODEL COACHES

8½ inches long.

AVAILABLE as follows:

Luggage and Guards Van
Continental Coach, 1st and 2nd
Continental Coach, 3rd
Mitropa Restaurant Car
Mitropa Sleeping Car
Wagons-Lits Luggage and Guard's Van
Wagons-Lits Restaurant Car
Wagons-Lits Sleeping Car

The lights in these Coaches can be switched on or off irrespective of whether the engine is on the train or not.

Fitted Electric Light, 10/6 per vehicle
Without Light - 7/6 ,,

Don't forget to VISIT US
AT THE
Model Railway Exhibition,
Central Hall, Westminster,
During Easter Week.
Opening TUESDAY, April 19th
Latest Productions on View,
and also our
USUAL BARGAIN STAND

Lighting Unit to fit all Coaches Nos. 20/161 to 167, with Two Bulbs, 14 volts, ·075 amps.

3/-

The "DIESEL FLYER"

2-COACH UNIT

SCALE GOODS ROLLING STOCK—Tank Loco, Continental Type, **15/6**; Long Open Trucks, 3½-in. long, Plain **1/6**; Extra Long Oil Tank Truck, 4½-in. long **3/-** ; Long Tarpaulin Trucks, 3½-in. long **2/3** ; Flatrol Truck, 4½-in. long **2/6**; Long Covered Van, 4½-in. long **2/3**.

Something Really New in 'OO' Gauge

The "DIESEL FLYER"—2-Coach Unit.

A scale model of the famous high-speed Trains on the Continent, showing to perfection the streamlines of its prototype. The special bogie motor units giving extra adhesion at high speeds and on curves. Scale length 17" overall, traversing with ease the standard T.T.R. curves and points.

Rails and Fittings extra **50/-** **The Two**

The feature of this train is that it is fitted with Headlight and Red Rear Light. These lights change automatically as the vehicle reverses

BASSETT-LOWKE LTD., - NORTHAMPTON, LONDON and MANCHESTER

Metallspielwarenfabrik Oppenheim & Co. GmbH. from 13 May 1938. However, as no business was allowed, the company was put into the hands of an official receiver, the liquidation being completed in May 1939. Payment to the partners for their company was tied up by the German financial authorities with so much red tape and legal obstacles, including securities for unpaid debts incurred outside Germany, that they were lucky to be allowed merely to emigrate to England.

In order that the partners could rebuild their lives in England, an application was made to allow them to retain shares in Trix Ltd to the value of £100. This was agreed, provided that S. Bing, in addition to all the securities amounting to over RM 100,000 deposited in the Nuremberg Foreign Exchange Bank and stipulated in a rider to the main purchase agreement, deposited £2,300 in hard cash in the Reichsbank credited to the account of Ernst Voelk. This sum of £2,300 had initially been credited to Trix Ltd on its formation in 1932. After all the financial requests of the authorities had been fulfilled, the final proviso for emigration was whether the Foreign Exchange Bank in Nuremberg would permit the transfer of the £100 in question! Fortunately it was allowed,

Trix Twin Railway layout in the News Theatre showcase on Waterloo station during 1937 to help with the promotion of 'Southern Electric' which was part of the Southern Railway system.

and emigration took place towards the end of June 1938. Although the hands of Ernst Voelk were tied by the harsh regulations and laws of Nazi regime, he was very helpful in many ways in trying to get the best deal for the previous owners of the company under very difficult circumstances.

As no money, apart from the £100 in shares, was allowed to be taken out of Germany, the partners just prior to emigrating to England started to arrange additional finance to enable

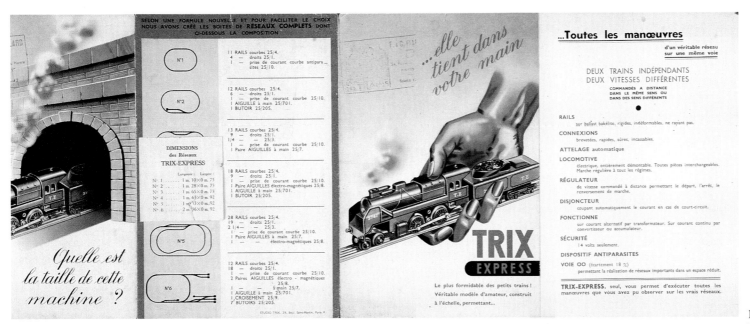

1938 French Trix Express catalogue.

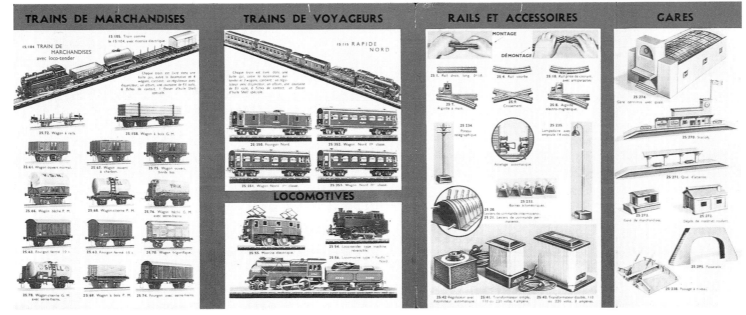

Trix Ltd to continue in business. Fortunately, H. Oppenheim by virtue of his previous banking position in Frankfurt had contacts with the New Trading Company in England, which was the forerunner of S. G. Warburg & Co. Ltd, and it was with them that an agreement was reached to cover all the liabilities of Trix Ltd.

During July 1938 Franz Bing was appointed as a director of Trix Ltd and took charge of the sales side of the business at a time when sales were booming, despite all the previously mentioned problems and the competition posed by the introduction of Hornby Dublo. Mrs Lilli Sommer joined her brother Franz Bing in 1939 taking an active part in sales and also taking charge of the administration at the registered office at Clerkenwell Road. Mrs Lilli Sommer had been on the sales force of her father's business in Nuremberg and had left Germany in 1933 to work at the Vereinigte Spielwaren-fabriken Andreas Förtner & J. Haffner's Nachf. GmbH agency in Brussels which was Bleyfuesz & Verboven. In view of the pending hostilities it was felt that it would be safer for her to join her parents in London.

Most of the production, packaging and distribution took place at the Winteringham factory in Northampton, although incorporated in the building housing the Trix Ltd office at Clerkenwell Road, London, was a small warehouse and a design and development workshop which was managed by Francis John J. Prior from March 1937 until the outbreak of war in September 1939, after which the design and development was moved to Northampton. This department was where the first sample products were made. Although not all the endeavours of the model makers resulted in actual production, the Trix management intended that the TTR system would always have something new to offer to the public. A part-time demonstrator and model maker was J. M. Catalani who can still remember the first samples of the remote-control semaphore signals and the remote-control level crossing being made in the workshop, the latter not going into production due to the war. He also recalls that, no doubt inspired by the Dinky Toy range, it was intended to produce a range of motor vehicles for which he made the first sample – a model of a 1 ton Morris van. In addition, all repairs were carried out at these premises by Messrs Gaskin and Best. Bill Best, who was also a part-time demonstrator, remained with Trix, except during the war years and a short time with the Southgate Hobbyshop in London, until ill health caused him to retire in circa 1970.

At this point it is worth noting that from the beginning of the Trix model railway system in Britain, all the motor chassis for the locomotives, including spares, were supplied by the Nuremberg factory right up to the advent of World War 2. There is even an unconfirmed suggestion that after the start of hostilities, spares were entering Britain via Switzerland. It may also be interesting to note that with the advent of the British outline locomotives, complete German outline locomotives were imported from Nuremberg, the German bodies were removed and the British outline bodies were fitted. These German bodies were discarded and sold to the local scrap merchant or thrown onto the local Council rubbish dump! This practice, which also included the 'Pacific' locomotives, continued until late 1939. The British-made 0-4-0 chassis was not planned until October 1939 at the earliest, and it is uncertain if any reached the market. It should also be noted that the chassis for the 2-4-2 and 'Pacific' AC locomotives were never made in Britain, and only a few were modified at Winteringham Ltd, later Precision Models Ltd, to suit the British types.

1939 promised to be a very good year for new models with the announcement of many exciting items including the LMS 'Coronation', three 4-4-0 locomotives and a 2-4-2 tank engine available in LMS, LNER and SR livery. Only the 'Coronation' and LMS and LNER 4-4-0 locomotives reached the shops in time for Christmas, the 2-4-2s in British outline and the SR 4-4-0 sadly never reaching the production stage. The 2-4-2 locomotives, which were on the British drawing board in the middle of 1939, were to utilise the remarkable Trix Express chassis as fitted to the German DR Class 71 Tank Engine, which became available in Germany in September 1940. This chassis provided a facility for coupling and remote-control uncoupling at both the front and rear. Incidentally, the introduction of this 2-4-2 locomotive became part of a German propaganda exercise to demonstrate to the German public that despite the problems of war, life in Germany was carrying on as normal!

THE WAR YEARS

The war altered the fortunes of Trix dramatically. After the pre-Christmas rush to produce new and existing models, the assembly lines in the Northampton factory were turned over to war-work during the beginning of 1940 and correspondingly during the latter part of 1940 in Nuremberg. In addition, the businesses on both sides suffered disruption due to bomb damage. The offices and workshop of Trix Ltd at Clerkenwell Road were damaged during the early part of 1941, and in March were moved to temporary premises at the Cascade Centre, Mount Pleasant, Alperton, Middlesex, where they stayed until transferred in June 1942 to more permanent premises at 91 Regent Street, London W1.

In Germany the Nuremberg factory and offices of Vereinigte Spielwarenfabriken Andreas Förtner & J. Haffner's Nachf. turned their skills to producing special gear-wheels. However, it was not long before Allied bombing disrupted production and use was made of temporary buildings in Spalt and Koppenhof on the outskirts of Nuremberg to provide relative safety for stock and tooling, plus a small amount of production. A severe blow was inflicted when in August 1943 the offices of the company in Schillerstrasse were totally destroyed. Due to continued disruption in Nuremberg, arrangements were made with the Spalt community to take over and expand the former HJ.-Heim, (Hitler Youth Building), which could be enlarged to house production. Vereinigte Spielwarenfabriken Andreas Förtner & J. Haffner's Nachf. took possession of this building in April 1944 into which some of the production was transferred from Nuremberg. It is still used to this day by their successors mainly for the production of Minitrix and certain items of the Trix International/Express range.

For most of the war the German company managed to sustain a profit and the thoughts of returning to model railway production was never far away. In March 1944 a shareholders' meeting was held to develop ideas for a French branch, possibly in the Jura province, which could assemble toys for export. Negotiations were also planned with Swiss companies with regards to shipment of parts for Trix Express.

In Britain it was a traumatic time for the Bing family and other personnel, as men of German

An insert in the 1938/39 TTR catalogue which shows the 'French Type 4-4-0 and Coaches' with the NORD locomotive and tender priced at 35/- (£1.75).

A letter sent to Trix dealers with the April 1940 price list. Although a brave promise was made to ensure the supply of goods, in reality it was only existing stocks that could be sold or items made up from existing parts as the actual manufacturing of parts had ceased. A catalogue was issued but it was only a reprint of the earlier 1939/40 version. *The TTR Gazette* was not to appear again until after the war.

origin at Trix were interned at the start of the war on the Isle-of-Man for a few weeks, just at a time when all their endeavours were required to run the business. All this disruption and worry took its toll, and Stephan Bing, the founder of Trix died of a heart attack on 19 April 1940. His daughter, Mrs L. Sommer took his place on the board of directors in June of that year.

In the early war years, plans for increased and

The front of an early 1938 leaflet/catalogue.

A pre-war MOTO TRIX Constructional Set produced after 1938. The end label of the box lid lists the restrictions as imposed by the 1938 changes in the Trix company structure.

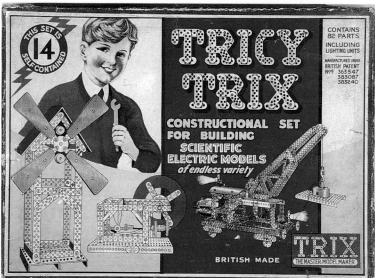

A pre-war post-1938 Tricy Trix Constructional Set.

Basic English translation

Nuremberg 10 June 1938.

President of Finance, Nuremberg.
   (Foreign Exchange)
   Contract No. C 8-50052.

To Stephan Bing.
        Acceptance Decree.

   With reference to an application of 31/5/1938 and in connection with my preliminary Decree of 10/5/1938 plus alteration on 13/5/1938, I hereby give permission to Vereinigte Spielwarenfabriken Nuremberg for the disposal of
        £100 - one hundred Pounds Sterling -,
        Shares in Trix Ltd., London.

   I also give permission to Stephan and Ida Bing of Kesslerplatz 7, Nuremberg, (with reference to certain German laws - author), for conversion of -
        £100 shares in Trix Ltd., London.

   Both permissions are given, subject to release procedures through the Reichsbank Head Office, Nuremberg. Application to the Reichsbank for release has to be made with this Acceptance Decree Document.

   According to section 2 paragraph 1 of my preliminary decree of 10/5/1938, the acceptance decree can only be executed by the German Bank, Nuremberg branch, in favour of the emigrants if the sum of £2,300 credit in favour of Mr Ernst Voelk has been paid at the Nuremberg branch of the German Bank. It is understood that Mr Voelk accepts this payment in Reichsmarks, but the £2,300 must be handed over to the Reichsbank in 'hard currency'.

   Duties mentioned in my preliminary decree of 10/5/1938 and amended 13/5/1938 are valid in connection with these final permissions and must be cleared as proof of permission for emigration.

   Both permissions are valid until 10/7/1938 inclusive.
Should the Acceptance Decree not be used within the time limit, it should be returned forthwith.

   Signed on behalf of the German Bank, Nuremberg Branch.

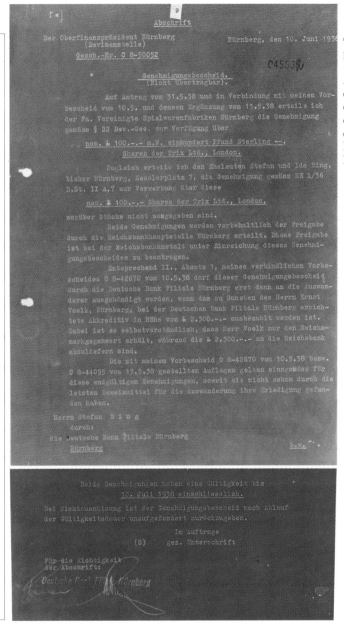

Official German pre-war photo-copy (number 045536) of an Acceptance Decree of certain conditions connected with the sale of VSN and the emigration of Stephan Bing and his wife to England.

almost exclusive production of Trix items by the Winteringham Ltd factory at Stimpson Avenue, Northampton went on undaunted. An application for the registration of Precision Models Ltd was made during February 1941 and the nominal capital was fixed at £20,000 divided into 12,000 'A' Ordinary shares of £1 each and 8,000 'B' Ordinary shares of £1 each. On 11 March Precision Models Ltd was Incorporated with the Registered Office situated at 107 Stimpson Avenue, and the Memorandum of Association states that the object of the company was: 'To acquire and amalgamate the whole or part of the undertakings and properties, assets, rights, powers, debts and liabilities of Winteringham Ltd and Trix Ltd...'. During June 1941, T. F. Smith, who was the major

shareholder acting on behalf of Vereinigte Spielwarenfabriken Andreas Förtner & J. Haffner's Nachf. GmbH., on the formation of Trix Ltd, relinquished his shares which were distributed to F. Bing, L. Sommer, H. Oppenheim and S. Kahn. The next month saw dramatic changes in the financial structure of the company.

The original 100 £1 shares were divided into 20 1/-(5p) shares creating 2,000 Ordinary 'B' shares, and £4,700 was used from the reserve fund provided by company profits to create 18,800 Ordinary 'A' shares of 5/- (25p) each and distributed to the above shareholders as a bonus on the basis of 188 'A' shares for every 20 'B' shares held. Through existing loans and new agreements which included a Debenture of

Pre-war TTR catalogue covers. At top left is the 1937/38 edition. All the others are 1938/39 editions including the Bassett-Lowke catalogue which is a basic Trix catalogue with a Bassett-Lowke cover.

1938 TTR dealer leaflet.

Pre-war Trix Express catalogue covers. From the left: 1938/39, 1937/38 and 1939/40.

1938 advertisement.

Samples of goods vehicles modelled and made in the Trix workshops by Michael Catalani which Trix Ltd were toying with the idea of producing. The van on the left was made in 1939 and the wagon complete with cover and clockwork motor in 1948.

£9,350 taken with the New Trading Company, the registered capital was increased from £100 to £18,500 represented by 25,600 Ordinary 'A' shares of 5/- (25p) each, 2,000 Ordinary 'B' shares of 1/- (5p) each and 12,000 6% Cumulative Preference shares of £1 each, the latter being shares that were never issued. Most of the newly created Ordinary 'A' shares were issued to the companies providing the finance, and Sir Andrew McFadyean was appointed as director of Trix Ltd representing the interests of the New Trading Co. Ltd.

On 11 July an Agreement was made with Precision Models Ltd for this company to purchase the assets and property, less exceptions, of Winteringham Ltd for £16,000 satisfied by £1,000 cash and 8,000 'A' and 7,000 'B' Precision Models Ltd shares of £1 each, also the plant machinery, tools, raw materials and partly finished goods of Trix Ltd for which the agreed purchase price was £4,000 satisfied by the allotment to Trix Ltd of 4,000 Precision Models Ltd 'A' shares of £1 each fully paid. It was agreed that Trix Ltd and Winteringham Ltd should act

as joint managers of the new company for a term of five years, but during September 8,000 Precision Models Ltd 'A' shares were transferred from Winteringham Ltd to Trix Ltd, and again in November 1942 Winteringham Ltd transferred 6,000 'B' shares to Trix Ltd making them the major shareholder and owner of Precision Models Ltd. Thus the exercise, begun in 1941 to raise sufficient capital for Trix Ltd to purchase the manufacturing facilities of Winteringham Ltd and form Precision Models Ltd for the virtually exclusive manufacture of Trix model railway items and other Trix products, was completed.

The new company was under the directorate

of W. J. Bassett-Lowke, who acted as advisor, R. Bindon Blood as Secretary and G. P. Keen. The latter was a wealthy and notable model railway enthusiast who had taken a financial interest in Bassett-Lowke Ltd to try to satisfy his amateur model requirements, and had become chairman of both Bassett-Lowke Ltd and Winteringham Ltd in 1927. He introduced R. Bindon Blood to Winteringham Ltd and for a while retained his position as director of that company whilst also being a director of Precision Models Ltd.

As mentioned previously, during the last few years before the war, production at the Stimpson

Avenue factory was at its peak with attention focussed almost entirely on Trix model railways, construction sets and equipment under contract to Bassett-Lowke Ltd. When the war began, the manufacture of precision gauges for the Admiralty became a major part of production. This work included highly accurate thread-measuring cylinders on which production continued well into the 1950s. In January 1940 the firm was running a night shift engaged entirely on war products including gears for aircraft instruments and parts for the gyros in submarine torpedoes, as well as instruments for petrol gauges in aircraft and specialised counters.

The latter items prompted the formation in April 1943 of Counting Instruments Ltd, a joint venture on a 50-50 basis between Trix Ltd and H. J. Thormann Engineering Ltd with the Registered Office also at 91 Regent Street, London W1. H. J. Thormann Engineering Ltd had done the development and arranged the man-ufacture of the castings required for the various types of counters produced by Precision Models Ltd, and it was felt that it would be a more viable proposition if production was integrated. The success of this venture can be measured by the fact that it was considered that Counting Instruments Ltd kept Trix and Precision Models solvent during the war.

Although no production of TTR or Trix Construction items of any kind took place over this period, the shops were supplied from items held in stock. As stocks ran low the few sets that were actually made up did not always correspond to the advertised contents, but full credit must be given to Trix and Bassett-Lowke for keeping interest going during this difficult time through periodic advertisements, some even containing special offers. Of special mention was the monthly magazine *Practical Mechanics* which carried an article on model railway topics every month. These articles were written by 'Motilus' who was really W. J. Bassett-Lowke and there was constant news concerning Trix trains and the description of many layouts extolled the

1938 advertisements.

The excellent Trix Twin Railway layout at the 1939 British Industries Fair.

TRIX LIMITED
Makers of Electric Trains & Constructional Sets.

DIRECTORS:
J. D. KILEY, J.P. (CHAIRMAN) H. OPPENHEIM (GERMAN)
W. J. BASSETT-LOWKE. S. BING (GERMAN)
S. KAHN (GERMAN)
SECRETARY: J. STEIN. BRITISH (BAVARIAN ORIGIN)

TRIX
TTR
TRADE MARKS

TELEPHONE:
CLERKENWELL 1522
TELEGRAMS:
TEETEEYAR, SMITH, LONDON.

· ST. JOHN'S HOUSE · 45 & 47, CLERKENWELL ROAD ·
· LONDON ·
E.C.1.

TRIX LTD. 45, CLERKENWELL ROAD. E.C.1.

20th October 1938.

Messrs. Bassett-Lowke Ltd.,
St. Andrews St.,
Northampton.

JS/SS

Dear Sirs,

In answer to your letter of February 3rd 1938 we have pleasure in informing you that our Board have now approved of the arrangement regarding the marketing of T.T.R. Scale Models as follows:

T.T.R. Scale Models of Locomotives and Coaches will be offered and sold by us, to the trade only, under the name of "Bassett-Lowke Scale Models" or under similar slogans.

For the use of your name in connection with these goods, and for any other assistance your Company may be able to give us from time to time, we reserve you a Royalty of 5% for a period of five years from January 1st 1938. This Royalty is payable for each calendar year not later than January 31st of the following year, on all net sales, excluding supplies to you, arrived at after deduction of trade discounts, cash discounts, returns and bad debts.

We shall supply you with these model goods for your own requirements at the regular terms agreed between us, and we are prepared to give you an extra discount of 10% in respect of all scale models which you will sell to your trade customers, provided you inform us about these sales in the same way as you are informing us regularly of your sales to the trade of Southern Railway Sets.

The first of the Bassett-Lowke Scale Models, the Southern Railway Set, will also come under this arrangement, and you will only take from us in future sufficient of this line for your retail trade.

It is understood that all models or articles sold by us as "Bassett-Lowke Scale Models", must have your approval before they are placed on the market, and it is also understood that you will not introduce any competitive lines during this arrangement, with the exception of special models you may build for private customers.

Yours faithfully,

288

A letter signed by J. Stein giving the trade terms between Trix Ltd and Bassett-Lowke Ltd.

The October 1940 edition of the *Trix Express Dienst* showing the 1-B-1 (2-4-2) Super Automatic DR Class 71 Tank Engine.

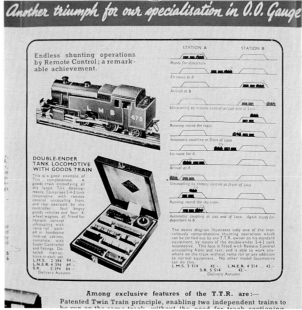

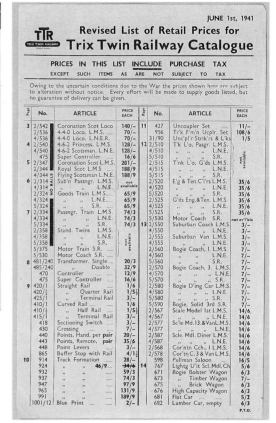

1939 trade catalogue showing many interesting items scheduled for that year. (K)

Extract from the Trix 1939 trade catalogue showing the 2-4-2 tank engine and its ability.

Part of the June 1941 price list.

Two views taken in 1990 of the German Trix factory in Spalt. Notice the old original part of the building to which modern extensions have been blended .

44

virtues of the TTR system. This somewhat made up for the loss of *The TTR Gazette* which was halted at the outbreak of hostilities.

Service back-up was provided from the Regent Street office throughout the war in so far as spares were available. Trix Ltd only occupied the third and fourth floors of this office building. The repair department, store and the office of H. Oppenheim, the finance manager, were on the third floor, while the fourth floor was occupied by the general office and smaller rooms taken up by S. Kahn and F. Bing. What clever planning and forethought took place between the walls of these offices at Regent Street is anyone's guess, but at least the directors had faith in the future and plans for consolidating their position were ready to be implemented at the end of the conflict; a conflict which had halted the rapid development of an exciting model railway system and split the production of Trix items into two separate but almost parallel paths which, in later years, were to merge once again.

A wartime picture of a group of workers outside the premises of Precision Models Ltd.
Frank Gratton (front row extreme right) was to become the works manager when the company was owned by Dufay Ltd.

An experimental livery change. This was an LNER 'Scotsman' disguised during 1942 at the Northampton factory as a Southern Railway Pacific. This shows that ideas for the Trix Twin model railway were being kept alive even through the dark years of the war.

Pre-war Trix Handbooks. The Belgian edition is on the left and the German on the right. The British edition was written by Henry Greenly, a famous miniature railway engineer and friend of W. J. Bassett-Lowke. This British edition continued to be printed with only a few up-dating details until 1955.

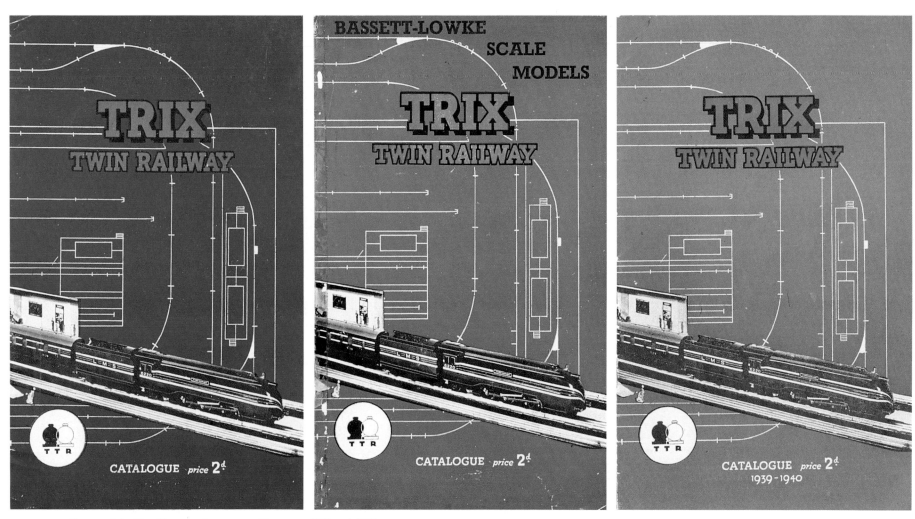

Covers of the Trix Twin catalogues issued between 1939 and 1941.

Pages 46–59: The complete TTR 1939/40 catalogue. >

The Coronation Scot

The world's most famous train

Turn to page 2 for a faithful Model by Trix

TRIX TWIN RAILWAY

Gauge 00 (16 mm.)   Radius 13½ ins.
for A.C. or D.C. Mains or for Accumulators.

A MINIATURE SYSTEM TRUE TO LIFE IN EVERY DETAIL, WITH AN AMAZINGLY COMPREHENSIVE SELECTION OF ACCESSORIES.

TO OUR NEW FRIENDS we extend a hearty welcome to the ever-growing Trix Twin Railway family. In the four years since its introduction, T.T.R. has grown to be the most popular and the most realistic model railway system yet devised.

The tremendous fascination for the operator in having two trains on one track under separate control—without the need for track sectioning—must be experienced to be fully realised. The trains can be run fast or slow, forward or reverse, switched on to sidings, stopped when the signal is at danger and started again when the "all clear" is given. Goods trains can be marshalled in sidings and all the operations of shunting can be performed with life-like precision. All this with the press of a knob or the turn of the controller.

Those who are already model railway enthusiasts will know how absorbing it can be to control and operate a miniature railway system—but with Trix Twin there is far more to it than that. The introduction of the patented Twin Train system has more than doubled the possibilities of this absorbing hobby. Previously, the running of two trains on the same track involved track sectioning, unnecessarily complicated wiring systems and hours of work spent in assembling and wiring up a small section of track. Even then two trains could not be separately controlled in the same

1

IMPORTANT ANNOUNCEMENT

OWING to the uncertain conditions created by the War, it has not been found possible to quote prices in the pages of this catalogue. The prices ruling at the date of issue of this book will be found on a separate sheet loosely inserted herein, but it must be distinctly understood that these prices are subject to alteration without notice.

The Manufacturers will make every effort to supply the goods listed in this catalogue, but regret that they can give no guarantee of delivery.

British Patent Nos. 451644, 459744, 465168, 469656, 471304, 488357, 498651.   *Further patents pending.   Numerous foreign patents.*

TRIX LTD., St. Johns House, 45, Clerkenwell Road, London, E.C.I.

Telephone : CLErkenwell 1521 (3 lines).

section. The Trix Twin system, by allowing two trains to run under separate control on the same section of track, has enormously increased the possibilities of model railway working, at the same time reducing the labour and technical skill needed in assembling.

So, for instance, it becomes possible with Trix Train material to reproduce in miniature a goods marshalling and shunting yard in every particular. You can start if you wish with the simplest goods shed and an oval of track. Then bit by bit you can add to it, a few small items at a time, and you will have the satisfaction of knowing that however much you add, however large your scale of operations becomes, no part of your equipment will ever be out of date or out of harmony with your newer purchases. The whole of Trix material is designed together as a system. It follows a consistent plan and nothing is an "afterthought" although its range increases year by year.

In the photograph on page 1, we present what is probably the world's most famous train, the "Coronation Scot" as it was shown at the New York Worlds Fair. It needs no words of ours to emphasize that this train is the pride of Britain, and in the illustration below it figures again as the pride of the Trix Twin Railway.

Notwithstanding the difficulties created by the war, our preparations for many of our new 1939 models were far enough advanced to secure the inclusion in this catalogue of the following new items.

"The Coronation Scot," a replica in miniature of the famous L.M.S. train shown at the World's Fair in New York. (Ready.)

L.M.S. 4-4-0 Compound Loco and Tender, a model very often asked for by our friends. (In preparation.)

L.N.E.R. 4-4-0 "Hunt" Class Loco and Tender, an excellent reproduction of its prototype. (In preparation.)

Scale Model Pullman Car. (Ready.)

Crane Truck Set and Crane on Base. (In preparation.)

Derelict Coach Hut. (Ready.)

Scenic Backgrounds and Miniature Posters. (Ready.)

Many other very interesting items were planned but had perforce to be put aside with a view to release when conditions permit.

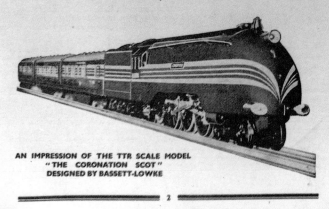

AN IMPRESSION OF THE TTR SCALE MODEL
"THE CORONATION SCOT"
DESIGNED BY BASSETT-LOWKE

2

NEW SCALE MODEL LOCOS

DESIGNED BY BASSETT-LOWKE

THE latest additions to the range of Scale Model Locos. are shown on this page. First there is the Model of the "Coronation Scot" Loco, a beautiful reproduction of its prototype; it looks and acts like the real thing. And then two 4-4-0 Engines; one of the well-known L.M.S. Compound, and the other the popular L.N.E.R. "Hunt" Class.

L.M.S. "CORONATION SCOT" LOCO AND TENDER

No. 2/542.

Length overall 10½ ins.

Latest T.T.R. six-coupled mechanism, precision made, all parts interchangeable, tender fitted with remote control uncoupling device, main axle bearings with continuous lubrication. 100 per cent. remote control. Special mechanism in tender makes it possible to detach the loco. from its train, anywhere on the track without railside devices. This uncoupling device is operated from the controller. With headlight and dummy bell. Hand-painted, lined and lettered in the correct lake and gold colours of the latest L.M.S. "Coronation Scot."

L.M.S. 4-4-0 STANDARD COMPOUND LOCOMOTIVE. No. 2/536

No. 2/536. Model of the famous 3-cylinder Compounds introduced on the Midland Railway and associated with the name of R. M. Deely. A large number of these engines is now working on the L M S Special Trix Twin Movement of latest type, body and tender pressure die cast from steel moulds, ensuring accurate detail. Loco and Tender hand painted in correct L.M.S. colours with lettering and lining according to latest practice.

L.N.E.R. 4-4-0 LOCO AND TENDER. No. 4/536

No. 4/536. A realistic model of the well-known "Hunt" Class Locomotives of the L.N.E.R. Special Trix Twin Movement of latest type, body and tender pressure die cast from steel moulds, ensuring accurate detail. Hand-painted in correct L.N.E.R. colour, with lettering and lining according to latest practice.

NOTE.—4-4-0 Locos.—In preparation. Delivery of these Models (L M S and L.N.E.R.) will commence as soon as the preparations are completed

3

SCALE MODELS TTR

DESIGNED BY BASSETT-LOWKE

TWO TRAINS ON THE SAME TRACK UNDER SEPARATE CONTROL ——— IDEAL SIZE FOR MODERN ROOMS

4-6-2 PACIFIC TYPE LOCOMOTIVES

L.M.S. "PRINCESS" CLASS
No. 2/540

L.N.E.R. "FLYING SCOTSMAN"
No. 4/540

Latest TTR six-coupled mechanism—precision made—all parts interchangeable—main axle bearing with continuous lubrication, 100 per cent. remote control. Fitted with remote control uncoupling device in the tender, which makes it possible to detach the locomotive from its train anywhere on the track without railside devices. This uncoupling device is operated from the controller. Body and tender pressure die cast from steel mould, ensuring accurate detail. Walschaert's valve gear. L.M.S. tender 6 wheels ; L.N.E.R. tender 8 wheels. The whole hand painted in correct Companies colours with lettering and lining according to latest practice.

REMOTE CONTROL UNCOUPLING

Tender | *Carriage*

Hook depressed & disengaged

This device makes the operation of a Trix Twin Railway much more realistic and interesting. By its use the locomotives shown can be detached from their trains **at any point on the track**, by remote electrical control, without the use of ramp rails and without alteration to the controller or circuits.

SUPER CONTROLLER

No. 475. Intended specially for the 4-6-2 "Pacific" type locos., this Super Controller has been designed and added to the T.T.R. range. Fitted with 24 stages of control (as compared with 16 on the standard Controller) it affords, quite obviously, considerably increased flexibility of control. The Locos. work with either the Super or the Standard Controller, but the possibilities for fine control are greater with the Super Controller. This also applies to its use with 0-4-0 Locos and 4-4-0 Locos.

No. 475

4

TTR SCALE MODELS

DESIGNED BY BASSETT-LOWKE

SCALE MODEL EXPRESS TRAINS

In Presentation Cabinets, comprising 4-6-2 Loco. and Tender with uncoupling device in tender, one First Class and two brake Third Class Coaches. Coaches fitted for uncoupling with ramp rail, Super Controller, Plugs, Wire and Instruction Book, all packed in handsome presentation cabinets.

No. 2/347. "Coronation Scot," a model of the famous L.M.S. streamlined train shown at New York Worlds Fair. Finished in standard L.M.S. lake colour with stripes in light buff.

No. 2/344. "Royal Scot," a model of the popular L.M.S. Express to the North, with "Princess" Class Loco.

No. 4/344. "Flying Scotsman," a model of the famous L.N.E.R. East Coast Express Trains, with "Flying Scotsman" Loco.

Rails, etc., packed separately. See pages 9-10-11.

The illustration below shows the "Royal Scot" Express Train as set up on the line.

For full individual specifications, see pages 3, 4 (Locomotives) and 13 (Coaches).

5

TRAIN SETS

Electrically operated from A.C. Mains through Transformers, from D.C. Mains through Converters, or from Accumulators.

TWO TRAINS ON THE SAME TRACK UNDER SEPARATE CONTROL—IDEAL SIZE FOR MODERN ROOMS

TRIX PERMANENT WAY is packed in self-contained complete formations *apart* from the trains. Eight layouts are available, suitably graded, complete with necessary Points, Levers, Plugs, Wire, Buffer Stops, ⅓ and/or ½ Rails, and Crossings, ready to lay down according to PLAN enclosed. Also included with each set is the T.T.R. PERMANENT WAY MANUAL, a fascinating treatise, profusely illustrated, written by a well-known Model Railway Expert.

All TTR LOCOS, without exception, are fitted and priced complete with Distant Control Reversing Gear built in with the mechanism.

No. 2/324—L.M.S. GOODS TRAIN

Supplied as shown in L.M.S. No. 2/324, L.N.E.R. No. 4/324, or S.R. No. 5/324.

RAILS EXTRA.

Goods Engine and Tender (Black with correct details), I high-sided open Truck, I Tank Truck, I low-sided open Truck and I Goods Brake Van. Automatic Couplings, fitted throughout for marshalling and shunting. Correct colours, lettering and lining. With Controller, 6 Plugs, Wire and Oil, and fully illustrated Book of Instructions, in handsome red box. Length of Train, 20 ins.

No. 2/314—L.M.S. SUBURBAN TRAIN

Supplied as shown in L.M.S. No. 2/314, or L.N.E.R. No. 4/314.

RAILS EXTRA.

Tank Locomotive Passenger Type in correct colours and details with 2 Standard Suburban Coaches and I Guards Van, correct colours, lettering and lining. With Controller, 6 Plugs, Wire and Oil and fully illustrated Book of Instructions, in handsome red box. Length of Train, 14½ ins. Automatic couplings throughout.

Rails are packed separately from the Train Sets. See pages 9, 10 and 11.

Owing to the variations of electric supply systems, Transformers or Converters are not included in the Train Sets, and should be ordered separately.

6

 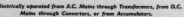

TRAIN SETS

Electrically operated from A.C. Mains through Transformers, from D.C. Mains through Converters, or from Accumulators.

No. 2/334—L.M.S. EXPRESS PASSENGER TRAIN

Passenger Engine and Tender in correct colours, lining and lettering, two bogie Brake Thirds and one bogie First Class Coach, the three of the latest all-steel type. Finished in correct colours, lettering and lining. Automatic couplings fitted throughout. With I Controller, 6 Plugs, Wire and Oil and a fully illustrated Book of Instructions. Packed in strong, handsome red box. Length of Train 28 ins.

Also supplied in L.N.E.R. No. 4/334 and S.R. No. 5/334.

RAILS EXTRA.

STANDARD TWINS

For the convenience of those who wish straightaway to take advantage of the unique " two trains on one line " feature, also for gift purposes, we provide sets with TWO trains and the necessary equipment (excepting rails). These sets contain I Passenger Express Train (as above), and I Goods Train (as facing page above), available in three Company's colours : L.M.S. 2/358, L.N.E.R. 4/358, S.R. 5/358. **RAILS EXTRA.**

THE OFFICIALLY APPROVED
SOUTHERN ELECTRIC
DESIGNED BY BASSETT-LOWKE

THE THREE-COACH TRAIN

consists of a model Third Class Motor Coach (7 in. long), containing a specially designed motor working off 14 volts A.C. or 12 volts D.C.; two Bogie Coaches (7 in. long, one First Class Corridor and one Brake Third Corridor) fitted with automatic couplings; 12 curved rails and 4 straight rails, making an oval track 28 in. by 42½ in. The motor is fitted in the front bogie of the motor coach and the reverser in the rear bogie. Controller for starting, stopping, and regulating the speed of the train, complete with Automatic Cut-out; Plugs and Connectors; Bottle of Lubricating Oil; and a complete Book of Instructions. Packed in an attractive Presentation Box covered with green enamelled paper, and smart label designed by the Southern Railway.

**Train Set No. 5/375. With rails.
MOTOR COACH only, No. 5/530**

THIS MODEL HAS THE OFFICIAL APPROVAL OF THE SOUTHERN RAILWAY.

7

CONTROL

How to Operate Trains from Mains and Accumulators.

POWER for operating T.T.R. Trains, Points and Lamps is obtained either from the Main Electricity Supply or from Accumulators. Where the Mains are Alternating Current (A.C.) which is the usual type of current, then a T.T.R. Transformer is used to reduce the voltage of the main to the 14 volts required by the T.T.R. engines.

Where the Mains are Direct Current (D.C.), sometimes also named Continuous Current, it is necessary to use a Converter. This converter delivers current at the correct voltage for the T.T.R. engines.

Where no mains are available, or in the case of D.C. supply where a converter is not wanted, it is possible to drive T.T.R. engines by means of Accumulators with an output of 12 volts, a pressure much in use for car lighting or ignition purposes.

Note.—For full instructions, see T.T.R. Instruction Book supplied with each Train Set, or separately.

TTR SINGLE TRANSFORMER

No. 481. For operating from A.C. Mains. Specially designed for T.T.R. Engines. Absolutely safe. Output 14 volts at 1 ampere. Complete with flex and adaptor.

TTR DOUBLE TRANSFORMER

No. 485. For operating from A.C. Mains. Specially designed for T.T.R. Engines. Absolutely safe. Output 14 volts at 3 amperes. Sufficient amperage for two Trains, Points and Lamps. Complete with flex and special plug adaptor.

TTR STANDARD CONTROLLER

No. 470. Neatly designed unit, giving perfect control from slow to fast. With Automatic Cut-out, ensuring perfect safety. Starting, stopping and reversing operated by button in centre of control ring.

TTR SUPER CONTROLLER

No. 475. Intended especially for the 4-6-2 "Pacific" type locos, this Super Controller has been designed and added to the T.T.R. range. Fitted with 24 stages of control (as compared with 16 on the Standard Controller) it affords, quite obviously, considerably increased flexibility of control. The Locos. work with either the Super or the Standard Controller, but the possibilities for fine control are greater with the Super Controller. This also applies to its use with 0-4-0 Locos and 4-4-0 Locos.

TTR CONVERTER

(Not illustrated)

No. 491/240. For operating from D.C. Mains. Specially designed for T.T.R. Engines. Absolutely safe. Output 40 watts. Complete with flex. When ordering, state voltage of mains supply.

8

TRACK UNITS

AS TTR Trains are now packed without track, we offer eight different Track Formations, each complete with all necessary parts to make the layout shown in the diagrams. (See Pages 10 and 11.) All parts for one formation are packed in one box. Included with each Set is a copy of the T.T.R. PERMANENT WAY MANUAL, written by a well-known Model Railway Expert, replete with illustrations and information.

At the same time, all Rails, Points, Crossings, etc., are also available separately as before.

Rails, Points and Crossings all mounted on real Bakelite Bases. Perfect Insulation—Rigid—Smooth —Non-Scratching—Non-Bending.

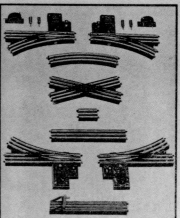

420/1	Straight Rail, 7¼ in. long.
420/¼	Straight Quarter Rail, 1⅞ in. long.
425/1	Straight Terminal Rail, 7¼ in. long.
410/1	Curved Rail, 7¼ in. long.
410/½	Curved Half Rail, 3⅝ in. long.
415/1	Curved Terminal Rail, 7¼ in. long.
430	Crossing, 7¼ in. long.
440	Points—Hand Operated, 7¼ in. long.
443	Points—Remote Control, Complete with Two Point Levers, Plugs and Wire, 7¼ in. long.
418	Permanent Switch for Track Sectioning or Lighting, Red.
448	Lever Section for Remote Points, Black.
865	Buffer Stop with Rail, 7¼ in. long.

Gauge 00 (16 mm.). Radius 13½ in

RAIL JOINT ENTIRELY NEW

Simply move one or both rails sideways or up or down, and they disconnect of their own accord. For joining, place one rail next to the other on the table and push together. Easy to join firmly, just as easy to take apart, but impossible to bend or damage in disconnecting. No long connecting pins or plates ; therefore no damaging of rail ends.

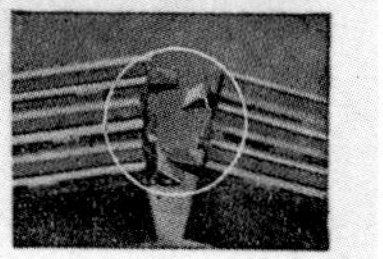

UNCOUPLER RAIL—See page 11.

9

PERMANENT WAY FORMATIONS

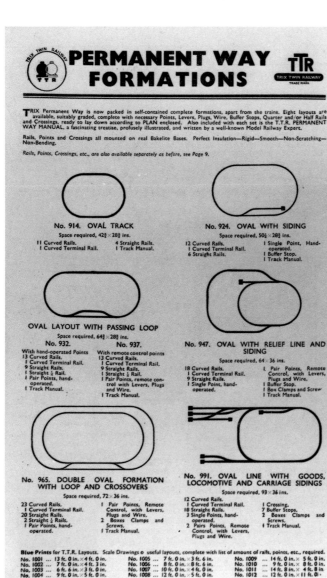

TRIX Permanent Way is now packed in self-contained complete formations, apart from the trains. Eight layouts are available, suitably graded, complete with necessary Points, Levers, Plugs, Wire, Buffer Stops, Quarter and/or Half Rails and Crossings, ready to lay down according to PLAN enclosed. Also included with each set is the T.T.R. PERMANENT WAY MANUAL, a fascinating treatise, profusely illustrated, and written by a well-known Model Railway Expert.

Rails, Points and Crossings all mounted on real Bakelite Bases. Perfect Insulation—Rigid—Smooth—Non-Scratching—Non-Bending.

Rails, Points, Crossings, etc., are also available separately as before, see Page 9.

No. 914. OVAL TRACK
Space required, 42¾ × 28¾ ins.

11 Curved Rails.	4 Straight Rails.
1 Curved Terminal Rail.	1 Track Manual.

No. 924. OVAL WITH SIDING
Space required, 50½ × 28¾ ins.

12 Curved Rails.	1 Single Point, Hand-operated.
1 Curved Terminal Rail.	1 Buffer Stop.
6 Straight Rails.	1 Track Manual.

OVAL LAYOUT WITH PASSING LOOP
Space required, 64¾ × 28¾ ins.

No. 932.   No. 937.

With hand-operated Points	With remote control points
13 Curved Rails.	13 Curved Rails.
1 Curved Terminal Rail.	1 Curved Terminal Rail.
9 Straight Rails.	9 Straight Rails.
1 Straight ½ Rail.	1 Straight ½ Rail.
1 Pair Points, hand-operated.	1 Pair Points, remote control with Levers, Plugs and Wire.
1 Track Manual.	1 Track Manual.

No. 947. OVAL WITH RELIEF LINE AND SIDING
Space required, 64 × 36 ins.

18 Curved Rails.	1 Pair Points, Remote Control, with Levers, Plugs and Wire.
1 Curved Terminal Rail.	1 Buffer Stop.
9 Straight Rails.	1 Box Clamps and Screw.
1 Single Point, hand-operated.	1 Track Manual.

No. 965. DOUBLE OVAL FORMATION WITH LOOP AND CROSSOVERS
Space required, 72 × 36 ins.

23 Curved Rails.	1 Pair Points, Remote Control, with Levers, Plugs and Wire.
1 Curved Terminal Rail.	2 Boxes Clamps and Screws.
20 Straight Rails.	1 Track Manual.
2 Straight ½ Rails.	
1 Pair Points, hand-operated.	

No. 991. OVAL LINE WITH GOODS, LOCOMOTIVE AND CARRIAGE SIDINGS
Space required, 93 × 36 ins.

12 Curved Rails.	1 Crossing.
1 Curved Terminal Rail.	7 Buffer Stops.
18 Straight Rails.	2 Boxes Clamps and Screws.
3 Single Points, hand-operated.	1 Track Manual.
2 Pairs Points, Remote Control, with Levers, Plugs and Wire.	

Blue Prints for T.T.R. Layouts. Scale Drawings o useful layouts, complete with list of amount of rails, points, etc., required.

No. 1001 ... 13 ft. 0 in. × 4 ft. 0 in.	No. 1005 ... 7 ft. 0 in. × 3 ft. 6 in.	No. 1009 ... 14 ft. 0 in. × 5 ft. 0 in.
No. 1002 ... 7 ft. 0 in. × 4 ft. 3 in.	No. 1006 ... 8 ft. 0 in. × 8 ft. 6 in.	No. 1010 ... 7 ft. 0 in. × 8 ft. 0 in.
No. 1003 ... 6 ft. 6 in. × 3 ft. 0 in.	No. 1007 ... 10 ft. 0 in. × 4 ft. 0 in.	No. 1011 ... 14 ft. 8 in. × 4 ft. 8 in.
No. 1004 ... 5 ft. 0 in. × 5 ft. 0 in.	No. 1008 ... 12 ft. 0 in. × 5 ft. 0 in.	No. 1012 ... 12 ft. 0 in. × 11 ft. 0 in.

10

UNCOUPLING BY REMOTE CONTROL

UNCOUPLER TRACK FORMATION

Uncoupler Track Formation. No. 956. Oval, with Relief Line and Uncoupler Siding. Space required, 64 × 36 ins.

18 Curved Rails.	1 Pair Points, Remote Control, with Levers, Plugs and Wire.
1 Curved Terminal Rail.	1 Buffer Stop.
9 Straight Rails.	1 Box Clamp and Screws.
1 UNCOUPLER SET.	1 Track Manual.
1 Single Point, Hand-operated.	

UNCOUPLER RAMP RAIL

UNCOUPLER SET

No. 427. Consisting of one Uncoupler Ramp Rail (illustrated), with electro-magnetic mechanism for raising and lowering ramp in centre of rail and one red "on" and "off" lever for operating the ramp, necessary plugs and wire, and with detailed illustrated instructions.

No. 31/90. UNCOUPLER PARTS

True to the principles upon which our range is developed, we also supply a set of Uncoupler Parts which put the T.T.R. owner in a position to convert in a very simple manner any vehicle in his possession into an Uncoupler Vehicle. The result is that existing rolling-stock does not become obsolete, but is brought up-to-date with this simple and inexpensive equipment. Full instructions for fitting the parts are included with each set.

The illustration shows the action of uncoupling just after the moment of impact of striker stirrup against raised ramp.

UNCOUPLING OF WAGONS AND CARRIAGES

With the addition of these Uncoupler Sets to any suitable layout, and by using vehicles fitted with Uncoupler Parts, remote control uncoupling can be performed in a trailing direction at the command of the operator at his control switchboard. The main principle of this wagon and carriage uncoupler is the use of an electrical remote control ramp, acting on a special lifting stirrup striker or trigger, fitted on the coupling and a new shaped coupling link. The ramp rail is fitted with a large number plate which both marks its position and identifies it with the switch, which can be similarly numbered. The rail ramp is a magnetic device inserted in a special length of straight rail in the centre of the middle conductor rail. The actual ramp-piece is of non-conducting material, and does not interfere with the electric propulsion system.

REALISTIC SHUNTING

The advent of these Uncoupler Sets and Parts, and their use in conjunction with the Twin Train principle and its manifold possibilities in the way of sectioning, means that real Railway shunting in all its many variations can now be added to all existing and projected T.T.R. layouts.

The introduction of well-planned Goods and Carriage Shunting Yards, coupled, where desired and where space allows, with Shunting Humps, will provide endless amusement and interest.

By reference to Chapter VII of the Permanent Way Manual, it will be possible to reproduce with T.T.R. all the intricate operations involved in receiving a mixed Goods Train, sorting out and marshalling the outgoing trains in a most realistic and workmanlike manner.

11

LOCOMOTIVES

 # ROLLING STOCK

All T.T.R. LOCOS.—without exception—are fitted and priced complete with Distant Control Reversing Gear built in with the mechanism.

IDEAL SIZE FOR MODERN ROOMS

No. 2/520. L.M.S. Passenger Engine and Tender. In correct L.M.S. Lake with appropriate lettering, numbering and lining.

No. 2/525. L.M.S. Goods Engine and Tender. Black with Red lining and correct lettering and numbering.

No. 2/510. L.M.S. Tank Loco-Passenger Type. Black with Red lining and correct lettering and numbering.

No. 2/515. L.M.S. Tank Loco-Goods Type. Black with correct lettering and numbering.

No. 4/520. L.N.E.R. Passenger Engine and Tender. In correct L.N.E.R. Green with appropriate lettering, numbering and lining.

No. 4/525. L.N.E.R. Goods Engine and Tender. Black with Red lining and correct lettering and numbering.

No. 4/510. L.N.E.R. Tank Loco - Passenger Type. Black with Red lining and appropriate lettering and numbering.

No. 4/515. L.N.E.R. Tank Loco-Goods Type. Black with correct lettering and numbering.

No. 5/520. S.R. Passenger Engine and Tender. In correct S.R. Green with appropriate lettering, numbering and lining.

No. 5/525. S.R. Goods Engine and Tender. Black with correct lettering and numbering.

No. 5/510. S.R. Tank Loco-Passenger Type. In correct S.R. Green with appropriate lettering and numbering.

No. 5/515. S.R. Tank Loco-Goods Type. Black, with Green lining and correct lettering and numbering.

For Scale Model Locomotives, see Pages 3 and 4.

SOUTHERN RAILWAY MOTOR COACH

No. 5/530. Realistic Model of the S.R. Motor Coaches. Motor fitted in the front bogie : the reverser is fitted in the rear bogie.

SCALE MODEL COACHES Designed by **BASSETT-LOWKE**

They are made throughout of best steel plate, accurately pressed from precision dies. All windows are glazed with transparent "Celastoid." Latest type bogies. Axle boxes to scale are fitted under the main frames. Fitted for automatic coupling and for remote control uncoupling (see page 11). Finish : lettering and lining are in the latest correct style. Length 8¾ ins.

L.M.S.		L.N.E.R.	
2/567	First Class.	4/567	First Class.
2/577	Brake Third.	4/577	Brake Third.
2/587	Dining Car.	4/587	Restaurant Car.

"CORONATION SCOT" COACHES,
L.M.S.
No. 2/568 First Class.
No. 2/578 Brake Third.

PULLMAN CAR—Saloon.

Excellent Model in correct colours. No 598.

All of the above 11 Scale Model Coaches are designed to take Coach Lighting Units, which enhance the realism of these models tremendously. Coach Lighting Units, No. 767, with instructions.

EXPRESS BOGIE COACHES

Modern All-Steel Type, perfect proportions, correct colouring, lettering and lining. "Celastoid" windows throughout. Automatic couplings. Length 7 ins.

L.M.S.	L.N.E.R.	S.R.
2/560 First Class.	4/560 First Class.	5/560 First Class.
2/570 Brake Third.	4/570 Brake Third.	5/570 Brake Third.
2/580 Dining Car.	4/580 Restaurant Car.	5/580 Restaurant Car.
		5/590 Solid Third.

The above Express Bogie Coaches (7 ins. long) do not lend themselves to interior lighting.

SUBURBAN COACHES & VANS

Correct colours, lettering and lining. Good proportions. Automatic Couplings. "Celastoid" windows. 3¼ ins. long.

L.M.S.	L.N.E.R.
2/550 Coach	4/550 Coach
2/555 Brake Van.	4/555 Brake Van.

12   13

BOGIE WAGONS
AND AMERICAN ROLLING STOCK

SCALE DIMENSIONS

IN compliance with frequent requests from our friends, we introduced a series of Bogie Goods Vehicles, particulars of which are set out below. They are constructed throughout of steel, very realistically, with the characteristic details of each type well brought out.

The British Types, Nos. 671, 673, 675, 676, are fitted with uncoupler parts ready to operate with the Uncoupler Ramp Rail (see page 11).

No. 675. Scale Model of the well-known L.N.E.R. Bogie Brick Wagon ; correct brick colouring and lettering ; 6 ins. long.

No. 673. Bogie Timber Wagon with uprights and load of timber ; 6 ins. long.
No. 671. Bogie Bolster Wagon similar to above, but without load ; 6 ins. long.

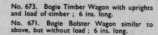

No. 676. Scale Model of the popular L.M.S. High Capacity Bogie Wagon ; correct L.M.S. colouring and lettering ; 6 ins. long.

AMERICAN MODELS

Although specially designed for the American and Canadian markets, these Models will, no doubt, be welcome to many of our friends. Length 6 ins.

No. 681. Flat Car.
No. 682. Lumber Car, empty.
No. 683. Lumber Car, loaded.
No. 684. Gondola Car.

No. 685. Box Car, Tuscan Red.
No. 686. Refrigerator Car, White.
No. 687. Fruit Car, Yellow.

 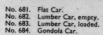 

No. 689. Texaco Oil Tank Car, aluminium colour.
No. 688. Union Oil Tank Car, Red.

No. 690. Caboose, excellent model.

14

GOODS VEHICLES
Correct colours, numbering, lettering and lining. Perfect proportions.
AUTOMATIC COUPLINGS fitted throughout for marshalling and shunting.

661 S.R. Refrigerator Van.
660 Assorted Company's Tarpaulin Trucks.
604 Private Owner, Trix.
605 Private Owner, Bassett-Lowke.

2/603 L.M.S. High-sided.
4/603 L.N.E.R. High-sided.
5/603 S.R. High-sided.

2/650 L.M.S. Goods Brake.
4/650 L.N.E.R. Goods Brake.

662 Timber Truck.

5/650 S.R. Goods Brake.
612 Container Truck, with removable container.

606 Coal Trucks with coal, assorted Co.'s.
609 Ballast Truck with ballast, assorted Co.'s.

627 L.M.S. Cattle Truck.
643 Shell Oil, red.
640 Esso-Tank, yellow.
645 United Dairies, green.

4/601 L.N.E.R. Low-sided.
2/601 L.M.S. Low-sided.

  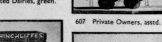

4/621 L.N.E.R. Covered Van.
2/621 L.M.S. Covered Van.

607 Private Owners, assorted.

607 Private Owners, asstd.
600 L.M.S. Platform or three-plank Truck.

15

ACCESSORIES

MODEL CRANE ON BASE

No. 715. Realistic *working* Crane, detachable. Base designed to fit into the system of " Many-Ways " Platforms. (*In preparation*)

DERELICT COACH HUT

No. 2/551. Realistic Replica of the Coach Retreat often seen at Country Wayside Stations. A fascinating addition to any layout.

MODEL BREAK-DOWN CRANE TRUCK SET

No. 615. Set of two Vehicles with Crane. Consisting of Crane Truck with working Crane, detachable, and companion Vehicle with rest for Crane Jib and Tool Box. Crane can be removed and placed on Platform. (*In preparation*)

SCENIC BACKGROUNDS

Scenic Backgrounds for 00 Gauge Railways, carefully designed so that all ends fit each other in all possible combinations. Best colour litho. work. Made in lengths of 36 in. × 9½ in. high. Three designs : No. 147 Fields ; No. 148 Hills ; No. 149 Sea.

Or in Sets of three different designs : No. 150.

MINIATURE POSTERS

No. 145. Comprehensive assortment of Miniature Posters, suitable for " Many-Ways " buildings and fences and for other 00 gauge buildings.

16

ACCESSORIES

IN order that the realism of the Trix Twin Railway shall reach the same high level within the station area as on the track, there is available a wide range of accessories and equipment, in the form of station staff, passengers, trackside signals and posts, etc., etc. These are all beautifully modelled and their dimensions are correct to scale.

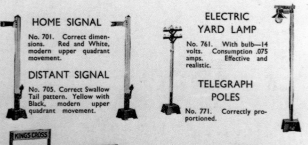

HOME SIGNAL

No. 701. Correct dimensions. Red and White, modern upper quadrant movement.

DISTANT SIGNAL

No. 705. Correct Swallow Tail pattern. Yellow with Black, modern upper quadrant movement.

ELECTRIC YARD LAMP

No. 761. With bulb—14 volts. Consumption .075 amps. Effective and realistic.

TELEGRAPH POLES

No. 771. Correctly proportioned.

STATION SEATS

Bench Type, correctly modelled, finished in Grey. Double seat has Station Nameplate, assorted names.
No. 142. Double Seat with station nameplate.
No. 141. Single Seat.

No. 143. Transfers of 12 different Station Names (for both sides), 2 Sheets of 12 Names each.

STATION FIGURES

Scale size Passengers, Railway Personnel, Platform Equipment and Merchandise. Made for T.T.R. Railway by BRITAIN'S of London. Of exact scale dimensions and finished in good taste. Sold in five assortments, viz. :

No. 101.	Railway Personnel	7 figures.
No. 111.	Passengers	7 "
No. 125.	Passengers	15 "
No. 131.	Merchandise	12 pieces.
No. 105.	Platform Equipment with Merchandise	20 "

SPARE PARTS

No. 31/1	Armature with Commutator.	No. 31/30	Motor Side Frame, etc.
No. 31/2	Piston Rods and Arms.	No. 31/36	Four pairs Bakelite Wheels.
No. 31/3	One Set Reduction Gear.	No. 31/40	One set Collector Shoes.
No. 31/5	Reversing Control Shaft.	No. 31/50	Six Plugs.
No. 31/10	Reversing Arm and Pawl.	No. 31/78	One Bottle Shell Trix Oil.
No. 31/12	Assortment of screws, Nuts.	No. 31/85	One Coil Wire.
No. 31/15	Five Coupling Hooks, 10 Links.	No. 31/94	Contact Shoes for Coach Lighting.
No. 31/20	25 Coupling Links.	No. 31/99	T.T.R. Instruction Book.
No. 31/25	25 each Clamps, Screws.	No. 31/200	Track Manual.
No. 31/27	Set Carbon Brushes.	No. 31/212	Many-Ways Handbook.

17

SIGNALS

REMOTE CONTROL SIGNALS WITH LIGHT.
SCALE DIMENSIONS FOR 00 GAUGE.
A REALLY REMARKABLE ACHIEVEMENT

THESE signals are certain to meet with the unqualified approval of all 00 Gauge Model Railway enthusiasts. Great ingenuity has been applied to the problems of remote control and of electric lighting, and as a result a real thrill is experienced in operating the red and green lights from a distance by throwing over the levers on the control switches. These latter are the standard lever frame units ; the black, No. 448, is a make-and-break switch for operating the semaphore arms and red and green spectacles, while the red, No. 418, is an on-and-off switch for the light behind the spectacles. In accordance with the latest railway practice, the semaphores are arranged to move in the upper quadrant.

The lamp supplied in these new signals is a marvel of ingenuity, fulfilling its purpose perfectly without appearing clumsy or out of proportion. This has been arranged by placing the minute glass bulb inside a brass tube ; the latter is fitted near the top of the signal pole and is provided with a small hole opposite the bulb filament. At the back of the bulb another small hole allows a white light to show to the rear, as in current railway practice. A cover plate is provided on the top of the tube to exclude unwanted light and to hold the bulb in position.

The signal relay and mechanism is of a new and ingenious design, fitting into the base of the signal realistically and without undue bulk.

No. 731. Home Signal with Red Semaphore, upper quadrant movement ; 4 in. high.

No. 735. Distant Signal with Yellow Semaphore, upper quadrant movement ; 4 in. high.

No. 738. Set of two, Home and Distant Signals, with Black Make-and-break Lever Frame Section, Plugs, Wire and Instructions.

18

BUILDINGS

MODERNITY has spread through all phases of Railway Buildings and all the new Signal Boxes are built in a style that reflects this treatment. Our Signal Boxes, which are quite up-to-date are in keeping with this tendency, and also match up with our "Many-Ways" Stations.

No. 62. COUNTRY SIGNAL BOX
This is a simple design of a Standard Box in use in small Wayside Stations and at points on the main line. Fitted with windows glazed with "Celastoid" and outside steps. Size : $4 \times 2\frac{1}{2} \times 3\frac{1}{2}$ in. high.

(NOT ILLUSTRATED)	
862	Footbridge—straight across.
863	Footbridge—angle approach.
805	Terminus Station, built of best hardwood.
847	Goods Shed, built of best hardwood.

No. 65. OVERHANGING SIGNAL BOX
This is the type in use at Junctions where ground space is of the utmost consideration. The Box is specially designed to have its foundation between two roads and overhanging the up and down line. Fitted with "Celastoid" glazed windows, entrance stairs, etc. Size : $6\frac{1}{2} \times 2 \times 4\frac{1}{2}$ in. high.

No. 67. GANTRY SIGNAL BOX
An attractive and striking design of a modern Signal Box, suitable for a terminus station. It is so arranged as to bridge one up and down road and one single road. The Box is fitted with glazed "Celastoid" windows. Size : $9\frac{1}{2} \times 2 \times 4\frac{1}{2}$ in. high.

No. 69. SQUARE WATER TOWER
The type of Tower in use in many Provincial Stations, finished in reinforced concrete and square tank on top. Size : $3\frac{1}{2} \times 2 \times 4$ in. high.

No. 71. CARRIAGE SHED
Plain roof, windows and posters on walls. Size : $7\frac{1}{2} \times 6$ in.

No. 73. ENGINE SHED
Shaped roof with chimneys, windows in walls. Size : $7\frac{1}{2} \times 6$ in.

19

56

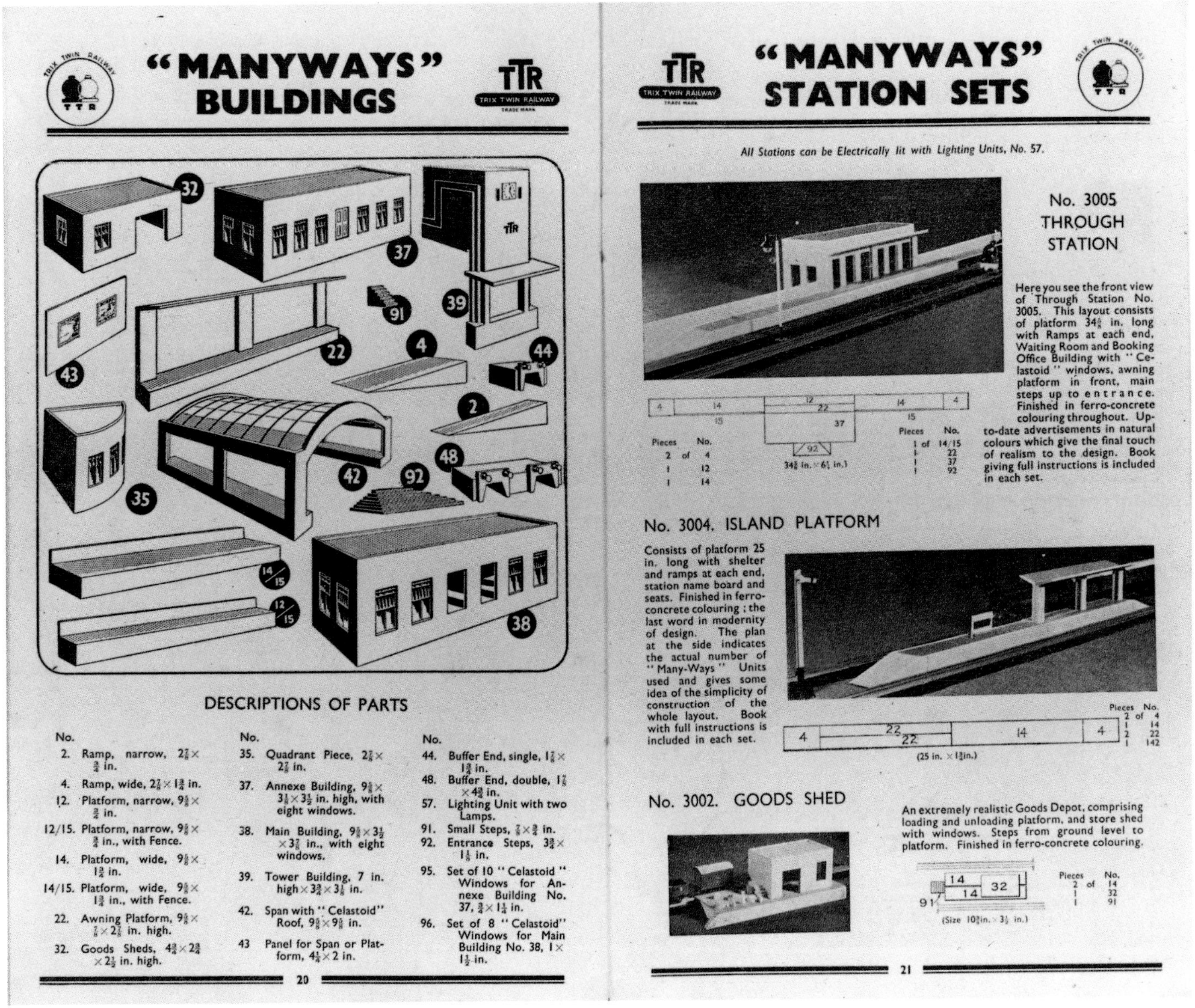

"MANYWAYS" BUILDINGS

TTR TRIX TWIN RAILWAY TRADE MARK

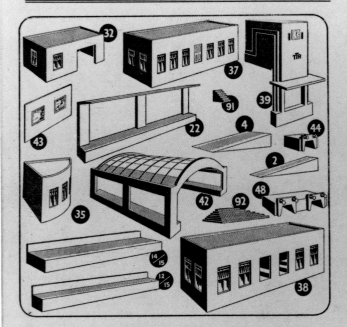

DESCRIPTIONS OF PARTS

No.		No.		No.	
2.	Ramp, narrow, $2\frac{7}{8}\times\frac{3}{4}$ in.	35.	Quadrant Piece, $2\frac{7}{8}\times 2\frac{7}{8}$ in.	44.	Buffer End, single, $1\frac{7}{8}\times 1\frac{3}{4}$ in.
4.	Ramp, wide, $2\frac{7}{8}\times 1\frac{3}{4}$ in.	37.	Annexe Building, $9\frac{5}{8}\times 3\frac{1}{8}\times 3\frac{1}{2}$ in. high, with eight windows.	48.	Buffer End, double, $1\frac{7}{8}\times 4\frac{3}{4}$ in.
12.	Platform, narrow, $9\frac{5}{8}\times\frac{3}{4}$ in.	38.	Main Building, $9\frac{5}{8}\times 3\frac{1}{2}\times 3\frac{7}{8}$ in., with eight windows.	57.	Lighting Unit with two Lamps.
12/15.	Platform, narrow, $9\frac{5}{8}\times\frac{3}{4}$ in., with Fence.	39.	Tower Building, 7 in. high $\times 3\frac{3}{4}\times 3\frac{1}{8}$ in.	91.	Small Steps, $\frac{7}{8}\times\frac{3}{4}$ in.
14.	Platform, wide, $9\frac{5}{8}\times 1\frac{3}{4}$ in.	42.	Span with "Celastoid" Roof, $9\frac{5}{8}\times 9\frac{5}{8}$ in.	92.	Entrance Steps, $3\frac{3}{4}\times 1\frac{1}{8}$ in.
14/15.	Platform, wide, $9\frac{5}{8}\times 1\frac{3}{4}$ in., with Fence.	43	Panel for Span or Platform, $4\frac{1}{4}\times 2$ in.	95.	Set of 10 "Celastoid" Windows for Annexe Building No. 37, $\frac{3}{4}\times 1\frac{1}{4}$ in.
22.	Awning Platform, $9\frac{5}{8}\times\frac{7}{8}\times 2\frac{7}{8}$ in. high.			96.	Set of 8 "Celastoid" Windows for Main Building No. 38, $1\times 1\frac{1}{2}$ in.
32.	Goods Sheds, $4\frac{3}{4}\times 2\frac{3}{4}\times 2\frac{1}{2}$ in. high.				

20

"MANYWAYS" STATION SETS

TTR TRIX TWIN RAILWAY TRADE MARK

All Stations can be Electrically lit with Lighting Units, No. 57.

No. 3005 THROUGH STATION

Here you see the front view of Through Station No. 3005. This layout consists of platform $34\frac{5}{8}$ in. long with Ramps at each end, Waiting Room and Booking Office Building with "Celastoid" windows, awning platform in front, main steps up to entrance. Finished in ferro-concrete colouring throughout. Up-to-date advertisements in natural colours which give the final touch of realism to the design. Book giving full instructions is included in each set.

Pieces	No.
2 of	4
1	12
1	14
1 of	14/15
1	22
1	37
1	92

($34\frac{5}{8}$ in. $\times 6\frac{1}{4}$ in.)

No. 3004. ISLAND PLATFORM

Consists of platform 25 in. long with shelter and ramps at each end, station name board and seats. Finished in ferro-concrete colouring; the last word in modernity of design. The plan at the side indicates the actual number of "Many-Ways" Units used and gives some idea of the simplicity of construction of the whole layout. Book with full instructions is included in each set.

Pieces	No.
2 of	4
1	14
2	22
1	142

(25 in. $\times 1\frac{3}{4}$ in.)

No. 3002. GOODS SHED

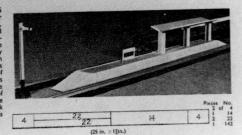

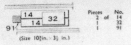

An extremely realistic Goods Depot, comprising loading and unloading platform, and store shed with windows. Steps from ground level to platform. Finished in ferro-concrete colouring.

Pieces	No.
2 of	14
1	32
1	91

(Size $10\frac{3}{8}$ in. $\times 3\frac{1}{2}$ in.)

21

"MANYWAYS" STATION SETS

No. 3021. SUBURBAN STATION

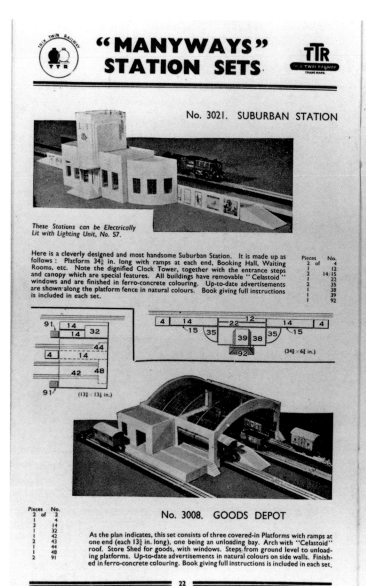

These Stations can be Electrically Lit with Lighting Unit, No. 57.

Here is a cleverly designed and most handsome Suburban Station. It is made up as follows : Platform 34¾ in. long with ramps at each end, Booking Hall, Waiting Rooms, etc. Note the dignified Clock Tower, together with the entrance steps and canopy which are special features. All buildings have removable " Celastoid " windows and are finished in ferro-concrete colouring. Up-to-date advertisements are shown along the platform fence in natural colours. Book giving full instructions is included in each set.

Pieces		No.
2	of	4
1		12
2		14/15
1		22
2		35
2		38
1		39
1		92

(34¾ × 6¼ in.)

(13¾ × 13¼ in.)

No. 3008. GOODS DEPOT

As the plan indicates, this set consists of three covered-in Platforms with ramps at one end (each 13¾ in. long), one being an unloading bay. Arch with "Celastoid" roof. Store Shed for goods, with windows. Steps from ground level to unloading platforms. Up-to-date advertisements in natural colours on side walls. Finished in ferro-concrete colouring. Book giving full instructions is included in each set.

Pieces		No.
2	of	2
3		14
1		32
1		42
2		43
1		44
1		48
2		91

22

"MANYWAYS" STATION SETS

No. 3025. TERMINAL STATION

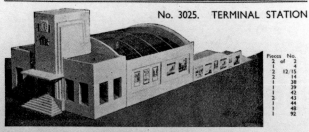

This Terminal Station is a typical example of the amazing realism achieved by the Trix " Many-Ways " Station Sets. It comprises two main line and one local Platform, each 27 in. long with correct shape Buffer Stops at rear, ramps in front, Booking Hall, Waiting Rooms and Clock Tower. All buildings have removable " Celastoid " windows and are finished in ferro-concrete colouring. Latest advertisements in natural colours complete the design. Platforms covered in by " Celastoid " arched roof. A very fine layout indeed. Book giving full instructions is included in each set.

(27 × 9½ in.)

Pieces		No.
2	of	2
2		4
2		12/15
2		14
1		38
3		39
2		42
2		43
2		44
1		48
1		92

No. 3043. THROUGH STATION

Comprises two main line and one local Platform, with ramps at each end and measuring 34¾ in. in length. Arch with " Celastoid " roof covers the platforms. The up side has Booking Hall, Waiting Room and Clock Tower with dignified entrance steps, etc. Down side has large Waiting Room. All buildings fitted with removable " Celastoid " windows. Up-to-date advertisements in colour along platform fences. Finished in ferro-concrete colouring throughout. Book giving full instructions is included in each set.

(34¾ × 19 in.)

Pieces		No.
4	of	2
2		4
2		12/15
3		14
2		22
2		35
1		37
1		38
1		39
1		42
1		43
4		44
1		48
1		92
2		142

All stations can be Electrically lit with Lighting Unit, No. 57.

23

"MANYWAYS" STATION SETS

TTR — TRIX TWIN RAILWAY — TRADE MARK.

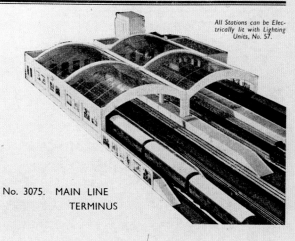

All Stations can be Electrically lit with Lighting Units, No. 57.

No. 3075. MAIN LINE TERMINUS

Comprises five Platforms with ramps at one end, 35¾ in. long. Correct shape Buffer Stops at end of all lines. Platforms covered in by four arches with "Celastoid" roofs. Buildings consist of Booking Hall, Clock Tower, Waiting Rooms and Enquiry Offices and have removable "Celastoid" windows. Large Steps to main entrance —two series of smaller steps to side buildings and Double Seats. Finished in ferro-concrete colouring and up-to-date advertisements in colour on platform walls. The parts in this set can be arranged in nine different alternative layouts. Book giving full instructions is included in each set.

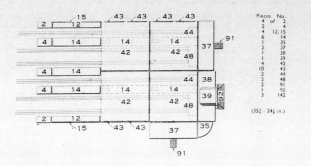

(35¾ × 24¼ in.)

OTHER TTR PUBLICATIONS:

Permanent Way Manual. A remarkable book written by a well-known Railway expert, dealing with the layout, planning and working possibilities of the Trix Twin Railway.

Instruction Book. Giving full illustrated instructions for the operation of the Trix Twin Railway.

T.T.R. Gazette. Issued at intervals **free to all registered** Trix Twin Railway owners, this magazine deals with all matters of interest to model railway enthusiasts. Do not forget—you must register your name and address to get it.

"Many-Ways" Handbook. Profusely illustrated, showing the possibilities for erecting "Many-Ways" Station Sets and Units.

Printed in England by De Vere Press, Ltd., London, W.C.1

24

REVISED TTR PRICE LIST — OCT. 1939

Owing to the uncertain conditions created by the War the prices shown here are subject to alteration without notice. The manufacturers will make every effort to supply the goods listed, but regret that they can give no guarantee of delivery.

No.	ARTICLE	Fixed Retail Price ea.
2/314	Sub'n Pass'ng'r L.M.S.	33/-
4/314	" L.N.E.	33/-
2/324	Goods Train L.M.S.	37/6
4/324	" L.N.E.	37/6
5/324	" S.R.	37/6
2/334	Pass'ng'r Bogie L.M.S.	43/-
4/334	" L.N.E.	43/-
5/334	" S.R.	43/-
2/344	Royal Scot	140/-
4/344	Flying Scotsman	140/-
2/347	Cr'n'tion Scot L.M.S.	140/-
2/358	Stand'd Twins L.M.S.	76/-
4/358	" L.N.E.	76/-
5/358	" S.R.	76/-
5/375	Motor Train S.R.	60/-
914	Track Formation	16/3
924	" "	27/-
932	" "	35/-
937	" "	44/-
947	" "	57/-
956	" " with uncplr set	64/6
965	" "	77/6
991	" "	110/-
420/1	Straight Rail	-/10½
420/	" Quarter Rail	-/9½
425/1	" Terminal Rail	1/8
427	Uncoupler Rail	7/6
410/1	Curved Rail	-/10½
410/	" Half Rail	-/9½
415/1	" Terminal Rail	1/8
418	Sectioning Switch	1/9
430	Crossing	4/-
440	Points, Hand, per pair	11/6
443	Points, Remote, pair	21/-
448	Point Levers	1/9
470	Controller	9/-
475	" Super	16/-
481/240	Transformer Single	12/9
485/240	" Double	27/6
491/240 DC	Converter	45/-
2/510 L.M.S.	Loco, Tank Passenger	18/6
4/510 L.N.E.	"	18/6
5/510 S.R.	" Green	18/6
2/515 L.M.S.	Goods, Tank	18/6
4/515 L.N.E.	"	18/6
5/515 S.R.	"	18/6
2/520 L.M.S.	Eng'e & Tender, Cols.	20/-
4/520 L.N.E.	"	20/-
5/520 S.R.	"	20/-
2/525 L.M.S.	Goods do. do. Black	20/-
4/525 L.N.E.	"	20/-
5/525 S.R.	"	20/-

No.	ARTICLE	Fixed Retail Price ea.
5/530 S.R.	Motor Coach	33/-
7/530 L.P.T.	London Transport Eng.	20/-
2/536 L.M.S.	4-4-0 Eng. & Tender	42/-
4/536 L.N.E.	4-4-0	42/-
2/540 L.M.S	4-6-2 Princess	97/6
4/540 L.N.E.	4-6-2 Flying Scot	97/6
2/542 L.M.S.	Coronation Scot Loco	97/6
2/550 L.M.S.	Suburban Coach	1/8
4/550 L.N.E.	"	1/8
2/551 L.M.S.	Der. Coach Hut	3/-
2/555 L.M.S.	Suburban Guards Van	1/8
4/555 L.N.E.	"	1/8
2/560 L.M.S.	Bogie Coach 1st	4/-
4/560 L.N.E.	"	4/-
5/560 S.R.	"	4/-
2/567 L.M.S.	Scale Model Coach 1st	8/6
4/567 L.N.E.	"	8/6
5/567 S.R.	"	8/6
2 568 L.M.S	Coronation	8/6
2/570 L.M.S.	Bogie Coach 3rd Compo	4/-
4/570 L.N.E.	"	4/-
5/570 S.R.	"	4/-
2/577 L.M.S.	Scle Mdl Cch 3rd & Van	8/6
4/577 L.N.E.	"	8/6
5/577 S.R.	"	8/6
2/578 L.M.S.	Coronation	8/6
2/580 L.M.S.	Bogie Dining Car	4/-
4/580 L.N.E.	"	4/-
2/587 L.M.S.	Scale Model Dining Car	8/6
4/587 L.N.E.	Scale Mdl Rest'rn't	8/6
5/590 S.R.	Bogie, 3rd Solid	4/-
598	Pullman Saloon	9/6
600	Platform Truck	1/6
2/601 L.M.S.	Open Truck low sided	1/3
4/601 L.N.E.	"	1/3
2/603 L.M.S.	Open Truck high sided	1/3
4/603 L.N.E.	"	1/3
5/603 S.R.	"	1/3
604	Open "Trix Ltd"	1/6
605	do."Bassett Lowke"	1/6
606	Coal Truck	1/6
607	Pte. Own's Assorted	1/6
609	Ballast Truck	1/6
612	Container Truck	1/9
615	Crane Truck Set	9/6
2/621 L.M.S.	Covered Van	1/9
4/621 L.N.E.	"	1/9
627	Cattle Truck	2/-
640	Tank ESSO, Yellow	2/3
643	" SHELL, Red	2/3
645	" "United Dairies"	2/3
2/650 L.M.S.	Goods Brake	2/-
4/650 L.N.E.	"	2/-

No.	ARTICLE	Fixed Retail Price ea.
5/650	Goods Brake S.R.	2/-
660	Tarpaulin Truck	2/3
661	Refrigerator Truck	1/9
662	Timber Truck	1/9
671	Bogie Bolster Wagon	3/6
673	" Timber "	3/-
675	" Brick "	3/6
676	High Capacity Wagon	3/6
681	Flat Car	3/-
682	Lumber Car Empty	3/6
683	" Loaded	4/-
684	Gondola Car	4/-
685	Box Car	4/6
686	Refrigerator Car	4/6
687	Fruit Car	4/6
688	Tank Car Red	5/-
689	Tank Car Aluminium	5/-
690	Caboose	6/-
701	Home Signal	1/3
705	Distant Signal	1/3
715	Crane on base	5/6
731	Rmte Home Sgnl with light	8/6
735	Rmte Distant Sgnl with lights	8/6
738	Remote Signal Sets Home & Distant with Fittings	18/6
761	Yard Lamp, electric	3/-
767	Lghtng units for Cches. 567-577-587	3/-
771	Telegraph Poles	-/7
862	Foot Bridge	2/3
863	" AngleApprch	2/9
865	Buffer Stop wich Rail	2/3
31/1	Armature with Com.	3/-
-/6	Piston Rods and Arms	/6 1set
-/3	1 Set Red'tion Gears	-/6
-/5	Reversing Cont. shaft	1/6
-/10	" Arm and Pawl	-/6
-/12	Ass. of Screws, Nuts	/- set
-/15	5 Cplg hooks, 10 Lnks.	-/6 set
-/20	25 Coupling links	1/3 box
-/25	25 ea. Clamps, Screws	1/3 set
-/27	Set Carbon Brushes	1/3 set
-/30	Motor side Frame etc.	1/-
-/36	4 prs, Bakelite wheels	1/3 4 prs.
-/40	1 set Collector shoes	1/6 set
-/50	6 plugs	-/8 set
-/75	2 spare El. Bulbs 14v.	1/9 for 2
-/78	1 Bot. Shell Trix Oil	-/4
-/85	1 Coil Wire	-/4
-/88	Bulb for Rmt. Signal	1/6
-/90	Uncplr Striker & Link	1/3 set
-/94	Contact Shoes for Scale Model Coach Lighting	
-/99	TTR Instruction Book	-/4
-/200	Track Manual	1/6
-/212	Many Ways Handbook	1/3

"TRIX" MANY-WAYS STATION BUILDING SETS and Single UNITS.

No.	ARTICLE	Price	No.	ARTICLE	Price	No.	ARTICLE	Price
3002	Goods Shed	5/-	38	Main Building	5/6	105	Platf'm Ac. & Mrchse.	2/4
3004	Island Platform	7/6	39	Tower	6/6	111	Passengers	1/2
3005	Through Station	12/9	42	Span with Roof	11/6	125	Passengers	2/4
3008	Goods Depot	23/6	43	Panel	-/3	131	Merchandise	1/2
3021	Suburban Station	27/6	44	Buffers, single		141	Seat Single	-/7
3025	Terminal Station	33/-	48	" double	4/3	142	Seat Double	-/7
3043	Up & Down Thro Stn.	54/-	57	Lghtng unit for 37 or 38	3/-	143	Transfers, 2 sheets of 12 each for	-/9
3075	Four Span Terminus	93/-	62	Country Signal Box	4/-	145	Posters set	1/3
2	Ramp, narrow	-/4	65	New style signl bx dble	6/-	147	Scenic Backgrounds	
4	" wide	-/6	67	" Gantry type	8/6		" single—Fields	1/10
12	Platform, narrow	-/9	69	Water Tower	2/9	148	" —Hills	1/10
12/15	" with fence	1/4	71	Carriage Shed	4/6	149	" —Sea	1/10
14	Platform, wide	1/2	73	Engine Shed	5/6	150	" Set of 3	5/6
14/15	" with fence	1/9	91	Steps, single	-/4			
22	Awning Platform	2/9	92	" Main Entrance	-/10			
32	Goods Building	2/9	95	Window, small Set of 10	-/9			
35	Quadrant	4/-	96	" large 8	-/9			
37	Annexe Building	5/-	101	Railway Personnel	1/2			

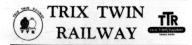

TRIX TWIN RAILWAY

To all registered T.T.R. enthusiasts

We have pleasure in sending you herewith a copy of our 1939/40 catalogue which, we feel sure, will be of great interest.

You will find in it many new productions, some of which are ready and others which are in preparation, the most outstanding being:

"THE CORONATION SCOT," a replica in miniature of the famous L.M.S. train shown at the World's Fair in New York.
L.M.S. 4-4-0 COMPOUND LOCO AND TENDER.
L.N.E.R. 4-4-0 "HUNT" CLASS LOCO AND TENDER.
SCALE MODEL PULLMAN CAR.
MODEL BREAK-DOWN CRANE TRUCK SET.
DERELICT COACH HUT.
SCENIC BACKGROUNDS and MINIATURE POSTERS.

All new equipment is designed to be interchangeable and to fit in with your present set. Nothing in it has become obsolete through these new additions.

When you are in any difficulty, or in doubt how to get the best results when operating your T.T.R. layout, do not hesitate to write to us. We shall be delighted to help you to solve your problems.

TRIX LIMITED.

1018/74/1139.

An insert included with the 1939 catalogue showing the intended program of new items for 1939.

October 1939 price list included with the 1939/40 catalogue.

A wartime advertisement.

THE EARLY POST-WAR PERIOD

With the end of the war in Europe in May 1945, the reorganisation of full-time production of Trix and Bassett-Lowke items quickly got under way at Precision Models Ltd, but progress in quantity production was hampered by the strict rationing of raw materials, and the pending supply to the home market was to be limited as the emphasis towards export was encouraged to help to reduce the war debt. The Trix reorganisation once again required financial restructuring and a consolidation of the manufacturing base.

During June 1945, the freehold factory occupied by Precision Models in Stimpson Avenue was purchased for £17,500 from George Green & Sons Ltd of Leicester. This latter company had occupied the premises for the manufacture of boots until 1931 when they vacated to allow Winteringham Ltd, (later Precision Models), to use it as a manufacturing base. This purchase was partly financed by a mortgage for £12,000 created with a local Building Society on the premises of Precision Models Ltd and land occupied by the factory. Thus, the manufacturing base for Trix items was now secure.

The following months saw a complicated restructuring and distribution of the shares and an increase in the company capital to £25,000. Although the Trix personnel holding shares remained the same, the major part of the issued shares were held by the Merchant Bankers, Rothschild (Nominees) Ltd and Nutraco (Nominees) Ltd, the latter being a subsidiary of S. G. Warburg & Co. Ltd. Shares to the value of £5,000 were unissued and held as capital reserve. Financial agreements made in 1938 and 1941 with the New Trading Co Ltd, (S. G. Warburg &

HOWARD & REGNIA, THE STUDIO   FELIXSTOWE

A Precision Models 'Works Outing' circa 1948.

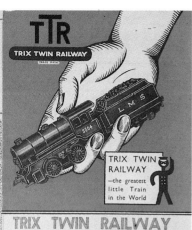

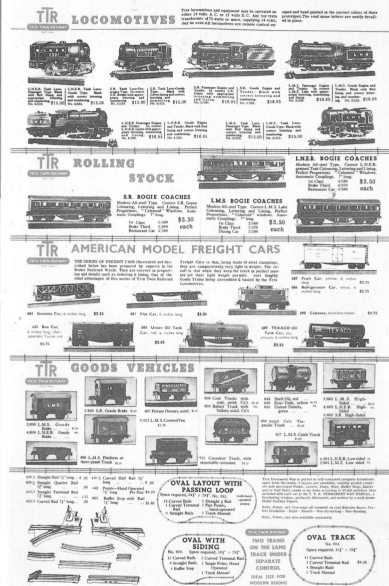

Special 1947
TTR catalogue
for America.

Co. Ltd), which enabled production to expand during the early years, were satisfied. Thus, the scene was set for the resumption of production in Britain of Trix Twin Railways and other Trix products.

The main driving force and policy maker behind the reorganisation of Trix Ltd and its factory at Stimpson Avenue was undoubtedly Siegfried Kahn. He was always involved in product design and development, and travelled every Thursday to Northampton to check on the various aspects of production. In fact, it has been mentioned that he, along with Franz Bing, were the only members of the Trix staff in London who wished to visit Precision Models Ltd. One very important decision that he made was to retain the 3-rail Trix Twin system with the very coarse flanged wheels for the locomotives and rolling stock instead of changing to a finer scale. His argument was that he had an obligation to his many existing customers and also that it worked well. In later years this unfortunate decision was to have a disastrous effect on the fortunes of Trix in the face of keen competition from other model railway manufacturers.

One factor for which the directors of Trix Ltd must have been very grateful was that Precision Models was an extremely harmonious factory with a family atmosphere. This no doubt helped to maintain high standards and a willingness to put just that little bit of extra effort into the work enabling orders to be met on time, subject, of course, to the restrictions on the supplies of raw materials imposed by the Ministry of Supply.

The latter part of 1945 and the first few months of 1946 were taken up with the com-

pletion of various War Office contracts, one of which was making a specialised part for the BTH Co. Ltd who produced electronic items including the transistor in its early form of development. This part required the boring of a 0.005" diameter hole down the middle of a 1/16" diameter mild steel rod. Another wartime contract of note was the manufacture of scale models of the famous Bailey Bridge, which were completed in their hundreds during the war and sent out in sets to Military centres so that training on the assembly of the model could be given in readiness for the assembly of the full size version

Post-war Trix Construction Unit Sets.

This advertisement appeared in a German Toy Trade magazine in February 1947. It states: 'To our friends. Our factory remained untouched. At the moment we work for export only and because of this please do not ask us any questions. We hope that it will not be long before we can supply you with what you require.' Which factory this statement refers to is unknown!

when the time arose. These Bailey Bridge models were produced on the second floor of the factory, and on completion of the contract this floor was taken up mainly with the assembly of TTR items under the watchful eye of the foreman, Frank Gratton.

The first Trix items to come off the post-war production line were the 'A', 'B' and Tricy-Trix Construction sets. No parts of the system produced at the factory before the outbreak of hostilities survived the needs of the war, except for a model of the Sydney Harbour Bridge which was subsequently donated to the children's ward of a Northampton hospital. The Construction set strips and other parts were produced by three special presses on the ground floor, but it was not until late in 1946 that the full range of Trix Construction parts became available, and then, incredibly, 4,000 of the 'A' and 'B' type sets were produced per day during the 1946/47 period. The stamping of the printed tinplate sheets ready for forming into rolling stock, and the forming of the tinplate rails ready for fixing to the bakelite bases were carried out by much larger presses installed on the same floor. These stamped and formed parts were then sent to the basement where the Construction sets were packed and the rolling stock and track assembled. Dick Walters was the man in charge of the basement and, being an ex-serviceman, he took pride in his and other's work. Also included on the ground floor alongside other types of machinery was the joiner's shop which, in the late 1930s, had produced the early TTR railway buildings and the later wooden 'Many-Ways' buildings.

The third floor was taken up with the paint shop under the expert and skilled guidance of George E. Cotton who had joined Winteringham Ltd in 1909 at the rate of 8d, (almost 3·5p), an hour. All the locomotive lining was done by hand, and the high quality of lining found on Bassett-Lowke and Trix engines was a tribute to the skill of this man and to the staff to whom he had passed on his skills. Most of the top floor was used for packing. Space was always at a premium within the factory and a warehouse in Adelaide Street was used as a goods in-and-out store for the Construction Set side of the business and as a packing store for all other Trix products, such as cartons, train boxes and inserts for the X-Acto products introduced in the 1950s.

Although most of the output of Precision Models Ltd was now involved with items for Trix Ltd, a significant percentage was still taken up with production for Bassett-Lowke Ltd, the directors of Trix Ltd taking a view that they owed W. J. Bassett-Lowke a debt of gratitude for all the help and kindness given to them in their hour of need before the war. The workforce was well looked after by Bindon Blood, but he was a Bassett-Lowke man and did not take too kindly to the 'toy' production for Trix Ltd with the result that he put a lot of his work load onto the shoulders of F. J. Prior, a good practical man who put ideas into practice.

By mid-1946 production of the Trix Twin

Bill Best at the controls of a Trix layout at the 1947 British Industries Fair.

Railway was well under way, but quantity was hampered by the lack of steel available and demand soon outstripped supply. The shop and store owners had to order their quota of three sets per quarter twelve months in advance, and many times the 'Trix Office', within the confines of Precision Models Ltd, had to juggle the despatch of sets so that all the shops in a particular town received their orders at the same time to keep everyone happy.

The situation in Germany was far more difficult, but Vereinigte Spielwarenfabriken Andreas Förtner & J. Haffner's Nachf. soon took the road to recovery despite severe bomb damage having caused the loss of many of the Trix working drawings and tooling. In addition, there were many peace-time restrictions imposed by the Allied authorities. A business manager, Max Epperlein, was appointed by the Allied Military Government in 1946 to act as executor for the company and to oversee Ernst Voelk.

No production took place in the year 1945-46, and turnover was achieved by the sale of war materials and existing parts. The small auxiliary buildings in Spalt and Koppenhof were sold and the gear-wheel tooling and machinery was sold to Johann Distler K.G. who were also based in Nuremberg and Spalt. Nevertheless, plans were well in hand for the expansion and development of the building acquired from the Spalt community in 1944.

Production started again in a small way in September 1946, although not on the Trix range but on small locks fashioned from existing raw materials and half-finished parts from the war-time production. It was not until the spring of 1947 that spasmodic production of the Trix Metallbaukasten and Trix Express range commenced. However, it was very quickly expanded to include nearly all the range that was available before the war, and this was shown in their first post-war catalogue published in 1949.

In France production of the Trix Construction system and the importation of TTR, and later Trix Express, was recommenced in 1947 by Maison Gobin-Daudé of Paris and continued up to the middle of the 1950s.

In Britain the main production drive was aimed at exports, with Trix Ltd exporting to many countries including South Africa, France, Australia, (sole distributors were Wee Folks Australian Productions Pty. Ltd, Melbourne), America using the agency of Model Trains Inc. of New York, Canada with Menzies & Co. Ltd of Toronto acting as sole distributors, and D. C. Sewell (PVT) Ltd of Salisbury, the distributors in Southern Rhodesia. During 1947/48 unsuccessful negotiations had taken place between Trix Ltd and Model Trains Inc for a joint manufacturing agreement.

1948 saw the introduction of the American style 0-4-0 locomotives and coaches plus the reintroduction of the matching wagons which were at this time only for the export market. The idea for the American locomotives was said to have originated from the daughter of F. J. Prior who settled in the USA after marrying an American serviceman. These locomotives were first shown in the 1948-1949 catalogue which was a folded broadsheet printed on both sides and published in small quantities in May 1948, and also in the 1948 'Export' catalogue published

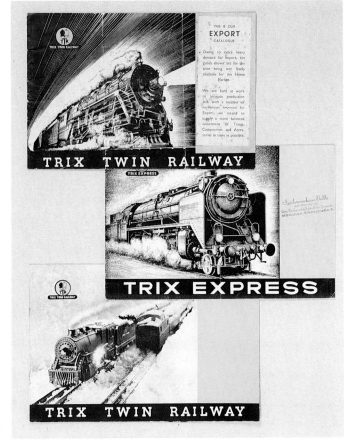

Top: 1948 Trix Twin Railway export catalogue.
Middle: 1949 Trix Express catalogue.
Bottom: 1950 Trix Twin Railway export catalogue.

later in the year but with a much larger printing run. The latter catalogue was a way of getting round the restrictions on the supply of paper, as unless it was to be used in connection with export production, the supply was very limited. These were among the first catalogues advertising the Trix Twin Railway after the war, the first being a single folded sheet published in 1947 for the American and Canadian markets and available from stockists in those countries.

These two 1948 catalogues mention for the first time the new self-lubricating bearings for the armature of the motors, and show the rolling stock and locomotives, which up to 1947 had been fitted with the pre-war style of coupling, now fitted with their 'new uncoupling couplers'. This coupling was a slightly modified version of one designed by S. C. Pritchard, who after the war approached Meccano Ltd, before they got into full production with their Hornby Dublo trains, with the idea of fitting his new design of coupling to their locomotives. Meccano Ltd immediately went into production, having first secured the manufacturing rights for the toy trade from S. C. Pritchard, and showed the coupling at the first Toy Fair after the war in 1946 which in those days was part of the British Industries Fair. At the following fair a year later Trix Ltd also showed the coupling, informing Meccano Ltd that a patent would never be granted. Unfortunately they were wrong as the patent was granted in 1948 in the name of S. C. Pritchard, and proceedings were taken against Trix Ltd in the High Court of Justice, Chancery Division, for the infringement of Letters Patent No.605283. After many years of costly wrangle

between the interested parties, terms of settlement were agreed in 1954, and although Trix Ltd had to pay all costs, they were granted a licence to continue manufacture by S. C. Pritchard in consideration of royalty payments of one farthing, (0.1p), per coupling.

Other interesting inclusions in the 1948 'Export' catalogue are the 'continental' (German-outline) locomotives, namely the Electric Locomotive, the Goods Tank Locomotive, and the Passenger Engine and Tender. All these locomotives were fitted with a British chassis and the new coupling, one interesting fact being that the tender coupled to the passenger locomotive was the British TTR type. These locomotives were assembled at Northampton, and the bodies were definitely among the very first Trix Express parts manufactured in post-war Germany. These 'continental' models were the direct result of a visit to Nuremberg by Siegfreid Kahn and his report to a Directors' meeting of Trix Ltd in February 1948 where it was proposed to place an order with the Nuremberg firm for locomotive bodies, tenders and coaches amounting to about £600. This would have enabled the Northampton factory to complete 2,000/3,000 locomotives of 'continental' type for export to European countries. In actuality only the locomotive bodies were provided. This saw the beginning of the post-war business relationship between the two 'Trix' companies leading to a successful but short reunification.

F. J. Prior, as a reward for all his hard work and technical innovations at Precision Models Ltd, was made director of this company in February 1948, while S. Kahn was made director

in 1949 which enabled the parent company, ie Trix Ltd, to have more control in production. Throughout this period reconstruction and reorganisation within the factory hampered normal trading activities and the drain on the meagre finances available necessitated the factory premises being remortgaged for £5,500 in June 1949. The directors of Trix Ltd must have been very grateful to the workforce at Precision Models Ltd as they showed great loyalty despite their relatively low wages and poor working conditions. In the severe winter of 1947 the factory had to endure many power cuts, sometimes up to three days in duration, and this was the time when the old gas lights were used again and even the old gas soldering irons.

In June 1947, Machinery (Smith's Patents) Ltd ceased to be shareholders of Trix Ltd and transferred their shares to J. D. Kiley who remained as chairman of Trix Ltd until his death in 1953. Thus ended a company relationship which had enabled the infant Trix Ltd to find its feet, a relationship founded on trust and friendship.

Production of Trix in Nuremberg had made a remarkable recovery under the guidance of a design engineer Rudolf Insam, despite the lack of raw materials and the burden of financial problems due to currency reforms. The latter was caused by the abolition of the Reichsmark and the formation on 21 June 1948 of the Deutsche Mark bringing with it a revaluation of monetary values. Rudolf Insam had entered the company in January 1939, taking over from Oswald Fischer as technical manager and was given a free hand as regards design of the Trix range by

The 1948/49
TTR domestic
catalogue.
(H)

TRACK FORMATIONS

TRIX Permanent Way is packed in self-contained complete formations, apart from the trains. Each formation includes the new type uncoupler rail. This is fully described on the back cover. Also included with each formation is the T.T.R. Track Manual, a fascinating treatise, profusely illustrated and written by a well-known Model Railway Expert. Details of the individual component parts, which can be bought separately, are given on the inside page.

915 OVAL TRACK
This is the first of the complete formations, and is a simple oval measuring 41 × 23½ ins. Even with this simple oval layout two trains can be run on the same line if desired.

925 OVAL with SIDING
With this formation simple shunting operations can be carried out. Space required 50 × 28½ ins.

935 OVAL with PASSING LOOP
This layout enables trains to be shunted and run in either direction. Space required 64½ × 36 ins.

939 As above, but with Remote Control Points and Remote Control Uncoupler Set complete with Levers and Wire.

945 OVAL with RELIEF LINE and SIDING
With this layout many realistic train operations can be carried out, including shunting, marshalling and normal running. Space required 64 × 36 ins.

949 As above, but with one pair of Remote Control Points and Remote Control Uncoupler Set complete with Levers and Wire.

949 DOUBLE OVAL with LOOP and CROSSOVERS
Two trains can either run side by side or in opposite directions can be run on this layout. Many variations are possible. Space required 72 × 36 ins.

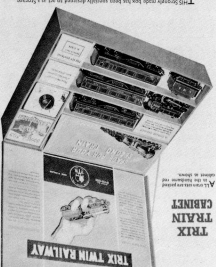

TRIX TWIN RAILWAY
TRAIN CABINET

ALL train sets are packed in the handsome red cabinet as shown.

THIS strongly made box has been specially designed to act as a Storage Cabinet. By removing the packing pieces, there is sufficient space to store two complete trains, plus additional locomotives and rolling stock.

TRAIN SETS

ALL Locomotives and Rolling Stock are in correct colours with appropriate lettering and lining. The new uncoupler couplings are fitted throughout. Packed in a strong, handsome red cabinet as shown on the centre page. Rails are not included in these sets, but are available either in complete formations or single units.

EXPRESS PASSENGER TRAIN
This set comprises Locomotive and Tender with three bogie Coaches, Controller, Plugs, Wire, Oil and fully illustrated Instruction Book. Length of train is 28 ins.
RAILS EXTRA.
Supplied in: 2 334 L.M.S.
2 334 L.N.E.R.
2 334 S.R.

GOODS TRAIN
This set comprises Locomotive and Tender with four Goods Wagons, Controller, Plugs, Wire, Oil and fully illustrated Instruction Book. Length of train is 20 ins.
RAILS EXTRA.

STANDARD TWINS
For the convenience of those who wish straightaway to take advantage of the unique feature of the Trix system whereby TWO TRAINS can run on the same track, we provide sets containing TWO TRAINS made up of one Passenger Train and one Goods Train as described above.

PASSENGER TRAINS—EXPORT ONLY
9 331 American Loco and Tender, 3 American No Rails. Freight Cars.
9 334 American Loco and Tender, 3 Standard No Rails. bogie Coaches.

FREIGHT TRAINS—EXPORT ONLY
9 351 2 American Loco and Tender, 3 American Freight Cars and 3 Standard bogie Passenger Cars. No Rails.

STANDARD TWIN TRAINS, EXPORT ONLY
10 324 Standard Loco and Tender, 3 No Rails. bogie Coaches.
10 326 Standard Loco and Tender, 4 No Rails. Goods Wagons.

TRIX TWIN RAILWAY

GAUGE 00 (16mm.) RADIUS 13½ ins.
ELECTRICALLY OPERATED
For A.C. Mains or for Accumulators

THE Trix Twin Railway provides a miniature system true to life in every detail. Since its introduction many years ago, the T.T.R. has grown to be the most popular and the most realistic model railway yet devised.

The unique feature of the Trix Railway which enables two trains to be run on the same track under separate control—without the need for track sectioning—has increased enormously the possibilities of model railway working.

The tremendous fascination of this independent dual control must be experienced to be fully realised. The trains can be run fast or slow, forward or reverse, switched on to sidings, stopped and started at will. Goods trains can be marshalled in sidings, and with the help of the new uncoupling couplers and uncoupler rails all the operations of shunting can be performed with life-like precision. All this by the press of a key or the turn of a knob.

So for instance, it will be possible with the Trix material to reproduce in miniature a goods marshalling and shunting yard in every particular. You can start with the simplest layout. Then you can add, as they become available, a few items at a time, and you will know that, whatever you add, no part of your equipment will ever be out of harmony with the additions. The whole Trix material is designed together as a system and follows a consistent plan.

British Patent Nos. 451644, 459744, 465168, 469656
471304, 488357, 498651, 545033
Further Patents pending. Numerous Foreign Patents

more popular than ever!

UNCOUPLING by REMOTE CONTROL

A new type uncoupler rail enables locos and rolling stock to be uncoupled at will without the vehicles being touched by hand. Ideal for use in marshalling and shunting yards, stations and for slip coaches. An uncoupler rail is included in all TRACK FORMATIONS. The uncoupler consists of a diamond set in the centre of the

track which can be raised or lowered at will, hand operated or by remote control, see Fig. 1. As the vehicles pass over the uncoupler, the leg on the lower side of the coupling is pressed sideways, see Fig. 2. In Fig. 3 the hooks have uncoupled as each is moved clear of the other.

Uncoupler in closed position for through running.
Uncoupler in raised position ready for action.

Automatic Coupling

ALL locomotives and rolling stock are fitted with the new TRIX coupling. Positive in action, it will not come undone during running periods and couples automatically as soon as two vehicles come lightly into contact with each other. A spur is provided so that where an existing vehicle is fitted with the original type hook, it will couple readily with the new type. Fig. 4 shows two wagons about to couple up. In Fig. 5 the two wagons have met and coupled up. The impact causes each coupling to move sideways until they pass each other when they move back into position making a perfect lock.

The new Uncoupler Coupling.

Snap Fixing Rail Joint

THIS unique fastening enables track to be laid rapidly with perfect fixing and electrical contact. For joining, place one rail next to the other on the table and push together. To disconnect, merely move one or both rails sideways or up or down and they will come apart at once.

MADE IN ENGLAND
TRIX LTD.
91, REGENT ST., LONDON, W.I.
Telephone: REGent. 0661-2-3

CATALOGUE 1948-49

TTR MAIN LINES

TRIX TWIN RAILWAY

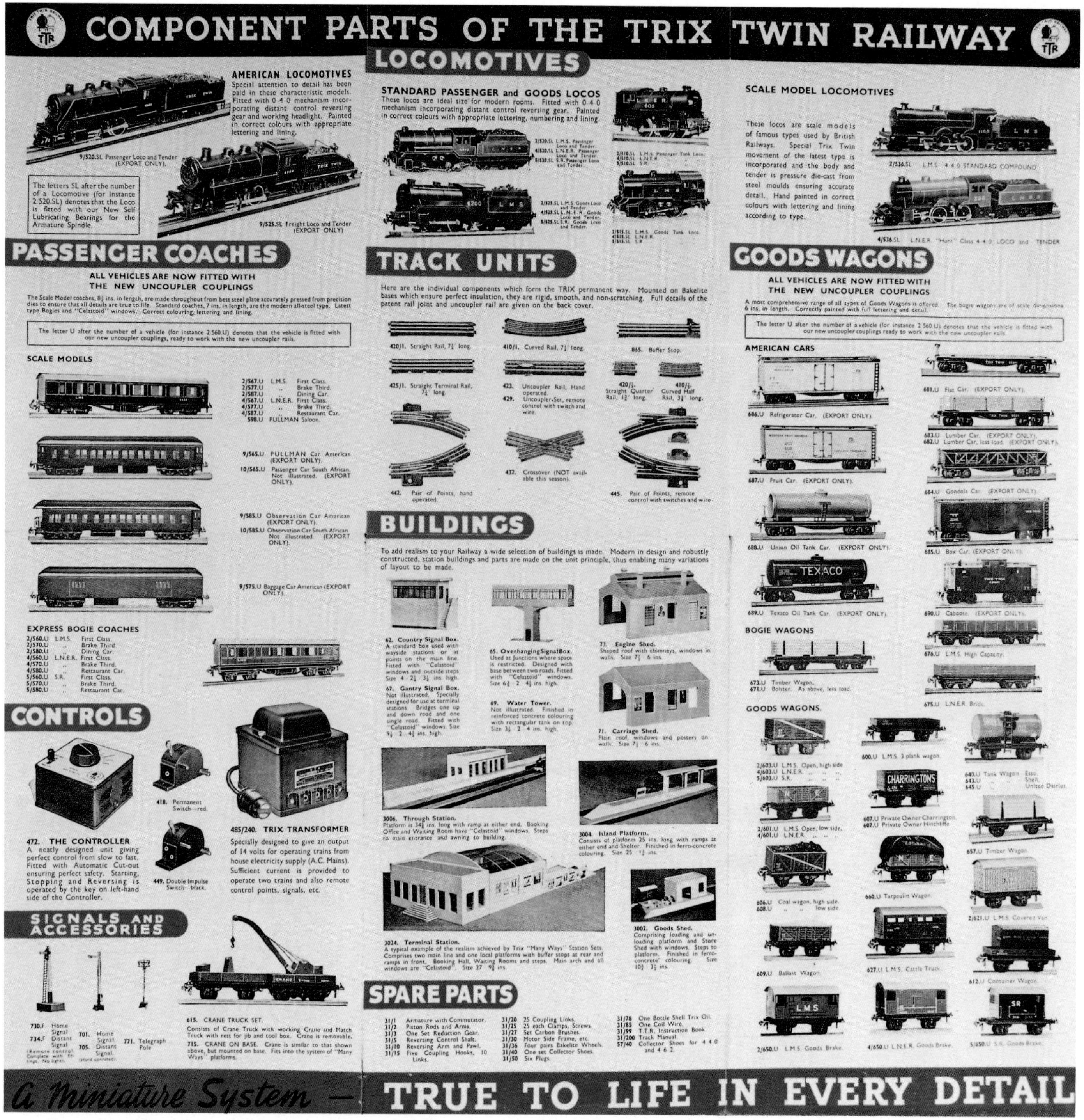

COMPONENT PARTS OF THE TRIX TWIN RAILWAY

LOCOMOTIVES

AMERICAN LOCOMOTIVES
Special attention to detail has been paid in these characteristic models. Fitted with 0 4 0 mechanism incorporating distant control reversing gear and working headlight. Painted in correct colours with appropriate lettering and lining.

9/520.SL Passenger Loco and Tender (EXPORT ONLY).

9/525.SL Freight Loco and Tender (EXPORT ONLY)

The letters SL after the number of a Locomotive (for instance 2/520.SL) denotes that the Loco is fitted with our New Self Lubricating Bearings for the Armature Spindle.

STANDARD PASSENGER and GOODS LOCOS
These locos are ideal size for modern rooms. Fitted with 0 4 0 mechanism incorporating distant control reversing gear. Painted in correct colours with appropriate lettering, numbering and lining.

2/520.SL L.M.S. Passenger Loco and Tender.
4/520.SL L.N.E.R. Passenger Loco and Tender.
5/520.SL S.R. Passenger Loco and Tender.

2/525.SL L.M.S. Goods Loco and Tender.
4/525.SL L.N.E.R. Goods Loco and Tender.
5/525.SL S.R. Goods Loco and Tender.

2/510.SL L.M.S. Passenger Tank Loco.
4/510.SL L.N.E.R. " " "
5/510.SL S.R. " " "

2/515.SL L.M.S. Goods Tank Loco.
4/515.SL L.N.E.R. " " "
5/515.SL S.R. " " "

SCALE MODEL LOCOMOTIVES
These locos are scale models of famous types used by British Railways. Special Trix Twin movement of the latest type is incorporated and the body and tender is pressure die-cast from steel moulds ensuring accurate detail. Hand painted in correct colours with lettering and lining according to type.

2/536.SL L.M.S. 4 4 0 STANDARD COMPOUND

4/536.SL L.N.E.R. "Hunt" Class 4 4 0 LOCO and TENDER

PASSENGER COACHES

ALL VEHICLES ARE NOW FITTED WITH THE NEW UNCOUPLER COUPLINGS

The Scale Model coaches, 8¾ ins. in length, are made throughout from best steel plate accurately pressed from precision dies to ensure that all details are true to life. Standard coaches, 7 ins. in length, are the modern all-steel type. Latest type Bogies and "Celastoid" windows. Correct colouring, lettering and lining.

The letter U after the number of a vehicle (for instance 2/560.U) denotes that the vehicle is fitted with our new uncoupler couplings, ready to work with the new uncoupler rails.

SCALE MODELS

2/567.U L.M.S. First Class.
2/577.U " Brake Third.
2/587.U " Dining Car.
4/567.U L.N.E.R. First Class.
4/577.U " Brake Third.
4/587.U " Restaurant Car.
598.U PULLMAN Saloon.

9/565.U PULLMAN Car American (EXPORT ONLY).
10/565.U Passenger Car South African. Not illustrated. (EXPORT ONLY).

9/585.U Observation Car American (EXPORT ONLY).
10/585.U Observation Car South African Not illustrated (EXPORT ONLY).

9/575.U Baggage Car American (EXPORT ONLY).

EXPRESS BOGIE COACHES

2/560.U L.M.S. First Class.
2/570.U " Brake Third.
2/580.U " Dining Car.
4/560.U L.N.E.R. First Class.
4/570.U " Brake Third.
4/580.U " Restaurant Car.
5/560.U S.R. First Class.
5/570.U " Brake Third.
5/580.U " Restaurant Car.

CONTROLS

472. THE CONTROLLER
A neatly designed unit giving perfect control from slow to fast. Fitted with Automatic Cut-out ensuring perfect safety. Starting, Stopping and Reversing is operated by the key on left-hand side of the Controller.

418. Permanent Switch—red.

449. Double Impulse Switch—black.

485/240. TRIX TRANSFORMER
Specially designed to give an output of 14 volts for operating trains from house electricity supply (A.C. Mains). Sufficient current is provided to operate two trains and also remote control points, signals, etc.

SIGNALS AND ACCESSORIES

730.F Home Signal
734.F Distant Signal
(Remote control Complete with fittings. No lights).

701. Home Signal.
705. Distant Signal.
(Hand operated).

771. Telegraph Pole

615. CRANE TRUCK SET.
Consists of Crane Truck with working Crane and Match Truck with rest for jib and tool box. Crane is removable.

715. CRANE ON BASE. Crane is similar to that shown above, but mounted on base. Fits into the system of "Many Ways" platforms.

TRACK UNITS

Here are the individual components which form the TRIX permanent way. Mounted on Bakelite bases which ensure perfect insulation, they are rigid, smooth, and non-scratching. Full details of the patent rail joint and uncoupler rail are given on the back cover.

420/1. Straight Rail, 7¼" long.

410/1. Curved Rail, 7¼" long.

865. Buffer Stop.

425/1. Straight Terminal Rail, 7¼" long.

423. Uncoupler Rail, Hand operated.

429. Uncoupler-Set, remote control with switch and wire.

420/¼. Straight Quarter Rail, 1¾" long.

410/½. Curved Half Rail, 3⅝" long.

442. Pair of Points, hand operated.

432. Crossover (NOT available this season).

445. Pair of Points, remote control with switches and wire.

BUILDINGS

To add realism to your Railway a wide selection of buildings is made. Modern in design and robustly constructed, station buildings and parts are made on the unit principle, thus enabling many variations of layout to be made.

62. Country Signal Box.
A standard box used with wayside stations or at points on the main line. Fitted with "Celastoid" windows and outside steps. Size 4 × 2¼ × 3¼ ins. high.

67. Gantry Signal Box.
Not illustrated. Specially designed for use at terminal stations. Bridges one up and down road and one single road. Fitted with "Celastoid" windows. Size 9¼ × 2 × 4¼ ins. high.

65. Overhanging Signal Box.
Used at Junctions where space is restricted. Designed with base between two roads. Fitted with "Celastoid" windows. Size 6¾ × 2 × 4½ ins. high.

69. Water Tower.
Not illustrated. Finished in reinforced concrete colouring with rectangular tank on top. Size 3½ × 2 × 4 ins. high.

73. Engine Shed.
Shaped roof with chimneys, windows in walls. Size 7½ × 6 ins.

71. Carriage Shed.
Plain roof, windows and posters on walls. Size 7½ × 6 ins.

3006. Through Station.
Platform is 34⅞ ins. long with ramp at either end. Booking Office and Waiting Room have "Celastoid" windows. Steps to main entrance and awning to building.

3004. Island Platform.
Consists of platform 25 ins. long with ramps at either end and Shelter. Finished in ferro-concrete colouring. Size 25 × 1½ ins.

3024. Terminal Station.
A typical example of the realism achieved by Trix "Many Ways" Station Sets. Comprises two main line and one local platforms with buffer stops at rear and ramps in front. Booking Hall, Waiting Rooms and steps. Main arch and all windows are "Celastoid". Size 27 × 9⅞ ins.

3002. Goods Shed.
Comprising loading and unloading platform and Store Shed with windows. Steps to platform. Finished in ferro-concrete colouring. Size 10¾ × 3½ ins.

SPARE PARTS

31/1 Armature with Commutator.
31/2 Piston Rods and Arms.
31/3 One Set Reduction Gear.
31/5 Reversing Control Shaft.
31/10 Reversing Arm and Pawl.
31/15 Five Coupling Hooks, 10 Links.
31/20 25 Coupling Links.
31/25 25 each Clamps, Screws.
31/27 Set Carbon Brushes.
31/30 Motor Side Frame, etc.
31/36 Four pairs Bakelite Wheels.
31/40 One set Collector Shoes.
31/50 Six Plugs.
31/78 One Bottle Shell Trix Oil.
31/85 One Coil Wire.
31/99 T.T.R. Instruction Book.
31/200 Track Manual.
57/40 Collector Shoes for 4 4 0 and 4 6 2.

GOODS WAGONS

ALL VEHICLES ARE NOW FITTED WITH THE NEW UNCOUPLER COUPLINGS

A most comprehensive range of all types of Goods Wagons is offered. The bogie wagons are of scale dimensions 6 ins. in length. Correctly painted with full lettering and detail.

The letter U after the number of a vehicle (for instance 2/560.U) denotes that the vehicle is fitted with our new uncoupler couplings ready to work with the new uncoupler rails.

AMERICAN CARS

686.U Refrigerator Car. (EXPORT ONLY).
681.U Flat Car. (EXPORT ONLY).
683.U Lumber Car. (EXPORT ONLY).
682.U Lumber Car, less load. (EXPORT ONLY).
687.U Fruit Car. (EXPORT ONLY).
684.U Gondola Car. (EXPORT ONLY).
688.U Union Oil Tank Car. (EXPORT ONLY).
685.U Box Car. (EXPORT ONLY).
689.U Texaco Oil Tank Car. (EXPORT ONLY).
690.U Caboose. (EXPORT ONLY).

BOGIE WAGONS

673.U Timber Wagon.
671.U Bolster. As above, less load.
676.U L.M.S. High Capacity.
675.U L.N.E.R. Brick.

GOODS WAGONS.

2/603.U L.M.S. Open, high side
4/603.U L.N.E.R. " " "
5/603.U S.R. " " "
600.U L.M.S. 3 plank wagon.
640.U Tank Wagon Esso.
643.U " " Shell.
645.U " " United Dairies.
2/601.U L.M.S. Open, low side.
4/601.U L.N.E.R. " " "
607.U Private Owner Charrington.
607.U Private Owner Hinchliffe.
657.U Timber Wagon.
606.U Coal wagon, high side.
608.U " " low side.
660.U Tarpaulin Wagon.
2/621.U L.M.S. Covered Van.
609.U Ballast Wagon.
627.U L.M.S. Cattle Truck.
612.U Container Wagon.
2/650.U L.M.S. Goods Brake.
4/650.U L.N.E.R. Goods Brake.
5/650.U S.R. Goods Brake.

A Miniature System — TRUE TO LIFE IN EVERY DETAIL

Ernst Voelk. Insam's skill is evidenced by the fine models that emerged from the German factory in the 1950s and 1960s, although the innovative technical ideas of Oswald Fischer continued to play a major role well into the 1950s.

The company was in the American Occupation Zone and it was to the War Compensation Court in July 1948 that a successful application was made by H. Oppenheim, F. Bing and his sister L. Sommer, (the latter two being the heirs to the estate of their late father, S. Bing), for a future court hearing to have the 1938 compulsory sale of their former business and resulting agreements declared null and void.

After prolonged negotiations in Nuremberg between H. Oppenheim and Ernst Voelk during the second week of February 1949, an agreement was reached which was submitted to the War Compensation Court in Munich. At the beginning of May the Court decided in favour of the original owners, and declared that a new limited company had to be formed to continue the business of Vereinigte Spielwarenfabriken Andreas Förtner & J. Haffner's Nachf. incorporating its assets and liabilities, and that H. Oppenheim, F. Bing and L. Sommer be allotted shares in the new company. The new limited company was registered on 19 January 1950, but was deemed to have taken effect from 21 June 1948. It was called Trix Vereinigte Spielwarenfabriken GmbH being formed with a capital of DM 260,000 represented by shares. Thus the year's trading of the limited partnership (Kommanditgesellschaft) under Ernst Voelk was taken as the first year's trading of the new limited company, (Gesellschaft mit beschränkter Haftung, or in short GmbH). The refugees were awarded a controlling interest of 152,000 shares of DM 1 each, but elected Ernst Voelk as General Manager. Ernst Voelk and his fellow shareholders from the former business, which was forced to change its name to Ernst Voelk KG on 19 January 1950, were allowed shares in the new company because part of the business which was conducted during the wartime period had nothing at all to do with the business of manufacturing toys, and thus could not be attributed to the enterprise of the refugees.

During February of 1949 a letter from S. Kahn of Trix Ltd to Ernst Voelk stated:

'In view of your talks with Herr Oppenheim at which you expressed concern as to the future of the new Trix company in Nuremberg, please be assured of the following:

'1) We will strive to coordinate the miscellaneous stocks of both firms to be extensively interchangeable and to produce a joint Export Catalogue which will allow the sale of German goods on the open market.

'2) It is planned to incorporate the stocks of both firms into a 'Distribution Company' to act as an Export Agency. Should this not work we will find another practical solution.

'3) It is self explanatory that we will have to make plans to safeguard your export activities, since protection laws only allow the use of the Trade Mark of the German company only in Germany.

'You can rely on us that we will consider the interests of the Nuremberg as well as the English companies and allow both companies to use the original Patents and Trademarks.'

One of the direct results of the above was that 'Polk's' of New York were recruited instead of Model Trains Inc. to act as sole distributors for the sale of the German and British Trix products in America, as shown in a combined catalogue produced in 1949 especially for the American market. This catalogue listed most of the products as shown in the corresponding catalogues for the respective home markets with certain interesting additions. On one of the leader pages it states that all items illustrated in the catalogue were made either in Germany, England or the United States. The items produced by the latter country were a twin AC controller and a street light complete with 18 volt bulb. (Why 18 volts when the Trix system used 14 volts is a mystery).

The first post-war Trix Express catalogue specifically for the German market was, as stated earlier, also issued in 1949, which was understandably of similar design, colour and layout to the TTR 'Export' catalogue of 1948 produced in Britain. This Trix Express catalogue showed nearly all the locomotives and rolling stock that were available before the war and in the same livery, except that the coaches were now without the Reichsbahn emblems, although the goods wagons still bore the words Deutsche Reichsbahn. Even the celebrated Class 71 2-4-2 Super Automatic tank engine was shown, which was also advertised in a German model magazine as being available during the autumn of that year. Although both of the above mentioned catalogues listed the coaches as being from the 'Bundesbahn', the German railway system did not change its name to Deutsche Bundesbahn until the 13 December 1951.

Up to the early 1950s, trade from the Trix Twin Railway was enjoying great success, and if Precision Models Ltd did not ship £1,000 worth of Trix goods a day questions were asked by Siegfried Kahn. A separate Trix Office was created within the Precision Models Ltd factory from where all the invoicing to customers took place. The two or three permanent staff at this office were separate to those of Precision Models Ltd, and each year during this period up to eight temporary typists had to be recruited to cope with the processing of the Trix invoices covering the very large Christmas sales. The staff worked some days from 7.30 in the morning until 10.00 at night.

In 1935 Bassett-Lowke Ltd had been awarded the position of sole concessionaire for Trix products in this country, but this had ceased on the formation of Precision Models Ltd in 1941, and W. J. Bassett-Lowke now only took the roll of advisor and signatory to both Trix Ltd and Precision Models Ltd with Bassett-Lowke now acting as Trix agents.

Head office was still at 91 Regent Street, London where the directors organised the day to day running of Trix, and it was also the address where the Trix locomotives were sent for repair. These repairs were still in the capable hands of Messrs Best and Gaskin assisted for a short time by Michael Catalani, until he em-barked on the task of developing the Trix Construction sets and designing a new range of models from the simple to the sophisticated. In the latter class was the working model of a grandfather clock. Siegfried Kahn told Michael Catalani that before the war he had such a model in his office in Nuremberg and it was his wish that a new model was to be built and the instructions for its construction included in a new manual. No details of the original were available and in addition M. Catalani had no details of the clock's mechanism, but after a seemingly impossible task the clock was duly built. It took pride of place at many British Industries Fairs and ticked away quite happily in its mahogany and glass case for many years. The new Trix Construction manuals were first published in 1947, the 112-page Engineering Manual taking pride of place which, with other Trix manuals, was also translated into German and published by Trix Vereinigte Spielwaren-fabriken GmbH at the turn of the decade.

Counting Instruments Ltd, which was, as mentioned previously, under a joint ownership between H. J. Thormann Engineering Co. Ltd and Trix Ltd, also had its sales office at 91 Regent Street and from there Paul Werner as sales manager, carried out his duties from a desk in the general office from 1945 until the middle of 1949. Although many types of commercial counters were manufactured jointly at Precision Models Ltd and at the H. J. Thormann Engineering Co. Ltd factory at Borehamwood, many cycle accessories were made available to the general public bearing the Trix trademark. These products were six and ten-in-one 'dumbell' spanners, cyclometers, a choice of six mascots, and two types of combination locks. The cyclometers were popular with cyclists, and were available for recording distance in miles or kilometres. Production of these cycle accessories was not hampered by the restriction on the use of steel, as the metal used was mainly the zinc based alloy called mazac, which was an unfortunate choice for the spanners as they had a habit of splitting when in use. The working parts for the cyclometers and locks were manufactured and assembled into the casings supplied by the Borehamwood factory at Precision Models Ltd.

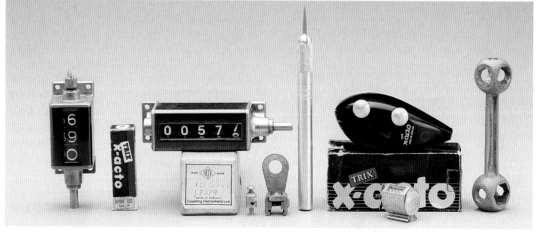

A selection of Trix Counters and Cycle Accessories plus Trix X-Acto handicraft tools.

1950 leaflet showing the Trix Cycle Accessories.

In the early part of 1950 relations between the H. J. Thormann Engineering Co. and Trix became difficult, as Trix required more production space at Precision Models Ltd to cope with increasing orders with the result that the manufacture of the Trix cycle accessories was transferred to Borehamwood. Shortly after, during April 1950, the joint manufacturing agreement between the two companies was terminated and the shares held by Trix Ltd were purchased by H. J. Thormann Engineering Co. Ltd. However, production of the accessories for Trix Ltd continued for several years.

Even with Trix being able to sell all that was produced, the profits of Precision Models in 1947 and again in 1948 were only £7 with Trix not showing much better figures. This lack of substantial profit was mainly caused by high overheads including development costs. The move of the Registered office of Trix Ltd in July 1949 to 11 Old Burlington Street, London W1 can only have aggravated the situation, although at the time it was felt that the new offices would in the long run suit their needs better.

Top: At a Bassett-Lowke 50 years celebration function in 1949. From the front left: F. J. Prior, H. Oppenheim (behind Mr. Prior), Bassett-Lowke's Holborn Branch shop sales manager, F. Bing, S. Kahn and R. Bindon Blood.

From left to right: Franz Bing, J. D. Kiley and W. J. Bassett-Lowke discussing the finer points of Trix in 1949.

SALES		TRIX	TRIX PROGRESSIVE	P.M.L. OTHER THAN TRIX	P.M.L. OTHER THAN TRIX PROGRESSIVE	TOGETHER	TOGETHER PROGRESSIVE
APRIL	1946	1956	1956	2040	2040	3996	3996
	1947	10088	10088	1433	1433	11521	11521
	1948	11932	11932	2656	2656	14588	14588
MAY	1946	5506	7462	2412	4452	7918	11914
	1947	6448	16536	1469	2902	7917	19438
	1948	13522	25454	2719	5375	16241	30829
JUNE	1946	6683	14145	1668	6120	8351	20265
	1947	6952	23488	2249	5151	9201	28639
	1948	12426	37880	2299	7674	14725	45554
JULY	1946	8769	22914	1088	7208	9857	30122
	1947	13499	36987	1776	6927	15275	43914
	1948	10611	48491	2046	9720	12657	58211
AUGUST	1946	5631	28545	1317	8525	6948	37070
	1947	7499	44486	1834	8761	9333	53247
	1948	10284	58775	2096	11816	12380	70591
SEPTB.	1946	5953	34498	1134	9659	7087	44157
	1947	10969	55455	3362	12123	14331	67578
	1948	17659	76435	3501	15317	21160	91751
OCTB.	1946	10683	45181	2127	11786	12810	56967
	1947	14492	69947	6423	18546	20915	88493
	1948						
NOVB.	1946	10309	55490	2839	14625	13148	70115
	1947	13080	83027	4905	23451	17985	106478
	1948						
DECB.	1946	11530	67020	1338	15963	12868	82983
	1947	19179	102206	2432	25383	21611	128089
	1948						
JAN.	1947	9194	76214	2303	18266	11497	94480
	1948	15124	117330	2069	27952	17193	145282
	1949						
FEB.	1947	6957	83171	1986	20252	8943	103423
	1948	8116	125446	2941	30893	11057	156339
	1949						
MARCH	1947	6977	90148	1887	22139	8864	112287
	1948	17667	143113	2518	33411	20185	176524
	1949						

Interesting sales figures for Trix and Precision Models in the early post-war period. It shows just how much Trix production dominated the output of the Northampton factory.

THE SWANSONG YEARS OF THE 1950s

By the end of 1950 reorganisation in Britain was complete and the joint profits of both Trix and Precision Models were looking healthier, fuelled by increased production and demand. The design and development section, which had been at Northampton since late 1939, was very busy working on new projects for the Trix Twin Railway and suggestions for the Trix Express models. However, the man behind most of the Patented technical innovations of the Trix Express models, (and consequently TTR models), was still Oswald Fischer who continued to provide many ideas well into the 1950s. Of the British inspired-designs, Werner Alton was a man who loved gadgets and abounded with a wealth of ideas which he applied to the TTR, ably assisted by F. J. Prior.

Restrictions on the supply of materials were now less severe and during 1950 Trix Ltd applied for a large allocation of steel to increase production capabilities about which they were optimistic. The area required for this expansion at Precision Models was occupied by the Trix office, and it was proposed that this be moved to premises in Abingdon Street in the town centre. Unfortunately, the plans fell through as their allocation request was refused as steel was in great demand and needed for more urgent requirements. It was the shortage of steelplate during this period that resulted in the decision not to proceed with South African models.

Trix Vereinigte Spielwarenfabriken GmbH were also having difficulties with the supply of materials, but nevertheless, according to the minutes of a Partners' meeting in October 1950,

The World's finest miniature railway

TRIX TWIN RAILWAY

PRICES ARE SUBJECT TO ALTERATION WITHOUT NOTICE AND INCLUDE PURCHASE TAX WHERE APPLICABLE.

There's twice the fun with T.T.R. You can run **two** Trix trains on the same track, at the same time, each controlled independently. While one continues on its journey the other can be speeded up or slowed down, stopped and even reversed.

It's the Trix system of fitting interchangeable shoes to the locomotives and the patented track on which they run that gives you this feature. Trix track can be taken apart and reassembled thousands of times—it always makes a perfect electrical contact: you can build a new layout or existing track could be relaid in a matter of minutes. Another feature that adds to the realism of T.T.R. is Trix automatic coupling and remote control uncoupling. With this you can carry out most of the functions of the full sized railway. T.T.R. operates on 12/14 volts from alternating current house mains through a transformer.

The gauge is "00" with 13¼" radius curves which gives you the most railway in the smallest space. T.T.R. is, in fact, the perfect table top railway.

Here is the latest T.T.R. product in service. This magnificent scale model of the 4-6-2 Pacific type locomotive in B.R. livery, incorporates the new remote control uncoupling device.

Cover of the 1951 TTR catalogue.

Lilli Sommer with the Trix sales manager Mr Masterton-Smith during the early 1950s.

TTR Owner's Badge which was first advertised in the Autumn 1952 *TTR Gazette* and was available for about one year. A later Trix Express Owner's Pin is also shown.

business was judged to be very favourable. By this time the workforce in Germany had grown to 276, but not all were working in Nuremberg, as part of the workforce was employed in the premises in Spalt.

During November 1951, Winteringham Ltd ceased to be a shareholder of Precision Models Ltd and transferred its remaining shares to Trix Ltd. The old-established company founded by George Winteringham in 1908 ceased trading shortly after. Also during November, Franz Bing was appointed as director of P. M. Ltd, replacing G. P. Keen who had resigned two months earlier.

The directors of Trix were always on the lookout for diversifications which might be connected with the hobby of creating and operating models. One such line was the production under licence from the X-Acto Company in America of a full range of handicraft knives and tools using the trade name of Trix X-Acto. This range of handicraft implements were of excellent quality and proved to be very popular. They were manufactured at the Precision Models factory until 1958 when the licence passed on to another interested party, namely, Dufay Ltd.

Large amounts of locomotives and rolling stock in British Railways livery were now on the market, and, in fact, during 1950 and 1951 it is estimated that between 300 and 400 0-4-0s were produced each working week. However the 'export only' range of American-outline locomotives and rolling stock were not on general release until 1952. Christmas 1950 saw the welcome return of *The TTR Gazette* which was produced at the London office, again with

1953 Trix X-Acto trade leaflet.

S. Kahn as Editor and with M. Catalani giving ample support. As with the pre-war editions it was used as a platform for advertising forthcoming products and included features on how to get the best out of the TTR model railway. For some reason, the first post-war edition of the *Trix Express Dienst* did not appear until December 1952.

In 1951 the British market saw the results of the shared ownership of the separate German and British Trix companies, firstly with the introduction of the Nuremberg-produced Class 71 advertised as a Mixed Traffic 2-4-2 Tank Locomotive, and also the 'Diesel Flyer' two-coach unit which was exactly the same as the model sold in German shops. The 2-4-2 locomotive was a different matter. Although basically identical to the German version, the uncoupling mechanism on each bogie had to be modified to suit the new type of coupling as used on TTR locomotives, and this was carried out at the Northampton factory where they were also reboxed.

The autumn saw the introduction of the BR 'Scotsman' 4-6-2 Pacific locomotive. This model was made at Northampton with the exception of the engine chassis which was once again, as in pre-war times, imported from Nuremberg. The uncoupling mechanism in the tender was of a new design patented by Werner Alton and based on the new motor fitted to the redesigned remote

Part of the 1952 catalogue.

The first post-war *TTR Gazette.*

CURRENT NEWS OF TTR PROGRESS

No. 1   CHRISTMAS NUMBER 1950   *GRATIS to Registered Owners*

EDITORIAL

AFTER 10 YEARS

... and as we were saying when the sirens went, the Trix Twin Railway, abounding in ingenious remote-control devices and designed to operate from a central control panel "as if by magic", simple to fit together, robust and easy to operate still represents the last word in home railways.

It is as true to-day as it was ten years ago and this, the first post-war issue of our Trix Gazette is here to tell you that by the time these lines appear in print, we ought to be within measurable distance of meeting some at least of our formidable list of outstanding demands.

To those of our keen users who must be asked to wait just a little longer, we can only extend our apologies. The past ten years have brought to us, in common with most people, times of difficulty, perplexity and the need to accommodate ourselves to unusual conditions.

Needless to say our plant, together with its highly specialised personnel, was called upon at the outset of the emergency to aid the national effort.

If space and circumstances permitted we could give an account of "Trix and the War effort" that would make romantic reading indeed. So far afield, in fact, did our activities lead us that at one time we wondered if we should ever again remember how to make miniature railways. And it was just about that time that we were called upon to divert part of our plant back to its original purpose and supply a railway that played its modest but necessary part in the model used for rehearsing the 'real thing'. And when, finally, the cause towards which we had contributed our mite, came to a successful conclusion a fresh set of strange circumstances confronted us.

It is true that we were permitted to turn our attention once again to the manufacture of the Trix Twin Railway. And it is true also that the experience gained in the war years was of great benefit, but only a fraction of our output was available for sale amongst the countless enthusiastic users in this country—the lion's share had to bear the label "For Export Only" and play its part in the equally vital struggle for market rehabilitation.

That struggle is by no means at an end as we all know and it must be a while yet before our quota for the Home Market can satisfy the demand. But we are able to arrange for part of our output to be

Realism in miniature.
Trix trains in action as shown on the cover of our Export Catalogue.

allocated for Home customers and it is our hope that a more plentiful supply will become available as time goes on.

Meanwhile, of one thing we can assure our readers: the Trix Twin Railway was designed in the first place to be essentially a *workable* railway—one from which *realistic operation* and fascinating enjoyment can be obtained in full measure. Our pre-war railway captured the imagination of innumerable enthusiastic users of all ages because we were able to produce a constant succession of new ideas and devices that gave increased operating realism.

During these ten years now past we have entered in our Development File a very useful number of ideas. Some of these you will find already on the market. Some are still in the production and experimental stage and others are scheduled for the programmes of the *next* ten years.

You can start with your Trix Railway to-day certain in the knowledge that the development of really practical ideas will be continuous; that the fascination of operating your Trix Railway will be maintained; and that each new component or accessory we introduce will substantially increase your operating facilities and pleasure.

TRIX is your assurance of sustained enjoyment through practical results.

The Precision Models factory in 1954.

Assembly of the American coaches.

Elevator Conveyor assembly section.

Inspection of Elevator Conveyor parts.

The paint-shop foreman George Cotton.

The spray booths.

A 1950s shop window display sticker.

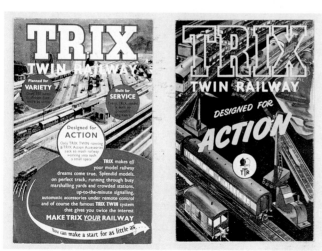

1953 and 1954 catalogue sheets.

control points which were made available earlier. The cost of this 'Pacific' model was rather high at £10, but it was a complicated piece of model engineering and the quality more than justified the price, even if the scale and appearance were somewhat off the mark. In former years correctness of scale had not mattered unduly but the taste of the public was altering and they were now more concerned with detail and nearer to scale dimensions. This was to be Trix's undoing as they persisted with their initial post-war policy of carrying on where they had left off in 1939-40.

Thus, while all their rivals were concentrating on producing near to scale models with much

The Trix Twin Railway Year books.

finer scale wheels, and also were almost universally using 12 volts DC as the operating voltage (with the notable exception of Märklin), Trix Ltd were developing more models for remote control action instead of new and nearer to scale locomotives. Even the range of diecast rolling stock fell into this category although they were exported to Germany for inclusion in the Trix Express catalogues from 1953 together with the excellent Elevator Conveyer from 1954.

After a climb back to relative success in 1950, Trix Ltd enjoyed a period of buoyancy up to 1952, but then it all started to go wrong again, as the company was faced with high development and production costs and decreasing sales due to the aforementioned changing fashions of model railway enthusiasts. In fact, at this time there was a general decline in interest in model railways which were being taken over by new lines including the introduction of slot-car racing.

H. Oppenheim had always been keen in maintaining ties with the German company, but the worsening financial problems of Trix Ltd was the deciding factor for the British shareholders of Trix Vereinigte Spielwarenfabriken GmbH. to sell their holding in the company. Just prior to the sale of the shares, an agreement was made on 1 April 1952 between the German enterprise and Trix Ltd in London, that full cooperation, including development work and the sale of each others goods, should be maintained for a period of 10 years so that the best possible commercial success could be achieved for both enterprises. The sale of the DM 152,000 shares were handled by S. G. Warburg & Company Ltd and a formal agreement was made, which included a further

settlement appertaining to Trademark and Patent rights, on 13 October 1952 thus terminating any controlling or share rights that S. Kahn, F. Bing, L. Sommer and H. Oppenheim had in Trix Vereinigte Spielwarenfabriken GmbH.

Once again, Ernst Voelk became the controlling executive of the company, although he preferred to transfer all the German Trix business to his existing company Ernst Voelk KG. As a consequence and resulting from a contract dated 31 December 1954, the partnership company of Ernst Voelk KG leased the right to continue the businesses of the former

A display of Trix Constructor sets in the early 1950s.

79

Trix 'Showing You The Way' booklet published in1955 with a pre-publication issue on the right corrected by Michael Catalani.

1955 publicity photograph of the Trix 'Junior Train'. Prototype models of the Hand Generator can be seen at the front and right-hand side of the picture.

A Junior Train leaflet included with the sets.

company Vereinigte Spielwarenfabriken Andreas Förtner & J. Haffner's Nachf. GmbH and the company Trix Vereinigte Spielwarenfabriken GmbH. As a further consequence Ernst Voelk K.G. changed its name to Trix Vereinigte Spielwarenfabriken Ernst Voelk K.G. which was registered in Nuremberg in April 1955. The letters KG after the company name are short for 'Kommanditgesellschaft' which translated into English means 'limited partnership'. Also during December 1954 it was decided to alter the name of Trix Vereinigte Spielwarenfabriken GmbH to Trix Spielwaren GmbH and use the company purely for distribution. At the end of May 1959 under liquidation laws, this company was absorbed by its only shareholding company, Johann Distler K.G. of Nuremberg.

1953 saw the beginning of the end of the

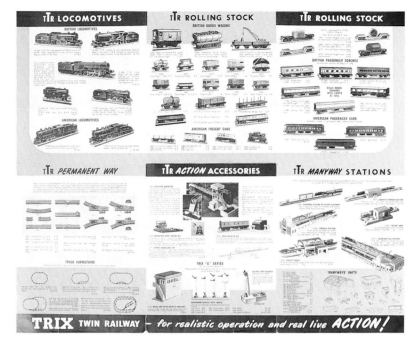

1956 Trix Twin Railway catalogue.

harmonious business relationship between Bassett-Lowke Ltd and Trix Ltd, as in March W. J. Bassett-Lowke resigned as director of Trix and Precision Models due to illness. Up to that time, the production of models at the Stimpson Avenue factory was split between Bassett-Lowke and Trix, which must have caused problems when the Trix directors were desperate for as much factory output in their favour as possible. Nevertheless, the personal obligation that had existed since before the war towards W. J. was totally honoured and only relinquished on his death in October 1953. Throughout his association with Trix Ltd, W. J. allowed his company name to be used in the promotion of

the Trix Twin Railway, using such words as 'TTR Scale Models Designed by Bassett-Lowke' or 'Bassett-Lowke Twin Train Table Railway', while in fact, contrary to popular belief, W. J. and his company only acted as advisors.

Without the influence of S. Kahn who always wanted to retain the old system, Trix Express started the change over from 14 volts AC to 12 volts DC in 1953 and immediately more realistic models appeared in the German shops. In the last months of 1955, Trix launched the 'Meteor' three-coach diesel unit again using 14 volts A.C. but with a superimposed 12 volts DC required for reversing. This was a freelance design with American influence and was of complicated

construction. The tooling costs for this alone must have been enormous as they also were for the Elevator Conveyer. Sales of the 'Meteor' were poor which were not helped by dubious reliability and its distinctly freelance appearance, and it was quickly reissued in DC form at a lower price to try to recoup some of the company's losses.

During 1953 Sir Andrew McFadyean took over as chairman from J. D. Kiley and with H. Oppenheim, the financial manager of Trix Ltd, (and also of P. M. Ltd from March of the same year), endeavoured to maintain the companies' finances against the tide of continuing lack of capital. To curb spending, a

An old wooden coach belonging to the New Zealand Railways used to house a Signal Instruction Layout put together using Trix Twin Railway items, (except for the special colour-light signals). This photograph was taken in 1954.

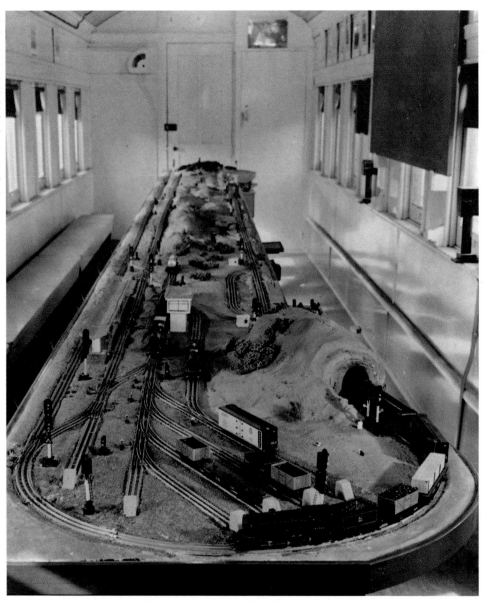

special resolution was passed restricting the borrowing or debt capacity of both companies to no more than three times the nominal share capital. The majority of the company's shares were still in the hands of the Merchant Bankers and that is why Sir Andrew McFadyean kept a tight reign of financial decisions. Maybe the worry was too great for H. Oppenheim as he died in February 1954, leaving the remaining original members of the company, namely Siegfried Kahn, plus Lilli Sommer and her brother Franz Bing to shoulder the responsibilities together with the long standing secretary of Trix Ltd – J Stein.

Events were not helped by the resignation and subsequent emigration to America of the much-respected F. J. Prior in December 1954 whose practical ability and inventive capabilities were to be sadly missed at Precision Models Ltd. By the end of 1955, the company accounts still showed a small combined profit, but large amounts of money were required for essential reorganisation and the continuation of the development programme to bring the products up to date. All these events were exacerbated by the additional cash demands of converting the Trix Twin Railway system to12 volts DC. The first positive venture into DC-controlled model railways was the 'Junior' train set introduced in the spring of 1955 but it was not generally available until the autumn. This Junior set could be bought in either passenger or goods form. The unique feature of the sets was that they could be driven by a 4.5 volt battery or by the Hand Generator that was included in the set. Its aim was to attract the young members of the public to the world of model railways and was completely safe in its operation. It was elaborately packaged and S. Kahn was heard to remark that the children would get more fun out of the box than the train set! Other DC items were being planned and developed to suit the more mature model railway enthusiasts for which the costs of this exercise were shown as a £15,000 development expenditure in the company accounts for 1956.

It was not unknown during this time for frequent disruption to production to be caused by the lack of supplies because accounts had not been paid, and it is known that on more than one occasion one of the staff from the factory paint shop had to slip to the local paint shop to buy a bottle of turpentine or paint.

In March 1956 S. G. Warburg & Co. Ltd, once again came to the rescue of Trix and Precision Models Ltd, making money available to the two companies by creating a Debenture for each company which stated 'To secure all monies due or to become due on any current or other account whatsoever'. The Debentures were secured on the properties and assets of the companies which helped to cover bank overdrafts and day to day operating expenses. A restructuring of the Trix Ltd shares took place, but the share capital still stood at £25,000. After the death of J. D. Kiley, the ex-chairman of the company, his shares were transferred to his wife who relinquished them during this year and consequently they were distributed to F. Bing, L. Sommer and S. Kahn. This meant that the final connection with Machinery (Smith's Patents) Ltd was broken. April 1956 saw the

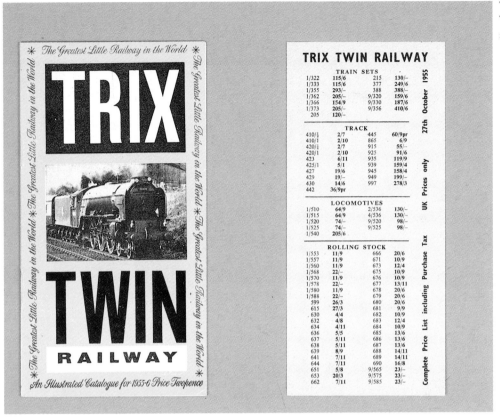

appointment of Frank D. Newman (a banker) as deputy chairman of Trix Ltd.

In October 1956 Precision Models Ltd purchased for £46,000 Manus Finance Co. Ltd in a scheme organised by Warburgs to secure added finances. It seems that this company had liquid assets of a similar amount to the purchase consideration. The directors of Precision Models Ltd changed the name of their acquisition to Northants Tools Ltd and appointed S. Kahn and Sidney George Birch as directors. S. G. Birch was the chief accountant of Trix Ltd.

Unfortunately all these manoeuvres did not prevent the company's overdraft from rising to over £112,000 at the end of December 1956. Selling the Trix group of companies became an inevitable next step.

A circular sent to registered owners in an attempt to reduce the large obsolescence stock inherited by Ewart Holdings Ltd.

TRIX LIMITED
Makers of Model Trains and Hobby Knives and Tools

TELEPHONE
LEGATION 2351
(3 LINES)

TELEGRAMS
TESTEEYAR, PHONE.
LONDON.

5, CONDUIT STREET, LONDON, W.1.

T/7/7/57

Dear Fellow Railwayman,

At last a Group of Railway Companies is actually going to REDUCE operating costs!

What makes this news really exciting is that YOUR Railway Company is included in this Group.

To every one of our existing members we of TRIX are offering certain items in our range at greatly reduced prices. These items are all standard T.T.R. goods, and this amazing economy drive will enable you to extend your layout to nearly TWICE its size for only HALF the outlay.

You'll find an illustrated leaflet and a list giving full details of the new prices with this letter. There's a C.O.D. Order Form included with the price list to make things easy for you.

We can't extend this offer beyond the end of September, and we are certain sure the response will be overwhelming, so get your stock requisitions in NOW!

Yours sincerely,

Guy S. Hibbs

Guy S. Hibbs,
Sales Director,
Trix Limited.

DIRECTORS:-A. E. JOHNSON. (CHAIRMAN). F. D. NEWMAN. B. H. WALLIS. SECRETARY:-H. A. MORRISS.

THE CHANGE OF OWNERSHIP.

The sale of the Trix Ltd group of companies was undertaken by S. G. Warburg & Co. Ltd, who were both acting on behalf of shareholders and themselves as creditors, by virtue of a Debenture, and shareholders through their subsidiary, Nutraco Nominees Ltd. In fact Trix Ltd and Precision Models Ltd were indebted to Warburg's in the sum of approximately £100,000. Ewart Holdings Ltd, an old-established company which in the 1920s and 1930s made gas appliances and in later years had diversified into many fields, purchased the whole of the issued share capital and debentures satisfied by the issue of 752,940 Ordinary shares of 1/- (5p) each of Ewart Holdings Ltd. The change of ownership took effect on 27 February 1957, which was also the day that the 'old team' of directors of Trix Ltd, Precision Models Ltd and Nuway Playthings Ltd (a W. J. Bassett-Lowke inspired retail company), retired.

Franz Bing and his sister Lilli seemed reluctant to let go of the old business completely, both having previously acquired 10,000 Ewart shares, and for a while acted as advisors until finally severing relations in May 1957. Apart from F. D. Newman, the only persons to remain in an official capacity with the new owners were the company secretaries, S. G. Birch of Precision Models Ltd, and J. Stein who had been associated with Trix Ltd since the beginning. However, even Mr Stein retired in April of that year and took up residence in Cornwall. Franz Bing started his own toy and hobby import-export business, F. Bing & Co. Ltd (located in Hammersmith), and was joined in later years by

The TRIX TWIN CADET gives you endless fun!
the perfect gift for any boy

1 Full speed control. At the touch of a switch, trains will run forward or in reverse, at any speed you choose.

2 Twin railway system. Two trains can be operated simultaneously on one set of rails!

3 New TRIX Track. Specially realistic, tough, with quick action assembly, easy to add to. Extra track costs only 1/3 per length.

4 Far more running time. TRIX TWIN CADET locomotives are fitted with new high-efficiency motors. They operate on two 4.5 volt standard bell batteries, which, in normal use, give over 100 hours actual running. Or you can use an inexpensive Transformer/Rectifier, enabling you to run your TRIX trains off the household electricity supply with complete safety.

5 Highly realistic rolling stock. Locomotives, passenger coaches, goods wagons, in great variety . . . all finely modelled, in exact British Railway colours.

6 Rail accessories of all kinds . . . to help you make your system still more lifelike and attractive.

GOODS SET 87/6

14 lengths of new TRIX TRACK
Speed control unit
Engine
Petrol Tank
Low Timber Truck
Guards Van

PASSENGER SET 92/-

14 lengths of new TRIX TRACK
Speed control unit
Engine
1st passenger coach
2nd passenger coach

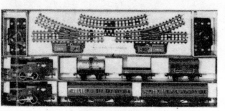

COMBINED SET 189/-

24 lengths of new TRIX TRACK with 1 pair hand points
2 speed control units
Goods Train Engine
Passenger Train Engine
Petrol Tank
Low Timber Truck
Guards Van
1st passenger coach
2nd passenger coach

The 1957 Trix Twin 'Cadet' Sets.

85

his sister Lilli Sommer. He died in 1978. Siegfried Kahn joined a finance company and R. Bindon Blood died from ill health in 1958.

F. D. Newman was now the chairman of the board of directors of both Trix Ltd and Precision Models Ltd and presided over his fellow directors Bernard H. Wallis, Guy S. Hibbs, (appointed during June 1957), and the chairman of Ewart Holdings Ltd, Albert E. Johnson. A. E. Johnson's associations with the toy trade went back many years. At the age of 14 he was successfully manufacturing and selling his own range of wooden animated toys. He is best known, however, for introducing the Grundig tape recorder to Britain in 1952. B. Wallis, the managing director of Ewart Holdings Ltd, was responsible for reorganising the manufacturing side of Trix Ltd. Sales direction was entrusted to G. S. Hibbs who had previous experience in the radio industry.

Apparently the workforce at the factory did not realise that the company had changed hands, only that one or two of the familiar faces had disappeared. The registered office of Trix Ltd moved to 5 Conduit Street, London W1 during July 1957.

Despite all these changes, the development of new items continued, emphasis being placed on the conversion of the Trix Twin Railway system to exclusive DC operation. The popular range of Trix X-Acto handicraft tools was retained, and also the unpopular, but cheap to produce, Trix Construction sets, of which large stocks of parts remained at the factory - a legacy of the previous management of Precision Models Ltd.

Due to economic difficulties a large part of the existing tooling was still employed, notwithstanding its obsolescence. However the new low profile fibre based 3-rail track, despite being a direct copy of that used by their German counterparts, had to be tooled-up for production at Northampton. This track made its first appearance in the revamped version of the 'Junior' train set which was now called the 'Trix Twin Cadet Railway'. This was shown at the International Toy Fair at Brighton which opened on 25 February 1957. At that time a lot of publicity was organised by their publicity director John Ridley to promote Trix's new image in the press and on Independent Television. Another line announced at the Toy Fair was the possible production of a working model of the famous 'Flying Bedstead', (the initial test-bed for the vertical take-off ability of the revolutionary Harrier jet aircraft), which would be powered by a new safety glo-motor from America. However this and other intended projects remained an unfulfilled dream.

Later during 1957, DC versions of the plastic-bodied 0-4-0 and the standard 4-4-0 locomotives were available, but still retaining the 3-rail method of control and the large flanged wheels. The design modifications for these locomotives were made by Michael Catalani. He did not agree with the policy of converting these old designs. However, as the tooling for the body castings was already in existence, only a new chassis needed to be designed, in the form of a pressing rather than a diecasting because the factory was now geared up to press work. The 12 volt DC. motor fitted to these new chassis was

the very robust and well-proved one made by Trix Vereinigte Spielwarenfabriken Ernst Voelk K.G. It was a motor which from 1954 was used in nearly all the Trix Express DC locomotives, and from 1957 in most of the Trix locomotives in Britain. A British version of this motor was later manufactured at Northampton, continuing until the factory closed in 1960.

Although the new owners were hampered by a large amount of obsolete stock and, as previously, a lack of finance, they were determined to create a new image by introducing a completely new range of models which were to be much nearer to scale proportions. The design of the models was mostly the undertaking of Michael Catalani, who with a small team started design and sample production during the end of 1957. Development costs were to be kept to a minimum, and with this in mind the first scale locomotive was that of the Ruston Hornsby diesel shunter. This locomotive was chosen as some of the chassis parts could be purchased from Trix in Germany to speed production in readiness for the Brighton Toy Fair in February the following year. In fact only six hand-made working samples were made in time for the Toy Fair along with mock-ups of two exciting new models, the BR 'Britannia' 4-6-2 and the BR Class 5 4-6-0. These models were very well received by the model press. Delivery to the shops was expected in June of 1958, but althoughwell advertised by Trix Ltd, only the Ruston Hornsby shunter actually reached the shops during that year due to the knock-on effect of the poor trading results of 1957. The poor performance in 1957 was blamed by Guy Hibbs on the inevitable transition period during which staff changes were frequent, factory and office reorganisation was extensive, and the overpricing of goods on the retailers' shelves had to be reduced and credit given for stocks held. At the end of 1957 a new catalogue made its appearance but was too late for effective use by many stockists. A new full-colour catalogue was to be available in early March plus other advertising literature for the retailer. Television advertising in peak spots was also booked for the end of the year to try and win the Christmas trade for all the Trix products. In January 1958, Trix Ltd became the sole selling agents throughout the world for Victory electric scale model cars which were to be used in conjunction with VIP roadways. This combined system was in direct competition to the Scalextric slot car racing sets of the time.

Many hopes and promises for 1958 were made, but few were fulfilled as the expansion and modernisation program required a large amount of finance. This requirement was partly met by an advance of nearly £178,000 taken as a loan and other sums from the group as well as a bank overdraft. During April, Ewart Holdings Ltd and eleven of its subsidiaries entered into an agreement to guarantee payment of any monies due to their common bankers by any of these companies. However, increased financial help was refused by the bank and problems soon arose at Precision Models as lack of money had resulted in production becoming unbalanced.

During June 1958 trade creditors obtained judgement against Precision Models Ltd for varying amounts, and especially for a sum of over £5,500 due under a dishonoured bill of exchange between a company who had manufactured transformers and other allied items for Precision Models Ltd. On 7 July this creditor presented a petition to wind up Precision Models Ltd but it was dismissed on 21 July as a large amount of this dishonoured bill was paid.

THE TRIX TWIN CATALOGUE

TTR

THE ONLY RAILWAY SYSTEM TO OPERATE TWO TRAINS SIMULTANEOUSLY ON THE SAME TRACK!

The '1957' Trix Twin catalogues.
The small temporary version was printed from August 1957 (see overleaf) and the coloured version actually appeared in this form in March 1958.
A few variations of each type exist.

To minimise the cash-flow problems a second mortgage on the Precision Models factory for £23,000 was created with Dufay Ltd. However most of this was used to reduce the bank overdraft. Dufay Ltd was a London-based company manufacturing medical and industrial X-ray films and films for black and white and colour photography. One of their popular products was the 'Coronet' camera for which sales were seasonal, and probably with this in mind they took the first step towards diversification via Trix who were happy to accept help from any quarter.

Nevertheless, the financial position of Trix Ltd and Precision Models Ltd worsened. In the case of the latter company there was an estimated deficiency with regards to creditors of almost £300,000 which included 260 outstanding trade accounts. This led during the latter part of September to the eventual petitioning for a winding-up order of Precision Models Ltd by a creditor backed by the company's bankers, Barclays Bank Ltd, who also petitioned against Trix Ltd.

By order of The High Court of Justice (Chancery Division), Precision Models Ltd was wound-up on 6 October 1958 and Trix Ltd, registered number 262881, was wound-up one week later. Over a similar period Ewart Holdings Ltd and the remaining ten subsidiary companies also suffered the same fate.

Every one of the 200 men and women employed by Precision Models Ltd were called into the canteen of the factory on the afternoon of 8 October and told that their employment had ceased. The announcement was a terrible shock to the staff as, despite being aware of the problems, most expected good news having been working overtime up to the night before to cope with the pre-Christmas rush of orders. The only compensation was 5/3d (26p) for each year worked paid out from the £300 in their own welfare and social club fund. Ironically it was later revealed that the factory had orders worth £100,000 on hand.

This marked the end of a pioneering and highly skilled era of commercial model engineering. The founders of Trix Express and Trix Twin Railway had been pioneers, but as is so often the case they were unable to consolidate. Later Hornby Dublo would suffer the same fate by falling into a similar trap of modernising too late.

TRIX

Twin Railway

14 pages of Trains and Action Accessories

TRIX LTD., 5 CONDUIT ST., LONDON, W.I.   EXPORT DIVISION : STANDBROOK HOUSE, 2 5 OLD BOND ST., LONDON, W.I.   CABLES : GOFFANIO, LONDON

TRIX Information Bureau is always at your service

THE 'DUFAY' PERIOD

With the collapse of the Ewart Holdings Group, the assets of Trix Ltd and its subsidiary companies were now in the hands of the Official Receiver. It was to this person that a succession of offers were made regarding the business and factory of Precision Models Ltd. One such interested company was Lines Bros. Ltd, who were so keen to purchase the company, and were so sure of being successful, that they even took on a few managerial personnel in readiness for the reopening of the factory. However it was not generally known that Dufay Ltd already had a vested interest in Precision Models Ltd by means of the mortgage on the factory premises, and it was not long before they made their intentions known, effectively blocking other offers.

Dufay Ltd was first registered in 1936 as Dufay-Chromex Ltd changing their name to the former in 1952. As mentioned previously, their main business was in the field of photography but they were experiencing difficulties in this area due to rising costs, poor export figures and, above all, according to company reports, the seasonal nature of their business and poor summer weather. It was felt that the purchase of the failed Trix business would help to even out the yearly business as camera production and sales peaked between April and July for the holiday trade, while Trix products peaked during October and November for the Christmas sales.

Thus on 10 November 1958 Dufay Ltd reached agreement with the Official Receiver for the purchase of the assets and good will of Trix Ltd for £56,000, and the freehold factory occu-pied by Precision Models Ltd for £32,000. The new management arranged for personal contact to be made with former key employees of Precision Models Ltd with a view to discussing re-employment. The new owners expected initially to absorb approximately half of the 200 dismissed workers who were given assurances by Commander R. H. Bristowe, the chairman of Dufay Ltd, that production of Trix model railway items would always take place at Stimpson Avenue. The new managing director of the Stimpson Avenue factory was Captain Ruck Keene, a personal friend of Commander Bristowe, who was well liked and very enthusiastic about the future prospects of the company. He was assisted by Doug Capple who came from the Birmingham factory of one of Dufay's subsidiary companies to act as production manager.

On Monday 17 November 1958 the factory reopened with 53 women and 40 men, the ex-Precision Models assembly foreman Frank Gratton taking the position of works manager. The immediate task was to concentrate on the production of Trix items that were ordered for the Christmas trade. Everybody was happy to get back to work at the factory which had always had a family atmosphere. However, the workshops and machines were covered in rust and dust which had accumulated in the five weeks that the factory had been closed.

Michael Catalani continued with the design and development of new models including the EM1 Bo+Bo electric locomotive, the GWR Class 66XX tank engine and a range of plastic-bodied wagons all of which had been started in the days of Ewart Holdings Ltd. The new management were very enthusiastic and keen to develop new products and these new items were shown at the Brighton Toy Fair in February 1959 but only in picture or mock-up form.

Spicer-Dufay (British) Ltd was a dormant wholly-owned subsidiary company of Dufay Ltd, using the address of its parent company at P & O House, 14-16 Cockspur Street, London, SW1 as the registered office. This company changed its name on 28 November 1958 to Trix Products Ltd (registered number 272812) and was used for promotion, design and development functions, although strangely from May 1960, Dufay Ltd were the registered proprietors of the trade marks originally held by Trix Ltd. The manufacture and distribution of the Trix products, including accounts, was handled by another subsidiary company called Dufay (B'ham) Ltd whose registered office was also at the parent company address. The Precision Models factory at 107 Stimpson Avenue, Northampton was renamed Dufay (B'ham) Ltd and was used as the service department and manufacturing base for all the Trix products, with the sales and accounts being dealt with from their other factory at 308-310 Summer Lane, Birmingham, the manufacturing base for the 'Coronet' camera.

The organisation of production, planning and progress at the Northampton factory was in the capable hands of Reg Thompson who had joined Trix Ltd in 1953. His task was difficult during the chaotic time after the factory reopening, and his efforts were rewarded by the release onto the market of the long-awaited 'Britannia' and Class V locomotives in the spring of 1959. Many other new items followed but problems were again just

200 SACKED AT A MINUTE'S NOTICE

WORKERS START THE "BIG HUNT" FOR JOBS

EVERY one of the 200 men and women employed by Precision Models Ltd., the Northampton model engineering firm, has been sacked—at a minute's notice.

They were all called to the canteen in the firm's Stimpson-avenue premises last night, and there they were told: "The business is closing down now. Your services are no longer required."

To-day the Big Hunt for jobs started, and the sacked workers have been flocking to the Employment Exchange in Grafton-street. Some, in fact, were waiting on the doorstep for it to open.

After they had registered, they stood in groups outside, discussing their prospects of getting work.

BOMBSHELL

Last night's announcement was made by a representative of the Official Receiver's office in London, who has been handling the affairs of the firm since it became the subject of a compulsory winding-up order in the Chancery Division earlier in the week.

It came as a complete "bombshell" to the employees, a number of whom have been with the firm for 50 years.

"A terrible and unexpected shock," was how Mr. T. F. Shaw, an employee of 37 years' standing described it to-day. He was the firm's head inspector and paint shop foreman.

"It still takes a lot to realise that it has actually happened," he said.

NO MONEY

The dismissed employees, he went on, had received no money, and were told they would not get any until after October 30.

Mr. James Catalani, 4, Greenlane, Wootton, a designer with the firm, with whom he was connected for 21 years, said: "Everybody from top to bottom got a minute's notice."

He thought an attempt should have been made to keep the firm going.

Mr. Catalani, who has five children at school, described the chances of specialists like himself of getting work as "pretty grim."

SUGGESTION

Mr. Fred Finch, of 63, Oxford-street, Northampton, assembly shop foreman, who has 30 years' service with the firm, estimated that the men were entitled to nine days pay, plus accumulated holiday pay.

He then put forward this suggestion: "Cannot groups of local business people club together and take over the firm and keep the name alive?"

Majority of the employees affected are women, and one of them, Miss A. E. Twisleton, who has worked at Precision Models for more than 30 years, said to-day: "I would not like to experience again the shock I had last night."

7TH OCTOBER 1958

She added: "What has happened is a great pity. It was such a happy firm."

SOMETHING AFOOT

Another woman, who was with her, said: "We new something was afoot, but I had an idea that what we were going to hear would be good news."

Besides being stunned by the news, the employees are also puzzled. For they say that up to last night they had been working overtime.

One explained: "We were just starting on the pre-Christmas rush."

They also say that they should have been given longer notice. A spokesman of the Official Receiver's Office in London told the Chronicle and Echo: "The dismissal dates from the time of the winding-up order, and is effective immediately."

He also said that an Official Receiver had no power to carry on a business unless sanctioned by the Court.

TOO EARLY

At the Employment Exchange it was stated that it was too early to say if they would be able to place all sacked workers.

"We hope to," said a spokesman. "We shall be contacting firms to see what openings they have."

He went on. "In the case of the women it may be difficult because they are mainly assemblers, and there is not a large demand for them."

PRECISION MODELS LTD.

4TH. NOV. 1958.

No decision yet on firm's future

—Receiver's spokesman

A "succession of offers"

THE firm which stated last week it had acquired the business of Precision Models Ltd., Northampton, was to-day named as Dufay Ltd., photographic equipment manufacturers, whose head office is in London.

But, at the office of the London Official Receiver — where the affairs of the Northampton model engineering firm are being wound up under a High Court order—the Chronicle and Echo was told that "a succession of offers" had been received for the business and that no decision had been made regarding the future of the firm.

More than 100 former members of Precision Models Ltd., last night attended a meeting at the Whyte Melville Hall, called by Dufay, Ltd., "to discuss their re-employment."

Chronicle and Echo representatives were refused admission to the meeting. But it is understood the workers were told that the future of the model engineering firm would be discussed at a meeting in London to-day.

The Official Receiver's spokesman to-day confirmed that a meeting was taking place this afternoon between the Official Receiver and the committee of inspection appointed at a creditors' meeting on October 30.

20TH APRIL 1960

DUFAY LTD.:

100 are given notice

ABOUT 100 men and women — all the people employed by Dufay Ltd., the model engineering firm of Stimpson-avenue, Northampton — were told to-day that they are to be given two weeks notice from this coming Friday.

Many of these employees were taken on by Dufay Ltd., when they took over the business of Precision Models Ltd., in November, 1958. When Precision Models went into liquidation the previous month they had been sacked at a minute's notice.

A spokesman for the firm which is part of a group, told the Chronicle and Echo that it had been decided in the interests of efficiency to combine the work at present being done at Northampton with that of another factory in the group, at Birmingham.

He confirmed that the factory employees had been given two weeks' notice from Friday this week, but added that certain of them would have their notice suspended while change-over details were completed. It was a move that had been under consideration for some time.

He agreed that certain people who had been employed by Precision Models had been taken on by Dufay Ltd., and added that it was hoped to offer some members of the staff work at the Birmingham factory, if they were willing to transfer.

10TH NOV. 1958.

Creditors of Trix Ltd. to meet

The first creditors' meeting of Trix, Ltd., parent company of Precision Models, Ltd., Northampton, is to be held in London on Wednesday.

Until then (writes a Chronicle and Echo reporter) it is thought unlikely that there will be any fresh developments in negotiations for the purchase of the Northampton model engineering firm.

Last week it was reported that there had been "a succession of offers" for Precision Models, Ltd., which is the subject of a High Court compulsory winding-up order.

One of the bids for the firm has been made by Dufay, Ltd., photographic equipment manufacturers, of London.

13TH. NOV. 1958

FACTORY STARTS AGAIN ON MONDAY

THE new company which has taken over the business of Precision Models Ltd., Northampton announced to-day that production of model railway equipment and construction sets at its Stimpson-avenue factory will restart on a "small scale" next Monday.

Captain J. H. Ruck Keene, managing director of the firm, told the Chronicle and Echo to-day: "From that start there will be a gradual expansion of production to full capacity."

The firm has already stated that it hopes to re-engage in the very near future most of the 200 men and women employees of Precision Models who were discharged when that firm closed down on October 8.

GETTING READY

News of the firm's intention to continue producing the same lines as its predecessor spread quickly yesterday and there was a steady stream of former employees calling on the new company, anxious to get their old jobs back.

Said Captain Ruck Keene: "There has been a very satisfactory response to our appeal for the former workers to return."

To-day at the firm's Stimpson-avenue premises, a small staff was busy making arrangements for the production wheels to start turning in four days time.

Newspaper cuttings from the *Northampton Chronicle & Echo* at the time of the problems at Precision Models Ltd.

round the corner.

As a result of the continued decline of interest in model railways, sales for 1959 were very disappointing, although the products met with general approval. At the same time production of the 'Coronet' camera in Birmingham suffered. Increasing costs and the loss of most of the overseas market necessitated a drastic solution. It was obvious that sales of the two diverse products were not sufficient to keep the factories at Northampton and Birmingham fully occupied. As the matter had to be resolved before the start of the 'Trix' season in July 1960 it was decided during April by the directors of Dufay Ltd (with the exception of the chairman Commander Bristowe) that production be integrated at the Birmingham factory and that the Northampton factory should close. Commander Bristowe argued that there were many years of hard-earned skills and experience at the Northampton factory, and that the staff had been given a personal promise when they were reinstated that Trix production would always be in Northampton. However, his recommendations were

Two editions of the 1959 Trix catalogue under Dufay Ltd. The lower illustration is the later catalogue which is the only edition to list the Engineer's Coach.

The cover from the 1960 and 1961 catalogue. The earlier edition has a stiff cover and a pocket at the back for the price list.

1959 publicity photographs intended for use in Trix leaflets.

not adopted and he resigned from the board with effect from 12 April. Soon after, Captain Ruck Keene resigned as the managing director of the Northampton factory for similar reasons. Harold Evans was appointed chairman as Commander Bristowe's successor.

All the employees at the ex-Precision Models factory, with the exception of a few key personnel, were once again given notice, but this time they were given two weeks grace instead of the notice taking immediate effect as had happened with Ewart Holdings Ltd. The factory closed its gates on Friday 6 May, and most of the remaining key personnel were on suspended notice until the change-over co-ordinated by Reg Thompson

was complete. Many employees were offered positions in the Birmingham factory but only a few took up the offer as there seemed to be too much uncertainty surrounding the move, plus the personal problems of relocating. The freehold factory at Northampton was put up for sale including the superfluous machinery, the goods and small tools being moved to a warehouse in the town.

The repair department was retained in Northampton, but moved from the factory into small premises called 'The Toll House' at 130 St James Road, St James's End, opposite the Mettoy factory. The repairs to Trix locomotives and other Trix items were carried out by Harry

Hymes, the successor to Bill Best who had refused to move to Northampton when the original Trix offices in London were closed. Bill Best took up employ-ment with Colonel Beattie at the Southgate Hobbyshop in London continuing repairs on Trix and other locomotives including a conversion service on the old AC chassis to 12 volts DC operation. Colonel Beattie was a very enthu-siastic Trix dealer enjoying excellent relations with the Trix companies, and in return always gave a lot of publicity to the products. In 1959 the Southgate Hobbyshop ordered a complete production run of the new GWR Class 66XX tank engine, which was specially produced for them with two-rail

Trix 1960 trade exhibition display. Notice the wall display of Coronet Cameras which were made by Dufay Ltd.

93

operation and offered to the public in October.

After a short absence from work with a Trix company, Michael Catalani rejoined Dufay (B'ham) Ltd and continued to design new products, working from the premises at St James Road, where he was to remain until August 1963.

It was intended that production of Trix model railways would be in full swing again at the Birmingham factory between July and Christmas, before switching back to cameras for the first half of 1961, and it was envisaged that the one plant and assembly lines could efficiently produce both products. However, moving from Northampton took longer than anticipated and proved very

Designer/draughtsman Michael Catalani in 1983 with a 'Britannia' which was one of his designs.

costly, causing production delays. These, coupled with a failure to obtain certain goods to balance stocks, exacerbated the very poor sales figures for 1960.

Events took a further turn for the worse in the following year when Trix made a substantial loss again due to poor sales aggravated by an appalling Christmas trade, and the realisation that the goods made in Northampton and Birmingham were too expensive and out of date. Sales for the last quarter of 1961 were only half those for 1960. Dufay Ltd, being the parent company, was forced to the decision in December 1961 that the manufacture of Trix model railway items be halted in order to avoid Trix Products Ltd pulling the whole group down, and that the assets be should be written off.

Prior to the decision to cease trading it had already been decided earlier in the year to sell the Trix business and with this in mind a 'ready made' company called Latflag Engineering Co. Ltd (registered number 698974) had been purchased by Dufay Ltd during the first week in October. A nominal sum was paid for the company and the chairman of Dufay Ltd, H. Evans, and a Swiss entrepreneur Friedrich E. G. Hanebeck were registered as company officials. On 1 November Latflag Engineering Co.Ltd changed its name to Trix Products Ltd, while on the same day the original Trix Products Ltd (registered number 272812), changed its name to Trix Products (Holdings) Ltd. For a very short while both companies had the same new registered office address of 71/73, Great Portland Street, London as that of Dufay Ltd, although one week later Trix Products Ltd changed its

registered address to the more familiar 205, Great Portland Street,London. F. E. G. Hanebeck was brought into the new company as a company 'doctor' to try and project a new image to replace that which over the past few years had not earned popular appraisal.

At this point Ernest Rozsa, who in future years was to play a very important role in the continued existence of Trix model railways in Britain, began his relationship with the Trix business. Ernest Rozsa, whose parents were Hungarian, emigrated to England from Austria in 1947 and, being interested in model railways, eventually set up an import business in 1958 called Miniature Constructions of London to supply the Austrian-made Liliput range of model railways to the British public. To lessen the effects of import restrictions, many of the wagons and other items were initially assembled from component parts at his home in London during the evenings by his wife and himself. He was then approached by M. Zang, a past executive of Britains Ltd, who at the age of 85 had started a moulding shop as he wished to be back in business. He liked the look of the Liliput model railway range and joined Ernest Rozsa in order to produce the full Liliput range under license in this country. They formed a company called Miniature Construction Ltd. Their finest achievement was the introduction in October 1960 of the only British-outline model in the Liliput range, the AEI Class E3000 electric locomotive. Most of the parts for this locomotive were manufactured in Austria and the model was later added to the Trix range in Britain when Miniature Construction Ltd ceased trading in

1961 due to production difficulties. The model continued in production in various forms until 1987, which was quite a remarkable achievement. Apart from the E3000, Miniature Construction Ltd only manufactured a small amount of track and one or two wagons in this country.

Approximately one week before Christmas 1961, F. G. Hanebeck got in touch with E. Rozsa with a request for help with the repair of the control system of a large demonstration layout in the famous Gamages toy shop in London. This layout was operated by Bill Best, who at that time had just re-established his relationship with Trix model railways, being in charge of the service department of Trix Products Ltd at 205 Great Portland Street. Between the two of them they sorted out the problems, and it was not long after the New Year that E. Rozsa was invited to join Trix Products Ltd, taking the very open position of general manager to run the company's office and showroom.

It was felt that the long and unbroken association with Trix in Nuremberg should be strengthened, and with this in mind Günter Kurz was invited to join the new company of Trix Products Ltd as a director, although strangely he was never listed as a director in the official documents of the company. Günter Kurz (son-in-law of Ernst Voelk), was the managing director of Vereinigte Spielwarenfabriken Ernst Voelk KG and a man with very forthright ideas. This move enabled a large part of the Trix Express range to be added to the rather poor range of British-outline models available, to which was also added the Wiad agency.

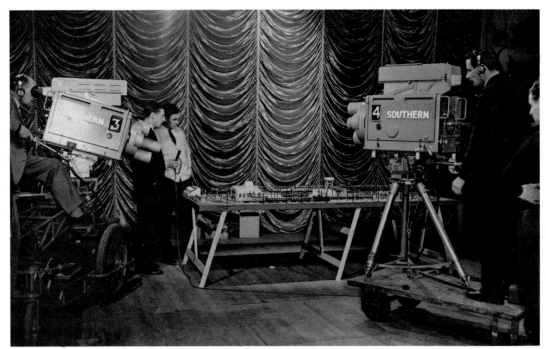

A Trix salesman being interviewed by Southern TV at the 1961 Brighton Toy Fair.

Dufay hoped that they would be able to sell this new company quickly. However, events did not work out as planned, and a large part of 1962 was taken up trying to complete a sale. Early in 1962, a finance company exchanged contracts with Dufay Ltd in order to purchase Trix Products Ltd with the result that Trix Products (Holdings) Ltd changed its name to Dufay (Holdings) Ltd, and H. Evans, the chairman of Dufay Ltd, resigned as director of the new company, Trix Products Ltd, thus severing ties with the parent company.

Unfortunately the purchasers failed to complete the deal due to a change of heart, which cannot have been helped by an article in the consumer magazine Which in December 1959 discussing the merits of the various model railway products and giving Trix a very unfavourable report. Thus Dufay Ltd were back to square one, and H. Evans was reinstated as director of Trix Products Ltd.

Through all these events, and even later, the new company continued to try and formulate different marketing and manufacturing

The layout used at
the 1961 Brighton
Toy Fair.

arrangements to attract customers to the virtues of Trix Twin Railways. When Dufay Ltd decided to cease the manufacture of Trix Twin Railways they were left with vast stocks. It was agreed that large amounts of completed sets and individual items, previously held in their many 'Polyfoto' shops in London should be processed in the Great Portland Street offices and dispatched to discount houses to be offered to the public at attractive prices. At one time Gamages took 5,000 sets containing the plastic BR 0-6-0 tank engine, and even large quantities of packs of Trix Construction parts and sets, including Trix X-Acto tools, were sold to the discount houses at greatly reduced rates. A warehouse belonging to Coronet Ltd also had large stocks of individual parts, including a few completed items, but Trix Products Ltd had no manufacturing base with which to capitalise on these parts.

During April, however, the shortage of completed track resulted in a large amount of rail parts being sent down from a Dufay (B'ham) warehouse to an old church hall in Almeida Street, Islington, London where the track was assembled on a balcony in the hall by a few girls. In fact this was the only product actually assembled by Trix Products Ltd in a large production run, a few other items being occasionally assembled in the company office and showroom premises.

Dufay Ltd now desperate to offload the company, made a loan of £34,000 during the latter part of June, which was the same time that H. Evans was reinstated, enabling the registered capital of Trix Products Ltd to be raised from £100 to £35,000 represented by 35,000 shares of

A Trix Products Newsletter dated April 1962.

Trix Express

No. 1 APRIL 1962   TRIX PRODUCTS LIMITED, 205 GREAT PORTLAND STREET, W.1.   LANGHAM 7593

PRICE REDUCTIONS ON TRIX RAILWAYS!

DRASTIC CUTS FOR 1962

This is the first news sheet to be issued by the new TRIX Company and it gives us a great sense of achievement to be able to open it with an announcement of price reductions. Not insignificant parings, but honest-to-goodness cuts which bring TRIX right back into the competitive market.

For years past the story has been an unending succession of increases to cover rising material and production costs. Through all this time the man behind the counter has fought a gallant rearguard action for TRIX in the face of fierce competition and for this we would like to express our sincerest thanks. In return we feel confident that our current re-organisation will bring you better products at a lower price and consequently a bigger turnover.

We appreciate that some of you may have a small quantity of goods left over from last year on which you must now take a reduced profit margin but you will certainly lose nothing in the process and the way will be clear for re-stocking at the new prices.

THE MAN BEHIND THE NEW TRIX

MR. E. G. HANEBECK

The motivating force of the new TRIX Company is Mr. E. G. HANEBECK. Of Swiss birth, he follows the tradition of his country in his skill and experience of small precision engineering. As Managing Director he has introduced to TRIX an unlimited store of new ideas, and technical know-how, some of the evidence of which will be seen in this and following news sheets.

We must also mention here that another new Director of TRIX Products Ltd. is Herr GUNTER KURZ who has for many years been a leading figure in the world's model railway business as Managing Director of TRIX EXPRESS of Nuremberg. This close association of the two Companies will provide some very interesting and no less beneficial developments in the very near future.

THE CHEAPEST TRAIN SET

When we speak of a cheap train set we must of course relate the price to the quality, at least in some measure.

TRIX can now offer a train set which on both price and quality will match anything at present on the British Market. This is the TRIX EXPRESS BEGINNER'S SET, available in either goods or passenger composition with 0-6-0 12V D.C. Locomotive, two goods wagons or two passenger coaches, a circle of track, connecting wires and a transformer complete with plug. This is packed in a plastic tray with transparent lid, and complete wiring instructions are enclosed with the set. The price— £4.19.6.

How easy it is to sell a train set which needs no explaining, no technical knowledge and most important of all, not one penny needing to be spent on extras before the train can operate. This set will not only be an easy seller for those who know the model railway business, but will be the answer to a frequently repeated prayer by the Departmental Stores who must rely, during the busy period, on non-technical staff whose main function in life is to sell a product rather than to know how it works. These sets are already in big demand, and if you want them, as you will, order them early. There will not be any left in December.

£1 each. On 9 November 1962 an agreement of sale was made for the purchase of Trix Products Ltd from Dufay Ltd which included the satisfaction of the above-mentioned loan account. From this transaction it emerged that the Alvus Investment & Trading Co. Ltd was the major shareholder with one of its directors, a solicitor named John J. Moreton, joining the board of directors of Trix Products Ltd. Morton then became the managing director on 4 February 1963. The remaining shareholders were four members of the Hanebeck family. It is worth noting that J. J. Moreton and the Alvus Investment & Trading Co. Ltd shared the same address.

J. J. Moreton and F. G. Hanebeck in the meantime had acquired South Bucks Tools Ltd in Lancaster Road, High Wycombe which was producing spark erosion equipment for the engineering industry, with the idea of expanding the production facilities to incorporate production of Trix components and the necessary tooling. This idea never materialised, with the exception of the moulding tools for the new scale plastic coaches designed by Michael Catalani. Earlier F. G. Hanebeck had taken Ernest Rozsa to the Mercedes car factory near the Bodensee in Baveria in the hope that Mercedes would produce the moulding tool for the coaches enabling parts for twenty coaches to be formed in one operation. As can be imagined, the weight of the tool would have been phenomenal and the idea was scrapped. Thus South Bucks Tools Ltd undertook to produce the moulding tool for these coaches which was the first attempt at a tool of this kind. Eventually it

was to prove a complete success, but unfortunately too late in the life of Trix Products Ltd for production use.

Although a brave face had been put on the company by the directors and many glowing promises were made to the public, the fact of the matter was that without a manufacturing base and with an inheritance of problems due to lack of continuity in production, Trix Products Ltd were finding it hard to be competitive and also to regain the public's confidence. The last public relations exercise was at the Brighton Toy Fair in

1963, when the company took the whole of the Winter Garden stage for a large Trix display seemingly as a pointer to the future. It was probably this display that caught the imagination of the directors of British Celanese Ltd, a member of the Courtaulds group of companies and a manufacturer of plastics, textiles and chemicals.

As a footnote to this era it might be marked that Dufay was to form the basis of the Slater Walker empire — but that is another story, albeit with a similar ending.

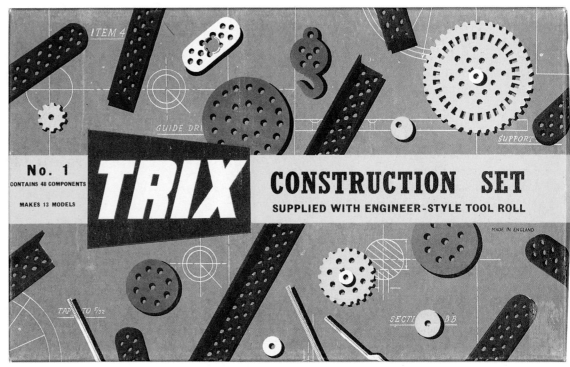

A No.1 Trix Construction Set manufactured under the Dufay banner circa 1959.

THE COURTAULDS PERIOD.

The Courtaulds group already partly owned British Lego Ltd, producers of the highly successful plastic building block sets for young children, and it was probably thought that a model railway company would be a natural progression. Events moved very quickly after the Brighton Toy Fair in February, so much so, that a subsidiary company of British Celanese Ltd (a Courtaulds group company), namely, British Transparent Containers Ltd (registered number 337171), changed its name to British Trix Ltd on 24 April 1963 with the registered office at 22/23 Hanover Square, London W1. There was no sale agreement relating to the business of Trix Products Ltd and it appears that the assets of the company were transferred to British Trix Ltd simply by the presentation and payment of an invoice. The goodwill of the business and the trademarks and patents, which had earlier been transferred from Dufay Ltd to Trix Products Ltd, were assigned to British Trix Ltd by an agreement dated 7 May 1963 for a payment of £1 in cash. It was decided that production and the general running of the business would take place from the British Celanese manufacturing complex at Wrexham, but the showroom was to remain at 205, Great Portland Street, London, W.1. until it was moved in 1965 to Silver City House, 62 Brompton Road, London SW3 with Ron Pordage as showroom manager. E. L. Rozsa believed very strongly in after sales service, and he decided that the customer would be best served if the service department was moved to Wrexham. Thus the longest serving Trix employee Bill Best, real name Thomas Campbell Best,

The Trix trade exhibition at the 1963 Brighton Toy Fair.

was persuaded to move with his family to Wrexham to take the position of service manager.

Trix Products Ltd were allocated 80,000 ordinary shares in British Trix Ltd with British Celanese Ltd holding a controlling issue of 342,600 ordinary shares with the residue from 520,000 ordinary 5/- (25p) shares and 1,500 preference £1 shares remaining unissued. One of the many stipulations of the agreement was that Trix Products Ltd must change its name to a title which did not contain the word 'TRIX' or anything similar to it, a ruling complied with in July 1963 when the company changed its name to Hanaton Ltd. J. J. Moreton and F. G. Hanebeck were appointed as directors of British Trix Ltd although they did not take any part in the general day-to-day running of the company.

Basically at the beginning of British Trix Ltd, E. E. Stimson, who was already a production executive of British Lego Ltd, was the managing director, E. Lampard was the production manager and E. L. Rozsa was in charge of design and development. One of the initial tasks was to transport the vast amounts of stock and tooling that remained in Birmingham and other places (all been painstakingly catalogued by Reg Thompson, the very efficient progress manager of Trix Products Ltd, who unfortunately at this point ended his services with the company, as he did not feel inclined to take up employment in Wrexham). It took over thirty lorry loads to transport all the Trix items to Wrexham.

British Celanese Ltd manufactured their goods predominantly in plastics and were not geared up to tinplate production, and thus a

Demonstration layout at a 1964/65 trade exhibition. Note the buildings and lineside features by Kibri and Wiad plus Trix Express locomotives and rolling stock used in conjunction with the British Trix range.

decision was made during 1964 to dispose of the unwanted and obsolete items. The responsibility for making this decision was taken by E. L. Rozsa. A mechanical digger was hired to dig a big hole in an industrial estate in Wrexham and a very large amount of AC locomotives, tinplate rolling stock including American Pullman coaches, LNER scale teak coaches and other now sought-after items were bulldozed into the hole. Of course the company had tried to find a buyer and a sale at greatly reduced prices was advertised in

the model press, but nobody was interested in purchasing the remnants of an obsolete system.

Initially the building allocated to production was number 208 in the British Celanese complex at Wrexham but it was more suited to assembly than anything else. This building was used to continue the production of the DC range inherited from Trix Products Ltd. There were various small improvements, including better wheels and the almost exclusive use of two-rail operation, although three rail versions were still

available to special order.

From the middle of 1964, the sales manager was J. Glynn who had previously been employed by Meccano Ltd and was well versed in this particular market, as at Meccano he had conducted a series of courses for dealers covering the technical and general aspects of model railways. Unfortunately his ideas did not always meet with general approval and he only remained for a few months. He organised the repackaging of the Trix Construction sets with limited success and tried to revitalise the 6-volt Trix Cadet sets but was unable to gain capital investment from British Celanese Ltd. As with Trix Products Ltd, E. L. Rozsa had pleaded with the management to invest in new products to increase the range available to the public, and it was for this reason that the agencies obtained by Trix Products Ltd with Wiad, Kibri, Schweiger, Liliput, Safiri SA and Schuco were renegotiated, although the Schuco agency was only retained for a short time. (Safiri SA were French-made veteran car models of approximately 7mm scale and plastic and diecast construction.) The long association with Trix Vereinigte Spielwaren-fabriken Ernst Voelk KG was maintained on a healthy basis which ensured the availability of a variety of locomotives and rolling stock for Trix customers in Britain.

Turnover for the first year of trading was very poor, and although a large amount of money had been spent by the parent company in extending the building used by British Trix Ltd, only a small sum was allocated to design and development. British Celanese Ltd, however, wanted to see a good return on their investments. The managing director, E. E. Stimson was replaced by J. R. S. Morris in June 1964 who, prior to joining British Trix Ltd, had been the factory manager of the very large Courtaulds Spondon Works at Derby and a director of many companies including G. & R. Wrenn Ltd. He quickly started to reorganise, with the result that the sales and production managers were replaced and overall control of the running of British Trix Ltd was given to E. L. Rozsa.

Apart from the new scale plastic coaches that were designed by Michael Catalani in Trix Products Ltd days, eventually getting onto the market during the early part of 1964, the only new item of note in the pipeline was the 'Western' diesel locomotive which was designed by E. L. Rozsa, who had persuaded Liliput of Austria to produce the model for British Trix Ltd. It was the total lack of new products that prompted Rozsa to include many related but selected products from continental manufacturers in the 1964 catalogue, including Liliput, Kibri, Wiad, Tempo from Yugoslavia and, of course, Trix Express. Most of the locomotives and rolling stock were repackaged by British Trix Ltd and fitted with the standard British type of Trix coupling.

1965 saw great improvements in the fortunes of the company and a substantial program of advertising took place. It was felt that in order to sell model railway sets track was essential, and as a result a new two-rail track system based on an existing Trix Express track was assembled in a small room in the building allocated to Trix production at Wrexham. Help in the production of this track was given by G. & R. Wrenn Ltd

A selection from the early German and British Minitrix range. Top four rows: The original diecast Minitrix push-along toy trains introduced in 1959. The wheels did not have any flanges. Bottom four rows: British Minitrix. Most of the items shown were manufactured at the British Trix factory in Wrexham.

New British Rail Coaches

Minitrix No 2928

Minitrix No 2927.

Minitrix No 2921

Minitrix No 2922.

Minitrix No 2923.

Minitrix No 2924.

Minitrix No 2926.

Minitrix No 2925.

Minitrix No 2928 Composite brake coach British Rail new blue/grey livery

Minitrix No 2927. Composite corridor coach British Rail new blue/grey livery

Minitrix No 2932 Corridor coach 2nd class Specification as above. *(Not illustrated)*

Minitrix No 2921. Composite corridor coach B.R. maroon • Moulded chassis and superstructure • Nylon bogies • Precision turned metal wheels • Fully printed and lined • Provision for interior lights • Length over buffers 5⅞ inches

Minitrix No 2929 Corridor coach 2nd class. Specification as above. *(Not illustrated)*

Minitrix No 2922. Composite brake coach B.R. maroon

Minitrix No 2923. Composite corridor coach Orig. Western region livery

Minitrix No 2930. Corridor coach 2nd class. Specification as above. *(Not illustrated)*

Minitrix No 2924. Composite brake coach Western Region livery

Minitrix No 2926. Composite brake coach Southern region livery

Minitrix No 2925. Composite corridor coach Southern Region livery

Minitrix No 2931. Corridor coach 2nd class Specifications as above. *(Not illustrated)*

New Tankwagons

Minitrix No 2957   Minitrix No 2958   Minitrix No 2955   Minitrix No 2956

Part of a 1970 Trix catalogue insert showing the British Minitrix range.

which at this time was also a member of the Courtaulds group of companies. Unfortunately the track was not a commercial success.

The unfortunate decision to retain a scale of 3.8mm instead of the more universal 4.0mm as used in Britain had a continuing adverse effect on the sales of the locomotives and rolling stock. Up to 1965 it seemed that British Trix Ltd had refused to progress with the times and adopt a system and scale that could be universally used with products from other manufacturers. A combination of this and other factors kept the sales of the 'Britannia', Class 'V', Warship diesel and other locomotives, including the new wagons and coaches at very low levels. The Footplateman, Coachbuilder, Wagonmaster and Platelayer series of assembly kits were thus introduced at very attractive prices to help bolster sales. This was a real shot in the arm for British Trix as very large quantities of locomotive kits were sold, including thousands of the coach kits.

1965 saw the introduction in Britain of a range of German-outline Minitrix Electric 'N' gauge locomotives and rolling stock developed by G. Kurz and his design team at Trix Vereinigte Spielwarenfabriken Ernst Voelk KG, which had been introduced a year earlier in Germany. This new system had earlier been rejected by J. Glynn but was seen to have great potential by E. L. Rozsa. Minitrix Electric was the natural progression from a range of push-along toy trains, with the trade name of Minitrix which were introduced in 1959. Initially the couplings were a Trix design and similar in operation to the British Triang coupling but changed a year later to a design by K. Arnold

GmbH & Co. of Nuremberg, which resulted yet again in the involvement of a Trix company in a dispute over the design of a coupling. However, it was not until 1967 that British-outline models were included in the Minitrix range, being tooled up and manufactured in Wrexham. After a slow start the range proved to be extremely popular.

With Ernest Rozsa at the helm British Trix Ltd was now beginning to put together a commendable range, and from 1966 to 1967 it saw the addition of a much-acclaimed range of plastic Private Owners and Whisky wagons plus the Inter-city DMU, most of them being tooled up by Liliput of Austria. Unfortunately even the excellence of the new products could not help the poor financial turnover of British Trix Ltd which did not come anywhere near to the hopes and expectations of the Courtaulds Group. The parent company, British Celanese Ltd, was not keen to invest more money in the company. In fact British Trix Ltd had made a substantial trading loss for each year of its existence. Once again the lack of popularity of model railways had taken its toll, but it was also felt that the lack of development money in the early days resulting in too few models in a highly competitive market was a contributing factor, as well as the popularity of other pastimes and hobbies in particular slot-car racing.

It was a sad day for the employees of British Trix Ltd when E. L. Rozsa was called to the managing director's office just prior to Christmas 1967 to be told that the company was to cease trading immediately. Consequently the interests of British Trix Ltd in model railways were disposed of on 19 January 1968, and British Trix Ltd changed its name back to British Transparent Containers Ltd on 24 February 1968.

1963 edition.

1964 edition.

The catalogues of British Trix Ltd.

1966 edition.

THE FINAL CHAPTER.

On a day at the beginning of January 1968 whilst tidying up the loose ends of British Trix Ltd, Ernest Rozsa received a call from Günter Kurz of Trix Vereinigte Spielwarenfabriken Ernst Voelk KG, asking him to get in touch with the Board of Trade as soon as possible as they wanted a factory in Great Britain. The idea was to set up a factory to build 'N' gauge models for the American market. At the time these were being manufactured for Trix Express by Roco Modelspielwaren GmbH & Co. KG of Salzburg. The Board of Trade agreed in principle and it was decided to continue production in the Wrexham area. For this reason the Welsh Development Board was contacted and was very keen on the idea of a new factory when it was realised that up to 200 people could be employed. There was even a broadcast on the local Welsh radio advertising the fact that a German toy manufacturer was going to set up a business in Wrexham. Trix could now indeed be termed a 'toy manufacturer' as during January 1966 the company had been purchased by The Schildkröt toy and doll company of Mannheim with the 'Turtle' trade mark who in turn was owned by Wasag-Chemie AG of Essen.

It was the middle of January 1968 that Trix Vereinigte Spielwarenfabriken Ernst Voelk KG entered into an agreement with British Celanese Ltd and British Trix Ltd to purchase the stock and tooling appertaining to Trix products, plus all trademarks and agency agreements. The purchase price was £28,247. Part of the agreement was that British Celanese Ltd should provide storage and production facilities until the new factory was completed.

Ernest Rozsa was instructed to find a company so that money from Germany could be transferred and business could commence. A ready-made company was purchased during March called Thernglade Ltd (registered number 903518), and Ernest and his wife were made the resident directors. With very little money production was started using building '208' in the British Celanese industrial compound with six staff, including the long serving Bill Best as service manager. Apart from providing the building, British Celanese Ltd were also helpful with other aspects, including security, fire services and the use of a machine shop.

During the early part of British Trix's last year, arrangements had been made with Liliput Spielwarenfabrik GmbH to supply the injection moulding tools for the LNER 'Flying Scotsman' locomotive and tender. This was the first really true 4.0mm scale locomotive to be produced with the Trix label. When British Trix Ltd ceased trading, the tooling had almost been completed with the exception of the valve gear which the German Trix company agreed to fund. Thus, after being initially announced by the model press in March 1967, the 'Flying Scotsman' was eventually assembled in Wrexham from parts supplied by Liliput and reached the shops in July 1968. This was the product that really made the model railway enthusiasts once again take a serious note of Trix.

All the range included in the 1967/1968 British Trix Ltd catalogue was retained including the agencies, but the Trix Construction sets made in Britain were slowly phased out as stocks diminished. The Trix Construction sets had done well to last from 1932 until this time, but had always had to compete with the ever-popular and sophisticated Meccano system and the same basic units had remained almost without alteration from the time of their introduction. In later years new parts and special finishes were added to the German Trix Construction sets which enjoyed a regained popularity.

As mentioned above, the first year of Thernglade Ltd was under the control of Ernest Rozsa and his wife, and it was not until the beginning of 1969 that Trix Vereinigte Spielwarenfabriken Ernst Voelk KG really took control of the company by creating and owning a total of 15,000 £1 shares and providing four German directors. Ernest's wife Terry resigned and took on the roll of secretary. Ernest was forward thinking and in tune with public taste. Thus the winter of 1970 saw the introduction of some very fine LNER 4.0mm scale models in the form of A2s and A4s which were just as good as their illustrious predecessor, the 'Flying Scotsman'. In addition, the range of British outline 'N' gauge was increased including the 'Britannia'. To complement the 4.0mm range of LNER locomotives, Gresley coach body card kits, and others such as station buildings in 4.0mm and 'N' gauge, were introduced in the autumn of 1971, produced for Thernglade Ltd by the successor company to Harris Edge Publications from designs by Roy C. Link. At the time it was felt that it would be too costly to produce the

THE GREAT TRIX TRAIN COMPETITION

£625
worth of prizes

MRC readers who have followed the Trix competition announcements should by now have collected the three Trix tokens that qualify them to enter the competition. The final token appears in this issue.

HOW TO ENTER

The competition is in two parts: the first tests the entrant's railway knowledge and the second, his (or her) skill in slogan writing. Complete clearly in ink or ballpoint the two parts and the declaration on the other side of this page. Cut along the dotted line and send the whole entry form, together with the three tokens, to this address:

**The Great Trix Train Competition
Norman Davis Limited
8, Thavies Inn
London E.C.I.**

The closing date is February 28th, 1969.

PRIZES

All prizes will be in the form of vouchers exchangeable at any Trix dealer for Trix products to the stated value, based on recommended list prices. The first, second and third prizes are vouchers for £100, £75 and £50. There will also be fifty other prizes consisting of five £20, fifteen £10 and thirty £5 vouchers. Prizewinners may choose from the entire Trix range. Vouchers can **only** be exchanged through accredited Trix dealers and only for Trix products. Prizes will be awarded to competitors who, in the opinion of the judges, submit the most meritorious entries, having regard for the correctness of the answers to Part I

and the aptness of the slogan. The complete list of prizewinners will be published in the May issue of **MRC.**

RULES

1 Entries can only be accepted from individuals.

2 Employees of Trix, their dealers, advertising agents, publishers, printer's or their families are not eligible to enter.

3 All entries will be examined but none will be returned.

4 It is a condition of entry that Trix acquire the copyright of all slogans submitted.

5 Entries are limited to one per person and each must be accompanied by the three consecutive tokens taken from the November, December 1968 and January 1969 issues of **MRC.**

6 Only the official entry form overleaf with all three parts completed and accompanied by three consecutive tokens will be accepted for judging.

7 The decision of the judging panel is final and no correspondence can be entered into.

8 The sponsors cannot accept (a) responsibility for entries lost, delayed or damaged in the post nor (b) proof of posting as proof of delivery.

9 Illegible entries or those which do not conform to the rules will be disqualified.

ENTRY FORM

Before you start, read the previous page carefully.

PART 1
Here are twelve straightforward questions to test your railway knowledge.
Please write the answers to each one clearly in the appropriate space.

1 Give the numbers carried by the locomotive "Flying Scotsman" during its life.

2 What do the initials BRT mean on the bulk grain wagons?

3 How many of the Bulleid pacifics were rebuilt?

4 How many miles did the "Flying Scotsman" cover on the non-stop run from Kings Cross to Edinburgh on May 1st 1968?

5 What is the horse power of the "Western" class diesel?

6 Name the locomotive which holds the world speed record, the speed and the date.

7 What class of locomotive was rebuilt by BR in 1951 to a design of 1898?

8 Give the full name of the designer of the "Flying Scotsman".

9 Name the first London terminal station opened to passenger traffic and in what year.

10 What is the code name of the covered motor car trucks as used on the Great Western?

11 What railway company absorbed the Merthyr, Tredegar and Abergavenny Railway?

12 Name the first tube railway in London and the date of opening.

PART II
Go for *authentrixity* is a familiar slogan which appears in all Trix advertisements. You are asked to invent a better one. There is no word limit, but remember that the best slogans are short, precise, memorable and do not necessarily rely on the pun.

My Trix Slogan is

PART III
DECLARATION
To: Great Trix Train Competition, Norman Davis Limited, 8, Thavies Inn, London, E.C.1. I have read the rules of the competition and agree to abide by them. I have completed Parts I and II and attached three consecutive Trix tokens (numbered 1, 2 and 3).

Signature   Date

Name and address of entrant (BLOCK CAPITALS)

Name and address of Trix dealer (BLOCK CAPITALS)

ix   x

Trix Trains Thernglade Ltd Industrial Estate Wrexham Denbighshire

Go for authentrixity

The Great Trix Train Competition. This was a competition run in conjunction with the magazine *Model Railway Constructor* which appeared in the November 1968 edition of that magazine.

tooling required for new plastic coaches, so the stop-gap answer was the card kits.

New model railway products were by this time eagerly awaited from Thernglade Ltd, marketed under the label of Trix Trains. For the first time the quality of these new British-outline mass-produced models was equal to those available on the continent.

To cope with the increased development and production costs and the pending move to the new factory premises during the spring of 1971, the capital of the company was increased by a

further £15,000 during October 1970, the shares again created and held by the parent company. The new factory, situated on the Wrexham Industrial Estate opposite the British Lego Ltd factory outside the British Celanese compound, provided ample room for offices and production facilities. Unfortunately by the time the factory was ready for production, the original intention of producing the American-outline Minitrix range for export had to be abandoned as the American Minitrix market had collapsed. Plans to ease production were concentrated on

manufacturing an increased number of components for the Trix Trains and the British-outline Minitrix range so as to reduce the dependency on continental imports, the cost of which had become prohibitive due to the fall in the value of the pound sterling. A great deal more moulding work was done in-house and it was hoped that eventually an uninterrupted production schedule would be maintained.

A long term objective of Ernest Rozsa, a dedicated model railway man, was the development of 100% British-designed and produced items which unfortunately never materialised. As a direct result of the involvement of Schildkröt Spielwaren GmbH, the other products associated with Thernglade such as Turtle toys and dolls and the French-made Bella dolls probably held back the progress of the Trix Trains.

The holding company, Wasag-Chemie AG who had initially had the idea of building a large toy empire, was at this time experiencing financial difficulties and the ultimate holding company, Böhlen Industria AG, called in a company 'doctor' to put matters straight, with the result that in June 1971 along with other holdings, Schildkröt Spielwaren GmbH was instructed to dispose of Trix Vereinigte Spielwarenfabriken Ernst Voelk KG, and Schildkröt Spielwaren GmbH became the direct shareholders of Thernglade Ltd. The model railway business was slowly phased out and a decision was taken to wind down the company. However, at the last moment it was given a reprieve as the German parent company introduced in May 1972 a new executive, H. W. Graham, who had previously worked for a large

1967/68 catalogue cover which started its days with British Trix Ltd. In 1968/69 the catalogue was reissued by Thernglade Ltd.

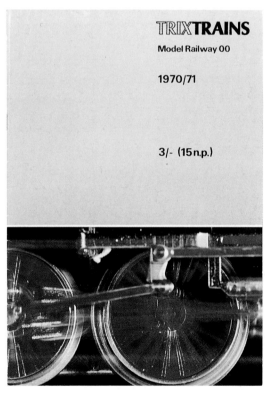

Trix Trains 1970/71 catalogue cover. This was to be the final catalogue published for British model trains with the trade name of TRIX.

Scottish toy manufacturer and had experience in the production of cheap mass-produced but expensively packaged toys.

The last official advertisement for the Trix side of the business actually appeared in the model press in November 1971, although various retail outlets continued to advertise Trix Trains, Trix Express and Continental and British-outline Minitrix during the following year.

When Trix Vereinigte Spielwarenfabriken Ernst Voelk GmbH was disposed of by Schildkröt Spielwaren GmbH, it was amalgamated with George Adam Mangold GmbH & Co KG, a toy manufacturer of renown established in 1882, to form the company Trix-Mangold GmbH On hearing that Thernglade Ltd was to close, prior to the later decision to continue with the toy side of the business, Trix-Mangold GmbH. procured all the Minitrix tooling so that the British range could be continued. Accordingly, on 1 January 1973 Rovex Ltd were appointed sole UK distributors for the British-outline Minitrix range and, although all the Minitrix items were manufactured in Nuremberg with the exception of a few plastic lineside buildings, they were packaged under the Hornby-Minitrix label — a clever exercise considering the respect for the name of 'Hornby' in the model railway world.

Thernglade Ltd continued toy production under Schildkröt until November 1973 when it was decided to close the factory due to constantly declining sales. Ernest Rozsa was instructed to start the winding up procedures for the company and to try and dispose of the lease on the factory premises. This was duly done when Thernglade Ltd and the factory were taken

Part of the Trix Trains July 1970 price list.

TRIX TRAINS
Price List—1st July 1970

NOTE—3 Rail Locomotives, track and accessories have been withdrawn and are not offered any longer. However, special orders for such equipment can be executed. When ordering 3 rail equipment please quote 2 rail catalogue numbers. Orders placed for 3 rail equipment CANNOT BE CANCELLED.

LOCOMOTIVES

Cat. No.	Description	Rec. Retail Price
1108	0-6-0 Tank loco, black	60/11
1120	Warship class diesel, green	123/8
1123	Warship class diesel, blue	123/8
1128	E-3000 class Bo-Bo loco, blue	133/3
1163	Western class diesel loco, blue	133/3
1165	Western class diesel loco, green	133/3
1167	Western class diesel loco, maroon	133/3
1169	Western class diesel loco, 2 mtrs.	199/10
1174	Intercity set blue/grey, no lights	161/7
1175	Intercity set green, no lights	152/3
1177	Intercity set blue/grey and lights	171/3
1178	Intercity set green and lights	171/3
1180	Flying Scotsman	180/9
1180DT	Flying Scotsman, 2 tenders	199/10
1182	Flying Scotsman, B.R. green	180/9
1183	4-6-2 (as above), black	171/3
1186	4-6-2 Steam loco and tender, Peppercorn	180/9
1188	4-6-2 " " " " Silver Link	180/9
1190	4-6-2 " " " " Mallard Blue	180/9
1195	4-6-2 " " " " Br. Green	180/9

FOOTPLATEMAN'S SERIES
(Construction Kits)

2118	Warship diesel kit, blue	104/8
2119	Warship diesel kit, maroon	104/8
2120	Warship diesel kit, green	104/8
2128	E-3000 class diesel kit, blue	114/2
2163	Western diesel kit, blue	114/2
2165	Western diesel kit, green	114/2
2167	Western diesel kit, maroon	114/2

COACHES WITH INTERIORS

1901	Composite, corridor, maroon	20/0
1902	Composite, corridor brake, maroon	20/0
1903	Buffet-miniature, maroon	20/0
1911	Composite corridor W.R. brown/cream	20/0
1912	Composite corridor brake, brown/cream	20/0
1913	Buffet-miniature W.R., brown/cream	20/0
1921	Composite corridor S.R., green	20/0
1922	Composite corridor brake, green	20/0
1923	Buffet-miniature S.R., green	20/0
1931	Pullman	20/0
1951	Composite corridor coach, blue/grey	20/0
1952	Composite corridor brake, blue/grey	20/0
1953	Buffet-miniature, blue/grey	20/0
1971	Intercity trailer, green	20/0
1972	Intercity trailer brake, green	20/0
1973	Intercity trailer, buffet, green	20/0
1975	Intercity trailer, blue/grey	20/0
1976	Intercity trailer brake, blue/grey	20/0
1977	Intercity trailer buffet, blue/grey	20/0

COACHBUILDER SERIES

1941	Composite corridor, maroon	15/3
1942	Composite corridor brake, maroon	15/3
1943	Buffet, maroon	15/3
1944	Composite corridor. W.R.	15/3
1945	Composite corridor brake W.R.	15/3
1946	Buffet W.R.	15/3
1947	Composite corridor, S.R., green	14/3
1948	Composite corridor brake, green	14/3
1949	Buffet S.R., green	14/3
1950	Pullman	15/3
1954	Composite corridor S.R., blue	14/3
1955	Composite corridor brake S.R., blue	14/3
1956	Composite corridor B.R., blue	15/3
1957	Composite corridor brake B.R., blue/grey	15/3
1958	Buffet B.R., blue/grey	15/3
1960	Pullman, blue/grey	15/3

WAGONS

1606	Mineral wagon, grey	7/7
1607	Mineral wagon, red	7/7
1610	Breakdown crane with truck	38/0
1613	Covered van, red	10/0
1614	Covered van, grey	10/0
1617	Container wagon	9/6
1618	Container wagon, white	9/6
1621	Brake van, grey	9/0
1622	Brake van, red	9/0
1623	Speedfreight container wagon	10/0
1641	Tank wagon, Shell B.P., red	10/6
1644	Tank wagon, Esso, silver	10/6
1645	Tank wagon, B.P., green	10/6
1648	Tank wagon, Total, grey	10/6
1652	Track cleaning wagon	34/3
1657	Private owner wagon, Spiers	10/0
1658	" " " Maltby	10/0
1659	" " " Salter	10/0
1661	" " " Young	10/0
1662	" " " Ocean	10/0
1664	" " " Hall and Co.	10/0
1665	" " " I.C.I.	10/0
1666	" " " Blue Circle	10/0
1667	" " " Charrington	10/0
1668	" " " Wilkinson	10/0
1669	" " " Abbott	10/0
1670	" " " Stewart and Lloyd	10/0
1671	" " " Chubb	10/0
1672	" " " Wm. Cordon Jameson	10/0
1673	" " " Roberts, Jenks	10/0
1674	" " " Sutton Manor	10/0
1675	" " " Nicholson	10/0

over on 1 April 1974 by the Park Toy Co. Ltd, which was based in nearby Chester and was a manufacturer of dolls' houses.

During the last year of Thernglade Ltd, Ernest Rozsa had been quietly and discreetly salvaging the model railway side of the business ready for the final closing down which he could clearly see coming. All the spares and stock, including those from manufacturers other than Trix, were purchased from Schildkröt and in 1973 he set up a mail-order business operating from a private address called 'Berwyn Hobbies Supplies' providing the modelling public with items which they thought had finally disappeared. During this same period, Liliput Spielwarenfabrik GmbH contacted Ernest with the idea of purchasing the HO/OO moulds from Trix in Germany and manufacturing the British outline locomotivs and rolling stock in Austria to be distributed by him in Britain, including the complete Liliput range. This was an exercise which was easily carried out as most of the tooling was already in Austria and the remaining moulds were still at the British Lego factory. Another private mail-order company operating from a private address was established by Ernest to distribute the Liliput items called 'E. L. Rozsa'. However, his business involvement with Liliput Spielwarenfabrik and other agencies increased to such an extent that in 1974 he decided to form a limited company called Liliput Model Railways (UK) Ltd, incorporating Kibri (UK) and Vollmer (UK) and operating eventu-ally from a building on the Industrial Estate at Bala, North Wales. He employed a handful of staff to assemble the ex-Trix British outline model railway items which were now sold under the name of Liliput British Series. Ernest was skilful in creating a demand for the ex-Trix locomotives by keeping supply to a restricted level, and over the years the technical details were improved tremendously.

Although his three companies were incorporated mainly to handle the products of Liliput, Kibri and Vollmer, Rosza also took on other agencies and renewed relationships with Trix-Mangold, handling the Trix HO and Continental outline Minitrix range as distributor. The entire range as issued by Thernglade Ltd was reissued under the British Liliput Series label and most items were at first readily available. However, the supply of parts again started to be erratic and unbalanced, with the rate of exchange for the pound as against the European currencies having an adverse effect on the cost of the end product. Although designs were modified to cope with the ever changing parts availability, in the end Ernest became disillusioned and by 1992 having become a one man business he decided to assemble his last batch of hand-made LNER/BR Peppercorn's during the summer of that year. He had already relinquished the Trix and Liliput agencies during the early part of 1987 to concentrate mainly on the retail side of the business which operated from the same building which had been renamed the Kivoli Centre.

It should be remembered that when Ernest Rozsa joined Trix Products Ltd he took with him the Liliput agency, which included the E3000 locomotive, and which over the years was a major contributory factor to the success of the British Trix range. Had it not been for him and

Ernest Rozsa in the assembly area of Liliput Model Railways (UK) Ltd in 1988.

him alone Trix in Britain may have disappeared into history long before it did. He pushed, persuaded and cajoled his masters to improve and expand, and at all times to strive for that perfection in quality which seemed to be the norm on the continent but not in Britain. Sadly, he was an idealist in a non-idealistic business world.

EPILOGUE.

The Trix model railway was the major pioneer for all small gauge commercially-produced systems. Although developed initially by the same team in both Germany and Britain, production in the latter country later relied heavily on an early winning formula, and for a long period it retained its toy-like image with a track system to suit. Germany was quick to realise the potential of a more realistic system, and was soon producing more and more scale models and accessories, whilst Britain produced items with the emphasis on action which were costly and only appealed to enthusiasts of the TTR system. Quality and reliability, although initially keenly adhered to in both countries, was later subject in Britain to severe financial constraints.

Production continuity after the middle of the 1950s in Britain was constantly hit by ownership changes, business politics, and the sometimes very poor and erratic supply of parts. All these factors contributed to the decline in sales, which was compounded by a general trend away from model railways into other interests. A brave effort was made between the mid-1960s to the early 1970s, but just when British Trix was once again regaining credibility, business politics determined otherwise.

On the German scene, despite changes within the ownership complexities of the Trix company, fortune looked kindly on the products which always strove for perfection within the constraints of the production techniques available. Indeed, the German company was always a pioneer of new technical innovations.

If cooperation in one form or another from Germany had not been available to the British Trix companies from the first to the last days of production, the *History of Trix HO/OO Model Railways in Britain* might have been a much shorter story to tell.

At the time of writing,(1993)Trix-Mangold GmbH remains a very important model railway company, enjoying tremendous success. Minitrix accounts for approximately 70% of production and supplies well over half the German 'N' gauge market, while remaining production is split between the two-rail HO gauge Trix International and the old three-rail Trix Express (DC) system for which there is still an enthusiastic following. Even the Trix Metallbaukasten is still produced in various set sizes. Production is based at two factories, one on the outskirts of Nuremberg at Spalt, and the other in Nuremberg itself. Together they employ well over 300 people.

British-outline Minitrix, produced by Trix-Mangold and supplied to Britain through a distributor, is still very popular, but as yet no HO gauge model has been specifically designed or produced for the British market.

Thus we come to the end of the somewhat rocky road of the British-produced Trix model railway items. Although I may have bored some readers with the history of complex and involved accounting manouevres, I think those who have stuck with the story will agree that the diverging fortunes of the German and British companies are highly instructive and tell us more than just the story of model trains.

The Trix-Mangold factory in Nuremberg.

THE LOCOMOTIVES

EARLY DAYS IN BRITAIN

Spring 1935 saw the introduction of the first Trix-Express locomotive at the Leipzig Fair in the form of a diecast German outline 0-4-0 engine and tinplate tender in black with the number 20 051 and TRIX EXPRESS embossed on the cab sides. This number, which was also embossed on the locomotive smokebox door, coincided with its catalogue number 20/51. For many years a running number on the cab side and smokebox door corresponding to a similar catalogue number was to be the norm for most Trix Express locomotives, a principle also applied to rolling stock. This 0-4-0 engine and tender, (German wheel classification 'B'), had a toy-like appearance as it must not be forgotten that the designers and manufacturers main aims were to cater for young children. Only after its highly

successful introduction in Germany, and later that year in Britain, was it realised that adults were taking a keen interest in the new Trix Express system and that even greater enthusiasm could be ensured if more realistic models were produced.

The backbone of the Trix locomotives for over 20 years were those designed around the basic 0-4-0 14 volt AC chassis which ran on a robust three-rail track. This chassis, from between 1937 and 1938 onwards, changed very little in its design and proved to be a very reliable and powerful unit, but its smooth operation relied greatly on the cleanliness of the rails and pick-up shoes. Although, strictly speaking, this chassis was capable of being driven from a 12 volt DC source as the motor design was universal, it is generally known and operated as an AC chassis.

Pre-production model of the Trix Express 0-4-0 ('B') engine and tender from which the backbone of the Trix AC locomotive range descended both in Germany and Britain. Note the lack of boiler detail and a different cab shape to the production version.

The first chassis, although smooth and efficient in its operation, was definitely toy-like in appearance with the four wheels, painted red according to German practice, being just plain flanged discs with no representation of spokes, and connecting rods which were decidely over scaled. The wheel flanges were of dimensions that allowed a child to enjoy running the locomotives fast over the track, often laid on an uneven surface, without the endless derailment experienced with finer scale wheels. Comparison between accepted modern day standards and those of coarse scale Trix wheels, reveals a flange depth on the Trix wheels of 2.00mm compared with 1.00mm for modern wheels, and a flange width of 1.50mm and 0.50mm respectively. Interestingly, at the time of writing, Trix-Mangold GmbH still manufacture a small percentage of their output to the old coarse scale for use with their three-rail track system, although the flange width is reduced somewhat.

The direction of the motor on the 14 volt AC chassis is governed by a sequence reverser relay, whose function is simple but was to cause many problems in use namely unscheduled stops and unplanned reversing! However, this basic design of direction control was used on all future Trix Express and Trix Twin Railway AC locomotive chassis, with certain refinements for special functions.

The common return for the current supply uses the centre rail pick-up shoes, insulated from the chassis frame, and the uninsulated outer pick-up shoes, which can be fitted to either side of the chassis, are used to collect the controlled current from an outside rail. This rail is fed from a specially-designed controller which incorporates a variable resistance and a combined safety cut-out and impulse switch. To explain the operation of the chassis, refer to the electrical diagram on the facing page, which assumes that the locomotive is travelling in a forward direction. As shown in section <1> of the electrical circuits, current passes from the common centre rail through the motor field coil 'F', then through the insulated brass sleeve on the contact shaft onto the wiper blade <B1> and through the carbon brush onto a segment of the commutator. The current then passes through the windings of an armature pole onto the next segment of the commutator <C>,

Original Twin Train promotional photograph. A hand holding one locomotive (later two), became a well known part of the decorative and publicity literature of the Trix Twin Railway. The hand in this picture is that of W. J. Bassett-Lowke.

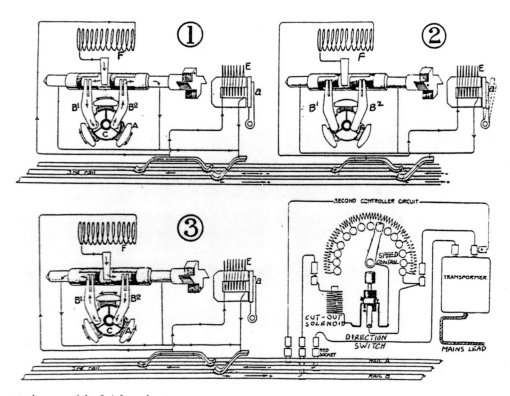

Schematic diagram of the 0-4-0 mechanism.

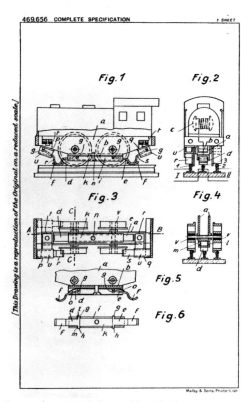

Extract from British Patent No.469,656,
(German origin), showing the pick-up arrangement.

through the carbon brush and then via the wiper blade <B2> and the uninsulated brass sleeve on the contact shaft to the chassis. From here it passes to the outer rail, completing the circuit which causes the motor armature <A> to revolve in a clockwise direc-tion. It will be seen from the same circuit that current also flows through the relay coil <E> which attracts the armature <a> to its pole.

Let us now assume that the operator wishes to change direction. Firstly the speed of the locomotive must be reduced to a standstill by the speed control knob on the controller, and then the combined safety cut-out and direction control switch is operated which has the effect of interrupting the current feed to the locomotive. This causes the relay armature to fall away from the pole. The direction switch is now released,

and due to special contacts on the switch assembly, a pulse of full current is momentarily applied to the relay coil before regulated current is restored as the switch returns to its normal position. This pulse of full current ensures that the relay armature operates in an efficient manner. Thus, the pole of the relay once again attracts the armature <a> which is mechanic-ally linked to the contact shaft causing it to rev-

113

olve one quarter of a revolution.

Referring to section <2> circuit, it will be seen that the contact shaft has turned to a position where the wiper blades <B1> and <B2> are in contact with an insulated section and thus no current can flow through the motor. The direction switch is operated again and the sequence of actions of the reversing relay results

in the contact shaft turning a further quarter of a revolution. As it can be seen from section <3> circuit, current once more flows through the motor, but because of the position of the brass sleeves on the contact shaft, the current flows through the commutator and the armature winding in a different direction causing the motor armature to revolve in an anti-clockwise

direction. Thus, the locomotive will now travel in the reverse direction when the current to the motor is increased by the action of the speed control. This sequence of operations is repeated to return the locomotive to forward movement.

Although the diagram shows the features of early pre-war locomotive chassis and controller, later versions of the 0-4-0 chassis were mechanically modified. However, the basic electrical circuit remained the same except that in 1938 instead of the centre rail current collector assembly being insulated from the chassis, it was now connected directly to it and the outside rail current collectors were insulated. This was called a 'C' type chassis which allowed two locomotives to be coupled together still under independent control of one another; an important feature and necessary refinement.

The Trix Express controller design basically remained unaltered until the demise of the 14 volt AC system in Germany in the early 1950s. After the war, as was mentioned in the preceding chapter, British-produced TTR sets were once again available, although a problem was that before the war the controllers had been supplied by Trix Germany and supplies had not resumed. TTR locomotives would not operate efficiently without a controller specifically designed for the job in question. The answer lay in a new British design which was launched in 1946/1947. This new controller had the direction control lever situated at the lower left corner of the assembly instead of being in the middle of the speed control knob, but the basic electrical circuit remained unaltered. The new TTR design was generally felt to be more efficient to operate,

1935 Trix Express 0-4-0 Electric Locomotive Cat.No. 20/52. The first version, note the protrusion on the buffer beam for mounting the coupling. (C)

The underneath of the 1935 Trix Express Electric 0-4-0 locomotive Cat.No.20/52 showing clearly the method of mounting the coupling. (C)

being much smoother in speed control due to a specially wound rheostat.

The question arises as to why Trix chose 14 volts AC? One reason is that during the early 1930s permanent magnets of the size required for small electric DC motors were prone to a rather fast magnetic decay rate. In addition, the technology of small rectifiers, used to convert AC to DC, could not handle the starting current of the motors. However, having to use a sequence reverser relay to change motor direction had the advantage in later years that the designers could add the unique feature of remote uncoupling anywhere on the track without the use of special rails, as well as head and tail lights which changed depending on the locomotive's direction of movement. All this was achieved without the use of modern electronics.

Returning to the locomotives, the next item to follow the 20/51 German outline 0-4-0 tender locomotive in 1935 was a representation of a German electric locomotive. This model had two fixed dummy tinplate pantographs and the basic 0-4-0 chassis which still retained the unspoked wheels. The diecast body was finished in dark green with a white roof and the number 20 052 was embossed on the sides of the body to correspond to a catalogue number of 20/52. The couplings fitted to each end of the locomotive were held in place by a plate which was fixed to the underside of the chassis by two screws. This early version had a very short production run before the body casting was modified, and only very few samples arrived on the British market. On later versions (catalogue number 20/55) produced from 1936, the couplings were retained

Trix Express Passenger set for the British market Cat.No.11/2.

115

Trix Express Goods set for the British market
Cat.No. 11/1. (D)

by a tinplate bracket held on to the modified body casting by the screwed buffers, this being the normal practice for nearly all the Trix Express and TTR locomotives up to the middle of the 1950s. The body always retained the number 20 052.

It is obvious that Vereinigte Spielwarenfabriken Andreas Förtner & J. Haffner's Nachf. GmbH had intentions of introducing and producing models for the British market at an early stage in the planning and development of the Trix Express system. In the latter part of November 1935 two sets were made available to the British public in time for Christmas. One was a goods set, Cat.No. 11/1, comprising an engine and tender, open wagon, refrigerator van, brake van and a 'Shell' tank wagon, (see The Rolling Stock Chapter). The other was a passenger set, Cat.No. 11/2, comprising an engine and tender, (the same model as for the goods set), two bogie first class coaches and a bogie guards van, the coaches being in a green livery and lined in yellow similar to Southern Railway livery. Both sets included four straight rails and 12 curved rails including the special controller. The initial cost of the goods set was 30/- (£1.50) and that of the passenger set 35/- (£1.75).

During the 1930s the British public had a somewhat negative attitude towards German-made goods and, accordingly, most of the advertisements only mentioned that 'The Big Sensation in Model Railways' was of foreign manufacture, although the actual models were identified as being manufactured by Trix Express in Germany. Even the English language instruction book stated that it was printed in Bavaria!

The set was in fact advertised as 'The Bassett-Lowke TWIN TRAIN Table Railway' and advertisements depicted the cab and tender sides of the locomotive as bearing the words TWIN TRAIN, although in actuality they did not.

The engine and tender supplied in the above sets was a 20/51 finished in a green Southern Railway livery, but without an SR number or insignia. The catalogue number allocated to this engine and tender was 21/51 which only differed in its pre-fix number. In fact Trix Express items that were destined or specifically manufactured for a country other than Germany were allocated an identifying prefix, namely 21 for Britain, 22 for Holland, 25 for France, 28 unknown (although used on a refrigerator van supplied with the 11/1 goods set), and 29 for the USA. The tender, which in these early models was semi-permanently coupled to the engine body by a split-pin, had the name TRIX EXPRESS and the number 5391 on each side, but careful inspection reveals that the word TWIN which was printed on to the tinplate has been hand-altered to read TRIX. Maybe there was an element of disagreement between Vereinigte Spielwarenfabriken and Bassett-Lowke Ltd, who acted as promoters, as to what name should be used. The launch of the 'Twin Train' was a huge success and the entire initial supply was sold out just before Christmas.

The design and production staff in Nuremberg were keen to develop and expand their model railway system, and it was with this in mind that an improved version of the chassis for the 20/51 and 20/55 was made available in Germany. These modifications were also passed on to the

21/51 reaching the British market in spring 1936. The nondescript disc-type wheels were replaced by spoked wheels and the representation of the coupling rods was improved in a form which was to survive up to the middle of the 1950s on models produced at both the Nuremberg and Northampton factories. The tinplate tender had a cast weight fitted to the underside of its chassis for extra stability supplementing the paper bag filled with little discs which represented waste metal from the punched holes in the Trix Construction components.

The summer of the same year brought further improvements as the body casting of the 20/51 0-4-0 German-outline tender engine was altered. The mounting of the front coupling was changed enabling a standard working diecast coupling to be fitted instead of the fixed tinplate hook. The

Early Trix Express 0-4-0s
as supplied to Britain.
From the top and left:
Cat.No.21/51 1935 version,
Cat.No.21/51 1936 version
with spoked wheels,
Cat.No. 21/53 late 1936 version
with black wheels,
Cat.No.20/51, 1935 version,
Cat.No.20/51, early 1936 version
with spoked wheels,
1936 Electric locomotive
Cat.No.20/55.

Trix Express 0-4-0 Tank Engines Cat.20/54. Left: 1936 model fitted with British type chassis. Right: Normal 1937 version as sold in Germany.

chassis-fixing plate and tender-coupling pin at the rear of the engine body were altered so that the tender could be uncoupled from the engine without having to remove a split pin. This resulted in a catalogue number change to 20/53 with the number on the cab sides changing to 20 053 accordingly. As before, these modifications were passed on to the British version, which at first nevertheless retained the red spoked wheels which were not British practice (black wheels only appeared on the engines late in 1936).

Although these green German-outline 0-4-0 locomotives were the only Trix Express items specially produced for the British market at this time, other Trix Express locomotives were available at various periods during 1936. The first was the 20/52 Electric-outline 0-4-0 of which as mentioned earlier only a few were actually distributed, and its successor the 20/55. This latter model was advertised as an 'Electric type locomotive...based on the standard design in use in Switzerland and other countries where electric traction has been adopted'. Once again there is evidence of an unwillingness to mention anything connected with Germany in advertising material. The latter part of 1936 saw the introduction of a new German-outline 0-4-0 tank engine in black with the number 20 054 on the cab sides and a catalogue number of 20/54. Apart from the chassis, strengthening ribs added in

1938 to the rear steps on the engine body and small variations in finish, this model remained virtually unchanged until production ceased in 1953.

During the autumn of 1936 the Bassett-Lowke 'Twin Train' leaflets and advertisements offered a 'Blue Train' (Cat.No. 11/6) for 45/-, stating it was 'a model of the famous Blue Train which runs from Calais to Marseilles'. Actually this set comprised a 20/53 engine and tender in black, together with three attractive short bogie coaches, namely a restaurant car, sleeping car and baggage car in the blue livery of the 'Compagnie Internationale des Wagon-Lits et des Grands Express Europeens' plus a controller and an oval of track. This set was available in Germany during 1935 with the 20/51 engine and the early versions of the Wagon-Lits coaches with yellow window frames. The sets sold in Britain mainly had the later version of these coaches, although a few sets retaining the old style coaches filtered through.

Many items of Trix Express rolling stock and accessories were available at this time to supplement the sets, but this is a topic for later chapters.

Early Trix Express 0-4-0 engine and tender hauling a rake of pre-production goods wagons. This locomotive was finished in green for the British market and still bears the words TWIN EXPRESS on the tender.

THE BIRTH OF BRITISH OUTLINE MODELS

In a Bassett-Lowke advertisement in the July 1936 edition of *Newnes Practical Mechanics* the following statement appeared:

'The Bassett-Lowke Twin Train Railway. Full supplies of the foreign-made article are now available. Place your order now. Although these will be withdrawn from sale when the British-made article is marketed next October, all parts, both British and foreign, will be interchangeable.'

True to the above statement, British-outline models started to appear in the shops during the latter part of October, and Trix Ltd advertised these for the first time during the following month in the model press and allied magazines, hailing the 'New OO Gauge TRIX TWIN RAILWAY' as perfectly proportioned miniature models. This was the first time that the name Trix Twin Railway had been used and it now became the official trade mark of Trix Ltd with regards to the model railway system. Bassett-Lowke, however, continued to advertise it as the Twin Train Table Railway right up to and during the Second World War. Even a very large store called 'Ravens' in Southend-on-Sea got in on the act, promoting the British outline Trix models as Ravens Twin Railway and even naming standard Trix items as RTR transformer, RTR controller etc. This raises the question as to what trading arrangements were made which would allow this misnaming of Trix products? The Trix Express 0-4-0s in green Southern Railway colours plus the matching coaches were quickly phased out.

1936 must have been a very busy time for the design staff and tool makers at George Winteringham Ltd in Northampton, as a credit-able range of British outline models were shown in the first leaflets published by Trix Ltd and the Bassett-Lowke catalogue published in November of that year. Three types of sets were initially available, each set being in either LMS or LNER livery. Set Cat.No. 2/335 was an LMS passenger set with 0-4-0 engine and tender, plus three matching bogie coaches, while the similar LNER set was Cat.No. 4/335. Both sets retailed at 45/-. Set Cat.No. 2/325 was an LMS goods set with 0-4-0 engine and tender plus four wagons, the similar LNER set being Cat.No. 4/325. Both cost 42/-. Sets bearing the catalogue numbers 2/315 and 4/315 were the LMS and LNER Suburban passenger coach sets containing an 0-4-0 tank engine and three four-wheeled coaches. All the above sets included controller and rails, the latter no longer being included in the majority of sets manufactured after 1936 until the post-war period.

The engines, which were always available separately, were of charming design catching the style of British locomotives well, which was quite an achievement when one recalls that the chassis was the standard 0-4-0 as fitted to the Trix Express locomotives. As mentioned earlier, the chassis for these British designs came from Nuremberg, and, initially, complete Trix Express locomotives were imported, the body castings removed and discarded, and the British style body fitted after the red wheels had been painted black. This practice did not last very long but Nuremberg continued to supply all the 0-4-0 chassis complete with black wheels for the TTR locomotives until the outbreak of hostilities in 1939. In fact during October of that year, the British Diecasting & Engineering Co. Ltd pro-

A 1936 Bassett-Lowke Ltd publicity picture advertising the Bassett-Lowke Twin Train Table Railway, no mention of Trix!

duced a batch of chassis castings for Trix Ltd with production continuing in the post-war period. Only very small parts were cast at the Northampton factory, larger items being sub-contracted to other companies. The 0-4-0 tender and tank engine bodies, excluding the later post-war American outline, were cast by Metal Castings Ltd of Worcester, who continued production until the withdrawal of the AC 0-4-0s in 1956. The tenders were constructed from tinplate in a similar fashion to the Trix Express models, but the coal was represented by moulded hard plastic instead of formed tinplate. The printed tinplate sheet used to fabricate these tenders was supplied by John Dale Ltd of New Southgate, London, who continued to supply the Northampton factory with high quality printed sheets for all wagons and coaches until tinplate was replaced by plastic. It is estimated from reliable sources that between 1936 and 1956 approximately 250,000 British outline 0-4-0 AC locomotives were produced.

The LMS passenger engine and tender, Cat.No. 2/520, was finished in LMS Crimson Lake with correct lining and lettering. Initially these had the number 6200 applied by transfer, but locomotives bearing different numbers were soon made available as was the case with nearly all the British outline 0-4-0s, the Southern Railway locomotives being the exception. The LMS transfers on the tender were available in pre-war days in two styles, serif and sans-serif, both with gold letters on a red background matching the numbers. An exception to this rule occurred on very early versions bearing transfers with gold number 6200 and LMS letters in sans-serif on a black background.

The LNER version of the passenger engine and tender, Cat.No. 4/520, was finished in LNER apple green and correctly lined, numbered and lettered, the first number being 4472. The colours and shading of the transfers were similar to those on the LMS locomotives, except that the letters were sans-serif only. The colour of the engine bodies and the printing of the tinplate tenders in both LMS and LNER versions suffered from shade variations which were more prevalent in the LNER locomotivs and particularly noticeable during the post-war period. The LMS and LNER goods engines and tenders, Cat.Nos. 2/525 and 4/525 respectively, were black with full lining in red. The number and letter transfers were gold on a red background and the style of the letters corresponded to the passenger

Pre-war LNER 0-4-0 Passenger and Goods Tender engines.

Pre-war LMS 0-4-0 Passenger Tender Engines Cat.No.2/520 with a Goods version Cat.No.2/525 on the bottom row. The early models have sans-serif LMS letters and later versions serif letters.

versions. Various locomotive numbers were used and in some cases the LMS and LNER numbers were the same which has led to confusion when matching tenders with engines. However it is safe to say that the factory at Northampton issued some goods engine bodies bearing a specific number with LMS or LNER tenders.

The LMS and LNER passenger and goods 0-4-0 tank engines, Cat. Nos. 2/510, 4/510, 2/515 and 4/515 respectively, were all finished in black. The passenger engines were fully lined in red but the goods engines were unlined. The transfers had gold letters and numbers on a red, (later maroon) background and the LMS letters were in serif or sans-serif. The tank engines were available with different running numbers of which a list of known numbers, together with those of the tender engines, is given at the end of this chapter.

On the rear of the diecast tank engine body was a transfer with the words 'Patents TTR Pending', also printed on the rear face of the tinplate tenders, which in addition bore the words 'Made in England'. The Patent Specifications that had been applied for were those initially instigated in Germany by Vereinigte Spielwarenfabriken Andreas Förtner & J. Haffner's Nachfolger GmbH and applied for in the United Kingdom during October 1935. They dealt with the invention of running and controlling two toy trains independently on one track, including the method of current collection. The Patent Specifications were granted in 1937 and given the numbers 465,168 and 469,656. From the second half of 1937 the wording of the transfers on the rear of the tank

engine body was altered to: 'British TTR Patents 465168 469656 Patented Abroad' The latter two words related to the Deutches Reich Patentschrifts 630,570 and 658,233 and to Patents granted in other countries. Apart from the British Railways models, these transfers continued on the tank engines until about 1950. The wording printed on the tinplate tenders was never altered and remained until the British Railways models appeared. However, the LMS and LNER goods tender engines produced from 1949 were exceptions to the rule and had Patent information transfers applied to the rear of the tender as used on the tank engines.

It is worth noting at this point that up to 1958 the British catalogue numbers used on locomotives and rolling stock were coded so that the first number corresponded to a railway company livery:

1/ = British Railways, 2/ = London Midland & Scottish, 4/ = London & North Eastern Railway, 5/ = Southern Railway, 7/ = London Transport, 9/ = all American style models. It is not known why certain numbers were left out. All other rolling stock were given general numbers. These coded numbers only related to items that were produced in Britain, while German imports usually retained the Trix Express catalogue number.

The pre-war LMS and LNER 0-4-0 Passenger and Goods 0-4-0 Tank Engines. Late versions of the LNER Goods Tank Engines are on the bottom row.

1937, THE YEAR OF MANY EXCITING NEW MODELS

Still on the theme of 0-4-0 locomotives, 1937 saw the introduction of the Southern Railway 0-4-0 passenger engine and tender in correct SR green livery, with the number and lettering on the tender incorporated in the tinplate printing. The goods version was finished in black, fully lined in green. The cab sides of both the passenger and goods engines bore a small oval-shaped red transfer lined in 'gold' with small indistinct lettering and the number 951, also in 'gold'. Unfortunately, with handling, the 'gold' was very prone to wearing off. The number on the sides of the tender of the passenger engine, Cat.No. 5/520, is 763, and on the goods engine tender, Cat.No. 5/525, 498.

The passenger and goods versions of the 0-4-0 tank engine in SR livery were introduced at the same time as the tender engines. The passenger engine was in green livery with full lining and the goods engine was finished in black with full green lining. Each engine had the word 'Southern' and a number in correct style applied by transfer to the tank sides. Again these transfers were very prone to wear as they were in a position invariably grasped when handling the locomotive. The catalogue numbers were 5/510 and 5/515 respectively. Both types of 'Patent' transfers were applied to the rear of the body but the 'Patent Pending' type was used only for a few months.

The first 'scale' locomotive to be introduced was the Motor Coach unit for the Southern Electric three-coach set, Cat. No. 5/375, available from February 1937. This Motor Coach unit in correct Southern Railway livery, Cat. No. 5/530, (shades ranging from olive green to an almost light blue/green), was completely manufactured in Nuremberg. The tinplate body shell, however, was formed from sheet printed in Britain in order to guarantee a correct colour match with the Northampton-produced coaches supplied in the set. The diecast front detail plate displaying the white number '8' was fitted to the body shell in Nuremberg. A few of these Motor Coach units were even available in Germany at the same time as they were released in Britain, although they were never specifically advertised.

Both bogies of this Motor Coach were utilised for current pick-up, the front bogie also forming part of the motor and drive gear assembly similar to the four-wheeled locomotives. The reverser mechanism assembly was rigidly attached to the

A selection of the pre-war 0-4-0 SR Tender and Tank Engines plus both sides of the SR Motor Coach.

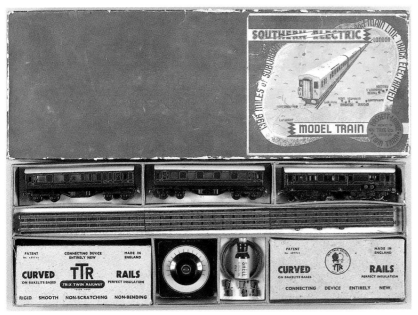

Experimental chassis for the
Southern Railway
Motor Coach.

Southern Electric Three Coach
Set Cat.No.5/375. (A)
Note – the right-hand curved
rail box is post-war.

chassis frame above the remaining bogie. The design of these bogies was entrusted to E. W. Twining who was a very versatile engineer and model maker who had undertaken much work for Bassett-Lowke Ltd. At one time he operated his own business, Twining Models Ltd, from the same premises as George Winteringham Ltd, before moving to new premises in Pike Lane, Northampton in 1931. He also designed the 'Many-Ways' station building units.

The method designed by Twining and refined by the engineers at Nuremberg for swivelling both the bogies was a feature which was new at that time. A central pivot was impracticable as most of the major parts from the 0-4-0 chassis had to be utilised, so instead each bogie casting and its associated side frame casting was

provided with four curved guides bearing on corresponding faces on the pressed steel underframe. The current pick-up shoes for both outside and centre rail were mounted in the centre of each bogie, the design for the outer rail shoe allowing it to extend beyond the centre line of the chassis.

The Southern Electric set was presented in an attractive box covered in bright green Celilynd enamelled paper with a label designed by the Southern Railway, which, as with some future sets, also incorporated the name Bassett-Lowke Ltd in its design. Clearly, the use of the name of 'Bassett- Lowke', synonymous with quality, must have been a great help to the sales department. The set comprised a Motor Coach, a First class coach, a Third Class Brake-end coach, a

controller, 12 curved rails, four straight rails, and the usual sundry items including a complimentary eight-page booklet from Southern Railway entitled *The Evolution of the World's Largest Suburban Electrified Railway*. Unfortunately this box, as with similar boxes for the 0-4-0 locomotive sets finished in red Celilynd, has not withstood the ravages of time as the Celilynd finish tends to peel away from the cardboard when handled frequently.

The *original* catalogue number allocated to the Motor Coach was 21/56. Individually boxed units were supplied from Nuremberg in plain cardboard boxes with 21/56 and FOREIGN stamped in ink on the white Trix Express box-end labels. Before being issued to the British public, normal white TTR labels were applied over the Trix Express labels stating the contents and the TTR catalogue number 5/530. The Trix Express catalogue number of 21/56 was a natural progression from that given to the previous German model – the modified design of the Electric 0-4-0 with fixed pantographs, Cat. No. 20/55. After the Southern Railway Motor Coach,

Pre-war Trix Express Diesel Electric Two Coach Unit, (or Diesel Flyer), Cat. No. 20/58. Top: 1939 version. Bottom: 1937 version with a single hole in the trailing coach for the wire connection.

the German models which followed were the Pacific locomotive, Cat. No. 20/57, the Diesel Flyer, Cat. No. 20/58 and the Pacific locomotive fitted with uncoupler, Cat. No. 20/59. However, at the same time the catalogue number of 25/56 was allocated to the NORD engine and tender. It was not until 1940 that the number /56 was used again by Nuremberg as part of a locomotive catalogue number and this was when the catalogue number of 20/56 was allocated to the DR Class 71 2-4-2 tank engine with remote control uncoupling at each end of the locomotive. What the reason was for reverting back to a previously used number is left for the reader to speculate.

A direct development from the Southern Electric Motor Coach was the Trix Express Diesel Electric Two Coach unit, Cat. No. 20/58, available both in Germany and Britain later in

the year. This unit was called a Diesel Flyer in Britain, but unfortunately acquired the totally incorrect name of 'Flying Hamburger'. This latter name probably came about as a result of a photograph of the 'Flying Hamburger' which appeared in an article in the spring 1938 edition of the *TTR Gazette* entitled 'The Fastest Trains in the World'. No doubt, in the eyes of the British railway enthusiast anything 'Foreign' was thought to bear a resemblance to the Diesel Flyer and hence the confusion. In fact the Diesel Flyer bears a close resemblance to the general outline of the Deutsche Reichsbahn Class VT137 series of Motor Coach units.

The construction of the bogies for the Diesel Flyer is more or less the same as that of the Southern Railway Motor Coach. The differences are that the pressed steel underframe is extended in the middle, the wheels have a thinner profile

and the motor side frames are cast rather than of fibre bakelite construction. One additional feature is that each of the two coach units were fitted with lights at one end that change from white to red depending on the direction in which the Diesel Flyer is travelling, these lights being operated by special contacts on the reverser contact shaft. The electrical connection between the two coaches is made by a twin flexible wire which, on early models, is fed through a single hole at the front of the trailing coach and then to the motor coach via a two-prong plug and socket. On later models after 1938 the single hole on the front end of the trailing coach and its chassis were modified to take a two-prong plug, the same as that used for the motor coach.

The bogie castings on early models were exactly the same as those used on the Southern Railway Motor Coach in that the two curved pivot guides formed part of the casting and 3.0mm axles were used. After 1938 the bogie casting was modified by removing the pivot guides and replacing them with adjustable pressed steel guide plates. The tinplate coach bodies were finished in red and pale yellow with the Reichsbahnadler emblem of the Deutsche Reichsbahn in the middle of each side. Each coach was given the number 20058. The initial production run had a single white light and two red lights at each end of the unit, whilst on all subsequent models the lights were changed to one red and two white lights at each end.

Unfortunately, as with other German outline models, they were not generally available in Britain after 1938 due to the unfavourable trading situation between the Nuremberg and London Trix companies, although the

Nuremberg constructed Southern Railway Motor Coach continued to be supplied from Germany up to the start of the war.

One of the intriguing features of the early days of the Trix model railway was the way in which the models designed for the German market were adapted for use in Britain without a huge expenditure on tooling. One such model in 1937 was the London Transport 0-4-0 locomotive, Cat. No. 7/530, which used a modified body casting from the Trix Express electric locomotive 20/55. Gone were the holes in the roof which were used to fix the pantographs, and the embossed words TRIX EXPRESS plus the number 20 052 were removed from each side of the body. The motor chassis used was the early type which incorporated a thin casting, this being changed in 1938 to the heavier type. The body was finished in dark maroon and red with yellow lining. The roof was a dark metallic grey. On each side of the body LONDON TRANSPORT transfers were affixed, together with the number 19 which was also applied to each end. Many pictures are shown in Trix literature of this locomotive with the number 17 instead of 19.

This number was only used on the prototype model and was never used in production. Sales of this locomotive were very poor and although it was still listed in the October 1939 TTR price list, was only manufactured for just over one year.

Probably the locomotive that is the most mysterious (the result of the joint effort between the Trix companies in Nuremberg and London, and Maison Gobin-Daudé in Paris) was a representation of a NORD Pacific, Cat.No. 25/56. In reality this was a 4-4-0 engine and tender with the diecast engine and tender bodies shaped in the general style of a Chapelon NORD Pacific. The body castings were painted a dark chocolate-brown with gold or yellow NORD transfers on the smoke deflectors and at the front end of the tender sides. The engine number on the cab sides and towards the rear of the tender sides, were also gold or yellow transfers. The known numbers applied to the engine and tender were 34289, 52896 and 68374, but cab and tender numbers did not always match as sometimes occurred in French railway practice.

The locomotive was assembled in the factory

of Maison Gobin-Daudé using a standard 0-4-0 chassis of early vintage from the Nuremberg factory with thin frame, but fitted with a cast motor side frame which became known as a 'B' type chassis. The connecting rods were again standard 0-4-0 type. The tender bogies, supplied from the Northampton factory, were the same as those used on the British pattern bogie coaches of that period. The engine and tender bodies were cast in France, with some of the engine castings having the words 'Made in France' applied just behind the front buffer beam. The mounting plate for the tender bogies also had the same marking stamped into the metal.

This locomotive, available in France during the latter months of 1937, could be obtained on its own or in a set, Cat.No.15/115, known as the 'Rapide Nord'. This set comprised a locomotive, a baggage coach, any two of either a first, second or third class coach, a controller and sundry items. Rails were not normally supplied with the set, but as with most Trix sets at this time, space for them was allocated in the box. Interestingly, the rails available in France were of French manufacture. The lid on the red box had a large

London Transport 0-4-0 locomotive
Cat.No.7/530. Both sides of the
locomotive shown.

NORD 4-4-0
Cat.No.25/56. (A)

Trix Express label depicting a hand holding the Trix Express NORD locomotive. When the locomotive alone was supplied, the engine and its tender were individually boxed and that is why it is possible to get a variety of engine/tender number combinations.

Unfortunately the full set was not advertised or on sale in Britain, but the locomotive and the full complement of matching coaches were available separately as advertised in the supplement to the 1938-1939 Trix Twin Railway catalogue. It did not achieve the popularity of its German or British counterparts, but sold steadily in France and Britain up to the outbreak of war.

Perhaps the locomotive which played the most important role in the transition from toy-like models to more realistic ones, was the Trix Express 2C1 (4-6-2) Pacific locomotive and tender, Cat. No. 20/57. Although it was probably based on the DR Class 01 Pacific, it was never advertised as such. This was the first commercially-produced OO gauge model railway locomotive with a fully working representation of Walschaert's valve gear. It started life in pre-production mock-up form during December 1936, and was first mentioned by way of a Christmas greeting from Siegfried Kahn presumably to W. J. Bassett-Lowke which was written on the back of a photograph of the model. The first production models appeared in Germany during November 1937 and in Britain the following month, just in time for the Christmas trade, but strangely the words TRIX EXPRESS and the number 20 057 on the cab side panels, including the smokebox door number, were omitted on the initial production run sold in Germany and Britain. The model continued in production for the German market until 1940, but only had a short advertised life in Britain.

Pre-war French and wartime (1940) German instruction books.

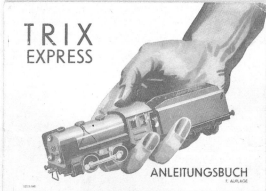

The special French Trix Express label depicting the Trix NORD 4-4-0 on the lid of the box of the 'Rapide Nord' set Cat.No.15/115. (G)

The diecast bodies of the engine and tender had a wealth of detail superbly capturing the style of a German Pacific locomotive. The smoke-box door was even fitted with a small plastic lens illuminated by a miniature bulb on the chassis. The latter was a completely new design although utilising some of the electrical parts used on the standard 0-4-0 chassis. The increased power for this locomotive was obtained by gearing down the high revolutions of the armature so that the result was a more realistic running speed coupled with good pulling characteristics. All the models using the standard 0-4-0 mechanism had the inherent disadvantage of excessive speed which often resulted in a failure to negotiate the tight curves of the Trix track. Although the length of the model was 27 centimetres, it negotiated the 34.2 centimetre, (13.5 inches) curves of the Trix track with ease thanks to flangeless centre driving wheels on the six-coupled mechanism and a floating mounting for the front four-wheeled bogie. Current pick-up for the outside rails was provided by shoes mounted on the pivot assembly for the two four-wheeled bogies. Pressed steel couplings of similar design to the cast couplings were provided at the front and rear of the locomotive. As the years went by, various changes took place in the construction of the chassis and the functions it performed, but the overall design lasted until 1956. Indeed, it was a design which lent itself admirably to the British models that were planned around this chassis.

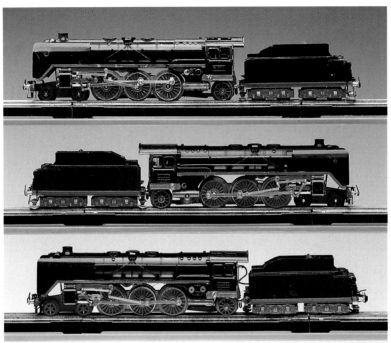

The Trix Express pre-war Pacific's. From the top:
First Cat. No. 20/57 version without any markings on the cab sides
Later 20/57 version with TRIX EXPRESS and 20 057 on the cab sides
Cat. No. 20/59 with the uncoupler mechanism in the tender.

The 1936 pre-production mock-up of the Trix Express German 4-6-2 Pacific.

THE EXPANSION OF THE BRITISH OUTLINE RANGE

A development from the basic 20/57 German Pacific in 1938 was the incorporation of an uncoupling device in the tender which enabled the operator to uncouple the locomotive from its rolling stock anywhere on the track without the use of special rails. The sequence employed in such an operation was as follows:

1) Forward motion.
2) Forward motion with uncoupler activated.
3) Stop.
4) Reverse motion.

An electrical pulse was taken from an additional contact on a modified version of the reversing contact shaft in the chassis of the engine. This pulse was then fed to an electromagnet housed in the tender (similar to that used on the remote control points), and then via mechanical linkages, causing the coupling hook to drop and disengage the following train. This device worked quite effectively providing the rails were kept clean to avoid unwanted uncoupling action.

By 1939 the diecast chassis had been modified by the addition of a support pillar containing the bearing for the rear end of the reversing contact shaft. Although the front end of this shaft was now allowed to float instead of being in a fixed bearing, a more positive action resulted without having to rely on the motor side frame contact blade pressure to keep the reversing contact shaft pinion in mesh with the ratchet wheel as on earlier models.

The catalogue number for this Pacific was 20/59, and as no other feature was altered it retained the number 20 057 on the cab sides. It was produced until 1950. Very few of these models found their way onto the British market

From the top: The 'American' 4-6-2 Pacific Cat. No. 9/198; two 0-4-0 Tank Engines in gloss and matt finish Cat. No. 9/32 (see text); 0-4-0 Tender Engines Cat. No. 9/252 (see text).

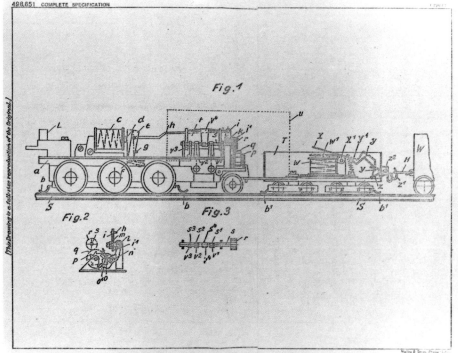

Extract from British Patent No.498,651, (German origin), showing the Pacific tender uncoupling mechanism.

but they were important to the British scene as they formed the basis for the British-outline Pacifics.

However, at about the same time as the introduction of the British Pacifics at the end of 1938, and as a direct result of the enforced agreement between the exiled former owners and new owners of Vereinigte Spielwarenfabriken Andreas Förtner & J. Haffner's Nachf., a Pacific locomotive was produced for the American market and advertised in the combined 1938/39 Trix Express/TTR catalogue as Cat. No. 9/198 'The 4-6-2 Pacific Express Locomotive of American type...'. Basically this was a 20/59 with the smoke deflectors removed, additional steps added to the front running board, a bell fitted to the front left-hand top side of the boiler, extended handrails and a cowcatcher cast from soft metal riveted to the front of the buffer beam on the bogie, plus a working 'headlight'. All the wheels and bogies, etc., were finished in black, and a white line was painted the length of the engine running board and along the bottom of the tender sides. Under one of the tender bogie frames was hand painted the words 'Made in Germany' in red. A very small quantity, maybe for promotional purposes, had the name TRIX TWIN LINES applied in white letters to the tender sides.

Not many models were produced, 50 being the figure suggested although this seems a little low for a catalogued production run. In addition to the quota for America, a few were made available in Germany and also in certain Bassett-Lowke shops in England. Finally, a small quantity were produced in the immediate post-war years.

The other Americanised locomotives available only for a short period were the standard Trix Express 0-4-0 tender and tank engines, Cat. Nos. were 20/53 and 20/54 respectively, to which a formed red tinplate cowcatcher was fitted to the front buffer beam. The wheels were not painted black as in the case of the Pacific. The 1937/38 joint export catalogue for the American market listed them as catalogue numbers 9/252 and 9/231 respectively, whilst the 1938/39 edition allocated the numbers 9/42 and 9/32. These export 0-4-0s can be distinguished from normal production by the word 'Germany' stamped in yellowish letters on the frame of the chassis, on the coupling retention plates, and, in the case of the tender locomotive, on the tender chassis weight. Interestingly, in America unlike in Britain there seemed to be no stigma attached to the German-produced models. The tender locomotive is known to exist with the early chassis fitted with disc type wheels.

And so to the British outline Pacifics. The first of the two locomotives chosen to be modelled was the 'Princess Elizabeth' from the LMS 'Princess Royal' class. This locomotive was famous for one of the greatest steam engine runs in British railways history, when, in November 1936, a special train of 260 tons was worked non-stop from Glasgow to Euston maintaining an average speed of 70mph – 401.25 miles in 344.75 minutes. It is not known how long the models of the Pacific locomotives were in the planning stage, but at the time when ownership of the Trix company in Nuremberg changed hands, most of the tooling for the LMS 'Princess' was done at the Northampton factory by N. Bray

An extract from the joint Trix Express/TTR 1938/39 catalogue.

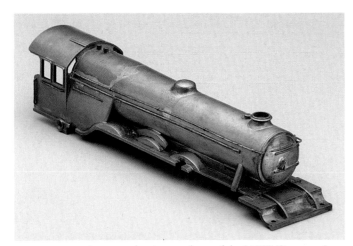

A pre-production mock-up of the LNER 'Scotsman' engine body. This was slightly different than the diecast version and interestingly in its finished state was used for the publicity photographs.

who had been a toolmaker with George Winteringham Ltd since 1925. The initial batch of engine body castings for the 'Princess' was done by Fry's Diecastings Ltd of London in time for its debut during November 1938.

The order for the die for the LNER 'Flying Scotsman' engine body casting was also received by Fry's Diecastings in May 1938 which enabled them to produce a batch of body castings ready for the introduction of the 'Scotsman' in December. This was an equally famous locomotive, whose full size counterpart survives to this day.

It is strange why the full names of 'Princess Elizabeth' and 'Flying Scotsman' were not cast instead of the shortened versions. However, although the shape of the model had to be

designed around the Trix Express chassis, the character of the locomotives was well captured.

The total number of bodies cast for the 'Scotsman' prior to the outbreak of war was 1,350. It is assumed, from the larger quantities surviving the ravages of time, that the quantity of 'Princess' locomotives produced was greater than that of the 'Scotsman'. In production arrangements that may seem ludicrous, complete German 20/59 Pacific locomotives were supplied by the Nuremberg factory only to have the chassis of the engines removed and altered to suit the British outline Pacific models. The uncoupling mechanism in the tender was also appropriately modified and fitted to the British tender chassis assembly in Northampton. The locomotive engine chassis was never produced in Britain and continued to be supplied by the Nuremberg factory until 1956, although in post-war days the chassis was supplied as a separate assembly. They were always marked 'Motor Foreign' on the centre pick-up shoe holder. The basic alterations included the replacement of the German pattern motor and gear side frames with parts suitable for British Pacific locomotives, and

the addition of suspension detail over the wheels of the rear pony truck. The main alteration to the chassis casting was the removal of the cylinder mounting lugs to facilitate the fixing of the British pattern cylinder assemblies, these being held in place by a keyed plate, which was in turn retained by a screw passing up into the front weight. All the British-pattern chassis parts were produced in Germany. The diecast tender bodies and chassis for these two Pacifics were produced by British Diecasting & Engineering Co. Ltd of London.

Both these locomotives were launched with a fanfare of publicity and were beautifully presented in a wooden attaché case style cabinet covered in dark blue rexine leather-cloth. The partitioned interior was lined with a soft light blue flannelette. The 'Princess' set, Cat. No. 2/344 priced at £6/6/-, comprised the LMS 'Princess' engine and tender number 6201 with three matching scale length coaches – first class, dining car and brake third. The usual bottle of Shell 'Trix' oil, plugs, wire, control unit and instruction book were also included. The locomotive was finished in LMS red and fully

Pre-production version of the LMS 'Princess' 4-6-2 Pacific. Apart from various small detail differences between this and the production version, Patent information transfers on the latter were applied to the engine cab end of the tender body and not to the rear tender face as shown in this photograph.

From the top:
Early LMS 'Princess' 4-6-2 Pacific in gloss finish with sans-serif letters.
LNER 'Scotsman' 4-6-2 Pacific.
Early LMS 'Coronation' 4-6-2 Pacific in gloss finish. (A)

Top, late LMS 'Coronation' 4-6-2 Pacific in semi-gloss finish. This finish is lighter than the earlier gloss version.
Bottom, later version of the LMS 'Princess' 4-6-2 Pacific in semi-gloss finish with serif LMS letters.

lined, although the red on all the LMS Trix locomotives never seemed to be quite the correct shade. The transfers applied to the cab and tender sides were gold on red, the early production models having sans-serif letters while later models adopted serif ones. This locomotive was available individually, Cat. No. 2/540, and manufactured in pre-war days only, although presentation sets of all the TTR Pacific locomotives were offered in the late 1940s by certain retail outlets who probably 'tucked them away for a rainy day' at the outbreak of the war.

The 'Scotsman' set, Cat. No. 4/344 also priced at £6/6/-, included the LNER 'Scotsman' engine and tender number 4472 with three matching LNER teak scale length coaches – first class, restaurant car and brake third. The locomotive, available individually as Cat. No. 4/540, was finished in LNER apple green with correct lining and gold on red transfers. Normally the cylinders were also in lined apple green, but a few were produced just prior to 1940 with black cylinders.

It is true that these Pacific models were greeted with a great deal of enthusiasm, but mainly by existing Trix owners, as at that time Meccano Ltd launched their Hornby-Dublo model railway which included a fine LNER 'Sir Nigel Gresley' Pacific locomotive operated by 12 volts DC. Their advertisements stated that their model railway system offered positive directional control of the locomotives at all times, implying that other model railways didn't! The new Hornby-Dublo model railway definitely took away the cream of expected sales of the new Trix miniature masterpieces.

The rumblings of war were gathering momentum, but these did not halt development. In the 1939 spring number of *The TTR Gazette*,

it was announced that a large number of new additions for delivery in the autumn were to be made available, all these new lines being shown in a trade catalogue printed in the form of a broad-sheet published later in the year. Sadly only a handful of the intended new items made it to the shops as the outbreak of war in September had an immediate effect.

One of the few new products that was actually manufactured was a set containing a model of a modified LMS streamlined Pacific locomotive 'Coronation' with matching coaches.

This famous Stanier-designed LMS 'Coronation' class Pacific was shipped across the Atlantic in 1939, with a train of new coaches, to represent British railways at the New York World's Fair. Although the engine carried the name 'Coronation' and the number 6220, it was actually No. 6229 'Duchess of Hamilton', the name and number-plates having been changed especially for the occasion. Seven coaches of the partly articulated 'Coronation Scot' type, including a 12-wheel sleeping car, accompanied the locomotive, which was in its streamlined

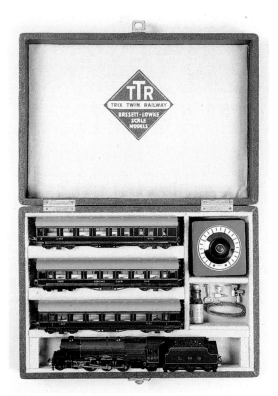

The 'Princess' Presentation Set Cat.No.2/344. (A)

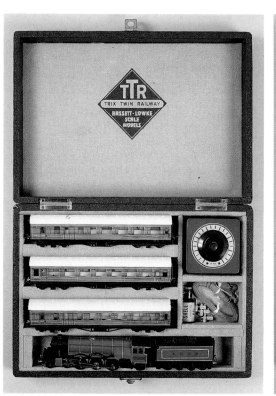

The 'Scotsman' Presentation Set Cat.No.4/344. (A)

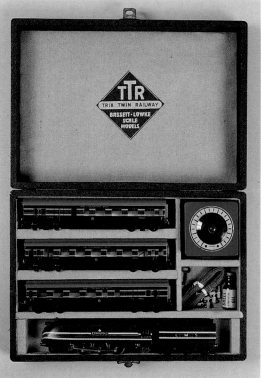

The 'Coronation' Presentation Set Cat.No.2/437. (A)

form and fitted with a bell and electric headlight as required by American law. This latter requirement lent itself admirably to the headlight fitting as used on the model of the Trix 'American' Pacific, and this was incorporated on a modified Trix Express chassis, as used on the two earlier TTR pacifics, which was fitted with a Coronation engine body casting. The castings for the tender body and chassis, which housed the uncoupling mechanism, were once again made by the British Diecasting & Engineering Co., while the order for the initial batch of engine body castings was received by Fry's Diecastings in June 1939.

The first production run produced an engine body which was very thin in places, resulting in a lightweight casting which did not add much weight to the chassis, thus not helping the adhesion between the driving wheels and the track. To overcome this, a lead lining was riveted around the inside surface of the casting to give the required weight. The second batch of body castings had a much thicker wall around the boiler area, thus eliminating the need for the lining. The factory production-line workers' bonus level of 1,000 models was not quite reached as remembered by a former employee of George Winteringham Ltd, Jack Percival, whose job was to drill the handrail split-pin holes in the engine body. The shortfall was caused by the fact that the chassis eventually became unobtainable from Germany due to the hostilities. However, after the war a small quantity of body castings were found in the attic

The 'Coronation' Presentation Set Cat. No. 2/347. This set is housed in the smaller dark green version of the case with fawn fabric lining. (B)

of Precision Models in an unpainted but unfortunately 'unusable condition'.

This was a handsome model finished in LMS red with the distinctive yellow lining, which, incidentally, was expertly applied by hand by a

few skilled women at the Northampton factory; the name-plate and crown were picked out in silver. Although the overall length fell short of a scale length, it seemed to capture the grandeur of the full size version.

It was available singly, Cat. No. 2/542 priced at £4/7/6, or in a presentation style set Cat. No. 2/347 priced at £6/6/-, complete with three matching coaches and the usual extras. It was never manufactured in the post-war era. The presentation cabinet was similar to that used for the earlier TTR pacific's, except that a few later models were presented in a slightly smaller cabinet lined with fawn flannelette with an exterior covered in a very dark green rexine leather-cloth. The catch was not lockable as with the general issue. Other small variations to the basic cabinet design for the Pacific sets also exist.

It has been rumoured that a small quantity of the TTR 'Coronations' were finished in the original colour of the full size version, namely blue with silver lining. However, after exhaustive enquiries of ex-employees of Trix Ltd and Precision Models, it is safe to say that this rumour is unfounded – a pity as this version would have looked magnificent hauling a train of matching coaches. Maybe someone along the line has mixed his, or her, gauges, as Bassett-Lowke did produce a gauge O blue and silver 'Coronation' in 1938.

Plans were well in hand and working drawings were being prepared by Machinery

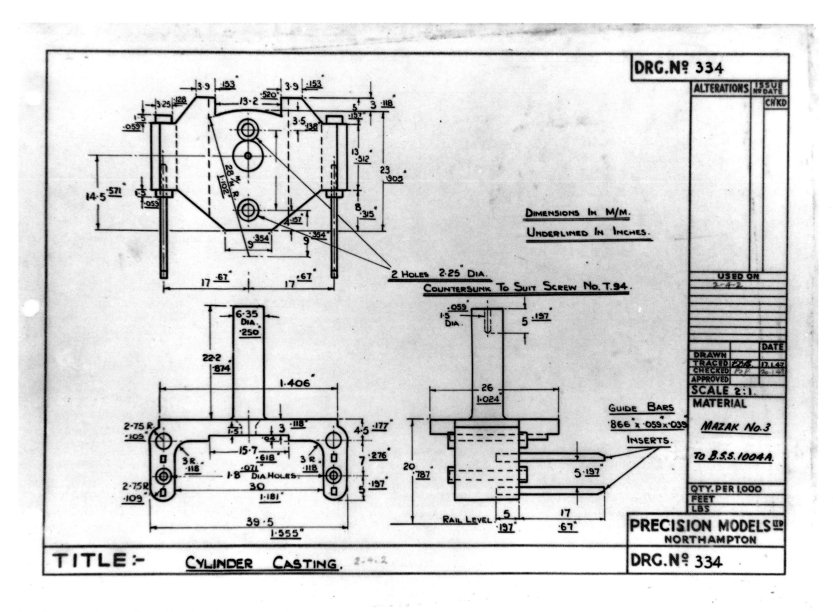

Cylinder casting drawing for the British outline 2-4-2 Tank Engine

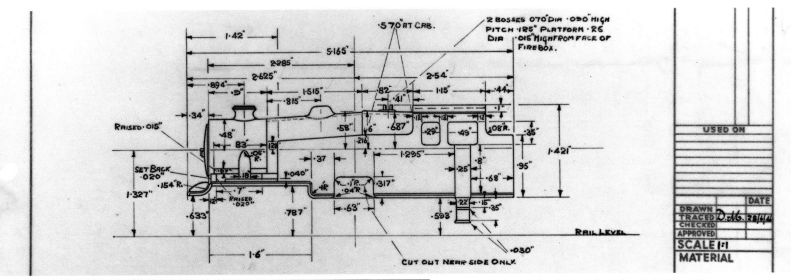

Body shell drawing for the British-outline 2-4-2 Tank Engine.

Top: The pre-war production model of the Trix Express 2-4-2 Super Automatic Tank Engine Cat.No.20/56. Note rivets instead of the later use of screws to locate the red cab step casting (broken on this model) plus a lip on the front of the rear bogie casting. The front bogie without this lip is a post-war version. The three British-outline 2-4-2s are fully working models constructed by the author based on official drawings of the locomotives proposed for production in 1939.

(Smith's Patents) Ltd during 1939 to manufacture a British outline 2-4-2 tank engine around the chassis of the Trix Express 1'B'1 tank engine, (Cat.No. 20/56), which was being developed in Germany and was made available to the German public in September 1940. The British model was projected in three versions, LMS, LNER and SR (Cat. Nos. 2/514, 4/514 and 5/514 respectively). Unfortunately, once again these well-founded plans did not bear fruit. This type of engine would have been a great asset to the TTR system allowing much greater scope in the quest for realism by incorporating remote control coupling and uncoupling facilities at both ends. Goods sets were planned for this 2-4-2

engine in each of the liveries, with catalogue numbers 2/394, 4/394 and 5/394 respetively, and they were to be presented in a cabinet similar to that used for the Pacifics. In addition to the engine, four 4-wheeled wagons and four bogie wagons plus controller were to be included in the sets.

Interestingly, after the war new drawings of the 2-4-2 were made by Precision Models from the Machinery (Smith's Patents) Ltd originals showing that the company wanted to retain the idea of this remarkable piece of mass-produced commercial model engineering. Sadly the high cost involved during this period sealed its fate until its appearance from the Nuremberg factory

in German outline in 1951.

Yet another Presentation Set which was a casualty of the war, was the intended set containing a Southern Railway 4-4-0 Schools class engine and tender named 'Dover', numbered 911. The catalogue number of the set was to have been 5/364 and that of the engine and tender, 5/536. Included in the set would have been three scale length coaches – SR First Class, Brake Third and a Pullman Saloon Car. Fry's Diecastings actually received an order for a batch of engine bodies in November 1939, but the order, as can be imagined, was never completed. This model locomotive eventually appeared in the shops with British Railways

1939 mock-up of the proposed Southern Railway 4-4-0 Schools Class 'Dover'.

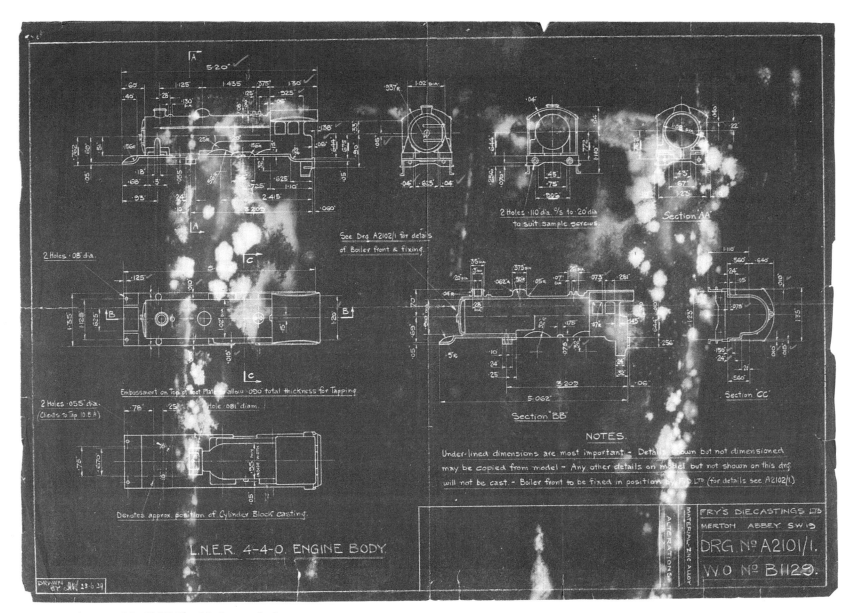

The casting drawing of the LNER 'Pytchley' engine body.

livery in the late 1950s, but with a modified casting to suit the 12 volt DC chassis. What a fine sight it would have made on a model railway layout with the Southern Railway version of the locomotive pulling a train of scale length Southern Railway coaches in their distinctive dark green livery. Two other models that actually went into production prior to the war were the LMS 4-4-0 Compound and the LNER 4-4-0 'Hunt' class locomotives. Both of these TTR models were produced in various liveries, and with modification, lasted well into the 12 volt DC period in the late 1950s, proving that they were popular in that they gave a good representation of the full-size locomotives

Pre-war 4-4-0s. From the top: LMS maroon 4-4-0 Compound; LMS black 4-4-0 Compound; LNER 4-4-0 Hunt Class 'Pytchley'.

without being too expensive. In fact when they first appeared in the shops they were priced at £2/2/-, being slightly more expensive than originally advertised. Nevertheless this was a much more affordable price than the £4/7/6 charged for the Pacific locomotives. It is a pity that Trix products were always classed as being expensive, but when one sees the amount of intricate engineering required for these models, and remembers that import duties had to be levied on the various parts from Nuremberg, one can begin to understand.

Prototype models of the two types of 4-4-0s were supplied by Trix Ltd to Fry's Diecastings in June 1939 from which they prepared drawings for the engine body and cylinder castings, the tender and chassis castings being prepared by British Diecasting & Engineering Co. Ltd. The official Trix photographs of all the 4-4-0s at this time showed the models with both front and rear driving wheels coupled. The production models were never constructed in this way and the connecting rod had a dummy pivot fitted in the front driving wheel position and was not connected to the front wheels in any way. Maybe this was due to cost cutting, or the geometry of the chassis to the cylinder assembly was not suitable.

Both models were made just in time for the Christmas trade after they had been well announced in the Trix literature for quite some time. The LMS Compound was first on the scene, and from records it is estimated that about 1,350 engine bodies were cast and that most were utilised. Not so the LNER Hunt class, as after the Christmas period, production of model

railway items came to an end and all work was concentrated on the war effort. Thus although approximately the same number of body castings were supplied as for the LMS Compound, the actual number of models completed was very small.

The TTR LMS 4-4-0 Compound engine and tender, Cat. No. 2/536, was based on the famous 3-cylinder Compounds introduced in large numbers on the Midland Railway. The passenger version was finished in LMS red and fully lined in yellow with serif style letters on the tender sides. The transfers used were gold letters and numbers on a red background; the number applied to the cab sides was 1168. The cylinders were also in lined LMS red with a small quantity appearing with unlined black cylinders probably at a time when parts were running low.

The main chassis used was a standard 0-4-0 chassis with most of the front portion 'sawn off', with just enough remaining to slide a small mounting plate into the channel that had been used to retain the insulated collector-shoe mount. The body of the engine was held on to the chassis at the rear by the usual screws, but these were extra long as they also located an additional lead weight to give stability, as without it the model was smoke-box-end heavy. The front of the chassis was screwed to the engine body by a special shouldered screw, which also acted as a pivot for the bogie which unlike that on the Pacific locomotives, was of British manufacture. Only the centre rail current pick-ups were fitted to the engine chassis, an electrical connection being made between engine and tender by the tender towbar. The arrangement of

'SquareDeal' instruction leaflet issued with the Spring 1939 TTR *Gazette*.

the outer rail pick-up shoes in the tender was similar to that of the Pacifics. Trix had initially intended that both types of 4-4-0s would be fitted with the remote control uncoupling mechanism in the tender, but unfortunately this did not materialise probably due to the lack of supplies from Germany and the need to get the models to the shops in time for Christmas.

In addition to the passenger version of the LMS Compound, a few were manufactured as goods locomotives finished in all black livery with red lining. The transfers and engine number were exactly the same as those used for the passenger version. Generally speaking, the black

paint applied to this engine and tender was of a much higher gloss finish to that used on its post-war sister.

The Trix replica of the LNER 4-4-0 Hunt class engine and tender, Cat. No. 4/536, was of pleasant appearance in its apple green finish with white lining. It carried the number 298 and the nameplate of 'Pytchley' surmounted by a fox picked out in silver, the nameplate being cast with the body. The transfers used for the numbers on the cab sides plus the sans-serif letters on the tender sides, were the usual gold on red. Apart from the different cylinder casting and the associated connecting rods, the chassis

and other parts were the same as used on the LMS Compound locomotive.

On both 4-4-0 models the wheel diameters were nowhere near scale size but the Trix models visually at least portrayed the sense of power that the full size locomotives possessed. Unfortunately, in operation this sense of power was not transmitted from the wheels to the track as the engine suffered badly from wheelspin and was not able to haul realistic loads. Nevertheless the models remained reasonably popular with Trix enthusiasts throughout their manufactured life.

After the rush at the Northampton factory to

The wartime black LNER 4-6-2 'Scotsman' Pacific. (B)

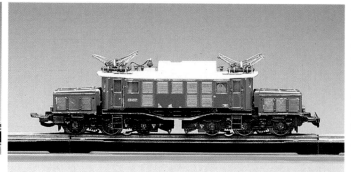

Trix Express Super Automatic AC DB Class E94 Cat. No. 20/60. This model was constructed from almost 500 parts!

produce TTR items in time for Christmas, New Year 1940 saw a total concentration on production for the war effort. A brave attempt was made to minimize the impact of the war during the first few months of 1940 by Bassett-Lowke, who occasionally used journalistic licence in the wording of their advertisements, and the flamboyant style of 'Motilus', the pseudonym of W. J. Bassett-Lowke, in his articles in the monthly magazine *Newnes Practical Mechanics* did wonders to keep alive the interest in model railways in general and the Trix Twin Railway in particular.

One such advertisement by Bassett-Lowke Ltd in the February 1940 issue of *The Model Railway News* stated:

'TO OUR NEW FRIENDS initiated into the mysteries of "OO" gauge at Christmas and in the New Year, we extend a hearty welcome. In the four years since its introduction, TTR has grown to be the most popular and the most realistic miniature railway system yet devised. AND NOTWITHSTANDING the difficulties created by the War the new productions for this season are BETTER THAN EVER.'

It then goes on to describe the new items actually made in the latter part of 1939. This advertisement was misleading, as in fact no Trix model railway production took place after the start of 1940.

Presumably this lack of production accounts for why Trix Ltd only did minimal advertising during the war, and then only the same advertisement each time showing the British outline 2-4-2 which was described as 'The double ender loco we didn't make' coupled with their vision of the future. However, they did manage to maintain a service department, and, depending on the availability of spare parts, repairs and occasional refurbishment took place.

It is with the above in mind that a TTR model of the LNER 4-6-2 'Scotsman' engine and tender finished in wartime unlined black is mentioned. A very small number of examples exist of this model on to which the usual Trix style of LNER transfers have been applied. These may have been models returned to Trix Ltd during the war after 1941 in a poor state for a complete overhaul and repaint, or contrary to

previous statements in this book, constructed from an odd collection of spares and exhibited in the Bassett-Lowke shops to help maintain interest during the dark hours of the war. One model examined was fitted with overpainted 'Coronation' cylinders which are rounded at the front so as not to foul the 'Coronation' body. Unfortunately the facts surrounding this model can only be conjectural, and after exhaustive enquiries, no evidence of a production run exists. On the real railways from November 1941 the distinctive LNER locomotive colours were abandoned in favour of overall plain black, and from July 1942 the initials NE replaced the full LNER legend on the tender and cab sides.

It is a pity that the war intervened at a time that development of the 14 volt AC system was progressing steadily, a development which was never to regain its momentum. In the early 1950s a brave effort was made with the TTR 'Meteor' and the Trix Express Class E94, Cat. No. 20/60, but production costs were prohibitive and the public were becoming accustomed to the much more reliable 12 volt DC system.

THE 0-4-0 AND 4-4-0 LOCOMOTIVES OF THE EARLY POST WAR PERIOD

During the period up to 1947 Trix Twin production was very sparse being confined to a small number of sets mainly for export made up in 1946 from a mixture of components started prior to the war and pieces manufactured during that year. Very few of these sets found their way into the home market, but those that did were strictly rationed. The only locomotives produced were the tank and tender engine 0-4-0s in three of the four British railway company liveries. The high gloss finish on the engine bodies and the retention of the cast coupling hook and wire link, made these locomotives indistinguishable from the pre-war production with the exception of the chassis and the tender coupling retainer channel.

The chassis at this stage was one built round the casting manufactured by the British Diecasting & Engineering Co., which continued to produce this chassis casting, with modifications, up to the cessation of the 14 volt AC locomotives. The material used in the casting of the chassis, engine body, wheels and other parts was mazak which, being an alloy could be used without restrictions compared with steel which was strictly rationed by the government. When viewed from underneath, the top end face of the tender coupling channel was now cut away at the edges for a short distance to allow the cast coupling to be easily changed, unlike previously when the tender had to be taken to pieces to replace a broken coupling. All further modifications to the 0-4-0 tender chassis followed those of the

4-wheel wagons described in the chapter dealing with rolling stock.

During each year since the introduction of the Trix Twin Railway, except for the war period, the model railway system was promoted more by way of demonstration than by advertisement, and at the various exhibitions and major departmental shops display layouts were shown. To help in the promotion of the trade name of Trix Twin Railways and TTR during this difficult period a handful of the British-outline 0-4-0 tender engines were specially finished. An all black goods version with no lining or markings whatsoever except for the words 'TRIX TWIN' in silver-white letters on the sides of the tender, plus the usual red printed Patent information on the rear face, was used mainly to haul a mixed train of available wagons. A passenger version was also provided which was very similar to the TTR Southern 0-4-0s, though painted in a very much darker green and unlined. However it still retained the red oval plate on the cab sides bordered in gold and with the number 951 in gold figures. Apart from the colour, the tender was exactly the same as the goods version. Both types of engine and tender used the diecast coupling and link plus hexagon-headed crank pins. Of the locomotives known to exist most used an early post-war pattern chassis, although a pre-war type 'C' chassis is also known to have been used. Short matching bogie coaches were provided in the same dark green colour as the passenger version and are known in first, second and third class versions. All have the letters TTR in the centre of each side.

With the advent of the Toy Fair in 1947, Trix

0-4-0 locomotive fitted with pre-war style coupling.

1948/49 pre-war pattern 0-4-0 locomotive body fitted with coupling conversion assembly. Note the widened gap in the buffer beam in comparison to the gap used for a pre-war diecast coupling.

Post-1949 modified 0-4-0 body and coupling. Note the use of a buffer beam plate.

Ltd showed off their new type of coupling which, as mentioned in the previous chapter, was almost identical to that employed by Meccano Ltd on their post-war Hornby Dublo locomotives and rolling stock. Initially in the latter part of 1948 the coupling was adapted in various ways to fit the existing location for the cast coupling hook on all the rolling stock and locomotives, although the coupling location gap in the 0-4-0 locomotive buffer beams had to be widened to allow correct movement of the new coupling. This latter feature will help collectors in distinguishing between pre or early post-war production, but care must be taken as locomotive bodies could always be 'doctored'. During this period there was an increase in the production of the 0-4-0s as the availability of parts and materials increased and the strict government controls eased, but most of the completed locomotives were earmarked for the export market.

It was at this point that the general quality of colour matching between the tinplate printing of the tenders and the paint used on the passenger

tender engine bodies started to deteriorate and a variety of shades appeared, predominantly on the engine bodies. The printing of the tender tinplate was much darker than that used in pre-war times, particularly noticeable on the LNER passenger engine and tender, whose engine was finished in a very bright apple green which did not match the much darker tender at all. The transfers on this LNER locomotive were similar to those applied to the pre-war model including the lining, except for the cylinders which were unlined.

The LMS passenger engine and tender now varied from a very deep maroon colour to an almost red-brown with the printing on the tender not always matching. The transfers were gold on

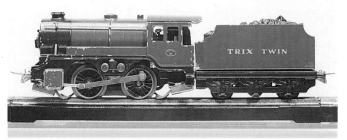

Early post-war demonstration 0-4-0 Passenger Tender Engine. (M)

The post-war demonstration 0-4-0 Goods Tender Engine (top row), plus a selection of post-war LMS 0-4-0 Passenger Tender Engine Cat. No. 2/520. Note the shade differences and the pre-1948 version on the second row.

a very deep maroon background, which from a distance looked almost black. These transfers were also used on the LMS goods tender and tank engines, including on some of the LNER tank engines a mixture of post- and the earlier pre-war type. The LNER goods engine and tender was still fully lined, but the equivalent LMS engine was only lined on the first boiler band, although still retaining a fully lined matching tender.

The LMS and LNER goods and passenger tank engines were finished in the same style as the pre-war versions with the exception of the transfers which appeared to be much brighter. The SR passenger tank engine was a much darker olive green, but apart from this, was identical to the pre-war model as was the goods tank engine and both versions of the tender engines.

It was during 1947 that a significant improvement was incorporated in the 0-4-0 chassis design in the form of a redesigned motor side frame into which was fitted a self-lubricating bronze bearing for the armature shaft with a corresponding bearing in the chassis casting. This was first advertised in the 1948 'Export' catalogue and then in the 1948/49 broadsheet catalogue where the locomotive catalogue numbers were given a distinguishing suffix, for example 2/510.SL to denote an LMS passenger tank engine with 'self-lubricating bearings'. The suffix SL was dropped with the publication of the 1950 TTR catalogue. The coupling rod 'crank pin' was now a hexagon-headed bolt instead of the cheese-head bolt as used on the pre-war imported Trix Express chassis.

Post-war LNER 0-4-0 Passenger Tender Engines Cat.No.4/520 showing the high degree of shade differences produced.

Both 0-4-0 tender and tank engine bodies had an inherent weakness where the cylinder joins the running board, which in many cases caused the cylinder to break off if the locomotive came off the track and fell to the floor! The steps below the tank engine cab often suffered the same fate. Trix Ltd clearly envisaged that the new coupling would endure long into the future and accordingly a much better and positive form of mounting was needed on the engine bodies. Thus in the early part of 1949 Metal Castings Ltd in Worcester altered the die for both tender and tank engine bodies, incorporating the following modifications which were put into immediate

Post-war L.M.S. A.C. 0-4-0 Goods Tender Engines: Top - Lining on front boiler band and tender: Bottom left - Lining on front boiler band only: Bottom right - Unlined.

production:

a) The tank engine steps had strengthening ribs added.

b) The wall thickness at the point where the cylinder meets the running board was increased.

c) The coupling hook mounting was altered in width and depth and a 10 BA internal thread was added to take a shouldered screw which retained the coupling hook.

To complete the modifications, a flat buffer beam plate, with a slot through which the coupling fitted, replaced the old style buffer beam plate which had acted as a pivot for the cast coupling hook.

It was after these modifications that the colours and finishes of the 0-4-0s altered. Not so much on the LMS passenger tender engine, which remained a very deep maroon, but the green of the LNER passenger tender engine

nearly matched that of its tender being a very dull shade. The locomotive numbers given to these engines were nearly all of three figure configuration, corresponding to the renumbering system adopted by the London & North Eastern Railway on 13 January 1946. Both the LMS and the LNER goods tender engines were now finished in unlined gloss black, which as production progressed changed to an almost matt finish; this included the tenders which were now sprayed instead of being tin printed. Patent information on the rear of the tender was conveyed by means of transfers. The LMS and LNER tank engines in both passenger and goods versions continued to be finished as earlier

Post-war LMS and LNER AC 0-4-0 Tank Engines.

models, except that Patent information transfers were omitted from the rear of the engine body. Then as the years went by, the paint gradually changed from a high gloss to an almost matt finish. The transfers used on all the above reverted to gold on a red background. In the case of the LNER goods locomotives, there were two sizes of letters used (including those on the printed tenders after 1947), 4mm high and 3mm high, but there appears to be no set pattern to their use except that the final production runs used the 4mm letters which were the same height as used on pre-war models.

The SR passenger and goods 0-4-0 engines presented a slightly different story. Both the passenger tank and tender engine bodies were finished in a shade of green very near to the malachite green used by the Southern Railway and were still fully lined. The goods tender engine body was in unlined black, whilst the goods tank engines were available either lined or unlined, with or without Patent transfers, depending on the luck of the draw! The oval shaped transfer with a red background and gold markings, as applied to the tender engine cab sides, was far more distinct than its pre-war

predecessor showing clearly the number 951.

The tenders for the above 0-4-0 tender engines deserve a special mention as they were the last of the fully printed tinplate tenders. Apart from the very different green of the passenger tender, each letter in the word 'SOUTHERN' and each number forming 763, and 498 on the goods tender, were slightly thinner giving the appearance of being less bold than the pre-war printing. Unfortunately the transfers used on the sides of the tank engines were still prone to wear. The chassis used for all the tenders were now generally a modified

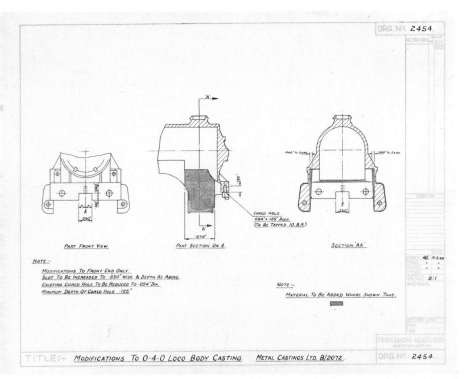

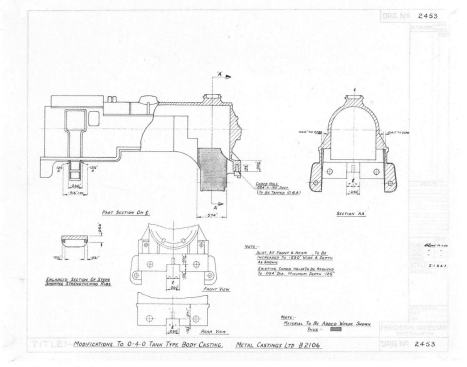

Drawings showing the strengthening modifications to the diecasting of the 0-4-0 tender and tank engine bodies.

Post-war LNER AC 0-4-0 Goods Tender Engines Cat. No. 4/525. Top and middle: Lined and unlined engines with lined tenders. Bottom: Unlined engines and tenders. In all cases notice the different size and style of the LNER transfer applied to the tender.

version which catered for the new rear coupling retainer and the pivoted tender-to-engine coupling bar.

Although the new livery of the nationalised British Railways was applied to TTR locomotives in 1950, the LMS, LNER and SR 0-4-0s in their various forms were generally available until 1952, although the former two predominated. After 1952, but no later than 1954, an occasional LMS or LNER tank engine would emanate from the factory at Northampton, but these were never advertised or mentioned in price lists or catalogues.

During 1948 a system of product dating was adopted, primarily to assist in the identification of the manufacturing date of 0-4-0 and other locomotives returned to the factory for repair or reconditioning. This dating procedure was devised by F. Gratton, the assembly foreman at Precision Models, and took the form of a single letter and number combination code stamped in white on the underside of the 0-4-0 chassis and

on the body casting of larger AC locomotives, with the letter denoting the month and the number denoting the year. For example, January 1949 would be shown as A9 and May 1950 as E0. The letter 'I' was not used presumably so as not to be confused with the figure 1, and thus December was denoted by the letter M. This coding continued to be used not only on locomotives but other selected TTR electrical products until May 1960 when production moved from Precision Models to Birmingham. No distinction was required between the code for 1950 and that for 1960 as the products were vastly different, and only 1956 saw a slight change in the code which used two figures for the year – June 1956 was coded F56.

This date code is very useful to the collector providing that the mechanism has not been changed. Two other slightly larger letters can also be found on the 0-4-0 type of AC chassis and these are 'R' and 'M'. The former denotes that the locomotive has been back to the factory for repair or renovation, whilst 'M' was only applied to 0-4-0 chassis made in 1948 and showed that the chassis was a modified version fitted with a brass reversing contact shaft retaining plate, part of which passed through a hole in the field coil laminations to fix it in place. The use of this latter coding soon vanished.

The early post-war period also saw the replanning of production for the LMS and LNER 4-4-0 locomotives. Consequently Fry's Diecastings Ltd received an order in June 1946 for 1,000 LMS engine body assemblies and corresponding cylinder and front bogie castings. It was not until early in 1947 that the first of the

LMS Compounds, Cat. No 2/536, the passenger version (locomotive number 1168), reached the shops. It was in very deep maroon similar to the LMS 0-4-0 passenger engine and tender of the same period. The lining was the same as the pre-war versions except that on some models produced circa 1949/1950 the letters of L, M and S on the tender were very widely spaced, the gaps normally being approximately 10mm. The couplings were still the pre-war pattern, and the transfers were gold on a red background with serif style letters.

A further order was received by Fry's Diecastings in June 1947 for another 650 Compound components together with 350 engine body and cylinder assemblies, including bogies, for the LNER 'Pytchley', Cat. No 4/536. Most of these early post-war 'Pytchley' 4-4-0 locomotives were finished in the very attractive LNER apple green, the very first few retaining the pre-war number of 298, but later they were given the number 2750 corresponding to the LNER renumbering. Unlike the LMS Compound they were only produced with the new coupling, as by this time it was well established on the production line and fitted to all locomotives and rolling stock. These early productions of the LMS and LNER 4-4-0s incorporated a tender coupling assembly similar to that used on the 0-4-0 engines produced at this time. This was accomplished by altering the tender chassis casting to accept the top pivot of the new type coupling with the addition of a tinplate keeper plate, held in place by the buffers, to locate the lower end of the pivot. This method was only in production for a short period.

During 1949 two limit pins were added to the top of the bogie buffer beam to restrict the

Post-war SR AC 0-4-0 Tank and Tender Engines. Note the shades of green on the passenger engines and the lack of lining on the engine body of the black goods tender engine.

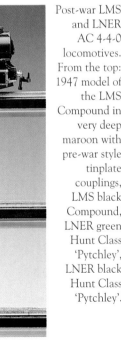

Post-war LMS and LNER AC 4-4-0 locomotives. From the top: 1947 model of the LMS Compound in very deep maroon with pre-war style tinplate couplings, LMS black Compound, LNER green Hunt Class 'Pytchley', LNER black Hunt Class 'Pytchley'.

sideways movement of the new coupling, and a spacer collar and screw was used to locate the coupling at the rear of the tender chassis. Unfortunately nearly all of these early LMS and LNER 4-4-0s were destined for the export market, as was most of the Trix production, until mid-way through 1949 when restrictions started to ease and the home market could have a slightly bigger 'slice of the cake'. By this time the LMS Compound was available finished in an almost matt black livery fully lined in red, retaining the number 1168 and an unchanged basic catalogue number of 2/536, although the suffix letters SL were used for a while. How smart this model looked!

1949 also saw the the introduction of the LNER 'Pytchley' Cat. No. 4/536, in a similar black finish, fully lined in red and bearing the number 2750 with the usual sans-serif letters on the tender. The nameplate was again picked out in yellow and surmounted by the silver fox.

After the initial quantities mentioned above, the approximate totals of LMS and LNER 4-4-0

locomotives produced prior to the introduction of the British Railways versions were approximately 2,000 and 1,200 respectively, with probably no more than 400 being produced of the LNER green 'Pytchley'. An interesting point regarding production figures is that a normal production run for most of the Trix range consisted of between 1,000 and 1,200 items, quantities which held true for most of the time from pre-war days up to the early 1960s.

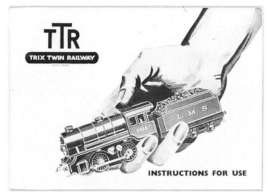

Instruction Books.
Top: 1935/36 Trix Express English edition.
Above left: Pre-war TTR edition.
Above: 1950s TTR edition.

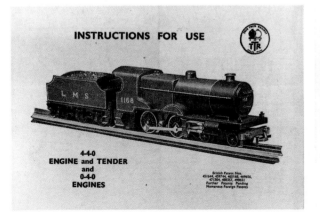

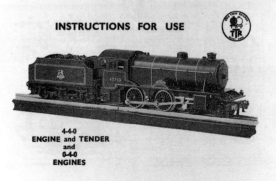

Far left: 1948 edition of the 4-4-0 instruction leaflet which continued in this style until circa 1954.
Left: 1955 edition of the 4-4-0 instruction leaflet.

THE INTRODUCTION OF NEW MODELS

Throughout the early post-war period, the design team always endeavoured to improve the Trix Twin Railway and even keep alive previous intentions as shown in the 1939 leaflet. As mentioned previously, this is evidenced by the drawings produced during 1946 and 1947 of the component parts for the body of the British outline 2-4-2 tank engine, which unfortunately never progressed beyond this stage. Even the 'Dover' of the SR 4-4-0 Schools class locomotive was planned, but maybe the fear that a further requirement would be matching scale-length SR coaches, and all that that implied in terms of tooling and costs, put paid to this project, which in any event would have appealed largely to the home market at a time when all effort was being put into the export drive.

It was for this export drive that the following two TTR locomotives were specifically designed in the spring of 1948 with America and Canada as the main target. American-style wagons had already been in production before the war, and although it was not possible to mass-produce another American Pacific for reasons of cost, it was essential that exports to the USA be achieved by offering suitable American-outline locomotives.

The result was that a few months later two 0-4-0 locomotives of freelance design based on the style of American steam locomotives were advertised for 'EXPORT ONLY' in the 1948 editions of the Trix Twin Railway catalogues, becoming available before the end of the year to overseas customers. The passenger locomotive and tender, Cat. No. 9/520.SL, and the 0-4-0

freight locomotive and tender, Cat. No. 9/525. SL, (commonly known as a Switcher), were initially finished in gloss black with white lining and the words TRIX TWIN on the passenger tender sides in white letters. Various engine numbers were applied to the cab sides initially using silver-white transfers and then quickly changing to white, the first batches using slightly smaller number transfers to those of 1949 and later. (See the list on page 214). Later models also had a wider space between the individual digits. Contrary to the pictures of the Switcher locomotive in various items of literature showing the tender with the words TRIX TWIN, it was never produced as such. This seems to be the case of the 'Chicken before the Egg', as invariably TTR catalogues were generally available before actual production of new models took place, and the pictures shown were either photographs of pre-production models or artists' impressions. This was not just peculiar to Trix Ltd as many other companies followed this procedure.

Up to 1950 the main component parts for the engine and tender bodies were cast by Sparklets Ltd, a subsidiary of the British Oxygen Co. Ltd which unfortunately closed down during that year. Their manufacture was then taken over by the British Diecasting & Engineering Co. Ltd. These later castings can be distinguished from those made earlier by Sparklets Ltd, by the letters BD embossed on the cow catcher, the cylinder casting, the inside top face of the tenders and the underside of the firebox on the engine body. It is safe to say that all the early production runs went for export, although in the 1949 and 1950 single sheet catalogue/price lists printed for the home

Publicity sheet aimed at Canadian retailers circa 1952.

The TTR American Switcher and Passenger AC 0-4-0 locomotives Cat. Nos. 9/525 and 9/520 respectively. Note the silvery finish to the number 2690 on the early Switcher.

The TRIX LOCO KIT Cat.No.81/51 (without 14 volt lamp).

market they were listed as being available without light (Cat. No. 9/519 for the passenger locomotive and Cat. No. 9/524 for the Switcher locomotive). One or two American 0-4-0s may have found their way under a shop counter, but it was not until 1950-51 that they filtered through onto the home market in any significant numbers becoming generally available by 1952.

The design of the engine body was cleverly executed to enable two types of engine to be produced with the minimum tooling and cost. The basic body shell for both passenger and Switcher engines was exactly the same, the only

difference occurring when either a passenger or Switcher smoke box door casting was assembled to the body shell. The other obvious difference was the addition of a buffer beam or cow catcher and associated hand rail wiring depending on which type of locomotive was to be depicted. The bogies used on both types of tender were the same as used on the various bogie goods wagons. One inherent weakness in both the main body shell and the two types of tender castings was the open fret steps, which were very prone to damage and on later versions were strengthened by filling in the open effect.

A freelance finish to a completed model DC American Switcher constructed from a TRIX LOCO KIT Cat. No. 81/50 or 81/51.

The chassis was the basic 0-4-0 mechanism manufactured at Northampton with the addition of a lamp socket and miniature lamp to illuminate the lens fitted to each type of smoke-box door. The only deviation, from 1949 for a period of about three years, was that the British chassis was sometimes replaced by one manufactured in Nuremberg, this practice also being extended to other locomotives. This took place during the time when Messrs Bing and Oppenheim together with Mrs Sommer were major shareholders in Trix Vereinigte Spielwaren-fabriken GmbH and full cooperation existed between the two countries for the benefit of both Trix companies. This German chassis can be distinguished from its British counterpart by the method of fixing the driving wheels to the axles. On a British chassis a bakelite insulating bush is used to locate the wheel on a 3.0mm diameter axle, whilst on a German chassis, a brass bush is pressed on to a 2.5mm diameter axle to which is fitted the wheel insulated from the bush by a moulded plastic spacer. These two American style locomotives continued in production until the end of 1956 and were offered for sale for a while by Ewart Holdings Ltd when they purchased Trix Ltd and Precision Models Ltd. Many thousands were sold worldwide and they even enjoyed a modicum of success in Britain despite it being the wrong outline for the British enthusiast.

An interesting attempt to gain the interest of overseas model railway enthusiasts using 16.5mm 2-rail scale track was the introduction during the last few months of 1949 of a TRIX LOCO KIT, Cat. No. 81/50. This was basically the compo-

Instruction leaflet for the TRIX LOCO KIT Cat. No. 81/51.

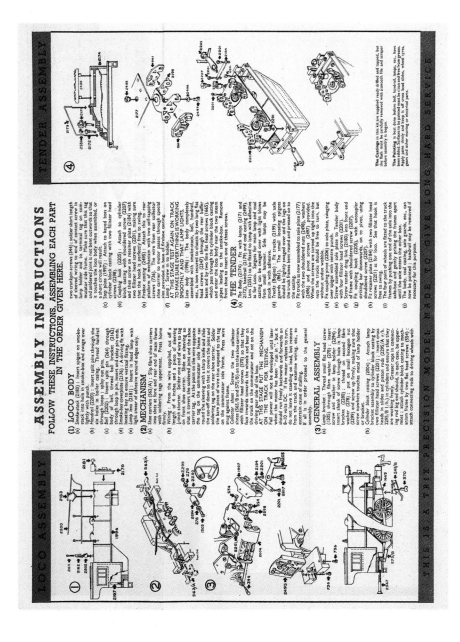

nent parts of the 0-4-0 American Switcher locomotive supplied unpainted in kit form which could be assembled very easily using only simple hand tools including a soldering iron. What was different was that the mechanism of the locomotive chassis was modified to operate on 12 volts DC only, having a permanent magnet instead of the usual AC components. The workings of the mechanism were also altered to such an extent that extra gearing was incorporated enabling high power and a more realistic speed to be transmitted to the specially turned down standard 0-4-0 wheels, which permitted its use on scale track. The chassis was supplied mechanically complete, and current from the two-rail track was taken via uninsulated wheels on one side and the normal AC type of shoes for the other rail. In place of the reversing relay on the AC versions, there was now a firebox casting depicting all the cab controls and dials which made the locomotive a little more realistic.

This was the first 12 volt DC model in the TTR range and, of course, was mainly for export being distributed in America by Polk's Modelcraft Hobbies, New York. However, a few kits were offered for sale on the home market with a small omission which was brought to the attention of the purchaser by a label stating:

'Due to import restrictions it has not been possible to include the 14 volt lamp in the TRIX Loco Kits offered for sale on the home market.'

Trix gave this home market version of the kit the catalogue number of 81/51. It was available until 1953 and was handled by some dealers in Britain, although strangely it was never mentioned in any of the general Trix catalogues or price lists.

THE RETURN OF GERMAN MODELS

Help was given by the British partners to the German company during the early post-war period by providing an export outlet for part of their limited production of model railway parts, an obvious move bearing in mind that a restitution agreement was in the process of negotiation. Finished cast bodies of the German-outline tender, tank and electric locomotives, catalogue numbers 20/52, 20/54 and 20/55 respectively, were fitted in Northampton to British 0-4-0 chassis with black wheels. The various language editions of the TTR 'Export' catalogues at this time listed these as continental locomotives which were given the catalogue numbers 20/52.SL, 20/54.SL and 20/55.SL respectively, the letters SL denoting self lubricating bearings.

The 20/52.SL tender locomotive was unique as it was supplied with a British pattern tender. In fact it was a normal 0-4-0 style tinplate tender sprayed with a satin black finish with no markings except for a red line painted along each side of the chassis frame. The tender chassis was of the early post-war pattern having the new post-1947 coupling riveted to a central channel as used on pre-war models. The engine body was finished in almost gloss black and physically no different from the German 20/52 version except that the gap on the front buffer beam was widened slightly to accommodate the modified coupling. This latter observation also applies to the buffer beams of the other two 'continental' models offered with the British range. The German 20/52 'B' (0-4-0) engine and tender were introduced in Germany in 1939 replacing

the earlier 20/51 and 20/53 models. An entirely new engine body casting was used on this model which was longer and looked more realistic than its predecessors. The smoke deflectors were now formed from sheet metal instead of being cast with the rest of the body, the coupling and piston rod assembly was more realistic, and two working headlights were also incorporated.

The 20/54.SL 0-4-0 tank engine was basically no different to previous German versions, being unlined with the letters of TRIX on each cab side and the number 20 0 54 on both cab sides and smokebox door picked out in yellow. Again the finish was in gloss black.

The 20/55.SL electric 0-4-0 engine was basically unchanged from pre-war days except that the roof was finished in light grey instead of off-white, and in most instances the 'bump' in the middle of the buffer beams was removed and the coupling slot widened for the new Trix coupling. The body was finished in dark green with yellow window frames together with black skirt, steps and buffer beams. The air cylinders were also dark green.

The above three models were available for only a short period, although the 20/55.SL was still shown in the 1950 general export catalogue but was deleted from later ones. According to

The 0-4-0 Electric Locomotive 20/55 SL and its box. Note the chassis on this model is that used for steam outline locomotives as one of the wheels is fitted with a crank. This frequently happened when the correct chassis was not available. (A)

Post-war Trix Express German outline models assembled in Northampton and fitted with TTR black-wheeled chassis. From the top: 0-4-0 Tank Engine Cat.No.20/54.SL; 0-4-0 Engine and Tender Cat.No.20/52.SL. Note the British outline tender; 0-4-0 Electric locomotive Cat.No.20/55.SL.

'Motilus' in the March 1949 *Newnes Practical Mechanics*, the 20/55.SL was intended for the Swiss market, whilst the 20/52.SL and 20/54.SL locomotives were aimed at the Belgian market.

The opening of a direct connection between the British and German Trix companies after the restitution agreement soon brought a locomotive onto the home market that had been promised for a long time. This was the 2-4-2 tank engine, which, although sadly not in British outline, was advertised as the 2-4-2 Mixed Duty locomotive and was available in the spring of 1951. Despite the fact that it was allotted the same catalogue number as the one manufactured for Germany, namely 20/56, it differed from the German model in that both the front and rear bogies incorporated an adaptation of the new coupling adopted by the Trix Twin Railway.

This model locomotive was cleverly constructed and incorporated various new features. Without the use of special fittings to the track, one could by operating the lever on the normal TTR control unit uncouple the front or rear of the locomotive from a train anywhere on the track. This was accomplished on the locomotive by two cams on the reversing contact shaft which revolved every time the reversing

relay was activated, and these cams operated a train of levers which in turn caused the coupling hook on the front or rear bogie to drop. The coupling hook returned to its normal position when the reversing relay was activated once again. The sequence of operations was as follows:

1) Forward.
2) Forward and uncouple.
3) Reverse.
4) Reverse and uncouple.

Another feature using electrical contacts on the reversing contact shaft was the automatic operation of the running lights which changed with the direction of the locomotive. Due to reduction gearing the model had a realistic operating speed and good pulling characteristics.

The cast engine body for the British market was fitted onto the normal red chassis and wheels as used for the German version and finished in a virtually matt black with the name TRIX EXPRESS and the number 20 056 embossed on the cab sides plus the corresponding number on the smokebox door. Earlier models for the German market had had an almost gloss black finish, but, as a result of complaints from model railway enthusiasts in Germany in the early post-war days that the finish on all the Trix

Express locomotives was not prototypical, the gloss finish was toned down. The locomotive was supplied ready boxed from the Nuremberg factory and underwent modification of the bogies plus general adjustment at Precision Models, including relabelling of the box. Apart from the special coupling assembly and British pattern buffers, formed tinplate steps and wheel guards similar to those on the pre-war TTR British Pacifics and the then current Trix Express Pacific locomotive were fitted. These were of a different pattern to those fitted on the 20/56 for the German market.

Although the aim of this book is primarily to describe the Trix products generally available or manufactured for or in Britain, it may be of interest to the collector to note the following information concerning the pre-war 2-4-2, Cat. No. 20/56, tank engine when compared to the post-war versions. It will be noticed on post-war models that the separate castings depicting the cab steps and other detail are attached to the main body casting by small screws; on the pre-war versions these separate castings are riveted to the body. On post-war models strengthening webs were added to the cylinder castings and the underside of each of the running board

Leaflet advertising the pending delivery of the 2-4-2 Tank Engine and the Diesel Flyer.

Post-war 2-4-2 Tank Engine instruction leaflet.

take care that the contact brushes (14) and the moving parts of the reversing mechanism are not bent or displaced. Finally, replace the three screws which serve to hold the body on the chassis.

Causes of possible troubles and how to remedy them

1. *If the engine does not answer the switch of the controller:*
First of all, find out whether the contact brushes (14) have been bent. If so, bend them back into their original positions as in paragraph (c). Then, if the engine has not been damaged by a fall you can seek the cause in the presence of dirt. In that case, remove the body, as mentioned above, and find out:
(a) if after first having pressed by hand the armature on the reversing magnet, the moving parts do not drop back freely, then all those moving parts must be cleaned with a dry cloth or rag. Do not in any circumstances use or apply oil to any part of the reversing mechanism.
(b) If the contact brushes or springs (14) should be dirty or over-oiled, or if the metal contacts on the reversing contact shaft (15) should have got dirty or over-oiled, the contact shaft will continue

turning in 90° steps, but the engine cannot respond because of the presence of dirt. Clean the reversing contact shaft and the contacts or springs with a dry cloth or rag—nothing else.
(c) Contact Brushes or Springs (14) are bent.
These must have very good electrical contact with the reversing contact shaft (15) but must be adjusted so that they lie against the contact shaft under slight pressure.
(d) There may be trouble in the Controller. This can easily be ascertained as follows: The Controller is taken out of circuit and the two free ends of the wires or the plugs are brought close to each other. By making short contacts between the two wire ends or plugs the reversing mechanism can be operated. If the engine does not respond, the trouble is in the engine. If it does respond, the trouble is in the controller.

2. *Insufficient power*
(a) **Adjusting the Carbon Brushes.** Put the engine on the track and holding the cylinders and the cab lift the engine slightly, so that the wheels can move freely, but the shoes should still

be in touch with the rails. Let the engine run with the controller full-on. Then turn the brushholder caps (9) slightly, and note how this affects the running. You can tell the speed by the sound produced by the armature. When the highest speed of the armature is reached, which is equivalent to the highest pitch, that is the correct position for the brush caps, or, in other words, that is the right compression of the springs behind the carbon brushes.
(b) **Cleaning the Commutator.** If after some time the engine develops insufficient power, then take it down, remove the armature and clean the commutator. This is easily done as follows: after removing the body unscrew the stator screws (16) less than ⅛ inch and remove the motor side-frame (17) very carefully. After that, you can draw out the armature quite easily. Then take a finely pointed piece of wood, such as a tooth-pick or a pointed matchstick—and remove any carbon dust or other dirt which may have got into the slots of the commutator. A dry cloth or rag should be used to clean the face of the commutator. Then replace the armature in its former position. Take great care that no wires of the commutator or armature are damaged or broken. Then remove the carbon brushes from the motor side-frame. After that, replace the motor side-frame in its proper position, put back the stator screws, giving one or two

turns, but not screwing them home completely. When doing this, observe that the field magnet is in its correct position and has not been moved upwards, because if that were the case, the armature would not be evenly influenced and it could, in fact, rub on the stator laminations. After all this, complete the screwing home of the stator screws (16) fully, so that there is no uneven tension on the chassis. Then replace the carbon brushes in their holders.

SPARE PARTS FOR ENGINE 20/56

30/57/1	Armature with commutator.
30/2/4	1 pair of cylinders.
30/2/5	1 pair of piston rods with cross-head and connecting rods.
30/5/4	Reversing contact shaft.
30/9/2h	Rear bogie.
30/9/2v	Front bogie.
31/10	Reversing arm and pawl.
30/12/2	3 screws for body and 2 long and 2 short screws for cranks.
31/27	2 carbon brushes and springs.
30/30/5	Motor side frame with carbon brush holders and caps therefor.
30/31/2	Right hand gear bearing plate.
30/40/4	1 set of collector shoes.
30/41v	Lamp holder, front.
30/41h	Lamp holder, rear.
30/72/1	Light bulb.

TRIX
LIMITED
11, OLD BURLINGTON STREET, LONDON, W.1

SCALE MODEL
2·4·2 TANK ENGINE
REMOTE CONTROL UNCOUPLING AT BOTH ENDS

20/56

PLEASE READ THESE INSTRUCTIONS BEFORE UNPACKING THE ENGINE

The Trix Loco 20/56 is fitted for remote control uncoupling at both ends. All possible shunting operations, including coupling-up or uncoupling in any part of the layout, can be performed by remote control.

In addition this model is fitted with lamps both at front and at rear. When the engine is running forward the front lamps are lit. When the engine is in reverse the rear lamps are lit.

This 2-4-2 Tank Engine, a masterpiece of small scale engineering, is precision made. Any parts subject to wear are easily accessible and interchangeable.

The model will run with a maximum of 14 volts alternating current or 14 volts direct current. It must, of course, never be connected directly to the mains. If that were done, a short-circuit would occur and the loco would be damaged beyond repair. To connect with the mains, proceed as follows: If the mains are alternating current, use a transformer with an input of the same voltage as your mains and with an output of not more than 14 volts. If your mains current is direct, then use a Rotary Converter, again with an

output of not more than 14 volts. The type of current and the voltage of your mains can be easily ascertained from your local electricity office. Transformers or Converters with less than a 30 watt output are not suitable for this model.

Speed control, direction control and uncoupling control are effected by means of the Trix Controller 472, which must be connected between the secondary outlet of the Transformer and the terminal rail.

This engine has been thoroughly tested both mechanically and electrically. If trouble arises in operating the loco, then it is probably due to handling other than in accordance with these instructions. We ask you, therefore, to proceed as follows:
Remove the engine carefully from the packing so as to avoid bending the piston and connecting rods. See that:
(a) the connecting rods which are fitted to the driving wheels sit loosely upon the crankshafts and that they have lateral play. Should they have been bent, they should be taken off and straightened out. To take them off, turn the screws of the crankshaft to the left,

---

extensions located above the cylinder. The electrical arrangement was modified to include two additional contacts on the field coil for the running lights, which on pre-war versions were connected directly to the carbon brush holders. Other pre-war differences in relation to later models include a shorter centre pick-up shoe

channel, short buffers, a raised lip on the front centre portion of each bogie buffer beam, and a thin aluminium disc added between the brass inner part of each driving wheel and its insulating disc which bears up against the inside of the wheel flange.

The 1949 combined catalogue for TTR and

Trix Express products for the American market, distributed by 'Polk's' in New York, listed a 2-4-2 under the following heading:

'Newest addition to the Trix line - The ultimate in realism-29-56-2 Super Automatic Tank Switcher-$29.95.'

Below this statement was a picture of the

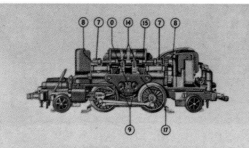
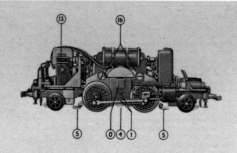
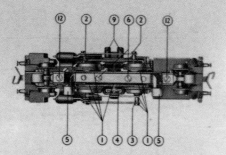

i.e. anti-clockwise, straighten and replace. The screw this time requires turning to the right. Screw them tight but take care not to strip the thread. Before doing this, please see that the tubular distance pieces between the coupling rod and the driving rod are not omitted.

(b) See that the wheels and all the rods move freely. This test should be made *only* by moving by hand the brass reduction gear (No. 4).

It will not be wise to push the loco *on* the rails or upon any other surface as moving it by force in that manner can only lead to damage.

Before using the engine it is advisable to perform the switching operations ordinarily brought about by electric impulse, by pushing the reversing armature (18) (the moveable plate visible through the right-hand cab window) several times to its stop. To do this, use a small screwdriver or a pencil. This ensures proper functioning of the reversing mechanism.

OPERATING

See that the two outside collector shoes (5) rest upon *that* outside rail for which they are intended, bearing in mind the twin running of the

engine. When required, the position of the two outside shoes (5) should be reversed. This can easily be done after loosening the holding screw (6). After changing over the shoes, the screws should, of course, be replaced and screwed home medium tight.

Testing the Engine

Turn the knob of the controller to a medium position and run through the switching sequences by moving the key of the controller towards yourself several times and observe what takes place. There are four distinct steps :

1. Forward.
2. Still forward, but uncoupled at the rear.
3. Reverse.
4. Still in reverse but un-

PLEASE NOTE—
Owing to the extra flexibility of the movement in this loco you may find it difficult, especially when running as a light engine, to bring it to a stop with the controller knob. If so, you can stop it by moving the controller key forward into the 'cut out' position.

All vehicle couplings should be examined, and, if necessary adjusted so that they are level with the couplings of the engine in their normal position.

performed and afterwards the locomotive will proceed in the original direction simply by turning the knob to the right.

IMPORTANT

With this model it is **essential** that the movement of the switching key is carried out very deliberately. If the key is moved quickly or suddenly the switching mechanism will not operate properly.

When you are sure that the engine responds correctly to all the movements of the controller, it is ready for normal operation.

Although every engine is carefully tested and " run-in " at the factory, it still requires a certain period of running-in just the same as any large engine or motor-car. It will reach its maximum efficiency only after it has been run-in for a distance of several miles. In other words, the engine should not be over-loaded and this with should not be asked to haul more than three bogie vehicles or their equivalent.

We call attention to the fact that the special feature of this engine is not high speed, but its unique flexibility at all speeds including dead-slow.

MAINTENANCE

1. **Moving Parts.** It is absolutely essential that all parts, moving or otherwise, be kept clean. Those parts of the engine which run fast, like the armature, act something like a vacuum cleaner and attract dust, fluff, etc., and pull these particles into the mechanism. The consequence is that the running is not as smooth as it should be and it is therefore advisable not to put lay-outs on carpets, or the like.

The cleaning should be done with a dry cloth or fluffless rag. When doing this make sure that no hairs or fibres remain in the gears.

2. **Oiling.** The engine was oiled at the factory. However, it will need further oiling from time to time. The important parts to be oiled are the bearings and other parts marked " O " on the illustrations. The oil can reach the bearings through two holes which will be found on top of the side water tanks. Points marked (1) must also be kept oiled. Only a light oil free from acid should be used.

The best way to do the oiling is to dip a wire into the oil and the small drop remaining at the end should be allowed to glide into the bearings or other positions as indicated above. Do not by any

means over-oil—especially the armature bearings between the brush caps (9). If too much oil is allowed to reach that part some will reach the commutator. This will in a short time lead to the motor getting dirty and ceasing to function. If the armature bearings are insufficiently oiled a grating noise will develop. The two cams (7) on the reversing contact shaft should only be touched with very little oil—of course, after removing the body.

Do N O T oil

The bearings (8) of the reversing contact shaft,
The uncoupling devices,
The reversing mechanism in the cab.

3. **Carbon Brushes.** The carbon brushes and their casings must be cleaned from time to time. Oil getting on to the carbon brushes causes clogging and will bring the engine to a standstill. To clean these parts, remove the brush caps (9), draw out the brushes gently, clean them ; clean the tubes in which they rest ; clean the brush caps with a dry cloth or rag and after they are completely clean, reassemble. *There is no need to remove the motor side frame in order to do this.* While cleaning, you

can also see whether the brushes require renewing. The brushes are useable down to a length of about 1/8 inch.

4. **Collector Shoes.** The collector shoes are subject to wear. They can be replaced by removing the screws (6 and 12). When fitting new shoes, please see that the curve of the shoe lies on the rail and that the springs behind them are not bent. Further, when the screws are tightened the shoes should remain springy. New collector shoes come in sets—spare part No. 30/40/4.

5. **Lighting, Removing Body.** The miniature bulbs, type 30/72/1 for the front and rear lamps, are interchangeable. First undo the two screws under the rear wall of the cab, and the screw in the funnel, and carefully lift the body up and off. Do not lift the spring on the lamps, but *slide* it away. When replacing the lamps under the cab, please be sure and see that the larger of the round openings on the lamp casing is against the lens. The spring, after it has been slid on again, must fit snugly. Before you replace the body please test the lighting by running the engine forward and backward. Then replace the body. When doing this,

2-4-2 tank engine.

The number 29 was the post-war German coding for goods destined for America. This model also differed from the normal 20/56 in the type of coupling and the method of uncoupling used. The front bogie was fitted with the normal 'inverted spoon' coupling, and another 'inverted

spoon' replaced the pivoted hook on the rear bogie. These couplings were operated by cams on the reversing contact shaft, but strangely, instead of the normal two cams operating alternately, cams of a new form were cast onto the shaft so that both couplings operated at the same time. Special guides were fitted to each buffer beam

around the coupling to help with the alignment of a new type of coupling fitted to Nuremberg-made rolling stock for America. In fact this coupling was almost identical to that adopted by the Trix Twin Railway with the exception of an extra small guide arm. This special coupling only had a very short life and disappeared when the controlling shares of the British co-partners were withdrawn.

The German version of the 20/56 first made its appearance during 1948, followed in 1951 by the modified version for the British market. Although it was available in Britain until 1954 and a year later in Germany, sales, apart from the original euphoria, were not very high, and due to a very poor type of mazak used to produce the castings for the chassis components, the chassis were very prone to fatigue. This is a great problem for the collector and not many 20/56 models have survived in one piece. Unfortunately this problem is prevalent on some other models produced at this time, and even on the occasional pre-war model produced by both Germany and Britain.

1951 also saw the reintroduction of the Nuremberg-produced two coach 'Diesel Flyer', Cat. No.20/58, for the home market. This was more or less the same as the pre-war version with the exception of certain refinements in the construction of the various electrical components, plus the omission of the Reichsbahnadler emblem of the Deutsche Reichsbahn. The number 20058 was printed on each side of each coach, together with certain inconsistencies in the use of the words TRIX EXPRESS-Germany which were sometimes printed on both end panels, on one of the end panels, or not at all. In contrast to the normal silvery metallic finish on the roofs of the coaches, the final production runs were finished in light grey. The couplings were always the German pattern as there was no need for the unit to couple with any TTR item. It was boxed in Nuremberg and sent to Northampton for relabelling and the addition of the English language instruction sheet. It remained on sale until 1954 and was quite popular. For the American market it was given the catalogue number of 29/58.

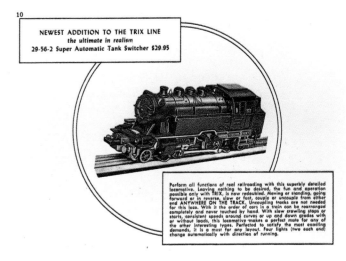

An extract from the Polk's 1949 Trix Express/TTR catalogue showing the 2-4-2 'Super Automatic Tank Switcher' Cat.No.29-56-2.

Top: The post-war Trix Express 2-4-2 Tank Engine; fitted with German couplings on the right and British couplings on the left. Both are Cat.No.20/56.
Bottom: The post-war Diesel Flyer Cat. No.20/58.

THE CHANGE OF THE 0-4-0 TO BRITISH RAILWAYS LIVERY

Following the nationalisation of the railway network in Britain on 1 January 1948, it passed through an experimental phase when, in an effort to ascertain the preferences of the public, locomotives and passenger stock changed colours with the rapidity of a chameleon. A decision was made in the autumn of 1949 that express steam and electric passenger locomotives were to be light blue with black and white lining. Selected express passenger steam locomotives were to be dark green with black and orange lining. Other passenger and mixed traffic locomotives were to be black with red, cream and grey lining, whilst goods locomotives were to be in unlined black.

It was always the policy of Trix Ltd to be competitive and innovative. Thus during the autumn of 1950, after the period of British Railways colour trials, Trix introduced their range of British outline 0-4-0 locomotives in BR livery.

The first 0-4-0 passenger engine and tender in BR livery, Cat. No. 1/520, was finished in light blue with white lining painted on the engine boiler bands and black cylinders, plus white and black lining on the tender applied as transfers. The new British Railways lion-over-wheel symbol was also applied by transfer to the sides of the tender and continued to be displayed on all TTR locomotives until and even after the introduction of a redesigned BR symbol in 1956.

The goods version of the 0-4-0 engine and tender, Cat. No. 1/525, was finished in black and completely unlined. Early production runs displayed the TTR Patent information on the rear of the tender, but this practice was quickly stopped and this was the last model locomotive to display such information. Again the goods version of the 0-4-0 tank engine, Cat. No. 1/515, was in unlined black, but the passenger version, Cat. No. 1/510, also in black had red lining on the boiler bands and grey lining on the tank and cab sides. The cylinders on these early versions were unlined.

The BR 0-4-0 Passenger Tender Engines Cat. No. 1/520. The early light blue model with small numbers can be seen at the left on the top row. On the left of the third row from the top is the green version with a green cylinder. The other green models are later versions with a modified coal moulding fitted to the tender.

BR 0-4-0 Goods Tender Engines Cat. No. 1/525. Top left: Early model with small cab numbers.
Top right: Note lining on the front boiler band and cylinder. Middle: Both locomotives have a gloss finish.
Bottom: 1956 models in matt finish.

Although these were the first BR locomotives in the advertised TTR range, it is known that 0-4-0 and 4-4-0 locomotives exist bearing the earlier BR markings introduced at the time of nationalisation, namely with the words BRITISH RAILWAYS applied to the tender sides. However, it cannot be substantiated with certainty whether Trix applied these transfers or whether they were applied by enthusiasts.

Certainly no Trix literature mentions locomotives finished in this way.

The running numbers on the cab sides of the locomotives were applied by individual numerical transfers which were bright yellow with a distinctive black edging. These were slightly smaller than those applied to models produced after the first few months of 1951, the latter being much bolder and in a dull yellow surrounded by a less distinctive black edging.

Spring 1951 saw the replacement of the light blue 0-4-0 passenger engine and tender with a dark blue version. The lining and markings were exactly as on the light blue locomotive except that the numbers were in the new pattern. This handsome dark blue 0-4-0 only had a slightly longer production life than its predecessor as it was phased out during the first half of 1952. For a while from December 1951, it was produced concurrently with a version finished in Brunswick green, which was by now standard British Railways colour for express passenger locomotives, and consequently this became the standard colour used for the 14 volt AC 0-4-0 passenger engine and tender locomotives.

During this period in which the 0-4-0 passenger engines were produced in both dark blue and Brunswick green concurrently, the cylinders were painted in the colour of the locomotive instead of black, as was the British Railways practice. However it was not long before Trix reverted to black for the cylinders, probably on the grounds of cost. These green 0-4-0s were lined in orange on the boiler bands and cylinders, with orange and black lining transfers applied to the tender. All colour variations of the passenger engine and tender retained the catalogue number 1/520.

Up to the withdrawal of 14 volt AC models from the TTR range, apart from the various electrical and mechanical modifications to the 0-4-0 chassis, the only major modification to the 0-4-0 engine and tender models, both in goods and passenger livery, was the alteration during 1954 of the coal moulding on the tender.

This latter version was much flatter in profile than the type which had been used from pre-war days, and was primarily produced for use on the new range of wagons incorporating diecast super-detailed under-frames introduced during the same year. With this new tender coal moulding came the change of lining on the tender to a single orange line.

During 1952 the goods 0-4-0 engine and tender, Cat. No. 1/525, was produced with the boiler band around the smoke-box lined in red, with and without the cylinders correspondingly lined. Again this practice only lasted for a short period, and soon these goods engines reverted to being unlined. Conversely, the passenger version of the 0-4-0 tank engine had red lining applied to the cylinders after circa 1952. Generally, the finish applied to all the TTR 0-4-0 AC locomotives in the early post-war days was almost gloss in appearance before gradually changing over the years to a definite matt finish by the end of AC production.

Autumn 1955 saw the end of production of the 0-4-0 tank engine using a diecast body, the latter being replaced with a plastic version. This was first used for the 4.5/6 volt battery locomotive included in the goods and passenger versions of the Trix 'Junior' train sets introduced at the Brighton Toy Fair earlier in the year, about which more information is contained in the section dealing with the introduction of DC models into the TTR system. This plastic body, which also incorporated a cylinder guide rod for the piston/connecting rod assembly, was an attempt to provide a more realistic outline on the very basic four-wheeled AC chassis. It was

available in two versions. One was advertised as a Mixed Traffic tank engine which was fully lined, similar to the cast body passenger tank engine, and retaining the same catalogue number, ie 1/510. The other version was unlined and classified as a goods tank engine, Cat. No. 1/515. Both versions were manufactured until the spring of 1957. It is a pity that the plastic used in the moulding of the body shell was of such poor quality that it soon distorted. Both versions have the BR lion-over-wheel symbol, but a few are known with the later design of the lion-holding-wheel-over-crown emblem introduced by British Railways in 1956.

Top three rows:
The BR Passenger
and Goods AC
0-4-0 Tank Engines with
diecast body.
Bottom two rows:
1956/57 production models
using a plastic body.

THE 'SCALE' TTR RANGE IN BR LIVERY

Although the 0-4-0 range of TTR locomotives were the 'bread-and-butter' of Trix Ltd and were produced in their thousands, it was most important that the interest of the more mature owner was kept stimulated by the continued inclusion in the range of models that could loosely be described as scale. Thus the 4-4-0 locomotives continued in production, making their debut in British Railway colours at the same time as the 0-4-0 during the autumn of 1950, although the reintroduction of the Pacific locomotive 'Scotsman' was not to take place until the following year.

Both the Midland Region Compound and the Hunt class 4-4-0 locomotives in black BR livery made their appearance in the shops at the same time. The black Hunt class 'Pytchley' was lined in red and grey on both engine and tender and carried the number 62750 with the nameplate and fox picked out in yellow. Strangely the catalogue number for this model, 4/536, remained the same as the LNER versions probably due to the fact that it was advertised as a 4-4-0 engine and tender, Eastern Region. This black 'Pytchley' was produced for a very short time and only approximately 350 were made.

A fun locomotive. An example of what can be done to a model that has lost most of its original paint to save it from the scrap box.

The AC BR 4-4-0 Hunt Class 'Pytchley' Cat. No.4/536. Note the small numbers on the early black version and the single orange lining on the tender of the late green model.

The AC BR 4-4-0 Compounds Cat. No. 2/536. From the top: Early model with small numbers and single lining on tender; version with larger numbers and double lining on tender; late 1953 model finished in Brunswick green; late version in matt finish.

The style and colour of the numbers on this model, and also on the Midland Region Compound, were exactly the same as those used on the BR 0-4-0 locomotives over the same period.

It was not until the latter months of 1953 that the 'Pytchley' was to appear again, this time in Brunswick green and lined in orange with the nameplate and fox also picked out in orange. The number was, of course, the same, but the numerals were in the latter 0-4-0 style. Approximately 6,850 were produced in this livery forming the backbone of many passenger sets, and apart from the minor mechanical and electrical modifications, it was never altered from the time of its introduction to its withdrawal from the official Trix listing in 1958, although production probably ceased during 1956.

The black BR Midland Region Compound, Cat. No. 2/536, enjoyed continuous production through to and during 1956, and was still offered for sale with its stable companion, the 'Pytchley', well into 1958. Both engine and tender were lined in red and grey. Again in the initial year of production, the running number numerals were slightly smaller and brighter than later production, and the lustre of the paint changed from an almost gloss finish to a near matt. There were only four engine numbers used — 41062, 41128, 41135 and 41162. What a pity the cast number of 1168 on the smoke-box door was never removed from the tooling for the body casting! Some of the early tenders were lined with a single grey line, while later tenders saw a modification to the body casting.

This modification, introduced during the first months of 1956, was to eliminate the need for a small spring contact on the coupling bar of the tender. Previously this had gripped the electrical and mechanical coupling pin on the engine body, thus ensuring good electrical coupling, which otherwise after constant use did not always act in an efficient manner. These modified tender body castings had a semi-circular hole just above the coupling bar into which was fitted a bakelite insulating bush containing a single electrical socket connected by wire to the pick-up shoe assembly. This socket connected with a plug and wire soldered to the coupling pin solder tag of the engine chassis. The modification was not fully implemented and the remaining production during 1956 reverted back to the original method, although the modified body casting of the tender remained. It was on a few of these tender bodies during the final stages of the production of the AC Compound, that the new British Railways emblem of 1956 was applied, making them the only AC TTR locomotive to carry this BR emblem.

A total of approximately 7,500 BR Midland Region 4-4-0 Compounds were manufactured, including a deviation from the normal black livery, when in the early autumn of 1953 a small batch were finished in Brunswick green and lined in orange similar to the green 'Pytchley'. There was no change in the catalogue number, while the number applied to the cab sides of this green Compound was 41162. A handful of green Compounds assembled in June 1953 found their way into the shops bearing the number 62750 on the cab sides. This was probably due to an error in the finishing departments of the factory which mistakenly gave the Compound a Hunt class livery.

A special offer made in the Spring 1954 TTR *Gazette* which enabled owners to trade in their old 0-4-0/4-4-0 AC mechanisms for a new one.

Application Form

NEW MECHS. FOR OLD

I wish to trade in my old loco mechanism for a new one and agree to pay an inclusive C.O.D. charge of 37/6 for this service according to the following conditions.

1. The offer applies to both 0-4-0 and 4-4-0 locos, manufactured from 1938 onwards.

2. Be sure to quote on your application any reference numbers and/or letters stamped on the underside of the frame, for us to check.

3. Young persons should have their application forms signed by their parent or guardian.

4. Please do not send your loco with the application form. We shall send you a "calling-in" card

5. The special "Trade-in" charge is 37/6 (post free), payable to the postman C.O.D., so please do not send any money with your application form.

6. We reserve the right to accept or refuse an application under this scheme in our sole discretion.

TRIX LTD., 11 Old Burlington St., London, W.1

NAME (In full use BLOCK LETTERS please) _____

ADDRESS _____

_____

REF. Nos. &/or LETTERS and DATE under loco _____

SIGNATURE OF APPLICANT _____ DATE _____
(PARENT/GUARDIAN) in the case of young persons.

THE REINTRODUCTION OF THE 'SCOTSMAN' PACIFIC

As a direct result of the restitution agreement and cooperation between the German and British Trix companies, the 4-6-2 'Scotsman' Pacific was reintroduced into the TTR range, and as it was now the period of the nationalised British Railways it was fitting that it should be made available in the livery of British Railways. It first appeared in the autumn of 1951 in dark blue livery expertly lined in white with the nameplate picked out in silver, but unlike its 0-4-0 stable mates, the tender was only lined with a single white line. It was a very handsome model and was listed under the catalogue number of 1/540, although at a retail cost of £10 it was a very expensive item and over twice the cost of comparable models by rival manufacturers.

The engine chassis, as in pre-war days, was supplied complete by the Trix factory in Nuremberg with the exception of the front bogie which was now the same as used on the 4-4-0 Compound and 'Pytchley' models. Nevertheless the chassis embodied many modifications, including the reduction of the driving wheel axle diameter from 3.0mm to 2.5mm and a much finer gear tooth pitch for the spur gear and the pinion of the reduction gear assembly which were now made from brass (the latter having previously been steel). There was also a spring-loaded reversing pawl actuator. The main modification was in the way that the uncoupling mechanism in the tender was constructed. This mechanism was now manufactured at the Northampton factory from a new patented design by Werner Alton to accommodate the new TTR coupling, and this in turn necessitated

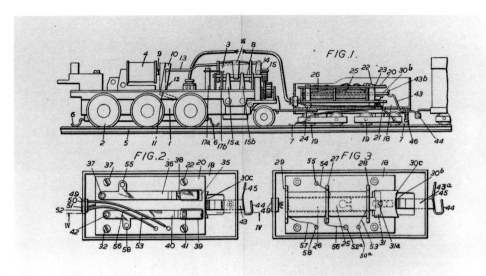

Extract from British Patent No.678,257 showing the new design for the Pacific tender uncoupling mechanism.

the alteration of the tender body and chassis castings.

Although mechanically efficient, one of the main problems with the pre-war uncoupling mechanism was that in its uncoupling mode, current was constantly fed to the coil of the electromagnet, this being usually accompanied by an irritatingly audible vibration of the armature on the core of the electromagnet. In 1948 the new TTR remote control points made their appearance, the point motors incorporating two solenoids end to end operating in push-pull with a common plunger mechanically connected to the point blades. It was this dual solenoid which was adapted for use in the 'Scotsman' tender for the uncoupling action using a pulse of current to operate the solenoids, instead of a constant current. The pulse of current was obtained by electrical and mechanical means and fed to

the selected solenoid whose plunger was mechanically linked to the tender coupling. Two solenoids were required, one to lower the coupling, the other to raise the coupling. As can be appreciated this necessitated the alteration of the reversing contact shaft and associated contact wiper blades. The uncoupling contact on the reversing contact shaft was now moved to the opposite end of the assembly adjacent to the drive pinion, and two sets of wiper blades were arranged around this contact at 90 degrees to each other with corresponding wires taken to a 3-pin socket on the chassis frame. These two wiper blades gave the necessary electrical feed for the push-pull operation of the solenoids in the tender. The electrical connections to the tender were carried by three wires twisted together whose ends were each terminated by a plug which fitted into corresponding sockets on the

The AC BR 'Scotsman' 4-6-2 Pacific locomotives. On the third row is the early green model which is finished in exactly the same way as the earlier blue 'Scotsman' except that the lining is now orange. The later 'Scotsman on the lower two shelves has larger cab numbers, orange nameplate and double lining on the tender. The driving wheels have fully represented spokes and not in relief as on earlier models.

engine and tender chassis. Although only two wires were used for the 'live' side of the solenoids, the third was used as a common electrical return replacing the electro/mechanical coupling between engine and tender as used in pre-war models.

The action of the locomotive mechanism was as follows:

1) Forward and coupled - coupling in raised position.

2) Forward and uncoupled - coupling in lowered position.

3) Stop - coupling in raised position.

4) Reverse - coupling in raised position.

This cycle of operations were repeated at each activation of the controller direction switch – in theory at least!

Spring 1952 saw the introduction of the 'Scotsman' Pacific in Brunswick green, lined exactly in the same way as the dark blue version, but this time in orange with the nameplate again in silver. The running number on the BR 'Scotsman' Pacifics was 60103, the blue and the early green versions using the same type of smaller transfers as on the early BR 0-4-0s and 4-4-0s. The 'Scotsman' in dark blue livery was phased out during 1952.

1953 saw the change in the tender lining to double orange lines interspaced with black, and in circa late 1954- early 1955 the nameplate was finished in orange instead of silver. Mechanically and electrically no major alterations to the engine or tender chassis took place, except that from 1955 more realistic wheels were fitted to the engine chassis. Up to this time the spokes on the driving and pony truck wheels had been represented in relief, but now they were fully modelled. These new wheels were first introduced on the Trix Express Pacific Cat. No.20/61 manufactured between 1951 and 1954, which was similar to the earlier Trix Express Pacifics but more detailed. However, the wheels fitted to the chassis for use on the 'Scotsman' were of a different and more stable metal than the mazak used for the wheels on the 20/61, the latter rarely lasting the ravages of time and usually found by the collector in a poor state.

The last batch of body castings were provided by Fry's Diecastings in February 1954, and the final 'Scotsman' Pacifics were manufactured during 1955, although, as with other AC Trix Twin Railway locomotives, they were catalogued and date coded until 1958. The total number of BR 'Scotsman' 4-6-2 Pacific locomotives produced was just over 4,500.

One may ask why the two pre-war TTR LMS Pacific locomotives were not produced in the post-war years. The fact of the matter is that unfortunately the tooling for the 'Princess' was damaged beyond practical repair, and the 'Coronation' with its streamlined form was out of date. In the immediate years after the war, the LMS 'Coronation' class locomotives had their streamlining removed, and Trix clearly felt that as they were always trying to keep up with modern practice, the 'Coronation' would not fall into this category. Furthermore, the historical significance of the additional bell and headlight on the front of the engine body would be lost on the youth of the post-war era.

THE METEOR DIESEL EXPRESS
THE LAST DEVELOPMENT IN THE
TRIX 14 VOLT AC LOCOMOTIVES

During the years between 1950 and 1956, the design team of Trix Ltd (and let us not forget Precision Models who were at the heart of production and development), endeavoured to improve the range of models with the emphasis on action, while in most cases retaining the basic operating and control voltage of 14 volts AC.

Many ideas were proposed which never reached the drawing board stage. Those that did were interesting, if not always practical. One major modification worth mentioning was that in 1951 the company planned that the American passenger and Switcher 0-4-0s, both the British outline 4-4-0 locomotives and a 'fabricated 0-4-0 tender engine' were to be fitted with an uncoupling mechanism in the tenders. (What the fabricated 0-4-0 tender engine was to look like and how it was to be constructed unfortunately remains a mystery as it is an item that did not reach the drawing board.) It was intended to fit the same uncoupling unit to the American 0-4-0 tenders as on the 'Scotsman' tender, but this was abandoned in favour of a system designed in

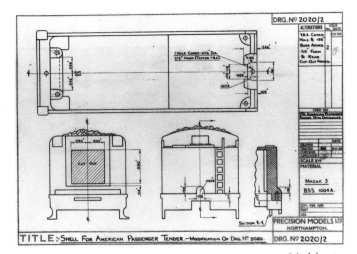

1953 which, looking at the component parts as drawn, was very similar to the reversing mechanism fitted to the Meteor diesel motor chassis introduced later.

The tender castings were to be modified accordingly, which included a diecast bogie assembly for the American 0-4-0 tenders, mainly to accommodate an electrical socket which was used to accept a special four-pin plug incorporating a ball joint to connect with the engine chassis. Trix attached sufficient importance to

Modification of the TTR American 0-4-0 Passenger tender shell for an uncoupling mechanism.

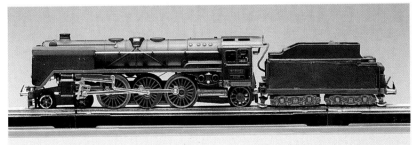

The early 1950s Trix Express AC Pacific with remote control uncoupling mechanism in the tender Cat.No.20/61.
The spokes on the driving wheels are fully formed.

the design of this plug for them to patent the idea (Patent number 734415). The principle was that the electrical leads from the engine chassis passed through the ball end of the plug and on to the pins, thus completely encasing the leads. The ball end of the plug was to be located behind a suitable hole in the rear plate of an engine body or chassis.

A further idea in 1953 was to incorporate the reversing mechanism of the 'Scotsman' Pacific in the tender. Although this would have simplified the engine chassis, the mechanism would have had to be similar to that used on the Meteor due to lack of space. All these ideas would have been costly to tool-up. Some may have worked efficiently and others not, but perhaps they may have created less of a problem than the production of the Meteor diesel express.

The Meteor 3-coach articulated diesel express was a freelance design based loosely on an American trans-continental high speed diesel finished in a distinctive red and yellow livery with the running number of 1394. It incorporated a remote control 'whistle', changing head and tail lights and a feature which Trix Ltd called positive direction control. The three articulated coaches riding on shared bogies were joined together by cleverly designed dummy corridor connections which gave good mechanical and electrical linkage. The bogies, with their plastic wheels, were advertised as Jacobs trucks and gave a good account of themselves being very stable when the unit was operated at high speed.

The centre coach was of tinplate construction, but the two end coaches were made up of diecast bodies mounted on a fabricated tinplate chassis, each chassis formed in a different way corresponding to its function. The motor coach chassis comprised a motor bogie, which was more or less the same as the one used in the Trix Express Diesel Flyer, and a rotary relay which controlled the direction of the motor. This relay was activated by a DC voltage superimposed on the normal controlled 14 volt AC supply fed from a special 'positive direction' control box incorporating a switched rectifier. The lights were also controlled by this relay.

The bogie on the trailing coach was again similar to that used on the diesel flyer. Housed in this trailing coach was the whistle mechanism which operated on every interruption of the supply current. The 'whistle' was a patented design by Siegfried Kahn and his team and was also used in the whistling coach and whistling signal box. Basically it was a magnetic sound generator mounted in a hollow metal chamber, which comprised a diaphragm, a coil and solenoid plus a self-interrupter contact. The sound generated by this unit was not what would normally be termed a whistle, being more of a screech, but an adjustment screw was provided to enable the operator to adjust the noise to his liking, or to make it completely inaudible if he or she so wished. This sound generator was operated by a rather sensitive relay which caused the unit to be switched on or off for every interruption of the supply current normally activated by the direction switch on the normal control unit. If, however, the rails over which the Meteor was running were dirty or, for any other reason the current to the Meteor was interrupted, the whistle would sound at random

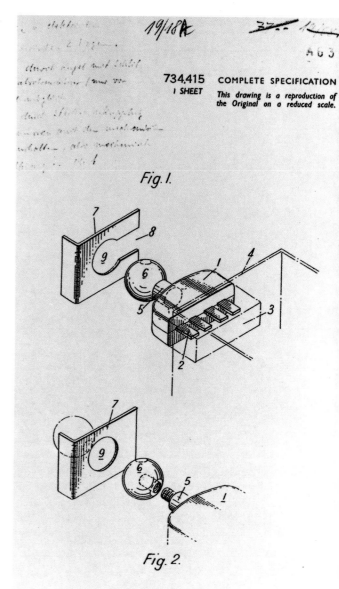

734,415 COMPLETE SPECIFICATION
1 SHEET
This drawing is a reproduction of the Original on a reduced scale.

Fig. 1.

Fig. 2.

Extract from British Patent No.734,415 showing the special ball joint proposed for TTR tenders with uncoupling mechanisms.

166

which did not make for an efficient system.

The design of the Meteor was started in the latter months of 1954, and a prototype model ran at the Brighton Toy Fair the following year. Photographs of this prototype model were shown in all the advertisements and literature for the Meteor. As this prototype model was, to coin a modern modelling phrase, scratch built, it differed externally and internally from the production models, and used parts of the chassis from the Trix express 12 volt DC VT 50 Diesel-Triebwagenzug which was produced at this time (this latter a direct descendant of the 20/58 Diesel Flyer). The castings in mazak for the motor coach and trailing coach bodies were ordered from Fry's Diecastings Ltd in April 1955.

The Meteor 3-coach diesel express, Cat. No.377, complete with positive direction control box was offered to the public in time for Christmas 1955 at a cost of £12/9/6, which was a very high price for a product which only had limited appeal. Nevertheless when everything was adjusted correctly and the track was clean, the Meteor made an impressive sight as it hurtled around the tight curves of the Trix track, shrieking who-o-o-o ! who-o-o-o ! as the whistle was activated on speeding through the station or tunnel. During the early months of the following year an additional middle coach, Cat. No.597, also became available. Under the ownership of Ewart Holdings Ltd it was decided to simplify the Meteor to operate on 12 volts DC, and by so doing reduce the cost to the public by a substantial amount. Again it was available in the shops just in time for Christmas 1957 in the same red and yellow livery at a cost of £7/7/-, but this time it was without whistle although it still retained the changing lights. It was given the catalogue number of 277. The AC version was

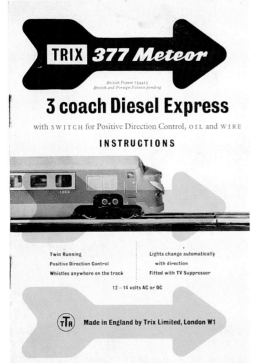

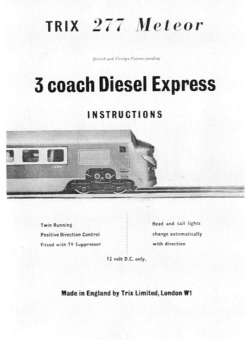

The front of the Meteor. Left: production model. Right: prototype model. Note the different size of the drivers windows.

The instruction leaflets for the AC and DC Meteor.

still available in 1958 although production had ceased early in 1957, and it was not long before the DC version was also available in blue and yellow with a choice of two running numbers, 2602 and 2782. The red and yellow version also had the number 2602. In an effort to kindle interest in the Meteor, Dufay Ltd, who purchased Trix in November 1958, produced a set, Cat. No. 278, in readiness for the 1958 Christmas trade containing the blue DC 3-coach Meteor and an oval of the new fibre-based track which included 18 straight rails, one of which was a terminal rail. Strangely no mention of this set is made in any known Trix catalogues or price lists and it can only have been available for a short time.

The motor bogie now had a permanent magnet in place of the field coil required for AC operation, and the lights were fed from a rectifier which electrically switched on the correct lights for the direction in which the train was travelling. Surprisingly this DC version of the Meteor was produced well into 1960 and advertised in Trix literature up to and including 1961. It was also offered for sale in the great Trix clearance sale of 1963 among many other items of rolling stock and AC and DC locomotives.

From 1957 until the end of 1960 additional middle Meteor coaches, Cat. No. 597, were available in red or blue livery. Interestingly, on a few middle coaches manufactured during 1959 and 1960, two rows of vents were depicted on the coach roof, whereas the roofs of all other Meteor coaches produced were plain.

An aborted design for a DC American-style diesel based on the Meteor.

The Meteor Diesel Express. From the top: The prototype model as shown at the 1955 Brighton Toy Fair; the AC version Cat.No.377; a blue DC version with running number 2782, Cat.No.277; a red DC version with running number 2602, Cat.No. 277.

Special AC chassis. From the top: Southern Railway Motor Coach, post-war Diesel Flyer, pre-war 'Scotsman' Pacific, post-war 'Scotsman' Pacific, Meteor motor and trailing units.

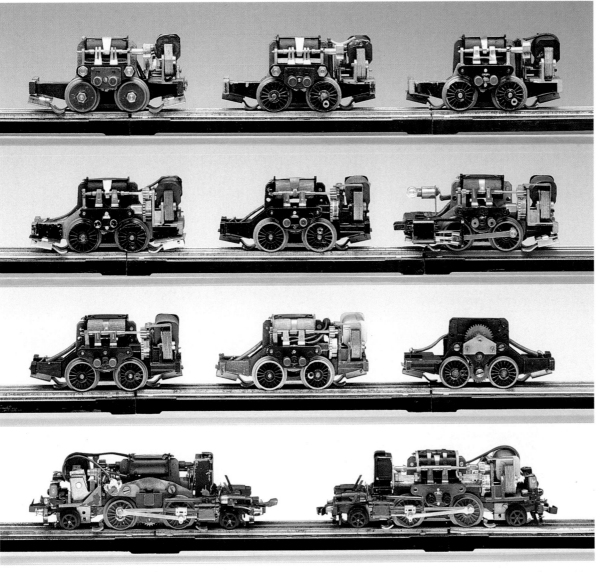

0-4-0 and 2-4-2 AC mechanisms.

Top left: 1935 Trix Express chassis with disc wheels which are keyed onto shouldered 3.5mm diameter axles. The reduction gear pivot screw depth can be adjusted by means of a nut.

Top middle: 1936 Trix Express for TTR 'A' type chassis. Wheels with bakelite bushes pressed onto 3mm diameter axles. Reduction gear pivot now a shouldered screw with a spacer washer.

Top right: 1937 Trix Express for TTR 'B' type chassis. Bakelite/fibre motor side frame replaced with a diecast version.

Second row, left: 1938 Trix Express for TTR 'C' type chassis. This was a major design change. The thin walled diecast chassis was replaced by a more substantial design. The reversing contact shaft star wheel and armature and pawl assembly was replaced by a pinion and ratchet wheel and a redesigned pawl assembly. The outside pick-up shoe assemblies were now insulated with the centre shoe assembly connected directly to the chassis frame. This is a reversal of the insulation arrangement on the earlier chassis.

Second row middle: Early TTR post-war chassis. Second row right: 1949/52 Trix Express for TTR chassis as used for the American and a few British-outline models. The wheels are held onto the 2.5mm axles with insulated brass bushes.

Third row left: 1950/55 TTR chassis. Note the addition of reversing contact shaft retainers which also provide a good electrical contact between the shaft and the chassis. The field coil contact is now behind the contact shaft instead of in front.

Third row middle: 1955/56 TTR chassis with the addition of a 500pF condenser for TV interference suppression.

Third row right: Basic 1949 TTR AC 0-4-0 chassis modified for DC operation with the American Switcher Trix Loco Kit. Note the permanent magnet in place of the field coil. The wheels flanges are turned down for use on scale track and extra gearing is cleverly incorporated.

Bottom row: Pre-war (left) and post-war Trix Express chassis for the 2-4-2 locomotive with remote uncoupling at each end. The post-war version is for the British market.

THE TRIX JUNIOR TRAIN

During the autumn of 1955 there was an attempt to entice young children into the world of model railways by the introduction in Britain of the Trix Junior Train Sets which were first shown at the Brighton Toy Fair at the beginning of the year. The idea was that because the locomotives contained in the sets could be operated by standard low voltage batteries, they were completely safe in the hands of young children. As early as 1952 the Trix design team had sought to provide some sort of toy train that young children could play with. This is substantiated by a Patent which was granted to Trix Ltd for an idea incorporating the remote stop/start and reversing functions of a clockwork toy locomotive by a simple electrical device mounted on the locomotive chassis. This idea was probably dropped in favour of the battery-driven locomotive because of the latter's simplicity and comparatively low cost.

This type of battery-operated locomotive was first introduced as an 0-4-0 tank engine in German outline by Trix Vereinigte Spielwaren-fabriken GmbH in the latter part of 1953. The highly efficient electric motor in these loco-motives (covered by a British Patent number 619481), is one which operates at a safe maxi-mum of 6 volts DC. It was manufactured by Johann Distler KG, a company with which Ernst Voelk of the German Trix company had a direct relationship. The chassis of the British outline 0-4-0 tank engine was basically a copy of the Trix Express chassis manufactured in Germany. There were differences in the gear train which reduced the high revolutions of the motor to an acceptable level at the driving wheels.

The black plastic tank engine body was the same as that used on the 14 volt AC version and the later 12 volt DC version. However, the Junior body did not have the piston guides fitted, just the simple piston rod and crank arm assembly. These Junior engines were completely unmarked, and even the moulded letters of

TRIX on the smoke-box door were not picked-out in white paint as was the tradition with all other TTR 0-4-0s. No individual catalogue number was quoted with respect to this Junior engine and they were not available as individual items, but only as part of a complete set.

Two sets were offered, a Junior Goods Set, Cat. No. 205, and a Junior Passenger Set, Cat. No. 215. The goods set comprised the loco-motive, two BR tinplate open wagons plus the BR guard's van, a 14-piece oval of the bakelite-based track and a hand generator. The passenger set contained two BR red suburban coaches instead of the goods wagons. Both sets were housed in identical attractive, but elaborate, cardboard display boxes with a label on one end of the box stating the type of set.

The main and most intriguing feature of the Junior Train Set was that no battery or transformer was required to run the locomotive. All the electrical power and control was provided by the special hand generator supplied with the sets. This hand generator was an approved model

The 4.5/6volt DC Junior 0-4-0 Tank Engines.

Junior Train Set
Hand Generator.

The Junior Train Passenger Set Cat. No.215. (E)   The Junior Train Goods Set Cat.No.205. (E)

of a GEC 30,000 KW generator, and a DC voltage was generated by turning the handle which was connected by a train of gears to an electric motor. The motor, which was exactly the same type as fitted to the locomotive, revolved at high speed, which in effect turned the motor into

a dynamo. The faster you turned the handle, the faster the locomotive went. Turn the handle in the opposite direction and the locomotive reversed its direction.

Unfortunately sales were not high, and although the sets were redesigned during 1956,

as was most of the TTR system for the forthcoming change to 12 volts DC, it was left to the new owners of Trix, Ewart Holdings, in 1957 to relaunch the product as the Trix Twin CADET Railway in a blaze of publicity at the Brighton Toy Fair. Gone was the hand generator replaced by a Speed Controller, Cat. No. 272. This was a simple rotary switch with on/off, forward and reverse positions coupled with a speed control knob. The unit fitted on to the screw terminals of one or two standard 4.5 volt batteries giving up to 100 hours of continuous use. The bakelite track was replaced by the new fibre-based track, and the packaging was completely redesigned although the old TTR practice of providing space for a second train was retained.

Three basic sets were now available, the Goods Set, Cat. No. 224, the Passenger Set, Cat. No. 234, and a Combined Set, Cat. No. 255, which included the goods and passenger trains, two controllers, 24 lengths of the new track together with a pair of points. The tank engines now carried the latest BR lion-over-wheel-over-crown crest on the sides of the tank and a '6V' transfer in white on the end of the engine body. This '6V' was a warning that the maximum voltage to be used on this locomotive was 6 volts. In 1958 these tank engines became available separately and were given the catalogue number of 201.

The passenger coaches included in the sets were still the BR Suburban type, Cat. No. 1/553, but the colour was now maroon. The pattern of goods wagons in the set varied, but basically three wagons were included, a tank wagon, a BR 3-plank wagon and a BR guard's van. All the wagons that found their way into these Cadet sets were simplified versions of the standard range, this simplification leading to the omission of the axlebox stampings over the ends of the wagon axles.

The Cadet Passenger and Goods Sets Cat.Nos.234 and 224 respectively. (A)

In addition to the three sets mentioned above, special Cadet Goods Sets were available through 'Gamages'. One known set contained an additional fourth wagon, a BR grey open highside wagon, numbered 168732, and another contained a red Shell tank wagon plus a Silver Shell tank wagon in place of the two 3-plank wagons. These content variations were 'advertised' using printed labels affixed to the boxes. All the wagons were fitted with the simplified chassis.

A mains-operated 4.5 volt DC transformer/rectifier, Cat.No.291/240, for use in conjunction with the Speed Controller was available from 1956, the output of which was raised to 6 volts during 1959.

The Cadet sets and the associated tank engine were still advertised in Trix price lists up to and including 1961.

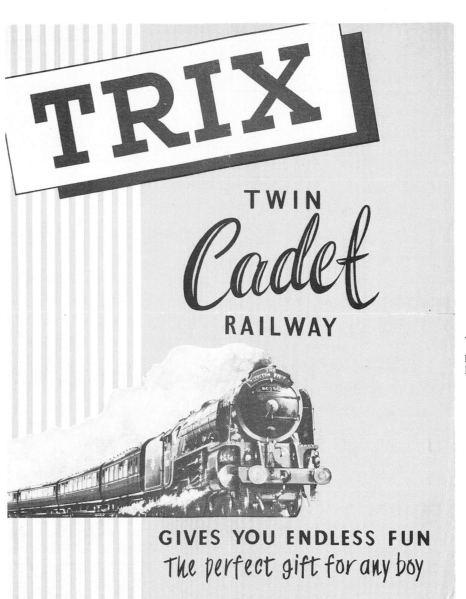

Trix Cadet promotion literature.

The cover of the Trix Twin Cadet instruction booklet.

THE HURRIED DESIGN CHANGES OF THE LOCOMOTIVES FROM AC TO DC

In October 1956, Michael Catalani moved from the Trix offices in London to Precision Models Ltd in Northampton where he was instructed by Siegfried Kahn to design the new range of DC-operated trains. As previously mentioned, Michael Catalani did not agree with the decision to up-date the existing AC 4-4-0 locomotives nor with the use of the plastic body as used on the Junior and AC Mixed Traffic tank engine. He would sooner have designed a completely new locomotive, or locomotives, especially as Trix was trying to create a brand new image. In fact, his ambition was to be granted in a very short period of time, shorter possibly than he may have wished given the amount of work a new design entailed to ensure the model was ready for the trade exhibitions.

In all fairness to Trix they were having a very poor trading period, and as the castings for the 4-4-0 engine bodies only required the cut-away for the carbon brush holders to be filled in and a

The Mixed Traffic DC 0-4-0 tank engines Cat. No.210.

reduction in the height of the bogie and front chassis mount, the cost was minimal. The new DC chassis was designed around the extremely powerful Trix Express 3-pole 'Perma-Motor' introduced into the Trix Express range during 1954. Instead of a new diecast chassis frame, it was of fabricated construction comprising plastic mouldings and pressed steel parts. The reason for this fabricated construction was again cost which was justified by the fact that the factory was geared up to press work.

The 3-rail system was retained including the same coarse scale wheels, and even the pick-up arrangement for centre and outside rails was

included on the engine chassis for the 4-4-0s, with no use being made of an electrical feed from the tender as with the AC versions. Thus, it can be seen there was no need for an elaborate tender, and, to reduce production costs even further an AC 0-4-0 tinplate tender was modified in its method of tender-to-engine coupling for use with the new DC 4-4-0 locomotives. It was unfortunate that this DC chassis suffered the same problems with wheel slip as did its AC predecessor, predominantly when used on the 4-4-0 locomotives. During the spring of 1958 wheel slip was reduced by adding plastic traction tyres to the driving wheels on one side of the chassis. The DC version of the Meteor Diesel Express also received traction tyres to the motor bogie driving wheels at this time.

Pre-production models of the DC versions of the BR Compound and BR Hunt Class 'Pytchley'

Pre-production model of the DC 4-4-0 BR Compound.

Pre-production model of the DC 4-4-0 BR Schools Class. Note the 'Pytchley' engine body!

4-4-0 locomotives, using unmodified engine bodies and coupled to diecast tenders, were shown at the February 1957 Brighton Toy Fair, together with the new 0-4-0 Mixed Traffic tank engine. The toy trade did not enthuse over the above which were overshadowed by the publicity the new owners showered on the Cadet sets and the new fibre-based track.

The plastic body of the AC Mixed Traffic 0-4-0 tank engine, without the cut-out for the carbon brushes, was fitted to the new DC chassis together with extra weights added for stability. Included with the new BR crest were running numbers of only two digits, but from circa 1958 more realistic numbers were applied containing five digits. This version of the 0-4-0 tank engine never appeared lined and was given the catalogue number of 210. In most of the catalogues and price lists, this engine was given the grand title of Main Line Tank Loco., although in reality the name 'Main Line' was the title given to the future series of DC sets. This tank engine was soon on the market after the Brighton Toy Fair and sold initially for £2/2/-.

It was not until spring 1957 that Fry's Diecastings Ltd received an order to modify the existing die and supply 7,000 of the 'Pytchley' engine bodies. Two versions of the BR Hunt Class 'Pytchley' were first available during the summer; a passenger engine and tender in Brunswick green, Cat. No. 230, and a goods version in black, Cat. No. 235. The lining and general finish on both passenger and goods engine bodies was exactly as on their AC predecessors, with the exception that the nameplate on the goods engine was picked out in

orange instead of yellow. The tenders were now tinplate and exactly the same as used on the old AC 0-4-0 locomotives, except that the tender coupling bar was now in the form of a flat upturned hook which located in a plastic spacer on the rear underside of the engine chassis. The tender lining for the passenger engine could be either double orange and black or just a single orange line, whilst red and grey lining was used on the goods engine tender. By now the latest BR lion crest was used on all models. As with other locomotives, the general finish in the first instance tended to be nearer to a gloss sheen, but during 1958 a few batches of passenger engines were produced with a matt finish to which smaller than normal cab side numbers were applied (2.3mm high). It was not long before production reverted back to a near gloss finish and regular size numbers (2.8mm high). The last order for 'Pytchley' engine bodies was for a quantity of 1,250 placed in the spring of 1958.

Spring 1959 saw an alteration to the casting of the 4-4-0 AC diecast tender chassis to accommodate a simplified plastic version of the axle retainer and the new tender coupling bar. Thus, a small quantity of the remaining 'Pytchley' engines were fitted with the diecast tenders, although the tinplate tenders were still used from time to time as stock varied. Single lining was used on these diecast tenders, orange for the green passenger engine and red for the black goods engine. A point must be made here that the date code on the underside of the engines does not signify that the locomotive was released to the shops at that time, but rather when it was assembled. Thus 4-4-0 engines will

be found with a date code which preceded the issue of its diecast tender.

All this took place a few months after Dufay Ltd had taken over the ownership of the TTR empire, and, although the design team lead by Michael Catalani was catapulted into producing something exciting for the 1959 Brighton Toy Fair, the policy for 1959 was to use existing assets as much as possible to help pay for development

DC versions of the BR 4-4-0 Hunt Class 'Pytchley'.

costs. The result was that in March 1959, Fry's Diecastings received an order to modify the dies of the BR 4-4-0 Compound and the pre-war Southern Railway 4-4-0 Schools Class 'Dover' engine bodies.

For the amount of modifications made, it is surprising that only 1,000 of each type of engine body were cast and supplied for production. The BR Compound, Cat. No. F101, was produced in

black as a goods engine and issued with tinplate or diecast tender as factory stocks dictated. As with the black 'Pytchley', the diecast tender was only lined in red, whilst the tinplate tender had the full red and grey lining. Only two running numbers were used, 1168 and 41168, applied to the cab sides with the usual style of yellow transfers, although the numerals used for 1168 were much larger in format than the normal size used for 41168, 'normal' meaning as used on nearly all TTR BR locomotives.

This DC version of the BR 4-4-0 Compound made its first appearance in the shops during May 1959, but it was a little later in the year when the BR 4-4-0 Schools Class 'Dover', Cat. No. F100, finally appeared. Strange to think that the die for the body castings of this locomotive in its original form was made twenty years earlier in 1939!

The 'Dover' was finished in BR Brunswick green and lined in orange, which was also the colour of the nameplate. The finish on this engine, and also on the Compound, was semi-gloss. Once again the engine was issued with either a diecast or tinplate tender, with single lining on the former and double lining on the latter. The running number on the cab sides was 30911 applied using the normal

The DC 4-4-0 models introduced during 1959.
Top two rows: BR Compounds with diecast tenders.
Third row: BR Compound with a tinplate tender.
Bottom row: BR Schools Class 'Dover' with diecast tender.

yellow numerical transfers. A distinguishing feature of this locomotive was the smoke deflectors which were of the correct pattern for an ex-Southern Railway locomotive. These were made from plastic mouldings, and not from metal as they would have been in pre-war days. Although the 'Dover' was available separately, it was mainly sold in a set, (F27), which included two short bogie coaches, a first class and brake second, especially finished in BR Southern Region green.

As a new chapter was opening with the introduction of a completely new range of scale 12 volt DC locomotive models, one can imagine why these modified AC designs produced concurrently were quickly phased out. In fact by the end of 1960 they were no longer listed in the official Trix literature. Interestingly, from the middle of 1958 for about two years, a conversion service was offered by a few retail outlets, but mainly by the Southgate Hobbyshop of London which was a very enthusiastic retail outlet for Trix products, and Eames of Reading who were conversion specialists. This service involved converting the old AC Trix locomotives to DC for use in conjunction with the new 12 volt DC system by fitting a permanent magnet in place of the motor field coil. It was found that the converted locomotives ran extremely well retaining the characteristic free-running qualities associated with the AC motor.

Despite everything, the dawn of the scale 12 volt DC Trix locomotives saw the end of the AC era, an era in which the designs for the locomotives were of a charming character that was uniquely Trix.

THE NEW SCALE MODEL DESIGNS

The 1958 Brighton Toy Fair was the venue for the introduction of the first of the new breed of DC models. The toy trade had awaited with anticipation to see what Trix Ltd had to offer in their much-publicised modernisation programme, and they were suitably impressed. Three new locomotives were on show – the 'Britannia', a Standard 5MT and a Ruston Hornsby 0-6-0 diesel shunter complete with shunter's truck. Unfortunately the models were only in mock-up form, although six hand-made models of the Ruston Hornsby diesel were in evidence with some operating on the demonstration layout. The trade gave approval to their general appearance and praised the excellence of the valve gear on the steam locomotives. The only misgivings were that Trix had retained the heavy style wheel flanges which were only suitable for running on Trix track or that specifically designed for Trix model railway items.

These new locomotives were promised for delivery to the shops during the summer of 1958, but due to the problems that Ewart Holdings were suffering, it was not until the following year that the 'Britannia' and Standard 5MT locomotives made their appearance, with the company under the new ownership of Dufay Ltd. However, the Ruston Hornsby diesel was available during the latter months of 1958.

Michael Catalani, who designed the subsequent locomotive models until his departure from Trix Products Ltd in April 1963, states that the only reason that the Ruston Hornsby diesel was chosen to be modelled was for cost and speed, as many of the parts could be purchased from the German Trix company. Although the production model had a diecast body, Ebonestos Industries Ltd, manufacturers of the Bakelite track bases, were asked to supply a sample and quotation for a body to be made from black general purpose cellulose acetate material (a cheap plastic) by one of their associate companies. This was the same company that made approximately 40,000 of the Junior/Cadet/AC/DC tank engine body from a similar plastic. Luckily for the modelling world, this idea was rejected in favour of the diecast body supplied in limited quantities by John Bruce (Engineers) Ltd of Bicester – their first and only venture into this type of diecasting.

The wheels, which were only available in coarse scale, were those as used on the Trix Express German Class V36 diesel locomotive, but unlike the centre driving wheels on this engine which were virtually flangeless, the centre driving wheels on the Ruston Hornsby were the normal flanged type but reduced slightly in diameter on a lathe to give a more realistic look to the chassis. The motor was the standard Trix Express 3-pole Perma-Motor which, as mentioned previously, was the power unit adopted for almost all subsequent models. The design of the chassis had to incorporate a current pick-up assembly suitable for twin running on the TTR three-rail system, and, as the chassis was much shorter than its Trix Express counterpart, the problem was where to mount the reversible outside shoes. This was solved by pivoting each insulated mount for the outside shoes on a driving-wheel axle.

The body was a well-detailed casting finished in dark green and lined in light green with the Ruston Hornsby emblem on the cab sides. The catalogue number allocated to this locomotive, including the shunter's truck which was always supplied with the engine, was 244. This shunter's truck, available separately, Cat. No. 620, was based on the new, short, super-detailed diecast wagon chassis to which had been fitted grey plastic mouldings depicting the platform and tool-box, plus added wire and tinplate details. From the summer of 1960 for probably less than one year, the Ruston Hornsby diesel shunter and truck were available as part of a Breakdown Set, Cat. No. F40, which contained a crane truck set (615), two 3-plank wagons (630), and a goods van (653). The diesel shunter did not sell very well and about 1,000 units were manufactured. It was no longer mentioned in the 1962 Trix catalogue

Beautifully crafted prototype models of the Class V and 'Britannia' locomotives. (A)

Top row: Ruston Hornsby Diesel Shunter complete with Shunters Truck Cat. No.244 with one of the pre-production models shown at the 1958 Brighton Toy Fair. Rows two and three: the BR green Class V 4-6-0, note the early number 73001 on the upper locomotive. Bottom rows: BR black versions with a Footplateman Kit version on the lower row.

or price lists.

The long-awaited BR Class 7MT 4-6-2 Pacific 'Britannia', Cat. No. 236 and the BR Class 5MT 4-6-0, (Class V), Cat. No. 237, were generally available in March 1959, although production had started at Precision Models under Ewart Holdings just prior to the collapse of the Ewart group of companies in October 1958. The choice of these two modern locomotive types was governed by trying to create an up-to-date image and controlling cost. The latter was reduced by the models sharing the same design of the chassis, tender and front bogie.

Top: BR Class 7MT 4-6-2 Pacific 'Britannia'. Bottom: A model of a BR Class 9F 2-10-0 'Evening Star' based on the component parts of the 'Britannia'. This was a study conducted, circa 1965, into the feasibility of the 2-10-0 wheel arrangement.

Unfinished Class V late engine body and tender diecastings. Note the cast hand rails on the tender top.

179

The major design problems associated with selecting these locomotives to model for the TTR system were firstly the thickness of the driving wheels, which at that time had to be the coarse Trix scale, and secondly the Trix Express Perma-Motor which was very wide. These two opposing factors made it impossible to fit the motor between the wheels and restricted the model to a shape which could accommodate the motor. In addition, the model had to have 3.8mm and not 4.0mm (OO gauge) proportions, and be able to negotiate the very sharp curves of the Trix track, necessitating the use of flangeless middle driving wheels.

The common chassis was designed to allow for different positions of the rear driving wheel axle on the two models, and the correct shape of the engine body of each engine was altered slightly to accommodate the size and position of the motor. The body castings of the engine and tender for both these models were well detailed, although the quality of the 'Britannia' engine body casting was superior to that of the Class V. The majority of these castings were produced by Silcoms Ltd, a company near Bolton.

On outside-cylinder locomotive models, the valve gear is one of the most important parts by which the realism, or lack of it, may be judged, and in the case of the 'Britannia' and Class V, after a lot of experimenting the resulting valve gear and associated connecting rods proved to be very realistic, although slightly marred by the flangeless centre driving wheels. The production of this valve gear involved intricate press work at which the staff at the Northampton factory were well skilled, and it also required careful assembly using very small rivets especially imported from

Switzerland.

Both the 4-6-2 'Britannia' Pacific and the 4-6-0 Class V were finished in BR green and fully lined in orange. The running number of the 'Britannia' was 70000, whilst that of the Class V was 73000, although a few are known with the number 73001. By the end of 1959 the Class V had been introduced in black livery fully lined in red, still with the same running number of 73000 and for a while retaining the same catalogue number. By the time the Brighton Toy Fair came round in 1960 the catalogue number had been changed to 237B with the green version adopting 237G.

The main news in the early months of 1960 was that the coarse scale Trix standard wheels on these two models had been replaced by finer wheels so they could run on scale 2-rail track. The pick-up shoes for one rail were still retained on the tender in the old AC tradition, but included with each model was a set of contact springs which could be fitted in place of the centre pick-up shoes thereby converting the model from 3-rail to 2-rail operation. These contact springs, held in place by the centre pick-up channel, made contact with the inside faces of two of the driving wheels running on the opposite rail to the tender shoes. Traction tyres were also retained. 'Scale' wheels were now fitted as standard, and if coarse scale Trix wheels were required by the customer they had to be specially ordered. These finer wheels were not what one would normally associate with 'scale', as the thickness of the wheel was maintained due to the chassis construction, and it was just the flange thickness and its depth that was reduced to enable the wheels to negotiate scale track.

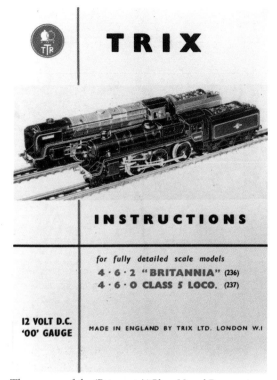

The covers of the 'Britannia'/ Class V and Ruston Hornsby Diesel Shunter instruction leaflets.

Interestingly, from April 1959, the Southgate Hobbyshop in London were providing a service to their customers by converting the 'Britannia' and Class V models to run on universal 2-rail track, similar to that supplied by Wrenn and other makes of track . These conversions were carried out by Bill Best, the ex-Trix service manager. Until 1963 no change took place in the allocation of catalogue numbers denoting any modification to scale wheels. The 1963 catalogue showed 'improved' versions of the 'Britannia' and

TRIX

DIESEL SHUNTER SET

No. 244

Comprises Diesel Shunter Locomotive
and Shunter Truck No. 620

12 volt D.C.   '00' Gauge

INSTRUCTIONS

Made in England by Trix Limited, London, W.I

1109   'Britannia', scale wheels, 2/3-rail
1110   'Britannia',Trix wheels, 3-rail
(withdrawn 1964)
1111   'Britannia', scale wheels, 2-rail
1112   Class V black, scale wheels, 2/3-rail
1113   Class V black, Trix wheels, 3-rail
(withdrawn 1964)
1114   Class V black, scale wheels, 2-rail
1115   Class V green, scale wheels, 2/3-rail
1116   Class V green, Trix wheels, 3-rail
(withdrawn 1964)
1117   Class V green, scale wheels, 2-rail

Correct fine-scale wheels were fitted to these locomotives during 1964, and although production of the 'Britannia' locomotive was discontinued in 1965, it was still available as a construction kit in the Footplateman's series in 1966 for about one year and reintroduced again for a short period in 1969. The black Class V, however, was still offered as a complete locomotive in 2 and 3-rail versions up to the end of 1966, although in the British Trix catalogue of 1966 they were incorrectly listed as being green in colour! Both Class V versions were available in the Footplateman's series of kits during the same years as the 'Britannia' kit.

During the period from 1964 to 1966, certain improvements and modifications took place. The main changes were that a redesigned sprung bogie was fitted, incorporating a new casting, and the tender casting was altered. On earlier models the handrails on the top of the tender body were formed from tinned wire and fixed with split pins, on these later castings from 1965 the handrails formed part of the casting. The chassis fixing screw holes on the tender body were also replaced by a central pillar containing a single

screw hole. These tender modifications were incorporated in an attempt to reduce production costs and as the result of an abortive idea to mould the body from styrene. In the early versions of the kits, the 'Britannia' and Class V bodies and tenders, except for the omission of lining and transfers, were painted exactly like the normal production versions. In the later kits, the 'Britannia' and green Class V engine and tender bodies were painted all-over green. There were other minor modifications to the locomotive, but mainly connected with the electrical wiring and the associated assemblies.

Locomotive productions built around the Class V and 'Britannia' models were intended. These included an ex-LMS 'Royal Scot' class, an ex-LMS Class 5MT and the BR class 9F 2-10-0 'Evening Star'. Mock-up models of the latter two were constructed in either 1965 or 1966 as a feasibility study. For the 'Evening Star' model, a 'Britannia' chassis was extended by the use of plastic side frames taken from a Kitmaster kit and fitted with wheels from an Austrian Liliput locomotive. The diecast 'Britannia' body was also suitably modified. The Class V/Britannia tender remained unaltered. The model was well proportioned, if not to scale, but the object of the exercise was to see whether a simple chassis in 2-10-0 wheel configuration would negotiate the tight curves of British proprietory track. Unfortunately, the answer was 'No' and so the project was abandoned. The Trix Express Class BR 42 introduced in 1959 with the same wheel configuration was a success and easily coped with the tight curves, but its wheel base was much shorter and the driving wheel diameters were smaller.

Class V locomotives. The improvement was brought about by the removal of the pick-up shoe assembly from the tender, this being replaced by contact springs which collected current from the inside faces of the insulated metal wheels, although the centre wheels remained as flangeless plastic mouldings. The engine chassis was similarly modified, except in the case of a 3-rail version which retained the centre pick-up shoes. From 1963 the following catalogue numbers were designated:

THE ADDITION OF A NEW DIMENSION

During the initial production phase of the 'Britannia' and Class V locomotives, an added problem was the change of ownership during 1958 and 1959. Michael Catalani was still resolutely working on his designs for new models which would enhance the TTR stable. New ground was broken with the announcement at the 1959 Brighton Toy Fair that Trix were in the process of producing an over-head electric locomotive modelled on the BR EM1 Bo-Bo built in 1950, for use on the 1,500 volt DC electrified Manchester to Sheffield railway line and the branch line to the great marshalling yards at Wath-upon-Dearne. Also in the pipeline was a model of the ex-Great Western Railway 5600 class 0-6-2 tank engine in BR livery plus a modern image diesel hydraulic locomotive, the BR Western Region 'Warship' class type 4 B-B.

It was not until October 1959 that the first of the EM1 Bo-Bo locomotives were released to the shops in black livery under catalogue number F105. The body shell for this electric locomotive was a one-piece casting of accurate scale and detail produced initially by Metlex Industries Ltd of Croydon, and then by Silcoms Ltd. The articulated bogies were based on the design adopted by Trix Express for use on their diesel and electric locomotives, and the outer frame and combined wheel drive and motor mount were also diecast. The buffers were mounted on the bogie frame which made it particularly suitable for operation on the sharp radii of the Trix track. The reversible pick-up shoes were mounted on an insulator sandwiched between the motor mount and the bogie outer frame. Working lights were fitted to each cab which also illuminated the headlights.

An important feature of this model was the working pantograph which took current from a catenary system enabling the independent control of three locomotives on one track. This was at a time when modern electronics were unheard of in the model railway world, and thus it added a new dimension to the realism of the TTR system. The spring-loaded pantographs were manufactured in the Northampton factory from tinplate and wire and were very effective and efficient in their operation. It was possible to switch the feed from these pantographs via a small plug in the roof so that the locomotive could be used on 2 or 3-rail track, without the provision of catenary equipment. Also on the roof were the plastic mouldings depicting ventilators; on early models the six ventilators were separate mouldings, but these were gradually phased out in favour of a single combined moulding.

The wheels were a new innovation and were classed as convertible. When purchased they were in a form which enabled the locomotive to be run on the coarse scale Trix track. By removing a plastic flange moulded onto the wheel it was converted to scale standards. Unfortunately the process was not reversible.

The inside of an EM1 Bo-Bo.

The black livery was lined in red and the locomotive carried the number 26010 applied with the usual sized black-lined yellow numeral transfers. The pattern of the red lining was not consistant as samples are known with lining applied to one (most common) or both sides of the vertical embossed lines on the locomotive body sides. It was not long before all versions of the EM1 were issued with scale wheels as standard, with once again the coarse wheel versions being available to special order.

By the spring 1960, the EM1 appeared in the orange-lined green livery of British Railways with the number 26056 and the name 'Triton' applied as a self-adhesive label. The name was highlighted on a red background, and stuck on the middle of each side of the locomotive body. This model was given the catalogue number of F105G, whilst the black version had F105B. The BR crest on the black version was the same size as that applied to the 'Britannia'/Class V tenders, but the transfers used for the green version were much smaller, as were the transfers used for the number 26056. In fact two sizes of the smaller BR crest transfers are known, the smaller of the two being used in conjunction with the name label, the other being applied when the locomotive appeared unnamed, circa 1962

A complimentary overhead catenary system was designed which was simple but efficient when used in conjunction with the Trix fibre-based track. However it could also be used with any other make of track. A full description will be given in the chapter dealing with track accessories.

Green BR EM1 Bo-Bo locomotives.
Top: Early version with small BR emblem, TRITON nameplate and individual roof ventilators Cat.No.F105G.
Middle: Similar version but with larger BR emblem Cat.No.F105G.
Bottom: 1962/3 EM1 with single combined ventilator moulding, no name, Cat.No.1125. (A)

Top: Early black EM1 Bo-Bo with convertible wheels and six individual ventilator mouldings on the roof.
Bottom: Later convertible wheel version with single combined roof ventilator moulding. Both Cat.No.F105B.

At the same time that the EM1 was released in October 1959, there appeared the BR Western Region Mixed Traffic 0-6-2 Collett Class 5600 tank engine. This model was described in the Trix literature as a Class 66XX, but in reality although the model depicted had the running number 6664, the GWR 5600 Class was first introduced in 1924 starting with number 5600 and carrying on to 5699. The modified class of 1927 continued from 6600 up to 6699. To eliminate confusion the Trix description of 0-6-2 Class 66XX will be used which was given an initial catalogue number, F103.

This was the first Great Western Railway locomotive to be modelled in the TTR range. Why no models were produced earlier in GWR livery must remain something of a mystery. Perhaps it was due to the fact that none of the previous TTR models looked remotely like any GWR locomotive.

The 5600 class was a completely new model incorporating a two-part diecast body, of which the main body casting was produced by Silcoms

Pre-production/ demonstration model of the 0-6-2 Class 66XX.

Top: Green BR Class 66XX 0-6-2. Note the half-length step beneath the cab on right-hand model. Bottom: Black BR Class 66XX 0-6-2. Both models have convertible wheels, but the right-hand version has pressed steel steps below the cab.

Ltd and the separate smokebox casting by Metlex Industries Ltd. Trouble was experienced in the formation of the steps below the cab sides which were subject to breakage as the body was being removed from the die. To cut down on expensive wastage, separate pressed-steel steps were screwed to the diecast chassis when a body shell lacked cast steps. Additional detail was added to the body, including a brass steam dome housing, and a plastic chimney top. The chassis was designed so that the pitch of the wheels corresponded to that of the Class V enabling the used of the same connecting rods. The centre driving wheels were again flangeless, but the remaining driving wheels were of convertible design.

The first batch was officially released by Trix at the beginning of October and was for 3-rail running only. An exclusive arrangement with Dufay Ltd, enabled Southgate Hobbyshop to order a full production run of the locomotive already converted for 2-rail running. These initial production runs were finished in black livery fully lined in red with the number plate picked out in gold-coloured paint. By February 1960 the Class 66XX was available in green livery, fully lined in orange and given the catalogue number F103G, and correspondingly the black version was allocated the catalogue number F103B. During 1960 the locomotives were beginning to be issued with 'scale' wheels for 2-rail running, with the coarse scale convertible type being provided to special order. At about this time Trix track became 'universal' with the introduction of points that would accept coarse and fine scale wheels. Until this time all Trix locomotives and rolling stock had been produced almost exclusively to run on Trix track, but to expand sales to a more discerning clientele, the ability to run on other makes of track was of paramount importance.

During the period in which the change of ownership was in the balance, no major locomotive alterations or innovations took place with the locomotives. However, after British Trix Ltd was formed in the spring of 1963, the casting of the 0-6-2 body shell was altered to incorporate a weight under the bunker (replacing the lead weight which had been fixed to the rear of the chassis). Also on later 2-rail models, the method of fixing the body shell to the chassis by use of a long screw through the chimney was dispensed with in favour of a short screw through the underside of the chassis on to the body, the chimney now being undrilled.

Another improvement initiated by British Trix was to dispense with the pick-up shoes, wherever possible, in favour of contact spring current collectors which made contact with the inside faces of the driving wheels. This meant redesigning the central current collector assembly, although the normal centre pick-up shoes were still used for 3-rail models. Accordingly, from 1963 through to 1964 inclusive, the catalogue numbers for the Class 66XX were changed to the following:

1100   Black livery, scale wheels, 3-rail
1101   Black livery, convertible wheels, 3-rail (1963 only)
1102   Black livery, scale wheels, 2-rail
1104   Green livery, scale wheels, 3-rail
1105   Green livery, convertible wheels, 3-rail (1963 only)
1106   Green livery, scale wheels, 2-rail

The Class 66XX was no longer listed in the Trix literature after 1964.

During the same period, similar modifications were made to the EM1 Bo-Bo, as the convertible wheels were phased out and the pick-up shoe assemblies were replaced by wheel contact springs to collect the current. The 'Triton' nameplate on the green version was no longer used and the 2 and 3-rail versions were now distinguished in the catalogues as listed below:

1121   Black livery, scale wheels, 3-rail
1122   Black livery, convertible wheels, 3-rail (1963 only)
1123   Black livery, scale wheels, 2-rail
1124   Green livery, scale wheels, 3-rail
1125   Green livery, convertible wheels, 3-rail (1963 only)
1126   Green livery, scale wheels, 2-rail

It is a pity that this model was withdrawn from the Trix range after 1964 as it was a fine model and proved to be moderately popular with modern image enthusiasts. Unfortunately, the tooling for the body shell had deteriorated and was beyond economical repair.

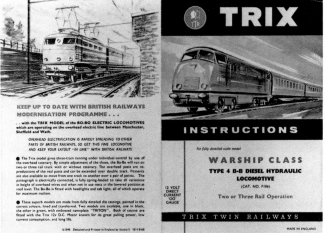

Covers from EM1 Bo-Bo, Warship Diesel and 0-6-2 Class 66XX locomotive instruction leaflets.

THE LAST TTR LOCOMOTIVE DESIGNED WITH A DIECAST BODY

This design was a model of the BR Western Region Class D800 type 4 B-B diesel hydraulic locomotive, later known as the 'Warship' Class, which officially entered regular service in 1958. The origins of the D800 series lay in the V200 Class of locomotive of the Deutsche Bundesbahn. The Western Region of British Railways purchased drawings and a licence to produce a suitably compressed version for the BR standard loading gauge, utilising the same 2,000 bhp power units carried on four axles, (B-B), and weighing less than 80 tons.

Luckily, Michael Catalani had finished the design and development work of the 'Warship' diesel before May 1960, the month which saw the closure of the factory at Northampton. Production was then moved to the Birmingham factory, and the official advertisements promised a July delivery date for the model. Unfortunately the management did not foresee all the delays relocation would cause. The expertise of the company's Northampton employees was not transferred to the factory at Birmingham, despite the offer of incentives.

Nevertheless, the first of the Trix 'Warship' Class models started to trickle through to the shops at the end of August. It was well detailed, and, apart from the roof in a well-moulded light grey plastic, the body shell was a one-piece diecasting, once again executed by Silcoms Ltd. The motor and trailing bogies were constructed in exactly the same way as the EM1, with the exception that the redundant idler gear mount

on one half of the diecast housing for the geared axles had to be removed to allow the bogie to swivel correctly inside the body shell. Nickel-plated oval buffers were mounted on the diecast bogie outer frame, which was of correct pattern. This was the first time that oval buffers had been used on TTR locomotives since the pre-war days of the 'Coronation'.

The internal lighting arrangement, which also illuminated the headlights, was similar to that used on the EM1. However the current pick-up arrangement differed slightly. On the rear of each bogie frame a brass spring-loaded plunger was mounted which, in 3-rail operation, was used to collect current from the centre rail. The outside pick-up shoe assembly was exactly the same as used on the EM1. Unfortunately the central studs caused problems of intermittent current collection over certain parts of the Trix track, and this method was discarded in favour of shoes mounted on the same insulated plate as the outside rail shoes. The former system was reintroduced in 1964 when the convertible wheels were no longer fitted. These central studs were also a feature of the Footplateman kits for this type of locomotive introduced in 1966

The locomotive was finished in semi-matt Brunswick green with a cream band along the waist. The number, D801, and the BR crests were transfers, the self-adhesive nameplate being made from stout metallised paper with the name 'Vanguard' and 'Warship Class' highlighted. It was allocated the catalogue number F106 and normally fitted with 'scale' wheels for 2 or 3-rail running with convertible wheels supplied to order until 1963, when both types were each

given a designated catalogue number. The scale-wheel version was given catalogue number 1118, whilst 1119 was designated to the model with convertible wheels, withdrawn in 1964.

From 1965 all the 'Warship' diesel locomotive models were fitted with new scale wheels, and the pick-up shoe assembly on each bogie was replaced by an assembly containing a single wheel-contact spring current collector. This model had quite a long life, and from 1966 started to appear in different liveries with distinctive markings of the then-current British Railways D800 Class diesel locomotives. Listed below are the catalogue numbers from 1966 associated with these variants:

1118   Green livery, 3-rail.

1119   Maroon livery, 3-rail. (This version was given the catalogue number of the withdrawn green version with convertible wheels.)

1120   Green livery, 2-rail.

1122   Maroon livery, 2-rail. (This version was given the catalogue number of the withdrawn black EM1. with convertible wheels.)

1123   Blue livery, 2-rail, introduced to the range in 1967.

From circa 1961, British Railways introduced a yellow warning panel around the route board on each end of the locomotive, but this was not incorporated on the Trix models until after 1964. During 1966 many marking variations on the British Railways stud were prevalent, including the replacement of the old BR crest with the circular type used for the coaching stock (applied to the maroon version in more cases than to the green or blue), the incorporation of the new British Railways totem of two white horizontal

lines and two arrow heads, plus the loss of the distinctive waist line. All the above were incorporated in one form or another on the Trix models. British Railways also introduced all-yellow ends during 1966, but this was not adopted on completed factory-produced models, and was left to individual choice on kit-built models from the Footplateman series.

The early green 'Warship' models carried the red nameplate 'Vanguard' which was used solely until 1965, but thereafter the models in all three colours carried the following additional names and corresponding numbers – 'Champion' D809, 'Daring' D811, 'Magnificent' D828, and 'Spartan' D844. The background of these nameplates was black, and in the latter life of the Footplateman kits these self-adhesive names were replaced by transfers.

From 1967 only the 2-rail models were available as factory-completed locomotives; the maroon version was withdrawn with the issue of the 1970 price list, the green version disappeared in 1971, and the last surviving blue liveried 'Warship' disappeared from the Trix range with the issue of the 1972 price list. The range of Trix 'Warships' was last shown in completed form in the Thernglade edition of the 1967/68 catalogue.

BR Western Region Class D800 Diesel Hydraulic locomotives.
From the top: 'Vanguard' D801 with large BR transfer Cat.No.F106 the yellow end panels were applied by a non-Trix source; 'Daring' D811 with convertible wheels Cat.No.1119, (pre-1964). The waist line on this model is pale green; maroon 'Champion' D809 Cat.No.1122; blue 'Champion' D809 Cat.No.1123.

THE LAST OF THE BRITISH TRIX STEAM LOCOMOTIVE DESIGNS TO A SCALE OF 3.8mm.

BR Class E2 0-6-0. On the left an early version with the spokes on the wheels in relief.
The model on the right has fully represented spokes.

This was an attempt at producing a cheap locomotive using a plastic body, and once again the the size of the Trix 12 volt motor was a governing factor. The locomotive chosen was the ex-Southern Railway 0-6-0 tank engine Class E2 which was first put into use in 1913 but was still running in British Railways days. Michael Catalani began the design during the summer of 1960, but it was not until late 1961 that production commenced in the Birmingham. The moulding of the plastic body shell was done at the Dufay factory in Birmingham who were proficient at plastic moulding from their experience with producing cheap cameras. The tooling for the mould was manufactured by a local company, Thomas Hales Ltd. The result was a very clean plastic moulding with only the safety valve and the chimney top moulded as separate items.

The chassis was a simple diecasting incorporating a weight at the front end and the Trix Perma-motor mounted at the rear, driving the centre pair of flangeless driving wheels through a brass worm and nylon pinion gear wheel. The wheels were made only for scale track, but the current pick-up arrangement allowed for 2- or 3-rail running using a similar assembly to that on the other 12 volt DC models. A spare wheel-contact spring was provided for this purpose to be used in place of the centre pick-up shoes when converting to 2-rail.

The wheels used on this model were sintered metal, that is, they were moulded from a metal powder subjected to high pressure and temperature. Unfortunately the spokes were only represented in relief, and the coupling rod was very crude in comparison to the well-detailed coupling rods and associated valve gear used on the steam outline models produced at the Northampton factory. The truth was that press-work expertise did not exist at the Birmingham factory. On the track the locomotive was extremely noisy, and due to the lack of traction tyres the considerable power of the motor was not converted into traction. The body shell was unpainted and left in its raw black moulded state, except for the embellishment of the BR crest and number transfers, of which the number 32103 was in the usual yellow colour with each numeral edged in black.

This model was not at first available on its own, but as part of a Goods Set, catalogue number F50, listed in the July 1961 Trix price list. The set was first advertised by dealers in December 1961 just in time for Christmas. Included with the tank engine were three of the latest goods wagons on the new style diecast chassis (two with plastic bodies and a goods brake van with diecast body), plus a 14-piece oval track. By the early spring of 1962 the 0-6-0 Class E2 was available on its own and given the catalogue number of F107.

A year later under the Courtaulds Group ownership of British Trix, the wheels were improved being fully spoked, and the catalogue number changed to 1107. However, by the time the 1964 catalogue had been published, two separate versions were available:

1107   2-rail
1108   3-rail

The 3-rail version was withdrawn in 1967, but the 2-rail model continued in production, or more correctly, was available until 1972. During its production life it was offered in a variety of sets, usually intended for the Junior end of the market including multiple stores. These sets are listed in the corresponding chapter.

Another attempt at providing a cheap 12 volt DC 'Toy Train' for the junior end of the market almost took off but was shelved at the last moment. This was to have been a simplified 0-4-0 version of the 0-6-0 Class E2 tank engine utilising a cut-down version of the E2 plastic body, a modified basic Cadet chassis with 0-6-0 wheels (although the 1964 catalogue stated a cast chassis), part of the coupling rod assembly from the Cadet, and the plastic cylinder assembly used by some of the German-outline steam locomotive models manufactured by Liliput of Austria.

A picture of this 'new' 0-4-0 tank locomotive was shown in the 1964 catalogue in which two versions were listed, the 2-rail Cat. No. 1165, and the 3-rail Cat. No. 1166. The corresponding catalogue listed the price for each type as 'to be announced'. It was a far cry from the other 'new' locomotive also shown in the same catalogue which was a scale model of BR Western Class diesel locomotive which helped to set the excellent standards of future products.

British Trix E3000 chassis.

THE FIRST LOCOMOTIVES
IN 4.0mm SCALE

For Trix to gain any appreciable foothold in the increasingly scale-conscious model railway market, the continued quest for the accurate portrayal of a particular type of full-size locomotive was paramount. Ernest Rozsa, who by now was holding the reins of the company, endeavoured to meet these standards and instigated various new designs, one of which was the 'Western' diesel-hydraulic locomotive. The assembly and design of the articulated bogies used on this model was based directly on the design of the BR E3001 electric locomotive introduced into the Trix range during the latter part of 1962.

This was a model of the British Railways 25kV AEI Class E3000 Bo-Bo electric locomotive which was one of a primary series numbered E3001-E3023 introduced in 1959 to run on the Manchester to Crewe electrified line. The model was initially manufactured to a partially-finished state in Austria by Liliput Spielwarenfabrik GmbH to a scale of 4.0mm from a design by Ernest Rozsa and imported by his company, Miniature Construction Ltd, eventually appearing in the shops in October 1960.

The model was completed on the premises of Miniature Construction by adding two simplified working versions of the Stone-Fairley pantographs and by a general adjustment of the locomotive to give a more efficient performance. The plastic body moulding was well detailed and all the windows were glazed with transparent plastic, producing an overall result that well conveyed the uncluttered appearance of the original. The roof was finished in grey with good cable conduit and insulator detail plus the addition of a plug which allowed the operator to change from overhead current collection to normal 2-rail operation. The body was finished initially in semi-gloss blue with black underframe, red bufferbeam, and rather strangely, silver-grey cab roof, cab window frames and grab-rail details instead of white. The embossed number E 3001, including the BR crest applied as a separate moulding, were also finished in silver. This crest was very clumsy in appearance and was formed from plastic using a brass mould.

Each bogie was formed from two main cast components, one of which was the support frame into which was slotted a chassis component housing the two axles, and in the case of the motor bogie, the idler gears and motor drive. The chassis casting was allowed to swivel in the frame by resting on its own pads, but restricted in its angular and lateral movement by a long brass bush which was located in a radial slot at the rear of the frame. The motor had five poles which gave very smooth running although it was not as powerful as the Trix Express Perma-Motor. The power from this motor was transmitted to the wheels via a two-start worm drive and reduction gears to the gear located on the front shaft. The lamp illuminating the headlights and headcode panel, for which route number transfers A123, 1A11, X100 and 3056 were provided, is situated on an insulated assembly on each bogie governed by a rectifier which decides which lamp is illuminated, depending on the direction of travel. Highly detailed black plastic bogie sideframes depicting suspension and wheel bearings, were clipped onto the support frames.

No current collector springs were used as only wheels on one side of each bogie were insulated, and thus each bogie assumed a different polarity insulated from each other by the plastic body into which each bogie frame clips. The wheels were suitable for scale track and are correctly detailed with part of the Alsthom quill-drive protrusions. The couplings at this stage were not to a Trix pattern, but to a standard European pattern. The model was given a Miniature Construction Ltd catalogue number of E3000.

During 1962, as stated above, the E3001 was purchased from Miniature Construction Ltd. by Trix Products Ltd, and so that it could be adapted to 'Trix' running a metal coupling designed for use on the new scale plastic coaches was fitted on to a special adapter. A 3-rail version was made available by machining screw threads in the base of the motor chassis casting to accept a centre contact shoe assembly as used on the Class V, Hornsby Diesel Shunter and similar models. In this version all the wheels on the motor bogie had to be insulated.

When British Trix Ltd was formed in April 1963 as part of the Courtaulds Group of companies, the E3001 was advertised in the new catalogue with the flamboyant statement of 'Liliput plus Trix co-operation'. It was part of an effort to increase the credibility of the Trix range with the known excellence attributed to most of the railway models manufactured on the European continent. By this time the main body and cab roofs plus cab window frames were finished in white, and the pantograph construction differed slightly. The blue of the body was now in a matt finish which seemed a little too matt, but it was not long before the finish took on an almost satin sheen. The E3001 was offered with Cat.No.1127 for 3-rail operation and Cat.No.1128 for 2-rail operation, both versions being fitted with scale wheels as shown in the 1963 catalogue.

This was also the period when a range of Trix Express locomotives, rolling stock and selected accessories were advertised in the catalogue to supplement the very small range of British Trix products. Where applicable, the German couplings were modified to the British type at the Wrexham factory. The imported range was increased with the introduction of the 1964 catalogue by the addition of other products from the Trix Express range and the Liliput factory in Austria, plus three locomotives and a goods wagon from Yugoslavia with the trade name of Tempo. The latter were soon discontinued as reliability was poor and spares were virtually unobtainable. It is felt that a detailed description of these imported models is irrel-evant to this publication.

By the middle of 1964, British Trix Ltd had purchased the tooling of the E3001 from the Liliput factory in Austria, although the bogie components were still manufactured at the Liliput factory. A few design changes took place during the following months including the re-designing of the tooling for the pantographs. Gone were some of the rather flimsy pantograph components constructed from wire, and in their place tinplate pressings and a skate assembly purchased from Trix Express. The result was a very efficient assembly with a good resemblance to the full size version. The main roof detail now incorporated switch gear detail and was finished in white as was the cab roof and window frames.

The body was now moulded at the British Lego factory, which at this time was part of the Courtaulds Group. Gone were the obnoxious BR crest mouldings to be replaced by silver coloured transfers, and included with the model were two self-adhesive yellow panels to fit on each end of the locomotive if the owner so wished. The metal coupling assembly was replaced by a new black Alkon plastic moulded coupling which was similar to the one fitted to the 3.8mm plastic scale coaches introduced earlier. The rectifier used for the directional control of the headlight was no longer fitted, and thus under operation the lights at both ends of the locomotive were permanently illuminated. 1965 saw the modification of the motor bogie to fit a new centre rail contact assembly supplied by Trix Express with a central fixing screw in the shoe retainer instead of the two screws as on the type previously used.

1965 also saw the addition of twin motor versions for both 3-rail and 2-rail, catalogue number 1129 and 1130 respectively, plus two kits in the Footplateman series. The June 1967 price list omitted both 3-rail versions, but the model with the single motor was relisted in the March 1968 edition corresponding to the 1967-1968 catalogue. With the introduction of this catalogue, the cast detail of the Alsthom quill-drive on the wheels had been replaced by moulded plastic inserts fitted into the recess on a plain disc pattern wheel, as used on the 'Western' diesel locomotive model. The 2-rail, two-motor version was now fitted with automatic light change but did not survive long, as by January

Lining the E3001 at Liliput Model Railways (UK) Ltd April 1982.

The BR 25kV AEI Class E3000 Bo-Bo Electric locomotive.
From the top: Ex-Miniature Construction model with adapted Trix couplings fitted Cat.No.1128. Note the large moulded BR crest.
The post-1964 Trix model Cat.No.1128 fitted with re-designed pantographs and BR crest transfers; Liliput (UK) single pantograph version Cat.No.1001;
Liliput (UK) BR Class 81 version Cat.No.1005.

1969, the only version being manufactured was the 2-rail single motor model, catalogue number 1128. This model was to remain virtually un-altered except for the reduction of the two pantographs to a single assembly during the early part of 1972.

After the collapse of Trix Trains under Thernglade Ltd in 1972, Liliput Model Railways (UK) Ltd continued to market the E3001 after the late summer of 1974. The tooling for the pantographs was purchased from the Courtaulds Group by Liliput in Austria who continued to manufacture the bogie assemblies, as well as the pantograph assemblies, although the body shell was still moulded at the British Lego factory in Wrexham. The final assembly was initially carried out at the private residence of Ernest Rozsa until more suitable premises were obtained in Bala North Wales the following year.

The catalogue number allocated by Liliput Model Railways (UK) Ltd. to this model was 1001. Three other variants were offered; Cat.No.1002, as 1001 but with changing headlights which used diodes instead of a metal rectifier, and Cat. No.1003, which was as 1001 but without head-lights. The third variant was Cat.No.1004 which was to have been the E3001 in kit form, but it never materialised and was withdrawn from the price list in 1976. After 1976 the E3001 was available with either the British Railways lion emblem or the later double arrow symbol.

By the end of 1976 the Liliput 5-pole motor was no longer produced, which necessitated a design modification to the motor bogie castings and drive gears to accommodate a new 3-pole motor manufactured by Bühler of West Germany. Although 3-pole, this was a very smooth motor and more powerful than its 5-pole predecessor. The model given Cat.No.1001 was now fitted with changing headlights, and Cat.No.1002 allocated to a model with two motor bogies which was available until 1982. The original model bearing this catalogue number was no longer available. A model finished in the new classification of British Railways, ie Class 81, was introduced at the same time, Cat.No.1005. This was technically the same as Cat.No.1001, but required the four sets of embossed number E3001 to be removed from the body prior to finishing in the normal blue colour, except for the ends which for this model were finished in yellow. Two running numbers were available, 81007 and 81014.

A marketing failure introduced in 1982 was the attempt to sell the E3001, including all other models in the British Series of Liliput Model Railways (UK) Ltd, fitted with the German Trix EMS system. EMS stands for Electronic Multiple train control System which allows the inde-pendent control of two trains on a 2-rail circuit or up to four trains utilising an overhead cate-nary system. Although the system is proficient, and has remained a popular form of multiple model train control in Western Germany, it requires the addition of a special controller which feeds electronically coded information to a special module fitted in the model. As the British model railway public at this time were not familiar, and also very wary of new electronic control systems, the relative high cost of the EMS system proved prohibitive. The models of the E3000 Class in various forms fitted with the EMS unit were given the general catalogue number of 1100 and remained in hopeful anticipation in the price lists until 1985, as did the rest of the British Series range.

1984 saw the reintroduction of the two pantograph versions of the E3001, Cat. No. 1001/0, and also the addition of two new running numbers, E3012 and E3018 which were applied by transfer after the removal of the embossed number E3001 on the body moulding. The new numbers were used on both the single and double pantograph versions of the E3000 Class. Production finally ceased in 1988 when parts from Liliput in Austria were no longer available.

It must be pointed out that from 1974 the models were never mass produced as the parts were assembled, and in some cases hand finished, by no more than four or five people, and in the last two years by Ernest Rozsa himself. Bearing this in mind, it is obvious that variations exist, and although every attempt has been made to record as many of the more important variations as accurately as possible, some of the minor details are omitted. This statement is common to all models produced from 1974. In fact one can say that all the British Series models produced under the banner of Liliput Model Railways (UK) Ltd were definitely limited issue productions.

The Western Diesels. The top three models are Trix and the lower two are Liliput (UK). The bottom Western is the track cleaning version Cat.No.1013.

THE WESTERN DIESEL - PENULTIMATE MODEL LOCOMOTIVE IN 3.8mm SCALE

The first of the BR D1000 Class 2700bhp 'Western' diesel-hydraulic locomotives, the D1000 'Western Enterprise', entered service on the Plymouth to Paddington line in December 1961. It was initially finished in a very distinctive 'desert-sand' (fawn) colour which by the time the Trix model was on the market had been repainted in maroon livery. The model of the 'Western' diesel helped to put Ernest Rozsa in a position of authority with British Trix Ltd, as he persuaded Liliput in Austria to develop the locomotive and provide the necessary tooling at a very creditable cost of £1,500 which delighted the controlling management. The body was produced to the design requirements of Ernest Rozsa and his team with the idea of producing the model to 4.0mm scale instead of to a scale of 3.8mm which in the past had restricted sales to enthusiasts with a less purist attitude. The cost of development was kept to a minimum by the adaptation of the motor and trailing bogie assemblies as used on the ex-Liliput BR E3001 electric locomotive. Unfortunately it was decided by British Trix Ltd that, as vast stocks of the plastic BR 3.8mm scale coaches existed, the company could not go to the expense of redesigning the coaches and would use the old 3.8mm scale for the 'Western' model.

The 'Western' was first mentioned in the 1964 edition of the British Trix catalogue published in January, but it was not until the latter part of the summer that the working drawings were started. The first batch of models went on sale during the early months of 1965 which was a little later than anticipated due to certain production problems at the Liliput factory in Austria where the first production samples were manufactured. Normal production took place at the British Trix factory in Wrexham to where the raw parts, burrs included, were air-freighted from Austria via Birmingham Airport. As the wheel arrangement of the 'Western' was C-C the centre idler gear on the motor bogie, as used by the E3001, was replaced by another geared axle and driving wheels. A corresponding wheel assembly was fitted to the trailing bogie. The lighting arrangement remained unaltered.

The body was mainly a one-piece plastic moulding with separate clear plastic windows and an excellently detailed separate roof moulding. Unfortunately the plastic bogie side frames were not to prototype pattern due to the need to mount them in the existing points on the chassis casting, thereby reducing the the 'open' effect of the inside framed bogies which was such a characteristic of the real engine. Both bogies and the underside central moulding are a clip-fit into the main body moulding. As with the E3001, only scale wheels with traction tyres on two of the motor bogie wheels were ever fitted to these models. All the other mechanical and electrical features were common over the same production period including the change of drive unit from a 5-pole Liliput motor to a 3-pole Bühler motor in 1976. One fault common to both models was the poor electrical pick-up qualities of earlier versions in which the current pick-up was by non-insulated wheels resulting in

each bogie chassis being electrically opposite. This was eliminated during the Liliput Model Railways (UK) production period by the use of wiper contact blades on the inside of the wheels.

Four basic versions were initially available from the first months of 1965:

Cat. No. 1165   2-rail   green
Cat. No. 1166   3-rail   green
Cat. No. 1167   2-rail   maroon
Cat. No. 1168   3-rail   maroon

These were available with a choice of colour and name:

D1000 Western Enterprise   maroon
D1002 Western Explorer   green
D1004 Western Crusader   green
D1038 Western Sovereign   maroon
D1045 Western Viscount   maroon
D1067 Western Vanguard   maroon

Each name and numberplate were separate plastic mouldings which clipped on to the body shell, and these were rather heavy in appearance. They were moulded in black plastic with the border, numbers and letters picked out in silver, except for those used on the green versions where the background was painted red with the raised features left as moulded. The circular coaching stock emblem is portrayed on the cab sides by correctly-detailed transfers. Thus it can be appreciated that a variety of colour and name/number combinations can exist, although factory-produced items kept to the advertised versions. The variations were usually the result of private individuals altering the existing name and/or colour combination of models constructed from the Footplateman's series of kits. As with other models in the Trix range it was deemed

necessary to issue the model in kit form to increase sales at a time when the model railway world in the United Kingdom was at a very low point. Details of these kits are given in a later chapter. Separate self-adhesive yellow warning panels and route number transfers (1C 40, 1C 88, 1A 17, 1F 55, 1F 60 and 3C 04) were supplied with each model for use at the owners' discretion. Some later models had the ends of each locomotive fully painted in yellow as befitting the British Railways practice at the time.

To increase the 'Western's' rather poor haulage qualities, British Trix Ltd introduced a maroon version with both bogies motorised, Cat. No. 1164 for 3-rail and Cat. No. 1169 for 2-rail. The 3-rail two-motor version was only available for a short period as by the time the June 1967 price list was published, it had been withdrawn along with the green 3-rail version Cat. No. 1166 to be followed in the latter part of 1968 by the maroon 'Western' Cat. No. 1168. It is interesting to note that although 3-rail versions were no longer standard production items, they could be obtained by placing a special order through a retailer. (This service was also available for other items in the Trix range up to 1972.)

From 1965 British Railways replaced the earlier livery styles and symbols with new corporate identity lettering and a modern double-arrow motif. The 'Westerns' began to appear in a new blue livery and it was only fitting that British Trix Ltd should keep up with the modern image. The first models finished in BR blue with the distinctive white double-arrow transfers on the cab sides were first announced in the January 1967 price list and given the catalogue number of 1163. Although only one catalogue number is listed, this blue version of the model was available with all six name and number combinations used in the Trix range, the numbers and letters picked out in silver on a black background.

Even after Liliput Model Railways (UK) Ltd had gone into production in 1974, it was still considered preferable for the models to be constructed on company premises, even with the small number of staff employed. This decision helped to increased the multitude of 'Western' variants available. Those locomotives manufactured under the Liliput Model Railways (UK) label can be distinguished from earlier versions by the underside central moulding which bears the inscription 'Liliput-made in Austria', whereas British Trix production bore the inscription 'British Trix - Great Britain' followed by mouldings with no inscription at all manufactured during the Thernglade period. Additionally, the body mouldings produced for British Trix had a slightly more glossy finish in comparison to later productions.

The Liliput Model Railways (UK)1974 price list presented the following 'Western' models which were still using the 5-pole motor:

Cat.No.1010 blue livery with yellow cab fronts
Cat.No.1011 green livery without yellow cab fronts
Cat.No.1012 maroon livery with yellow cab fronts
Cat.No.1013 blue livery, yellow cab fronts, no lights
Cat.No.1014 As above but in kit form
(discontinued after the start of 1976).
Cat.No.1015 blue livery with yellow cab fronts,

two motor bogies and changing headlights.
Followed in 1975 by:
Cat.No.1016 blue livery with yellow cab fronts and changing headlights.

1976 was the year that the tooling for the motor bogie had to be altered to accommodate the new 3-pole motor which coupled with new gearing gave a much smoother performance. All current 'Westerns' in the range at this time were fitted with the new motor. By January 1977 the 'Western' in maroon or green livery without lights had been added to the blue version under the general catalogue number of 1013, but, by the end of the following year, Cat. No. 1016 was deleted from the range.

1979 saw the addition of what was undoubtedly the most handsome model in the 'Western' range – the D1000 'Western Enterprise' finished in the desert-sand livery of the prototype on first entering service. The roof moulding was matt black and the correct British Railways 'Lion-on-Crown' silver emblems were applied to the cab sides by transfers. As an additional feature to the headlights which changed with direction, a coupling converter in the form of a wire loop was located in the lower part of the body moulding. This enabled couplings of other designs fitted to rolling stock to be used with this model, and this modification continued to be a feature of all subsequent 'Western' models. Also at this time, the wheels were detailed with the addition of a plastic insert fitted to the recessed face of each wheel. This proved to be a very popular model and was given the catalogue number 1009, but unfortunately

production quantities were low due to the special finish required.

The same year saw the reintroduction of two-motor versions, Cat.No.1017 in blue, green or maroon livery and Cat. Nos 1010, 1011 and 1012 with the same specifications as the desert-sand liveried model described above. Models with specifications for Cat. No. 1017 were deleted from the range in 1982. Throughout the production life of this model, the green-liveried versions were only ever issued with the names, D1002 'Western Explorer' and D1004 'Western Crusader'.

The first, and only, catalogue published by Liliput Model Railways (UK) Ltd was issued in 1980 and was rather ambitious, or over-optimistic, in the range of variations offered for most models in the catalogue. The 'Western' fell into this category with nine extra number/name combinations offered, namely:
D1010 'Campaigner', D1013 'Ranger', D1021 'Cavalier', D1040 'Queen', D1042 'Princess', D1051 'Ambassador', D1057 'Chieftain', D1062 'Courier' and D1066 'Prefect'. All the names were naturally pre-fixed with the name 'Western'. Unfortunately although the mouldings for these number/name combinations were produced, they never appeared on the models. Incidentally the 'Western Vanguard' was given the incorrect number of D1067 in the catalogue instead of D1069.

In the summer of 1982 an unusual 'Western' model was produced. This was Cat. No. 1013 which was advertised as a Western class diesel with a motorised track-cleaning device. The actual cleaning apparatus was a circular abrasive pad mounted on the underside of a modified trailing bogie driven by a vertically-mounted small electric motor which could be electrically disconnected by means of a small plug located in the middle of the roof moulding. The pad could then be easily removed from its self-adhering backing and the locomotive used normally, although there were no couplings fitted. A coupling could have been fitted to the cleaning motor bogie, but its position on the main motor bogie was taken up with a spring-mounted pad which 'brushed' the rails during operation. An extra weight was located in the roof of the body moulding which helped with rail-to-wheel adhesion. The writer's version was finished in maroon with yellow cab fronts and given the name D1069 'Western Vanguard'. It was a very unsuccessful model and inefficient in its operation. No more than the trial production batch was made and it was discontinued within the same year of its introduction.

Also during 1982, the Trix Express EMS System was arbitrarily installed in 'Westerns' of varying liveries. This EMS version was given the catalogue number1110 and was manufactured for about two years only. As with other models in the Liliput Model Railways (UK) range the 'Westerns' were made by a very small team and

as they aimed to improve where possible this naturally resulted in minor variations to finish and mechanical details. It was a successful model of which large numbers were manufactured over the years, and only ceased production in the early part of 1987 due to the non-availability of parts.

THE INTERCITY DMU - THE LAST MODEL LOCOMOTIVE IN 3.8mm SCALE

The existing range of plastic coaches was to once again govern the scale of a new model – this time that of the Intercity Diesel Multiple Unit which was fixed at 3.8mm. The primary reason for this decision was that in this scale

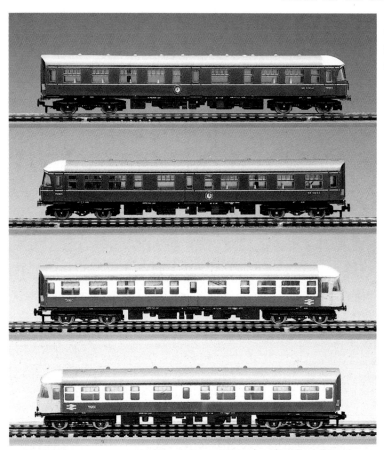

The Trix Diesel Multiple Units
Cat.Nos 1178 (green)
and 1177 (blue/grey).

196

tional coaches could be made available so that six-car units could be used on a model railway layout as in British Railways practice. These BR six-car Inter-City diesel units were employed on the Trans-Pennine service from Hull to Liverpool and were introduced in 1960 to offer high-quality business travel with first class accommodation and buffet car service. The existing Trix plastic coaches could meet this requirement after the application of a suitable livery.

The model reached the drawing board stage in July 1965 and Liliput in Austria were once again called upon to provide some of the tooling, principally the moulds for the superstructure and bogie outer frames. To save on tooling costs it was decided to use a motor-bogie assembly manufactured by Trix Vereinigte Spielwaren-fabriken Ernst Voelk KG for use on their Dutch ELD 2 and VT 08 electric and diesel twin car sets introduced in 1962 and 1963 respectively. This used the standard Trix 3-pole motor and thus adequate power was assured. The design of the non-powered bogie casting was also based on that used for the Trix Express ELD 2 and VT 08 twin car units which used a similar method for fixing the plastic outer frame mouldings depicting suspension details, etc. These bogie castings were manufactured by Silcoms Ltd of Farnworth, a company who had provided many of the diecast parts for previous models in the Trix range.

The moulding of the motor and trailing coach was carried out at the Lego factory in Wrexham, together with most of the other larger plastic parts. The smaller plastic parts were moulded by

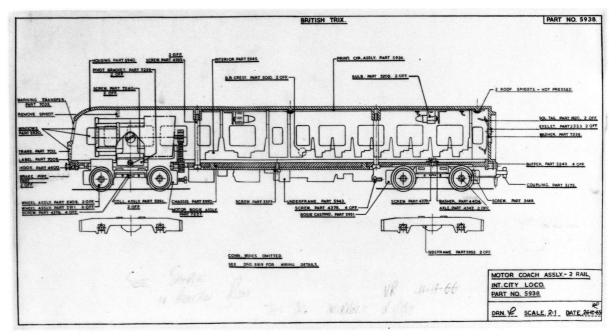

Intercity DMU 2-rail motor coach assembly drawing.

Tresco Plastics Ltd of Earls Barton, another company who for many years had manufactured plastic parts for Trix in the UK.

The model first made its appearance in October 1966 in dark green lined in cream, which was the BR multiple unit standard colour when the original was introduced. A yellow self-adhesive warning panel was supplied with the model which could be applied to each end of the unit at the discretion of the owner. Route and interior lights were included together with cream coloured interior fittings. The designers had intended that the two units should be electrically

coupled by means of a twin plug and wire set, but this idea was abandoned in favour of inde-pendent pick-up assemblies for each coach. Two holes in the corridor ends of the body mouldings show where the wire leads would have been located. The main chassis detail was accurate with good legible lettering, and this included the bodies of the motor and trailing coaches which carried the numbers NE 51953 and NE 51954 respectively. Two versions were initially available – Cat. Nos. 1178 2-rail and 1179 3-rail. Headcode transfers IM75 and IM80 were provided with each set.

197

By the middle of 1967, the model of the DMU appeared in BR blue/grey livery with yellow ends and supporting the new BR arrow symbol and the running number 51960 on both coach units. The green and blue/grey versions were now available without lights, the additional catalogue numbers being:

1174   2-rail blue/grey livery, without lights.
1175   2-rail green livery, without lights.
1176   3-rail green livery, without lights.
1177   2-rail blue/grey livery, with lights.

Followed in the spring of 1968 by:

1173   3-rail blue/grey, without lights.
1177/3   3-rail blue/grey, with lights.

The 3-rail versions were not popular, and by the middle of 1970 the range of DMUs had been reduced by withdrawing from production, firstly, at the beginning of 1969, two 3-rail models (Cat. Nos. 1176 and 1177/3), followed in summer 1970 by two further 3-rail versions (Cat. Nos. 1173

and 1179). This left only the 2-rail versions in green or blue/grey livery available with or without lights until Liliput Model Railways (UK) took over production in 1974.

Although the 3.8mm scale of the Trix DMU was a little on the small side for the British purist, it proved to be very popular and sold very well. With this knowledge in mind, Liliput Model Railways (UK) produced a range of six versions catalogued in 1974 as follows:

1020   blue/grey, no lights.
1021   blue grey with route lights.
1022   blue/grey with route lights and two motors.
1025   green, no lights.
1026   green with route lights.
1027   green with route lights and two motors.

Interior lighting was omitted from the above models until 1979 when it was once again fitted,

but only to the versions with route lights. In the two motor versions, both the leading and trailing coaches had a motorised bogie. In fact the only difference between the two units in green livery was the running number, which did not apply in the case of the blue/grey units which carried the same number even in the standard versions.

The model was available from 1982 until 1985, fitted with the Trix Express EMS module – Cat. No. 1120 in grey/blue and Cat. No. 1125 in green livery. During 1984 the models in blue/grey livery were deleted from the range due to the poor finish obtained with the tooling used in the spraying and letter-printing process.

The basic differences between the models produced earlier and those produced under the Liliput Model Railways (UK) banner are that the roof of the latter is a much lighter grey, the interior fittings were generally grey instead of cream as in former productions, and the coaching stock round transfers applied to the sides of the coaches in green livery had a red border, whilst earlier transfers had a yellow border with slightly different format. Production of all versions ceased in 1988.

The assembly of the DMU motor coach.

THE FIRST OF THE 4mm SCALE PACIFIC LOCOMOTIVES

From the mid-1960s on it was intended to produce a variety of scale locomotive models for the British enthusiast, but unfortunately many of the plans came to nothing. One such model that was actually depicted using an artist's impression and a photograph of the real-life original in the 1967/68 catalogue was the Brush-Sulzer Type 4 2750 h.p. diesel electric locomotive. This model never got past the rough drawing stage, although given two catalogue numbers 1170 and 1171 for intended differing liveries.

Also shown in the 1967/68 catalogue was a photograph of the Gresley A3 4-6-2 Pacific No.4472 'Flying Scotsman' in LNER livery. This locomotive, at the time, was privately owned by Alan Pegler and used to haul enthusiasts' special trains after rescue and restoration from the scrap heap. It was fitted with two corridor-type tenders, the second one converted to carry only water in order to overcome the lack of watering facilities resulting from the demise of steam on the British Railways network. It was announced by British Trix Ltd in March 1967 that a model of this locomotive would be available in the autumn.

The news of this pending model was greeted with enthusiasm and eagerly awaited with interest. For the first time, thanks to the persistence of Ernest Rozsa, a new Trix design was to be manufactured to a scale of 4.0mm. This decision immediately increased its prospective clientele, as the model could be

matched with rolling stock manufactured by other British companies who had adopted 4.0mm as the standard scale many years previously. The development costs allowed for the model were in the region of £5,000, and Liliput Spielwaren-fabrik GmbH in Austria were once again

Trix 2-rail models of the Gresley A3 Pacific 'Flying Scotsman'. From the top: Early pale green LNER model with the body shells finished in Austria; later model finished in Wrexham in a deeper green and note also the addition of a handrail on the front of the tender side; double tender version; BR tender drive model.

assigned to provide the tooling and supply the parts for assembly in Britain.

Although most of the tooling was complete at the time British Trix Ltd ceased trading, the valve gear was the one major assembly yet to be tooled, and it was left to the new company, Thernglade Ltd, to persuade their new owners, Trix Vereinigte Spielwarenfabriken Ernst Voelk KG to agree to fund this. It can be imagined from the above that production delays were inevitable, and it was not until summer 1968 that the model of the 'Flying Scotsman' appeared in the shops, although the first production model had been given to Alan Pegler to promote during the British Trade Tour of the restored 'Flying Scotsman' in America in 1969. Thernglade were offered a special coach to promote their products on the American tour but the cost was prohibitive and so the offer was declined. Unfortunately it was an ill-fated tour and the 'Flying Scotsman' was stranded in the USA due to lack of funds, becoming one of the few locomotives in history to have a writ attached to its boiler!

The weighted diecast chassis was fitted with the standard Liliput 5-pole motor which was coupled to the front driving wheel axle by the usual worm-and-gear wheel. The wheels were the correct pattern and of scale proportions with the important feature that all the wheels were flanged, the centre drivers having enough side play to allow the locomotive to run without trouble on the tight curves of proprietory track. In fact, this was the first time that flanged, centre-driving wheels had been fitted to a British mass-produced, six-coupled model. The diecast front bogie was functional in that it was sprung loaded which helped to keep the wheels on the track, and also take some of the weight of the model. Adequate track adhesion was provided by traction tyres. The Walschaert valve gear was based on that used on the 'Britannia' model and in fact used many of the latter model's parts in its construction. The coupling rods were fluted and picked out in the same green of the wheels. The two front lamps on the model were illuminated, via two clear pieces of perspex, by a bulb assembly fitted to the front weight.

The moulded plastic engine body was well detailed, featuring separate scale metal handrail knobs to support the handrail wires along the boiler. There were glazed cab windows and metal safety valves. The tender was basically made up from two plastic mouldings, the chassis and the body, with a small additional moulding giving hand wheel and coal-shoot detail at the cab end. The detailed chassis moulding was fitted with a lead weight for stability and utilised the wheels from the 'Western' diesel model. Facilities were also provided for fitting a Tri-ang coupling as well as the standard Trix pattern; no coupling was fitted to the front of the engine except for a small hook suitable for a chain and, on occasion, this item was omitted.

The single tender version in LNER livery was the first on the market followed shortly by the restored double tender version. The high-sided version of the Pacific tender with corridor connection was chosen as it could be used with other types of LNER Pacific models including the A2s and A4s. On a note of interest, in 1927 some of the A3 locomotives hauling the non-stop run of the 'Flying Scotsman' train between London and Edinburgh were fitted with these corridor tenders so that the crew could be changed during the trip. This was the first time that such tenders had been used on any British railway.

The engine body and tender shells arrived from Austria in a finished condition, but the shade of the green used was too light and made the model look as though the paint had become faded by the sun, although the printing on the tender and cab sides was superb and to scale. It was not long before the paint spraying of the body and tender shells was executed at the Wrexham factory in the correct shade of LNER green, the printing of the letters and number 4472 eventually appearing slightly shorter and much brighter. The LNER 'Flying Scotsman' was lined in black, which was a departure from the lining on the original which was white/black/white, and the finely-detailed, moulded plastic nameplate had a red background with the letters picked out in gold. The buffer beam number and the LNER coat of arms on the cabsides of the double tender version were applied by transfer, and it is interesting that the 'Flying Scotsman' was one of the only two locomotives in this class to carry this coat of arms between the years 1924-1928. On the double-tender model, the first tender carried the letters LNER, whilst the second water-carrying tender carried the number 4 4 7 2. Initially, this water-carrying tender was issued with the top detail exactly the same as the normal tender. This of course was incorrect, but it was not until the early part of 1970 that this tender body was

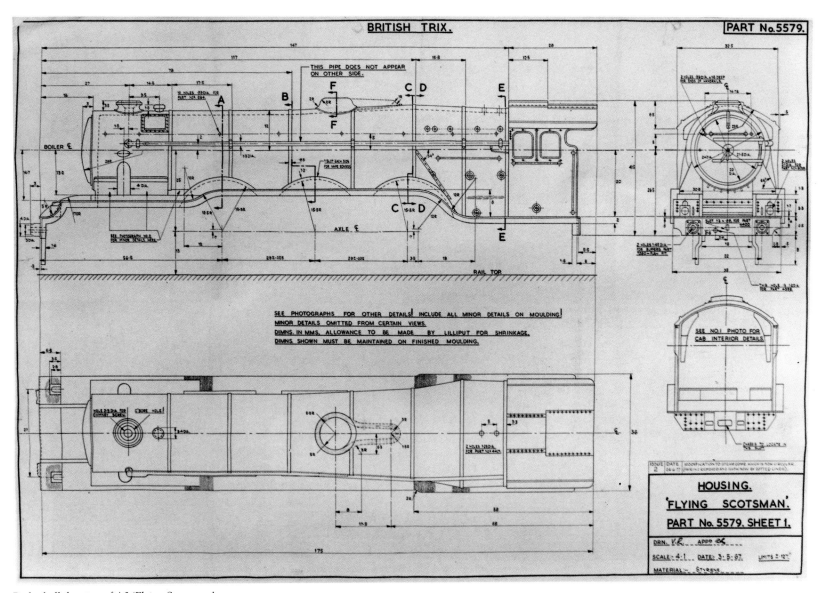

Body shell drawing of A3 'Flying Scotsman'.

fitted with a rounded top, moulded in plastic and glued in place over the original tender top detail. It had been intended to remove the corridor connection from the moulding of the water-tender body but this was abandoned, as was the idea of fitting a light in both types of tender, although the perspex lense continued to be fitted. One criticism of the tender was that no handrails were fitted to the front of its sides, although depicted on the original drawings by Vernon Rogers of British Trix Ltd. This was duly rectified in 1970 by altering the moulding to incorporate handrails. In addition, the top corner of the recessed front side panel, which in earlier mouldings was sharp and had to be removed with a file, was now rounded off.

The BR version with black wheels went on sale at the end of the year, and was finished in Brunswick green with orange lining and the number 60103 printed on the cab sides. The BR symbol on the tender sides was applied by transfer which looked as though it had been added as an afterthought. The single tender LNER and BR models were available for 2-rail or

3-rail operation, the latter being withdrawn from the price lists after 1970, although still available on a special non-cancellable order until 1972. The catalogue numbers were as follows:

1180	LNER green, 2-rail.
1180DT	LNER green, double-tender version, 2-rail.
1181	LNER green, 3-rail.
1181DT	LNER green, double-tender version, 3-rail.
1182	BR green, 2-rail.
1182/3	BR green, 3-rail.

By the time the January 1969 price list had been published, an all-black A3 was introduced without number or railway company markings in 2-rail only, Cat. No.1183. The 'Flying Scotsman' nameplates still remained on the model, but they were easily removed, enabling the owner to name and number the model to his or her choice. The only departure from the basic black finish was the engine buffer beam and the sides of the running plate which were painted red. This model is also known with gold-on-red 4472 cab and NER tender transfers issued as a very limited

production run.

Reliability problems occurred with the 5-pole motor to such an extent that it was decided in 1970 to design and produce a motorised tender chassis around the well-proven and powerful German Trix 3-pole motor. The design, tooling and production of parts was executed at the Trix Vereinigte Spielwarenfabriken Ernst Voelk KG factory in Nuremberg, and the new tender drive, now using a diecast chassis, was incorporated in the models during the winter of the same year. The non-motorised engine chassis now had an improved current pick-up assembly which was fitted in the position formerly occupied by the old motor. The tender drive, although noisy, was very powerful and track adhesion was assured by the use of traction tyres. It was initially fitted to the BR and black versions of the 'Flying Scotsman', with very few of the LNER versions receiving this tender drive.

Under the label of Liliput Model Railways (UK) Ltd both engine-chassis and tender-chassis drive versions were available for a short period, but the latter became predominant. The following variations of the A3 with corresponding catalogue numbers were available from 1974:

1030	LNER green.
1031	LNER green, without lights.
1035	LNER green, double-tender version.
1037	BR green.
1038	BR green, without lights.
1039	black without lights.

By January 1976, catalogue numbers 1031 and 1038 were withdrawn from production. During

Trix black Ex-LNER Class A3 4-6-2 Pacific Cat.No.1183.

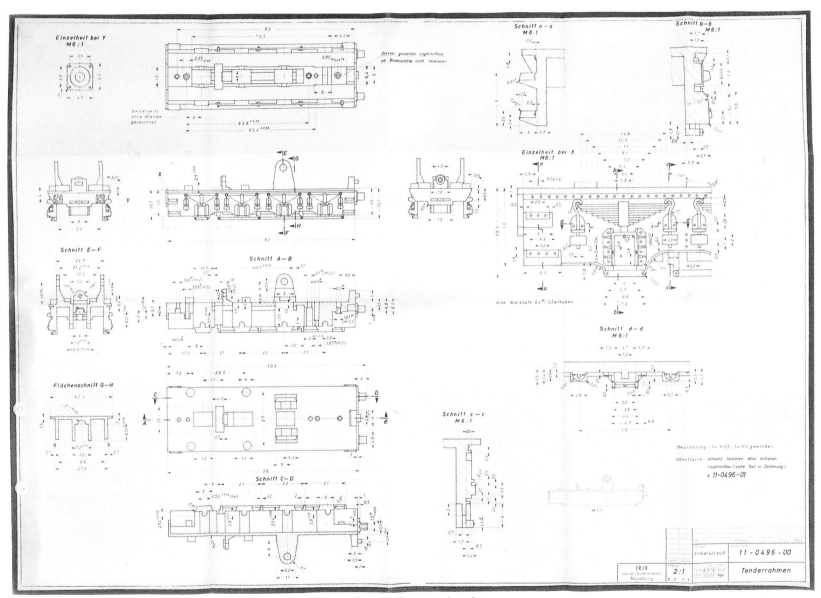

Trix Vereinigte Spielwarenfabriken drawing of the chassis for the 'Flying Scotsman' motorised tender.

203

the middle of 1976, a water tender for the LNER 'Flying Scotsman' bearing the number 4 4 7 2 was available separately, Cat. No. 1035T. For some reason this failed to appear on later price lists until its reintroduction in 1979 when it was given the new catalogue number of 1071.

During 1976 the German Trix parts for the tender drive were no longer supplied and it was necessary for this unit to be redesigned. This was duly carried out by Liliput Spielwarenfabrik GmbH who also tooled and produced the necessary parts except for the motor which was manufactured in Hong Kong. This new chassis

was based on the Liliput Deutschen Reichsbahn Class 05 model. The main part of the chassis reverted to plastic and supported a diecast motor mount and geared drive unit powered by a 3-pole motor with flywheel, giving a much smoother and quieter drive to the model. This motor was manufactured in Hong Kong with the Japanese trade name of Mabuchi. In 1986 a very small number of models were produced to special order incorporating a 3-pole motor without flywheel in the tender. This motor was the same as used in the 'Western' diesel models and was made by Bühler of West Germany.

The supply of correctly patterned driving wheels ceased around 1982, and a compromise was reached with wheels as used by Liliput on their German Pacific models. These had web detail at the end of each spoke and also incorrectly patterned counterweights. Apart from the driving wheels, bogie wheel diameters (the first batches were too small) and a few minor constructional and cosmetic details, the outward appearance of each model from 1971 did not change right up to the cessation of volume production in 1987. It was proposed in 1977 to replace the existing banjo steam dome with the earlier round type, but this idea never got past the drawing board stage.

From 1982 for three years the Trix Express EMS control system was fitted to two 'Flying Scotsman' models:

Cat. No. 1130   LNER green, single-tender model.
Cat. No. 1137   BR green.

A direct derivative of the water tender as used with the double-tender version of the 'Flying Scotsman' was the Snowplough, Cat. No. 1070, introduced in 1978. The actual snowplough was that fitted and produced by Liliput for their model of a German Bundesbahn snowplough. The free-wheeling A3 tender with rounded top was finished without markings in matt black with the red snowplough connected at the engine coupling end. It continued to be available throughout the Liliput Model Railways (UK) period.

Trix Vereinigte Spielwarenfabriken assembly drawing of the motorised 'Flying Scotsman' tender.

THE LNER CLASS A2 AND A4 PACIFICS

The success of the 'Flying Scotsman' encouraged Thernglade to continue with their intended program of introducing a creditable range of scale model locomotives. During the latter six months of 1969, Michael Catalani designed and drew the plans for the LNER Class A2 and A4 models to the requirements of Ernest Rozsa of Thernglade. Initially two models of the Gresley streamlined Class A4 Pacific locomotives in LNER liveries (blue and grey), 'Mallard' and 'Silver Link', together with the 'Merlin' in BR livery were planned and eventually produced. It was fortunate that the engine chassis, including the complete tender as used for the 'Flying Scotsman', could also be used for the Class A4 models without modification, except for two extra detail mouldings fitted to the top front and rear of the tender. Thus all the technical alterations and variations appertaining to the 'Flying Scotsman' engine chassis and tender hold good for the A4 models, except for the front lights which were omitted.

Two types of body-shell mouldings for the A4s were produced, with valances for the LNER versions and without valances for the BR version. The valances were removed from the prototypes during the war to facilitate ease of servicing, and were never refitted. A double chimney was a feature of the body-shell mouldings, although strictly speaking the 'Silver Link' did not receive its double chimney until the late 1950s. This had been noted during the design of the models, but cost had to be kept to a minimum and the modification of the mould

From the top:
Trix LNER Class A4 'Mallard' Cat.No. 1190;
Trix LNER Class A4 'Silver Link' Cat.No. 1188;
Liliput (UK) BR Class A4 'Merlin' Cat.No. 1050;
Liliput (UK) LNER Class A4 Cat.No.1046;
Liliput (UK) Snowplough Cat.No.1070.

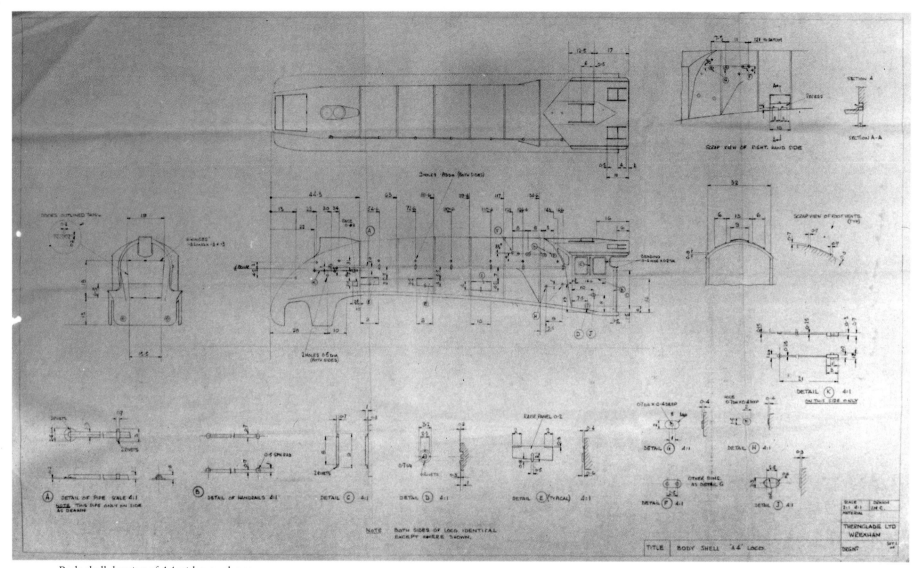

Body shell drawing of A4 without valances.

for this model was dropped. The handrail knobs, handrails along the boiler, safety valves and whistle were metal fittings, whilst the nameplates and cab-window glazing were separate plastic mouldings. The tooling and production of parts was once again completed by Liliput in Austria with the final finishing organised by Thernglade.

The A4s were first shown at the 1970 Brighton Toy Fair, but it was not until the end of the year that the first of the range appeared in the shops. This was the 'Mallard' in LNER garter blue livery with red wheels and the catalogue number 1190. The engine, number 4468, is famous for holding the all-time speed record for steam-traction of 126mph, achieved on 3 July 1938, hauling a seven-coach train weighing 240 tons. The number on each cab side and the tender letters were again 'printed' in the style and brightness of those used on the model of the LNER A3 produced during the same period. The nameplate was yellow on a black background.

The above model was soon followed during February 1971 by 'Merlin', number 60027, in BR green livery, without valances. This model was finished in exactly the same colour and lining as the BR version of the A3 and allotted catalogue number 1195. In the spring there followed the 'Silver Link', number 2509, resplendent in its grey and silver-grey livery plus grey wheels and with the same style and type of number and letter printing as the 'Mallard'. The LNER 'Silver Link' also held a position of distinction as it was the first of the A4s, and on 27 September 1935 broke the existing world-speed record for steam, reaching 112.5mph twice on the same run, hauling the scheduled 'Silver Jubilee' train

comprising a seven coach train weighing 230 tons. More significantly on the same journey an average speed of 107.5 mph was maintained for 25 miles, a record for steam traction that still stands today. The catalogue number of the above model was 1188.

The range was continued with Liliput Model Railways (UK) Ltd without any outward change except for slight shade differences in the livery. The designated catalogue numbers were:1040 Silver Link, 1045 Mallard and 1050 Merlin.

In 1978 it had been intended that the A4 range would be extended by the introduction of locomotives with different name and number combinations for the above three liveries. In anticipation, they were given the following catalogue numbers:
In 'Silver Link' livery – 1041 Silver Fox, 1042 Silver King, 1043 Quicksilver; in garter blue livery – 1047 Sir Nigel Gresley, with valances, 1048 Sir Nigel Gresley, without valances; and in BR livery – 1051 Falcon, 1052 Golden Fleece, 1053 Golden Shuttle, 1054 Kestrel, 1055 Seagull.

The drawings and tooling for the new plastic nameplate mouldings had been executed as far back as 1969, and in fact the different nameplates were actually moulded, but the cost of other tooling, including masking tools, for the completion of each new version proved to be prohibitive, and so the idea was dropped. Nevertheless, the models continued to be mentioned in the price lists for a few years, probably more in hopeful anticipation than anything else.

However, in 1978 a new A4 model, Cat. No.1046, was introduced which did not require

expensive tooling. This was the 'Mallard' finished in wartime matt black with the letters NE in white printed on the tender sides. The cab sides were numberlesss, again perhaps to save money. In 1982/3 a few of these models were issued with cab 'fire-glow'. This effect was achieved by drilling a hole in the fire-box door, placing a piece of orange plastic behind and illuminating it by means of a lamp mounted on the engine chassis. This looked quite effective but did not help to sell many more models, even when it was extended to include all the A4s, and was soon discontinued. At about this time for a short period only, the safety valves, which since the introduction of the 'Flying Scotsman' had been almost flat with only a small pip in the middle of the diameter, were replaced with brass plugs as used on the E3001 for changing the feeds to the pantographs.

In 1982 for three years the EMS system was installed in the following:
Cat. No.1140 Mallard.
Cat. No.1145 Silver Link.
Cat. No.1150 Merlin.

In passing it should also be noted that the 1975 price list listed various non-powered models for display only:
1071, the LNER 'Flying Scotsman' (the water tender for the 'Flying Scotsman' carried this catalogue number from 1979).
1075, the double-tender version of the above.
1078, BR 'Flying Scotsman'.
1080, the LNER 'Silver Link'.
1085, the LNER 'Mallard'.
1090, BR 'Merlin'.

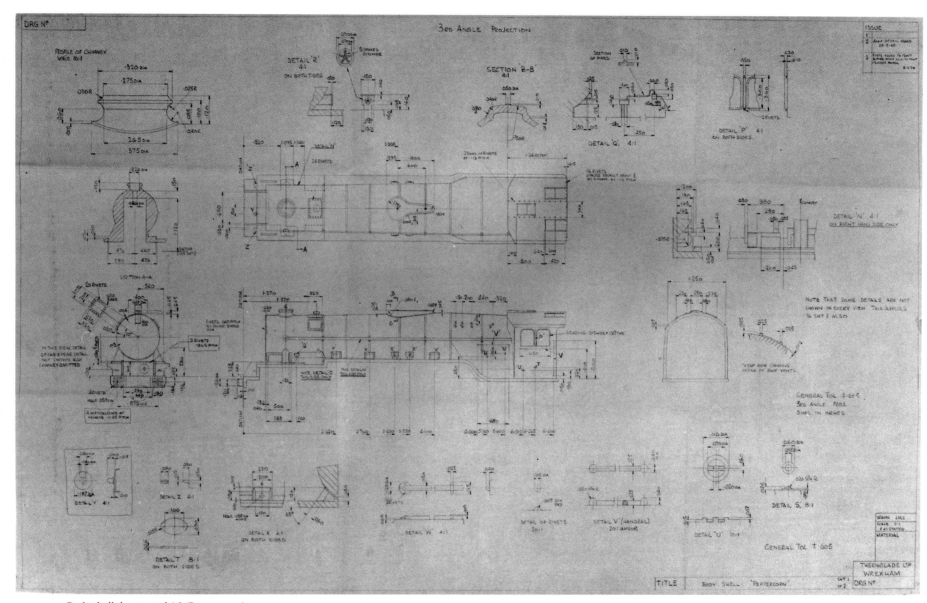

Body shell drawing of A2 'Peppercorn'.

This was at a time when the young Liliput Model Railways (UK) Ltd was still finding its feet and an organised flow of necessary parts had not yet been established. This exercise was repeated in 1990 when a small amount of the above models were assembled using the few remaining parts. They were constructed with non-motorised versions of both engine chassis and tender chassis, together with a fabricated rear bogie-assembly.

Perhaps the most successful model during the latter years of the Trix production in Britain was that of the LNER Class A2 Pacific number 525 'A. H. Peppercorn'. The prototype locomotive was produced by the Doncaster Works at the end of 1947 and was the first of its class and also the 1,434th and last locomotive to be built by the LNER before nationalisation in 1948. The model was designed at the same time as the A4 models but actually reached the shops before them in October 1970.

The A2 model used the same tender as that for the A4 except that there was no additional moulding on its top rear tender. The engine was a complete departure from the general construction of the latter Pacific models, as it used a modified Trix Express/International chassis from the DB Class BR 18 Pacific. This diecast chassis used the standard German Trix 3-pole Perma motor, driving, through gears and a long double-ended worm shaft, the front and rear driving wheel axles. The top part of the cylinder castings and part of the slide bars including the front light assembly were removed, while the chimney screw hole was repositioned. Apart from the addition of a lead weight at the front and the

repainting of the wheels and fluting on the valve gear, no other alterations were made. The front bogie was also unaltered although the original drawing had asked for the removal of the suspension detail. The rear bogie was similar to that used on the A3 and A4 models except that the body casting was altered to facilitate the addition of a metal tow bar. This modification

was to eliminate the need to alter the main chassis casting which would not have allowed the mounting of the normal A3/A4 rear bogie assembly.

Normal production models used the Trix International scale wheel chassis wired for 2-rail operation although 3-rail versions were available to special order. Also to special order were A2s

From the top:
Trix LNER Class A2
4-6-2 'Peppercorn'
Cat.No.1186;
Trix BR Class A2
4-6-2 'Peppercorn'
Cat.No.1185;
Liliput (UK) Wartime black LNER Class A2
4-6-2 'Peppercorn'
Cat.No.1064;
Trix LNER 'Peppercorn' with coarse scale wheels.

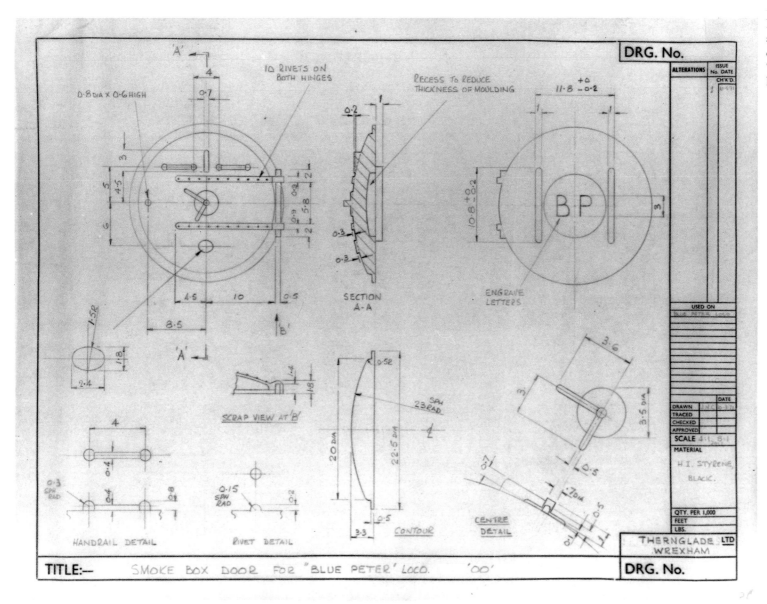

Drawing of smoke-box door for 'Blue Peter' locomotive.

made to 3-rail Trix Express standards using the coarse-scale flanged wheels and a method of current pick-up exactly the same as used on the German Trix Express 3-rail models. No special catalogue numbers were ever issued for these variants.

The engine body shell was basically a one-piece moulding with added detailing such as sand boxes, window glazing and smoke deflectors provided by separate mouldings. The injection mould for this body shell was provided by Universal Tools Ltd of Mitcham in Surrey. It was the first time that this company had attempted this form of tooling, and the resultant 'Peppercorn' body shell moulded at the British Lego factory in Wrexham was a complete

success. Unlike the A3 and A4 models, the nameplate was not a separate moulding but integral with the mouldings of the smoke deflectors, and the boiler handrails, knobs and safety valves were separate metal fittings similar to those used on the A3 and A4 models.

The first model of the 'Peppercorn', Cat. No.1186, was available in October 1970 in LNER green and numbered 525. As with the 'Flying Scotsman' it was lined in black only with a red buffer beam and red line along the running plate, plus green wheels and valve gear fluting. The BR version was not available until the late summer of the following year and was given the catalogue number 1185. It was finished in Brunswick green and lined in orange with an

orange line along the running plate and a red buffer beam. The wheels, etc. were in black. The 'works-plate' below the 60525 cab-side running number was usually picked out in gold, but many examples exist where this gold paint has been omitted.

The A2 with the name of 'Blue Peter' in British Railways livery was also projected for 1971 from designs that had already been drawn up earlier by Michael Catalani, and was listed in the 1971 price list as catalogue number 1187. Unfortunately as with many ideas, nothing came of this intention *officially*. However, a batch of BR 'Peppercorn's were purchased by a company in England and altered accordingly to be sold to special order.

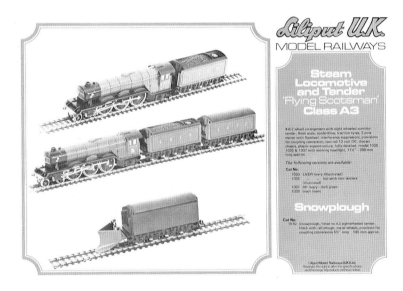

Part of the 1980s Liliput Model Railways (UK) Ltd catalogue.

Under the Liliput (UK) banner the catalogue numbers changed to 1060 and 1061 for the LNER and BR versions respectively. From 1978 the customer had a choice of either engine or tender drive, the tender drive being exactly the same as that used for the A3 and A4 models with, of course, the motor and all gearing omitted from the Trix Express/International engine chassis. The decision to provide tender drive may have been prompted by the knowledge which was highlighted in a later instruction sheet:

'The model is somewhat noisy at full speed or in the initial period due to the motor and transmission unit employed. Whilst thus extremely powerful the noise level can be reduced considerably by removing the securing screws from the chimney and also from below the cab. The superstructure will still be held firmly against the chassis by the double-sided tape strips fitted...'

1982 once again saw the usual EMS versions, Cat. No. 1160 LNER, and Cat. No. 1161 BR, but of greater interest was the introduction of the 'Peppercorn' in wartime black livery. Two versions were available, Cat. No.1064 engine drive and Cat.No.1065 tender drive. Apart from the metal handrail fittings, other handrails and the nameplate were picked out in silver with white N E letters on the tender sides. Once again the running number on the cab sides were omitted. Over the years the black finish varied between matt and gloss. The wheels and fluting on the valve gear were also finished in black. In the latter days of production the Trix Express/International front bogie was replaced by the pattern used on the A3 and A4 models, but as previously stated, small variations are always evident once volume production had ceased in favour of construction by Ernest Rozsa alone, with occasional assistance from others including the author in 1990 when I provided white metal castings for the rear bogie. The 'Peppercorn' was a fine model, which combined the best of German Trix and small quantities continued to be produced up to and including 1992.

'Peppercorn' chassis.

LOCOMOTIVE NUMBERS APPLIED TO AC AND DC MODELS

The known locomotive numbers listed below have not been taken from catalogues or other Trix literature, but are those that have been reported by owners and later verified. Every endeavour has been made to provide a complete list, but it is possible that other number/finish combinations exist hitherto unknown. Other locomotive numbers are detailed in the text of the chapter preceding this list. With regard to post-war locomotives, if not stated otherwise, all numbers are large format, and BR 'Lion' emblems are the early type. The small and large format numbers are approximately 2.5mm and 3.2mm high respectively.

Cat.No.   AC

1/510 BR black 0-4-0 Passenger tank engine, fully lined.
Small format number - 40, 63.
Large format number - 48, 50, 85.
Also known without BR emblem and number, (not an oddity).

1/510 BR black plastic 0-4-0 Passenger/Mixed traffic tank engine, fully lined.
Early BR emblem - 85.
Late BR emblem - 85.

2/510 LMS black 0-4-0 Passenger tank engine, fully lined.
Pre-war - 58, 63, 91, 121, 141, 191.

4/510 LNER Black 0-4-0 Passenger tank engine, fully lined.
Pre-war - 2901, 9276.
Post-war - 396, 7693.

5/510 SR green 0-4-0 Passenger tank engine.
Pre-war - 520, 1923.
Post-war - 951, 1923.

1/515 BR black 0-4-0 Goods tank engine, unlined.
Small format number - 30, 60, 63, 781, 914, 1109.
Large format number - 84, 97, 98.

1/515 BR black plastic 0-4-0 Goods/Mixed traffic tank engine, unlined.
Early BR emblem - 84.
Late BR emblem - 98, 30951.

2/515 LMS black 0-4-0 Goods tank engine, unlined.
Pre-war - 5, 20, 31, 39, 58, 62, 63, 91.
Post-war - 5, 11, 20, 30, 31, 62, 63, 68.

4/515 LNER black 0-4-0 Goods tank engine, unlined.
Pre-war - 6178, 7693, 8403.
Post-war - 298, 605, 7693, 8403.

5/515 SR black 0-4-0 Goods tank engine.
Pre-war - lined - 91, 490, 951.
Post-war - unlined - 91 only.

1/520 BR light blue 0-4-0 Passenger engine and tender, fully lined.
Small format number - 46231.
Large format number - 46256, 60100.

1/520 BR dark blue 0-4-0 Passenger engine and tender, fully lined.
46256, 60100.

1/520 BR green 0-4-0 Passenger engine and tender, fully lined.
Double tender lining- black cylinders - 30782, 46256, 46258, 60089.
Double tender lining - green cylinders - 60100.
Double tender lining - green or black cylinders -73029.
Single tender lining - black cylinders -30782, 46258, 60089.

2/520 LMS crimson lake 0-4-0 Passenger engine and tender.
Pre-war - 5647, 5670, 5724, 5876, 6138, 6200.
Post-war - 5647, 6138.

4/520 LNER green 0-4-0 Passenger engine and tender.
Pre-war - 2581, 2876, 4472.
Post-war - light green - 2876.
Post-war - light green with black cylinders - 693.
Post-war - dark green - 103, 447, 465, 2876.

1/525 **BR black 0-4-0 Goods engine and tender.**   ·
Lining on front boiler band and cylinders - 48427.
Lining on front boiler band only - 48152 small format.
Unlined - small format numbers - 6201, 48152.
Unlined - large format numbers - 2750, 30846, 31829,
46201, 48427, 63950.

2/525 **LMS black 0-4-0 Goods engine and tender.**
Pre-war - fully lined - 5049, 6138, 8046, 8067, 8209.
Post-war - front boiler band and tender lined - 5049,
6138, 8209.
Post-war - front boiler band lined, tender unlined - 6138.
Post-war - engine and tender unlined - 5124, 8032.

4/525 **LNER black 0-4-0 Goods engine and tender.**
Pre-war - fully lined - 2394, 3451, 4472, 8048.
Post-war - fully lined - 2394, 3451.
Post-war - lining on tender only - 2394, 3451, 4472.
Post-war - engine and tender unlined - 103, 620, 693,
4472, 5124.

2/536 **BR black 4-4-0 Midland Compound** - double lining on tender.
Small format numbers - 41062, 41128.
Large format numbers - 41135, 41162.

2/536 **BR black 4-4-0 Midland Compound** - single grey lining
on tender - small format number - 41128.

2/536 **BR black 4-4-0 Midland Compound** - double lining on
tender - late BR 'Lion' emblem - large format numbers
- 41135, 41162.

4/536 **BR black 4-4-0 Hunt Class 'Pytchley'** - single grey lining
on tender, or double grey and red lining on tender -
small format number - 62750.

4/536 **BR green 4-4-0 Hunt Class 'Pytchley'** - single
or double lining on tender - large format number - 62750.

9/520 **American Outline 0-4-0 Passenger engine and tender.**
Silvery small format number (1948/49 only) - 4826.
Larger white numbers (after 1949) - 4638, 4762, 5986, 8612.
Cat.No.9/519, without light, would not carry numbers
5986 or 8612.

9/525 **American Outline 0-4-0 Switcher engine and tender.**
Silvery small format numbers (1948/49 only) - 2690, 4681.
Larger white numbers (after 1949) - 3747, 3812, 4701,
5647, 5986, 8612.
Cat.No.9/524, without light, would not carry numbers
3747, 3812, 5986, 8612.

Note: It is possible that some Passenger and Switcher engines
received the same numbers.

25/56 **French NORD 4-4-0 engine and tender.**
Numbers normally in yellow but also known in gold - 34289,
52896, 68374.

It is not necessary for engine and tender numbers to match
as this was the practice on French railways.

DC

210 **BR black plastic 0-4-0 Mixed Traffic tank engine**
late BR emblem - unlined - 84, 30951, 41218, 67611.

277 **Meteor Diesel Express** - red - 1394, 2602.

277 **Meteor Diesel Express** - blue - 2602, 2782.

TRIX EXPRESS, LILIPUT AND TEMPO LOCOMOTIVES IN THE BRITISH TRIX CATALOGUES

These locomotives were intended to supplement the rather sparse range of British locomotive models and were listed over a period of approximately three years from 1963. They were fitted with British Trix couplings when applicable. The 3-rail versions have coarse wheel flanges and the 2-rail versions have scale flanges.

The first catalogue number in the list below is that shown in the 1964 British Trix catalogue and the 1965 Release leaflet, the numbers in the 1963 catalogue being slightly different for the same items. The number in brackets is the corresponding Trix Express, Trix International or Liliput catalogue number. The original Tempo catalogue numbers are not known. The prefix TE, TI, L or T denotes Trix Express, Trix International, Liliput or Tempo respectively. Trix Express/International were available from 1963, Liliput and Tempo from 1964.

Tempo models as shown in the 1964 British Trix catalogue.
Top; US BL2 Western Maryland diesel Cat.No.1176. Bottom: DB Class V 160 diesel Cat.No.1177.

Cat. No.
1130 (TE 1530) 'Der Adler' train – 3-rail.
1131 (TE 2243) DB Class E.10 Electric locomotive – 3-rail.
1132 (TE 2232) BLS Class Ae 4/4 Electric locomotive Green – 3-rail.
1133 (TE 2233) DB Class E.50 Electric Goods loco – 3-rail
1134 (TE 2234) DB Class E.40 Electric locomotive – 3-rail.
1136 (TE 2236) BLS Class Ae 4/4 Electric locomotive Brown – 3-rail.
1137 (TE 2204) DB Class BR 01 4-6-2 Pacific – 3-rail.
1138 (TE 2207) DB Class BR 18 4-6-2 Pacific – 3-rail.
1139 (TI 1532) As 1130 but 2-rail.
1141 (TI 2443) As 1131 but 2-rail.
1142 (TI 2432) As 1132 but 2-rail.
1143 (TI 2433) As 1133 but 2-rail.
1144 (TI 2434) As 1134 but 2-rail.
1146 (TI 2436) As 1136 but 2-rail.
1147 (TI 2404) As 1137 but 2-rail.
1148 (TI 2407) As 1138 but 2-rail.
1150 (L 105) DB Class BR 38 4-6-0 Black – tender permanently coupled – 2-rail.

1151 (L 102A) DB Class BR 38 4-6-0 Green – 2-rail.
1152 (L 103) DB Class BR 62 4-6-4 Tank engine – 2-rail.
1153 (L 102) As 1151 but black.
1154 (L 110) ÖBB Class 1010 Electric loco – 2-rail.
1155 (L 119) DB Class E.40 Electric loco – 2-rail.
1156 (L 112) Swiss Emmental-Burgdorf-Thun Railway electric Bo-Bo – 2-rail.
1160 (TE 2260) DB V.200 Diesel locomotive – 3-rail.
1170 (TI 2460) As 1160 but 2-rail.
1171 (TE 2266) DB Class V 100 diesel shunter – 3-rail.
1175 (T —) US 'Sante Fe' Diesel locomotive – 2-rail
1176 (T —) US BL2 'Western Maryland' diesel – 2-rail
1177 (T —) DB Class V 160 diesel loco – 2-rail.
1181 (TI 2466) As 1171 but 2-rail.
1184 (TI 2284) Dutch ELD.2 two-car unit Green – 2-rail.
1195 (TI 2295) DB Class VT 08 two-car unit.
1996 (TI 2296) Centre coach for 1195.
1997 (TI 2285) Centre coach for 1184.

P.609
MINERAL WAGON
WITH IRON ORE

P.604
20-TON
PIG IRON WAGON

P.641
SHELL TANK
WAGON

P.613
12-TON
COVERED VAN

P.605
20-TON
PIG IRON WAGON

P.612
16-TON
COAL WAGON

SHELL LUBRICATING OIL

P.601
OPEN WAGON
3-PLANK

P.614
12-TON
COVERED VAN

P.602
OPEN WAGON
3-PLANK

620
ENGINEER'S
TRUCK

P.619
CON FLAT 'B'
WITH INSULATED
CONTAINERS

P.616
CON FLAT 'A'
UNLOADED

P.606
16-TON
MINERAL WAGON

P.617
CON FLAT 'A'
WITH B.R.
CONTAINER

P.615
CRANE TRUCK SET

P.618
CON FLAT 'A'
WITH INSULATED
CONTAINER

P.607
16-TON
MINERAL WAGON

ENGINEERS
DEPT

P.608
16-TON
COAL WAGON

P.603
OPEN WAGON
WITH STEEL PLATE
AND TRESTLE

666
DUMP WAGON
(OPERATING)

P.646
ESSO
TANK WAGON

P.660
16-TON
WITH COVERED LOAD

T R I X

ESSO   ESSO

B.R.
317420

P.621
GOODS BRAKE

P.644
SHELL
TANK WAGON

TRIX
TWIN
RAILWAYS

'WELTROL'
WITH CABLE
P.680
WAGON
DRUM

TRIX
TWIN
RAILWAYS

P.611
MINERAL WAGON
WITH BALLAST

P.622
GOODS BRAKE

SHELL

BRITISH INSULATED CALLENDER'S CABLES LIMITED

WELTROL WH

P.678
'WELTROL' WAGON
WITH MARINE BOILER

BRING YOUR LAYOUT
TO LIFE—

P.677
'WELTROL' WAGON
UNLOADED

—WITH TRIX
ROLLING STOCK

P.674
'WELTROL' WAGON
WITH GRANITE BLOCK

WELTROL WH

WELTROL WH

WELTROL WH

MADE IN
ENGLAND

673
BOGIE TIMBER
WAGON

ASK FOR FULL
DESCRIPTIVE
LITERATURE

671
BOLSTER WAGON
UNLOADED

TRIX TWIN RAILWAYS
BIRMINGHAM

'WELTROL' WAGON
P.679
WITH TRANSFORMER

MADE IN
ENGLAND

PRINTED IN
ENGLAND

WELTROL WH

ROLLING STOCK

THE PATTERN SET BY TRIX EXPRESS

Since the introduction of the first Trix Express tinplate wagons and coaches in 1935, the style and construction methods of the rolling stock in Britain remained unchanged for many years. Both wagons and coaches had a charming simplicity typical of an earlier tradition of toy railway manufacture and yet were functional in their operation.

Throughout the entire range of Trix wagons produced in Britain, including the later plastic models, the 4-wheel wagon chassis had only two basic lengths, apart from those used for special wagons. Similarly the tinplate coach chassis was produced in two basic lengths. As could be expected from the common ownership of the Nuremberg and London Trix companies the

pattern and construction of the TTR range of wagons was almost identical to the early Trix Express range. This was not quite the case with the coaches, where, although the construction methods were the same, the style of the German coaches would not have fitted correctly with the British range of locomotives.

With regard to the Trix Express rolling stock advertised in the Bassett-Lowke Twin Train leaflet of April 1936, the lengths of the actual wagon chassis frames were 61mm and 71mm. The shorter chassis provided the platform for the lithographed tinplate bodies of the Open wagons, with or without loads, and the shorter Covered van plus Timber wagon, whilst the longer chassis catered for the Shell tank wagon and Refrigerator van. These wagons duplicated the range available in Germany, but the catalogue

numbers, as shown in the British leaflet, were given the prefix of 21 instead of 20 as used in Germany. The chassis had spring and axle box detail embossed in the tinplate, with each recess, caused by the raised axle box, providing a location for the ends of the axles. These axles did not rotate but were used as a spindle for the free-wheeling bakelite wheels retained in place by 'pinching' the circumference of the axles. The wheels were of very coarse proportions with deep flanges, for the reasons stated in the Locomotive chapter, and although the wheel 'mechanics' changed over the years, these Trix Express wheels set the pattern for the TTR range and only changed slightly in dimension until the introduction of scale wheels.

On the underside of the chassis an enclosed channel housed the automatic coupling assembly. Each cast coupling pivoted in holes provided in the channel and chassis base, with a single centralising spring joining the two couplings. There has been speculation as to the function of the two extra holes on the tinplate channel; these were tooling holes used during assembly only, and it will be noticed that the pitch between the two holes is the same for both short and long chassis. A pivoted wire link on each cast coupling completed the assembly. The buffers on these early Trix Express wagons were much larger than the later British pattern and were cast in a lead alloy.

Only seven types of Trix Express wagon were shown in the Bassett-Lowke Twin Train leaflets of 1935 and 1936 of which the Open wagon Cat. No. 21/61 was available in two colours, dark red with black and yellow lining, and dark green lined in black and light green. The red wagon carried the number 2061/67 on each side with the name of Trix Express Germany on each end. The green wagon was similar but with the number 2066. The Coal wagon Cat. No. 21/67 was one of the open wagons with an embossed tinplate imitation coal load. The Tarpaulin wagon Cat. No. 21/66 again used the open wagon with a inverted tinplate 'U' shape supporting a white cotton cover gathered together at the ends with cotton thread tied around the buffers. V S N in large black letters were printed on each side of this cover, V S N being an abbreviation for Vereinigte Spielwaren-fabriken Nuremberg.

The load for the Timber wagon Cat. No. 21/69 was a block of wood grooved to represent planking, held on to the chassis with two pins and with tinplate or copper cross-strapping added to each side of the block. The Covered van Cat. No. 21/62, lithographed in red with black and yellow markings, including the number 2062, was mistakenly listed as a Brake van 21/63. The latter catalogue number applied to a similar wagon but with a longer wheelbase. The van was fitted with a white roof which was a sliding fit onto the body. This method of fixing the roof to the body

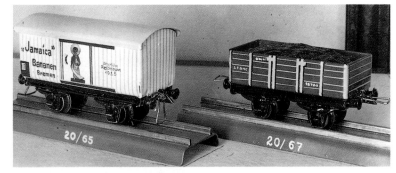

A selection of pre-production models of the Trix Express goods wagons and the passenger luggage van.
Only the Banana van, the Tucher Bier van and the Timber wagon resembled actual production models.

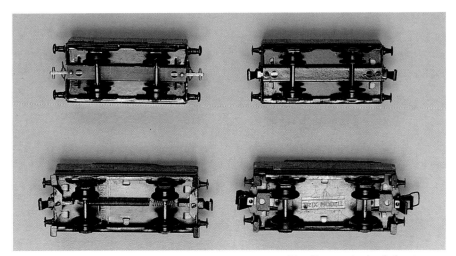

was retained until the finish of the TTR tinplate era. Each end of the van body was marked with Trix Express Germany.

The two following wagons were fitted to the longer chassis. The first was a Refrigerator van Cat. No. 21/70, again mistakenly listed as 21/64. Fitted with a white roof, it was finished in a straw colour lined in grey, black and yellow with the number 28/70 and Trix Express marked on each side. The second wagon fitted with the longer chassis was a yellow Shell tank wagon Cat. No. 21/68, yet again incorrectly listed as 21/64. Each side had the name and two Shell symbols in red, plus a ladder and platform assembly on one side only leading to a small cast filler cap. The number 2068/SH was printed on one side with Trix Express on the other. The tank was formed from a roll of tinplate with push-on caps at each end, a method of assembly which did not change throughout the many variations of Trix Express and TTR tinplate tank wagons.

Trix Express 4-wheel chassis. From the top and left: 1935/36 short wheelbase; 1937 short wheelbase; 1937 long wheelbase; 1939 long wheelbase.

The Trix Express wagons as shown in the Bassett-Lowke Twin Train leaflet of 1935. From the top and left to right: Cat.Nos. 21/68, 21/61 (red), 21/70, 21/69, 21/62, 21/66 (green), 21/66 (red), 21/67 (green with coal load), 21/67 (red with coal load), 21/61 (green).

The bogie passenger coaches in Southern Railway colours shown in the 1935 Bassett-Lowke leaflet were especially prepared for the British market, although the physical shape was no different to the Trix Express range offered in Germany. The length of these coaches over the buffers, (the buffers as used on the wagons), was

136mm. The windows were formed with celluloid-type strips (later Celastoid), held in place with tabs behind the window cut-outs. The overall appearance of the coach was typically 'continental' with the doors at each end recessed back from the sides of the coach and with steps leading up to them. The formed tinplate bogie

Pre-production models of the 'Mitropa' Speisewagen (Dining car) and the DR 1st/2nd Class passenger coach. Note the windows in the end panels of the coaches. On production models these windows were only to be found on scale length coaches.

acted as a location for the fixed axle wheel assemblies, using the same method of construction as for the wagons. The cast coupling was located on the bogie frame but was held rigid, unlike the wagon couplings which were pivoted. The white roof was a sliding fit with five raised contusions representing ventilators.

There were only two types of bogie coach listed – the Baggage coach, (or Brake van), Cat. No. 21/151 and the Passenger coach Cat. No. 21/152. Both were finished in a green similar to that used on the Southern Railway and lined in yellow with broad white window frames. Apart from the usual Trix Express Germany printed on each end of the coaches, the Baggage coach was fitted with two sliding doors, long steps in the centre of each side and the number 21/151, whilst the Passenger coach carried the number 21/152. Both types of coach are known with or without a 'I', (a Roman 1), on the end doors, due to a mix-up during assembly (it certainly is not usual to have a 1st class coach with large sliding doors for baggage!).

The above two coaches were produced until approximately the end of 1936, by which time the coupling had been changed for a more substantial casting. The coupling was by then self-centring by means of a spring, which in fact had been introduced during the use of the original type of coupling. At about this time the export of the Trix Express range in conjunction with the TTR range was being planned, and as a direct result the Trix Express Southern Railway coaches were slightly modified accordingly. The yellow lining at the top of the large windows on the Baggage coach given square corners as opposed to the original rounded ones, the white window frame was much thinner and the number printed on the sides was changed to 21/159 corresponding to the catalogue number. On the Passenger coach the white window frames were also much thinner and the printed number on each side changed to 21/160, again corresponding to the catalogue number. The coach roofs were initially white, but later changed to light grey. Both coaches are known with or

without the 'I' on the doors. It is not certain how long these coaches remained in production but definitely until the end of 1938. Although they were issued in a set containing the 0-4-0 Electric locomotive Cat. No. 20/55 for export to America as shown in the combined Trix Express/TTR catalogues of 1937/38 and 1938/39, they were more likely aimed at the Swiss market whose railway livery was finished almost in the shade of green they used. They were not generally available in Britain.

In the Bassett-Lowke Twin Train leaflets for 1936 and 1937, a 'Blue Train' set was advertised. Together with the locomotive, a set of three short bogie coaches in the dark blue livery of the International Sleeping Car Company – Wagon-Lits were included. Two versions of these coaches were supplied – a first series from 1935 and a second series from 1937. Each set version included a Sleeping car, a Dining car and a Baggage car. The construction of the first series of coaches was exactly the same as the previously-mentioned Southern Railway coaches. The lining, lettering and numbers were in bright yellow on all three, with the exception of the Baggage car which had the coach number in black figures on a white background plus extra black lining. The Baggage car Cat. No. 20/155 had the number I/151 printed on the sides of the coach, the Dining car Cat. No. 20/156 had number I/153, and the Sleeping car Cat. No. 20/157 had number I/154 on each side. All roofs were white.

The second series of coaches were constructed in the same way and style except for the couplings which were formed tinplate on a steel

Top two rows, the 1935/36 Trix Express coaches for the British market, Baggage coach Cat.No.21/151 and Passenger coach Cat.No.21/152. Note the wrong doors on the right - hand Baggage coach. The bottom row contains the later and slightly different versions with the numbers 21/159 and 21/160 on the Baggage and Passenger coaches respectively.

Early and late pre-war Trix Express 4-wheel coaches. Top row from left: Cat.Nos. 20/101, 20/103 (2nd class), 20/103 (3rd class). Bottom row 1939/1940 period: Cat.Nos. 20/101E, 20/103E (2nd class), 20/103E (3rd class).

1935/36 Trix Express short bogie coaches. From the top and left to right: Cat.Nos. 20/151, 20/152/1, 20/152/3, 20/153, 20/154, 20/155, 20/156 and 20/157.

pivot in the style of the cast couplings, and the roof of the Baggage car which was without the imitation ventilators. The blue was much deeper, and in addition to the main black lining on the Baggage car, all the lettering, numbers and feature lining were in gold. Although the catalogue numbers stayed the same, the numbers printed on the coaches were different. The Baggage car now carried the number 20155, the Dining car the number I/156 and the Sleeping car the number I/157.

Reverting to the 1935 Bassett-Lowke leaflet, a small 4-wheel Suburban coach in Southern Railway colours was also shown and given the catalogue number of 21/103. This coach was

no different to those available in Germany under catalogue number 20/103. It was dark green and marked as a 3rd class coach with yellow window frames plus various other markings including the number 20103 on each side. The body was mounted on the longer wagon chassis and fitted with a white roof with three 'ventilators'. The open windows were not glazed. A 2nd class version was available in Germany with the same catalogue number, but, as the

Trix Express 1937/38 scale-length coaches. From the top: Cat.Nos. 20/161, 20/162/1, 20/162/3, 20/164, 20/163. The coaches on the second and fourth rows have the modified higher bogie-assembly frame.

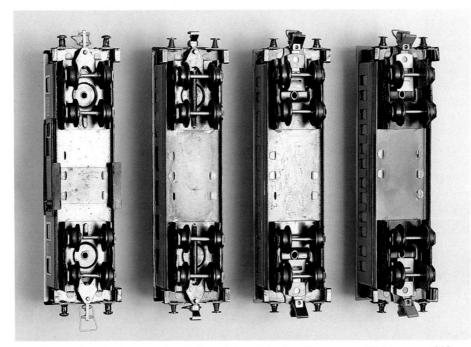

Trix Express short bogie coach chassis. From left to right: 1935/36 pattern, 1937 pattern, 1939 pattern, 1949 pattern.

railways in Britain at that time did not cater for 2nd class travel, there was no point in promoting this coach.

With the introduction of the excellent Trix Express German 4-6-2 Pacific locomotive in 1937 came a range of scale tinplate model coaches, which were a far cry from the earlier toy-like ones and could now be classed as models. They made their British debut in the TTR 1937-38 catalogue and were to a continental pattern of that period, with recessed doors at each end of the passenger coach, similarly adopted by the British Pullman coaches. The main chassis of each coach was 214mm long over the turned metal buffers and was used for all models, with only the baggage cars having different central underframe detail. Due to the length of these coaches and the small radius of the Trix track, the buffer beam was part of the bogie assembly and swivelled with the movement of the bogie, as did the formed tinplate coupling and wire link assembly with its own freedom of movement. The bogies were of formed tinplate construction with additional embossed side-frame detail. The bakelite wheels were by now a press fit onto the axles, unlike their predecessors which revolved on fixed axles. However, at the end of one of the two axles on one of the bogies, zinc alloy wheels were fitted instead of bakelite ones. These zinc alloy wheels were used as an electrical pick-up for a light unit that could be fitted in the roof of the coaches. The other pick-up was a sprung, split-roller assembly located in the middle of the other bogie which made contact with the centre rail.

Each bogie frame was electrically insulated

from the chassis by pivoting the sides of the bogie on a central spindle containing two bakelite bushes which in turn were located in the main bogie assembly. Connections to the light fitting were completed by sliding a small brass plug over pins soldered to the bogie frame located through large holes in the chassis base. The light unit was fixed to insulated spacers at the top of the coach sides. The light unit could be purchased as a separate item and was given the Cat. No. 30/78. To help with the illumination given off by the light unit, reflective white paper was fitted on the inside of the base and coach roof, the latter being a clip-fit onto the coach sides. Each coach end had door markings, three unglazed windows and corrugated tinplate corridor connection detail. All the windows in the side panels of the coach body were glazed, except the end doors, with loose-fitting clear Celastoid strips which were frosted at the ends and held in place with large tabs. In operation these scale coaches were very stable even on uneven track laid on the carpet.

Three coaches in the dark green livery of the Deutsches Reichsbahn were available – Baggage car Cat. No. 20/171, (20/161), Combined 1st and 2nd class coach Cat. No. 20/172/1, (20/162/1) and 3rd class coach Cat. No. 20/172/3, (20/162/3). The first catalogue number was for a coach with lights, while the bracketed number was for a coach without lights. The Baggage car was equipped with two sliding doors on each side, fitted with neat wire handles and lined black with additional yellow and black detail, including the Reichsbahnadler symbol and the number 20161. The roof was in very light grey, as were all the scale coaches in this early series,

1939 version of the Trix Express DR Suburban coach Cat.No. 20/114.

with a guard's look-out at one end. Two small embossed ventilator details completed the roof. The two passenger coaches were lined in a similar fashion with added black, white, red and yellow markings. Both coaches carried the same number 20162 plus the Reichsbahnadler symbol. The Combined 1st and 2nd class coach, Cat. No. 20/172/1, had eight large windows on each side plus eight ventilators and other embossed detail in the roof, whilst the 3rd class coach, Cat. No. 20/172/3, had 10 large windows on each side with 10 roof ventilators and embossed detail.

Two model coaches in the bright red livery of the German Mitropa Company (Mitteleuropäische Schlafwagen und Speisewagen Aktiengesellschaft) were produced. Both coaches were lined and detailed in gold with the Mitropa coat of arms and 'Mitropa' displayed in the middle of each side. The Speisewagen (Diner), Cat. No. 20/173, (20/163) displayed the number 20163 on the coach sides with eight unequally spaced ventilators in the roof, and the Schlafwagen (Sleeping car), Cat. No. 20/174, (20/164) displayed the number 20164 with 11 pairs of ventilators in the roof. Both coach roofs had the same extra embossed detail at each end, but the window configuration was different for each. A full train of these coaches hauled by the

Trix Express German Pacific made a fine sight on a Trix layout.

The final three coaches in this range were produced in the dark blue livery of the Compagnie Internationale des Wagons-Lits et des Grands Express Européens. The Baggage car Cat. No. 20/175, (20/165) had the same physical features as the green Reichsbahn Baggage car plus the black vertical planking lines. The roof on the initial production during 1937 was completely plain, but in the same year it started to appear with shallow embossed detailing at each end. The decorative lining, lettering and numbering were in gold of which the distinguishing number for this model was 20165. It did not carry any reference to Wagon-Lits.

The Wagon-Lits Dining car, Cat. No. 20/176, (20/166), which carried the number 20166, and the Wagon-Lits Sleeping car, Cat. No. 20/177, (20/167), similarly carrying the number 20167, were very handsome models with excellent lining and lettering in gold including the very decorative Wagon-Lits coat of arms. The configuration of the windows and other physical details were exactly the same as the Mitropa coaches. The early Wagon-Lit coaches were more generally available in Britain than in Germany, but it is strange that all these early scale Trix Express coaches were only listed in the 1937/38 TTR catalogue with special numbers relating to the models fitted with the light unit.

In the 1938/39 TTR catalogue, the 3rd class DR passenger coach 20/172/3, (or 20/162/3 without lights), was no longer listed. The remainder of the range was, although only in the versions without lights. More importantly, by the time the 1938/39 catalogue was on the market, certain modifications had taken place. A minor one was the alteration in the embossed detail at each end of the coach roofs, whereby the raised pip in the centre of the 12mm square embossing was omitted. A much more significant modification was the alteration in the construction of the bogie in order to compensate for the mismatch between the height of the coach buffers (lower) and the locomotives and other rolling stock (higher). This necessitated the redesign of the bogie support assembly, effectively lifting the buffer beam and coach body almost 3mm. The coaches with this modification can be easily distinguished from earlier versions by the addition of embossed ribbing on the sides of the bogie location pillars and raised portions at the front and rear of the two cut-outs for the bogie support pillars in the base of the bogie frame. A further modification was made at a later time during 1938 by adding a centralising spring to each coupling anchored on the bogie pivot plate by a tab.

The other new items of 'continental' rolling stock listed in the 1937/38 TTR catalogue were eight types of wagon and a Suburban coach. This 4-wheel Suburban coach, Cat. No. 20/114, was 123mm long and in the dark green livery of the DR with white, black, red and yellow markings with the Reichsbahnadler symbol on both sides and the number 20114. The formed tinplate couplings pivoted in extension pieces to the main chassis which formed the buffer beam and balcony assembly plus the location for the wheel axles which were free to rotate in the chassis frame. The ends of the axles were covered by a separate embossed plate representing the coach springing and axle box detail. The plain light grey roof was a sliding fit onto the main body.

The new wagons were far more realistic in their appearance and were in a variety of lengths appropriate to the wagon types depicted. However, it would appear that not many were sold in Britain, which is perhaps why they and the Suburban coach did not reappear in the 1938/1939 edition of the TTR catalogue, although political problems in Germany at that time may also have been a reason.

Three of the wagons were based on the DR 'Halle' low-sided wagon, the models using a common red-brown and well-detailed lithographed body with the inscription Deutsche Reichsbahn – Halle – 2071. The basic wagon, Cat. No. 20/75, was 83mm long over the buffers whilst the version with a Brakeman's Cabin, Cat. No. 20/71, was 90mm long. The Tarpaulin wagon, Cat. No. 20/76, was the same as the version with the Brakeman's Cabin but with the addition of a tarpaulin fashioned from a piece of medium brown cotton cloth, supported by an inverted tinplate 'U', with TRIX printed in broad white letters on either side. The inside of the wagon bodies was finished in a duck-egg blue.

A large Covered Goods van with Brakeman's Cabin, Cat. No. 20/74, was finished in the same colour and lined in a similar style as the Halle wagons but this time with the inscription Deutsche Reichsbahn – Kassel – 2074. It was 123mm long over the buffers and had a very light grey roof. A simple-looking Rail Transporter, Cat. No. 20/72, had duck-egg blue base and inside end faces, the latter changing later to red-

Trix Express goods wagons offered in the TTR 1937/38 catalogue. From the top and the left: Cat.Nos. 20/158, 20/78 St, 20/78 L, 20/78 SH, 20/78 O, 20/75, 20/76, 20/71, 20/74, 20/72.

Later series Trix Express wagons listed in the 1937/38 and 1938/39 joint Trix Express/Trix TwinRailway catalogues. From the top and left: 20/68 (Shell), 20/68 (Standard), 20/61, 20/63 (bright red), 20/63 (dull red), 20/66: (V S N), 20/67, 20/66, (TRIX), 20/72, 20/62.

brown, inside and outside. The construction was far more complicated than a quick glance suggests, as all the stanchions and chassis support frame in wire had to be individually soldered in place. The length of the model at 123mm was the same as the Covered Van.

One of the finest tinplate model designs to be produced over the pre-war and post-war years in the Trix Express range was that of the Oil Tank wagon which appeared in various liveries. The first of these models was the PB Olex Tank wagon, Cat. No. 20/78, which was listed in the 1937/38 TTR catalogue as an Extra Long Oil Tank truck. The tank was constructed in the same way as the earlier shorter tank wagons, but was 98mm long with a ladder and platform on each side instead of just the one. It was finished in bright yellow with inscription and BP shields in blue including the number 2078. On each side of the tank and in front of the cradles were two plates, one inscribed Deutsche Reichsbahn – Altona – 524152, and the other Olex – Berlin. On one end of the black chassis was mounted a red-brown Brakeman's Cabin. In 1938 Trix Express changed the catalogue number to 20/78O to distinguish it from similar tank wagons produced in different liveries during the same year. It is probable that some, if not all, of these tank wagons found their way into the Trix Ltd distribution system during 1938. All bore the number 2078 on the tank, and it was only the livery and the inscription of the plates that altered for each model as follows:

Leuna Tank wagon, Cat. No. 20/78 L, which had a silver tank with the lettering of 'Leuna' in red and black. The inscription on the plates was Deutsche Reichsbahn – Karlsruhe – 547 558 and Deutsche Gasolin Akt.Ges.– Berlin.

Standard Tank wagon, Cat. No. 20/78 St, with silver tank and red, white and light blue emblems of which the Standard emblem was on the left of the steps and the Essolub emblem on the right. The plate inscriptions were Deutsche Reichsbahn – Altona – 526 662 and Deutsche-Amerik-Petroleum Gesellschaft – Hamburg.

Shell Tank wagon, Cat. No. 20/78 SH, with yellow tank and red lettering. The Shell emblem was a red circle superimposed with a yellow and red shell. The inscriptions on the plates were Deutsche Reichsbahn – Köln – 567 054 and Rhenania Ossag – Hamburg.

The chassis of the wagons described above were of the same style of construction as the 20/114 Suburban coach, incorporating the formed tinplate coupling with a centralising spring connecting the two couplings on the shorter chassis models. The final available wagon advertised in the 1937/38 TTR catalogue was the

Bogie Timber truck, Cat. No. 20/158, originally introduced in Germany in 1936 but in Britain only in 1937. This wagon comprised two short 72mm-long wagon chassis, (measured over buffers), each chassis fitted with revolving axles and complete with four buffers and two couplings with a central spring channel. A pair of stanchions were pivoted in the centre of each chassis with a length of chain between the two. The single wood load, 152mm long, was located and pinned to each stanchion in a position which made the overall length 169mm.

All the above different types of wagons enjoyed a long life until the middle of the 1950s, although the livery changed slightly as a result of commercial and political changes together with production improvements. All the post 1936 Trix Express pre-war rolling stock can be distinguished from their post-war counterparts by examining the gold TRIX MODELL transfer on the underside of the chassis. The pre-war version was 22mm long with 2.6mm high letters between lines 5.2mm apart, whilst the early 1949 transfer was approximately the same length with 3.5mm high TRIX EXPRESS letters between lines 8.5mm apart also enclosing GERMANY in 2.4mm high letters. Later in 1949 the transfer was changed again with TRIX EXPRESS letters 3.5mm high between lines 4.5mm apart plus GERMANY in small letters beneath the lower line. In many instances the word 'Foreign' was applied to the models especially around 1937-38, when German products were frowned upon in the British community. The final 'foreign' wagon listed in the 1937/38 TTR catalogue was a Long Cattle truck 20/80. This model was never

Trix Express 4-wheel chassis. From the left: 1949 long wheelbase chassis; Post-1949 long wheelbase chassis.

produced and its number was eventually given to a 'Lederer-Bräu' Beer wagon in the 1950s.

When a model railway system such as Trix Express and TTR have the same roots but subsequently diverging paths, it is very difficult to know where to draw the line in describing models not generally on sale in Britain. However in this instance it has been decided to give a brief description of the Trix Express rolling stock listed in the joint Trix Express/Trix Twin Railway catalogues of 1937/38 and 1938/39. Most of the items were as described with the addition of a few different models. The equivalent Trix Express catalogue number is given with the 1937/38 and the different 1938/39 joint catalogue numbers in brackets, followed by the Americanised description. The models which were fitted with Uncoupler Strikers and Special Links, as listed in the 1938/39 catalogue, are marked with an asterisk:

A departure from the type of construction

Trix Express coaches as listed in the joint 1937/38 and 1938/39 Trix Express/Trix Twin Railway catalogues. From the top and left: 20/155, 20/157, 20/165, 20/166, 20/167.

20/61 (9/258, 9/48) Open Freight car First produced in 1937 – red-brown with the number 2061 and black and brown lining.

20/62 (9/259, not 1938/39) Box car 3" long First introduced in 1937 – red-brown with number 2062, light grey roof and black and brown lining.

20/63 (9/260, 9/49) Box car 3.375" long First introduced in 1937 – red-brown with number 2063, Deutsche Reichsbahn and black and brown lining with light grey roof.

20/66 (9/261, 9/123) Covered car Introduced 1937/38 with white supported cotton cover with the letters V S N on both sides. Wagon as 20/61 above.

20/67 (9/262, 9/50) Coal car First introduced in 1937/38 – green with the number 20667 and tinplate coal load.

20/68 (9/240, 9/124) Shell Oil car Yellow. New chassis introduced 1937.

20/68 (9/241, 9/40) Standard Oil car Red. Introduced with chassis as above in 1937. (Initially produced 1935).

20/71 (9/263, 9/125) (*) Open Gravel car with Braker's Hut.

20/72 (9/264, 9/51) (*) Rail Transport car.

20/74 (99/265, 9/126) (*) Box car 5" long.

20/75 (9/52, not 1937/38) (*) Open Gravel car without Braker's Hut.

20/76 (9/267, 9/127) (*) Covered car 3.5" long.

20/78 (9/268, 9/53) (*) 'Olex' Oil car 5" long Yellow. The oil car shown in the 1937/38 catalogue was a mock-up, the 5" long Shell Oil car was not produced until 1938.

20/158 (9/272, not 1938/39) Lumber car 6.5" long First issued with this type of coupling 1937.

20/155 (9/269, 9/128) Wagon Lits Baggage car 1937 short series bogie coach.

20/156 (9/270, 9/129) Wagon Lits Dining car 1937 short series bogie coach.

20/157 (9/271, 9/130) Wagon Lits Sleeping car 1937 short series bogie coach.

20/163 (9/273, 9/131) Mitropa Dining car Scale bogie coach.

20/164 (9/274, 9/132) Mitropa Sleeping car Scale bogie coach.

20/165 (9/275, 9/133) Wagon Lits Baggage car Scale bogie coach.

20/166 (9/276, 9/54) Wagon Lits Dining car Scale bogie coach.

20/167 (9/277, 9/134) Wagon Lits Sleeping car Scale bogie coach.

30/78 (9/281, 9/135) Lighting set to fit scale bogie coaches.

used by the German factory for their Trix Express coaches was that used by the French company Maison Gobin-Daudé of Paris in the construction of their replicas of the passenger coaches and luggage van of the Chemins de Fer du Nord produced to compliment their NORD locomotive. The chassis for these coaches were supplied to the French company by Trix Ltd and were the same type as used on the standard LMS, LNER and SR short bogie coaches (described later), except that the Battery Box detail on both sides of the chassis was removed. The bodies of both the passenger coach and baggage car were a one piece diecasting, with the windows glazed by a celastoid strip cleverly held in place by the internal handrail running the length of the coach. This handrail wire passed through to the exterior of the coach body at the inside edge of the door frame, at each end of the coach, forming the handrails for the entrance doors. Although holes were drilled on the outside edge of the door frames ready to receive a handrail, they were rarely fitted. A similar glazing and handrail assembly was executed on the luggage van, but unlike the passenger coach, it is known with and without the handrail fitted to the outside door frame.

Three passenger coach classes were available – 1st class (Cat. No. 25/351), 2nd class (Cat. No. 25/352) and 3rd class (Cat. No. 25/353) with the Luggage van given Cat. No. 25/350. The passenger and luggage van were painted in dark green with the NORD and the coach passenger classification markings in roman numerals applied in yellow print. Two slightly different styles of transfers/printing exist corresponding to

French Trix Express NORD coaches.

an internal casting modification. The earlier style is much lighter with the tops of each roman 'I' on the second and third class coaches joined together, whilst on the later versions each 'I' is separated. This latter style is accompanied by the addition of internal roof ribbing either side of the central chassis mounting pillar in the coach body casting. The chassis of the early NORD coaches was marked 'BODY MADE IN FRANCE' and 'Exporte d'Angleterre', whilst the chassis on later versions was stamped 'Made in France' These French items reached the markets in the latter part of 1937 and were listed on a separate leaflet inserted in the 1938/39 TTR catalogue with each coach costing 6/9d (nearly 34p). Sales in Britain were very poor but steady in France where the

NORD locomotive and set of coaches were available until 1939.

The TTR 1938/39 catalogue was the last time that part of the Trix Express rolling stock range was listed as available through the normal advertising channels of the TTR catalogue until 1964, when once again Trix Express and other Continental rolling stock were offered as a supplement to the British range. However, Polk's Model Craft Hobbies Inc. of New York produced a catalogue in liaison with Trix Ltd of London during 1949 listing the normal TTR range plus a selection of post-war Trix Express rolling stock. This was the direct result of the offer by Trix Ltd to help the German Trix company at a very difficult time with their exports.

THE INTRODUCTION OF THE TRIX TWIN RAILWAY ROLLING STOCK AND THE BASIC 4-WHEEL CHASSIS

After the general acclaim of the Twin Trains in 1935 and 1936, it was apparent that the impetus of popularity in Britain would only be sustained if the outline of the range became British instead of retaining and expanding the existing 'continental' outline range. Another plus for Trix Ltd would be the ability to advertise the products as 'British Made'. Plans must have been well ahead during the early months of 1936, as by the autumn of the same year the first of the wagons and coaches in British outline were available to the public, and more importantly at this particular time they were advertised as being MADE IN NORTHAMPTON.

The TTR wagons used two basic lengths of chassis, the construction and general dimensions being exactly the same as the Trix Express chassis of 1936 except that the buffers were machine-turned brass of much smaller and realistic proportions than the Trix Express pattern. The frames acting as bearings for the revolving axles were also slightly different in their basic shape, and the separate tinplate stampings depicting spring and axle box detail which were fitted over the axle ends retained by tabs folded over the chassis frames, bore a distinctive 'English' pattern.

Diecast mazak couplings were used throughout the pre-war period except for a few isolated cases of rolling stock and 0-4-0 tenders together with the range of American-style wagons introduced in 1938 which used the formed tinplate type supplied by the German company.

The various printed tinplate bodies were 32.0mm wide compared with the Trix Express bodies of 30.7mm width, with the interior of each wagon finished in black.

Vereinigte Spielwarenfabriken Andreas Förtner & J. Haffner's Nachfolger GmbH in Nuremberg had applied for the necessary British Patents to cover their inventions, and these were pending at the time of the introduction of the new British range of wagons and coaches. As a result the early range of wagons had the following printed on each end:

'TTR Patents Pending
Made in England'

with a shortened version on the coach end-panels.

The early pre-war range of LMS goods wagons.

The first of the new British wagons and coaches made their appearance during October/November 1936 and were shown in the Bassett-Lowke Twin Train catalogue dated November 1936, although most of the illustrations were artists' impressions. Wagons in the livery of three of the main railway companies were offered, LMS, LNER and SR, but initially the catalogue numbers did not distinguish between one company livery or another. Both LMS and LNER Goods Brake vans had the same catalogue number - 650. This was partially solved in 1937 by adding a prefix number, where applicable, to the main number. Thus the LMS Goods Brake became 2/650 and the LNER version became 4/560. However, it was not long before there was a change in the colour and tinplate printing of the LMS and LNER wagon designs, unfortunately not accompanied by a change in the catalogue number. Why Trix Ltd did not issue an exclusive catalogue number for each type and variation in the TTR rolling stock range is a mystery. This results in some uncertainties regarding the production dates of these pre-war wagons and coaches. Nevertheless all is not lost thanks to the British Patents granted to the TTR system applied for by the German Trix company. Three of the Patent numbers, 465168, 451644 and 471304 were inscribed on the wagons (and coaches), in various forms, the latter two always appearing together. Patent number 465168 refers to the basic concept of two toy trains running on one track under independent control and was granted on 30 April 1937. The Patent number 451644 was granted on 10 August 1936 and relates to the coupling and uncoupling device on the locomotives and rolling stock. Patent number 471304 was granted on the 1 September 1937

and covered the associated uncoupling device fitted to a length of track. Initially the Patent inscriptions were printed in white letters on the coupling channel on the underside of the wagons as shown below:

A) 'Brit. Pat. 465168
Other Brit. Pats. Pdg.
(Used after June 1937) Patd. Abroad.'

B) 'Brit. Pats. 451644
471304 Patd. Abroad.' (Used after 1/9/1937)

Thus any of the early wagons bearing these inscriptions were definitely in production until at least the end of 1937, any wagon bearing the Patent number 465168 in the tinplate printing was designed and produced after April 1937, and the wagons bearing the Patent numbers 451644 and 471304 together were designed and produced after September 1937.

Following is a list of 4-wheel wagons produced up to and including 1939, (excluding the Crane

Truck Set), with approximate inclusive production dates (not to be confused with availability dates), based on a combination of Patent information and information contained in the various pre-war catalogues. Although some of the pre-war styles were continued after the war, a separate listing for these wagons is given later in this chapter due to modifications in the design of the chassis and couplings.

To avoid confusion, only the later standardised catalogue numbers are used in the descriptions which follow. Those marked with an asterisk (*) were originally shown in the Bassett-Lowke Twin Train catalogues for November 1936 and March 1937 without a prefix number. Unless otherwise stated the lining on the LMS, LNER and SR wagons was light grey and black with the main lettering in white, the Private Owner wagons also falling into this category. The number in the description is the wagon number printed in the design, and S/C or L/C denotes short or long wagon chassis respectively.

A rake of early 'Bassett-Lowke' Private Owner wagons with an unadopted style of printing which omits the yellow background to the 'Bassett-Lowke Ltd' diagonal lettering.

Later pre-war range of LMS goods wagons.

Cat.No.

600 LMS Platform truck, (3-plank wagon) Dark brown – 472870 – L/C (1937-end of 1939).

2/601 LMS Open low side (*) Light grey – 247185 – S/C (1936-ca 1938).

2/601 LMS Open low side Brown – 33550 – S/C (1937-end of 1939).

4/601 LNER Open low side (*) Red-oxide – 140721 – S/C (1936-ca 1938).

4/601 LNER Open low side Red-oxide – 174651 – S/C (1937-end of 1939).

2/603 LMS Open high side (*) Light grey – LOCO COAL ONLY – 93631 – S/C. (1936-ca 1938).

2/603 LMS Open high side Brown – 604707 – S/C (1938-end of 1939).

2/603 LMS Open high side Brown – LOCO – 63084 – S/C (1938-end of 1939).

4/603 LNER Open high side (*) Grey – 142690 – S/C (1936-ca 1938).

4/603 LNER Open high side Grey – 171312 – S/C (1938-end of 1939).

4/603 LNER Open high side Grey – 10687 – S/C (1938-end of 1939).

5/603 SR Open high side (*) Dark brown – 40037 – S/C (1937-end of 1939).

604 TRIX Private Owner wagon high side Yellow – black letters – 7372 – original catalogue number in Nov.1936 and March 1937 Twin Train catalogues was 605 – S/C (1936-end of 1939).

605 BASSETT-LOWKE Private Owner wagon high side Light grey – black letters on a yellow background – 6285 – S/C (1936-ca 1937).

605 BASSETT-LOWKE Private Owner wagon high side Dark grey – black letters on a yellow background – 6285 – S/C (ca 1937 - end of 1939).

606 Both low and high-sided wagons in any livery were eligible for addition of a coal load made up from an injection moulding mounted on a tinplate support – S/C (1936-end of 1939).

607 HINCHLIFFES Private Owner wagon high side Red – 236 – S/C (late 1937-end of 1939).

607 CHARRINGTONS Private Owner wagon high side Red – 451 – S/C (late 1937-end of 1939).

The pre-war Private Owner wagons with and without coal load.
Notice the two different shades of grey on the Bassett-Lowke Ltd wagons.

609 Ballast wagon Ballast load fitted to LMS and LNER low side wagons – S/C – ballast is coal load overpainted in grey. Light grey ballast 1937-ca1938. Blue-grey ballast ca 1938-end of 1939.

609 Ballast wagon Ballast load fitted to LNER high-side wagons – not known officially fitted to high side LMS wagons – blue-grey ballast – S/C (ca 1938-end of 1939).

612 LMS Container wagon with removable 'Carter Paterson' container (see below) – the wagon is the basic LMS Platform truck 482870, Cat.No.600 – L/C (1938-end of 1939).

2/621 LMS Covered van Light grey with white roof – 81548 – S/C (1937-ca 1938).

2/621 LMS Covered van Brown with white roof – 61253 – S/C (1938-end of 1939).

4/621 LNER Covered van (*) Red-oxide with white roof – 24296 – S/C (1936-end of 1939).

627 LMS Cattle truck Brown with white roof – 14549 – L/C (Late 1937-end of 1939).

640 ESSO Tank wagon Yellow – ladder and platform assembly with small black undetailed filler cap, (see below) – markings in red and black – L/C (1936-1938).

640 ESSO Tank wagon Pale yellow (shades) – ladder and platform assembly with large pale yellow detailed filler cap – markings in red and black – L/C.(1938-end of 1939).

643 SHELL OIL Tank wagon Red – ladder and platform assembly with small black undetailed filler cap – markings in yellow, black and white – L/C (1936-1938).

643 SHELL OIL Tank wagon Red – ladder and platform assembly with large red detailed filler cap – markings in yellow, black and white – L/C (1938-end of 1939).

645 UD Tank wagon Green – ladder and platform assembly with small black undetailed filler cap – markings in yellow and black – L/C(1936-1938).

645 UD Tank wagon Dark green – ladder and platform assembly with large green detailed filler cap – markings in yellow and black – L/C (1938-end of 1939). (UD denotes United Dairies).

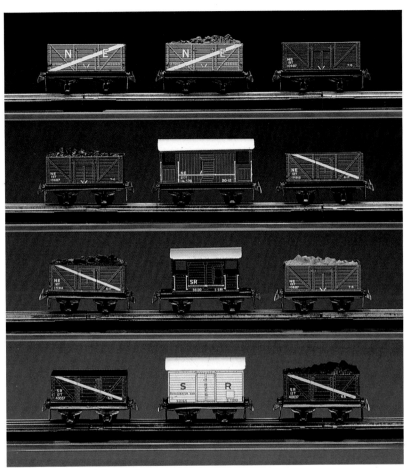

Pre-war LNER and SR goods wagons.

2/650 LMS Goods Brake van (*) Light grey with white roof – grey 134900 on black background – L/C (1936-late 1937).

2/650 LMS Goods Brake van Brown with white roof – 730274 – L/C (1938-end of 1939).

4/650 LNER Goods Brake van (*) Red-oxide with white roof – 140351 – L/C (1936-late 1937).

4/650 LNER Goods Brake van Red-oxide with white roof – 141578 – L/C (1938-end of 1939).

5/650 SR Goods Brake van (*) Dark brown with white roof – 56130 – L/C (see below) (Early 1937-end of 1939).

660 LMS Tarpaulin wagon Tarpaulin, (see below) only known officially fitted to brown LMS open low-side wagon 33550 – S/C (1937-end of 1939).

660 LNER Tarpaulin wagon Tarpaulin, (see below) – only fitted officially to LNER open low-side wagons – S/C (1936-end of 1939).

661 SR Refrigerator wagon Straw coloured with brown main lettering and black lining White roof – 50165 – S/C (1936-end of 1939).

662 Timber wagon Wood load representing 29 planks as used on Trix Express model with cross strapping – load painted deep cream – S/C (1936-1937).

662 Timber wagon Wood load representing 29 planks as used on Trix Express model without cross strapping but retaining strap pin holes – load painted off-white – pressed steel couplings – S/C (1937-1938).

662 Timber wagon Wood load representing 25 planks with two thin up-and-over card straps – load painted off-white – S/C (1938-end of 1939).

The diecast 'Carter Paterson' container was probably made for Trix Ltd by the British Diecasting & Engineering Co Ltd of London, although no definite evidence to this effect exists. However, the company was actively producing other castings for Trix Ltd at the time and continued to do so after the war. The container diecastings were received by the Northampton factory in the raw state and were then finished. The blue background of the design on each side of the pre-war container is much darker than the post-war version, whilst the lettering on the latter is much bolder and slightly larger. The grey of the roof has many shades. The pre-and post-war catalogues show the container load with various markings, but the only container supplied and sold officially with the wagons was the 'Carter Paterson'.

The tarpaulin covers were fashioned from starched cloth dyed black initially until approximately 1937 and then dark brown for the latter part of the pre-war period. The tarpaulins were marked on each side with either N E and the number 270341 or L M S and the number 304721 in white. There were also white diagonal lines which up to 1937 were broken at the centre to form an 'X'. On later types the diagonal lines were unbroken. The applied letters and numbers varied in their form, ranging from very thin to heavy with some 1936 versions having a stencilled appearance. The tarpaulins were attached to the wagons by passing a loop of elasticated cotton through a sewn fold at each end of the tarpaulin and then over the wagon buffers. The wagon bodies were filled with kapok (occasionally straw), and then wrapped in tissue paper to obtain the required shape for the tarpaulin. A tarpaulin for the SR wagon was never produced.

The tooling for the main cylinder and end caps which formed the tank wagon bodies was supplied by the German Trix company. However, the step and platform assembly was supplied in completed form by the Nuremberg factory for assembly onto the tank wagons in Northampton. As can be expected, after the war no supplies of the step assemblies were available from Germany, thus new tooling had to be made in Britain resulting in the production of steps to a new but much simpler form. This also removed the need for special location slots in one side of the chassis formerly used for the tabs at the bottom of the ladder .

The long chassis was not only used for the various wagons but also for the 4-wheel Suburban coaches that were issued from 1936, and it was with this in mind that the slots for the superstructure tabs were elongated where necessary and placed in a manner which would serve all the rolling stock using this chassis. One exception to the rule was the long chassis used for the SR Brake Van, Cat.No.5/650, which was produced minus the long latitudinal slots at each end as these would not have been covered by the very short brake van body. The attention to detail seen in the pre-war products was not continued in the post-war era as the chassis used for the SR Brake Van was issued complete with unsightly end slots.

The 4-wheel Suburban coaches were introduced in 1936 and continued in production up to the end of 1939. They were available in LMS and LNER livery and in two patterns – 1st/3rd class and Luggage van as listed below:

Cat. No. 2/550 LMS 1st/3rd class coach LMS Lake – grey roof – coach number 3012.
Cat. No. 4/550 LNER 1st/3rd class coach Teak – white roof – coach number 3120.
Cat. No. 2/555 LMS Luggage van LMS Lake – grey roof – van number 7401.
Cat. No. 4/555 LNER Luggage van Teak – white roof – van number 3316.

The shade of the tinplate printing on the LMS coaches varied from an LMS lake to maroon and almost brown, whilst that of the LNER coaches remained more or less stable. The colour crimson-lake was adopted by the LMS during the period from 1928 to 1939 and dubbed LMS lake. The coach and van windows were glazed with celastoid windows which were

retained in place by the now standard tinplate tab method. The lining detail depicted by the tinplate printing was quite superb for these simplified short coaches and typified the excellence of such printing at that time. A train of these coaches behind the relevant TTR 0-4-0 tank engine in LMS or LNER livery made a charming sight and one wonders why these coaches were never reissued after the war.

Pre-war LNER goods wagons. Note the different styles of tarpaulin covers.

THE PRE-WAR BRITISH & AMERICAN OUTLINE BOGIE WAGONS

The realism of the wagon range was improved in 1938 by the addition of British and American-outline goods wagons built upon, with one exception, a basic 152mm long chassis (over buffers), incorporating two 4-wheel bogies. These bogie assemblies used shoelace-eye rivets as attachment pivots to the main body of the chassis, and separate diecastings located over the axle frames depicting suspension detail. Initially the British-outline wagons were fitted with diecast couplings together with special uncoupling strikers and modified coupling wire links, whilst the American-outline models were fitted with formed tinplate couplings later to be replaced with the standard TTR diecast coupling. The tinplate couplings were provided by the German factory at a time when the joint export venture to America was at its height, and as by this time the entire Trix Express range used this type, it was felt that uniformity should be maintained by fitting them to the TTR American wagons.

The range of British outline bogie wagons up to the end of 1939 consisted of the following:
Cat. No.671 Bogie Bolster wagon without load Black – marked in white 6713 with 20T directly below – early production.

Pre-war TTR bogie and special goods wagons.
From the top and left: Cat.Nos. 673 (two with different numbers), 643 (small black cap), 645 (small black cap), 643 (large red cap), 640 (small black cap),
645 (large green cap), 640 (large yellow cap), 675, 676, 662 (late version), 671, 612.

Cat. No. 671 Bogie Bolster wagon without load Black – marked in white 46713 with 20T to the left – late production.

Cat. No. 673 Bogie Timber wagon with timber load Black – marked in white 6713 with 20T directly below – early production – timber load painted cream with 20 planks represented. When the timber load was first introduced its length was 5.437" (138mm), too long to use on the American models due to the hand-brake assembly. To reduce production costs it was then produced at 5" (127mm) long so as to be used on both the British and American versions. The post-war bogie timber load was standardised at 5.125" (131mm) long.

Cat. No. 673 Bogie Timber wagon with timber load Black – marked in white 46713 with 20T to the left – late production – timber load painted cream with 25 planks represented.

Cat. No. 675 LNER Bogie Brick wagon Red-oxide – wagon number 163551 and marked BRICK Return to Fletton.

Cat. No. 676 LMS High Capacity Bogie wagon Dark brown – wagon number 10468.
Both the last two wagons listed above have grey and black lining with the lettering and numbering in white.

The American-outline wagons introduced concurrently with the above were primarily intended for the American and Canadian markets but soon found their way into the British shops where they gained moderate popularity. Although they used the same basic chassis as the British range but without buffers, the superstructure of the Box Cars, Caboose and Oil Tank Cars captured the style of American Freight wagons well. On each model, except the

Pre-war American goods wagons.

Caboose, was fitted a hand-brake assembly made up with a handwheel and a long shaft. This was mounted on an end panel of the Box cars and a short version mounted on the chassis of the Lumber cars, Oil Tank cars, Gondola car and Flat car. The roof of each Box Car, including the Caboose, supported a walk-way which also helped to stylise the models as did the ladder located on the right of each side. The Caboose was a fine model and arguably the best of the tinplate rolling stock produced in the TTR range. The body of the Caboose was mounted on a chassis 110mm long and it incorporated many separate tinplate parts forming the required detail, including the chimney for the guard's fire. This chimney assembly was also used at a later date on the track-side Derelict Huts. Listed below is the range of TTR American outline models with the joint Trix Express/TTR Export catalogue number in brackets:

Cat. No.
681 (9/182) Flat car Black – wagon number T.T.64681 – white markings.
682 (9/183) Lumber car empty Black – wagon number T.T.96823 – white markings.
683 (9/184) Lumber car with load Black – wagon number T.T.96823 – white markings – timber load painted cream with 20 planks represented.
684 (9/185) Gondola car Black with light grey lining – wagon number T.T.1684 – white markings.
685 (9/186) Box car Red-brown roof, ends and sides – wagon number T.T.37685 – white and black markings.
686 (9/187) Refrigerator car Red-brown roof and ends, white sides – wagon number T.T.20686 – black main markings with red and blue lining – not available until late in 1938 or early 1939.
687 (9/188) Fruit car Red-brown roof and ends, yellow sides – wagon number W.F.E.X.53687 – black markings.
688 (9/189) Union Oil Tank car Red – wagon number U.T.L.X. 50689 – golden markings.
689 (9/190) Texaco Oil Tank car Aluminium – wagon number TCX 3688 – black markings.
690 (9/191) Caboose Red-brown all over – marked TRIX TWIN and number 482690 in white.

All these wagons were marked TTR MADE IN ENGLAND in one form or another, but surprisingly no patent information was given. The tank wagons were constructed in a similar style to the smaller British outline 4-wheel versions but with a ladder assembly located on each side of the tank leading up to a large 18mm diameter cast filler cap. All the markings were applied by transfer, except the lining on the Gondola car which was part of the tinplate printing, and the main markings on the Box car are known in silver-grey in addition to the normal white transfers. Two styles of the TTR transfers were used, the second differing from the first by the fact that the first T and the R were much smaller and less distinct, and the first transfers were 3.5mm high while the second were 3.0mm. The use of the second style corresponded approximately with the introduction of the diecast couplings.

THE PRE-WAR TTR BOGIE COACHES

Unlike the TTR 4-wheel wagons where the British superstructure was mounted on a chassis based on the Trix Express production, the construction of the first bogie coaches was completely new. Although they were not to scale length they were longer than their Trix Express counterparts and measured 168mm over the buffers. The chassis of these coaches was basically a platform with buffers at each end with the tinplate folded at the sides to form a continuous step. A 4-wheel bogie of similar construction to the later bogie wagons, but longer, was mounted at each end of the chassis using a shoe-lace eye rivet as a central pivot. Additional bogie side frame white-metal detailing 42mm long was added to each side of the tinplate assembly. Each cast coupling was located on the bogie assembly and kept central by a spring anchored at the bogie's rear. A slot in the shape of an arc was formed in the chassis frame to accommodate the top spigot of the cast coupling to eliminate fouling, modified during 1937 by removing the metal in front of the slot. Coach battery box detail was provided by separate tinplate pressings.

There were only two styles of body pressings, that used for the Brake 3rd coach and the other for the 1st class coach, the latter pressing also being used for the Dining/Restaurant cars and the later SR Solid 3rd coach. The glazing for the windows was provided by printed Celastoid strips attached to the inside of the body with tabs, the printing on the Celastoid taking the form of ventilation window detail. This detailing has not been found on Southern Railway coaches and was discontinued during 1937. The slide-on roofs were without any detail. The following is a list of coaches introduced in the latter part of 1936, except where stated, and produced until the end of 1939:

Cat. No. 2/560 LMS 1st Class coach LMS lake – coach number 7495 – yellow and black lining.

Cat. No. 4/560 LNER 1st Class coach Teak – coach number 1134 – black and white lining.

Cat. No. 5/560 SR 1st Class coach Dark green – coach number 12232 – yellow and black lining – introduced early 1937.

Cat. No. 2/570 LMS Brake 3rd LMS lake – coach number 5542 – yellow and black lining.

Cat. No. 4/570 LNER Brake 3rd Teak – coach number 1263 – black and white lining.

Cat. No. 5/570 SR Brake 3rd Dark green – coach number 11012 – yellow and black lining – introduced early 1937.

Cat. No. 2/580 LMS Dining car LMS lake – coach number 2074 – yellow and black lining.

Cat. No. 4/580 LNER Restaurant car Teak – coach number 1433 – black and white lining.

Cat. No. 5/580 SR Restaurant car Dark green –

coach number 7621 – yellow and black lining – introduced mid-1937.

Cat. No. 5/590 SR Solid 3rd class coach Dark green – coach number 10055 – introduced late 1937.

The shade of the Trix LMS lake varied considerably and was never quite correct, being nearer to a metallic red-brown than anything else. On the other hand the shade of the teak colour on the LNER coaches remained more or less constant. The plain roof of the LMS coach ranged from a blue-grey

LNER and LMS 4-wheel Suburban coaches.

Early and late pre-war LMS short bogie coaches.
The early coaches have printed Celastoid windows.

238

to a medium grey, whilst that of the LNER and SR coaches remained white. Apart from the chassis, dating of the coaches can be determined by examining the interior colour of the coach bodies including the Patent information stamped in white letters on the underside of the chassis. All LMS coaches fitted with printed Celastoid windows, but which do not have Patent information, have a brown interior and date from late 1936 to the middle of 1937. Similarly LNER coaches produced over the same period have an interior very close to the exterior teak colour. Early SR coaches had a brown interior until the middle of 1937, but Patent information was not given until about the same time, thus coaches exist with both Patent information and brown interiors.

From the middle of 1937 to the end of 1939 the interiors of the LMS, LNER and SR short bogie coaches were light brown, with all coaches carrying Patent information. There is an exception to the rule, however, in that between 1938 and the end of the pre-war period, LMS coaches are known to exist with a white interior and SR coaches with a dark cream interior.

To complement the LMS 'Princess' and LNER 'Scotsman' Pacific locomotives in 1938, scale-length coaches were introduced their construction based on the Trix Express scale-length coaches introduced the year previously. The bogie assemblies, although using the same method of pivoting and insulation, were far more robust than their Trix Express counterparts. Each bogie side-frame detail was formed from a separate white metal diecasting, and the diecast couplings were held in place on the integral swivelling buffer beam and ribbed main frame by a rectangular 'U' piece. The turned buffers

LNER and SR short bogie coaches.
Note the early LNER Restaurant car on the left.

239

Pre-war scale
length LNER
coaches. Notice the
Uncoupling Striker
fitted to the right
hand coupling
on the 1st class
coach.

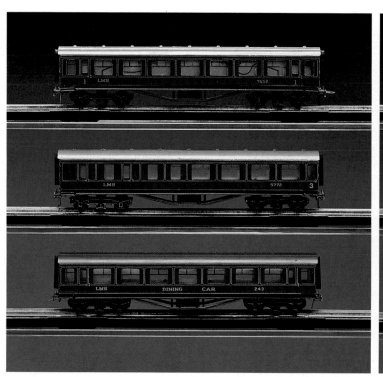

Pre-war scale -
length LMS
coaches.

on the early scale coaches were 7mm long, whilst those on coaches produced in 1939 were 6mm long and not as heavy in their appearance. The length of the early coaches over the buffers was 230mm. The battery box detail in the centre of the chassis was formed from a single stamping, unlike the short bogie coaches which utilised a separate stamping for each side, held in place by the body tabs.

The construction of the body was uncomplicated with the printed Celastoid window glazing held in place by long body tabs, and the side body panels were kept rigid at the top by four insulated spacers which were used as mounts for a lighting unit when

fitted. The white paper on the floor of the coaches acted as a reflector for the lighting unit as did the off-white/cream interior body finish. The coaches were fitted at each end with a black formed tinplate pressing representing a corridor connection which framed the printed Patent information. The roof, which was a clip fit onto the body, had nine small embossed equally-spaced ventilators. As in the case of the short bogie coaches, initially only two patterns of body stamping were used, that for the Brake 3rd type of coach and the other which was used for the 1st class and Restaurant/Dining cars.

The following is a list of scale model coaches

available in 1938 which were first shown in the TTR 1938/39 catalogue. Note the mock-up pictures of the LMS coaches without corridor connections as shown in the catalogues, which were never produced in this form:

Cat. No. 2/567 LMS 1st Class coach LMS lake – coach number 7652 – grey roof.

Cat. No. 4/567 LNER 1st Class coach Teak – coach number 31876 – white roof.

Cat. No. 2/577 LMS Brake 3rd LMS lake – coach number 5772 – grey roof.

Cat. No. 4/577 LNER Brake 3rd Teak – coach number 4942 – white roof.

240

Cat. No. 2/587 LMS Dining car LMS lake – coach number 243 – grey roof.

Cat. No. 4/587 LNER Restaurant car Teak – coach number 3587 – white roof.

The notes regarding the LMS lake finish on the short bogie coaches also applies in the case of the above scale LMS coaches. Unlike the smaller bogie coaches the shade of the teak finish on the LNER coaches varied. A Lighting Unit, Cat. No. 767, was available for these and subsequent scale-length coaches and, located on the centre of two insulated body spacers, it was connected to the two bogies in the same fashion as that used on the Trix Express

coaches. The current pick-up for the lighting unit was via the two diecast mazak wheels on one bogie, and the Trix Express type of roller pick-up located around the central latitudinal bogie pivot bar on the other. The blade providing the springing for this roller pick-up was fitted as standard to the coaches and held in place on the frame of the bogie by a 10BA screw and washer.

By 1939 certain modifications were being introduced to improve the general characteristics of the coaches. These included the addition of a slotted frame at each end of the coach which fitted over the bogie support frame restricting the angular

movement of the bogie, plus the addition of a plate located in slots in the 'front' buffer beam which stopped the link of the cast coupling lifting too high during the coupling operation. These special buffer-beam plates were never fitted to the 'rear' of the coach which was reserved for the uncoupler striker assembly. With regard to the above improvements, the author has yet to find them incorporated in the pre-war LNER coaches. The centre current pick-up assembly for the coach lighting unit now incorporated a cylinder riveted at one end of the sprung blade instead of the loose roller assembly, the latter having a habit of working free from its mount and falling off in a place where it could not be found !

All these modification found their way onto the new scale-length coaches introduced during the latter part of 1939. To complement the LMS 'Coronation' Pacific locomotive, the 1st class and Brake 3rd pattern coaches were finished in the style of the distinctive livery applied to the locomotive and tender. Although the tinplate stamping for the 1st class coach sides was unaltered, the second (medium) and third (small) windows at the guard's end of the Brake 3rd were not formed leaving only eight windows on each side. Again the comments concerning the shade of LMS lake used on the short bogie coaches apply here, but generally only to those coaches that were supplied with the 'Coronation' Presentation Set, as most of the 'Coronation' coaches available separately were of a much darker shade much nearer to reality. One cannot say that the latter coaches were maroon in colour, as there is no evidence that the LMS ever officially used maroon for their stock in the pre-war period, and thus there was no need for Trix Ltd to think otherwise. Both 1st and Brake 3rd coaches were lined in a dull

TTR Lighting Unit for coaches, Cat.No.767. (A)

golden-yellow with the lining on the darker-liveried coaches being closer to a bright yellow. Each coach bore the words 'THE CORONATION SCOT' and the LMS circular crest. The grey roofs were as the normal LMS scale coaches, while the interiors were finished in a dark cream colour. The centre portion of the chassis deviated from the normal pattern by having a formed 'skirt' fitted in place of the battery box detail. It was on the underside of this that Patent information was printed instead of incorporating it in the end panel printing. The 'Coronation' 1st class coach was given the catalogue number 2/568 and carried the number 56001, whilst that of the Brake 3rd was 2/578 and carried the number 56501.

Probably the most striking of the pre-war TTR scale coaches was the Pullman Car Saloon, Cat.No.598. This coach, along with the 'Coronation' coaches, was one of only a few items advertised as being available during the autumn of 1939 that actually made it to the shops before the war spoilt the programme. The pattern of the body was completely different from the other standard TTR scale coaches and captured the grandeur of the prototype completely with recessed end doors containing the characteristic oval windows and wire handrails, plus a white roof with elliptical ends. The livery was dark brown and yellow with the various decorative markings in gold, including the name PULLMAN above the windows and a panel containing the name TRIX TWIN below the windows. This latter panel was the only serious deviation from the prototype which normally carried a classical name. The interior of the body was finished as per the 'Coronation' coaches in dark cream, but the printed markings on the Celastoid

'Coronation Scot' coaches. Note the later darker versions. Bottom row - the pre-war Pullman coach.

glazing were different in the way the ventilator windows were portrayed. The centre panel on the underside of the chassis was again different from any of the previous coaches and was used to display the Patent information not included on the coach end panels as on the standard LMS and LNER scale coaches.

What a pity that the proposed SR 1st class, Cat. No. 5/567, and the Brake 3rd Cat.No.5/577, scale-length coaches, advertised along with the Pullman coach as being available during the autumn of 1939, were never produced. These would have made handsome models in the rich green livery of the Southern Railway, but the greater war needs of the nation took precedent.

General Trix Twin Railway wagon and coach chassis. From the top and left: 1938 American wagon chassis; Standard short wheel-base chassis; Short bogie coach chassis; Scale-length coach chassis with 1939 style lighting current pick-up assembly; Scale-length coach chassis fitted with post-war lighting current pick-up; Trix Express 1938 scale-length coach chassis fitted with loose roller type of lighting current pick-up.

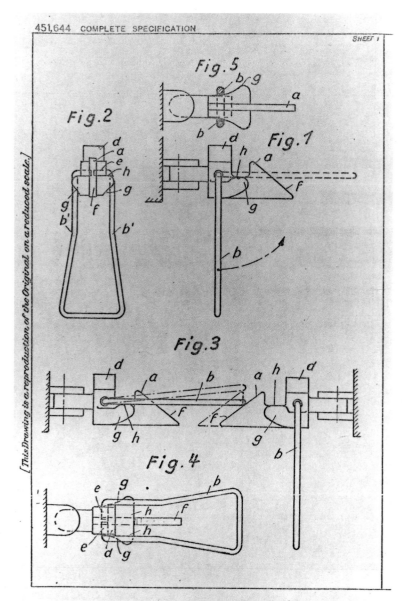

Extract from British Patent Specification 451,644 showing the idea of the early Trix pre-war coupling.

1935/36 Trix Express/TTR diecast coupling.

1936/37 Trix Express/TTR diecast coupling.

1937/38 Trix Express/TTR tinplate coupling. This coupling continued to be used on selected TTR and Trix Express locomotives up to 1948 and 1954 respectively.

TTR diecast coupling from 1938.

TTR diecast coupling as used from 1938 fitted with uncoupler striker link from Uncoupler Set Cat. No. 31/90.

'Coronation' coach fitted with link movement restrictor plate.

1939/40 Trix Express coupling. This type of diecast coupling continued to be used after the war until 1961.

TTR tinplate coupling used from 1948 up to and including 1959.

1948 LNER scale coach with the coupling loosely riveted to the holder. On later scale coaches the coupling was fitted to a shouldered shaft. Note the slots remaining in the buffer beam for the now redundant restrictor plate.

1949 Trix Express coupling to a TTR pattern for the American market during the joint Trix Express/TTR promotion.

Tinplate coupling used from 1960 to 1964 inclusive.

Plastic coupling used from 1965 including the Liliput (UK) range.

THE EARLY POST-WAR ROLLING STOCK
(Excluding scale-length coaches and American rolling stock)

The few wagons and coaches that were produced in the period from 1946 up to the introduction of the new coupling in 1948 were built on the pre-war style chassis incorporating the diecast coupling and link. On the goods wagons the only way of distinguishing pre-war and post-war, except with the tank wagon, is to examine the coupling channel which has a high gloss finish and much sharper bends in the metal. This applies to the long and short wagon chassis. It is not certain how many different goods wagons were produced using the pre-war style of chassis, but the author remembers receiving an LMS Goods Set for Christmas 1947 comprising goods engine and tender, LMS brown Goods Brake van, three red Shell tank wagons, all with the diecast couplings, plus the new British Controller. Patent information was no longer applied to the underneath of rolling stock in the post-war period.

These Shell tank wagons were different from the pre-war pattern as the ladder and platform assembly was no longer available from Nuremberg. Tank wagons were a popular and attractive item and so it was in the interest of Trix Ltd to design tooling to enable a suitable ladder to be produced. This was duly carried out, and a curved ladder was fitted to one side of the tank using new slots in the tank body and an existing slot on the platform of the chassis. The red filler cap remained the same as that used just before the war and was to be used on all subsequent 4-wheel tinplate tank wagons.

A small quantity of short bogie coaches were available in LMS and LNER livery, and even fewer in SR livery, finished in the style of the pre-war versions with diecast couplings and wire links. These were intended for export only although a few of the LMS and LNER coaches found their way onto the home market. Three versions of each livery were available, 1st class, Brake 3rd and Restaurant/Dining car. The Solid 3rd class coach of the Southern Railway was not produced.

The post-war versions can be distinguished from those produced pre-war from observing the following:

The chassis of each coach carries no Patent number information and the buffer head diameters are 4.4mm as against 4.8mm as used on pre-war chassis, both figures are approximate and apply also to the wagon chassis. The lining on the post-war LNER coaches is off-white although there is no change in the shade of the Teak colour. The livery of the LMS coach is almost brown with a dark brown interior and yellow, black and 'green' lining. The 'green' colour is formed by the yellow lining being printed over the black lining which from a distance looks as though the coaches had been lined in green. There was no change in the catalogue numbers.

To compliment the green TRIX TWIN demonstration 0-4-0 passenger engine and tender, a set of three coaches was produced. These were finished in a similar green with a single dark grey line along the underneath of the windows. The chassis was the

Post-war LMS short bogie coaches. The earlier coaches in an almost brown livery are on the left and note the pre-war style coupling on the Brake 3rd.

The post-war TTR tinplate wagon chassis. Top left: pre-1948. Top right: converted pre-1948 chassis to new coupling. Bottom left: 1948/1950. Bottom right: post-1950.

The post-war TTR tinplate short bogie coach chassis. Centre: pre-war style bogie with new coupling riveted to the coupling pivot plate. Left: early short coupling assembly with no embossed rib. Right: later coupling assembly with embossed rib generally used from 1950.

same as used for normal production, and the pattern of the body was the same as the standard LMS/LNER/SR 1st class coach. The roofs were painted grey and the body interior matched the exterior green. The position of the end doors and associated handles was marked with thin black lines, and the class of the coach was indicated at each end using silver-white number transfers. Three classes were produced, 1st, 2nd and 3rd all with a TTR transfer in the middle of each side. This transfer was white and the same pattern as used on the later pre-war American wagons, in other words 3.0mm high. These coaches can also be found with a later chassis fitted with the redesigned coupling introduced in 1948, but have never been seen in the shape of a Brake 3rd coach. As these coaches were not normal production models, no catalogue number exists.

By the end of 1948 most of the rolling stock was fitted with the new coupling as mentioned in the chapter dealing with the early post-war history. On the long and short pre-war style wagon chassis, the mounting arm of the new coupling was reduced in width and loosely riveted to the central channel using the tooling holes on the channel of the long

chassis and new holes provided on the short chassis channel, the rivet acting as a pivot. On the short bogie coaches and bogie wagons, including the American wagons, the new coupling was riveted to the former diecast coupling mount, some retaining the pivot hole for this coupling, others not. All the catalogue numbers of rolling stock fitted with these

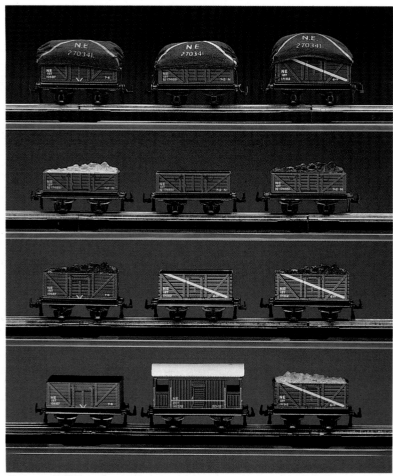

Post-war LNER goods wagons.

Post-war LMS wagons.

he TTR post-war bogie wagon chassis. From left to right: coupling riveted to pre-war tyle coupling mount; new style coupling ssembly; TTR MADE IN ENGLAND amped in chassis; pre-war coupling spring ook at the rear of the bogie removed; o bogie spring hook or chassis inscription.

Top row: Post-war TTR demonstration coaches. Second and third rows: circa 1948, coaches intended for the Swiss or Belgian market to compliment the 'Continental' outline locomotives introduced in the TTR export catalogues at the same time.

'new uncoupler couplings' for use with the new uncoupler rail, were given the suffix 'U' but by 1950 this suffix had been dropped. Only the 1948/49 domestic and export catalogues listed rolling stock with 'U' numbers.

By 1950 all wagon and short bogie coach chassis were modified to take a new mounting assembly for the new coupling which was first introduced mainly on the short bogie coaches. However, it also appeared on some 0-4-0 locomotive tender

chassis. The initial assembly took the form of a shortened version of the open ended wagon channel to which the coupling was riveted, and in turn this was tabbed to the basically unchanged bogie chassis. This tended to give the couplings too much vertical freedom, as the couplings on the wagons, necessitating a further modification to the rolling stock for efficient operation.

The buffer beams of the long and short wagon chassis pressings were altered so that when the short

channel assembly, complete with coupling, was tabbed to the chassis only a narrow slot remained through which the coupling passed. The channels now incorporated an internal embossed rib allowing the coupling to pivot more smoothly. Similarly coach and large wagon bogie frames were altered to give a resultant narrow slot for the coupling. It is strange that the short wagon chassis retained the fixing pin holes for the wood load on the timber wagon almost until the BR wagon days.

Among the first short bogie coaches to be fitted with these modifications were the green TTR demonstration coaches introduced earlier and described above along with coaches finished in exactly the same livery, only this time with a black-edged white square in place of the TTR transfer with the names PARIS-STRASBOURG-BASLE-ZURICH inscribed. These coaches were produced concurrently with the introduction of the 'continental'-outline 0-4-0 locomotives in 1948/49 but were never listed in any known literature and only produced for a very short time, hence no catalogue number is available. They were introduced to complement the 0-4-0 Electric loco Cat. No. 20/55.SL intended for the Swiss market and the German-outline steam locos intended mainly for the Belgian market. One must bear mind that cooperation with the Trix company in Nuremberg was once again taking place. Coaches are also known to exist with TTR in the middle of each side together with panels containing PARIS-STRASBOURG-BASLE-ZURICH at each end of both sides of the coach. Why these coaches were produced in this way is a mystery.

Most of the pre-war wagon and short bogie coach designs were gradually phased out during 1950/51 in favour of BR liveries. It was at this time that the short and long wagon chassis underwent a further modification, this time in the shape of the axle-box stamping produced with clearer detail and the addition of small 'wings' at the base. A new buffer was also gradually introduced with a head diameter of 4.75mm, an increase of 0.35mm, and a length of 4.9mm, an increase of 1.1mm. This new buffer was far more realistic in appearance and was incorporated on all rolling stock where required with the

Post-war tank wagons and early bogie wagons. From the left:
Top row: Shell tank wagons with red and black filler caps; the very early version on the extreme left has pre-war type couplings.
Second row: Esso tank wagons with yellow and black filler caps plus early UD tank wagon.
Third row: UD tank wagon on late chassis with 'wings' on the axle box detail.
Fourth and fifth rows: early bogie wagons.

exception of the scale model coaches. During the latter part of the life of the LMS, LNER, SR and Private Owner wagons and during the introduction of the BR range, the tinplate printing took on a matt finish resulting in a less rich-looking colouring. However, the white lettering was much brighter than some of the earlier lettering which had a distinctly orange tinge. During 1950 the bakelite wheels of all rolling stock took on a slimmer appearance by reducing the flange width by 0.5mm, and the rolling diameter of the wheel by 0.4mm. Unfortunately the new wheel was not as immovable on the axle as its predecessor.

The following wagons were produced after the war with pre-war liveries (excluding the Crane Truck Set). The letters in brackets relate to notes following this list, and L/C and S/C denote long and short chassis respectively. The letter 'U' has been omitted from the catalogue numbers for clarity, and the date quoted for each wagon is the final year of production:

Cat. No.

600 LMS 3-plank wagon Brown – wagon number 472870 – L/C (A,B,C). 1951

2/601 LMS open low side Brown – wagon number 33550 – S/C (A,B,C). 1951

4/601 LNER open low side Red-oxide – wagon number 174651 – S/C (A,B,C). 1951

2/603 LMS open high side Brown – wagon number 604707 – S/C (A). 1948/49

2/603 LMS open high side loco Brown – wagon number 53084 – S/C (A,B). 1949/50

4/603 LNER open high side Grey – wagon number 10687 – S/C (A,B,C). 1951

4/603 LNER open high side Grey – wagon number 171312 – S/C (A,B,C). 1951

5/603 SR open high side Dark brown – wagon number 40037 – S/C (A,B,C). 1951

2/606 Coal load fitted to any of the above high side wagon, including the following Private Owner wagons. S/C Up to early 1954 depending upon wagon

607 Charingtons Private Owner wagon Red – wagon number 451 – S/C (A,B,C). Early 1954

607 Hinchliffes Private Owner wagon Red – wagon number 236 – S/C (A,B,C). Early 1954

608 Coal low side LMS Brown – wagon number 33550 – S/C (A,B,C,D). 1951

608 Coal low side LNER Red-oxide – wagon number 174651 – S/C (A,B,C,D). 1951

609 Ballast wagon Ballast load only known fitted to LMS and LNER low side wagons and LNER high side wagons. – S/C. Up to 1951

612 LMS Container wagon with Carter Paterson diecast container – LMS brown 3-plank wagon number 472870 –L/C (A,B,C). 1951

2/621 LMS Covered van Brown – white roof – van number 61253 – S/C (A,B,C). 1951

627 LMS Cattle truck Brown – white roof – wagon number 14549 – L/C (A,B). 1949/50

640 Esso tank wagon Yellow – yellow filler cap – L/C (A,J). 1948/49

640 Esso tank wagon Yellow – black filler cap – L/C (A,B,J). 1949/50

643 Shell tank wagon Red – red filler cap – L/C (A,J). 1948/49

643 Shell tank wagon Red – black filler cap – L/C (B,C,J). Early 1954)

645 UD tank wagon Green – black filler cap – L/C (B,C,J). Early 1951

2/650 LMS Goods Brake van Brown – grey roof – van number 730274 – L/C (A). 1948/49

2/650 LMS Goods Brake van Brown – white roof – van number 730274 – L/C (A,B,C). 1951

4/650 LNER Goods Brake van Red-oxide – white roof – van number 141578 – L/C (A,B,C). 1951

5/650 SR Goods Brake van Dark brown – van number 56130 – L/C (A,B,C). 1950

657 Timber wagon Black – L/C (A,H). 1950

660 Tarpaulin wagon Tarpaulin fitted to any LMS and LNER short chassis low or high side wagon except LMS LOCO and SR high side wagons (A,B,C with F or G). 1951

671 Bogie Bolster wagon Black – no number (H,K). 1948/49

671 Bogie Bolster wagon Black – no number (L,M). 1950

673 Bogie Timber wagon Black – no number – unpainted wood load representing 20 planks (H,K). 1948/49

673 Bogie Timber wagon Black – no number – unpainted wood load representing 20 planks (L.M). 1950

675 LNER Bogie Brick wagon Red-oxide – wagon number 163551 (K,L). 1950

676 LMS High Capacity bogie wagon Brown – wagon number 10468 (K,L). 1950

Notes relating to bracketed letters

(**A**) Central channel with new couplings.

(**B**) Two short channels with new coupling and pre-war style axle box stamping.

(**C**) Two short channels with new coupling and modified axle-box stamping with 'wings'.

(**D**) Cat.No.608 was a new catalogue number created for the low-side coal wagons.

(**E**) Cat.No.657. This timber wagon replaced the pre-war short chassis model. Mounted on the platform of the chassis were two pairs of stanchions, as used on the bogie timber wagons, to which the wood load was pinned. The unpainted wood load was grooved to represent 20 planks. This model was only produced for a short period.

(**F**) LMS tarpaulin of stitched black cotton with elasticated cotton or ordinary cotton ties. Diagonal lines, LMS and 304721 screen-printed in white.

(**G**) LNER tarpaulin. As the LMS tarpaulin above but with the letters NE and the number 270341.

(**H**) TTR Made in England stamped in white letters on the underneath of the chassis. The middle T of TTR was 6mm high. This may have been applied to more models than listed above.

(**J**) Ladder assembly without platform, large filler cap.

(**K**) Pre-war pattern bogie with new coupling.

(**L**) Modified bogie to take coupling with short channel.

(**M**) TTR Made in England applied by transfers. Small letters.

According to the 1948/49 British domestic TTR catalogue, the short bogie coaches, given the name 'Express Bogie Coaches', were available with the new coupling in LMS, LNER and SR liveries.

Post-war Private Owner and SR goods wagons.
The early versions are on the left. The Timber wagon, Cat.No.657, on a long wheel-base was only produced for a short period.

Post-war LNER short bogie coaches, gloss finish on the left and matt finish on the right.

Notes relating to bracketted letters
(**P**) Pre-war pattern bogie with new coupling. 1948/49
(**Q**) Plain short coupling channel fitted to pre-war pattern bogie frame. 1949
(**R**) Short coupling channel with embossed line fitted to modified bogie frame. 1949/50
The roofs of the LMS coaches were painted various shades of grey and those of the LNER coaches white. The interiors of the LMS coaches were dark brown whilst those of the LNER coaches almost matched the exterior teak finish. These coaches were no longer listed in the 1951 catalogue.

However, after exhaustive enquiries, it can be assumed that the short bogie coaches were not put into production with the new coupling in Southern Railway livery, even for export. If one looks carefully at the picture of a Southern Railway set in the general 1948 and 1950 export catalogues, it can be seen that the coaches shown have pre-war pattern diecast couplings. This is yet another example of the fact that what catalogues present should not always be taken as gospel.

At right is a list of short bogie coaches made prior to the change to British Railways livery. Letters in brackets refer to the bogie and coupling mount:

Cat. No.
2/560 LMS 1st class coach Brown – coach number 7495 (P,Q,R).
2/560 LMS 1st class coach Almost crimson lake – coach number 7495 (R).
4/560 LNER 1st class coach Teak, gloss finish – coach number 1134 (P,Q).
4/560 LNER 1st class coach Teak, matt finish – coach number 1134 (Q,R).
2/570 LMS Brake 3rd Brown – coach number 5542 (P,Q,R)
2/570 LMS Brake 3rd Almost crimson lake – coach number 5542 (R).
4/570 LNER Brake 3rd Teak, gloss finish – coach number 1263 (P,Q).
4/570 LNER Brake 3rd Teak, matt finish – coach number 1263 (Q,R).
2/580 LMS Dining car Brown – coach number 2074 (P,Q,R)
2/580 LMS Dining car Almost crimson lake – coach number 2074 (R).
4/580 LNER Restaurant car Teak, gloss finish – coach number 1433 (P,Q).
4/580 LNER Restaurant car Teak, matt finish – coach number 1433 (Q,R).

THE BRITISH RAILWAYS RANGE OF TINPLATE WAGONS

During 1950/51 the BR range of tinplate 4-wheel and bogie wagons were being introduced. The basic shape of the body and chassis for each type of wagon was the same as used on the preceding range with the numbers and design letters also in white. Each wagon, where applicable, was lined in black and grey, and Patent information was once more incorporated in the tinplate printing of which most of the 4-wheel wagons bore the inscription:

'TTR Brit. Pat. 465168
Pat. Pendg.
Made in England'

The Cattle truck and 3-plank wagons bore the inscription:

'TTR Patents Pending
Made in England'

The bogie wagons were inscribed:
'TTR British Patents
451644   471304
Made in England'

The aluminium-coloured Esso and Shell tank wagons just carried the words:
'TTR Patents
Made in England'

During the autumn of 1952 the bogie wagons started to appear with 'TTR Made in England' stamped on the underside of the chassis frame, a practice which was to continue until 1959.

BR goods wagons on tinplate chassis.

The BR range comprised:

Cat. No.

600   **3-Plank wagon** Light grey – wagon number 481760.

600   **3-Plank wagon** Red-brown – wagon number 481760.

600   **3-Plank wagon** Light grey – wagon number 49736. This wagon uses the body of the Crane Set match truck – only a few were produced.

1/601 **Open low-side wagon** Red-brown – wagon number 183724.

1/603 **Open high-side wagon** Light grey with short white diagonal strip – wagon number 168732.

1/603 **Open high-side wagon** Light grey – wagon number 12738.

606   **Coal wagon, high side** – Both high-side wagons numbered 168732 and 12738 respectively.

608   **Coal wagon, low side** Red-brown – wagon number 183724.

609   **Ballast wagon** Both high-side wagons 168723 and 12738 and low-side wagon, number 183724, were used.

612   **Container wagon** Light grey 3-plank wagon number 481760 with diecast Carter Paterson container.

612   **Container wagon** Red-brown 3-plank wagon number 481760 with diecast Carter Patersoncontainer.

627   **Cattle truck** Red-brown, white roof – truck number 15263. This truck was produced with a white roof during 1950/51 only and issued in an LMS box.

627   **Cattle truck** Red-brown, grey roof – truck number 14263.

627   **Cattle truck** Light grey, grey roof – truck number 14263.

640   **Esso tank wagon** Aluminium – two red, white and blue Esso symbols on each side of tank, other markings in yellow and black, tank number 1591, black filler cap, produced up to 1953.

640   **Esso tank wagon** As above but tank number 2591 – produced early 1953.

643   **Shell tank wagon** Aluminium – red Shell letters plus other yellow and black markings.

1/650 **Goods Brake van** Light grey, grey roof – van number 743126.

1/650 **Goods Brake van** Red-brown, grey roof – van number 743126.

660   **Tarpaulin wagon** Light grey high-side wagons numbered 168723 and 12738 plus red-brown low-side wagon number 183724 used. Tarpaulin numbers: 278304, 287430, 317420, 317521 and 321704. The figures on the tarpaulin 317521 are in the style as used on the LMS and LNER tarpaulins, whilst the others have a 'type written' style.

675   **Bogie Brick wagon** Red-brown – wagon number 164132. The early post-war pattern of bogie stamping used on this wagon continued in use until 1953. (See following list for continuation of this model).

676   **High Capacity bogie wagon** Light grey – wagon number 12640. The above notes also apply to this wagon.

In 1953 the prefix 1/ was omitted from the wagon catalogue numbers. Production of the above listed 4-wheel models ceased during the early part of 1954 with the exception of the 3-Plank wagon and its derivative, the Container wagon, which continued to be produced well into 1955. 1953 also the introductions of plastic-moulded spoked wheels, which were an even worse fit on the axles than the previous ones and caused eventual operational problems as they had a tendency to slide along the axle. The coal and ballast mouldings were of the same pattern as used for the previous railway company wagons until late in 1953 when they were changed for a much flatter version with less coarse 'lumps'.

It was unfortunate that the 4-wheel wagons still retained a toy-like appearance, and in the latter part of 1952 the design team endeavoured to make them more acceptable to the increasingly critical public. The result of their deliberations was that both the long and short tinplate 4-wheel chassis were replaced by highly detailed mazak diecast chassis during 1954. The design of these was very similar to those produced for the Operating Dump wagon and the Lighted Goods Brake van introduced during 1953. For a very short period in 1953 (unannounced), the tinplate bodies from the 4-wheel wagons listed above were fitted to an early version of these new chassis with open fret axle box detail, a main frame depth of 0.25" (6.35mm) and a measurement of 0.141" (3.58mm) from the centre line of the axle to the bottom of the axle box, which made the bottom of the axle box very close to the level of the rails. It was intended to incorporate tinplate stampings riveted to the underside of the chassis to represent brake detail, but unfortunately the tooling was not ready in time to allow production of this detail to be fitted to these wagons. The coupling and axle assembly at each end of the wagon were held in place by a specially-shaped long screw which also allowed the axle to 'float'.

It was only a few months after the introduction of the wagons with the new diecast chassis that Trix Ltd felt a need to modify their design which incorporated a reduction in the main frame depth of 0.04", (1.02mm). The axle centre height to base of

BR goods wagons on tinplate chassis. Note the two different numbers on the Esso tank wagons.

BR goods wagons on the diecast chassis introduced in 1954. Note the two shades of grey plastic on the centre and right three-plank wagons on the top row. Note also the early deep chassis on the left wagon row two, centre wagon row three, and the Goods Brake to the left of row four.

axle box dimension was also reduced by the same amount, and the axle box fret was filled in, plus other minor alterations. This modification can be easily spotted as the earlier chassis had vertical rows of three rivets, whilst the later one has vertical rows of only two. These modifications were incorporated in the general release of the wagons in the latter part of 1954, but problems still existed with the production of the tinplate brake detail for the long chassis, and for a while it was omitted from these wagons. (Occasionally one can also find modified short chassis without brake detail). The factory at Northampton must have had a slight problem with quality control, as this brake-detail stamping is found bent in two ways in which one is the mirror image of the other, with the result that some brake details fitted to wagons seem back to front with reference to other wagons.

1954 also saw the introduction of the Patent number 605283 stamped into the metal of all the couplings, this being one of the requisites of the agreement which allowed Trix to continue its manufacture.

For some unexplained reason the Bogie Bolster wagon, Cat. No. 671, and the Bogie Timber wagon, Cat. No. 673, disappeared from the lists from 1951 until 1953 when they reappeared, although the American Lumber Cars using the same chassis continued to be manufactured during this period. The reappearance of the Bogie Bolster and Bogie Timber wagons coincided with the introduction of the diecast Weltrol wagons (see later section for description), which was fitted with a modified bogie frame. So that the bogie frame used on previous wagons could be used on the Weltrol wagon, the rear edge of the frame was rounded thereby removing the spring anchor tab used on pre-war models. This modified frame was used on all subsequent bogie wagons.

Below is a list of the BR tinplate 4-wheel wagons with a diecast chassis introduced during 1954 and the post-1953 BR tinplate bogie wagons. The date at the end of each description denotes the final year of production:

Cat. No.

630 Open wagon 3-plank Light grey – wagon number 481760 – not introduced until 1955. 1959

630 Open wagon 3-plank Light grey plastic body – wagon number B457434. This body was fitted to this type of chassis in 1959 prior to its use with a new range introduced in 1960 using plastic wagon bodies fitted to a diecast chassis of new design. 1960

630 Open wagon 3-plank As above but in medium grey. 1960

632 Open wagon low side Red-brown – wagon number 183724. 1960

634 Open wagon high side Light grey – wagon number 12738. 1959

634 Open wagon high side Light grey – wagon number 168732. 1959

636 Cattle wagon Red-brown, grey roof – wagon number 15263. 1960

637 Coal wagon Coal load fitted to high side light grey wagons 12738 and 168732. 1959

638 Ballast wagon Ballast load fitted to above high-side wagons plus red-brown low side wagon number 183724. 1959

639 Container wagon with Carter Paterson container 3-plank Light grey wagon number 481760. Not introduced until 1955. 1959

641 Esso Tank wagon Aluminium – tank number 2591. 1959

644 Shell Tank wagon Aluminium. 1959

646 Shell Tank wagon Red. Not introduced until 1957. 1960

651 Goods Brake van Light grey, grey roof – van number 743126 – brake detail not fitted to this model. 1959

651 Goods Brake van Red-brown, grey roof – van number 743126 – brake detail not fitted to this model. 1959

662 Tarpaulin wagon Tarpaulin fitted to high-side light grey wagons 12738 and 168732 plus red-brown low-side wagon number 183724 – tarpaulin numbers 278304, 287430, 317420 and 321704. 1960

671 Bogie Bolster wagon Black – wagon numbers 46713 and 58209. 1959

671 Bogie Bolster wagon Black – wagon number 59382. This wagon is known with and without a block of 'inscriptions' in the centre and also 'inscriptions' right of centre on each side of the wagon. 1959

671 Bogie Bolster wagon Black – embossed detail on wagon sides – no number. Introduced 1959 and catalogue number changed to 1671 in 1963. 1963

673 Bogie Timber wagon Black – wagon numbers 46713, 58209 and 59382 – wood load has 20 planks and is unpainted. Comments regarding the Bolster wagon number 59382 also apply here. 1959

673 Bogie Timber wagon Black – embossed detail on wagon sides – no number. Introduced 1959 and catalogue number changed to 1673 in 1963. 1963

675 Bogie Brick wagon Red-brown – wagon number 164132. 1960

676 High Capacity Bogie wagon Light grey (shades) – wagon number 12640. 1959

Large quantities of the Open 3-plank wagon with a grey plastic body, Cat. No. 630, were produced and a surplus was carried well into British Trix Ltd days. This resulted in the wagon being issued in a red and green box in the early part of 1963 bearing catalogue number 602, (plus 603 with Trestle and Plate), and later a red and blue box with catalogue number 1602 on the end flap. Only coarse Trix wheels were fitted to this wagon together with the older style coupling. It must be noted here that the position of the fixing lugs on the body had to be altered for the later series of diecast chassis.

In early 1957 the diecast wagon chassis were altered to give better running. This alteration took the form of a reduction in the diameter of the axle ends which located in the bearing slots of the chassis. To eliminate excessive sideways movement of the axle, the bearing slot in the chassis was reduced in width. In 1958 the white metal axle box casting on the bogie wagons was replaced with a plastic moulding.

1957 also saw the introduction of the Cadet sets. The wagons included in the Goods Sets were completely tinplate using the tinplate chassis as used on the original BR wagon series. However, the slots in which the axles ran were suitably punched to take the new reduced axle end diameters. Unfortunately these chassis looked very crude as there were no axle-box stampings fitted to give a small amount of authenticity to the appearance. No catalogue

Bogie Bolster wagons and special wagons on the 1954 style diecast chassis.
Top row left: Note the embossed chassis detail on this 1959 version.
Third row left: Note the deep early chassis on the Esso tank wagon.

A selection of the tinplate wagons without axle box detail included with the Cadet sets, plus a privately produced wagon celebrating the 50 years of Trix between 1935 and 1985.

numbers were ever published for these wagons, and the following is a list of the types known to exist:

BR 3-plank wagon Light grey – wagon number 481760.

BR Goods Brake van Red-brown, grey roof – van number 743126.

BR Open wagon high side Light grey – wagon number 168732.

Esso Tank wagon Aluminium – tank number 2591.

Shell Tank wagon Aluminium.

Shell Tank wagon Red.

These wagons were only supplied with the Cadet sets and were not available separately. The Cadet sets continued until 1961.

Fry's Diecastings Ltd were the company responsible for producing the diecast wagon chassis, for which they received their first order in October 1952. After a short gap, orders were again received in January 1954, and by the time the last order had been executed in the winter of 1957, 88,800 long and 47,000 short chassis diecastings had been supplied to Trix Ltd.

Using the same short diecast chassis as the BR open wagons, the Shunter's Truck, Cat. No. 620, was produced in 1958 and usually supplied with the 'Ruston Hornsby' Diesel Shunter, Cat. No. 244, although it was available and listed separately. The chassis was modified to take a grey plastic moulded platform and tool box assembly, plus a tinplate running board in place of the usual brake detail. In 1960 it received the new coupling and scale wheels. The Shunter's Truck remained in the official Trix literature up to and including the 1965 price list having received a new catalogue number of 1620 in 1963.

THE FULLY DIECAST WAGONS

At the same time that the tinplate wagons with diecast chassis were being developed, three basic fully diecast models were also being designed. These included a well trolley wagon or Weltrol as it became known, a lighted Goods Brake van and an Operating Dump wagon, the latter primarily for use with an Elevator Conveyor described in the later chapter dealing with accessories.

The main body of the Weltrol wagon was a highly-detailed magnesium alloy diecasting produced for Trix Ltd by Fry's Diecastings Ltd who received their first order in October 1952 for 10,000 wagon bodies. The wagon was to prove a popular model as a little over 89,000 wagon bodies were supplied by the diecasters up to the completion of the last order in 1961. The Weltrol wagon, along with the Operating Dump wagon and associated equipment, formed part of the marketing cooperation between the German and British Trix companies. As a result the Weltrol models were listed in the British catalogues from 1953 up to and including 1965, and in the Trix Express catalogues from 1953 until 1961, the latter showing models suitably modified for the German coupling system.

The bogie assemblies used on the Weltrol wagons were exactly the same as used on the tinplate bogie wagons produced during the same period, with the exception that for the German market a Trix Express coupling assembly was provided and fitted by the Nuremberg factory, including slightly larger diameter Trix Express wheels with reduced diameter axle ends. The body of the tinplate frame for these bogies was normally rounded on the rear edge, but it is known that an earlier pattern was used containing

A leaflet included with the Spring 1953 *TTR Gazette* showing the new 'Well Trolley Wagons'. Note the real block of granite and a pre-production boiler which is shorter than the production version.

a coupling spring anchor bent to miss the body of the Weltrol. Initially the main body of the wagon was matt grey, but in 1954 this changed to matt black with the grey wagon gradually being phased out over the same year. Over this initial period the cut-away at each end of the body in which the coupling swung, had a large back taper (15.24mm opening to 18.24mm). On subsequent models this back taper was almost non-existent. As a general rule the turned buffers were screwed into the buffer beam on the early grey Weltrols, while on all later versions they were a press fit into the buffer beam.

The Weltrols were available with various loads with the first Weltrol advertisement in spring 1953 showing three models. One was an unloaded version, one had a Marine Boiler and the other was loaded with a Granite Block. It was a long time after this advertisement that the Granite Block load actually appeared on a actual wagon. In fact it was not until 1960 that it was on sale, and it is known that Siegfried Kahn was never happy with the design of the block and thus the idea was put to one side until long after he had severed his ties with the Trix company. Exhibition and promotional models of the Weltrol wagon with granite Block were actually fitted with a piece of real Granite which is somewhat different from the eventual production load made from a moulded block of plastic.

General changes and modifications followed the rest of the Trix bogie wagon rolling stock, including

Weltrol wagons. From the top and left: Cat.Nos. P674, 680 (black), 680 (grey), 680 (late version), 20/93C, 1679, 20/93T (1953 version), 679, 678, 677 (yellow letters and numbers).

plastic axle-box mouldings in 1958, and scale running plastic wheels and a modified coupling in 1960 on the British versions indicated by the use of the prefix letter 'P' in the catalogue number. The modification to the coupling was the removal of the vertical hook which had enabled pre-war style couplings to be used with its modern counterpart.

Below is a list of the Weltrol wagons produced. All wagons carried the inscription 41900 WELTROL WH 45T in white unless otherwise stated. The catalogue numbers with the prefix 20/ were modified for the German Trix system and listed in the Trix Express catalogues. The dates in brackets are inclusive years of production:

Although the basic British Weltrol catalogue numbers were prefixed with the letter 'P' in 1960, it was not long before the 'P' was replaced by the figure '1' towards the latter months of 1963 giving a four-figure catalogue number. However, for a brief period at the beginning of 1963, the catalogue numbers reverted to a three digit figure as Trix Products Ltd dropped the prefix letter 'P'.

Cat.No.

P674 **Weltrol with Granite Block** Black – introduced in 1960. (1960 to 1963)

677 **Weltrol unloaded** Light grey – large back taper in buffer beam cut-aways. (1953 to 1954)

20/93 As above but for Trix Express operation. (1953 to 1954)

677 **Weltrol unloaded** Black – known with orange or white letters and figures – large back taper in buffer beam cut-aways. (1954 only)

20/93 As above but for Trix Express operation. (1954 only)

677 **Weltrol** Unloaded – black – introduced in 1955. (1955 to 1965)

20/93 As above but for Trix Express operation – catalogue number changed to 488 in 1959. (1955 to 1961)

678 **Weltrol with Marine Boiler (Cat. No. 878)** Light grey – large back taper in buffer beam cut-aways. (1953 to 1954)

20/93K As above but for Trix Express operation. (1953 to 1954)

678 **Weltrol with Marine Boiler (Cat. No. 878)** Black – Weltrol as produced in 1954 only. (1954 only)

20/93K As above but for Trix Express operation. (1954 only)

678 **Weltrol with Marine Boiler(Cat. No.878)** Black – Weltrol as produced from 1955. (1955 to 1965)

20/93K As above but for Trix Express operation Catalogue number changed to 489 in 1959. (1955 to 1961)

20/93T **Weltrol with Transformer (Cat.No.879)** Grey – large back taper in buffer beam cut-aways. Known with TRIX EXPRESS GERMANY transfer applied to the underside of the wagon. (1953 to 1954)

679 **Weltrol with Transformer (Cat.No.879)** Black – Weltrol as produced in 1954 only. (1954 only)

20/93T As above but for Trix Express operation. (1954 only)

679 **Weltrol with Transformer (Cat.No.879)** Black – Weltrol as produced from 1955. (1955 to 1960)

20/93T As above but for Trix Express operation. (1955 to 1957)

1679 **Weltrol with Siemens Transformer** Black – introduced in 1963. Transformer supplied by the Nuremberg factory. (1963 to 1965)

680 **Weltrol with BICC Cable Drum (Cat.No.880)** Light grey – large back taper in buffer beam cut-aways. (1953 to 1954)

20/93C **Wetrol with Siemens Cable Drum** Basic wagon as above but for Trix Express operation. (1954 only)

680 **Weltrol with BICC Cable Drum (Cat.No.880)** Black – Weltrol as produced in 1954 only. (1954 only)

20/93C **Weltrol with Siemens Cable Drum** Basic wagon as above, but for Trix Express operation. (1954 only)

680 **Weltrol with BICC Cable Drum (Cat.No.880)** Black – Weltrol as produced from 1955. (1955 to 1965)

20/93C **Weltrol with Siemens Cable Drum** Basic wagon as above but for Trix Express operation. Catalogue number changed to 490 in 1959. (1955 to 1961)

A pre-production
demonstration version
of the diecast
Lighted Goods
Brake.

From 1954 some of the loads for the Weltrol wagons were available separately and were catalogued accordingly. Changes in the method of production were evident of which the main alterations are included in the following list. Dates in brackets refer to last listing in the official price lists or last year of use on the Weltrol wagons:

Cat. No.

878 Marine Boiler Red plastic and tinplate construction - located on Weltrol using two brown (shades)or from white (circa 1960) plastic chocks and secured with twisted wires. The plastic boiler ends were initially moulded from brown (occasionally green or white) plastic and sprayed a similar red to the tinplate part of the boiler. In circa 1960 a self-coloured red plastic was used for these boiler ends. (1962)

879 Heavy Duty Transformer Dark grey plastic moulding (shades) with three brown 'insulators' produced from1953 for and by the Nuremberg factory but supplied to Northampton from 1954 fitted with white moulded 'insulators'. The brown ones were initially taken from the Trix Express pantograph assemblies fitted to the Electric locomotive models. The transfer moulding clipped into place on the Weltrol body. (1962)

'Siemens' Heavy Duty Transformer Cream and dark brown plastic moulding - Produced by and supplied by Trix Express - not available as a separate item. Applied in Britain on Weltrol Cat. No. 1679 only - located on Weltrol using two screws through the wagon body. (1963-1965)

880 'British Insulated Callender's Cables Limited' Cable Drum Diecast outer shell with plastic moulded faces - yellow-ochre outer, black end faces with white letters - cradle brown (shades) - secured on Weltrol using red chord and twisted wire. (circa 1960)

'Siemens' Cable Drum Details as above but end faces moulded with the name and symbols of 'Siemens' for use on Weltrol Cat.No.20/93C - although produced by TTR, not available as a separate item. The letters TTR are moulded onto the inside faces of the mouldings. (circa 1960)

880 'British Insulated Callender's Cables Limited' Cable Drum White plastic outer shell and cradle - secured to Weltrol with twisted wire only - other details as diecast version. (circa 1960-1965)

'Siemens' Cable Drum White plastic outer shell and cradle - secured to Weltrol with twisted wire only.(Used on German version of Weltrol circa 1960 only)

Granite Block Moulded mottled-grey plastic - not available separately. Secured to Weltrol with single-strand wire. (1960-1963)

The Marine Boiler and 'Siemens' Cable Drum were used by Trix Express as loads for their highly detailed Tiefladewagen between 1962 and 1965.

A popular model was the scale model of a standard BR Goods Brake van with internal light, Cat. No. 653, released during the Autumn of 1953 as part of the TTR concept of 'design for action'. The body of the van was a detailed magnesium alloy diecasting mounted on a modified long diecast mazak chassis as used for the later tinplate wagon range. The van was finished in matt grey with hand-rail detail picked out in white. The van number was 31595, the same as the telephone number of the Northampton TTR factory!

A feature of the model was the incorporation of a light fitting which illuminated the frosted windows of the internal partition assemblies, including the plastic tail lamp illuminated by a perspex cylinder which reflected the light from the lamp. A current pick-up assembly was fitted to the underside of the wagon chassis on which the position of the pick-up shoes could be altered to suit 2 or 3-rail running. This pick-up assembly was a rather bulky affair hidden by a tinplate skirt. Running qualities were poor mainly due to the pressure exerted on the rails by the pick-up shoes, and thus it could not be used at the end of a long train of tinplate wagons because of the possibilities of the wagons being toppled on curved track sections. From 1959 the chassis casting was modified slightly and fitted with reduced diameter axles which helped to improve running characteristics. This model was listed up to and including 1961, with the catalogue number changing to P653 in 1960.

In 1960 a new diecast 'scale' chassis formed the backbone of a new range of wagons. Most of these were fitted with plastic bodies, of which the full range is described in a later section. However, two Goods Brake vans with diecast bodies formed part of this range. These bodies were the same as used on the earlier model, Cat. No. 653, with the exception that the buffer beam overhang at both ends of the body

was removed. In addition there was a reduction in the length of the body locating pillars to facilitate the fixing of a chassis mounting plate. No light unit was fitted although the tail lamp remained. The diecast chassis used for these models, (fully described later), is known with or without vacuum tank.
The two models were:
Cat. No.P621 Goods Brake van Light grey – van number 31595. (1960-1962)
Cat. No. P622 Goods Brake van Light brown (officially listed as red) – van number 31595. (1960-1962)

The final basic model in this diecast series was the Operating Dump wagon, Cat. No. 666. This was another 'design for action' model with the ability to tip its load of coal, or similar, onto a suitable

receptacle at the side of the track, such as the Coal Bin, Cat. No. 868, which was part of the Operating Dump wagon and Elevator Conveyor system.

The wagon was remotely operated by shunting the wagon over an electro-magnetic rail, Cat. No. 427, which was then activated. By the resultant magnetism acting on an armature coupled to levers, the wagon body tipped sideways discharging its load.

Fry's Diecastings Ltd were once again given the task of manufacturing the necessary dies for which they received the order during March 1953. The first batch of wagon diecast parts were manufactured in September of the same year in readiness for Trix Ltd to prepare for the important Christmas market. The wagon chassis was based upon the early design of the diecast chassis introduced in 1953. This had a main frame depth of 0.25" with added underframe detail in the form of pipes and cylinders used to camouflage two hollow locating frames acting as guides for the operating armature assembly. The wheel and coupling assembly was the same as used on the normal wagons of the period. An unfortunate reaction due to the tipping action of the wagon when operated, was that the complete wagon would tend to tip in sympathy. To overcome this problem the hollow location frame opposite the load discharge side was modified to a solid casting, thus providing extra weight and stability. The modification to the die took place in the spring of 1954. In 1962 the catalogue number was changed to P666, but by 1963 the Operating Dump wagon had disappeared from the price list.

A few months later during 1954 an alternative die core was used to produce the wagon chassis without buffers. This was to suit the American market for which Aristo Craft Miniatures of

Diecast Lighted Goods Brake with the German version of the Operating Dump wagon on the left and the British version on the right.

Specially boxed and modified Operating Dump Wagons for Aristo Craft Miniatures of America.

America applied their name together with the Trix Action Series logo, to the packaging and instruction leaflet, although interestingly all the packaging and instruction leaflets were printed in England. The body of the wagon remained grey although boxed examples are known finished in bright red. (The author cannot vouch for the authenticity of these wagons finished in red.) The Aristo Craft Dump wagon was widely advertised in the American model railway journals by Polk's Model Craft Hobbies of New York who acted for Trix Ltd and Trix Vereinigte Spielwarenfabriken GmbH as their exclusive agents in America. The trade name of Aristo Craft Miniatures was the idea of Nathan Polk, who also designed the artwork for the packaging, and was purely a marketing exercise as part of the Polk's trading company.

The American model also had a slightly larger coupling slot enabling a special Knuckle coupling to be fitted, but this could be changed for a coupling to NMRA standards included in the packaging. The special wheel assemblies fitted to these wagons were to the same standard. It was boxed with or without a special electro-magnetic unit adapted to fit between the rails of any propriety track in place of the standard Trix magnetic rail. This model was available in America from 1954 until approximately 1958. No catalogue number is available.

Another variant of the standard British model was that supplied to the German Trix company who included it in their Trix Express catalogues from 1954 until 1957 inclusive. The only difference to the model supplied to the home market was that the chassis was adapted to take couplings suitable for the Trix Express system. Each coupling assembly took the form of a special hook and centralising spring designed and manufactured in the Northampton factory, fitted with an uncoupling striker supplied by the Nuremberg factory. The Trix Express catalogue number for this model was 20/89.

From official records, approximately 34,000 of the British and German versions of the Operating Dump wagons were produced collectively, of which only about 9,500 of these had the heavier chassis. From 1955 no orders were placed with the diecasters until the final order in 1961 for approximately 1,000 units, a unit comprising chassis, wagon front and wagon body. The total number of the American versions of the Operating Dump wagon was 11,000 produced mainly during 1954.

As with early mazak diecastings, the magnesium alloy diecastings which were used for the main body components of the above diecast range, suffered from the effects of poor storage, especially damp conditions. The latter condition acted as a catalyst helping magnesium oxide to form on the surface as a white powdery growth causing pitting of the diecast surface. It is wise to remove this oxide growth and touch up the affected area if possible, before ensuring that the models are stored in a dry environment.

THE POST-WAR AMERICAN WAGONS

With the relatively small production pro-gramme in operation after the war, it was inevitable that the few American-outline models that were produced should be for export only, with naturally the emphasis on the American market, although Australia was also considered a possible market. Even though a slightly reduced range of the pre-war versions of the American wagons was shown in the 1947 catalogue distributed in America (no Lumber Car with or without load), it is doubtful if many of these wagons were delivered for distribution prior to the change to the new coupling in 1948.

1948 was the year of the first general TTR export catalogue including that issued by Polk's Model Craft Hobbies Inc. of New York. These listed the full range of American wagons and, as mentioned previously, each catalogue number was given the suffix letter 'U' denoting that a new-style coupling was fitted. However, during 1948/49 a few were fitted with the 1939 post-war Trix Express coupling especially for the Swiss market. It was not until 1951 that the wagons were shown in a domestic TTR catalogue and even then they were listed as for EXPORT ONLY. By 1952 they were on general release and remained fairly popular for a few years. They were still listed in the 1959 TTR literature, but by 1961 they had been phased out.

The general comments of previous chapters regarding the pre-war versions, and the subsequent general post-war modifications to the British-outline bogie wagons also apply to these wagons. Due to possible shortages and/or difficulties in meeting production requirements during the early 1950s, it was possible to find a hybrid chassis. For example, one may find an American-outline body on a chassis

with buffers, or on a chassis punched to accept buffers as well as other anomalies which also affected the BR bogie wagons. The first post-war American-outline wagons carried the same numbers as their pre-war predecessors, but it was not long before the various wagons appeared with different numbers helping to stimulate sales. The wagons listed on the following page, except the Gondola Cars and some early Flat Cars, have 'TTR Made in England' applied by transfer to either the underside

TTR American goods wagons. Note the slots in the left-hand Texaco Oil Tank Car chassis as used for the Box Cars, and the shade differences in the two Box Cars with the same number.

of the chassis or to the end of the wagon body. In the majority of cases the transfers are white, but where they occur on the end caps of the Texaco and Union oil tank cars they are black and golden yellow respectively. Black transfers are known to have been applied to the end of the body of the Refrigerator cars. Later wagons had 'TTR Made in England' printed in white or golden yellow letters on the underside of the chassis. The list, which includes wagons produced up to and including 1952, omits the suffix 'U' from the catalogue numbers as this was dis-continued after 1949:

Cat. No.

681 Flat Car Black – wagon numbers T.T.64681 and T.T.68341.

682 Lumber Car without load Black – wagon numbers T.T.64681, T.T.94618 and T.T.96823.

683 Lumber Car with load Black – unpainted wood load represents 20 planks – wagon numbers T.T.64681, T.T.94618 and T.T.96823.

684 Gondola Car Black with light grey lining – wagon numbers T.T.1684 and T.T.1732.

685 Box Car Early models were a deep maroon to almost dark brown with later models in varying shades of red-brown – wagon numbers T.T.37685, T.T.38246 and T.T.38492.

686 Refrigerator Car White – wagon numbers T.T.2086 and T.T.21734.

687 Fruit Car Yellow – wagon numbers W.F.E.X.53687 and W.F.E.X.54536.

Note: On the above three Box Car type wagons, panels at both ends of the bodies have been found with slots for the hand-brake shaft support frame location. Normally only one end is slotted.

688 Union Oil Tank Car Red – wagon numbers U.T.L.X.50689 and U.T.L.X.51375 – early chassis can be found with Box Car type body tab-location slots on the side frames.

689 Texaco Oil Tank Car Silver – TCX3688 and TCX3768 – early chassis can be found with Box Car type body tab-location slots on the side frames. Markings on very early post-war production models with diecast couplings display MADE IN ENGLAND on one side only in place of the square of inscriptions.

690 Caboose Early models varied from deep maroon to almost dark brown with later models in

TTR American goods wagons.

varying shades of red-brown – wagon numbers 482690, 564701 and 463812.

Below is listed the remainder of the series in which the underside of the chassis was punch marked TTR MADE IN ENGLAND, in place of the varied use of transfers. These were produced from 1952 until the cessation of the range in 1961. Plastic axle-box mouldings were fitted in 1958. Only essential details are given as the all main features, unless otherwise stated, are as previously listed:

681 Flat Car Wagon numbers T.T.56443 and T.T.58814.

682 Lumber Car without load Wagon numbers T.T.94621 and T.T.98734 – both these are also known with buffers but without handbrake.

683 Lumber Car with load Details as Lumber Car without load.

684 Gondola Car Grey with dark grey lining – wagon number T.T.1735.

685 Box Car Red-brown (shades) – wagon number T.T.39624.

686 Refrigerator Car Wagon numbers T.T.23465 and T.T.24683.

687 Fruit Car Wagon numbers W.F.E.X.56387, W.F.E.X.61723 and W.F.E.X.64301.

688 Union Oil Tank Car U.T.L.X.35162 and U.T.L.X.63157.

689 Texaco Oil Tank Car Wagon numbers TCX3614 and TCX3876. •

690 Caboose Red-brown (shades of) – wagon numbers 374762 and 598612.

It is worth noting that the four digits at the start or finish of the number transfers applied to the Caboose were used on the American Passenger and Switcher locomotives:

THE POST-WAR TRIX EXPRESS RANGE FOR AMERICA

With the pending restitution agreement between the former owners and the owners of the German Trix company 1948/49, help with exports to America for the German products was given by the British company in liaison with Polk's Model Craft Hobbies Inc. of New York who produced a comprehensive catalogue listing all the TTR and a good selection of the Trix Express products. The Trix Express range shown in the catalogue was almost the same as that produced just prior to the war with a few basic modifications and additions. Unfortunately this joint promotion only lasted approximately two or three years.

Although most of the early pre-war Trix Express rolling stock is described elsewhere in this book, these descriptions do not include certain modifications to the rolling stock which were introduced during 1939. One such modification was the replacement of the tinplate bogie side-frames of the scale-length coaches by more authentic-looking diecast versions. Although these new bogie side-frames were incorporated on all the scale-length coaches, the pattern, a representation of the American 'Swan-neck' bogie, was unfortunately only correct for the Wagon-Lits coaches. In contrast, the tinplate pattern used in pre-war days depicting the Görlitz-3 bogie was absolutely correct for the Deutsche Reichsbahn and Mitropa coaches but not for the Wagon-Lits coaches.

Another improvement was a a new type of diecast coupling assembly and integral uncoupling striker subsequently fitted to all post-war Trix Express rolling stock for the domestic market. However, a special tinplate coupling based on the new TTR

Top row: Trix Express 1939/40 Mitropa Speisewagen with diecast bogie side frames. From the second row: Trix Express post-war coaches Cat.Nos. 20/164, 20/165, 20/166 and 20/167 from the 1948/53 period.

coupling introduced in 1948 was fitted to the Trix Express rolling stock for export to America in place of the improved diecast coupling assembly. This had a 'heel-and-foot' striker incorporated in the design which was positioned to the lower left of the coupling when viewed from the front to improve alignment of the unit during the act of coupling. (This coupling was only fitted to the rolling stock for the duration of the joint promotion.)

Also in 1939 a set of three short bogie coaches in a new Deutsche Reichsbahn light green livery with less elaborate markings than their predecessors was introduced into the Trix Express range. This included a Baggage Car, 1st/2nd Class coach and a 3rd Class coach. The Reichsbahn Adler emblem was still retained at this time but omitted in the 1949 productions, as it was from all post-war coaches produced from 1949.

On the post-war wagons and coaches the diameter of the running-wheel axle ends was reduced to improve running characteristics, and the diameter of the filler caps on the long wheelbase oil tank wagons was increased from approximately 9.1mm to 12.7mm overall. One of the problems with the gold markings on the Wagon-Lits and Mitropa coaches had been a tendency to dull with handling, and this was eliminated on the post-war versions of the scale Wagon-Lits coaches by incorporating the markings in the tinplate printing, although these appeared almost green in colour. A small quantity from the very early stages of post-war production still retained the gold markings. This process was used on the short bogie and scale-length Mitropa coaches, which kept the gold markings. The roof ventilators on the post-war scale length coaches were formed from turned brass and were much

Post-war Trix Express coaches as listed in the 1949 Polk's catalogue.
From the top and left to right: 20/151 (note special TTR post-war style coupling), 20/152-1, 20/152-3, 20/153 (with special TTR style coupling), 20/154, 20/162-3.

smaller and neater than their pre-war counterparts.

Overleaf is a list of known Trix Express rolling stock prepared for export primarily to the USA and fitted with the modified post-war TTR-style coupling. All the goods wagons retained the inscription 'Deutsche Reichsbahn'. The normal Trix Express catalogue number is given first, with the export catalogue number for the American market

269

given in brackets. Detailed information is only given in this list when the item is not described elsewhere. The American style description is based on that printed in Polk's catalogue:

Cat. No.

20/74 (29-74) Box car (with braker's cabin) Red-brown – car number 2074.

20/76 (29-75) Covered car (with brown tarpaulin) Red-brown – car number 2071. The American number 29-75 quoted in the catalogue is probably a mistake and should be 29-76.

20/78-O (29-78) Olex Tank car Yellow – car number 524 512.

20/78-L (29-78) Leuna Tank car Silver – car number 547 658.

20/78-ST (29-78) Standard Tank car Silver – car number 526 662.

20/78-S (29-78) Shell Tank car Yellow – car number 567 054.

20/79 (29-79) Box car (without braker's cabin) Red-brown – car number 2074.

20/151 (29-151) Continental Baggage car (Bundesbahn short bogie Luggage van) Green lined in light green and black, grey roof with dome – car number 20151.

20/152-1 (29-152) First and Second class coach (Bundesbahn short passenger bogie coach) Green with black lining, grey roof – coach number 20152.

20/152-3 (29-152) Third class coach (Bundesbahn short passenger bogie coach) Green with black lining, grey roof – coach number 20152.

20/153 (29-153) Mitropa Diner (Short bogie coach) Red with gold markings, grey roof (various shades), without Mitropa coat of arms – coach number 20153.

20/154 (29-154) Mitropa Coach Sleeper (Short bogie coach) Red with gold markings, grey roof (various shades), 12 windows each side, without Mitropa coat of arms – coach number 20154.

20/162-3 (29-162) 3rd Class coach (Scale Bundesbahn coach) Green with black and grey lining, grey roof (varous shades) with 10 ventilators – coach number 20162.

20/163 (29-163) Mitropa Diner (Scale coach) Red with gold markings, grey roof (various shades) with 8 ventilators, without Mitropa coat of arms – coach number 20163.

20/164 (29-164) Mitropa Sleeper (Scale coach) Red with gold markings, grey roof (various shades) with 22 ventilators, without Mitropa coat of arms – coach number 20164.

20/165 (29-165-2) Continental Baggage car (Scale Wagon-Lit baggage car) Dark blue with vertical black lining and yellow-green markings, grey roof (various shades) with a small raised area at each end – coach number 20165.

20/166 (29-166) Wagon-Lit Diner (Scale coach) Dark blue with yellow-green markings, grey roof (various shades) with 8 ventilators – coach number 20166.

20/167 (29-167) Wagon-Lits Sleeper (Scale coach) Dark blue with yellow-green markings, grey roof (various shades) with 22 ventilators – coach number 20167.

With the collapse of the post-war joint ownership of the German enterprise, the German and British Trix companies went their own ways both in export sales and their relationship with Polk's.

BR AND SPECIAL SHORT BOGIE COACHES

The 1950 Christmas edition of *The TTR Gazette* showed for the first time the short Express bogie coaches in the new BR livery of carmine and cream. A train of these coaches looked very striking on a layout when coupled up to a matching 0-4-0 engine and tender in the new experimental light blue passenger livery. The construction of these coaches was exactly the same as their LMS and LNER predecessors except that the previously plain, grey (various shades) roof was embossed with seven raised dimples representing ventilators.

One of the factors governing the continued production of these toy-like coaches was that the TTR system at this time was governed by financial dictates. In addition, it was essential that it continued to appeal to a world-wide toy-train market in which it had a good foothold. It was also vital that the cost of the TTR rolling stock was within the reach of young children. This was accomplished with these coaches as the tooling was already available and they could be produced in great quantities moderately cheaply, although the retail price was almost 3 shillings dearer than an equivalent Hornby-Dublo coach.

The short BR carmine and cream bogie coaches were first available during the early part of 1951. Three versions were available:

Cat.No.1/560 1st class coach number 4135.
Cat.No.1/570 Brake 3rd coach number 27104.
Cat.No.1/580 Restaurant car coach number 19.

The coaches were lined in black and yellow, the latter colour taking on a green hue depending upon the accuracy of the tinplate printing, a characteristic that also applied to the coaches which were later produced in other liveries. The tinplate printing on the early coaches had a dull rough textured finish. Both black end panels bore the words 'TTR BRIT PATS 451644 471304 MADE IN ENGLAND' in yellow letters which took up almost the entire area. In 1952 the quality of the tinplate printing was far superior to that of the earlier versions and, as well as being much brighter, was also a shade lighter. The wheels also took on an improved appearance with spokes in place of the plain discs as used on early post-war rolling stock. In 1956 the coaches were fitted with a chassis as used by the Whistle coach (described later), on which the cast bogie side-frames were replaced with black plastic mouldings. These coaches continued to be listed in the official price lists up to and including the end of 1958.

During the summer of 1956 British Railways changed their coach livery to maroon. Trix soon followed in 1957 by producing the short bogie coaches in the new livery with the added refinement of shouldered axles fitted to a modified bogie frame. These axles replaced the parallel versions and had freer running characteristics. However, the latter axles are known to have been fitted to these new coaches in a few cases. In addition, the now standard black plastic bogie side-frame mouldings were fitted. Patent information was now only normally printed on one of the black end panels and can be found in much smaller lettering than was previously used. The lining was again yellow and black, and occasional use was made of the Whistle coach chassis in either aluminium or pressed steel sheet, although for normal production the standard chassis as used throughout this range prevailed.

BR carmine and cream short bogie coaches. Early models with a dull finish on the right. The bottom row contains a 1st. class coach with plastic bogie side-frames.

271

It was felt that the spur, enabling pre-war style coupling links to be used with post-1948 couplings, had become redundant and a modified coupling was incorporated into the construction of the coaches during 1960. This also corresponded to a time when the coaches could be purchased fitted with standard Trix wheels or scale plastic wheels, although there was no distinction between the two versions with regards to catalogue numbers. The short BR maroon bogie coaches were listed in the official price lists up to and including 1962. Three types were available:

Cat. No. 1/561 1st class coach number 4135.

Cat. No. 1/571 Brake 2nd coach number 27104.

Cat. No. 1/581 Restaurant Car coach number 19.

To compliment the 12-volt DC BR Southern Region Schools Class 4-4-0 'Dover' locomotive contained in the passenger train set F27 introduced during 1959, it was essential that coaches with correct livery were included. These were duly produced to the same pattern and construction as the previous short BR maroon coaches except that the livery was changed to BR Southern Region green and only Brake 2nd and 1st Class coaches were manufactured. The interior of each coach was finished in white instead of the light brown of their predecessors. During 1959 the coaches were only available in the passenger set and it was not until spring 1960 that they became available separately.

The early production models were completely without any markings or lining except for one of the black end panels displaying patent information in small print. However, the coaches soon acquired black door frame markings and the figure '1' on the doors of the 1st Class coach. Later the number

S 31595 was applied by yellow transfer to both types of coach (this was the same basic number as given to the diecast lighted Goods Brake van). A second number S 33289 was planned for one or other of the coaches at the same time but never used. In the final version with coach numbers, patent information was printed on both of the end panels and took on a larger format as used for the early BR coaches. Control of the transfer application on the coach sides must have been poor as the transfers on each side of the coach can be found at

corresponding or opposite ends of the coach.

As with the previously-mentioned coaches, scale wheels were fitted to the coaches during 1960 as well as the modified coupling but the number transfers were no longer applied. The coaches were listed up to and including the spring of 1962 and were as follows:

Cat. No. 5/560 1st class coach number (when applied) S 31595

Cat. No. 5/570 Brake 2nd coach number (when applied) S 31595

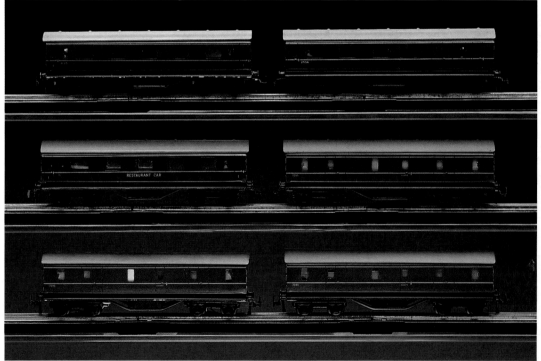

BR short bogie coach from the left Top row: Maroon 1st class and Brake 3rd. Middle row: Maroon Restaurant car and Parcels and Guard's van Bottom row: Whistle coach and crimson lake Parcels and Guard's van

These BR Southern Region coaches were first issued individually in red boxes with yellow labels which were printed with Cat. Nos. 5/561 and 5/571 respectively. To the author's belief this was the only time that these coaches were associated with these catalogue numbers as they do not appear in any of the TTR price lists or catalogues bearing these numbers. The BR Southern Region coaches were to be the last produced to a pattern first introduced in 1936.

One of the most intriguing coaches of the TTR system was the Whistle coach which started life on the drawing board in 1954. The concept was that by means of a remotely-controlled device, a sound would emit from the coach on command from the operator to mimic a train whistle. Unfortunately, as with the Meteor Diesel Express which used the same sound generator, the sound in question was more of an excruciating screech than anything else. The sound generator and associated relay, which was actually the reversing relay from the Meteor, were mounted on a modified standard short bogie coach

chassis whose bogies were also modified to take the necessary current pick-up assemblies and which were first fitted with the diecast bogie side frame, changing to plastic in 1956. Initially the framework of the chassis was made from pressed-steel sheet but shortly after changed to aluminium for the duration of the coach production.

The tinplate body of the coach was of new design formed to represent a British Railways parcel and guards van which was finished in crimson lake with yellow and black lining and numbered 7055. Through a rubber grommet, mounted in one of the black ends of the coach, protruded a small screw which was used to adjust the tone and volume of the sound generator. Printed on the other end of the coach was 'TTR BRITISH AND FOREIGN PAT'S PENDING. MADE IN ENGLAND'. Soon after the introduction of this Whistle Coach in the autumn of 1955, the latter-mentioned coach end received two windows. The grey coach roof was usually formed from aluminium sheet although tinplate roofs are known.

The coach was presented as part of the Train Whistle Set No. 274 together with a special Train Whistle Control Box, two trackside Whistle Boards, coil of wire and instruction booklet, all attractively packed in a special red display box. The 'whistle' was activated by the special on/off control switch which fed a DC current superimposed over the normal AC current used for the trains. This DC current operated the relay allowing AC to be fed to, or cut off from the track to the sound generator depending upon the operation of the special control unit. The set was listed up to and including the autumn of 1958.

Whether the Whistle coach prompted the production of a BR Parcels and Guard's Van, Cat.

R Southern Region short bogie coaches, Cat.Nos. 5/560 and 5/570. The coaches on the top row have no markings whilst those on the second row have markings but no numbers.

No. 1/557, or the other way round is open to question, but they were both issued at approximately the same time. The van used the same crimson lake body side panels with both ends displaying the same patent information as on the Whistle coach. Initially the chassis was the same as used on the BR carmine and cream range with diecast bogie side-frames but soon acquired the same chassis and bogies, less pick-up attachments, as the Whistle coach with plastic bogie side-frames. As the financial situation during 1956 caused severe production problems, Whistle coaches, without the sound unit and pick-up assemblies, were passed off as Parcels and Guard's vans and boxed accordingly.

After the change in ownership of Trix Ltd in 1957, the Parcels and Guard's van disappeared from the official lists for a few months but reappeared in the autumn of the same year in a maroon livery with exactly the same lining and markings as the crimson lake version. The chassis by now was the same as fitted to the normal production versions of the standard BR maroon short bogie coaches. The maroon Parcels and Guard's van is known with one end only printed with early type patent information, and also with both ends printed in a smaller format giving patent information. Although this coach was officially listed up to and including the spring of 1962, not many were sold in line with all the other short bogie coaches, this mainly due to the ever-increasing desire of the public for accurate model railways instead of the toy railway image of which Trix Ltd had difficulty in escaping from.

The final coach in this category is the BR 1st/3rd Class Suburban short bogie coach Cat. No. 1/553 which along with the Parcels and Guard's van made its debut in 1955. This was yet another new body

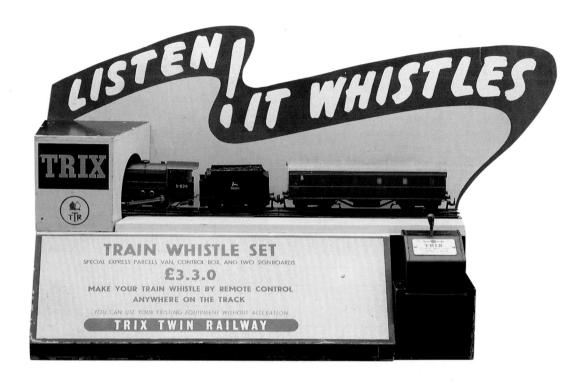

Dealer's display.

design mounted on the standard short bogie chassis which captured the style of full-size suburban coaches quite well. It was finished in crimson lake and lined in yellow and black with the customary Celastoid window strips glazing the 21 windows on each side of the coach. It carried the number 6301. Either one or both of the black end panels displayed patent information in the smaller format. The grey roof and the chassis for this coach were usually the aluminium versions as used on the Whistle coach, but as this was clearly a period when 'anything will do as long as the label is correct', variations in the material and method of construction will exist as with other items of rolling stock at this time.

During the latter part of 1957 the livery was changed to BR maroon and acquired the more

274

robust pressed-steel chassis and roof although occasionly in the early stages of production an aluminium chassis frame was used. The crimson lake version continued to be available for approximately two years. Both versions of the 1959 catalogue when describing the contents of the BR Western Region passenger set F23, gave the catalogue number of the Suburban coach as 1/554. This was probably because the crimson lake version was shown in the catalogue with the number 1/553, and, as with the other maroon passenger coaches in the series, to

avoid confusion with earlier issues, the catalogue number was raised by adding '1' (one) to the last number. For example the BR 1st class coach, Cat. No. 1/560, was altered to 1/561 when the livery changed to maroon. However this situation did not last long and later catalogues showing the BR Suburban coach reverted back to 1/553. Strangely the Suburban coach did not receive the catalogue number of 1/554 in any of the official price lists, although this number appeared on boxes containing the coach. As with other similar coaches the

Suburban coach was listed up to and including 1962.

As sales of the maroon BR Parcels and Guard's van and the Suburban coach never really excelled themselves, many items remained unsold on the shelves for long periods, and thus there was no necessity to produce updated versions with the modified coupling. In fact, the quantitiy of Suburban coach body and chassis stampings in the factory at Birmingham became something of a problem. A decision was made to spray the coach sides black and

Train Whistle Set No 274. (A)

convert them into an Engineer's Department Breakdown coach. A mock-up model was shown in the later edition of the 1959 catalogue, the latter being identified by the price tag of 6d printed in the bottom right-hand corner of the cover, whilst the price tag of the earlier edition was printed in the top right-hand corner of the cover.

Unfortunately it was not until the spring of 1961 that the Engineer's coach emerged from the factory unannounced, with not even a mention in any of the price lists or the model press. The basic model was exactly the same as the maroon BR Suburban coach except that the coach sides had been sprayed matt

black with the yellow number ED 94528 applied to the left-hand end of each side. Both formats of patent information are used on the coach ends even at the same time. No catalogue number was given and the label on the box just stated ENGINEER'S COACH. It was not until 1963 that the catalogue number of 1688 was listed under the Courtauld's Group banner who showed it in their 1963 catalogue in dark blue livery. This colour version was never manufactured and it is doubtful if it ever appeared in the Courtauld's style of packaging. As can be expected, the Engineer's coach is a hard-to-find model.

Thus an era of basic coach construction and design which started in 1936 came to a close. How many thousands of coaches were produced to this basic design is anyone's guess, but it served the Trix companies, and more importantly, the customers well.

Engineer's Coach. This is probably a pre-production model as the number ED 94732 is the same as shown in the 1959 catalogue. (L)

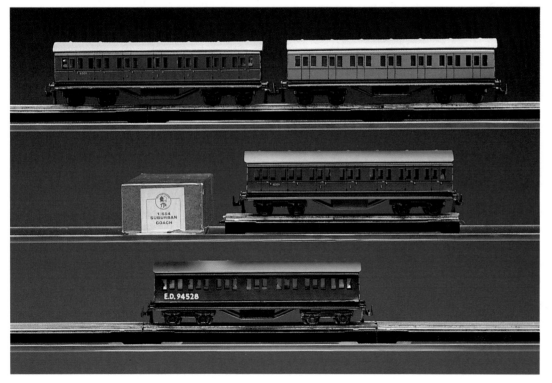

Top row: BR Crimson Lake Suburban coach Cat.No. 1/553 next to an example of what can be done with a little imagination. Middle row: BR Maroon Suburban coach with the initial Cat.No. 1/554. Bottom row: Engineer's Department Breakdown coach Cat.No. 1688.

THE POST-WAR SCALE-LENGTH TINPLATE COACHES

It was not until 1948 that the scale-length coaches once more started to appear in the British shops, at first in very small numbers due to export commitments, although it was not long before quantities increased to an acceptable level. Three versions of the standard LMS and LNER coaches were produced, with the Pullman coach appearing during 1951, but although the latter was advertised in the earlier export catalogues it is doubtful if production commenced prior to this date. To add credibility to this statement, Pullman component drawings inspected by the author are dated around this time. The most exciting news was that a range of American-style coaches had quickly been developed to compliment the American 0-4-0 Passenger engine and tender released during the latter months of 1948. Unfortunately these American coaches were for export only and did not become generally available to the British public until 1952.

The construction of the post-war British-outline scale coaches was basically no different to that used in pre-war days, including modifications applied in 1939, apart from certain details. A full description of the basic construction details is given in the earlier section dealing with the pre-war coaches. The couplings fitted to these post-war coaches were the type introduced in 1948, and on the LMS and LNER coaches were loosely riveted to the coupling retainer 'U' piece, the rivet acting as a pivot. This new coupling eliminated the need for the special coupling link deflection plate fitted to one end of some late pre-war coaches, although for a while the location slots in the buffer beam remained. Initially

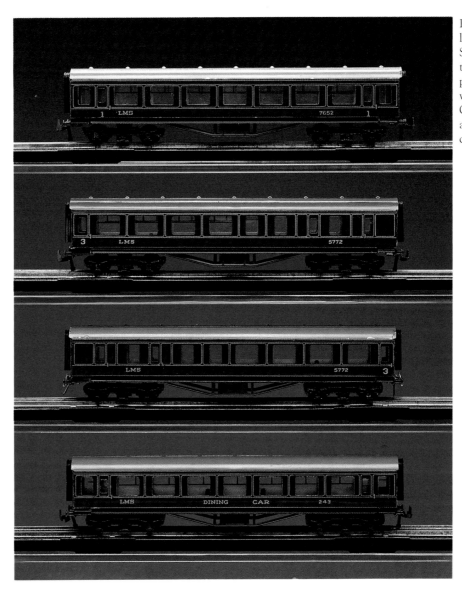

Post-war LMS scale-length coaches. Second row from the bottom: Early pre-1948 Brake 3rd with plain Celastoid windows and pre-war style couplings.

277

Post-war LNER
scale-length
coaches.
Note shade
differences.

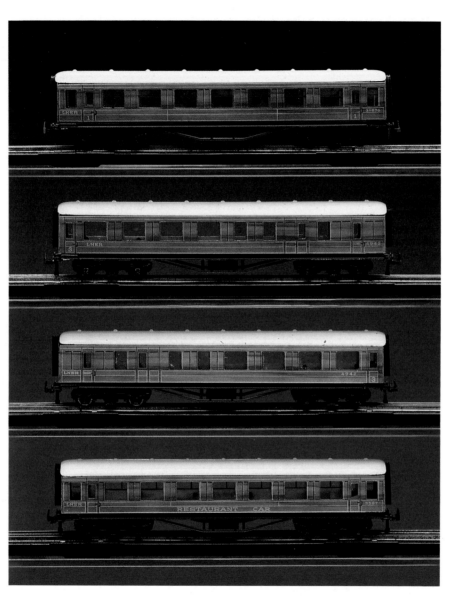

the Celastoid window strips fitted to the LMS and LNER coaches were without markings which lasted until circa 1949 when they were replaced with a printed version giving representation of ventilator windows.

In a departure from the standard plain type of roof fitted to the pre-war LNER coaches, the post-war versions had a white elliptical roof as fitted to the Pullman coaches which was more in keeping with the style of an LNER Gresley coach. What a pity that the bogie side-frame diecastings were not altered from the LMS pattern which was used for all British-outline scale-length coaches right up to the finish of the tinplate era. For a while the tinplate printing of the LNER coaches had an almost matt finish and was much paler than pre-war productions, but around 1949/1950 it regained its rich teak colour although still without the high-gloss finish of the late 1930s production. As regards to the tinplate printing on the LMS coaches, apart from slight shade differences there was no real distinction between pre- and post-war production. The suffix 'U' was initially added to all catalogue numbers denoting that the coaches had been fitted with the new uncoupling coupler.

Cat. No. 2/567 LMS 1st class coach
Coach number 7652.
Cat. No. 4/567 LNER 1st class coach
Coach number 31876.
Cat. No. 2/577 LMS Brake 3rd
Coach number 5772.
Cat. No. 4/577 LNER Brake 3rd
Coach number 4942.
Cat. No. 2/587 LMS Dining car
Coach number 243.

Cat.No. 4/587 LNER Restaurant car
Coach number 3587.

The above were produced from 1948 to circa 1951 inclusive.

The mazak wheels, used for the outside rail current pick-up as part of the coach lighting system on the above coaches, were replaced by more efficient turned brass wheels in 1950 which were fitted to a modified bogie frame in readiness for the reintroduction of the coach lighting unit. However it was not until the autumn of 1952 that the coach lighting unit, Cat. No. 767, with its associated centre rail pick-up assembly was once more available. One of the reasons for the delay in the reintroduction of the coach lighting unit was that miniature bulbs were not available in the early post-war days from the specialist manufacturers. The centre rail current pick-up shoe assembly was of a new and more efficient design with the actual shoe mounted at the centre of a sprung blade anchored at one end of the modified bogie frame by a 10 BA screw, with the other end free to slide along an added longitudinal member. The actual lighting unit and electrical connections were no different to those produced in pre-war days.

As mentioned earlier, to stimulate export orders and to compliment the American outline 0-4-0 passenger engine and tender, three types of American-outline coaches were produced and introduced to the TTR range probably towards the middle of 1950. The three types were:

Cat. No. 9/565 American Pullman Day
coach Dark green body and roof.
Cat. No. 9/575 Baggage car Dark green body
and roof.

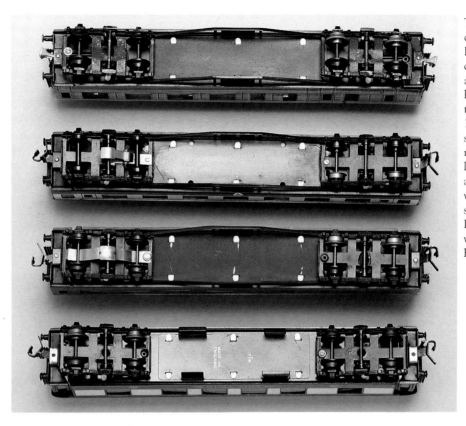

TTR scale-length coach chassis. From the top: Pre-war version for comparison, note the addition of a central longitudinal member on the post-war bogie frames; 1961 version fitted with scale wheels and re-designed centre lighting pick-up shoe assembly; 1952 version with lighting pick-up shoe; Pre-1952 Pullman chassis with TTR MADE IN ENGLAND transfers.

Cat. No. 9/585 American Pullman
Observation car Dark green body and roof.

It is very difficult to pin down exactly when these American-outline coaches were first manufactured for the export market, but all the mechanical details point to 1950 more than any other date. The basic method of construction was the same as other scale-length coaches in the TTR range, but the American-outline design necessitated completely new tinplate body pressings, including the bogie-mounting frame.

The main chassis frame was the same as used on the British-outline Pullman coach but with the various mounting slots in different positions. The roof shape was one which could be called 'curved domed' and was typically American, but unlike the inside of the bodies of these coaches, was not finished in white. The Day coach and the Observation car were similar with 16 windows on each coach side but with different spacing, symmetrical on the Day coach and asymmetrical on the Observation car. In addition, on

American scale-length
coaches. From the top;
Observation car, Day
coach and Baggage car
in gloss finish,
Day coach and Baggage
car in matt finish.

Post-war Pullman
coaches.
From top to bottom:
Cat.Nos. 598 (1947/48
export version), 598
(1950 version), 599 (1953
version, note finer
printing),
P599 (ZENA), P599
(SHEILA), both the
latter two 1960/62
models.

the latter the door pressing at one end was replaced by a set-back glazed end panel and a gold-coloured verandah. The glazing on the above two coaches was provided by unmarked Celastoid strips held in place by white tinplate strips running the full length of the coach and tabbed to the main chassis frame. This was far superior to the old method of long body tabs holding the window strip in place. Unfortunately this new method was not applied to later BR coaches.

The bogies were fitted with a completely new design of bogie side-frame diecasting which captured the style of the American pattern very well. The coupling was now assembled onto a shouldered pivot instead of being riveted to the 'U'-shaped support bracket, but strangely the end of the coupling guide arm was partly cut away. The author has no idea why this was done, but if buffers had been fitted to the coaches they would have stopped the coupling guide arm from catching the underside of the buffer head. However this was discontinued just prior to the introduction in 1954 of the practice of stamping the patent number 605283 on the coupling.

Underframe detail on the passenger coaches was restricted to two separate but identical pressings, probably depicting battery boxes. On the Baggage car this was reduced to one. Early production models were marked with TTR MADE IN ENGLAND in white transfers on the underside of the chassis, whilst later models from the autumn of 1952 had this information stamped on one of the underframe-detail pressings.

The plain sides of the Baggage car were broken by two separate but fixed glazed doors let into the side panels. This was the only detailing done on

what was a very uninteresting looking model, but having said this, it was true to the American pattern for this item of rolling stock.

The only markings applied to the coaches were in the form of gold transfers. The name PULLMAN was assigned only to the passenger coaches and as each letter was a separate transfer, the spacing over the years was not consistent with some Pullman names being longer than others. All the coaches received numbers at each end of each side, of which a variety exist. The coaches were sprayed dark green and had a high gloss finish up to about 1953 when this was changed to matt until production ceased. Baggage cars exist with a mixture of parts in gloss and matt finish.

The known American coach numbers are as follows:
Day coach Gloss finish – 2407, 2513, 2531. Matt finish – 2407, 2513, 2602.
Baggage car Gloss finish – 1093, 1125, 1186, 1241. Matt finish – 1093, 1241, 1394.
Observation car Gloss finish – 2513, 8273, 8568, 9106. Matt finish – 9106, 9473.

The American coaches were last shown in the 1957 catalogues but still mentioned in the official price lists up to and including the middle of 1960. It is a fact that many of them remained in the factory warehouse unsold with the result that when Courtaulds took over in 1963 a large quantity were bulldozed into a large hole in the ground along with other tinplate items.

The TTR export catalogues of 1948, 1949 and 1950 all mentioned that South African scale model passenger coaches were being designed and would be shortly in production. These coaches were to be produced using the American-outline Day coach and

Early 1960 Pullman coach. (A)

the Observation car but finished in South African railway colours. They were to be given the catalogue numbers of 10/565 and 10/585 respectively. Unfortunately they were never produced.

The British-outline Pullman coaches, Cat. No. 598, were once again generally on sale from 1950, (although a few were available in 1947/48 for export only), but with various small changes from pre-war days. These include a grey elliptical roof instead of white, a single line on the window strips instead of full detailing and the various post-war modifications applicable to this time. One very noticeable feature was that the tinplate printing on these post-war Pullmans was far inferior to that produced in pre-war days. This was highlighted by the printing of the gold designs which was very heavy and blurred although of the same pattern.

Trix Ltd must have been unhappy with the printing on these Pullman coaches as in 1953 they were issued with gold markings of a new and much finer design. The letters of the words PULLMAN and TRIX TWIN were not as heavy looking and the design box around the words TRIX TWIN was about 1.25mm deeper. The basic colour of the earlier post-war Pullman coach was dark chocolate brown, but the later version was much lighter. As with other items, many shades exist with some of the panels not quite matching others. The roof was now white and a light unit was fitted prompting Trix to change the catalogue number to 599. This version continued to be available up to and including 1959 after which extensive modifications took place.

During 1960 the main chassis frame of the Pullman coach was altered to enable furniture to be fitted. This took the form of a single white plastic moulding depicting seats and tables as in a full-size coach. Each table was graced with a turned brass table lamp topped with a red plastic lampshade. On this version the name TRIX TWIN, as printed on the sides of the earlier coaches, was eventually replaced with a plain panel on which a choice of names could be applied using printed labels of which only the following are known, namely ZENA, SHEILA or CAR No. 34 (named coaches being 1st class and numbered coaches, 2nd).

To enable the furniture moulding to be fitted

the body stretchers, by now uninsulated, had to be removed although the stretchers at each end were occasionally retained. As a consequence, the existing coach lighting unit could not now be used. This Pullman coach, without lights and produced during 1960, was given the catalogue number of P599. The following year the later style coupling was fitted together with a choice of scale or standard Trix wheels, and the catalogue number reverted back to 599. This Pullman coach continued to be listed only until 1962.

Various lighting units. The unit directly in front of the German box is a pre-war coach lighting assembly, and the one in front of that is the 1961 version. The 1950s coach lighting unit is on the right. The German light assembly and the TTR unit on the left are for illuminating station buildings, etc.

A new lighting unit was designed in 1961 for use with these new style coaches which clipped into the vacated slots used previously for the centre two body stretchers. At the same time the bogie frame was modified so that a solder tag could be bolted to one bogie, and a newly-designed centre rail pick-up shoe assembly bolted to the other, both of which received a connecting wire from the light unit. The central bogie pin which in the past was used for the very same connections was now not fitted. This new lighting unit was not advertised as being available as a separate item. Pullman coaches fitted with

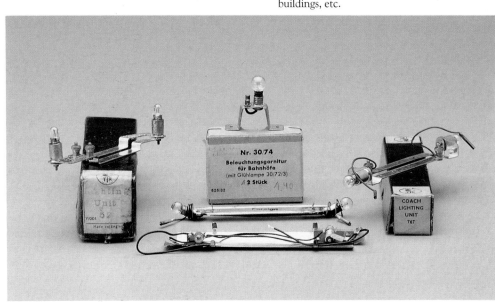

Scale-length BR carmine and cream coaches with lights. From the top: Cat.Nos. 1/568, 1/578 (without tail light), 1/588.

furniture and the new lighting assembly were given the catalogue number FL 599 but were listed for only one year.

1951 saw the introduction of the first TTR British Railways scale-length coaches to compliment the magnificent model of the dark blue BR 4-6-2 'Scotsman' Pacific locomotive. The coaches looked smart in their carmine and cream livery with black and yellow lining. The roof was the same pattern as used on the LMS coaches but finished in matt grey as were all the following BR coaches. The basic constructional details were no different than any other of the TTR coaches at this time, except that in

the first year of production, one could occasionally find a mixture of the old and new pattern bogie frame on one coach, the latter bogie frame being used for the lighting unit. Each coach type utilised the same tinplate stampings as the previous LMS/LNER coaches, and either one or both of the black end panels contained the relevant patent information. The three models were:

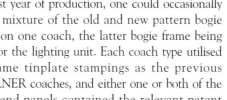

Scale length BR Maroon coaches with furniture. From the top: Cat.Nos. 562, 572, 572 with Guards enclosure, 582.

Cat. No. 1/567 BR 1st class coach Carmine and cream - coach number 3963.

Cat. No. 1/577 BR Brake 3rd coach Carmine and cream - coach number 27316.

Cat. No. 1/587 BR Restaurant car Carmine and cream - coach number 23.

1953 saw a change in the catalogue numbers brought about by the addition of the lighting units as

Scale length BR maroon coaches. From the top: Cat.Nos. 1/569, 1/579 and 1/589.

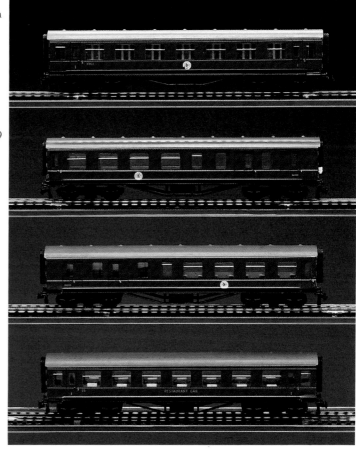

283

a standard item, and followed one year later by the addition of an illuminated white and red plastic tail light fitted to the Brake 3rd coach.

The revised catalogue numbers were:

Cat. No. 1/568 BR 1st class coach with lights.

Cat. No. 1/578 BR Brake 3rd coach with lights, (up to 1954).

Cat. No. 1/578 BR Brake 3rd coach with lights and tail light, (from 1954).

Cat. No. 1/588 BR Restaurant car with lights.

In the 1967 catalogue, the 1st class and Brake 3rd coaches were shown as part of the Night Express set 1/373, which was the last time that any of the BR carmine and cream scale length coaches were shown in a catalogue, although the Brake 3rd and the Restaurant Car continued to be listed during 1958, whilst the 1st Class coach continued to be listed in the price lists up to and including July 1960.

The livery of the above coaches was updated in 1957 to BR maroon with yellow and black lining, but to distinguish them from the carmine and cream models the following catalogue numbers were applied:

Cat. No. 1/569 BR 1st class coach with lights Maroon – coach number 3963.

Cat. No. 1/579 BR Brake 2nd coach lights and tail light Maroon – coach number 27316.

Cat. No. 1/589 BR Restaurant car with lights Maroon – coach number 23.

Physically they were no different from the carmine and cream models up to 1960 from which time they were fitted with furniture, although the above basic coaches with light unit remained listed until the middle of 1961. The addition of furniture, and later the redesigned light unit, necessitated constructional modifications which were exactly the same as those applied to the Pullman coaches during this 1960/1961 period plus the general updating modifications which included the replacement on all coaches of the diecast bogie side-frames with plastic mouldings during 1961.

The furniture fitted to the 1st class coach, Cat. No. 562, took the form of double and single seat mouldings in blue plastic with a tinplate corridor partition clipped to the side of the single moulding to form the side corridor. All body stretchers were removed. Round BR coaching stock crest transfers were applied to the centre of each side, but the main lining on the coach was simplified with only the yellow remaining.

The Brake 2nd coach, Cat. No. 572, was an interesting coach. Initially in 1960 two short rows of light brown plastic seating were fitted up to the guards van section, with a gap between forming the walk-way between the two rows. The two end body stretchers remained. In the following year a light brown guard's van enclosure was added complete with white packing cases and blue barrels. At one side of the enclosure a finely printed Celastoid screen was fitted. In this version of the coach no body stretchers were fitted at all. In both versions BR coaching stock transfers were applied to the centre portion of the passenger section of the coach sides, and the main lining only consisted of a yellow line below the window level, the upper lining being completely omitted, including the coach number.

The last coach in this series was the Restaurant car, Cat. No. 582, fitted with blue seating as used in the 1st class coach, but the two mouldings were separated to form a gangway, with white plastic tables fitted between the seats. The coach was not fitted with body stretchers. Unlike the 1st Class and Brake 2nd coaches, there was no alteration to the printing of the body lining, nor were any BR coaching stock transfers applied.

With the availability of the new lighting unit in 1961, the catalogue for that year listed the above coaches fitted with this lighting unit as an alternative addition to the range as follows:

Cat. No. FL 562 BR 1st class coach with lights and furniture – coach number 3963.

Cat. No. FL 572 BR Brake 2nd with lights and furniture – no coach number.

Cat. No. FL 582 BR Restaurant car with lights and furniture – coach number 23.

Apart from the Pullman coach, the most attractive of the post-war scale-length standard pattern tinplate coaches were those in the chocolate and cream livery of the BR Western Region, lined with a single yellow line under the windows. It is strange that no running numbers were ever applied to these or subsequent models in the same livery. These coaches first made their appearance in 1959 with the issue of the 1st class and Brake 2nd coaches complete with the old style lighting unit. From a distinguishing point of view with regards to the price lists and catalogues, the catalogue numbers were no different to the BR maroon coaches and were as follows:-

Cat. No. 1/569 BR Western Region 1st class coach with lights. Available 1959 to 1960 inclusive.

Cat. No. 1/579 BR Western Region Brake 2nd coach with lights and tail light. Available 1959 only.

Scale length BR Western Region coaches.
From the top: Cat.Nos. 1/569, 1/579, 563, 583, 573.

The previous two coaches, and those described below, were physically exactly the same as the BR maroon versions available during the same periods, even down to the same internal fittings.

BR coaching stock transfers were applied only to the coaches fitted with furniture and this included the Restaurant, or Dining car as it was listed. The word 'Restaurant' was not printed on the coach sides, in fact outwardly the Dining car had exactly the same markings as the 1st class coach and could only be recognised as such by observing if tables were present. Listed below are the Western Region coaches with furniture:

Cat. No. 563 BR Western Region
1st class coach with furniture.
Cat. No. FL 563 BR Western Region
1st class coach with furniture and lights.
Cat. No. 573 BR Western Region
Brake 2nd with furniture and and tail light.
Cat. No. FL 573 BR Western Region
Brake 2nd with furniture, lights and illuminated tail light.
Cat. No. 583 BR Western Region
Dining car with furniture.
Cat. No. FL 583 BR Western Region
Dining car with furniture and lights.

The Western Region coaches with furniture but without lights were listed from 1960, and with furniture and the new lighting unit from 1961. Both sets were withdrawn or sold out in 1962. Thus 1962 brought to an end the long-running range of Trix Twin Railway scale-length tinplate coaches whose standard basic design had not altered since the introduction of the LMS and LNER coaches in 1938. A fine achievement.

THE DEVELOPMENT OF THE PLASTIC WAGONS

Dufay Ltd were very keen to improve and expand the Trix Twin system and designs for a new range of wagons were well under way during the early part of 1959. The design team, inspired by the long-serving Michael Catalani, drew plans for the new range which was an attempt to portray actual British Railways rolling stock. This was a time when the first step was taken to bridge the gap between the 'toys' of the past and the 'models' of the future. All the new 4-wheel wagons were built on a short or long version of a new highly-detailed diecast chassis fitted with scale plastic three-hole disc wheels, (or standard coarse Trix wheels to order), and the standard Trix coupling. The new range was announced at the Brighton Toy Fair in February 1960 but did not reach the shops until the summer of that year.

Along with good brake detail, the two types of chassis were made available with or without a vacuum tank. The initial intention was to mould this tank in plastic and assemble it to the chassis. However, it was found to be more cost effective to include it as part of a chassis diecasting. Each tinplate wagon axle retainer was normally riveted in place, the axle retainer also acting as a washer holding the wagon coupling on its pivot. The problem with the axle retainer was that once fitted it was permanent and stopped customers changing the wagon wheels for a pattern of their choice. To overcome this problem, a new type of axle retaining plate was fabricated in 1961 from spring steel; this clipped over the axle and could be pulled back to release the axle when the need arose.

Dealer's display set.

These chassis were in use with the various plastic bodies well into 1964, after which they were replaced by even more highly-detailed plastic versions which will be described later. Each chassis had the markings TTR MADE IN ENGLAND cast into the underside. Listed below are the known chassis variations in approximate order of production:

AS) Short chassis with hole in foot of L -shaped centre member for plastic vacuum tank which was not fitted. Holes drilled in casting for coupling/tinplate axle retainer rivets. Very early production.

AL) As AS but long chassis.

BS) Short chassis as AS but with coupling/axle retainer rivet replaced by an 8 BA screw. This was normally used when Trix standard wheels were fitted in place of scale wheels, but may have been a legacy of the original intention of using an axle-retaining screw as on the earlier type of diecast chassis. 1960 only.

BL) As above but long chassis.

CS) Short chassis as AS but separate rivets replaced by rivets cast into chassis. General early 1960 production.

CL) As CS but long chassis.

DS) Short chassis with vacuum tank cast into L-shaped centre member. Other details as CS. General 1960/1961 production.

DL) As DS but long chassis.

ES) Short chassis with vacuum tank cast into L -shaped centre member. No tinplate axle retainer, but axle slots on diecasting nipped to retain axles, and washer used with rivet to retain coupling. Used for a short time only during 1960.

EL) As ES but long chassis.

FS) Short chassis with L -shaped foot of centre member containing vacuum tank cut away. Rivet detail as CS. General 1960/1961 production.

FL) As ES but long chassis.

GS) Short chassis as DS but rivets replaced by 10 BA screws. Known to be used on Tarpaulin wagons only.

HL) Long chassis as DL but all brake detail removed. Used on Brake vans only. 1960/1961 production.

JS) Short chassis with vacuum tank cast into L -shaped centre member. Spring steel coupling/axle retainer enabling axles to be removed easily. Introduced during 1961.

JL) As JS but long chassis.

KS) Short chassis with L -shaped foot of centre member containing vacuum tank cut away. Spring steel coupling/axle retainer. Introduced during 1961.

LL) Long chassis as JL but all brake detail removed. Used on Brake vans only.

Apart from the tank wagons, all the different types of plastic goods wagon bodies were clipped into place on the relevant chassis. The well-detailed plastic superstructures were moulded from self-coloured plastic, light grey or light brown, the latter colour being listed as 'red' in the catalogues. The tank wagons have the earlier series printed tinplate tanks in which the blanks were suitably altered to take the new method of mounting plus the various new fittings. The tank was mounted on a plastic cradle with the end caps held in place with plastic end supports held rigid by wire stays. A new finely sculptured metal ladder was fitted to one side leading up to a plastic platform and filler cap. The above assembly was mounted on a long chassis using a central self-tapping screw.

In the descriptive list following, the only information given regarding the chassis will be whether it was short (C/S), or long (L/C), and whether it was fitted with vacuum tank or not in normal production. Just to confuse the situation, all of the later models fitted with spring steel axle retainers can be found with a vacuum tank. An approximation of the period of manufacture can be made from the information given in the above list in relation to the chassis variations:

Mock-up model of a BR 16-ton Mineral wagon fitted with opening end door.

Pre-production model of the BR 12-ton Covered van.

Cat. No.

P601 BR Open 3-plank wagon Light brown –wagon number B457434 – with vacuum tank – (L/C).

P602 BR Open 3-plank wagon Light grey –wagon number B457434 – (L/C).

P603 BR Open 3-plank wagon with trestle and plate (Cat.No.883) Light grey – wagon number B457434 – (L/C).

P604 BR 20-ton Pig Iron wagon Light brown – wagon number B744083 – with vacuum tank – (S/C).

P605 BR 20-ton Pig Iron wagon Light grey – wagon number B744083 – (S/C).

P606 BR 16-ton Mineral wagon, unloaded Light grey – wagon number B68174 – (S/C).

P607 BR 16-ton Mineral wagon, unloaded Light brown – wagon number B68174 – with vacuum tank – (S/C).

P608 BR 16-ton Mineral wagon with coal load Light grey – wagon number B68174 – (S/C).

P609 BR 16-ton Mineral wagon with iron ore load Light grey – wagon number B68174 – (S/C).

P611 BR 16-ton Mineral wagon with ballast load Light brown – wagon number B68174 – with vacuum tank – (S/C).

P612 BR 16-ton Mineral wagon with coal load Light brown – wagon number B68174 – with vacuum tank – (S/C).

P613 BR 12-ton Covered van Light brown body and light grey roof (shades) – two sliding doors fitted – van number B753500 – with vacuum tank – (S/C).

P614 BR 12-ton Covered van Light grey body and roof (shades) – two sliding doors fitted – van number B753500 – (S/C).

P616 BR Container Flat A Light brown body – wagon number B735103 – with vacuum tank – (S/C).

P617 BR Container Flat A with BR Standard Container (Cat. No. 882) Light brown wagon body – wagon number B753500 – with vacuum tank – (S/C).

P618 BR Container Flat A with BR Insulated Container (Cat. No. 885) Light brown wagon body – wagon number B753500 – with vacuum tank – (S/C).

P619 BR Container Flat B with 2 Bird's Eye Containers (one only Cat. No. 881) – light brown wagon body – wagon number B740367 – with vacuum tank – produced after August 1960 – (L/C).

P621 BR Goods Brake van Light grey body and roof (shades) with two glazed internal partitions – van number M731528 – with vacuum tank but no brake detail – also known without glazing – first produced in plastic during the winter of 1960 – (L/C).

P622 BR Goods Brake van Light brown body and light grey roof (shades) with two glazed internal partitions – van number M731528 – with vacuum tank but no brake detail – also known without glazing – first produced in plastic during the winter of 1960 – (L/C).

P641 Shell Tank wagon Red tinplate tank with markings the same as the previous series – with vacuum tank.

P644 Shell Tank wagon Aluminium coloured tinplate tank with markings the same as the previous series – with vacuum tank.

P646 Esso Tank wagon Aluminium coloured tinplate tank with markings the same as the previous series – with vacuum tank, tank number 2591.

P660 BR 16-ton Mineral wagon with BR black tarpaulin Light grey wagon – wagon number B68174 – tarpaulin numbers used were 278430, 287430 317420 and 321704, style of printing, cloth and method of fixing to wagon as previous series.

The information regarding the remainder of the wagons in this range is given elsewhere in this book. P621 and P622 Goods Brake vans with diecast bodies, together with P674, P677, P678, P679, P680 Weltrol wagons are described in the section 'The Fully Diecast Wagons'. The P615 Crane Truck Set is described in the section dealing exclusively with this subject.

In the Trix Products January 1963 price list, the catalogue number prefix letter 'P' had been dropped, but later in the same year when Courtaulds had formed British Trix Ltd each catalogue number was prefixed with the number '1'. No change in the construction of the wagons took place until 1965 when both sizes of diecast chassis, representing 10 ft and 12 ft BR wagons , were replaced by finely detailed moulded black polypropylene versions. These were tooled and moulded by the Liliput factory in Austria, a company with which British Trix Ltd became more and more involved as they attained a level of quality expected of Continental model railway products which was not usually found in British mass-produced models at this time. Each chassis had BRITISH TRIX, and GREAT

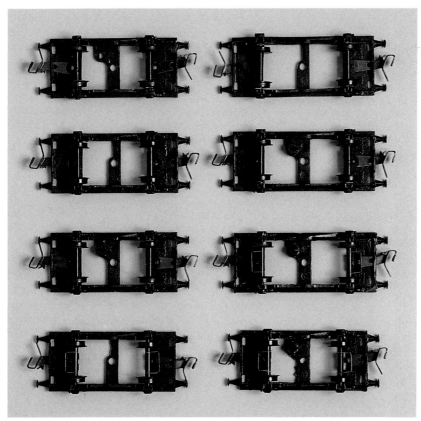

The 1960s diecast chassis. From the top and left: AS, FL, FS, DL, DS, JL, KS, JS. For an explanation of the key letters refer to the text.

BRITAIN plus a part number moulded into the underside.

The chassis was fitted with extremely free-running scale metal wheels with needle point bearings. This allowed very long trains of wagons to be hauled without derailing on the corners of the track. To enable these wagons to be used with other proprietory makes, provision was made for Tri-ang

The range of goods wagons introduced during 1960 with the highly detailed diecast chassis. The two Goods Brake vans on the top row Cat.Nos. P622 and P621 respectively are fitted with diecast bodies. The other wagons are fitted with plastic bodies. From the second row and the left - Cat.Nos. P601, P603, P602, P604, P620, P605, 3 of P660, P608, P611, P609.

Goods wagons introduced during 1960 plus two Liliput (Austria) produced Track Cleaning Tank wagons on the bottom row both Cat.No.1652 listed from 1963 in the British Trix catalogues. The three tank wagons on the second row still retain tinplate bodies. From the top row and the left: Cat.Nos. P614, P618, P613, P644, P641, P646, P622 (plastic), P619, P621 (plastic), P612, P617, P616 (middle bottom row).

couplings to be fitted in place of the new 'Alkon' plastic Trix ones. With these new plastic Trix couplings the patent number was no longer marked on the guide arm.

All the wagons in list on page 288 (except for the unloaded BR Container Flat A and the Tank wagons with tinplate tanks, the former discontinued in 1964 and the latter in 1965), were fitted with the new chassis and retained the same catalogue number as allocated in 1963, for example, P601 became 1601 etc. The only noticeable difference between the bodies of the earlier production and this range was that the white diagonal lines, printed on corresponding ends of each side of the BR Mineral wagons, ceased to be applied after a short period. The BR Open 3-plank wagon with Trestle and Plate was available with either a light brown or light grey body but was withdrawn by the end of the year,

The plastic chassis first introduced in 1965. From left to right, the versions are Liliput Made in Austria for the Private Owner wagons etc: all names blanked out for the Liliput Model Railways (UK) range of BR wagons with long wheel-base: British Trix wagons.

and two years later only the following wagons were still listed in the official literature. The date in brackets gives the last official listing:

Cat.No.
1606 BR 16-ton Mineral wagon, light grey. (1971)
1606 BR 16-ton Mineral wagon, very light grey – no white diagonal lines. (1971 to 1972 only)
1607 BR 16-ton Mineral wagon, light brown. (1972)
1613 BR 12-ton Covered van, light brown. (1972)
1614 BR 12-ton Covered van, light grey. (1972)
1617 BR Container Flat A with BR standard container.(1971)
1618 BR Container Flat A with BR insulated container.(1972)
1619 BR Container Flat B with two Birds Eye containers. (1969)
1621 BR Goods Brake van, light grey. (1972)
1622 BR Goods Brake van, light brown. (1972)

In 1966 a BR Container Flat B wagon was fitted with a BR London Midland Region 'Speedfreight' container, (Cat.No. 1482), finished in silver with black and yellow markings. This was a another finely-detailed plastic moulding produced by the Liliput factory. The catalogue number allocated to the Container Flat B wagon with Speedfreight container was 1623. It was withdrawn in 1971.

The autumn of 1966 saw the introduction of the BR Goods Brake vans fitted with lights:
Cat. No. 1653 Goods Brake van, light grey with lights for 2-rail operation.
Cat. No. 1654 Goods Brake van, light brown with lights for 3-rail operation.
The 3-rail version was only produced for one year, but the 2-rail version continued until 1969. Both versions had metal scale wheels which were used for current pick-ups via a contact wiper-blade assembly. The 3-rail version had a centre pick-up shoe assembly in place of one set of contact wiper blades.

The loads fitted to the above wagons were at one time or another available as separate items, as suggested by the catalogue numbers given in the wagon description. These, plus other loads, excluding those previously listed, were as follows: (Where a second catalogue number is given in brackets, it relates to a change in the original number from 1963. The dates in brackets relate to the years listed.)
Cat.No.
863 (1463) Bag of coal This was small pieces of loose black plastic waste. Two sizes of bag known. (1960 to 1963)
864 Bag of Iron Ore This was small pieces of loose light red-brown plastic waste. Two sizes of bag known.(1960 to 1962)
865 (1465) Bag of Ballast This was small pieces of loose grey plastic waste. Two sizes of bag known. (1960 to 1963)
881 (1481) 'Birds Eye' container Silver-grey plastic container with stuck-on printed foil design. Shade of printing varies – two containers per Con. Flat B wagon – container number AFP66358B. (1960 to 1969)

The pick-up assembly for the plastic Lighted Goods Brake Cat.No.1654. (B)

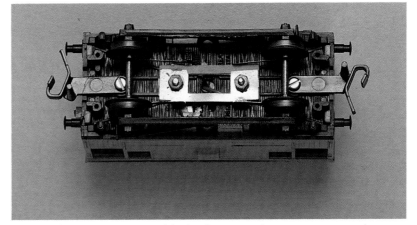

Showing the poor construction of the 2-rail current pick-up arrangement on the chassis of the grey plastic Goods Brake with Lights Cat.No.1653.

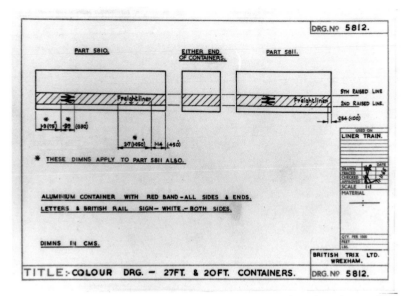

A marking drawing for the proposed model of a BR Freightliner.

882 (1482) BR Standard 4-ton container
Initially dark red plastic with dark grey roof and small yellow 'Huntley & Palmers' labels on each side. Container number BD6062B. (1960 to 1963)

883 Trestle and Plate Cream plastic trestle – tinplate 'plate' but later manufactured from aluminium. (1960 to 1962)

884 Six Asbestos Pipes White plastic sleeves, 3.8mm diameter x 48mm long. (1960 to 1962)

885 (1485) BR Insulated container Same mould as the BR Standard container but in white plastic with dark grey roof. (1960 to 1963)

886 7-piece Goods Wagon Load Set Comprising two small, one medium and one large off-white plastic packing cases plus three blue plastic barrels. These were used in the tinplate. Brake 2nd coaches with furniture. (1960 to 1962)

Private Owner Tank wagons.

1482 BR LMR Speedfreight container Plastic moulding finished in silver with black and yellow markings – container number BA4326B. (Catalogue number is a reissue. (1966 to 1970)

1483 Load Set, Coal, Ballast and Iron Ore These were the plastic mouldings as used for the loads in the 16-ton Mineral wagons. Each was self coloured, black for the coal, red-brown for the iron ore and fawn for the ballast. The red-brown load is also known over-sprayed to represent a ballast load. (1967 to 1969)

1484 Container Set One each of the red and white plastic containers in unpainted condition – originally items with catalogue numbers 882 and 885 respectively. (1967 to 1969)

During November 1965 plans were drawn for BR Freightliner container wagons with the intention that the special wagons would be permanently coupled by special link, so forming a Liner Train. Two sizes of containers were to be manufactured, 20 ft and 27 ft, each finished in aluminium with red bands carrying the BR logo and the letters of FREIGHTLINER in white. Most of the parts were to be manufactured at the Liliput factory and then shipped to Wrexham for assembly. The designated catalogue number was 1655 for release in the autumn of 1966. The reason that the design was never put into production was that British Trix Ltd, after carefully weighing up the situation, felt that as the Freightliner would only have limited appeal it was far more important to concentrate company efforts, and limited finances, on wagons with general appeal and variety that could be based on common plastic mouldings.

During the period from spring to autumn 1966, British Trix reintroduced a range of Private Owner tank wagons based upon the new polypropylene long chassis but using the existing tank cradle, end supports and top fittings as used on the previous range. The tinplate tank was replaced with one moulded from plastic, the whole assembly held on to the chassis by two fine metal ladders, each one hooked into a slot in the tank platform and to the underside of the chassis frame. Below is the list of Tank wagons available, with the date in brackets representing the last year they were officially listed. The basic tank colour is given, together with the colour of the stars where 'two-star' transfers were used in conjunction with the main ones. All the colour combinations and related transfers are taken from British Trix production documents:

Most of the proprietory ranges of goods rolling stock in the mid 1960s did not include many Private Owner wagons. It was the intention of British Trix Ltd to redress the balance with the introduction of two such ranges. The first was a 7-plank open wagon fitted to the short new polypropylene chassis and finished in the liveries of many private companies. The second was a range of BR Bulk Grain wagons carrying the names of Whiskey distillers. Liliput in Austria produced all the tooling and most of the finished parts for these two ranges.

The drawing for the basic Private Owner wagon body was started during February 1966, but it was not until August that Liliput received copies of the

Cat. No.
1638 REGENT tank wagon Grey with black stars. (1969)
1639 REGENT tank wagon Black with white stars. (1966 only)
1640 SHELL tank wagon Aluminium with black stars. This tank wagon had a single large Shell transfer and not the combined BP/Shell transfer as Cat. Nos. 1641 and 1642. (1966 only)
1641 SHELL/BP tank wagon Red with black stars – tank number 1198. (1972)
1642 SHELL/BP tank wagon Black with white stars.(1966 only)
1643 ESSO tank wagon Black with white stars. (1966 only)
1644 ESSO tank wagon Aluminium with black stars. (1972)
1645 BP tank wagon Green with small BP transfer (larger transfer usually found on kit version) and black stars. (1972)
1646 BP tank wagon Black with small BP transfer (larger version usually found on kit version) and white stars. (1966 only)
1647 FINA tank wagon Aluminium with black stars. (1969)
1648 TOTAL tank wagon Grey with black stars. (1971)
1649 MOBIL tank wagon Aluminium with black stars. (1969)
1650 FINA tank wagon Black with white stars. (1966 only)
The MOBIL tank wagon was also available in black, but only in the Wagonmaster series. As most of the above tank wagons were available in the Wagonmaster kit series, it is inevitable that many unofficial variations exist.

basic drawing superimposed with the details of the markings for the different private companies. The wagon body was based upon the wooden 7-plank wagon seen in large quantities on the railways prior to nationalisation. One complaint by purists was that the chassis incorporated a vacuum tank which was non-prototypical. However, this could be removed with a sharp knife. At 7/11d (almost 40p) they were good value. An interesting memo dated 11 May 1967 from Ernest Rozsa of British Trix to Mr A. H. Davies of British Lego Ltd gave the following production statement:

'Re PRIVATE OWNER WAGON
PRODUCTION.

The production of the above wagons involves
the following processes:
(Average times quoted)

Wheel assembly Bush two wheels and assemble same to axle. 20 sec./unit, ie 40 secs.
Wagon assembly Fit coupling, check for free movement, clip in wheels and test. Clip on body and inspect. 45 secs.
Packing Wagon to be inserted in the box and secured by two cardboard rings and a yellow self-adhesive descriptive label fixed to one end of the box. 20 secs.
Total time on average = 105 seconds, or say 2 minutes.'

It must be remembered that at this time British Trix and British Lego were under the same ownership, namely the Courtaulds Group. Thus the Private Owner wagons were designed by British Trix Ltd, the parts manufactured by Liliput Spielwaren-fabrik GmbH and initially assembled in the Lego factory.

Below is a list of the Private Owner wagons produced, the dates in brackets refer to the inclusive official production/availability period:

Cat.No.
1657 Wallace Spiers & Co. Ltd Yellow – wagon number 347 – black markings. (1967 to 1971)
1658 Maltby Red-oxide – wagon number 11 – white markings, main letters edged in black. (1967 to early 1972)
1659 A. J. Salter & Co. Red-oxide – wagon number 122 – white markings. (1967 to 1972)
1661 Young & Co. Brown – wagon number 25 – white markings. (1967 to 1972)
1662 Ocean Black – wagon number 17107 – white markings. (1967 to 1972)
1664 Hall & Co. Grey – wagon number 510 – white markings. (1967 to 1972)
1665 ICI Bright red – wagon number 326 – white markings (late 1967 to 1972)
1666 Blue Circle Cement Wagon number 173 – white and blue markings. (late 1967 to 1971)
1667 Charringtons Red-oxide – wagon number 257 – white and black markings. (late 1967 to 1972)
1668 Isaac Wilkinson Ltd Bright red – wagon number 35 – white and black markings. (late 1967 to 1972)
1669 Abbott & Co. Ltd Black – wagon number 3510 – white markings. (late 1967 to 1972)
1670 Stewarts and LLoyds Ltd Dark green – wagon number 6534 – white and black markings. (late 1967 to 1971)
1671 Chubb Red-oxide – wagon number 181 – white markings.(late 1968 to 1972)
1672 Wm. Gordon Jameson's Yellow – wagon number 51 – black markings. (late 1968 to 1972)
1673 Roberts, Jenks & Co. Ltd Black – wagon number 100 – white markings. (late 1968 to 1972)
1674 Sutton Manor Grey (shades) – wagon number 1075 – white and black markings. (late 1968 to 1972)
1675 Nicholsons' Black – wagon number 1 – white and red markings. (late 1968 to 1972)

By popular demand, the above basic wagons were finished in the livery of the four pre-nationalised railway companies, plus an unmarked version, as follows:
1631 LMS 7-plank Red-oxide – wagon number 259484 – white markings. (mid-1971 to 1972)
1632 GWR 7-plank Very light grey – wagon number 109453 – white markings. (mid-1971 to 1972)
1632 GWR 7-plank Medium grey – wagon number 109453 – white markings. (mid-1971 to 1972)
1633 SR 7-plank Very light grey – wagon number 32277 – white markings. (mid-1971 to 1972)
1633 SR 7-plank Medium grey – wagon number 32277 – white markings. (mid-1971 to 1972)
1634 NE 7-plank Red-oxide – wagon number 91528 – white markings. (mid-1971 to 1972)
1656 7-plank wagon Sprayed black – no number or markings. (1972 only)

The draughtsman, Michael Catalani, stipulated on the design drawings that the LMS wagon should be grey and the S.R wagon brown. Why the colours were changed by the manufacturers is unknown.

Most of the wagon bodies from the Private Owner wagons could be purchased separately, the first six available during the summer of 1967 and six

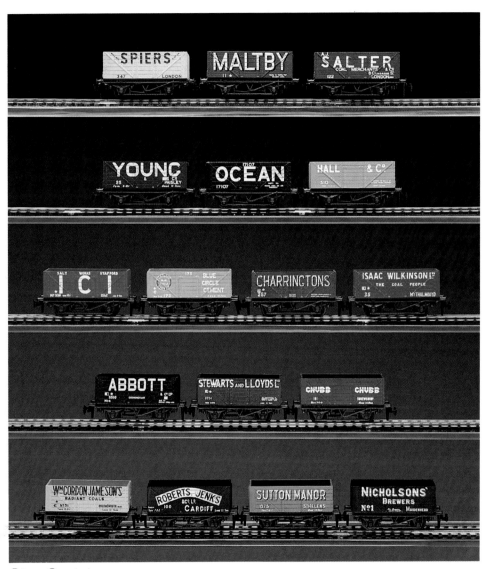

Private Owner wagons.

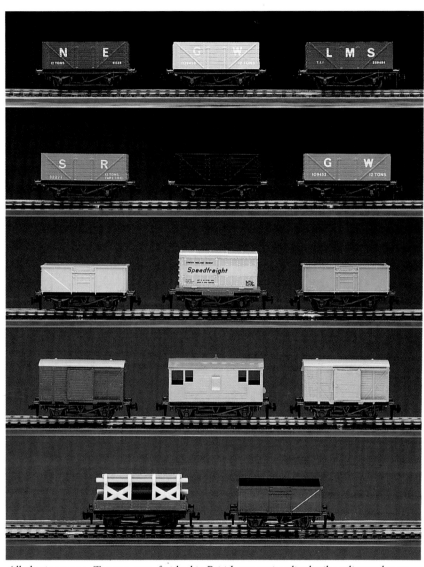

All plastic wagons. Top two rows finished in British pre-nationalised railway livery plus an unmarked version. The next three rows are Trix and Liliput(UK) models. From the left: Cat.Nos. 1307, 1623, 1606, 1313, 1621, 1322, 1603, 1306 (grey over-sprayed brown).

others from the spring of 1968. The last two digits of the catalogue number of these wagon bodies corresponded to the catalogue number of the complete wagon. Thus the wagon body for the Cat. No.1658 Maltby wagon was Cat. No.1458. The following bodies were available: 1457-Spiers, 1458-Maltby, 1459-Salter, 1461-Young, 1462-Ocean, 1464-Hall, 1465-ICI, 1466-Blue Circle, 1467-Charringtons, 1468-Wilkinson, 1469-Abbott and 1470-Stewarts and Lloyds. These separate wagon bodies were not listed after 1968.

Probably the finest range of wagons to carry the Trix name were the BRT 35-ton Bulk Grain vans. These models were built to a scale of 4mm to the foot using various highly-detailed plastic mouldings, with a special graphite impregnated nylon for the chassis which when fitted with the needle point axle and metal wheel assemblies gave extremely free running characteristics. These special vans carried either long or short nameboards depending upon the design of the sign used.

British Trix Ltd were endeavouring to reflect the modernisation of British Railways, and with this in mind, design and livery detail enquiries were begun in the spring of 1966 by Vernon Rogers, a designer/draughtsman who had joined British Trix in the latter part of 1963. These enquiries were made long before the vans were in general service with the whisky distillers. Unfortunately this created problems, and it was not until February of 1967, after prolonged correspondence with the various companies involved in operating the vans, that the final decorative details were made known to British Trix.

Unadopted Private Owner wagon designs.

Nevertheless, van constructional details had been obtained from the makers, Rootes Pressings (Scotland) Ltd, in good time for the design of the basic model to be drawn and submitted to Liliput for manufacture in October 1966. Eventually the first production samples of six of the models were ready in May 1967, but the full range was not available in the shops until the late summer, well after the time that Vernon Rodgers had left the company.

The full size Bulk Grain vans were owned by the British Railway Traffic & Electric Co. Ltd (BRT) and leased to various private whisky distillers in the Scottish Malt Distillers group (blue van bodies), and to The Maltsters' Association of Great Britain (yellow van bodies). British Railways also operated this type of Bulk Grain van which was finished in grey.

On the model, provision was made on the chassis to enable Tri-ang couplings to be fitted in place of the normal Trix ones. The buffers were separate mouldings and were a push fit in the buffer beam housing; the vacuum tank was also a separate moulding. The chassis and body were held together by two plastic rivets, and a stabilising weight was glued in place inside the body. The roof moulding was a loose fit on the body. Apart from the various company signs, three details were printed on each side, one was a black 'C' on a yellow square together with a yellow star on a black square, or a black 'C' on a white square together with a white star on a black square, and the last was a label in black and white giving the name of British Railway Traffic & Electric Co. Ltd. A red and black BRT self-adhesive label was also applied to each side plus a range of individual white van number transfers. The numbers

Bulk Grain vans. Note Crawfords signs with and without red stars, and different shades of yellow in the Maltsters vans.

on these transfers were correct at the time for the full-size vans in service with the various distillers. The following is the list of the BRT 35-ton Bulk Grain Vans produced which were introduced in the summer of 1967. The date in brackets refers to the last time is was officially listed:

Cat.No.

1680 Johnnie Walker Blue – small printed sign with self-adhesive label – van numbers 5817, 5820, 5822, 5825, 5829, 5833, 5837, 5842, 5846, 5847, 5850, 5853, 5854, and 5857 to 5861 inclusive. (1972)

1681 Haig Blue – small printed sign – van numbers 5815, 5823, 5826, 5830, 5834, 5839, 5843, 5862, 5863 and 5864. (1972)

1683 Vat 69 Blue – small printed sign with self adhesive label – van numbers 5814, 5819, 5824, 5827, 5831, 5835, 5840, 5844, 5848 and 5851. (1969)

1684 King George IV Blue – small printed sign with self-adhesive label – van numbers 5816 and 5878. (1969)

1685 Dewar's Blue – large printed sign – van numbers 5810, 5811, 5812 and 5838. (1972)

1686 Crawford's Blue – small printed sign normally with three red stars, but early production are without stars – van number 5899. (1971)

1687 White Horse Whisky Blue – large printed sign – van numbers 5813, 5818, 5821, 5828, 5832, 5836, 5841, 5845, 5849, 5852, 5855, and 5856. (1972)

The van numbers applied to the following models have no set pattern, and many of those numbers listed for the above models, plus others up to 5900, were used. For this reason, van numbers for the following are not listed.

1688 Jamie Stuart Blue – small printed sign. (1972)

1689 The Maltsters Association of Great Britain Yellow (various shades) – large sign – not introduced until late 1967. (1972)

1690 Abbot's Choice Blue – large sign. (1971)

1691 BR 35-ton bulkcarrier Grey – no sign. (1971)

1692 BR 35-ton open bulkcarrier Grey – no sign. (1968)

In many instances the number transfers and the self-adhesive BRT label are found to be missing. It is inevitable that as the Bulk Grain vans were available in the Wagonmaster kit series, anomalies will exist.

In 1968 British Trix Ltd supplied a quantity of Bulk Grain wagons to Lines Bros. Ltd for inclusion in their Tri-ang range. The four types supplied were Dewar's, Johnnie Walker, Vat 69 and Haig, (Tri-ang Cat. Nos. R647, R648, R649, R650 respectively), of which 1,000 of each were ordered. Each wagon was fitted with standard Tri-ang couplings. During 1969 a few of the wagon bodies were supplied and fitted to Tri-ang China Clay wagon chassis.

From 1963 a range of Trix Express and Liliput wagons and coaches, plus one wagon from Tempo, were included in the British Trix catalogues. This was an attempt to increase the range on offer and thus make it more attractive to customers. All the rolling stock were fitted with scale metal wheels and British Trix couplings. After careful consideration it was felt beyond the scope of this book to describe these items in detail. However, the range of rolling stock that was offered in the British Trix catalogues is listed elsewhere in this book together with actual Trix Express and Liliput catalogue numbers.

After Trix Trains were gradually phased out during 1973 by Thernglade Ltd, the range was taken over and continued from 1974 under the banner of Liliput Model Railways (UK) Ltd. Basically the goods wagons remained the same with a few minor alterations. The remains of the Trix Trains stock, as well as spares, were purchased by Liliput Model Railways (UK). These included short polypropylene wagon chassis bearing the inscriptions BRITISH TRIX and GREAT BRITAIN. It was intended to use these for the BR wagon range whose bodies were moulded by Lego Ltd, but as they were not now strictly 'Trix', the name TRIX was removed from the chassis. The long version of this chassis for use on the remainder of the BR wagons, plus the tank wagons, received similar treatment initially, but it was not long before it became necessary for the chassis to be specially moulded by Liliput with the inscriptions BRITISH TRIX and GREAT BRITAIN blanked out leaving no manufacturer's identification at all.

As the Private Owner wagon bodies, including the other 7-plank wagon bodies produced from the same mould, were manufactured by Liliput in Austria, the short chassis for these wagons now bore the apt inscriptions LILIPUT and MADE IN AUSTRIA. The chassis for the Bulk Grain vans were modified enabling a more efficient method of mounting the body and securing the stabilising weight. This was achieved by blanking off the two rivet holes in the chassis and providing a central spigot over which the body and two circular weights were fitted, all retained by a push-on fastener on the central spigot. The roof of the Bulk Grain vans was glued in place instead of being a loose fit, and the practice of fitting van numbers was generally discontinued.

Overall, the grey plastic used in the moulding of the BR wagon and van bodies was much lighter than that used during the Trix era with the roofs of the vans being even lighter than the main body moulding. After a very short time, the brown plastic mouldings of the 16-ton Mineral wagon bodies were replaced with grey mouldings over-painted with matt brown, although on both grey and brown versions of the Mineral wagon the white diagonal line was reinstated.

New catalogue numbers were allotted, which bore a direct relationship with those used by British Trix/Trix Trains except in certain instances where a corresponding catalogue number relating to a grey or brown version were changed around. All the ex-Trix goods vehicles listed below were reintroduced by Liliput Model Railways (UK) Ltd in the late summer of 1974. The date in brackets refers to the last official listing:

Cat. No.
1301 BR Open 3-plank wagon Brown.
1302 BR Open 3-plank wagon Light grey. (From 1986 the above two wagons were given the same catalogue number of 1301 and were not available after 1988.)
1306 BR 16-ton Mineral wagon Brown plastic – later versions were grey wagons over-sprayed matt brown. (1985)
1307 BR 16-ton Mineral wagon Grey. (1985)
1313 BR Covered van Brown. (1984)
1314 BR Covered van Grey. (1984)
1321 BR Goods Brake van Brown.
1322 BR Goods Brake van Grey. (From 1986 the above Goods Brake vans were given the same

catalogue number of 1321 and were not available after 1990.)
From 1978 all the above wagons were made to special order only, except for the Goods Brake vans which once again became stock items from 1986.
1340 Shell tank wagon Red. (1983)
1344 Esso tank wagon Silver. (1983)
1345 BP tank wagon Green. (1983)
From 1978 the above tank wagons were made to special order only
1346 LMS 7-plank wagon Red-oxide. (1975 to 1976 only)
1347 NER 7-plank wagon Red-oxide. (1975 to 1976 only)
1348 GWR 7-plank wagon Very light grey. (1975 to 1976 only)
1349 SR 7-plank wagon Very light grey. (1975 to 1976 only)
1356 7-plank wagon Matt black. (1985)
1357 Wallace Spiers & Co. Ltd private owner wagon. (1983)
1358 Maltby private owner wagon. (1983)
1359 A.J. Salter & Co. private owner wagon. (1983)
1361 Young & Co. private owner wagon. (1978)
1362 Ocean private owner wagon. (1983)
1364 Hall & Co. private owner wagon. (1978 but re-introduced 1984 until 1988)
1365 ICI private owner wagon. (1983)
1366 Blue Circle Cement private owner wagon. (1978 but reintroduced 1984 until 1988)
1367 Charringtons private owner wagon. (1983)
1368 Isaac Wilkinson Ltd private owner wagon. (1983)

1369 Abbott & Co. Ltd private owner wagon. (1978 but reintroduced 1984 until 1988)
1370 Stewarts & Lloyds Ltd private owner wagon. (1978)
1371 Chubb private owner wagon. (1978 but re-introduced 1984 until 1988)
1372 Wm. Gordon Jameson's private owner wagon. (1978 but reintroduced 1984 until 1988)
1373 Roberts, Jenks & Co. Ltd private owner wagon. (1978 but reintroduced 1986 until 1988)
1374 Sutton Manor private owner wagon. (1984)
1375 Nicholsons' private owner wagon. (1978 but re-introduced 1984 until 1988)
From 1978 all the above wagons, when listed in the range, were available to special order only, except for catalogue numbers 1364, 1366, 1369, 1371, 1372, 1373 and 1375 which once again became stock items from 1986.
1380 Johnnie Walker bulk grain van. (1983)
1381 Haig bulk grain van. (1983)
1383 Vat 69 bulk grain van. (1985)
1384 King George IV bulk grain van The inscription OLD SCOTCH WHISKY on the van sign was in yellow letters, whilst that on the Trix version was in white letters. (1985)
1385 Dewar's bulk grain van. (1985)
1386 Crawford's bulk grain van. (1985)
1387 White Horse Whisky bulk grain van. (1983)
1388 Jamie Stuart bulk grain van. (1985)
1389 Maltsters' Association of Great Britain bulk grain van. (1983)
1390 Abbot's Choice bulk grain van. (1983)
1391 BR 35-ton bulk carrier. (1985)

THE PLASTIC MODELS OF THE BR STANDARD AND PULLMAN RANGE OF COACHES

It was in 1961 that Michael Catalani was entrusted with the design of a new range of TTR coaches which were to be a complete departure from the previous method of construction, and as near as possible to scale proportions based upon British Railways Standard coaches. The chosen scale was 3.8mm to the foot, as the initial intention was to offer the coaches in both the TTR and Trix Express catalogues, appropriately modified to suit Trix Express running. However, such a choice of scale proved to be a disastrous decision as it impeded sales in Britain, despite the quality of the coaches receiving very favourable comments from the modelling press. In point of fact, when the coaches eventually went into mass production three years later, the planned German outlet was dropped.

The construction of the coaches was on the principle of separate underframe (or chassis), sides, roof, interior and bogie frame mouldings. The same styrene chassis moulding, incorporating the coach ends, was used for the Miniature Buffet car, Composite Brake and Composite Corridor coaches, with a different moulding for the Pullman Kitchen car. The moulded coach ends on the Pullman chassis were parallel, much narrower and with different detailing to those on the chassis used for the other coaches. This was to accommodate the recessed doors on the Pullman coach sides. Each chassis was fitted with Commonwealth-pattern bogie-frame mouldings and separate buffer-beam mouldings complete with oval buffers, the latter moulding being a clip fit into the ends of the chassis.

The proposed version for the German market made use of a swivelling buffer beam and Trix Express-style coupling mounted on the bogies, in turn fitted with coarse wheels to enable the coaches to be used on the standard Trix Express track. Both the British and German versions were on show at the 1963 British Toy Fair at Brighton, but it was not until the summer of 1964 that the first of the mass-produced coaches reached the British model shops.

As mentioned above, four basic patterns of coach were produced – a Composite Corridor, a Composite Brake, a Miniature Buffet car and a Pullman Kitchen car. The first two patterns were also used for coaches finished in LMS and GWR livery introduced in 1971. The tooling for the moulds was produced by South Bucks Tools Ltd with the injection mould for the coach sides being a very ambitious affair capable of producing a pair of sides for each of the three standard pattern coaches with one injection of styrene, (plastic). Each of these three coaches had a different patterned roof which was also produced from one mould. The Pullman coach parts were formed in different moulds. During Trix days, the basic coach sides were produce from self-coloured styrene sprayed with a different colour as and when required, as for example the yellow band on the Western Region coaches, while in the Liliput Model Railways era, almost all the coach sides were black oversprayed with the appropriate colour.

Lining and marking of the coach sides, except in the case of the Pullman cars as used on the British Railways East Coast route, was kept to an acceptable minimum. It had been the intention to apply an additional heavy yellow line above the First class compartment windows and a red line above the

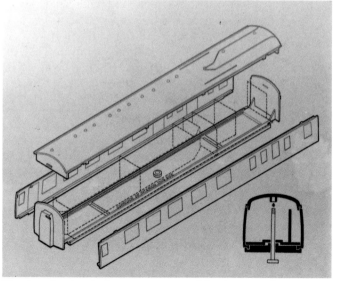
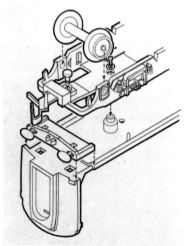

Drawings showing the basic construction of the plastic coaches.

300

Pre-production model of the BR Midland Region Composite Brake Coach.

Pre-production model of the Pullman.

Pre-production model of the BR Western Region Composite Corridor Coach.

Pre-production model of the BR Southern Region Miniature Buffet Car.

windows on the Buffet cars, but these details were dropped until the introduction of de-luxe versions some years later. For these de-luxe versions, machine printing trials for the additional lines proved to be a failure, and the production staff had to resort to hand painting. Understandably this was not a cost-effective exercise, and the additional lining was soon abandoned.

The interiors of the coaches were single mouldings in cream styrene (including a version with inferior quality plastic) until around 1969 when there was a gradual change to light grey. Each coach had a different layout of seats and tables, with turned brass table lamps fitted to the Pullman interior. These mouldings were a close fit between the sides of the coach which helped to retain the Celastoid window strips in place, although a plastic cement was also used. The window strips were 'whitened' in appropriate places such as the toilet windows.

All the main parts were interlocking and held together by a special 6 BA screw passing through the centre of the chassis and interior mouldings, and secured in the roof moulding. A metal plate was inserted between the chassis and the furniture to give added stability. The bogies were moulded in black polypropylene and initially fitted with spring steel couplings, and moulded scale-profile styrene wheels on needle-point axles. The bogie assemblies were held in place on the coach chassis pivots with self-tap screws.

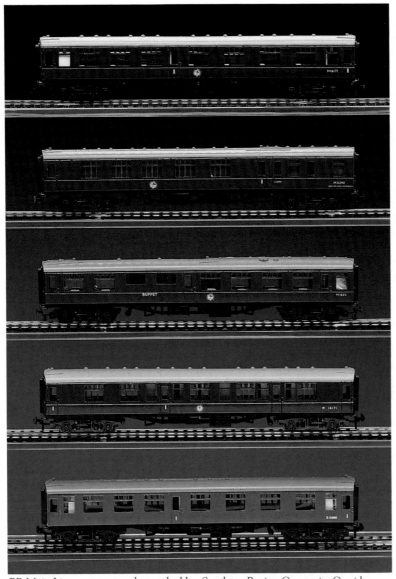

BR Main Line maroon coaches and a blue Southern Region Composite Corridor coach available only in 'Coachbuilder' kit form. From the top: Cat.Nos. 1901, 1902, 1903, 1201 [Liliput (UK)], 1954.

BR Southern Region coaches. From the top: early demonstration model Composite Brake, then Cat.Nos. 1921, 1922, 1923, 1222 [Liliput (UK)]. Notice the different finish on the latter in comparison to the other coaches.

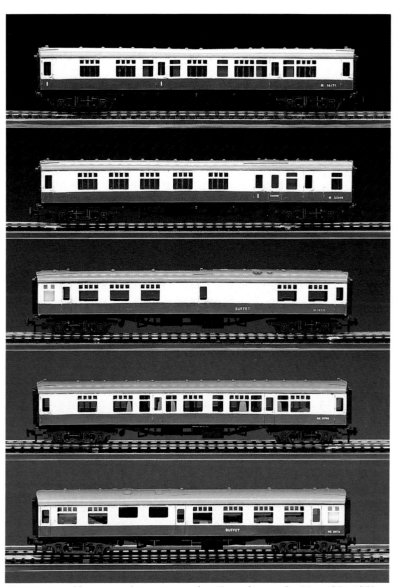

BR Western Region coaches. From the top: Cat.Nos. 1911, 1912, 1912 with additional markings, 1913, 1213 [Liliput (UK)].

BR Main Line blue/grey and Intercity coaches. From the top: Cat.Nos. 1951, 1952, 1953, 1975, 1977.

Cat. No.

1901 BR Composite Corridor, Midland region maroon Lined in yellow – coach number M 16171. (1964 to 1972)

1902 BR Composite Brake, Midland region maroon Lined in yellow – coach number M 21240. (1964 to 1972)

1903 BR MR Miniature Buffet Car, Midland region maroon Lined in yellow – coach number M 1820. (1964 to 1972)

1905 As catalogue number 1901 but fitted with lights 2-rail. (1965 to 1967)

1906 As catalogue number 1902 but fitted with lights 2-rail. (1965 to 1967)

1907 As catalogue number 1903 but fitted with lights 2-rail. (1965 to 1967)

1908 As catalogue number 1901 but fitted with lights 3-rail. (1966 to 1967)

1909 As catalogue number 1902 but fitted with lights 3-rail. (1966 to 1967)

1910 As catalogue number 1903 but fitted with lights 3-rail. (1966 to 1967)

1911 BR Composite Corridor, Western region yellow/brown Unlined – coach number W 16198. (1964 to 1972)

1912 BR Composite Brake, Western region yellow/brown Unlined – coach number W 21194. (1964 to 1972)

1913 BR Miniature Buffet Car, Western region yellow/brown Unlined – coach number W 1816. (1964 to 1972)

1915 As catalogue number 1911 but fitted with lights 2-rail. (1965 to 1967)

1916 As catalogue number 1912 but fitted with lights 2-rail. (1965 to 1967)

1917 As catalogue number 1913 but fitted with lights 2-rail. (1965 to 1967)

1918 As catalogue number 1911 but fitted with lights 3-rail. (1966 to 1967)

1919 As catalogue number 1912 but fitted with lights 3-rail. (1966 to 1967)

1920 As catalogue number 1913 but fitted with lights 3-rail. (1966 to 1967)

1921 BR Composite Corridor, Southern region green Unlined – coach number S 15900. (1964 to 1972)

1922 BR Composite Brake, Southern region green Unlined – coach number S 2301. (1964 to 1972)

1923 BR Miniature Buffet Car, Southern region green Unlined – coach number S 1852. (1964 to 1972)

1925 As catalogue number 1921 but fitted with lights 2-rail. (1965 to 1967)

1926 As catalogue number 1922 but fitted with lights 2-rail. (1965 to 1967)

1927 As catalogue number 1923 but fitted with lights 2-rail. (1965 to 1967)

1928 As catalogue number 1921 but fitted with lights 3-rail. (1966 to 1967)

1929 As catalogue number 1922 but fitted with lights 3-rail. (1966 to 1967)

1930 As catalogue number 1923 but fitted with lights 3-rail. (1966 to 1967)

1931 Pullman Car, dark brown/cream Markings and lining in gold.
The name PULLMAN initially printed in gold lettering but from 1971 applied by transfer. Names used were: ADRIAN, ARIES, CARINA, EAGLE, HAWK, HERON, IBIS, JOAN, LYDIA, ORION, RAVEN, PLATO, ROBIN, SNIPE, WREN.

The coach was initially supplied with a name, but later with a blank name panel plus sheet of name transfers. (late 1964 to 1972)

1932 LMS 1st/3rd Class Corridor, maroon Yellow lining and markings – known with black or white roof – coach number 1670. (1971 to 1972)

1933 LMS Composite Brake, maroon Yellow lining and markings – known with black or white roof – coach number 5531. (1971 to 1972)

1935 As catalogue number 1931 but fitted with lights 2-rail (1965 to 1967)

1935 GWR Corridor, brown and cream Known with black or white roof – unlined – coach number 2017. (1971 to 1972)

1936 GWR Brake, brown and cream Known with black or white roof – unlined – coach number 3148. (1971 to 1972)

1938 As catalogue number 1931 but fitted with lights 3-rail (1966 to 1967)

1951 BR Composite Corridor, blue and grey Unlined – coach number M 16171 – white inscriptions and number. (1966 to 1972)

1952 BR Composite Brake, blue and grey Unlined – coach number M 21240 – white inscriptions and number. (1966 to 1972)

1953 BR Miniature Buffet Car, blue and grey Unlined – coach number M 1820 – white inscriptions and number. (1966 to 1972)

1954 BR Composite Corridor, Southern region blue Unlined – coach number S 15900 – white markings and number – available only from Coachbuilder kit. (1968 to 1970)

1955 BR Composite Brake, Southern region blue Unlined – coach number S 2301 – white markings and number. Available only from Coachbuilder kit. (1968 to 1970)

1971 BR Intercity Composite Corridor, dark green Yellow lining – coach number NE 59766 – early models had the following inscriptions on the chassis solebar in white:
EMERGENCY LIGHTING POINT   S.H.O. 2033   BO 11.3.66
This chassis inscription ceased to be applied in circa 1970. (1967 to 1972)

1972 BR Intercity Composite Brake, dark green Yellow lining – coach number NE 51976 chassis comments as for catalogue number 1971. (1967 to 1972)

1973 BR Intercity Miniature Buffet Car, dark green Yellow lining – coach number NE 59774 – chassis comments as for catalogue number 1971. (1967 to 1972)

1975 BR Intercity Composite Corridor, blue and grey Unlined – white letters and number – coach number NE 59766 – chassis comments as for catalogue number 1971 (1967 to 1972)

1976 BR Intercity Composite Brake, blue and grey Unlined – white letters and numbers – coach number NE 51970 – chassis comments as for catalogue number 1972. (1967 to 1972)

1977 BR Intercity Miniature Buffet Car, blue and grey Unlined – white letters and numbers – coach number NE 59744 – chassis comments as for catalogue number 1971. (1967 to 1972)

1978 Pullman Car, blue and grey Unlined – white PULLMAN letters and number 342. This coach was first available in 1968 but only from a Coachbuilder kit and not in completed form until 1971. (1968 to 1972)

By the spring of 1965 the spring steel coupling had been replaced by an Alkon plastic version and was held in place with a self-tap screw instead of a rivet, although some coaches are known with the plastic coupling riveted in place. During the same period the bogie mouldings were modified at one end to take a Tri-ang coupling if required, the latter in an endeavour to widen the scope of prospective sales. 1966 saw the introduction of the metal wheel assemblies, although the plastic wheels continued to be issued in the Coachbuilder kits well into the following year. These metal wheels, coupled with the bogie frames, by now impregnated with graphite and identifiable by their smokey-black appearance, gave the coaches a remarkable, virtually unrivalled, free-running characteristic.

To increase realism, coaches with lighting units were available during the autumn of 1965 for 2-rail versions, and the spring of 1966 for the 3-rail versions. The fitting of the lighting units necessitated modification to the roof, interior and chassis mouldings which became standard and used on all coaches. The modification to the roof moulding took the form of two extra studs used to locate the Tufnol printed circuit strip on which the lights were mounted. The height of the partitions on the interior furniture moulding had to be reduced to accommodate the lighting unit, and the inside face of the chassis at the point of the bogie pivots had to be recessed to allow the use of solder tags as part of the electrical circuit between the current pick-ups and the lights. Current pick-up on the 2-rail versions was by means of brass wheels and spring contacts on the axles, and in the case of the 3-rail versions one bogie was fitted with a centre pick-up shoe assembly similar to that used on the tinplate coaches, the other

bogie being the same as the 2-rail version.

This series of coaches was listed in the 1962 and 1963 Trix price lists, furnished and unfurnished, which also listed the furniture moulding as being available separately. The unfurnished coaches and the furniture packs were never issued, and it was not until the middle of 1964 that the following range was made available to the public. All coaches, except where stated, had light grey roofs plus yellow inscriptions. The coach letter/number combination was printed in two ways; firstly, with the letter close to the number as in M21240 which was used up to 1966, and secondly, the letter spaced from the number as in M 21240 which remained in constant use from 1966. The first style of printing was much finer than the later style. In addition during 1965, for approximately one year only, the words –

LOAD 1 TON EVENLY DISTRIBUTED were applied to the brake-end of the Composite Brake coaches below the coach number. The Midland, Southern, Western Region and later dark green Intercity coaches normally carried round British Railways coaching stock transfers, but as large quantities of Coachbuilder kits were sold, many coaches, other than the Intercity coaches, can be found with these transfers missing. With reference to the list of coaches shown on page 304 the dates in brackets indicate the inclusive period that they were supplied to the retail outlets. (Coachbuilder kits are described fully in the chapter dealing with the Railway Construction kits).

The BR standard coaches introduced in Intercity livery were intended to be used as intermediate coaches for the DMU Intercity 2-car sets. Correct pattern intermediate coaches, although designed,

were never introduced due to the low demand for the DMUs at the time.

Listed in the 1967 to 1969 price lists were BR Composite Brake coaches fitted with illuminated tail lights, catalogue numbers 1981 and 1982 respectively. These never went into mass production due to the relatively high cost of the proposed Trix Express light unit and its insertion into the coach. This high cost is seen in the published price in 1967 of 30/4d as against 17/8d for a standard coach. A handful of these coaches were made to special order only.

Shown on the rear inside cover page of the 1967/1968 catalogue was a selection of British Railways coaches in blue and grey livery intended for the Trix range. Although allocated catalogue numbers and even listed in the 1968 price list, they were not produced. For reference they are listed below:

Cat. No.
1906 Coach 2nd class open. Mark 2
1907 Coach Mark 2.
1933 Pullman Parlour Car 1st Class.
1934 Pullman Parlour Brake Car.
1935 Pullman Parlour Kitchen Car.

Coach lighting units were available separately from 1966 to 1970 with the following catalogue numbers:
1451 for 2-rail
1452 for 3-rail,
1951 for 3-rail, listed in 1964 but not produced.

Most of the coaches reappeared under the Liliput Model Railways (UK) banner from 1974 onwards. After the exhaustion of the ex-Trix parts, the roofs and interiors were moulded from much lighter grey plastic, and the coach sides were sprayed with the appropriate colour which resulted in the Midland and Southern region coaches having a much richer-looking finish. The embossed letters TTR on the underside of the chassis were obliterated to indicate that they were Liliput Model Railways (UK) Ltd items, the moulds for the chassis remaining unaltered from the Trix period. All the markings were the same as the normal Trix production, except the chassis solebars which were devoid of inscriptions. In the list on the right the number in brackets after the main catalogue number is the corresponding Trix catalogue number, and the dates correspond to the inclusive availability period:

For a few years most of the coaches produced by Liliput Model Railways (UK) Ltd, excluding the Intercity range, were only available to special order. On nearing the end of coach production during the latter part of the 1980s, some of the Intercity coaches were fitted with correct DMU bogies consisting of a diecast unit and plastic bogie frame as the Commonwealth bogie frame tool used previously was no longer available.

This range of coaches introduced during 1964 probably holds the record as the longest-running production period for any proprietor model railway coach range. Many thousands were manufactured and sold in completed form or in the popular Coachbuilder kit form.

Cat.No.

1201 (1901) BR Composite Corridor Maroon. (1974 to 1988)

1202 (1902) BR Composite Brake Maroon. (1974 to 1988)

1203 (1903) BR Miniature Buffet Car Maroon. (1974 to 1988)

1211 (1911) BR Composite Corridor Yellow and brown. (1974 to 1988)

1212 (1912) BR Composite Brake Yellow and brown. (1974 to 1988)

1213 (1913) BR Miniature Buffet Car Yellow and brown. (1974 to 1988)

1221 (1921) BR Composite Corridor Green. (1974 to 1988)

1222 (1922) BR Composite Brake Green. (1974 to 1988)

1223 (1923) BR Miniature Buffet Car Green. (1974 to 1988)

1230 (1932) LMS Corridor Maroon, black roof only. (1974 to 1983)

1231 (1933) LMS Brake Maroon, black roof only. (1974 to 1979)

1235 (1935) GWR Corridor Brown and cream, white roof only. (1974 to 1987)

1236 (1936) GWR Brake Brown and cream, white roof only. (1974 to 1979)

1251 (1951) BR Composite Corridor Blue and grey. (1974 to 1988)

1252 (1952) BR Composite Brake Blue and grey. (1974 to 1988)

1253 (1953) BR Miniature Buffet Car Blue and grey. (1974 to 1988)

1271 (1971) BR Intercity Composite Corridor Green. (1974 to 1988)

1272 (1972) BR Intercity Composite Brake Green. (1974 to 1988)

1273 (1973) BR Intercity Miniature Buffet Car Green. (1974 to 1988)

1275 (1975) BR Intercity Composite Corridor Blue and grey. (1974 to 1988)

1276 (1976) BR Intercity Composite Brake Blue and grey. (1974 to 1988)

1277 (1977) BR Intercity Miniature Buffet Car Blue and grey. (1974 to 1988)

1278 (1931) Pullman Car Brown and cream. (1974 to 1985)

1279 (1978) Pullman Car Blue and grey. (1974 to 1985). E3000 locomotive roof plugs fitted as table lamps in late models.

1291 BR Intercity Composite Corridor with lights Green. (1978 to 1985)

1293 BR Intercity Miniature Buffet Car with lights Green. (1978 to 1985)

1295 BR Intercity Composite Corridor with lights Blue and grey. (1978 to 1985)

1297 BR Miniature Buffet Car with lights Blue and grey. (1978 to 1985)

BR Pullman and green Intercity coaches. From the top: Cat.Nos. 1931 (without name), 1978, 1971, 1272 [Liliput (UK)], 1973.

Great Western and LMS scale plastic coaches. From the top: Cat.Nos. 1235 [Liliput (UK)], 1236 [Liliput (UK)], 1933 (Trix), 1231 [Liliput (UK)], 1230 [Liliput (UK)].

ROLLING STOCK

THE BREAKDOWN CRANE TRUCK SETS

The popular Break-down Crane Truck set, catalogue number 615, comprising crane unit and match-truck was introduced during the autumn of 1939 and was one of the few new items advertised for that year which was actually produced and delivered to the retailers. A removable working diecast crane was located by a central pivot on a circular brass plate mounted on a special tinplate base. The whole unit fitted into a wagon body with the same measurements as a normal 3-plank wagon. The chassis for this wagon body was the same as that used for the 0-4-0 tinplate tenders, including central weight, rear coupling and front draw-bar, except that in most cases, the steps from the chassis side panels were removed.

The diecast crane finished in matt grey, was a well made unit capable of lifting light loads, but governed by the stability of the wagon on which it was mounted. The jib could be put into three locked positions by means of captivated wire stays locating in notches on the jib. The jib itself was fitted

TTR Break-down Truck sets. From the top and left:
(1) Early production with no 'TTR 10 TONS' on the side of the jib.
(2) Normal pre-war production with crank handle extension on row below.
(3) Early post-war version.
(4) 1948 version.
(5) 1952 version.
(6) Diecast chassis version.
(7) 1961 production using wagons with plastic bodies and the late series diecast chassis.

308

with a turned brass pulley over which the cord attached to a small hook passed. The brass winch was geared to a small winding handle and also to a ratcheting spring which restricted the free movement of the hook. An extension handle was provided in the pre-war sets to ease the operation of the crane. The jib sides on early units were unmarked, but the die was soon altered to include the formation of the inscription 10 TONS TTR embossed on both sides, the numbers and letters being picked out in white. The angle of the casting below the ratchet spring was also increased at the same time. After these initial modifications, the crane remained unaltered for the residual period of its long production run.

The match-truck was also the same proportions as a 3-plank wagon and was fitted with a tinplate insert complete with diecast tool box and jib support, this insert again being finished in mat grey. At one end of the match-truck was the normal diecast coupling for use with other items of rolling stock, and at the other end a wire bent into the shape of a U was fixed into the coupling channel which engaged with the draw-bar of the crane truck.

Both wagon bodies were in dark grey with the number 83610 and ENGINEER'S DEPT. on the crane wagon body and the number 49736 on the match-truck body. When the crane truck set was re-introduced just after the war, lithographed tinplate sheets were initially not available and the set was issued with the wagon bodies sprayed in matt dark grey with no markings at all. This situation did not last for long, and corresponding to the use of the new type of coupling in 1948, the lithographed wagon bodies made their reappearance which were indistinguishable from the pre-war models except for the inscriptions. The numbering and lettering on

the post-war models was slightly bolder and a fraction larger than the pre-war versions. This can be readily seen by comparing the '0' in the number 83610 on the pre-war crane truck body which is round in contrast to the post-war version which looks almost oval.

The crane truck and match-truck chassis followed the modifications introduced on the 0-4-0 tenders and the normal wagons respectively, and with the demise of the central coupling channel, the U shaped coupling pin was replaced with a small and less conspicuous vertical hook. The dark grey tinplate printing on the wagon bodies was replaced during 1952 by a much lighter shade of grey, but with no alteration to the markings. Although the first series of diecast chassis were introduced in 1954, it was not until the beginning of 1956 that the diecast chassis was used for the crane truck set. The

chassis of the crane truck was the same as that used for the lighted goods brake van except that a weight was fitted to the underside of the chassis in place of the pick-up assembly and the diecast chassis used for the match-truck was standard. However in both cases the buffers on each chassis were removed on the ends which coupled together.

In 1961 the wagons used for the crane and match-trucks were identical BR Open 3-plank wagons of the 'P' series in either light brown or light grey. No weight was fitted to the crane truck, thus reducing stability, and no buffers were removed. The base inserts for the crane and match-truck were now moulded light grey plastic. Instead of the location for the crane pivot being in the centre of the base, it was now off-set towards one end with an additional moulded plastic ridge located at the opposite end. The match-truck used the same insert, except that

Liliput for Trix Breakdown Crane and Match truck Cat.No.1610 together with one of the colour variations.

the moulded jib support was located in the crane pivot hole, and the moulded tool box used the same location holes as the ridge on the crane truck insert. This crane-truck set was only in production for one year and was given the catalogue number of P615.

1963 saw a completely new design of Breakdown Crane introduced into the Trix range. This was of mainly plastic construction manufac-tured by Liliput of Austria with certain parts modified to make it identifiable with Trix and was first introduced in Britain during the Christmas period of 1958 by Miniature Construction. It was given the catalogue number of 1610, which slightly reflected the original British Liliput catalogue number of 210, and was offered complete with match truck. The model was based on a German Federal Railways Steam Crane used for building bridges and the clearance of wreckage after derailments, hence the letters DB and the German town name of Essen moulded into the chassis side frames plus the crane number 734054.

The model was fully operating with facilities for raising or lowering the jib and hook independently by means of suitable chains activated by small removable knobs at the side of the cabin. On versions of the Liliput crane for inclusion in the Trix range, the Liliput trade mark on the underside of the diecast metal base of the swivelling cabin was omitted, and normal Trix plastic couplings were fitted to opposite ends of the crane and match truck chassis, the coupling between match truck and crane in the majority of cases being effected by standard Liliput couplings. The brown plastic match truck was the same as the Low-Sided Gondola wagon listed in the 1964 catalogue, Cat.No.1698, except

that a jib support was inserted towards one end of the wagon. This wagon had the markings of the Austrian Federal Railway, ÖBB, and the number 415 505. It was listed in the official price list of 1972 as a separate item with the catalogue number of 204.

The crane unit was available with a variety of cab colours – red, yellow, silver plus light and dark blue and of course as a kit in the Wagonmaster series, Cat.No.2010. The wheels for the match-truck and the two six-wheeled bogies on the crane were initially the same plastic versions with needle point axles as used on the plastic scale coaches, introduced during the same period. Later all metal wheel assemblies were fitted. As a marketing exercise in the late 1960s, a coach was issued with the crane unit which represented the Engineer's Dept. coach as seen on British Railways at the time. This coach was a standard Buffet Car from the Trix range of scale

plastic coaches overpainted in bright red with the round B.R. coaching stock transfer applied on both sides at the position where the word BUFFET would have been. Each of the six doors on the coach had the figure 1 in gold applied by transfer. No boxes were specially made for this coach, nor did it have a catalogue number. Only a handful, a maximum of 20, were made and due to a less than enthusiastic response the exercise was not continued. The Crane Unit was available until 1972 under the Trix banner and then from 1974 until 1978, Cat.No.1310, with Liliput Model Railways (UK) Ltd. Although it was not to a British pattern, this plastic crane unit proved to be quite popular.

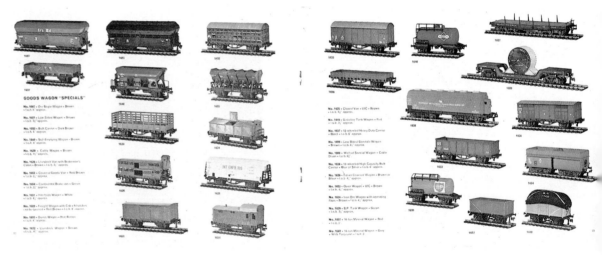

Extract from the British Trix 1964 catalogue showing some of the German Trix and Austrian Liliput wagons offered.

TRIX EXPRESS AND LILIPUT ROLLING STOCK IN THE BRITISH TRIX CATALOGUES

These were items imported by British Trix Ltd from 1963 over a period of approximately three years in a endeavour to increase the rather small domestic range. Unfortunately, the fact that the British public were not over-enthusiastic about continental-outline models at this time was not taken into consideration, and this additional range was discontinued with the issue of the 1966 catalogue except for certain items listed separately.

The first catalogue number in the list is that shown in the British Trix catalogues, whilst the number in brackets is the corresponding Trix Express International or Liliput catalogue number. The prefix TE or L denotes Trix Express or Liliput respectively.

Cat. No.

1624 (TE 3624) **DB Lime wagon with cab** Brown, diecast.
1626 (TE 3626) **DB Livestock wagon V with cab** Brown, diecast.
1630 (L 230) **SNCF Open cattle wagon** Brown, plastic.
1631 (L 221) **DB or FS Interfrigo refrigerator wagon** White, plastic.
1632 (L 232) **DB cattle wagon** Brown, plastic.
1633 (L 231) **SBB Open wagon, UIC** Brown, plastic.
1634 (L 220) **DB Hopper wagon OOfz** Brown, plastic.
1635 (L 235) **DB Goods van Type Gms-54** Brown, plastic.
1636 (L 236) **FS Covered wagon** Brown, plastic.
1637 (L 212) **DB 12-wheeled heavy duty carrier SSym-46** Black and brown, plastic.
1638 (L 239) **ÖBB 12-wheeled high capacity bulk carrier** Blue, plastic.
1639 (L 225BP) **ÖBB BP tank wagon** Green, plastic.
1640 (L 225G) **ÖBB Gasolin tank wagon** Red, plastic.
1648 (TE 3648) **DB Dump wagon Fd-52** Brown, cast chassis, plastic body.
1651 (TE 3651) **DB low-sided wagon Omm** Brown, plastic.

1653 (TE 3653) **DB Covered van G** Brown, plastic.
1654 (TE 3654) **DB Brake van Pwg** Green, plastic.
1655 (TE 3655) **DB Dump wagon F-v-51** Brown, plastic body, diecast chassis.
1657 (TE 3657) **DB Container wagon Lbs-50** with three open containers Plastic containers, diecast chassis.
1658 (TE 3658) **DB Container wagon Lbs-50** with three closed containers Plastic containers, diecast chassis
1663 (TE 3663) **DB Car-carrier Laes 55** Brown and black, tinplate superstructure, diecast chassis.
1681 (TE 3671) **Jünkerath pig-iron wagon** Green, plastic body, diecast chassis.
1682 (TE 3672) **Jünkerath slag carrier** Grey, plastic body, diecast chassis.
1683 (TE 3683) **DB large capacity carrier Uad-v-57** Dark brown, plastic body, diecast chassis.
1684 (L 242) **ÖBB large capacity goods van** Brown, plastic.
1687 (TE 3687) **DB large capacity bogie wagon Fad-50** Brown, plastic body, diecast chassis.
1688 (L 224) **FS Migros refrigerator wagon** White, plastic.
1689 (L 229) **ÖBB Aproz refrigerator wagon** Green, plastic.
1690 (L 241) **SBB special service wagon with flaps** Brown and silver, plastic.
1691 (TEMPO) **US Great Northern livestock car type MKT** Initially red but later various colours, plastic.
1692 (L 214) **DB Covered van with brakeman's cab** Brown, plastic.
1693 (L 215) **DB Löwenbräu beer wagon** White, plastic.
1696 (L 240) **DB VAW 12-wheeled hopper car** Silver, plastic.
1697 (L 238) **DB VAW 12-wheeled hopper car** Brown, plastic.
1699 (TE 3499) **DB Bogie stanchion wagon type SSa** Black, diecast.
1960 (L 280) **ÖBB 1st/2nd class coach type AB 4üh** Green, plastic.
1961 (L 261) **Dining car of the CIWL** Blue, plastic.
1962 (L 260) **Dining car of the CIWL** Brown - plastic.

1963 (L 266) **Sleeping car of the CIWL** Blue - plastic.

1964 (L 265) **Sleeping car of the CIWL** Brown, plastic.

1965 (L 294) **Prussian luggage van type Pw 4ü Pr 07** Green, plastic.

1966 (L 295) **Prussian 1st/2nd class coach type AB 4ü Pr 09a**
Green, plastic.

1967 (L 291) **DR Mail coach with brakeman's cab** Green, plastic.

1968 (L 290) **Prussian 3rd class coach** Green, plastic.

1969 (L 290/3) **Prussian 3rd class coach with brakeman's cab**
Green, plastic.

1970 (L 270) **DB 4-wheeled coach type Ci 25** Green, plastic.

1971 (L 271) **DB 4-wheeled baggage car type Pwi 29** Green, plastic.

1980 (TE 3780) **DB Touropa express coach** Blue, plastic.

1982 (TE 3782) **DB Intercity traffic coach** Green, plastic.

1983 (TE 3783) **DSG Sleeping car** Red, plastic.

1984 (TE 3784) **DSG Dining car** Red, plastic.

1986 (TE 3786) **DB Express 1st/2nd class coach type AB 4ümg** Green,
plastic.

1987 (TE 3787) **DB Express luggage van type Pw 4üm** Green, plastic.

1988 (TE 3774) **DB 1st/2nd class Suburban coach** Green, plastic.

1989 (TE 3776) **DB 2nd class Suburban coach** with luggage compartment
Green, plastic.

1990 (TE 3777) **DB Intercity 1st/2nd class coach** Silver, plastic.

1991 (TE 3779) **DB Intercity 2nd class coach** with luggage compartment
Silver, plastic.

1992 (TE 3725) **DB 1st/2nd class 6-wheeled coach** Green, plastic.

1993 (TE 3727) **DB 2nd class 6-wheeled coach** with luggage
compartment   Green, plastic.

1994 (L 272) **ÖBB 4-wheeled mail coach** Green, plastic.

1998 (TE 3798) **BLS luggage van** Dark green, plastic body, diecast chassis.

1999 (TE 3799) **BLS 1st class coach** Dark green, plastic body, diecast
chassis.

The following items were made available at the same time, but continued in use after the range listed previously was no longer listed in the British Trix catalogues:

1652 (L 252) Operating track cleaning tank wagon Various liveries.

1698 (L 204) ÖBB open low-sided (gondola) wagon Brown plastic.

The operating track-cleaning tank wagon incorporated a metal tank containing cleaning fluid housed within the superstructure. By adjusting the valve on the top of the tank, fluid flow to a weighted felt pad was controlled. This replaceable pad was constructed in such a way as to give constant pressure to the rails. The wagon continued to be listed during the 'Trix' period from 1963 until 1972, then under Liliput Model Railways (UK) Ltd with a new catalogue number of 1352 until 1978. It was available with the following liveries:

Esso-silver, **Shell**-yellow, **BP**-green, **Aral**-blue and **Gasolin**-red.

The open low-sided (gondola) wagon was removed from the price lists in 1967, although it was also used as a Match-Truck for the Liliput Breakdown Crane in made-up and Wagonmaster form. The wagon reappeared in the 1972 price list with the catalogue number of 204 as a Crane Match-Truck.

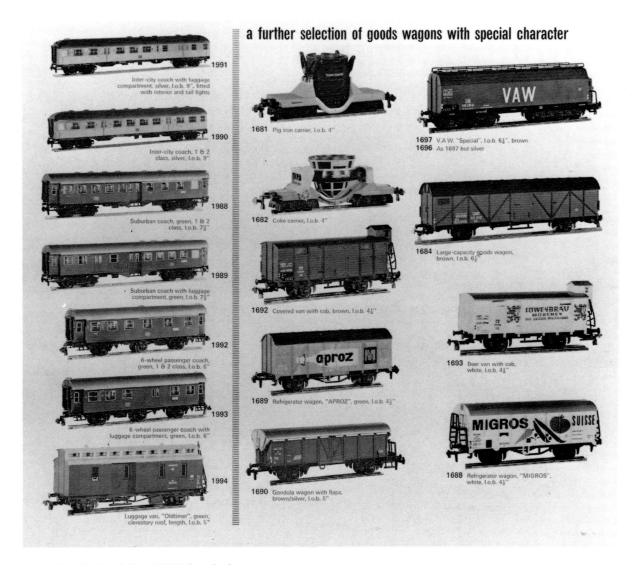

a further selection of goods wagons with special character

1991 Inter-city coach with luggage compartment, silver, l.o.b. 9", fitted with interior and tail lights

1990 Inter-city coach, 1 & 2 class, silver, l.o.b. 9"

1988 Suburban coach, green, 1 & 2 class, l.o.b. 7¾"

1989 Suburban coach with luggage compartment, green, l.o.b. 7¾"

1992 6-wheel passenger coach, green, 1 & 2 class, l.o.b. 6"

1993 6-wheel passenger coach with luggage compartment, green, l.o.b. 6"

1994 Luggage van, "Oldtimer", green, clerestory roof, length, l.o.b. 5"

1681 Pig iron carrier, l.o.b. 4"

1682 Coke carrier, l.o.b. 4"

1692 Covered van with cab, brown, l.o.b. 4¼"

1689 Refrigerator wagon, "APROZ", green, l.o.b. 4½"

1690 Gondola wagon with flaps, brown/silver, l.o.b. 5"

1697 V.A.W. "Special", l.o.b. 6½", brown
1696 As 1697 but silver

1684 Large-capacity goods wagon, brown, l.o.b. 6½"

1693 Beer van with cab, white, l.o.b. 4½"

1688 Refrigerator wagon, "MIGROS", white, l.o.b. 4½"

Extract from the British Trix 1965 Release leaflet.

Late 1936 Trix Express Goods Set Cat.No. 11/4 for the British market. Note the black wheels on the locomotive instead of red as in earlier versions. (A)

Late 1936 Trix Express Passenger Set Cat.No.11/5 for the British market. Note the black wheels on the locomotive instead of red as in earlier productions. (A)

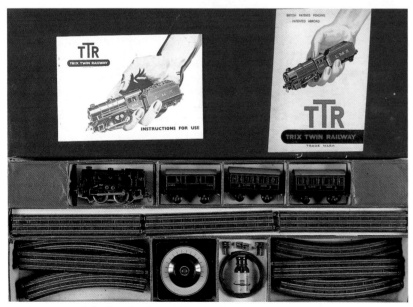

LMS Passenger Suburban Set Cat.No.2/315. (A)

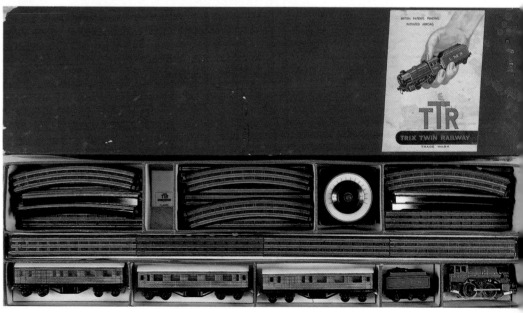

LNER Passenger Set Cat.No.4/335. Extra rails included in this box. (A)

TRAIN SETS & KITS

TRIX TRAIN SETS

The sets are listed in the approximate order of production and not in numerical order. The first table lists the 14 volt AC sets normally available in Britain, the second table lists the 14 volt AC sets prepared in Britain or in cooperation with the German Trix company for export. The export sets were not generally available in Britain. Most of the sets prepared for the British home market were also available in other countries especially during the early post-war period when all production was destined for export. The third table lists the DC sets available of which none were especially produced for the export market.

The first set of figures represents the catalogue number, and the dates at the end of the description give the years of initial and final listing in official Trix literature. Only the main items are listed. It is difficult to give an exact description of the rolling stock contained in each set, as over the years there were many alterations brought about by stock availability and product changes coupled with no hard and fast rules as to the contents. These comments are particularly associated with the goods sets. All the AC sets included wire, connecting plugs, bottle of oil and instruction book, and when included, the rails are on Bakelite bases. A suitable terminal rail was included as part of the complete number of rails supplied with a set. All AC and early DC sets are 3-rail unless otherwise stated. All AC pre-war sets, except where a Super Controller is included, should contain a Trix Express Controller Cat. No. 20/42 which had the British Cat.No. 470. The Super Controller Cat. No. 475 contained in the presentation sets is a Trix Express Controller Cat. No. 20/45. All post-war AC sets should contain the British Controller Cat. No. 472.

Pre-war SR Passenger Set Cat.No.5/334. (A)

Post-war SR Goods Set
Cat.No.5/324. (A)

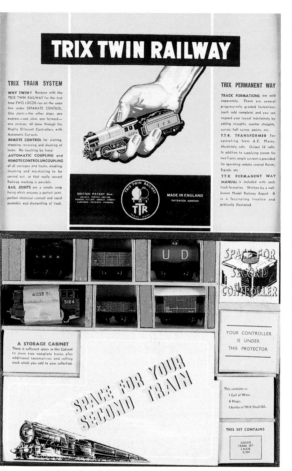

Post-war LNER Goods Set
Cat.No.4/324. (A)

Post-war LNER Passenger Set
Cat.No.2/334. (A)

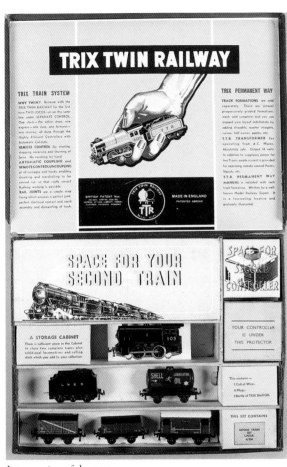

Late version of the post-
war LNER Goods Set
Cat.No.4/324. (A)

Post-war LMS Passenger Set
Cat.No.2/334.

BR Passenger Set
Cat.No.1/334.
This set contained
the earlier
light blue locomotive.

AC SETS FOR THE BRITISH MARKET

11/1 German set prepared for the British market with a German-outline 0-4-0 engine and tender (21/51) in green with four German-outline wagons, 21/61 open wagon, 21/62 goods van, 21/70 refrigerator van and 21/68 Shell tank wagon, controller and 16-piece oval track. 1935-1936.

11/2 German set prepared for the British market with a German-outline 0-4-0 engine and tender (21/51) in green with German-outline coaches, two 21/152, one 21/151, controller and 16-piece oval track. 1935-1936.

2/335 LMS Passenger set with maroon LMS 0-4-0 engine and tender (2/520), one 1st class (2/560) and two brake 3rd (2/570) bogie coaches, controller and 16-piece oval track. 1936 only.

4/335 LNER Passenger set with green LNER 0-4-0 engine and tender (2/520), one 1st class (4/560) and two brake 3rd (4/570) bogie coaches, controller and 16-piece oval track. 1936 only.

2/325 LMS Goods set with black LMS 0-4-0 engine and tender (2/525), four assorted wagons, controller and 14-piece oval track. 1936 only.

4/325 LNER Goods set with black LNER 0-4-0 engine and tender (4/525), four assorted wagons, controller and 14-piece oval track. 1936 only.

2/315 LMS Suburban passenger set with LMS tank engine (2/510), two 1st/3rd (2/550) and one luggage (2/555) 4-wheel coaches, controller and 14-piece oval track. 1936 only.

4/315 LNER Suburban passenger set with LNER tank engine (4/510), two 1st/3rd (4/550) and one luggage (4/555) 4-wheel coaches, controller and 14-piece oval track. 1936 only.

10/3 Continental Blue Train set with black German outline 0-4-0 engine and tender (20/53), Wagon-Lit dining car (20/156), sleeping car (20/157) and baggage car (20/155) bogie coaches, controller and 14-piece oval track. Produced with first and second series coaches. Listed in Britain 1936-1937.

2/334 LMS Passenger set, as in 1936 set 2/335 but without rails. 1937-1950.

4/334 LNER Passenger set, as in 1936 set 4/335 but without rails. 1937-1950.

5/334 SR Passenger set with green SR 0-4-0 engine and tender (5/520), three bogie coaches, [usually 1st class (5/560), brake 3rd (5/570) and all 3rd class (5/590) but make-up varies], controller. No rails. 1937-1940. No post-war sets known to exist although listed in early post-war catalogues.

2/324 LMS Goods set, as in 1936 set 2/325 but without rails. 1937-1950. Due to production difficulties during 1946 to 1948 a tank engine could be substituted for a tender locomotive. In this case an extra wagon was included.

4/324 LNER Goods set, as in 1936 set 4/325 but without rails. 1937-1950. The comments relating to the above 2/324 set also apply to this set.

5/324 SR Goods set, with black SR 0-4-0 engine and tender (5/525), four assorted wagons and controller. No rails. 1937-1949.

2/314 LMS Suburban set, as in 1936 set 2/315 but without rails. 1937-1940.

4/314 LNER Suburban set, as in 1936 set 4/315 but without rails. 1937-1940.

2/358 LMS twin set comprising contents from sets 2/334 and 2/324. 1937-1950.

4/358 LNER twin set comprising contents from sets 4/334 and 4/324. 1937-1950.

5/358 SR twin set comprising contents from sets 5/334 and 5/324. 1937-1940.

5/375 Southern Railway three-coach Electric Train, comprising motor coach (5/530), 1st class (5/560) and brake 3rd (5/570) bogie coaches, 16-piece oval track plus controller in special long green box. 1937-1940.

2/344 LMS 'Princess' Pacific (2/540) with one 1st class (2/567), two brake 3rd (2/577) LMS scale coaches and Super controller, all in special presentation cabinet. No rails. 1937-1941.

4/344 LNER 'Scotsman' Pacific (4/540) with one 1st class (4/567), two brake 3rd (4/577) LNER. scale coaches and Super controller, all in special presentation cabinet. No rails. 1937-1941.

2/347 LMS 'Coronation' Pacific (2/542) with one 1st class (2/568), two brake 3rd (2/578) Coronation coaches plus Super controller, all in special presentation cabinet. No rails. 1939-1941.

5/364 SR 'Dover' 4-4-0 engine and tender (5/536) with SR 1st class (5/567) and brake 3rd (5/577) scale coaches plus Pullman scale coach. All in presentation cabinet with Super controller. Listed in 1939 but not produced.

2/394 LMS 2-4-2 tank engine (2/514) with remote uncoupling at both ends including an assortment of four 4-wheel wagons and four bogie wagons plus Super controller in presentation cabinet. Listed in 1939 but not produced.

4/394 As above 2/394 set but in LNER livery. Listed in 1939 but not produced.

5/394 As above 2/394 set but in SR livery. Listed in 1939 but not produced.

5/384 Southern Electric 4-Car Main Line set, four scale SR coaches, the front coach being the motor coach and the rear had the outline of the motor coach, front and rear lights changed with direction of train. Three coaches lighted. In presentation cabinet with Super controller. (The front and rear units were based on the Trix Express 20/58). Listed in 1939 but not produced.

1/334 BR Passenger set comprising BR blue 0-4-0 engine and tender (1/520) with two 1st class (1/560) and one brake 3rd BR (1/570) carmine and cream short bogie coaches, plus controller. No rails. Initially the engine and tender were light blue later changed to dark blue. 1950-1953.

1/324 BR Goods set comprising BR black 0-4-0 engine and tender (1/525) with four assorted wagons, plus controller. No rails. 1950-1953.

1/358 BR twin set comprising the contents of sets 1/334 and 1/324. 1950-1953.

9/321 American Freight set with Freight engine and tender (9/525), gondola car (684), caboose (690), box car (685) and controller. 1950-1953.

9/331 American Passenger set with Passenger engine and tender (9/520), baggage car (9/575), observation car (9/585), day coach (9/565) and controller. 1950-1953.

9/351 American twin set comprising the contents of sets 9/321 and 9/331. 1950-1953.

1/323 BR Goods set comprising BR 0-4-0 Goods engine and tender (1/525) with five assorted wagons. No rails or controller. This was the last basic set containing BR wagons which were all constructed with tinplate chassis. 1953 only.

1/336 BR Passenger set with BR green 'Pytchley' 4-4-0 engine and tender (4/536) with two 1st class (1/560) and one brake 3rd (1/570) BR carmine and cream short bogie coaches. No rails or controller. 1953 only.

1/336 As the above set but with BR green 4-4-0 Compound engine and tender (Cat. No. 2/536) Late 1953 only.

1/354 BR twin set comprising the contents from sets 1/323 and 1/336 plus master switch 464 and two controllers. No rails. 1953 only.

9/320 American Freight set with Freight engine and tender (9/525), caboose (690), gondola car (684) and box car (685). No rails or controller. 1953-1957.

9/330 American Passenger set with Passenger engine and tender (9/520), baggage car (9/575), observation car (9/585) and day coach (9/565). No rails or controller. 1953-1957.

9/356 American twin set with contents of sets 9/320 and 9/330 plus master switch 464 and two controllers. No rails. 1953-1957.

1/366 Operating mineral train set comprising BR 0-4-0 tank engine (1/510), two operating dump wagons (666), one scale goods brake with light (653), magnetic rail and switch (427), fireman's shovel (867) and bin (868)

plus sack of plastic 'coal' (866). This set is known to exist with an extra dump wagon in place of the goods brake when the latter was not available. No rails or controller. 1953-1957.

766 Operating dump wagon set with operating dump wagon (666), magnetic rail and switch (427), fireman's shovel (866) and coal bin (868) plus sack of plastic 'coal' (866). 1953-1956.

388 Trix Portable set. This contained the Operating Mineral Train set 1/366, Elevator Conveyor 788, 20 track units including an uncoupler and magnetic rail plus a table-top plan, all housed in a special hardwood carrying cabinet. 1954-1957.

1/362 Fast Night Freight set comprising black BR 4-4-0 Compound engine and tender (2/536), two 4-wheel wagons, three bogie wagons and lighted goods brake van (653). No rails or controller. This was the first set to contain wagons with a super-detailed cast chassis. 1954-1957.

1/373 Night Express set comprising green BR 4-4-0 'Pytchley' engine and tender (4/536), BR carmine and cream scale 1st class (1/568) and brake 3rd (1/578) coaches and scale Pullman coach (599) all with lights. No rails or controller. 1954-1957.

1/322 BR Goods set comprising black BR 0-4-0 engine and tender (1/525), five 4-wheel wagons and one bogie wagon. No rails or controller. 1954-1957.

1/333 BR Passenger set comprising green BR 0-4-0 engine and tender (1/520), one 1st class (1/560) and two brake 3rd (1/570) carmine and red short bogie coaches. No rails or controller. 1954-1957.

1/355 Twin set comprising sets 1/322 and 1/333, plus two controllers 472 and master switch 464. No rails. 1954-1957.

377 'Meteor' articulated 3-coach Diesel Express in red and cream with special directional control switch. No rails. 1955-1957.

274 Train Whistle set comprising Express Parcels van in crimson lake, (similar to Parcels van 1/557), incorporating a whistle device, special switch unit and two lineside 'Whistle' boards. 1955-1958.

Notes regarding the above sets:
The class of coaches contained in the 'Princess', 'Scotsman' and 'Coronation' presentation sets varied occasionally from the normal. They are known to include two 1st class coaches and one brake 3rd, or even a Dining/Restaurant car in place of a 1st class coach.

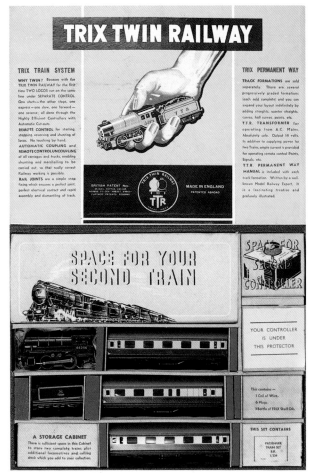

BR Passenger Set Cat.No.1/334.
This set contained the
later dark blue locomotive.

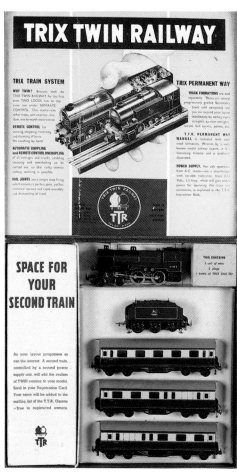

BR Passenger Set Cat.No.1/336.
Note the green BR 4-4-0
Compound. (A)

American Passenger Set
Cat.No.9/330. (A)

American Freight Set
Cat.No.9/320.

Night Express Set
Cat.No.1/373. (A)

Fast Night Freight Set
Cat.No.1/362. (A)

AC SETS FOR EXPORT

11/158 (9/105) Goods set comprising 9/231 (9/32) German-outline 0-4-0 tank engine with cowcatcher, 9/258 (9/48) open wagon, 9/252 ((9/50) coal wagon, 9/240 (9/124) Shell Oil tank wagon, 9/260 (9/49) goods van plus controller. No rails. 1937-1939.

19/104 As above but German-outline 0-4-0 tender engine in place of the tank engine. Circa 1938.

11/159 (9/106) Passenger set comprising 9/252 (9/42) German-outline 0-4-0 engine and tender with cowcatcher, two 21/160 1st class passenger bogie coaches, 21/159 baggage car plus controller. No rails. 1937-1939.

11/160 (9/107) Passenger set comprising 9/232 (9/116) German-outline 0-4-0 Electric locomotive, two 21/160 1st class passenger bogie coaches, 21/159 baggage car plus controller. No rails. 1937-1939.

The actual catalogue number printed on the box label was 19/135 which apart from the prefix number corresponds to the catalogue number given in the Trix Express catalogues. More confusion!

11/161 (9/108) International Express set comprising 9/252 (9/42) German outline 0-4-0 engine and tender with cowcatcher, three Wagon-Lit bogie coaches – 9/270 (9/129) Dining car, 9/271 (9/130) Sleeping car and 9/269 (9/128)

Baggage car including controller. No rails. 1937-1939.

The actual catalogue number printed on the box label was 19/106, the latter three digits correspond to the catalogue number given in the Trix Express catalogues.

11/156 (9/103) Combined Passenger and Goods set containing the contents from sets 11/159 (9/106) and 11/158 (9/105). 1937-1939.

11/157 (9/104) Combined International Express and Goods set containing the contents from sets 11/161 (9/108) and 11/158 (9/105). 1937-1939.

19/560 Twin Set containing contents from 19/104 and 19/106. Circa 1938

Notes regarding the above sets

These sets appeared in the special combined Trix Express and TTR catalogues for the American market. The catalogue numbers without brackets relate to the 1937/38 edition, whilst the catalogue numbers in brackets relate to the 1938/39 edition. It is not known why these catalogue number changes took place. The 21/159 and the 21/160 bogie coaches are almost identical to the 21/151 and 21/152 bogie coaches made for the British market. Apart from

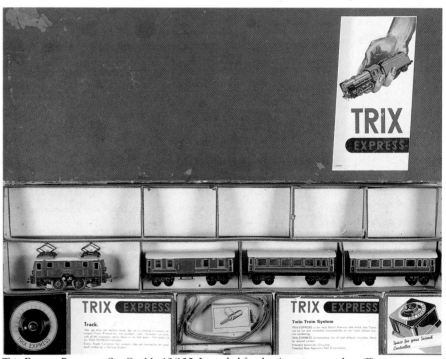

Trix Express Goods Set Cat.No.19/104. Locomotive has a cowcatcher fitted and the set was intended for the American market. (F)

Trix Express Passenger Set Cat.No.19/135. Intended for the American market. (F)

the printed number on these coaches only the lining around the windows is different, being more rounded on the British pattern.

Below is a list of Trix Express (20/) catalogue numbers corresponding to the numbers given in the 1938/39 special catalogue:

Locos: 9/32 = 20/54 plus cowcatcher, 9/42 = 20/52 plus cowcatcher, 9/116 = 20/55.
Wagons: 9/48 =20/61, 9/49 = 20/63, 9/50 = 20/67, 9/124 = 20/68.
Coaches: 9/128 = 20/155, 9/129 = 20/156, 9/130 = 20/157, all second series.

The first four sets were made up in France for that market with the assistance of certain parts and complete assemblies exported from Britain and Germany:

15/115 Rapide Nord comprising NORD 4-4-0 'Pacific Type' engine and tender 25/56, baggage coach 25/350, 1st class coach 25/351, 2nd class coach 25/352, 3rd class coach 25/353 plus controller. No rails. 1937-1939.

15/104 Goods set comprising German outline 0-4-0 tank engine 25/54, four assorted German wagons plus controller. No rails. 1937-1939.

15/105 As the above set but with German-outline 0-4-0 Electric locomotive 25/55. 1937-1939.

15/200 Combined set with contents of Sets 15/104 and 15/115. 1938-1939.

8/328 Goods set with 20/54 German-outline 0-4-0 tank engine. Other contents unknown. No rails. Listed in TTR 1948 price list for Swiss market.

8/337 Passenger set with 20/52 German outline 0-4-0 engine and tender, (with lights), plus standard TTR 1st class-type short bogie coaches in dark green livery with a Paris/Basle/Strasbourg/Zurich destination panel in the middle of each side. Coaches known in 1st, 2nd and 3rd class. Quantity of coaches unknown. No rails. Listed in TTR 1948 price list for Swiss market.

8/357 Twin set containing sets 8/328 and 8/337. Listed in TTR 1948 price list for Swiss market.

10/326 Engine and tender, (0-4-0 in any livery except BR) with three bogie Goods wagons. No rails. Contents uncertain. Intended for South African market. 1948-circa 1950.

9/331 American Passenger set consisted of American passenger engine and tender (9/520), observation car (9/585), day coach (9/565), baggage car (9/575)and controller. No rails. 1948-1953. Available in Britain in 1950.

9/321 American Goods set consisted of American Freight engine and tender (9/525), caboose (690), box car (685), gondola car (684) and controller. No rails. 1948-1953. Available in Britain in 1950.

9/351 Combined set with contents of sets 9/321 and 9/331. No rails. 1948-1953. Available in Britain in 1950.

9/334 American Passenger set consisted of American Passenger engine and tender (9/520) with three short bogie coaches as per either the LMS, LNER or SR British passenger sets. With controller but no rails. 1948-circa 1949.

9/324 American Freight set consisted of American Freight engine and tender (9/525) with an assortment of British 4-wheeled goods wagons plus controller. 1948-circa 1949.

9/358 Combined set with contents of sets 9/324 and 9/334. No rails. 1948-circa 1949.

Set #1 Made up by Polk's Model Craft Hobbies Inc. of New York and contained LMS 0-4-0 Goods tank engine 2/510, four assorted goods wagons and 14-piece oval track. No box. 1948- ?

Set #2 As above but comprising German-outline 0-4-0 Electric locomotive 20/55, 29/151 baggage car, two 29/152 passenger coaches and 14-piece oval track. 1948- ? (The coaches above were in the green German Bundesbahn livery).

No other sets produced for export only are known.

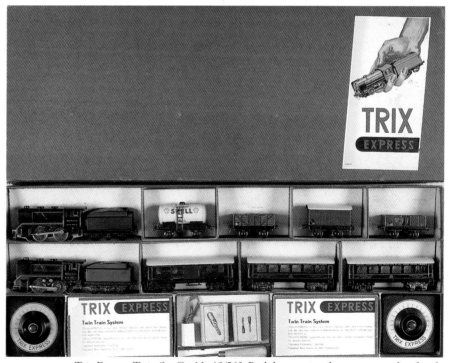

Trix Express Twin Set Cat.No.19/560. Both locomotives have a cowcatcher fitted. This set was intended for the American market. (F)

DC SETS

All sets are for 12 volt DC operation unless otherwise stated, and where rails are included they are the 3-rail with a fibre base unless otherwise stated.

205 Trix 'Junior' Goods train set comprising BR 0-4-0 tank engine with plastic body and special 4½/6 volt motor, two open wagons, goods brake van, (all three on tinplate chassis), special hand driven generator plus 14-piece oval track on bakelite bases. Housed in special, (and complicated) cardboard display box. 1955-1956.

215 Trix 'Junior' Passenger train set as above but with two crimson lake BR Suburban coaches 1/553 in place of the wagons . 1955-1956.

224 'Cadet' Goods set with BR 0-4-0 tank engine with plastic body and special 4½/2/6 volt motor (201), three goods wagons on simplified tinplate chassis, speed control unit for use with two or one large 4½ volt batteries, (272) and 14-piece oval of track. 1957-1961.

224 Special. As the above 'Cadet' Goods set 224 but with an extra wagon. (BR Open grey high side, wagon number 168732). Box lid has a red 'Special' label above the name 'Trix' on one end and a blue and white contents label rubber-stamped '4 wagons' on the other. This set was sold by the Gamages Mail Order company.

224 Special. 'Cadet' Goods set as 224 but containing a red Shell tank wagon and a silver Shell tank wagon, both using the simplified chassis), in place of the two Open wagons. Box lid has a red 'Special' label and a blue and white contents label rubber-stamped '2 Shell'. This set was sold by the Gamages Mail Order company.

Note. Both the above special sets also had a standard yellow Trix Twin Railway catalogue identification label applied to the end of the box lid.

234 'Cadet' Passenger set. As above 224 set but wagons replaced with maroon BR Suburban (1/553) and Parcels van (1/557) short bogie coaches. In later sets the Parcels van was replaced with another Suburban coach. 1957-1961.

255 'Cadet' Twin Set. A combination of sets 224 and 234 complete with 24 pieces of track plus one pair of hand points. 1957-1961.

277 'Meteor' Diesel Express articulated three-coach unit, red and cream. No rails or controller. 1957-1960.

277 'Meteor' Diesel Express articulated three-coach unit, blue and cream. No rails or controller. 1957-1961.

278 Main Line Diesel Express containing 'Meteor' articulated three-coach unit in blue and cream, 12 curved rails (704), 17 straight rails (701) and one straight terminal rail (711). No power unit/controller. This set was not listed in the general Trix literature and was probably produced especially for the Mail Order business. 1958-1959. (From date codes on set items).

251 Main Line Goods Set. This set comprised BR 0-4- 0 tank engine (210), 3-plank open wagon (630), high-side open wagon (634), Shell red tank wagon (646), bogie brick wagon (675), goods brake van (651),16 items of track including an uncoupler rail (705), and a whistling controller (275). 1957-1958.

273 Main Line Passenger Set. This set comprised green BR 4-4-0 Hunt Class 'Pytchley' engine and tender (230), one 1st class (1/561) and one brake 2nd (1/571) BR maroon short bogie coaches, 16 items of track including an uncoupler rail (705), and a whistling controller (275). 1957-1958.

260 Fast Night Freight. Comprising black BR 4-6-0 Class V engine and tender (237B), tarpaulin wagon (662), bogie brick wagon (675), Esso silver tank wagon (641), Weltrol wagon with marine boiler (678), bogie timber wagon (673) and goods brake with light (653). No rails or power supply unit. 1958 only.

258 Night Express. Comprising BR 4-6-2 'Britannia' engine and tender (236), BR maroon coaches – 1st class (1/569), brake 2nd (1/579) and Diner (1/589) all with lights. No rails or power supply unit. 1958 only.

F21 0-4-0 Goods Set. This set was similar to set 251 except for packaging and contains BR 0-4-0 tank engine (210), 3-plank open wagon (630), high-side open wagon (634), Shell red tank wagon (646), bogie brick wagon (675), goods brake (651), 14-piece oval track which includes hand uncoupler rail. 1959 only.

F22 0-6-2 Goods Set. Comprising black BR 0-6-2 Class 66XX tank engine (F103B), 3-plank open wagon (630), Shell red tank wagon (646), goods brake (651) and 14-piece oval track. 1959 only.

F23 0-6-2 Passenger Set. Comprising green BR 0-6-2 Class 66XX tank engine (F103G), two BR maroon Suburban short bogie coaches (1/553) and 14-piece oval of track. Initially for a very short period only the black Class 64XX was used in this set, also the original intention was to use coaches 1/560 and 1/570. The catalogue number of the Suburban coaches was quoted as 1/554 in the description of this set in the 1959 catalogue. 1959-1963.

F24 .4-4-0 Eastern Region Passenger Set. This set comprised BR green 4-4-0 Hunt Class 'Pytchley' engine and tender (230), two Suburban coaches (1/553) and 14-piece oval track. 1959-1960.

F25 4-4-0 Eastern Region Goods Set. This set comprised BR black 4-4-0 Hunt Class 'Pytchley' engine and tender (235), 3-plank open wagon (630), Esso silver tank wagon (641), Weltrol wagon (677), goods brake van (651) and 14-piece oval track. 1959-1960.

F26 4-4-0 Midland Region Passenger Set. Containing BR black 4-4-0 Compound engine and tender (F101), 1st class (1/561) and brake 2nd (1/571) BR maroon short bogie coaches and 14-piece oval track. 1959-1960.

F27 4-4-0 Southern Region Passenger set with BR green 4-4-0 Schools Class 'Dover' engine and tender (F100), 1st class (5/560) and brake 3rd 5/570 BR green short bogie coaches and 14-piece oval track. 1959-1960.

F28 4-6-0 Class V Goods Set. This set comprised BR black 4-6-0 Class V engine and tender (237B), 3-plank open wagon (630), Shell silver tank wagon (644), Weltrol with marine boiler (678), lighted goods brake van (653) and 14-piece oval track. 1959 only.

F29 4-6-0 Class V Passenger Set with BR green 4-6-0 Class V engine and tender (237G), 1st class (1/569) and brake 2nd BR maroon scale coaches with lights and 14-piece oval track. 1959 only.

F30 4-6-2 Britannia Set. This set was made up of a BR green 4-6-2 Britannia Class engine and tender (236) together with two Pullman lighted coaches (599) and 14-piece oval track. 1959-1963.

F40 Diesel Breakdown Set. Comprising Ruston Hornsby diesel shunter (244) without shunters truck, two 3-plank open wagons (630), crane truck set (615) and an Engineer's coach (later cat.No.1688). No rails. 1959-1960.

F32 0-6-2 Goods Set with three wagons, 3-plank open (P. 601), Iron Ore mineral wagon (P. 609), goods brake van (P. 622), with BR black 0-6-2 Class 66XX tank engine and 14-piece oval track. 1960-1963.

F33 0-6-2 Goods Set with six wagons, Con.Flat B with two 'Bird's Eye' containers (P. 619), Shell red tank wagon (P. 641), 12-ton covered van (P. 614), 20-ton Pig iron wagon (P. 604), 3-plank wagon with trestle (P. 603), goods brake van (P. 621), with black 0-6-2 Class 66XX tank engine and 14-piece oval track. 1960-1963.

In the above set the wagons were sometimes packed in long red and blue Trix Products Ltd coach boxes, three wagons to a box.

F34 4-6-0 Class V Goods Set. This comprised a BR black 4-6-0 Class V engine and tender (237B), 12-ton covered van red or grey (P. 622 or P.621), Con. Flat A unloaded (P. 616), Shell red tank wagon (P. 641), 20-ton pig iron wagon (P.605), 16-ton mineral wagon (P. 607), goods brake van (P. 621) and 14-piece oval track. 1960-1963.

F35 4-6-0 Class V Passenger Set with BR green 4-6-0 Class V engine and tender (237G), two maroon BR Suburban coaches (1/553), one maroon Express Parcels and Guards van (1/557) and 14-piece oval track. 1960-1963.

F36 Bo-Bo Mineral Train Set. This set was made up with a black EM1 Bo-Bo Electric locomotive (F105B), O1 Overhead Catenary set, (not Cantenary set as printed in the 1960 Trix catalogue!), two mineral wagons with Ore (P. 609), mineral wagon with ballast (P.611), mineral wagon with coal (P. 608),

goods brake van (P.622) and 14-piece oval of track. 1960-1963.

F37 Bo-Bo Passenger Train Set comprised green EM1 Bo- Bo Electric locomotive (F105G), BR maroon 1st class (562) and brake 2nd (572) scale coaches, O1 Overhead Catenary set and 14-piece oval track. 1960-1963. Note:- The O1 Catenary Sets supplied with the above two sets comprise the following: 11 standard posts, one terminal post, one set of overhead wires, 12 track clips and one coil of connecting wire 31/85.

F38 'Vanguard' Western Region Express Set. This set included Warship Class Diesel locomotive named 'Vanguard' (F106) together with BR Western Region 1st class (563) and brake 2nd (573) scale coaches plus 14-piece oval track. 1960-1963.

F50 0-6-0 Goods Set with BR 0-6-0 Class E2 tank engine (F107), 12-ton covered van (P. 614), 3-plank open wagon (P.601), goods brake van (P. 621) and 14-piece oval track. 1961-1963.

Note regarding above set: The Class E2 tank engine was not available separately until 1959. In 1963 'Gamages', the mail order company, were also advertising the set with a different set of wagons which were the old tinplate variety as used in the 'Cadet' sets.

F52 0-6-0 Passenger set with BR 0-6-0 Class E2 tank engine (F107), BR maroon 1st class (562) and brake 2nd (572) scale coaches plus 14-piece oval track. 1963 only.

The catalogue numbers quoted below for the locomotives are for the scale wheel variety only.

1200 0-6-2 Passenger Set. This set contained Class 66XX 0-6-2 tank engine (1100), BR Western region composite corridor (1911) and composite brake (1912) scale coaches plus 14-piece oval track. 1963 only.

1201 4-6-2 Britannia Pullman Set. Comprised Britannia Class 4-6-2 engine and tender (1109), two Pullman coaches (1931) and 14-piece oval track. 1963 only.

1202 4-6-2 Britannia Express Set. Comprised Britannia Class 4-6-2 engine and tender (1109), BR maroon composite corridor (1901) and composite brake (1902) scale coaches plus 14-piece oval track. 1963 only.

1203 0-6-2 Goods Set (3 wagons). As set F32 but catalogue numbers of contents changed. For example Mineral wagon with Iron Ore was P. 609 now changed to 1609. 1963 only.

1204 0-6-2 Goods Set (6 wagons). As set F33 but catalogue numbers of contents changed. 1963 only.

1205 4-6-0 Class V Goods Set (6 wagons). As set F34 but catalogue numbers of contents changed. 1963 only.

1206 4-6-0 Class V Passenger Set. This set comprised BR green 4-6-0 Class V 4-6-0 engine and tender (1115) with BR maroon composite corridor (1901) and composite brake (1902) scale coaches plus 14-piece oval track. 1963 only.

1207 Bo-Bo Mineral Train Set. As set F36 but catalogue numbers of contents changed. 1963 only.

1208 Bo-Bo Passenger Train Set. Green EM1 Bo-Bo Electric locomotive (1124) with BR maroon composite corridor (1901) and composite brake (1902) scale coaches plus 14-piece oval track. 1963 only.

1208 Bo-Bo Passenger Train Set. As above but with 'Trix Control' power/control unit Cat.No.1805. 1964 only.

1209 'Vanguard' Western Region Express Set. This set comprised Warship Class Diesel 'Vanguard' (1118) with BR Western Region composite corridor (1911) and composite brake (1912) and with a 14-piece oval track. 1963 only.

1210 0-6-0 Goods Set. As set F50 but catalogue numbers of contents changed.

1963 only.

1211 0-6-0 Passenger Set. As set F52 but catalogue numbers of contents changed. 1963 only.

1212 E 3000 Express. This set contained AEI E3000 electric locomotive (1127) together with BR maroon composite corridor (1901), composite brake (1902) and 14-piece oval track. 1963 only.

1232 Trix Express 'Der Adler'. Imported set, no rails. Listed in British catalogues 1963 only.

1285 Trix Express Dutch ELD Electric Railcar Set, green. Imported set, no rails. Listed in British catalogues 1963 only.

0-6-0 Goods Set. This set was especially packaged for the Australian market. It was essentially an F50 0-6-0 Goods Set as produced between 1961 and 1963 except that an oval of 2-rail track was included instead of the 3-rail track. A highly decorative sleeve was fitted over the box. Circa 1964-1965.

1255 Complete Starter Set, (later called De luxe Goods Train). This set comprised BR Class E2 0-6-0 tank engine (1108) together with six assorted wagons, 12 curved rails, five straight rails, two hand uncoupler rails, two buffer rails, pair of hand-operated points, and Trix Express power/control unit (later changed to a British Trix power/control unit 'Trix Control' Cat. No. 1805 made for British Trix by Hammant & Morgan Ltd). As in earlier AC sets the types of wagons varied with availability. The loco and rails are for the 2-rail system. 1964-1968.

1256 De luxe Goods Train Set. As set 1255 but for the 3-rail system. 1965-1968.

1265 Euston (Blue Flash) Express Set. This set comprised E3000 Electric locomotive (1128), BR maroon composite corridor (1901), composite brake (1902) and Buffet (1903) scale coaches. 12 large radius curved rails and six straights. From 1967 the BR maroon coaches were replaced with BR blue/grey coaches. Loco and rails for 2-rail system. 1965-1971.

1266 Euston (Blue Flash) Express Set. As set 1265 but for 3-rail system. 1965-1966.

1275 Western Express Set. This set included maroon Class D1000 diesel locomotive (1167), and initially BR Western Region composite corridor (1911) composite brake (1912) and Buffet (1913) scale coaches but later sets could have either the above or the BR maroon versions. Also included were 12 large radius curved rails and six straights. Loco and rails for the 2-rail system. 1965-1971.

1276 Western Express Set. As set 1275 but for 3-rail system. 1965-1966.

1277 0-6-2 Goods Set. Listed in 1965 but not produced.

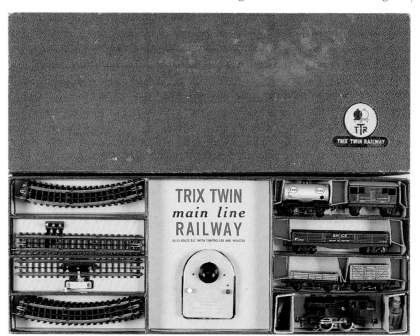

Main Line Goods Set Cat.No.251. (A)

4-4-0 BR Southern Region
Passenger Set Cat.No.F27.(A)

EM1 Bo-Bo Mineral Train Set Cat.No.F36 The Catenary
Set 01 supplied with this train set was packed separately. (A)

Diesel Breakdown Set Cat.No.F40.

0-6-0 Passenger Set Cat.No.F52. (A)

1278 0-6-2 Passenger Set. Listed in 1965 but not produced.
1285 0-6-0 Goods Set. Comprised of BR Class E2 0-6-0 tank engine (1108), four assorted goods wagons, 14-piece oval track and 'Trix Control' power unit/controller (1805). Once again the types of wagons included with the set varied. Loco and rails for 2-rail system. 1965-1968.
1286 0-6-0 Goods Set. As set 1285 but for 3-rail system. 1965-1966.
1295 0-6-0 Passenger Set. Comprised BR Class E2 0-6-0 tank engine (1108), BR maroon composite corridor (1901) and composite brake (1902) scale coaches, 14-piece oval track and 'Trix Control' power unit/controller (1805). Loco and rails for 2-rail system. 1965-1968.
1296 0-6-0 Passenger Set. As set 1295 but for 3-rail system. 1965-1966.
1218 Diesel Passenger Set. Comprised of green Warship diesel locomotive (1118), BR Western region composite corridor (1911), composite brake (1912) and Buffet (1913) scale coaches plus 12 large radius curved rails and six straights. Loco and rails for 3-rail system. 1966 only.
1220 Diesel Passenger Set. As set 1218 but for 3-rail system. 1966 only.
1251 Goods special – 2-rail. Listed in 1966. No information available.
1252 Goods special – 3-rail. Listed in 1966. No information available.
1261 Freightliner set – 2-rail. Listed in 1966 but not produced.
1262 Freightliner set – 3-rail. Listed in 1966 but not produced.
1263 Midland Goods set. This set included E3000 Class Electric locomotive (1128) with six assorted wagons, 12 large radius curved rails and six straights. For 2-rail operation. 1966-1971.
1264 Midland Goods set. As set 1264 but for 3-rail operation. 1966 only.
1273 Western Goods set. This set comprised D1000 'Western Enterprise' Diesel locomotive (1165) with six assorted wagons, 12 large radius curved rails and six straights. Loco and rails for 2-rail operation. 1966-1971.
1274 Western Goods set. As set 1273 but for 3-rail operation. 1966 only.
1287 Speedfreight Set. Contents were BR Class E2 0-6-0 tank engine (1108), three Speedfreight wagons (1623), goods brake van (1622) and 14-piece oval track. Loco and track for 2-rail operation. 1966 only.
1288 Speedfreight Set. As set 1287 but for 3-rail operation. 1966 only.
1299 Two Train Super Set. This was an imported Trix Express twin set comprising the following German-outline items. All catalogue numbers are Trix Express and for 3-rail operation:
30 straight rails (4304), 24 curved rails (4312), terminal rail (4372), pair of remote control points (4362), diamond crossing (4358), two power units

(5599), two 4-wheel passenger coaches (3303), 4-wheel baggage coach (3302), dump wagon (3455), open wagon (3414), Shell yellow tank wagon (3427), container wagon with three containers (3457), Class V 100 diesel locomotive (2266), DB Class 24 2-6-0 engine and tender (2202) plus connecting wire; all housed in a carrying case. 1966-1967.
1257 Britannia Goods Set. Comprised BR Britannia Class 4-6-2 engine and tender (1109) and six assorted wagons plus 12 large radius curved rails and six straights. Loco and rails for 3-rail operation. 1966 only.
1258 Britannia Goods Set. As set 1257 but for 2-rail operation. 1966 only.
1259 Britannia Passenger Set. Comprised BR Britannia Class 4-6-2 engine and tender (1109), BR maroon composite corridor (1901), composite brake (1902) and Buffet (1903) scale coaches with 12 large radius curved rails and six straights. Loco and rails for 3-rail operation. 1966 only.
1260 Britannia Passenger Set. As set 1259 but for 2-rail operation. 1966-1967.
1290 Private Goods Set. This set included BR Class E2 0-6-0 tank engine (1108), Spiers Private Owner wagon (1657), Maltby PO wagon (1658), Salter PO wagon (1659), Young PO wagon (1661), Ocean PO wagon (1662), Hall & Co PO wagon (1664), goods brake van (1621), 12 large curved rails and six straights. For 2-rail operation. The types of Private Owner wagons included in the set changed as the range increased. 1967-1971.
1292 Special Goods Set. Included in this set were the BR E2 0-6-0 tank engine (1108), six assorted Bulk Grain wagons, 12 large radius curved rails and six straight rails. For 2-rail operation. 1967-1971.
1298B Intercity Set. This set contained Intercity blue/grey DMU without lights (1174), blue/grey composite corridor coach (1975), blue/grey composite brake (1976), 12 large radius curved rails and 12 straight rails. For 2-rail operation. 1967-1969.
1298G Intercity Set. This set contained Intercity green DMU without lights (1175), green composite corridor coach (1971) and composite brake (1972), 12 large radius curved rails and 12 straight rails. For 2-rail operation. 1967-1968.
1297 Intercity Set. As set 1298G but with lights. 1967 only.

Note: Many of the above later DC sets were not held as stock items in the shops but supplied to order. In the period immediately prior to Liliput Model Railways (UK) Ltd sets were made up to the special requirements of the customer.

EM1 Bo-Bo Passenger Train Set Cat.No.1208.
This is the 1964 version with the Power Unit
Cat.No.1805. (A)

Western Express Set
Cat.No.1275. (A)

THE RAILWAY CONSTRUCTION KITS

These kits were introduced in 1965 in an attempt to increase the sales of the Trix range. Due to the relatively high cost of Trix products, and the fact that other interests were increasingly occupying the public's leisure time, the quantity of stock-piled parts was building up and required to be moved. The plastic coaches to a scale of 3.8mm were one of the problems; not many customers were prepared to pay the moderately high price even for this excellent product, as it was considered to be to the 'wrong' scale. Nevertheless, as soon as these coaches appeared in kit form at a much lower price (for example, at the time of the introduction of the kits a factory-produced coach cost on average 14/-, against the cost of the kit which was 9/11d), the sales increased dramatically. This also held for all the other items in the range, showing that if the price was right, the scale, within reason, did not matter. The assembly of the kits was kept as simple as possible with the minimum of tools required to complete the model. There were four ranges altogether – the Footplateman Series, the Coachbuilder Series, the Wagonmaster Series and the Platelayer Series. Each kit was boxed in the yellow and black style of boxes used by British Trix Ltd with a general black and white line drawing showing Trix locomotives, coaches, wagons and track on their respective boxes. Later packaging for the coaches and wagons used clear plastic bags to hold the loose contents. Detailed easy-to-follow instructions were included with each kit.

The Footplateman Series

All the assemblies for the models that required special tools and skill in their construction, for example, the valve gear for the steam locomotives, were supplied fully made-up. The main locomotive bodies, and where applicable, tender bodies, were supplied already painted but unlined and without transfers. There were small minor details in the construction of the model that differed from the production version, but these were only to ease assembly for the customer. Below is a list of Footplateman kits available together with corresponding catalogue numbers:

2102 (U) Class 64XX 0-6-2 Tank engine. (1965 only)
2108 (U) Class E2 0-6-0 Tank engine. (1965 only)
2111 (U) 4-6-2 Britannia. (1965 to 1966 and in 1969 only)
2114 (U) 4-6-0 Class V, black. (1965 to 1966 and in 1969 only)
2117 (U) 4-6-0 Class V, green. (1966 and 1969 only)
2118 (U) Warship Diesel, blue. (1967 to 1971)
2119 (U) Warship Diesel, maroon. (1966 to 1970)
2120 (U) Warship Diesel, green. (1965 to 1970)
2127 (3) E-3000 Class. (1966 to 1968)
2128 (U) E-3000 Class. (1965 and again in 1969 only)
2128 (2) E-3000 Class. (1966 to 1971)
2163 (2) Western Diesel, blue. (1967 to 1972)
2163DL (2) Western Diesel, blue, De Luxe kit. (1968 only)
2165 (2) Western Diesel, green. (1966 to 1972)
2165DL (2) Western Diesel, green, De Luxe kit. (1968 only)
2166 (3) Western Diesel, green. (1966 only)
2167 (U) Western Diesel, maroon. (1965 only)
2167 (2) Western Diesel, maroon. (1966 to 1972)
2167DL (2) Western Diesel, maroon, De Luxe kit. (1968 only)

The box lid of a Footplateman kit.

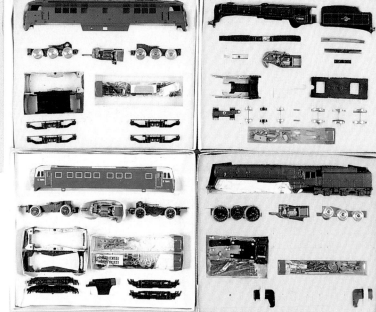

Footplateman Kits. Top left: Western Diesel Cat.No. 2167. Top right: Black BR Class V Cat.No.2114 with the body in finished condition. In later kits the body was just painted black. Bottom left: E3000 Cat.No.2128. Bottom right: BR 'Britannia' Cat.No. 2111. (A)

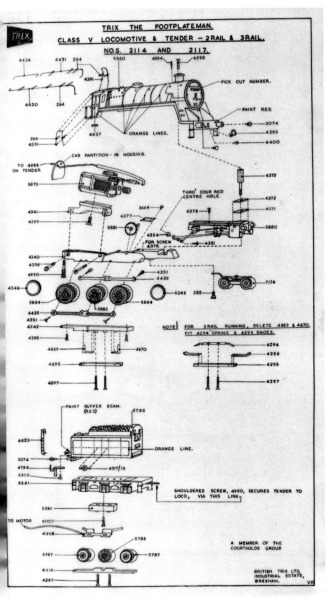

Instruction sheet for Footplateman Kit for the Class V.

2168 (3) Western Diesel, maroon. (1966 and 1968 only)
2183 (2) 4-6-2 Class A3, black. (not produced)
2186 (2) 4-6-2 Class A2 'Peppercorn', LNER green. (not produced)
Note: (U) denotes 2 or 3-rail, (2) only 2-rail and (3) only 3-rail.
The above dates are inclusive. The De Luxe kits included the body shell completely finished plus an extra weight for the trailing bogie, whereas the body shell supplied in the normal kits was finished in just the basic colour. The break in the sequence of dates of certain kits was due to the erratic production of parts.

An attempt was made in 1982 by Liliput Model Railways (UK) Ltd to resurrect the Footplateman Series but it was an unsuccessful exercise. This was mainly due to an inadequate flow of parts above the normal requirement needed for production of complete models. Although most of these kits continued to be included in the price lists up to 1988, less than five of the A4 kits were ever produced and that included a black war-time version which was not even listed!

Below is a list of planned kits that were not issued:
1180 E3000
1181 Western
1183 Intercity, blue/grey
1184 Intercity, green
1185 LNER Flying Scotsman
1186 BR Flying Scotsman
1187 LNER A4 Silver Link
1188 LNER A4 Mallard, blue
1189 BR A4 Merlin
1190 LNER A2 Peppercorn
1191 BR A2 Peppercorn

The Coachbuilder Series
When the coaches from these kits were made up correctly they were more or less indistinguishable from factory-produced items. Initially plastic wheels were issued with the kit which were replaced after 1968 with metal wheel assemblies. The coach sides were lined and numbered and only the appropriate transfers needed application. The De Luxe kits (1967-1968) contained metal wheel assemblies and additional weights.

The unlisted Liliput (UK) wartime black LNER A4 kit.

Below is a list of Coachbuilder kits available with their corresponding catalogue numbers. All dates are inclusive:

1941 BR Composite corridor, Midland Region maroon.
1942 BR Composite brake, Midland Region maroon.
1943 BR Buffet car, Midland Region maroon.
1944 BR Composite corridor, Western Region yellow/brown
1945 BR Composite brake, Western Region yellow/brown.
1946 BR Buffet car, Western Region yellow/brown.
1947 BR Composite corridor, Southern Region green.
1948 BR Composite brake, Southern Region green.
1949 BR Buffet car, Southern Region green.
1950 Pullman car, dark-brown/cream.
All the above kits were produced from 1965 to 1972.

1954 BR Composite corridor, Southern Region blue.
1955 BR Composite brake, Southern Region blue. Both the above produced 1968 to 1970.

1956 BR Composite corridor, Midland Region blue/grey.
1957 BR Composite brake, Midland Region blue grey.
1958 BR Buffet car, Midland Region blue grey. The above produced from September 1966 to 1972.

A selection of Coachbuilder and Wagonmaster Kits. (A)

1959 BR Composite corridor, Western Region blue/grey. Produced from 1968 to 1969.

1960 Pullman car, blue/grey. Produced from 1968 to 1972.

1961 BR Composite corridor, Midland Region maroon.
1962 BR Composite brake, Midland Region maroon.
1963 BR Buffet car, Midland Region maroon.
1966 BR Composite corridor, Midland Region blue/grey.

1967 BR Composite brake, Midland Region blue/grey.
1968 BR Buffet car, Midland Region blue/grey. The above six kits are all De Luxe kits and were produced from the middle of 1967 to 1968.

The Wagonmaster Series

The wagon kits were initially retailed at 3/11d each, a saving of almost 2/- on the factory-produced wagon, which provided modellers with an inexpensive method of equipping their model railway with rolling stock displaying detail that was formerly only found on continental models. The assembly used the clip-together principle with no painting required and only the transfers to apply where appropriate. Below is the list of Wagonmaster kits with catalogue numbers. All dates are inclusive:

2001 Open wagon, red. (1965 to 1966)
2002 Open wagon, grey. (1965 to 1966)
2004 Pig iron wagon, red. (1965 to 1966)
2005 Pig iron wagon, grey. (1965 to 1966)
2006 Mineral wagon, grey. (1965 to 1970)
2007 Mineral wagon, red. (1965 to 1971)
2008 Coal wagon, grey. (1965 to 1966)
2009 Ore wagon, grey. (1965 to 1966)
2010 Crane unit. (1966 to 1969)
2011 Ballast wagon, red. (1965 to 1966)
2011 Mineral wagon with load. This was a general kit and could be supplied with a red or grey wagon body, and a load of ore, coal or ballast. (1968 to 1970)
2013 Covered van, red. (1965 to 1971)
2014 Covered van, grey. (1965 to 1970)
2017 Container wagon, red with red container. (1965 to 1971)
2018 Container wagon, red with white container. (1965 to 1971)
2019 Bird's Eye container wagon. (1966 to 1969)
2021 Brake van, grey. (1966 to 1971)
2022 Brake van, red. (1966 to 1971)
2023 Speedfreight wagon. (1968 to 1969)
2024 Tank wagon, grey, REGENT, TOTAL. This kit contained transfers to make up either version. (1967 to 1971)
2025 Tank wagon, black, SHELL/B.P. (1966 only)
2025 Tank wagon, black, SHELL/B.P., FINA, ESSO, MOBIL. This kit contained transfers to make up any one of the four versions. (1967 to 1971)
2026 Tank wagon, black, ESSO. (1966 only)
2027 Tank wagon, black, FINA. (1966 only)
2028 Tank wagon, grey, TOTAL. (1966 only)
2029 Tank wagon, black, MOBIL. (1966 only)
2030 Tank wagon, black, BP. (1966 only)
2057 Private Owner wagon, Spiers. (1968 to 1970)
2061 Private owner wagon, Young. (1968 to 1971)
2062 Private owner wagon, Ocean. (1968 to 1970)
2064 Private owner wagon, Hall. (1968 to 1971)
2065 Private owner wagon, ICI. (1968 to 1971)
2069 Private owner wagon, Abbott. (1968 to 1971)
2080 Bulk grain wagon, Johnnie Walker. (1968 to 1969)
2081 Bulk grain wagon, Haig. (1968 to 1969)
2083 Bulk grain wagon, Vat 69. (1968 to 1969)
2084 Bulk grain wagon, King George IV. (1968 to 1969)
2085 Bulk grain wagon, Dewars. (1968 to 1969)
2086 Bulk grain wagon, Crawford. (1968 to 1969)
2087 Bulk grain wagon, White Horse. (1968 to 1969)
2088 Bulk grain wagon, Jamie Stuart. (1968 to 1969)
2089 Bulk grain wagon, Maltsters' Association. (1968 to 1969)
2090 Bulk grain wagon, Abbott's Choice. (1968 to 1969)
2091 Bulk grain wagon, BR. (1968 to 1969)

The Platelayer Series
These were kits were to make up units of the British Trix Ltd 2-rail track system. They were not very successful and had a very short life:

2301 Straight track kit, one yard. (1965 to 1966)
2302 Curved track, small radius, half circle. (1965 to 1966)
2303 Curved track, large radius, half circle. (1965 to 1966)
2304 Straight track assortment. (1965 only)
2305 Curved track assortment. (1965 only)
2306 Buffer and uncoupler. (1965 to 1966)
2307 Left-hand point. (not produced)
2308 Right-hand point. (not produced)

Platelayer Kit Cat.No.2302. (A)

CARD COACH KITS

These card coach kits were introduced in 1971 to compliment the fine 4mm LNER model locomotives produced at that time. Unfortunately the finances of Trix Trains would not allow the development and tooling costs to produces a new range of LNER coaches. Three Trix Trains coach kits were available, all modelled on a Gresley coach:

Cat. No. C1 all 1st.
Cat. No. C2 Brake 3rd.
Cat. No. C3 1st/3rd Composite.

Prototype model of the Trix 1800 Series Card Kits: The GWR Class 57XX Pannier Tank Engine Cat. No. SC7.

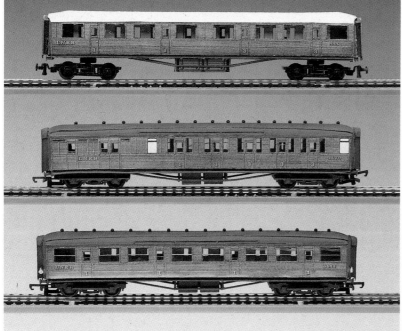

Coaches constructed from the Trix Card Coach kits.
From the top: 1st/3rd Composite, Brake 3rd, all 1st.

The coach sides were embossed and well printed with all the relevant detail, but the parts had to be cut out and carefully assembled. They were extremely difficult to build correctly and definitely not for unskilled hands. When built they captured the Gresley style very well but in use required very careful handling. Correct pattern Gresley bogies could be built from the parts contained in the kit, except for the wheels which were not included, or bogies assemblies as used on the BR range of 3.8mm scale plastic coaches could be purchased separately. The kits were available for a few years from various outlets.

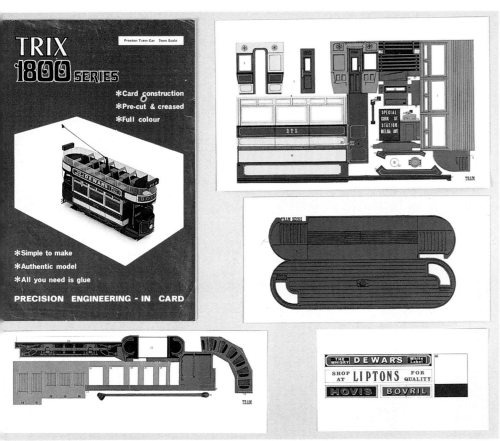

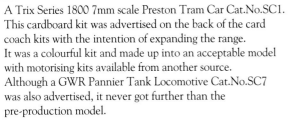

Prototype model of the Trix 1800 Series Card Kits –
the Preston Tramcar Cat. No.SC1.

A Trix Series 1800 7mm scale Preston Tram Car Cat.No.SC1.
This cardboard kit was advertised on the back of the card
coach kits with the intention of expanding the range.
It was a colourful kit and made up into an acceptable model
with motorising kits available from another source.
Although a GWR Pannier Tank Locomotive Cat.No.SC7
was also advertised, it never got further than the
pre-production model.

'Trixstad' Station Cat.No.20/270.

Trix express Goods Shed 20/273.

Twin Engine
Shed
Cat.No.844.

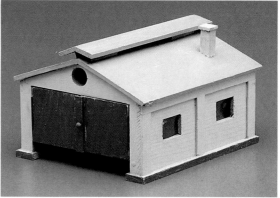

Trix Express
Locomotive
Shed
Cat.No.20/272.
(A)

A layout in early 1935 displaying the full Trix Express range available. The goods train in the centre of the picture is made up from mostly pre-production models hauled by a locomotive finished for the British market. Note the words Twin Express on the tender.

ACCESSORIES

STATION BUILDINGS AND LINESIDE FEATURES

Early Wooden Buildings

During the early 1930s, Bassett-Lowke offered the latest in model railway station designs with an O gauge model of a single platform station which incorporated all the features and finish of a ferro-concrete Overground through station of the London Underground Railway network. This model was given the station name of 'Ashfield' and was designed by Henry Greenly, the well-known model engineer, in collaboration with the London Passenger Board. It was constructed from wood and made in the workshop of Winteringham Ltd in Stimpson Avenue, Northampton.

It was this model station that caught the eye of Stephan Bing during the development period of the Trix Express system, and he instructed his design team, with sanction from W. J. Bassett-Lowke, to copy the basic features resulting in the model Station 'Trixstadt' Cat. No. 20/270, together with an Island Platform, Cat. No. 20/271. These station buildings were offered together with a Locomotive Shed with opening doors, Cat. No. 20/272, and a Good's Shed with sliding doors, Cat. No. 20/273, in the first German Trix Express catalogue of 1935.

The model buildings were manufactured in the German Trix factory from wood using simple pinned and glued butt-joints suitably finished in the colour of reinforced concrete, with certain features picked out in a bright colour. They were imported into Britain to be included in the TWIN TRAIN range during the 1935/36 period with the prefix digits of the catalogue numbers changing from 20 to 21. Basically there was no change to the models intended for the British market, including the resplendent tinplate TRIX EXPRESS flag flying above the clock tower on the station, but the name-boards at each end of the platform initially bore the name TRIX CITY instead of TRIXSTADT, and the miniature posters pasted to the walls of the platform were decidedly British. The name TRIX CITY was very quickly changed to TWIN CITY with the corresponding omission of the TRIX EXPRESS flag.

Winter 1936 saw the introduction of a new extended range of TWIN TRAIN wooden buildings and structures fabricated in the workshops of the Winteringham factory replacing those imported from Germany. The basic finish for all the following wooden models was a matt dull yellow representing ferro-concrete. The design of the TWIN CITY Station and the Island Platform remained the same except that the yellow finish was much paler than the German version, the latter having a greenish-grey tinge. The catalogue numbers were changed to 804 and 807 respectively.

The new Twin City Engine Shed, Cat. No. 844, was much larger than the German version as was the Twin Goods Shed, Cat. No. 847, although the latter was rather crude looking in comparison with its flat grey roof and large green sliding doors. A welcome addition was the Twin Carriage Shed, Cat. No. 848, constructed in a way which allowed two or more units to be placed end-to-end to house a train-length of coaches, especially the short types available at this time. The pictures in the Trix literature depicting this Carriage Shed showed it to have a base plinth to match that of the Engine Shed, but it was never produced with a plinth as this would have prevented the close end contact of two units.

A well-proportioned but simple Twin Terminus Station, Cat. No. 805, was introduced which provided two long platforms accommodating three roads of track. It had a large, lined Celastoid span roof together with a clock tower and entrance steps at the terminus end. T T R in large dark blue letters was applied above the entrance canopy. The total length of the station was 27 inches. Also on sale in

Britain, but in small quantities, was the Trix Express Terminal/Through Station named TRIXBURG, Cat. No. 20/274. This was a much larger and heavier structure than the British version with the main span 2.5 inches wider but still only accommodating three roads of track. Again a printed Celastoid-type of span covering was provided. The entrance building and clock tower structure was a separate unit which could be placed in any position, thus creating either a through, or terminal, station to be formed. This TRIXBURG station was readily available up to and including 1939 in Germany, but it is doubtful if many units were sold in Britain after 1937. This Trix Express station was only provided with the letters T T R beneath the printed cardboard clock face for Bassett-Lowke publicity photographs.

An essential feature of any railway system is the signal box, and in the Twin Train range this was provided in the form of the Twin Signal Box, Cat. No. 822. It was a basic and simple design with a set of steps leading to a recessed door at the left-hand side when viewed from the front and had a Celastoid-glazed full-length window. The 'handrail'

of the steps and the door were painted bright yellow. The remaining items in this early wooden Twin Train range were two footbridges – a straight-over span entitled the Twin Footbridge, Cat. No. 862, plus a Footbridge With Angle Approach, Cat. No. 863. As with the steps of the Twin Signal Box, the tops of the bridge sides were painted bright yellow.

The above Twin Train range of buildings remained in the catalogues only until the middle of 1937, when they were replaced with a completely new and innovative system. However, the two types of Footbridge, the Terminus Station, Cat. No. 805, and the Goods Shed were listed, but not illustrated, in the 1939/1940 TTR catalogue and price list. In fact, in the TTR January 1941 price list the Island Platform also made a reappearance, but this was to be the very last time any of the early series of structures were listed. One must conclude that the relisting of these items was due to large stocks remaining on the shelves of Trix Ltd. It is interesting to note that the two types of Footbridge supplied at this time were now finished in light grey, with or without the tops of the bridge sides in dark grey, to match the existing range of buildings. One can see evidence in many instances of the original yellow finish being over-sprayed with grey. The straight-across Footbridge, Cat. No.862, was also listed in the French Trix Express catalogue, but given the catalogue number 25/295.

Tinplate Buildings and Lineside Features for the American Market

During 1936 the Trix company in Germany employed the expertise of Kindler & Briel of Böblingen, who at this time specialised in tinplate railway accessories under the trade name of Kibri, to

Mock-up of Twin Terminus station (Cat.No.805). Note difference in the tower to the production version.

Twin Goods Shed Cat.No.847.

Top: 'Twin City' Station Cat.No.804.

Above: Twin City Island Platform Cat.No.807.

Twin Carriage Shed Cat.No.848.

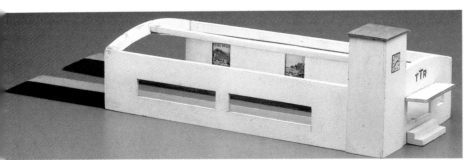

Twin Terminus station Cat.No.805. (A)

Trix Express 'Trixburg' Terminal/Through Station Cat.No.20/274.

Twin Signal Box Cat.No.822.

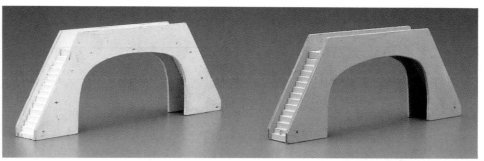

Twin Footbridges Cat.No.862.

Kibri for Trix Express Guard
House Cat.No.20/301.

Twin Footbridges with Angle Approach Cat.No.863.

A selection of pre-war Kibri tinplate lineside
accessories shown in the joint Trix Express/TTR
pre-war export catalogues.

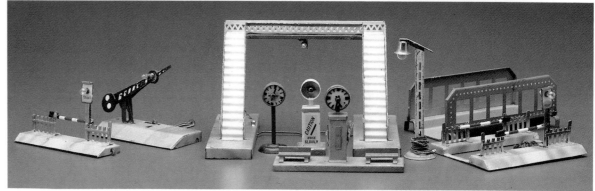

Three views of an interesting Trix Express layout in 1936 which displays the full range available at that time including the large TRIXBURG station and the remotely controlled Level Crossing Gates. The tinplate Signal Boxes, Signal Gantry and wooden Embankments were produced by Kibri for Trix.

supply a range of items suitable for use with the Trix Express model railway system. By agreement, the Kibri tinplate and wooden accessories manufactured for Trix were supplied without the Kibri trademark and given Trix catalogue numbers as shown in the various pre-war Trix Express catalogues. A variety of items were produced for the German market up to 1940 but it is beyond the scope of this book to list them.

However, between the inclusive period of 1937 to 1939, the joint Trix Express /TTR catalogues for the American market showed a moderately large range of these Kibri-produced accessories advertised as 'Miniature Accessories – Scaled for Trix Express (TTR) Electric Table Trains'. In many cases the accessories were specially adapted for this market by using signs and inscriptions in English, as well as the addition of American features on a few of the items such as the barriers on railway crossing gates.

A detailed description of this series of Kibri accessories is beyond the scope of this book, but a list of items included in the 1937/1939 joint catalogues is given below. Unfortunately, the catalogue numbers given in the 1937/1938 catalogue were entirely different to those given in the 1938/1939 version, and thus for reference both sets are given, the 1937/1938 catalogue numbers being listed first. The 1938/1939 catalogue had an amended range. Where the same item is listed in a normal Trix Express catalogue the corresponding catalogue number is given after the description.

Cat. Nos.

9/180, 9/1		Illuminated Signal Tower.
9/181, 9/2		Illuminated Bench with Clock.
9/182, 9/3		Tunnel, wood 5½" long. (20/291).
9/183, 9/4		Guardhouse.
9/184, –		Passenger Station, 9" long, 5" high.
9/185, 9/6		Warning Signal.
9/186, –		Railroad Gate, single barrier.
9/187, 9/8		Passenger Bridge, 9½" long.
9/188, 9/9		Signal.
9/189, 9/10		Overhead Derrick.
9/201, 9/17		Illuminated Clock.
9/202, –		Illuminated Railroad Crossing, two barriers.
9/204, 9/195		Arc Light.
9/205, 9/19		Freight Station with Derrick.
9/208, 9/22		Illuminated Signal Bridge. (20/294).
9/286, 9/60		Corner Tunnel, wood 17" long, 17" wide. (20/295).
9/287, 9/61		Water Tower.
9/288, 9/62		Passeger Station, 13" long, 5½" high.
9/289, 9/196		Double Platform, 8" long. (20/297)
9/290, 9/63		Derrick, Arc Lamp, Bunker and Water Tower on base.
9/291, 9/64		Freight Depot, 6½" long.
9/292, –		Illuminated Railway Crossing, 3" high.
9/293, –		Illuminated Signal.
9/294, 9/66		Overhead Passenger Bridge, with automatic light.
9/295, 9/67		Automatic Drop Gate.
9/296, 9/193		Automatic Twin Drop Gate.
9/299, 9/68		Single Span Railroad Bridge, 6" long.
–, 0/52/17		Station with Tower and adjoining platform, 10¼" long, 8¼" wide, 5½" high. (20/303).
–, 0/53/2B		Illuminated Double Platform with wireglass roof, 19" long. (20/310). (wireglass is a fine square wire mesh dipped in clear plastic to form a continuous surface.
–, 0/53/3B		Illuminated Triple Platform with wireglass roof, 19" long.
–, 0/61/21		Bridge, 20" long.

Above: Trix Express Banking, Tunnel and Pedestrian Bridge Cat.Nos.20/290, 20/291, 20/292 respectively. A few of these items found their way into many countries.

Below: Kibri for Trix Stations for the American market. On the left Cat.No.9/288 and on the right Cat.No.9/184.

The Many-Ways System, including Complimentary Buildings and Accessories

Based on the initial idea of Siegfried Kahn, E. W. Twining was entrusted with the task of working out a scheme whereby all kinds of station formations could be built from a range of basic units, ranging from a single short platform and shelter of a wayside halt to terminal and through stations as seen in large towns and cities. The design and drawing of each of the units, together the master models from which the moulds, etc., were prepared for manufacture, were accomplished in the architectural modelling department of E. W. Twining's own company, Twining Models Ltd, situated in Pike Lane, Northampton. The complete system was granted a Patent in 1938, (number 485,170) in the names of Siegfried Kahn and Trix Ltd. It was an excellent system and enjoyed a long production life from 1937 up to and including 1960.

The individual units were finished in a way which was supposed to resemble ferro-concrete, with the pre-war units being painted a light grey, the early post-war units light khaki and the late post-war units almost a desert-sand colour. Different production runs gave shade variations for each basic finish. The roofs of all the units were painted dark grey, the windows were glazed with Celastoid with printed red frames, and the large span covering was a printed Celastoid sheet with dark grey (pre-war), or grey (post-war) framework. Complimentary to the basic Many-Ways system was a range of railway buildings and structures including station accessories. The buildings, constructed from wood, were always finished in light grey although many shades exist, the post-war versions taking on a decidedly green tint. The vast majority of Many-Ways items and complimentary buildings were manufactured by various companies for Trix Ltd.

After the war, it was not until 1953 that full production of the Many-Ways units resumed and the complete range of individual units could once again be purchased. Until then, the Many-Ways units could only be purchased as part of a set (except for a few selected individual units in 1948). These sets were in short supply and occasionally contained some surviving units of pre-war production.

The actual production range was slightly different to that initially envisaged as it had been intended to produce separate platform fence units for the ramps and platforms, as well as a Tunnel Mouth, Subway Head and End Panel for the Span, none of which materialised. Two other interesting items that were mentioned in the Patent specification but never got any further were a narrow and wide Distance Piece. These were to be used in conjunction with a Span (42) to position, as required, a Span platform to a track, between two tracks, between track and Wide Platform (14), between Wide Platform and track and then track to other Span platform, thus filling up the gaps and positioning the tracks.

On the front cover of the 1939 spring edition of the *TTR Gazette* was a picture of a large Many-Ways Terminus Station, as shown at a recent British Industries Fair Exhibition. The forecourt was surrounded by a range of shop-fronts which were to be offered as part of the 1939 releases, which were to be illuminated and manufactured from a pressure diecasting. Two shop lengths were to equal the length of a Many-Ways Main Building unit. Unfortunately, this unit, as with many other TTR items at this time, was a casualty of the priorities of war and was never produced. In general, all pre-war wooden platform units were stamped in ink on the ends with 'TRIX "MANY WAYS" STATION SETS Made in England', while the corresponding post-war marking was 'TTR Made in England'.

The cover of the 1937 Trix Many-Ways Station Set instruction book and guide.

Above: pre-production Many-Ways units.

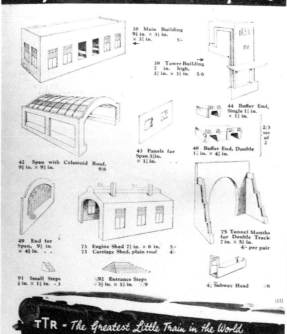

The component parts of the Trix Many-Ways Units as shown in an early 1937 Trix booklet. Not all the items shown were actually produced.

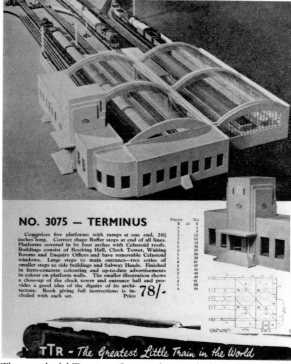

The wonderful Terminus Station that can be built from the Many-Ways Units in set No.3075 as shown in the early 1937 Trix leaflet. The Span End Panel was never produced.

Below is a list and brief description of the Many-Ways units and other structures and accessories listed in order of their catalogue numbers. Some of the items listed here do not form part of the units that make up the Many-Ways stations, but they were manufactured to be complimentary to the system and form part of the overall picture. The catalogue numbers in brackets with the prefix 9 are those given to the same items as shown in the joint Trix

Express/TTR 1938/1939 American catalogue. Pre-war terminology is used and all platform heights were 0.875".Unless otherwise stated, all the following items were produced from1937until1960:

2 (9/155) Ramp, narrow, 2.875" long x 0.875" wide.

A white line marking the platform edge was painted on one side only resulting in left-and right-hand versions. Up to 1953 it was made of hardwood,

usually poplar or lime. From 1953 formed hiduminium, (aluminium-manganese alloy)was used.

4 (9/156) Ramp, wide, 2.875" long x 1.75" wide.
A white line was painted on each side marking the edge of the platform. Manufacturing details as for the Narrow Ramp.

5 Fence for Ramp, 2.875" long x 1.5" high.
This short fence was shown and listed as a separate item in the first booklet of 1937 describing the new

Trix Many-Ways Station Sets, and was intended to be fitted to the side face of a Ramp. Some of the photographs in this booklet show this fence in position. It was never produced.

12 (9/157) Platform, narrow. 9.625" long x 0.875" wide.

A white line marking the edge of the platform was applied to one side only. Hardwood was used in the manufacture of the platform until 1948 when an aluminium alloy extruded section was employed. Nevertheless the wooden platforms continued to be available for a year or two until stocks were depleted. The aluminium alloy was changed during 1953 in favour of a formed-hiduminium alloy section.

12/15 (9/158) Platform, narrow with Fence. 9.625" long x 0.875" wide x 1.5" high.

In pre-war versions, a mild steel Fence 1.5" high was pinned to the side of the wooden platform. In post-war versions, dural was used for the Fence, later changing to hiduminium in 1953, which was riveted to the platform side. During the pre-war production period, miniature posters were often applied by the manufacturers to the outside face of the Fence, while

Extract from Patent No.485,170 showing the proposed Many-Ways Station unit system.

2 485,170

other, and means may be provided whereby they are locked together in the required positions.

Dated this 12th day of November, 1936.

H. GARDINER & SON,
Chartered Patent Agents,
173—4—5, Fleet Street, London,
E.C.4,
Agents for the said Applicants.

COMPLETE SPECIFICATION

Improvements in or connected with Toy or Model Buildings or Structures for use with Toy Railways

We, TRIX LIMITED, of St. John's House, 45, and 47, Clerkenwell Road, London, E.C.1, a British Company, and SIEGFRIED KAHN, of the Company's address, a German Subject, do hereby declare the nature of this invention and in what manner the same is to be performed, to be particularly described and ascertained in and by the following statement :—

This invention relates to toy or model buildings or structures for use with toy railways, in which the vehicles provided with flanged wheels run on rails secured to track sections, the track sections being formed in lengths and adapted to be joined together end to end, and has for its object to provide means whereby the railway track or tracks can be properly positioned in relation to the buildings or structures which are constructed in sectional form.

It has been proposed in a model tunnel which could also be used as a packing for a toy locomotive to construct same from a sheet of corrugated paper which was curved to shape and had the curved edges clipped to curved strips, and to further maintain the curved shape of the tunnel and also to centralise it in respect to the track rails, a spacing device was employed, consisting of a straight strip of flat metal having end flanges for engaging the lower edges of the tunnel and punched up inner fins between which the rails were located.

According to this invention, various buildings and structures are constructed in sectional form, and loose distancing pieces are provided for locating between the side walls or edges of the railway track or tracks and the buildings or structures, whereby the railway track or tracks can be properly positioned in relation to the buildings or structures.

The invention will be clearly understood from the following description aided by the accompanying drawings, in which :—

Figures 1 to 17 are perspective views of various sectional buildings and structures and in which Figure 1 is a span roofed station building, Figure 2 a main building, Figure 3 an annexe building, Figure 4 a quadrant piece, Figure 5 a tower building, Figure 6 a platform, Figure 7 a platform ramp, Figure 8 a narrow distancing piece, Figure 9 a wide distancing piece, Figure 10 entrance steps, Figure 11 an end wall for the span roofed building shown in Figure 1, Figure 12 a panel for use in some of the buildings, Figure 13 a fence for a platform, Figure 14 a single buffer end, Figure 15 a double buffer end, Figure 16 a tunnel mouth, and Figure 17 an awning platform.

Figure 18 is a plan of a through platform showing one example of employing some of the buildings and structures shown in Figures 1 to 17, and Figure 19 is an end view of same.

Figure 20 is an end view on an enlarged scale of a double track and two platforms.

Figure 21 is a plan of an example of a terminus station and Figure 22 an end view of same, and Figure 23 an end view of a single buffer and with a track in place.

The span roofed station building 1 in Figure 1, comprises side walls *1a*, end spans and columns *1b*, two platforms *1c* constructed with the building, one inside each side wall *1a*, and a non-inflammable transparent roof *1d*, apertures *1e* being provided in each side wall *1a*.

The buildings 2 and 3 and quadrant 4, (Figures 2, 3 and 4) are each constructed with apertures *2a*, *3a* and *4a* respectively, at a little distance from the bottom edge, that is at a height corresponding to the height of the platforms, and in such apertures are detachably inserted filling in pieces marked to represent windows or doors. The roof of each building is at a little distance below the top edge so as to provide walls *2b*, *3b*, *4b* respectively at the top of each building.

The tower 5 (Figure 5), is constructed with a main tower body having a depending portion *5a* formed with an aperture *5b* and canopy *5c*, the aperture *5b* being at a little distance above the bottom edge, and in the lower edge of the main portion and next to the depending portion is formed a slot *5d* of a size to engage over the wall *2b* or *3b* of the buildings 2 or 3.

The platforms 6 and ramps 7 are shown in the drawings comparatively wide for a double platform, and platforms 6 and ramps 7 of less width are also supplied for single platforms.

485,170 3

The single buffer member 14 (Figure 14) is formed with a cut-away portion *14a* of a width at its lower end to accommodate a rail track, and the member is of a width outside the cut away portion *14a* corresponding to the distance the track should be from a platform.

The double buffer member 15 (Figure 15) is constructed with two cut-away portions *15a*, *15a* to accommodate two rail tracks and at the proper distance apart for a double track.

The tunnel mouth wall 16 (Figure 16) around which a tunnel is positioned, is formed with an opening and portions *16a* of a width apart to accommodate a single or double rail track, or such portions *16a* may be separate from the wall.

The awning platform 17 (Figure 17) comprises a wall *17a* formed with a platform *17b*, and an awning *17c* or roof, apertures *17d* being formed in the wall *17a* above the level of the platform *17b*.

The rail tracks comprise sections of material A (Figures 20 and 23) joined end to end and having angled depending side walls Al, the running rails B being secured to the track in any suitable manner, and in the case of electric railways a current rail C is also provided.

For building a span roofed through station having three rail tracks, as shown in Figures 18 and 19, a span-roofed building 1 is employed, and between the platforms *1c*, *1c* is positioned from one side a distancing piece 8, a rail track A, a distancing piece 8, a double platform 6, a distancing piece 8, a rail track A, a distancing piece 9, a rail track A and a distancing piece 8, thus filling up and locating the rail tracks A and platform 6 between the fixed platforms *1c*, *1c*.

The platforms *1c*, *1c* and 6 are extended at each end by positioning other single platform sections *6a* end on at the ends of the platforms *1c*, *1c* and double platforms 6 at the ends of the double platforms 6, single ramps *7a* being positioned at the ends of the platforms *6a* and double ramps 7 at the ends of the platforms 6.

On one side of the span roofed building 1 is positioned a main building 2 with a quadrant building 4 on each side.

On the other side of the span roofed building is positioned an annexe building 3 and on the outside of each of the buildings 2 and 3 is positioned an entrance steps 10 under the central aperture of each building, and on the outside edges of the single platforms *6a*, *6a* and on each side of the buildings are positioned fences 13.

For a simple span-roofed terminus station with three rail tracks Figures 21 and 22, the distancing pieces 8, 9 may be dispensed with and the buffer end members 14, 15 employed for distancing the rail-tracks apart.

In this case positioned between the platforms *1c* at one end of a span-roofed building 1 is a single buffer member 14, the end of a double platform 6 and a double buffer member 15 filling up the distance between the platform *1c*. The end sections of three rail tracks A are inserted in the cut-away portions *14a*, *15a*, *15a* of the buffer members 14 and 15, as will be understood from Figure 23, the buffer members 14 and 15 correctly positioning or locating the rail tracks in relation to each other and to the platforms.

The platforms *1c* and 6 are extended on one side of the building by additional platforms *6a* and 6, and end ramps *7a*, 7 as already described, and the buffer end of the building 1 may be closed by inserting an end 11 (Figure 11) in the open end of the building 1, and buildings 2, 3 and 4 may be positioned on each side of the building 1 as described with reference to Figures 18 and 19, or as shown in Figures 21 and 22, a main building 2 can be positioned at the buffer end of the span roofed building 1 and a tower building 5 placed on the main building 2 with the depending front *5a* over the centre of the front of the building 2, entrance steps 10 being placed in front of the tower 5.

In both examples, in place of the extending platforms *6a* and fences 13, awning platforms 17 (Figure 17) could be employed and the apertures *17d* filled in with panels 12 (Figure 12).

For a single platform wayside station, an awning platform 17 could be employed and the apertures left open and an annexe building 3 placed against the back of the awning platform 17 with an entrance steps 10, the awning platform 17 being extended on each side by single platforms *6a*, ramps *7a* and fences 13. The various parts are made to scale for the tracks and trains with which they are to be employed, so that proper positioning is ensured.

For a large station, two or more span-roofed buildings 1 may be employed placed end to end, and a greater number of platforms employed to give the longer platforms to suit the length of the buildings.

For stations in which more than three tracks are required, two or more span-roofed buildings 1 or lines of buildings would be placed side by side, one building or line of buildings for each set of tracks.

The buildings and various members are painted or otherwise ornamented or decorated to suit the various structures they are to represent.

In some cases, such as for example, engine sheds, the platforms would not

4 485,170

necessarily be used, in which case where end buffers are employed distancing pieces would be positioned between the buffers or several single buffers could be employed next to each other, and in some other cases, such as with the tunnel mouth 16, or a bridge or fly-over, the distancing pieces *16a* could be shaped to represent banks or ground.

Various other sectional members can be added, such as out-buildings, goods sheds and the like, and the various members may be simply placed in relation to each other, or means may be provided whereby they can be locked together in placed positions.

Having now particularly described and ascertained the nature of our said invention and in what manner the same is to be performed, we declare that what we claim is :—

1. Toy or model buildings or structures for use with toy railways, in which the vehicles provided with flanged wheels run on rails secured to track sections, the track sections being formed in lengths and adapted to be joined together end to end, comprising various buildings and structures constructed in sectional form, and loose distancing pieces for locating between the side walls or edges of the railway track or tracks and the buildings or structures, whereby the railway track or tracks can be properly positioned in relation to the buildings or structures.

2. Toy or model buildings or structures for use with toy railways, as claimed in claim 1, wherein a distancing piece for positioning the track or tracks comprises an end buffer member provided with a cut-away portion or portions in which the end or ends of the track or tracks can be properly positioned in relation to the buildings or structures.

3. Toy or model buildings or structures for use with toy railways as in claim 1, constructed substantially as described with reference to the accompanying drawings.

Dated this 12th day of November, 1937.

H. GARDNER & SON,
Chartered Patent Agents,
173—4—5, Fleet Street, London,
E.C.4,
Agents for the said Applicants.

Leamington Spa: Printed for His Majesty's Stationery Office, by the Courier Press.—1938.

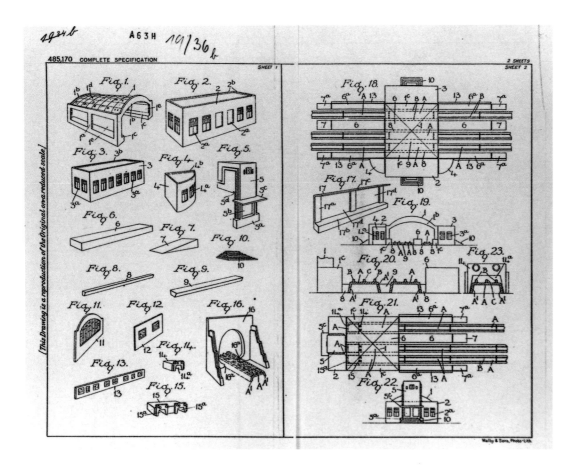

part of Platform units 12/15 and 14/15.

22 (9/161) Awning Platform. 9.625" long x 0.875" wide x 2.875" high at the rear face.

A pair of these units, when used back-to-back, formed the centre piece of Island Platform station layouts. Each unit was diecast from mazak and the design was loosely based on the platform and awning of the earlier wooden Twin City station. Each unit could be applied to many uses. The outside edge of the platform had a white line.

32 (9/162) Goods Shed. 4.75" long x 2.75" wide x 2.5" high.

This was a completely wooden building widely used in all manner of goods depot layouts. Both sides were identical containing a cut-out and a small glazed window, (¾" x 1¼"). On all pre-war and most post-war versions, an additional window was inserted in one end wall of the building. In some post-war versions, this end window was omitted, and on others the corners of all the apertures were rounded instead of being square.

35 (9/163) Quadrant Piece. 2.875" x 2.875" x 3.5" high.

This unit was diecast from mazak and was, as the description suggests, in the form of a quarter circle. Three windows, the bottoms of which were at platform level, were fitted to the front curved face and glazed by a continuous, printed Celastoid strip located by slots on the inside faces of the casting. A push-fit piece of cardboard in the base of the unit held the window strip in place.

37 (9/164) Annexe Building. 9.625" long x 3.125" wide x 3.5" high.

The sides and base were constructed from mild steel sheet with a removable plywood roof. The centre of the front face contained a large window opening

post-war these were usually supplied in packets to be affixed by the owner.

14 (9/159) Platform, wide. 9.625" long x 1.75" wide.

A white line was applied to each side marking the edge of the platform. Manufacturing details as for the Narrow Platform.

14/15 (9/160) Platform, wide with Fence.

9.625" long x 1.75" wide x 1.5" high.

The comments regarding the Fence used on the 12/15 Platform also apply here, although only the outside edge of the platform was marked with a white line.

15 Fence for Platform. 9.625" long x 1.5" high.

Initially this Fence was to be available separately, but it was never issued as such and can only be found as

Goods Sheds. Pre-war on extreme right.

Pre-war Many-Ways buildings.

A Many-Ways 'Southern Railway' station. This picture shows the good use of platforms between the tracks.

Late post-war Many-Ways buildings.

347

(1" x 1½"), which could also be used as a door opening, and on either side were three small windows, (¾" x 1¼"). There were also two small windows in each of the end faces and six large windows on the rear face. Each large window could be used as a door opening. The internal floor and the bottoms of the window openings were at platform level. Convenient small openings at the base of each end, plus corresponding holes in the floor, provided passage for the wires for the Lighting Unit 57. The Annexe Building was supplied with the correct number of printed Celastoid windows, held in place by internal grooves formed in the mild steel sheet at each window opening. This unit was the same height as the Quadrant Piece but could not be used with the Clock Tower. It was not as widely used as the Main Building, and production was not continued after the war.

38 (9/165) Main Building. 9.625" long x 3.5" wide x 3.875" high.

The general construction was exactly the same as that of the Annexe Building, except that large windows were symmetrically placed around the building; six on each side plus two at each end. This was a widely-used unit and together with the Tower Building provided the centre piece for many station layouts.

39 (9/166) Tower Building. Approximately 3.125" wide x 3.75" deep x 7" high.

This Tower Building was a very heavy mazak diecast unit (over 1 kilogram in weight), and was used to provide a very imposing entrance to the larger of the station layouts when placed in conjunction with a Main Building. It was made in such a way that it located on the flat wooden roof and roof ridge of the Main Building, the open space below the canopy

Shade differences in Many-Ways buildings. The Main building and the Steps are early post-war, the other items are pre-war.

Wood and composite Many-Way Tower and Span ends used just after the war as substitutes for diecast units.

locating over two of the windows. The Tower Building could be placed in any position around the Main Building. The raised letters of TTR and two decorative lines, on the front and rear face were highlighted with red paint, and the two clock faces were affixed using transfers. The times shown on these clock faces were either 11.37 or 8.22

depending which way round the square transfer was applied. It is possible to have the clock showing two other times, but in these instances the hour hand would not be in the correct position.

Due to production difficulties immediately after the beginning of World War 2, it was not possible to produce the diecast Tower Building and a substitute was provided. This was manufactured from wood and supplied in two pieces; the tower unit and the canopy framework. The shape of the tower was a simplified design with a clock face and red TTR transfers on the front only. It located on the Main Building roof in the same way as the diecast version. The canopy unit could be located over any two of the windows of the Main Building and held in place by two clips which fitted to the inside top of two of the window openings. This wooden Tower Building is known to have been included in the 1941 Many-Ways sets 3021/O, 3043/O and 3075/O, and may

also have been available as a separate unit just after the war. Although 'engineering' production of the TTR system ceased at the beginning of 1940, the manufacture of wooden 'toys' was still permitted. By the middle of 1949 the diecast version was once again available but supply was very limited until 1953.

42 (9/167) Span with Celastoid Roof. 9.625" x 9.625".

This was a fine unit which could embrace three roads of track allowing realistically large terminal stations to be built when several units were used

together. The Span was constructed from four individual diecast mazak parts to facilitate packing, transport and storage. The individual diecast parts consisted of two platform members and two span ends keyed into each another and held together by four 4 BA bolts, as used in the Trix Constructor sets. The Span was completed by adding the printed Celastoid roof which fitted into special locating grooves on the platform members.

As with the Tower Building, war-time production problems caused the introduction of a substitute design for the span ends and the preceding comments regarding the wooden Tower Building also apply here. These span ends were constructed from laminating leatherboard, plywood and tinplate, the assembly clipping into place on the platform members. The assembled unit was not secured by bolts. By 1949 the diecast span ends were once more in production, although production was limited until 1953.

43 (9/168) Panel for Span or Platform. 4¼" long x 2" high.

This was a cardboard insert usually decorated on both sides with miniature posters. It was a press fit in the large apertures of both the Awning Platform and

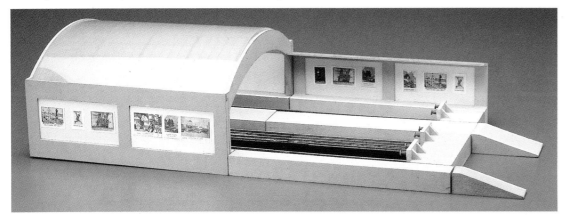

A post-war Many-Ways Covered Span Cat.No.42 with other units from various periods.

Overhanging Signal Boxes Cat.No.65. Pre-war on the right, post-war on the left.

Many-Ways Buffer Stops. The units at the centre and right are for the fibre-based track.

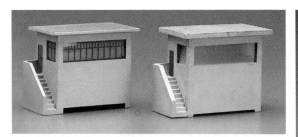

Country Signal Boxes Cat.No.62. Post-war version on right.

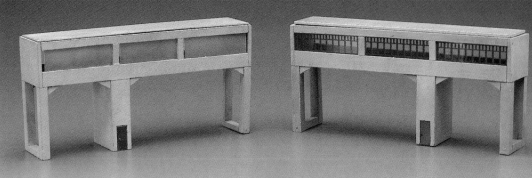

Gantry Signal Boxes Cat.No.67. Pre-war on the right, post-war on the left.

Pre and Post-war Square Water Towers Cat.No.69.

Span platform sides. The panels were supplied in a packet of two with, in pre-war days, miniature posters already fixed to the panels. However, after the war a packet of posters was supplied with the panels so that they could be affixed as desired. The cardboard used for the pre-war panels was almost light grey in colour whilst that used for the post-war versions was cream.

44 (9/169) Buffer Stop and Platform End, single. 1.75" x 1.75" (platform).

This mazak diecast Buffer Stop and Platform End fitted over the the bakelite track in a terminus station or station siding to form part of the platform system.

In 1957 the diecasting was modified to accommodate the fibre-based track introduced at that time. This had the effect of reducing the platform height to ½".

48 (9/170) Buffer Stop and Platform End, double. 4" long x 1.75" wide (platform).

The comments relating to the single unit 44 above apply here, except that the spacing between the track apertures corresponds to the TTR track geometry.

The Buffer Stops 44 and 48 were sold together as a set and were an exact fit between the two platforms of a Span when used in conjunction with a wide (14) platform unit. Both units are known with

factory fitted screw-in locomotive buffers and 0-4-0 style buffer beam plates on 0.875" high platform versions manufactured in the late 1950s. On these versions the upper cast webbing was altered by machining.

49 End for Span. 9.25" x 4.625".

This was a panel to fit at the end of the Span to seal the opening. It was to have been glazed with printed celastoid. Although never produced it would have been a useful item.

57 (9/171) Lighting Unit with two lamps.

This was constructed from parts used for the Coach lighting unit, except that the bends of the contact strips enabled the bulb holders to hang down when the unit was mounted on the wood roof of the Annexe and Main Buildings. It was available from 1938. (See photograph of lighting units in chapter dealing with post-war scale tinplate coaches.)

62 Country Signal Box. 4" long x 2.25" wide x 3.25" high.

This signal box was similar in design to the earlier Twin Signal Box except that the steps were now on the right-hand side. It was constructed from hardwoods and introduced in 1938. The large window at the front, plus the small window at each end, were glazed with printed Celastoid. In pre-war versions the red door at the top of the steps was slightly recessed, whilst the door on the post-war version was produced flush and much smaller, and the windows were glazed with plain frosted Celastoid. In general, the post-war version was rather crudely constructed. Production of the Country Signal Box ceased in 1949.

65 Overhanging Signal Box. 7" long x 2" wide x 4.5" high.

This was the type of signal box used at junctions where ground area was at a minimum. Constructed from hardwoods, it had a central column, mounted on a mild steel plate for stability, and was designed to locate between two adjacent tracks. The main body of the box, containing eight printed Celastoid windows, overhung the two tracks. The post-war version contained only six windows with plain end panels in place of the glazed end faces of the pre-war version. These six windows were glazed with plain frosted Celastoid. The plywood roof on some of the latter signal boxes overhung the body of the box, whilst those produced at all other times were slightly

smaller than the body of the box. The roof was held in place by long screws passing through the base. Production ran from 1938 to 1949.

67 Gantry Signal Box. 9.5" long x 2" wide x 4.5" high.

This signal box constructed from hardwoods was designed for use with terminal stations, and was capable of bridging one up and down track plus a single track. The main support column was the same design as that used for the Overhanging Signal Box. Three long windows at the front and rear of the box were glazed with printed Celastoid windows, which in the post-war war period of production were with plain frosted Celastoid. The end panels did not have windows. The roof was slightly smaller than the body of the box and held in place by long screws passing through the base of the box. The post-war signal boxes were 0.125" shorter than the pre-war versions. Manufactured from 1938 to 1949.

69 Square Water Tower. 3.125" x 2" x 4" high.

This model, made from wood, was based on the type of water tower used in many provincial stations. It contained a glazed Celastoid window on each long side and a representation of a red double door

on one end. The water tank was finished in dark grey, and on the post-war version the bottom of the tank sides were more rounded than on earlier versions. The windows on the post-war version were glazed with plain frosted Celastoid. Manufactured from 1938 to 1949.

71 (9/176) Carriage Shed. 7.5" long x 6" wide x 4" high.

The Carriage Shed was open at both ends and took two roads of track. The three windows on each side of the building were glazed in the usual way by large, (1" x ½"), Celastoid windows which were printed in pre-war days but plain frosted in post-war days. The glazing was held in place by slots provided in the jambs of the window openings, as was the case with all the wooden buildings in this range. The sloping roof was symmetrical in design, and the sides were usually embellished with miniature posters. This Carriage Shed was first produced in 1937 and manufactured until 1949.

73 (9/177) Engine Shed. 7.5" long x 6" wide x 5" high.

This Engine Shed was exactly the same construction as the Carriage Shed except that a clerestory roof and

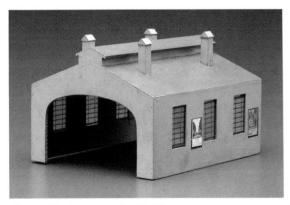

Engine Shed, pre-war, Cat.No.73.

Pre- and post-war Carriage Sheds Cat.No.71.

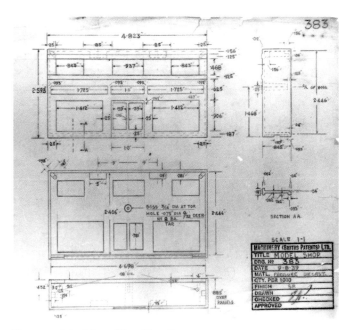

Drawing of the Many-Ways Shop Front.

Proposed Many-Ways Shop Front. (A)

The layout at the 1939 British Industries Fair showing the Shop Fronts.

CURRENT NEWS OF TTR PROGRESS

No. 5   SPRING NUMBER, 1939   *GRATIS to Registered Owners*

The Many-ways Terminus Station on our layout at the recent B.I.F. Exhibition. Note the pleasing appearance of the forecourt surrounded by the range of shop-fronts which form part of our new season's releases. The shops are arranged for internal illumination, and the gaily coloured window displays contribute an effect which is both pleasing and convincing.

EDITORIAL

WHEN we set a competition in the form of a Questionnaire in our last issue of the *Trix Gazette* we congratulated ourselves.

It was all going to be so sublimely simple to read through the answers and pick out the lucky winners. Little did we know !

No sooner had we made a start on the first few entries than we began to realise something of what we were in for.

True there were some forms which hardly contained anything beyond a simple YES or NO to the questions asked. But what of the many hundreds which offered suggestions for improvements and descriptions of the readers' circuits, and occupied anything from a few lines to (in one case) sixteen pages of typescript ?

There were diagrams, sketches and layout plans, some just roughly drawn in pen or pencil, and some that would do credit to any engineer's office.

There were photographs, beautifully painted views of scenic effects, and even, in some cases, carefully packed samples of home-made gadgets for the railway. And the replies themselves hailed from all over the world : from Rangoon, from Rhodesia, from Trinidad, from Tooting—and every one of them mustard keen. No stronger proof of the firm hold. The hold which the Trix Railway has upon the public imagination could never have been more strikingly demonstrated ! So what ?

How could we show our appreciation of such overwhelming and magnificent enthusiasm ?

There appeared to be only one way.

Apart from judging the competition and selecting the winners—their names appear on another page—we went through each of those replies again, and wherever there was an idea for a new accessory that could make the Trix Railway more complete and more fascinating, or wherever there was a suggestion for improvement to our existing equipment, we jotted it down on a list. Then we tabulated the results and compared the requests with the programme of new lines upon which we had already decided for next season.

To say that this comparison was interesting is to put it mildly.

There were some things asked for that we had not contemplated making ; where possible we have extended our programme to include these items.

There were some things which we had decided to make which were not asked for—they will be pleasant surprises when we release them.

But the great majority of the requests corresponded identically with what we ourselves had already put in hand for the coming season, and there can now be no doubt that when this programme is in full swing the Trix Railway will have established a lead which will make it more than ever unapproachable.

And, finally, one request that was by no means uncommon was that we should increase our *Trix Gazette* both in size and in frequency of publication.

This also is a step which we have been contemplating for some time. And although it may not be possible to do this just at the moment, we are nevertheless doing the next best thing.

We are attempting to pack each issue with useful and instructive information, giving you only such articles as will actually help you to get the best out of your Trix Railway.

It would require a fat magazine to do full justice to all the points that have been raised, so if you find that your pet theme has received little or no attention in this issue, bear with us awhile.

Meantime, if you find this issue more to your liking, drop us a card —it will be appreciated.

A selection of pre- and post-war Railway Personnel, Passengers, Platform Equipment, Merchandise and Seats. Seated figure is a Master Models product.

A pre-war W. Britain trade display showing the range of passengers, station staff and equipment produced specially for Trix Ltd. (A)

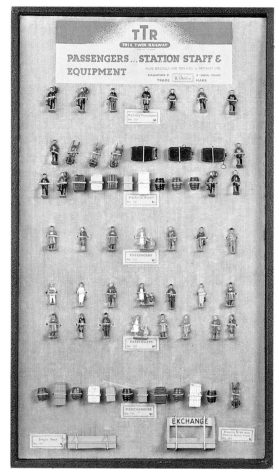

four chimney stacks were added. All other comments regarding the Carriage Shed also apply to the Engine Shed.

75 Tunnel Mouths for Double Track. 7" high x 5.625" wide.

This was another item that was not produced. It was intended for this item to provide the framework for a tunnel entrance spanning a double track .

91 (9/178) Small Steps. 0.75" wide x 0.875" deep x 0.875" high.

These steps were designed to be placed at the end of a narrow platform or in any other desired position on the station layout. In the pre-war and early post-war periods they were manufactured from a lead-alloy by Britains Ltd. From 1953 they were manufactured by another company using diecast mazak which resulted in a much 'cleaner' product. The mazak steps can be found with or without the embossed

inscription 'TTR Made in England'. They were usually packaged as a pair, but in the latter period they were packed singly.

92 (9/179) Entrance Steps. 3.875" long x 1.125" deep x 0.875" high.

Designed primarily to fit in front of the Tower Building entrance or any other suitable double entrance on the Many-Ways buildings. All other details are as for the Small Steps, except that the lead-alloy castings carried the inscription 'Made in England Britains Ltd'. These steps when diecast in mazak can be found with or without the embossed inscription 'TTR Made in England'.

94 Subway Head.

This was a small unit listed in the first Many-Ways booklet of 1937. It was meant to be placed on a platform to represent the entrance to a subway giving access to platforms on the other side of the

track. It was never produced.

95 (9/180) Celastoid Windows for Annexe Building No. 37.

This was a set of 10 small windows, ¾" x 1¼", for the Annexe building. In the 1937/1938 domestic and 'American' catalogues, the packet quantity was listed as eight, but this was an error as there were 10 small window openings in the Annexe building. These packaged windows were not listed or generally available after the war, although they were still used in the Goods Shed.

96 (9/181) Celastoid Windows for Main Building No. 38.

This was a set of eight large windows, 1" x 1½", for the Main Building. After the war, this packaged set of windows was not generally available separately and was only listed in the 1954 Trix literature. However, they continued to be supplied with the Main Building.

98 Many-Ways Shop Front. 4.812" long x 0.875" deep x 2.593" high.

The spring 1939 number of the *TTR Gazette* showed a picture of a Many-ways Station on a Trix layout as seen at a British Industries Fair Exhibition earlier that year. Of special interest was the remark in the picture caption which drew attention to the range of Shop Fronts which was to form part of the new releases for that year. Each shop unit was to be manufactured from diecast mazak, plywood and cardboard with facilities for added illumination and different window displays. The length was such that two shop units were equal to the length of a Main Building. The drawing for the diecast body of the shop was dated August 1939. What a pity it became yet another victim of the war effort, never reaching the production stage even in peacetime.

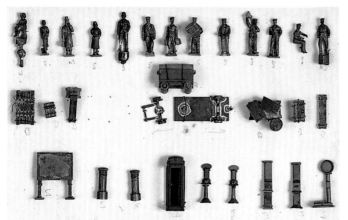

Master models of a proposed new range of Trix figures and platform accessories circa 1954.

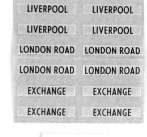

Station Names. Transfers (bright yellow) Cat.No.143 and self-adhesive labels Cat.No.144.

141 (9/148) Single Seat.

Made by Britains Ltd for Trix from a lead alloy casting until 1953 after which another company produced the Seat using mazak which gave much better results. Up to 1953 the Seats were embossed with 'Britains TTR Made in England', after which they were embossed with 'TTR Made in England'.

142 (9/149) Double Seat with Station Nameplate.

Production and inscription details as for Single Seat 141. In 1937 this Double Seat was supplied with Station Name Transfers enabling the randomly-supplied name to be affixed, or a different name taken from a sheet of Name Transfers available separately. In 1939 the Double Seat was supplied with the Station Name Transfers already fixed in place. Transfers continued to be used after the war until 1953 when they were succeeded by adhesive labels.

143 Transfers of 12 different Station Names.

Transfers were used from 1937 until 1953 for use with the Double Seat 142. The station names were in black on a buff background. Two sheets of 12 different names were supplied – MANCHESTER, EDINBURGH, SOUTHAMPTON, LONDON ROAD, LIVERPOOL, GLASGOW, EUSTON, St. PANCRAS, KINGS CROSS, WATERLOO, EXCHANGE and CENTRAL.

144 Station Names (adhesive)

This was a packet of 24 pairs of assorted self-adhesive Station Names for use with the Double Seat 142. The sheets were available from 1953. The station names supplied were – EDINBURGH, SOUTHAMPTON, LONDON ROAD, LIVERPOOL, GLASGOW, EUSTON, EXCHANGE, CENTRAL, BRADFORD, BIRMINGHAM, BRISTOL and VICTORIA.

145 Miniature Posters.

This was a packet of assorted miniature posters as used on the Many-Ways buildings and platforms. They depicted the actual railway posters that were in use on full-size stations throughout the British railway system, and thus in their own right are of historical interest. The packets were first introduced in 1939 but did not reappear after the war until 1954. The posters were affixed using Seccotine glue or similar.

176 Station Notices.

These were first introduced in 1955 as an attractively boxed set of diecast items containing four station nameboards with self-adhesive names (as included in Station Names 144), timetable board and small notice board for choice of either 'PASSENGERS MUST CROSS THE LINE BY THE BRIDGE' or 'TRESPASSERS WILL BE PROSECUTED' label. The set appeared for the last time in the 1960 price lists.

Pre-war Miniature Posters.

715 Model Crane on Base. Base 2.625" x 1.75" x 0.875" high.

This unit was designed specifically to fit into the Many-Ways system. The removable working crane was exactly the same as that used on the Breakdown Crane Truck set described in an earlier chapter. The underside of the base was embossed with 'TRIX TWIN RAILWAY Made in England'. It was first introduced in late 1939 being one of the lucky few of the planned items to actually be produced in that year. After the war it continued to be available from 1948 until 1960 and was included in the post-war Many-Ways sets where applicable.

THE MANY-WAYS STATION SETS

Listed opposite are the Many-Ways Station sets and contents. The contents are given by catalogue numbers, their description having been given in the preceding section. The sets were attractively packaged in bright yellow boxes with a large red, black and white label showing a Many-Ways Station layout. The inclusive dates in brackets relate to the period the set was included in the official Trix price lists with the contents listed below. (Although no sets were manufactured after the end of 1939 until peacetime, a few sets were still available up to and including 1942 through the Bassett-Lowke retail outlets). Unfortunately the 1957 to 1960 catalogues gave a list of parts included in each set which was not quite accurate as certain items were omitted from the list.

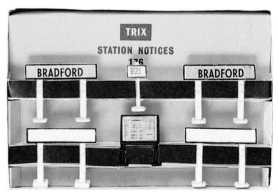

Station Notices Cat.No.176.

Post-war Miniature Posters.

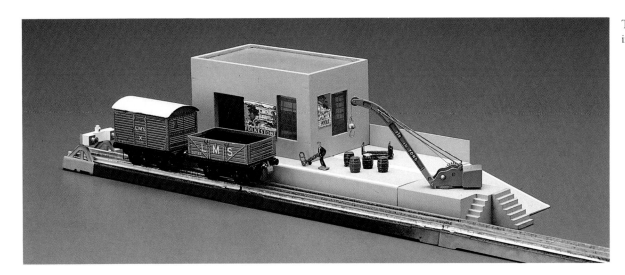

The Model Crane on Base Cat.No.715 in its correct setting.

3002　**Goods Shed.** 2 x 14, 1 x 32, 1 x 91. (1937 to 1960)

3003　**Suburban Station or Island Platform.** 2 x 4, 2 x 14, 2 x 22, 2 x 142. (1953 to 1960)

3004　**Island Platform.** 2 x 4, 1 x 14, 2 x 22, 1 x 142. Part number 142 was not included after 1951. (1937 to 1952)

3005　**Through Station.** 2 x 4, 1 x 12, 1 x 14, 1 x 14/15, 1 x 22, 1 x 37, 1 x 92. (1937 to 1941)

3006　**Through Station.** 2 x 2, 2 x 12/15, 1 x 22, 1 x 38, 1 x 92. (1948 to 1952)

3007　**Country Through Station.** 2 x 4, 1 x 14, 2 x 14/15, 1 x 22, 1 x 38, 1 x 92, 1 x 142, 1 x 145. (1953 to 1960)

3008　**Goods Depot.** 2 x 2, 1 x 4, 3 x 14, 1 x 32, 1 x 42, 2 x 43, 1 x 44, 1 x 48, 1 x 91. (1937 to 1941)

3009　**Freight Depot.** 2 x 2, 3 x 14, 1 x 32, 1 x 42, 2 x 43, 1 x 91, 1 x 715, 1 x 145. (1953 to 1960)

3021　**Suburban Station.** 2 x 4, 1 x 12, 2 x 14/15, 1 x 22, 2 x 35, 1 x 38, 1 x 39, 1 x 92. (1937 to 1940)

3021/0 **Suburban Station.** Contents as above but without 2 x 35 (Quadrant Pieces). (1941 only)

3024　**Terminal Station.** 2 x 2, 1 x 4, 2 x 12/15, 2 x 14, 1 x 38, 1 x 42, 2 x 43, 1 x 44, 1 x 48, 1 x 92. (1948 to 1952)

3025　**Terminal Station.** 2 x 2, 1 x 4, 2 x 12/15, 2 x 14, 1 x 38, 1 x 39, 1 x 42, 2 x 43, 1 x 44, 1 x 48, 1 x 92. (1937 to 1952)

3026　**Terminus Station.** 2 x 2, 1 x 4, 2 x 12/15, 3 x 14, 2 x 22, 1 x 38, 1 x 39, 1 x 42, 8 x 43, 1 x 44, 1 x 48, 1 x 92, 1 x 142, 3 x 145. (1953 to 1960)

3043　**Through Station.** 4 x 2, 2 x 4, 2 x 12/15, 3 x 14, 2 x 22, 2 x 35, 1 x 37, 1 x 38, 1 x 39, 1 x 42, 4 x 43, 1 x 44, 1 x 48, 2 x 92, 2 x 142. (1937 to 1940)

3043/0 **Through Station.** Contents as above but without 2 x 35 (Quadrant Pieces). (1941 only)

3057　**Grand Central Station.** 1 x 2, 5 x 4, 2 x 12/15, 9 x 14, 2 x 14/15, 5 x 22, 1 x 32, 2 x 35, 2 x 38, 1 x 39, 2 x 42, 6 x 43, 1 x 44, 1 x 48, 2 x 91, 2 x 92, 4 x 145, 1 x 715. (1953 to 1960)

3075　**Main Line Terminus.** 4 x 2, 2 x 4, 4 x 12/15, 6 x 14, 1 x 35, 2 x 37, 1 x 38, 1 x 39, 4 x 42, 10 x 43, 2 x 44, 2 x 48, 2 x 91, 1 x 92, 3 x 142. (1937 to 1940)

3075/0 **Main Line Terminus.** Contents as above but without 1 x 39 (Quadrant Piece). (1941 only)

BRITAINS LILLIPUT 00 SCALE PEOPLE AND RAILWAY ACCESSORIES FOR TRIX LTD

The Britains range of Lilliput 00 lead-alloy people and railway accessories was established in the mid-1930s shortly before Britains were asked to provide similar products for Trix in 1937. Various sets were offered in small red boxes with a distinctive dark green and yellow label with the TTR logo and contents, the W. Britain trademark and the statement 'Made specially for Trix Ltd by Britains Ltd'. The pre-war boxes were covered in red Celilynd, whilst the post-war boxes were formed from ordinary red-coloured card. The larger pre-war sets, for example the 12-piece set of Platform Equipment with Merchandise, Cat. No. 105, were supplied in boxes 4" (102mm) long, whilst smaller sets including all the post-war ones used 2½" (63.5mm) boxes. Lister below are the figures, merchandise and platform equipment with the corresponding Britains Lilliput catalogue number and known colour combinations supplied in the Trix sets. No doubt other colour combinations may exist especially for the passengers.

LB/517 Nurse and Child. (In all cases the nurse has a white front).

Nurse	Child	Case
Dark blue	tan	green
Dark blue	brown	green
Grey	blue	grey
Grey	red	green
Grey	red	grey
Grey	pink	grey
Red-brown	green	yellow
Red-brown	green	red
Cream	green	grey
Light blue	red	grey
Light blue	green	grey
Light blue	brown	green
Green	yellow	grey
Green	pink	grey
Green	pink	grey
Tan	pink	grey

LB/533 Porter with barrow (two pieces). The barrow ranged from medium to dark brown)

Trousers	Jacket and hat
Navy blue	red
Navy blue	navy blue

LB/534 Guard Navy blue uniform, green flag.

LB/535 Station master, navy blue uniform.

LB/537 Porter with luggage (luggage which was always brown was on shoulder, under one arm and in one hand).

Trousers	Jacket and hat
Navy blue	red
Navy blue	navy blue

LB/538 Newsvendor.

Uniform and hat	Papers and shoulder strap
Navy blue	light grey
Navy blue	dark grey
Navy blue	brown
White	blue

LB/539 Lady with case (in right hand, standing still).

Suit	Case and hat
Yellow	red
Yellow	green
Navy blue	red
Navy blue	brown
Navy blue	black
Light blue	orange
Red	green
Red	black
Grey	red
Red-brown	black
Dark green	orange
Light green	red
Light green	yellow

LB/540 Man with book (case on ground).

Coat	Case and hat	Book
Brown	black	red
Dark brown	black	white
Red-brown	black	white
Grey	red-brown	white
Blue	black	white
Olive-grey	brown	white
Dark grey	brown	white

LB/541 Man with umbrella.

Suit	Case and hat
Red-brown	black
Dark grey	black
Light grey	black

LB/542 Lady with hatbox (walking with box in left hand).

Coat	Hat and box
Light blue	orange
Light blue	black
Navy blue	orange
Navy blue	red
Red	black
Green	black
Green	blue
Green	yellow
Grey	red
Yellow	red
Yellow	black
Yellow	brown
White	black
White	red

LB/543 Golfer

Sweater	Plus fours	Hat, club and socks
Tan brown	tan brown	coffee
Dark brown	dark brown	tan brown
Navy blue	grey	tan brown
Brown	brown	khaki
Grey	navy blue	tan brown
Brown	grey	brown

(Various shades of brown exist)

LB/544 Barrel.

Barrel body	Ends
Black	black
Black	white
Black	light grey
Red-brown	red-brown
Very dark brown	very dark brown

LB/545 Hamper, red brown, pale tan, dark brown, cream, shades of light grey

LB/546 Large packing case, pale tan, cream, shades of light grey

LB/547 Small packing case, pale tan, cream, shades of light grey and brown

LB/549 Electric Trolley, black

4-Wheel hand Trolley with wire handle, black. (No Britains catalogue number exists for this item which was manufactured exclusively for Trix).

Both the Electric trolley and the 4-Wheel hand trolley were marked BRITAINS LTD TRIX TTR MADE IN ENGLAND. The Hand trolley was only supplied in the pre-war sets. It is difficult to make hard and fast rules for distinguishing pre- and post-war production, but there are certain indicators.

1. Porters with red jackets are pre-war.

2. Guards' shoulder strap and bag picked out in brown are pre-war. These details were not highlighted post-war.

3. Newsvendor in white is pre-war. Strap detail painted on all versions.

4. Golfer and man with book were only finished in shades of brown post-war.

5. For the rest, it can only be said that more care was taken with the various details in the pre-war era. The colour of the bases were usually a shade of grey, although green and occasionally brown were used. It is not possible to tell with certainty from the colour of the bases whether an item is pre- or post-war although green bases were used with much greater frequency post-war.

The TTR sets are detailed below. The catalogue numbers in brackets are those given for the same item in the joint Trix Express/TTR 1938-39 American catalogue.

100 Railway Personnel (equivalent Lilliput set LP/510)
This was a set of six items including Station Master, Guard, Newsvendor, Porter with bags, Porter with barrow (two pieces). It was produced for Trix from 1948 until 1952.

101 (9/143) Railway Personnel
This was introduced in 1937 and contained six items as in the post-war set above. In 1938 the set had the addition of one extra item which was probably the barrow or a Porter and remained as such until the war period.

105 (9/147) Platform Equipment with Merchandise
Introduced in 1937 with 12 pieces comprising two each of the Hamper, Large packing case, Small packing case, Barrel and Porter's Barrow together with an Electric trolley and the 4-Wheel hand trolley. By 1938 the number of pieces included in the set had been increased to 20 with four of each of the items of merchandise plus the Platform Equipment.

110 Passengers (equivalent Lilliput set LP/511)
The six passengers included in this set were the Nurse and Child, Golfer, Man with book, Woman with hatbox, Woman with case and Man with

umbrella. The set was produced from 1948 to 1952.

111 (9/144) Passengers

In 1937 a set of six was made up from one of each of the passengers. In 1938 until the war period an extra passenger picked at random from the six types was included in the set making seven pieces in total.

125 (9/145) Passengers

A large set, introduced in 1937 containing 12 figures taken from the six designs, which was enlarged to include 15 figures from 1938 until the end of 1939.

130 Merchandise (equivalent Lilliput set LP/512)

This post-war set produced from 1948 to 1952 comprised Electric trolley, Barrow, two Large packing cases, two Small packing cases, two Barrels and two Hampers.

131 (9/146) Merchandise

This pre-war set contained only Barrels, Hampers and both types of packing cases. In 1937 the set contained nine pieces which were increased to 12 from 1938.

Derelict Coach Huts. The pre-war version is second from the right. The coach fitted with a terminal block is an experimental version with light fitting.

MISCELLANEOUS BUILDINGS AND LINESIDE FEATURES

Scenic Backgrounds

In 1939 a set of three Scenic Backgrounds were produced, each 36" long x 9½" high and so designed that when placed end-to-end the picture designs blended together in whatever combination was used. The three designs available separately and printed in full colour on heavy quality paper were:

Cat. No. 147 Fields Pastureland with undulating country.

Cat. No. 148 Hills Mountains with heather foreground.

Cat. No. 149 Sea Sea coast with cliffs, and gorse in the foreground.

They were also available as a complete set of the three different designs, Cat. No. 150. The Scenic Backgrounds were still available in 1942 but failed to reappear after the war.

Derelict Coach Hut.

This was a model of a Coach Retreat often seen at country wayside stations which did not have covered platforms or waiting rooms. The model, introduced in the latter part of 1939 and listed until 1941, used the body of an LMS 4-wheel 1st/3rd class Suburban Coach fitted to a special floor which was mounted on a diecast mazak base. The body was overpainted

in dark red in such a way that the printed features of the LMS coach could be faintly seen. The roof, ends and base were finished in black. A doorway was cut into one side of the body and a chimney, as used on the American Caboose, added to the roof, plus ribbed cardboard fitted behind selected windows to represent wooden boarding. The catalogue number of this pre-war version was 2/551. It was not produced in pre-war days using an LNER Suburban Coach.

It was not until late in 1952 that it was reintroduced. Due to the fact that Suburban Coaches were no longer produced, the style of finish on the body of the Derelict Coach was different to that of the pre-war version. The Derelict Coach was now available in both LMS and LNER colours with the roof painted grey and the diecast base coloured to represent ferro-concrete, the latter now having the words 'TTR Made in England' embossed on the underside (the pre-war version had no inscriptions). The sides and ends of the body of the LNER version were formed from plain teak-effect printed tin-plate, whilst the body for the LMS version was completely sprayed with dark maroon with no markings applied. The catalogue number for these post-war models was 551 and they were last listed in the November 1959 price list.

Telegraph Pole

The Telegraph Pole available in 1935/36 was the Trix Express version, Cat. No. 21/234, with a heavy ¾" square light grey diecast base with a small diameter recess on the underside. It was usual to find the word 'FOREIGN' stamped in ink on one side of the base. The pole was hardwood topped with two tinplate cable carriers. During the latter part of 1936

Trix Expre pre-productio Telegraph Pole.

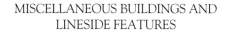

Scenic Background: Fields Cat.No.147. (A)

Scenic Background: Hills Cat.no.148. (A)

Scenic Background: Sea Cat.No.149. (A)

a British version, Cat. No. 771, replaced the German one, the only difference being that the base was now a hollow whitemetal diecasting with a hole in the top enabling a small wood screw to pass through for fixing to the layout board.

In 1948 the design of the Telegraph Pole changed although the base remained unaltered, except for the addition of the inscription 'Made in England' in the hollow of the base. The pole was now mild steel and the two cable carriers had lost the 'V' struts. The height (4"), and the catalogue number remained the same for both British versions. The Telegraph Pole remained in the Trix price lists until 1959.

Electric Yard Lamp

The latter part of 1936 saw the introduction of the Electric Yard Lamp, Cat. No. 761, which was fitted with a 14 volt miniature screw-in bulb. The lamp head was a white-metal diecasting which fitted onto a copper tube which in turn was a press fit into a hollow white metal base. This base contained one insulated and one non-insulated electrical socket which accepted the Trix plugs. The unit was 5" high.

After the war there was a shortage of miniature bulbs due to import/export restrictions, and it was not until 1952 that the Electric Yard Lamp was once more available. Slight changes had taken place, the tube was now aluminium alloy and the hollow of the base had the same inscription as the Telegraph Pole. The diecasting of the lamp head was slightly different, the radius on the top face of the arm being less pronounced than its pre-war counterpart. This particular Yard Lamp was listed until 1960.

In the American Polk's catalogue of circa 1948/1949, on the controls and accessories page, a Street Light was shown. This was obviously an

Pre and post-war TTR Yard Lamps and Telegraph Poles with the early Trix Express Telegraph Pole Cat.No. 21/234 in the middle.

Below left:
A range of pre-war Trix Express lineside accessories.

Below right:
Trix Express signals and lamps. From left to right: Cat.Nos.1499, 1489, 1498, 1488.

attempt at copying the TTR item, which, as mentioned previously, was not available at this time. The electrical connections on the base look rather crude, and the 18 volt long-life miniature bulb would look on the dim side when used with the Trix standard 14 volt supply. No wonder the bulb was long-life if used with a 14 volt supply!

In 1963, as a result of the introduction of Trix Express models to the Trix range in Britain, two quite splendid Yard Lamps were made available, one with a single lamp and the other with a double lamp fitting, Cat. Nos 1488 and 1489 respectively. The corresponding Trix Express catalogue numbers were 6601 and 6602 to which the British catalogue changed to in 1969. They were to disappear from

the price list one year later. The ladder type uprights and lamp arms were finely diecast items which were set into a plastic base containing two 'quick-fit' wire connectors and a tinplate cover. Both were 7" high.

Cat. No. 178 Trackside Notices

This set was boxed in the same style as the Station Notices set, Cat. No. 176, and contained five gradient posts, WHISTLE board, speed restriction board and small double-sided notice post for choice of either CATCH POINTS or BEWARE OF TRAINS label. A label with '30 mph ON CURVE' was applied to the speed restriction board, but the inscriptions on the gradient posts and the Whistle board were cast into the design. All items were diecast mazak. The set was introduced in 1955 and

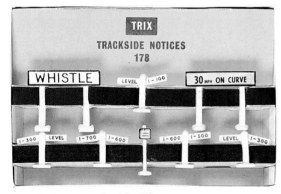

Trackside Notices Cat.No.178.

An extract from the Polk's 1949 catalogue showing the strange Street (Yard) Lamp and the special twin controller.

appeared for the last time in the 1961 price list.

Cat. No. 276 Signal Box with Whistle and Light

Part of the Trix Action range of 1955 was the Whistling Signal Box complete with black double-impulse switch, Cat. No. 449. The switch was used to operate a Whistle unit fitted to the removable base of the Signal Box which was similar to that fitted to the Meteor diesel set and the Whistling Coach. The signal box was of contemporary design

for the 1950s and was constructed from tinplate and plastic, the latter being the material used for the roof, steps and well-detailed window mouldings. A floor was fitted at the correct height in the cabin of the signal box which also contained a light unit. Electrical connections were made via a terminal block situated under the staircase moulding. The window mouldings were in white with the remainder of the signal box sprayed in a ferro-concrete colour. Self-adhesive station name labels,

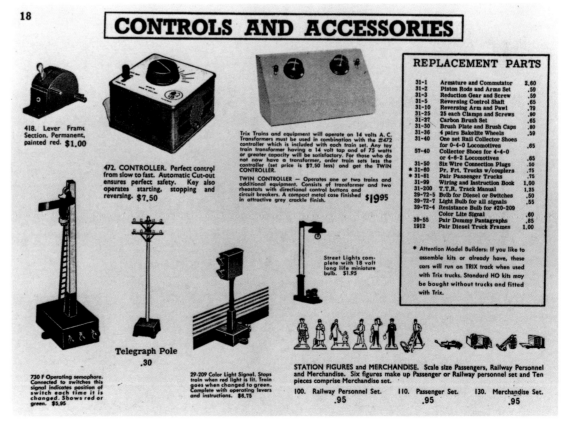

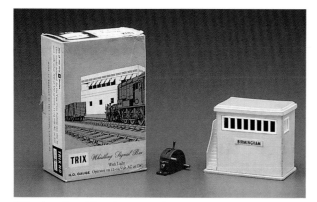

Whistling Signal Box Cat.No.276.

Lineside Accessories Set.

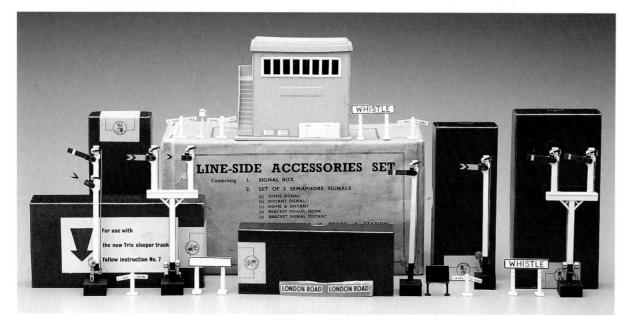

as used for the Many-Ways Double Seat, were included for applying to a panel just below the main window moulding. The top surface of the roof on early models was painted grey, but it was not long before this too became the same colour as the rest of the unit.

Between 1956 and 1957 the Whistling Signal Box appeared in the Trix Express catalogues with the catalogue number 20/405. It was packaged in Germany and as can be expected neither contained the British station names nor a TTR switch. In 1963 the British catalogue number was changed to 1476, but just one year later the Whistle unit was removed and a new catalogue number of 1478 allocated. It was destined to redundancy and failed to appear in the 1965 price list. In 1960 a Lineside Accessories Set, (detailed below), included the signal box but it was without any of the electrical fittings.

Lineside Accessories Set

During 1960 without any publicity the Lineside Accessories Set made its debut and strangely it was never allocated a catalogue number. Apart from the Signal Box mentioned above it contained the following items: two Whistle boards, Nameboard, five Gradient Posts, Small Notice Post and Timetable Board (all items from a part combination of Notice sets 176 and 178); Home signal, Distant signal, Double signal, Home Bracket signal and Distant Bracket signal. These were the basic signals, without any light fittings or base mounts, corresponding to signals with catalogue numbers 722, 723, 725, 726 and 724 respectively.

Level Crossing Gates

Unfortunately, a level crossing with typically British opening gates for use on Trix layouts was not manufactured by Trix Ltd pre- or post-war. However, Trix Express manufactured a Level Crossing, Cat. No. 20/238, in 1936 which was only available until 1940. The design was based on the continental practice of raising barrier arms either side of the track, subsequently adopted by the British railway network in the 1960s and 1970s. The level crossing was in two halves, each half comprising a tinplate ramp on which was mounted a barrier arm operated by a separate solenoid located under the ramp.

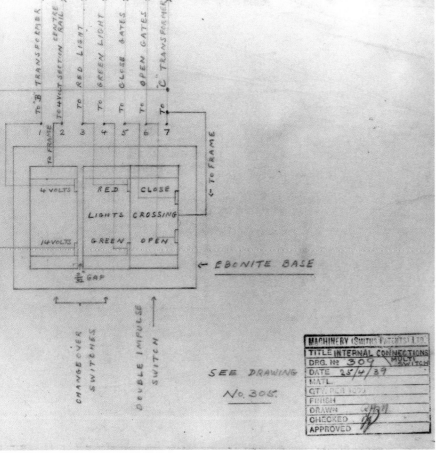

The wiring diagram for the planned Level Crossing.

Trix Express Level Crossing Cat.No.20/238 and a simple wooden version by Hugar British Models.

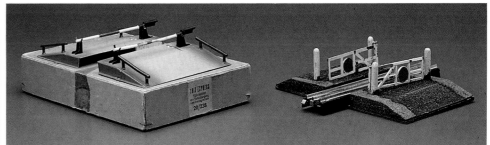

Trix Ltd had intended to introduce a British version in 1939 with the usual pattern swinging double gates, but once again, although advertised as a new feature in the 1939 trade catalogue, it never went into production. A pre-production version was shown in operation at the British Industries Fair in February and met with awed approval. The description in the 1939 trade catalogue was as follows:

'Equipped with a new electric operating mechanism. In conjunction with impulse rails the gates will automatically open to permit the passage of train and close again when it has passed. It is easy to arrange that the gates function correctly whichever direction the train may be travelling. If the correct setting of the gates is interfered with, the approach of the train will automatically effect a correction, rendering a collision with the gates impossible. Remote control can also be carried out by manual operation of a special lever frame section. The position of the gates is definitely identified with the position of the lever frame, and this relationship cannot be upset. Complete with two impulse rails and one lever frame section. Cat. No. 741.'

The impulse rails were to be yet another new item, Cat. No. 428, never to be produced.

On many of the private pre-war and early post-

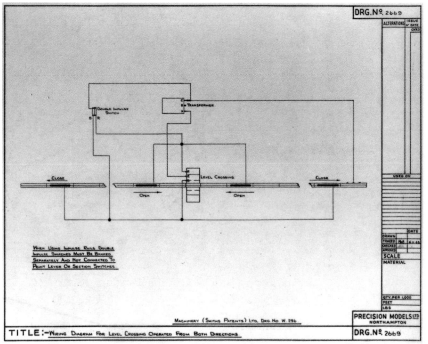

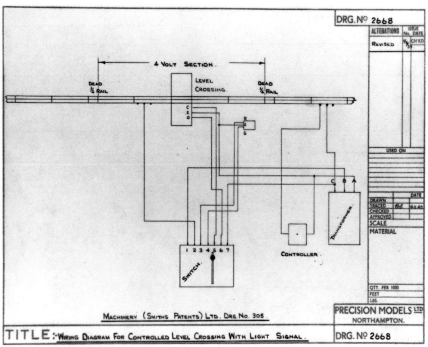

The arrangement of an idea in 1949 to introduce a remote controlled level crossing.

war Trix layouts one could find a level crossing produced by a small company manufacturing under the trade name of Hugar British Models. This was of simple wooden construction, complete with two opening gates cast in lead alloy, in which the Trix bakelite track sat in a central channel. In the early 1950s another make of level crossing produced exclusively for Trix track, and manufactured in tinplate, was distributed by Hammonds of London.

An attempt was made in 1949 to resurrect the pre-war design for the British-pattern level crossing gates but it got no further than the drawing board.

During the summer of 1958 a further design for a level crossing gate unit was drawn, the gates of which were to have opened and closed in a realistic manner by means of rods and pulleys operated by the expansion of a 'Vacrom' 80/20 resistance wire when an electric current was applied. Unfortunately the system was not reliable and the idea was dropped.

Wiad and Kibri Buildings and Accessories

It is felt that the description of the large amount of Wiad and Kibri items shown in the 1964 British Trix catalogue is beyond the scope of this book and

does not form a relevant part of the Trix story, although British Trix Ltd continued to stock and sell these items as a service to their clients.

Cardboard Building Kits

Six kits were offered – 00-1 Station, 00-2 Platform, for use with Station, 00-3 Signal Box and Huts, 00-4 Goods Shed, 00-5 Engine Shed, 00-6 two Platform Shelters.

The designs were printed on partly pre-cut and creased heavy card. The colours used were predominantly yellows, browns and greys with

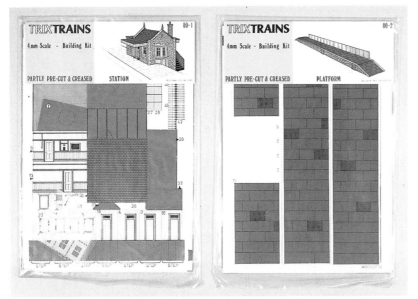

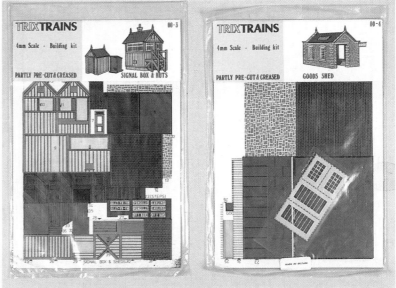

Top left: Cardboard Building Kits 00-1 and 00-2.

Above: Cardboard Building Kits 00-3 and 00-4.

Left: Cardboard Building Kits 00-5 and 00-6.

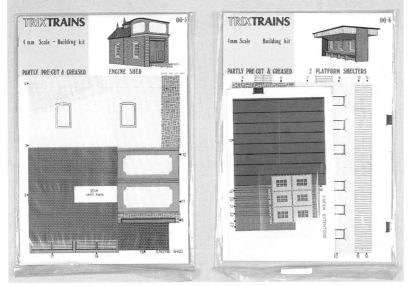

Signal Box and Huts from the Cardboard Building Kit 00-3.

The pre-production Elevator Conveyor.

The Trix Portable Set. (A)

The Elevator Conveyor and associated parts. Notice the British and German versions of the Sack of Coal.

separate printed Celastoid glazing sheets. The kits only made their appearance in the 1972 Trix price list. However, they sold well and made up into very realistic and sturdy models.

Elevator Conveyor and associated items

Probably the most ambitious accessories ever produced by a British toy or model railway manufacturer in the 1950s was the well-engineered Trix Elevator Conveyor system. The Elevator Conveyor itself was designed to fit between two lengths of track, the width between them corresponding to the diameter of a full circle of the bakelite track, and used in conjunction with the Operating Dump Wagons, Cat. No. 666, and associated items available separately or in sets. The operation of the system was as follows:

Coal was caused to tip from a Dump Wagon into the hopper of the Elevator Conveyor by remotely operating a special Magnetic Rail, Cat. No. 427. When an empty wagon was positioned under the loading shoot, the Elevator Conveyor was set in motion causing the coal to be raised from the hopper by the elevator belt and onto the conveyor belt, and hence to the loading shoot where it fell into the waiting wagon.

It was designed by Siegfried Kahn and Werner Alton, and it was in these names that the British Patent number 726723 was granted in 1955. The designs for the whole system, including associated accessories, was started in late 1952, to form part of the TRIX ACTION MODEL series. The base and hopper unit, tower, hut and conveyor support were all diecast mazak parts manufactured in the raw state by Fry's Diecastings Ltd who received an order in October 1953 for 5,000 of each of the above parts.

No further orders were ever received and the dies were returned to British Trix Ltd in 1966. The motive power hidden under the removable hut was provided by a 12/14 volt AC/DC motor assembly very similar to that used in the AC locomotives, except that it had an extended shaft on to which a 2-start worm gear was fitted. This engaged with a nylon helical gear mounted on a vertical shaft which at the top had two further nylon helical gears meshing with worm gears driving the elevator and conveyor belts. The various sub-assemblies were bolted together, but the conveyor arm and separate support could be easily removed for ease of packing or storage. The stepped elevator belt was made from extruded vulcanised rubber section, and the conveyor from lap-jointed fabric/rubber belting.

As has been stated earlier, the Elevator Conveyor unit was well engineered and included brass bearings, special conveyor belt tensioners and support rollers . Many of the parts were made of heavy gauge sheet metal. When it was first introduced in 1954 the cost of the basic Elevator Conveyor was £7/10/6d, and, bearing in mind the high cost of tooling for this

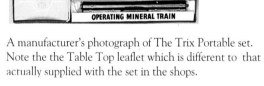

Operating Mineral Train Set, Cat.No.1/336.

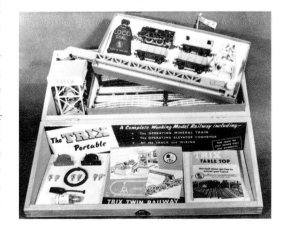

A manufacturer's photograph of The Trix Portable set. Note the the Table Top leaflet which is different to that actually supplied with the set in the shops.

system, it cannot have been a very profitable product. The sales were also not very high, remembering that the total number of diecast units made were 5,000 and it was still available in 1959, it is doubtful if the full production figure of 5,000 was ever reached. Sales were boosted slightly by offering the Elevator Conveyor as part of the Trix Express range in 1955, plus in 1954-55, under the Aristo Craft label and distributed by Polk's Model Craft Hobbies of New York. Although the Polk's advertisements listed the Elevator Conveyor as being available in assembled or kit form, it has been confirmed by Nathan Polk that the kit form was never issued.

Below is a list of sets and accessories associated with the Elevator Conveyor. The dates in brackets give the inclusive periods that the items were listed in the catalogues.

Cat. No.
388 The Trix Portable (1954 to 1957)

This was a wonderful set made up from the Elevator Conveyor, Operating Mineral Train set, an oval of track consisting of 20 units of bakelite rails, (which included the Magnetic and Uncoupler rails), oil, plugs, etc. and Table Top Plan, all housed in an excellent hardwood carrying cabinet measuring 21" x 8¾" x 9". The top and bottom of the box were split on an angle and hinged in such a way that when the box was opened an attractive display met the eye, and gave easy access to the parts. The cabinet with leather carrying handle had permanent value as a storeplace for any of the Trix range. The Table Top Plan shows the Elevator Conveyor on layouts complete with wiring details using the Ready-wired Table Top, Cat. No. 1085, as the base.

At £18/17/6d, (£18.87), it was a very expensive set and no doubt could only be afforded by the more fortunate, and for this reason not many were sold.

427 Magnetic Rail Set with Fittings (1953 to 1960)

This special Magnetic Rail rail was similar to the normal straight bakelite rail, except that the base moulding was modified to take a twin magnetic coil assembly mounted at the centre of the rail. The ensuing gap in the centre rail was bridged by a flat blade allowing smooth passage of locomotive pick-ups. When an Operating Dump Wagon, Cat. No. 666, was centred over the electro magnets they caused it to tip its load by means of a magnetic field caused by an impulse of current, via a Black Switch, passing through the electro magnets. When the Fibre-Based Track was introduced it was necessary to use two Transition Rails, Cat. No. 20/15, to join the Magnetic Rail to the new track system. The Fittings in the set comprised a Black Switch 449 and a coil of wire.

766 Operating Dump Wagon set (1953 to 1960)

This consisted of the following – Operating Dump Wagon, Magnetic rail with Black Impulse Switch 449, Sack of Coal, Fireman's Shovel and Lineside Coal Bin.

20/401 Operating Dump Wagon set (1954 to 1956)

This set was shown in the Trix Express catalogues. The Dump Wagon was fitted with Trix Express couplings, the inscriptions on the Coal Sack

As a temporary measure, this set is supplied with a third Operating Dump Wagon in place of the Goods Brake with Lights specified in our catalogue. No extra charge is made.

TRIX LTD.

The notice contained in some Operating Mineral Train Sets supplied without the Goods Brake with Lights.

appertaining to the German system and the Impulse Switch, Cat. No. 20/27, part of the Trix Express range.

788 Elevator Conveyor (1954 to 1959)
This was the basic unit.

20/402 Elevator Conveyor (1954 to 1957)

Up to and including 1956, only the basic Elevator Conveyor unit was included in the packaging. However, in 1957 as the German Operating Mineral Train set , Cat. No. 7/1015, was not available, two Transition Rails, Cat. No. 20/15P, and two suitable switches, Cat. Nos 20/26 and 20/27 were included.

799 Coal Loading Set (1954 to 1956)

This set contained the Elevator Conveyor and the Operating Dump Wagon set.

866 Sack of Coal (1953 to 1959)

It was essential that the 'coal' used on the Elevator Conveyor was suitable for correct operation and led to the special production of this plastic coal. It was supplied in black cloth bags on which the inscription '866 - LOCO COAL - Made in England' and the TTR trademark were printed in white.

30/35 Sack of Coal (1956 only)

As above but the bag was inscribed with '30/35 - LOK-KOHLEN' and the Trix Express trademark. It was produced in Britain by Trix Ltd.

867 Fireman's Shovel (1953 to 1962)

This was a small diecast model based on a Fireman's Shovel as used on steam locomotives, but could be practically used for shovelling the Trix 'coal' on the Elevator Conveyor or Lineside Bin.

868 Coal Bin (1953 to 1962)

Made from pressed-steel sheet, this Coal Bin held the stock of plastic 'coal' at the side of the Elevator Conveyor so that the load in the hopper could be replenished when used in conjunction with the Fireman's Shovel or other small scoop. The Coal Bin was 7.25" x 4" x 0.375".

1/336 Operating Mineral Train Set (1953 to 1957)

The locomotive in this set was the fully lined AC BR 0-4-0 passenger tank engine, Cat. No. 1/510, which on reflection seems rather odd as goods wagons are normally hauled by a goods engine. Even stranger given that the supply of Trix AC goods tank engines were ample. The set also included two Operating Dump Wagons, a Lighted Goods Brake Van, Magnetic Rail, Sack of Coal, Fireman's Shovel, Black Impulse Switch and Coal Bin as well as the usual oil, wire, plugs and instructions. When the Lighted Goods Brake Van was not available, an extra Dump Wagon was included in the set.

7/1015 Operating Mineral Train Set (1954 to 1955)

This Trix Express version included the following: Operating Dump Wagon set, (Cat. No. 20/401), an extra Dump Wagon, an oval of Fibre track complete with two Transition rails, (Cat. No. 20/15P), and the Magnetic Rail, together with an excellent Transformer/Rectifier DC controller, (Cat. No. 745). To complete the set, a German outline DC 0-4-0 Tank Engine, (Cat. No. 754), was included. Apart from the chassis mechanism, this DC Tank Engine was similar to the Cat. No. 20/54 AC version except that the diecast body had more detailed markings. This was at a time when Trix Express had just made the change from AC to DC and the models were more or less a compromise. Later, a very similar situation arose with the change of the TTR system from AC to DC in 1957/58.

Signals

Signals were not usually a predominant feature on a toy train layout, but most manufacturers, Trix included, offered one sort or another in their range. In pre-war days the range of signals manufactured and offered by Trix Ltd was very basic. However the situation improved in the 1950s with more realistic semaphore and colour light signals being added to the range. Below is a list of British pattern signals produced. The dates in the brackets are the inclusive years that the signals were listed in official Trix literature.

Cat. No.
21/203 Manual Home Signal (1935 to 1939)

This was a Trix Express signal fitted with a British pattern red 'home' semaphore arm and the post painted accordingly. The tinplate post was fixed to a heavy cast metal base on which the word 'Foreign'

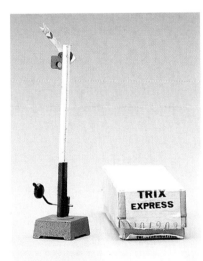

Trix Express Signal Cat.No.21/203 modified for the French market.

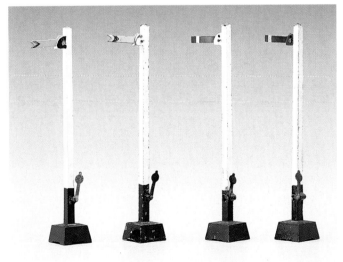

Pre and post-war TTR Signals. Post-war signals have a black spectacle plate.

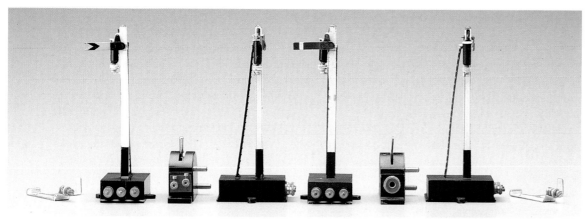

Remote Control Signals complete with fittings. Post-war to the left pre-war to the right.

was stamped. The operating lever was weighted giving positive action to the movement of the signal. The signal is also known with a yellow 'distant' semaphore in place of the 'home' without any change to the catalogue number. However, this latter signal was for the French market. The 'home' signal remained in the British catalogues only until 1936, but reappeared in the 1937-38 and 1938-39 joint Trix Express/TTR American catalogues with catalogue numbers 9/220 and 9/29 respectively.

701 Manual Home Signal (1936 to 1956)

The signal post and base were cast in one piece from mazak and fitted with tinplate semaphore arm and operating lever. No distinguishing marks were to be found on the base until the early post-war period when a round black and white sticker with 'TTR Made in England' was applied. In 1952 the die for the post and base casting was altered to include the words 'TTR Made in England' on the underside of

the base. Between 1947 and 1952 a total of 24,500 posts were diecast by Fry's Diecastings Ltd for use with this and the Distant Signal mentioned below.

705 Manual Distant Signal (1936 to 1956)

Physically this signal was exactly the same as the one described above except that a 'distant' semaphore arm was fitted.

731 Remote Control Home Signal with Light (1938 to 1941)

Trix were always enthusiastic to produce 'action' models which helped to nurture interest in progressing from a basic oval of track to layouts which were more interesting to operate. The Remote Control Home Signal with Light fell into this 'action' category. The mechanism installed in the diecast mazak base was quite ingenious and was activated by feeding an impulse of 14 volts to a pair of electromagnetic coils. This resulted in the

attraction of a flat armature and special spring-plate assembly which in turn tilted a special lever in one direction causing movement of the semaphore, through linkages. By the action of an armature return spring, the armature assembly returned to the normal position ready for the next voltage impulse. When this happened the special lever moved in the opposite direction causing the semaphore to return to the original position. To add further realism, the semaphore spectacles were illuminated by a special bulb assembly which consisted of a very small 10-volt bulb encased in a brass tube and illuminated the spectacles through a hole in the side of the tube. A much smaller hole at the rear of the tube allowed white light to show as in real railway practice.

In 1939 the diecasting of the integral signal post and base unit was modified at the points where the ladder locates at the top of the post and on the top face of the base. This was to overcome a problem whereby the bottom of the ladder escaped from the location holes in the base, and to provide a more efficient form of location for the top of the ladder. The top of the post was given an upturned hook instead of a pinch-slot on which to locate the top rung of the ladder, and on the base a small raised area was added which effectively increased the depth of the ladder location holes. The ladder itself was improved from being a completely flat stamping to one with raised sides.

The fittings included with the signal were a coil of wire, a centre rail connector and a Black Switch, Cat. No. 448. The Black Switch controlled the movement of the semaphore, whilst a Red on-off Switch, Cat. No. 418, was required for the light. The signal was shown as Cat. No. 9/136 in the Trix Express/TTR 1938-1939 American catalogue.

711 Model Colour Light Signal

As seen elsewhere, 1939 was an important year for new designs and innovations aimed at improving and whetting the appetite of TTR owners. This was to have been a two-bulb, two-colour (red and green), Colour Light Signal with planned additional use with the proposed Level Crossing Gates. It was advertised as having a special wiring scheme included showing how to stop and start a train through the Signal. Although never produced, a further abortive attempt was made in 1947, the idea getting as far as the drawing board stage.

730F Remote Control Home Signal without Light (1948 to 1950)

This was manufactured mainly for export at a time when miniature light bulbs were not generally available to the toy trade. The heading is rather misleading as the signals that found their way into the export trade were fitted with a bulb, only those destined for the home market were without. See

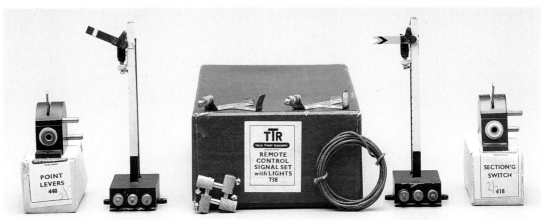

Pre-war Remote Control Signal set Cat.No.738. (A)

below under Cat. No. 732F for general comments regarding this post-war signal.

732F Remote Control Home Signal with Light (1950 to 1954)

This was the post-war version of the pre-war Remote Control Home Signal with Light, Cat. No.

731. Basically there was no difference at all between this and the 1939 model with the better ladder and ladder locations, and it is difficult to distinguish pre- and post-war versions except that the end of the pivot pin for the semaphore on the latter was soldered instead of just being pinched as in the case of pre-war models. Even the slide-on base cover was

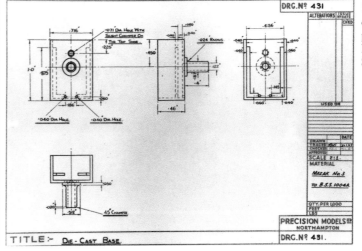

1947 copy drawings of parts of the planned pre-war Model Colour Light Signal Cat.No.711.

made from either aluminium or tinplate as in the pre-war version. One wonders why the catalogue number was changed from 731 to 732F. The Black Impulse Switch included was the new type, Cat. No. 449. The catalogue number was changed from 732F to 732 in 1953 at a time when spare bulbs, Cat. No. 31/88, also became available with a change in the voltage rating of the bulb from 10 to 14 volts.

735 Remote Control Distant Signal with Light (1938 to 1941)

Except for the Distant pattern of semaphore and the fact that it was not listed in the joint 1938-1939 Trix Express/TTR catalogue, the comments regarding Cat.No.731 also apply here.

734F Remote Control Distant Signal without Light (1948 to 1950)

See Cat. No. 730F for general comments.

736F Remote Control Distant Signal with Light (1950 to 1954)

See Cat.No. 732F for general comments. The catalogue number was changed from 736F to 736 in 1953.

738 Set of two Home and Distant Remote Control Signals with Light (1938 to 1941)

A combined set containing Remote Control Home, Cat. No. 731, and Distant, Cat. No. 735, signals with fittings.

752 Home Colour Light Signal with Fittings (1953 to 1959)

This was a very neat and compact Colour Light signal 2¾" high with a single lamp head showing either a red or green light remotely changed using a new type of two-way Yellow Switch with central off position, (Cat. No. 438). Two bulbs with red and green filters were located in the diecast base unit over which the base cover, post, ladder and lamp head assembly were a slide fit. Up the centre of the post tube and into the lamp head a shaped perspex rod was fitted which transmitted the red or green light from whichever bulb was lit. As it was difficult to distinguish between Home or Distant signals without removing the base, a Home or Distant sticker was applied from 1955 to the underside of the base. The base cover was painted to represent ferro-concrete. The 1960 price list stated that the signals were 'Temporarily Unavailable' and they were never again listed. The Yellow Switch and Centre Rail Connector were included. This signal was also listed in the 1954 and 1955 Trix Express catalogues as Cat. No. 20/226.

756 Distant Colour Light Signal with Fittings (1953 to 1959)

This signal was exactly the same as the Home Colour Light Signal described above, except that the bulb filter colours were amber and green.

758 Colour Light Signal Set, Home and Distant with Fittings (1953 to 1959)

This set was a combination of the Home, Cat. No.752, and Distant, Cat. No. 756, Colour Light Signals.

777 Block Signalling set (1953 to 1959)

This was a predetermined train control system comprising a Home and a Distant Colour Light Signal set, (Cat. Nos 752 and 756 respectively), and an Indicating Check Switch and fittings, (Cat. No. 439). By combining the colour light signals with the indicating check switch (see the section on Power Supplies and Control Equipment for details), automatic control of trains was obtained. It worked in the following manner:

An isolated section of track, approximately four or five rails long, was arranged at a required position immediately preceding a Home colour light signal. The isolated section was wired in series with the Indicating Check Switch which contained a resistance lamp. When a locomotive entered the isolated section with the check switch in the 'stop' position, the lamp in the switch was illuminated consuming most of the current from the section, the remaining current being not sufficient to move the locomotive. With the switch in the 'go' position the isolated section was connected directly through the switch to the live part of the track following. The Distant signal could be placed at a suitable distance before the isolated section, with the Yellow Switches for both signals plugged into the side of the Indicating Check Switch with the switch levers joined by the special link-bar. This ensured that the signals operated in the correct manner in relationship to the position of the Indicating Check Switch.

Although discontinued at the end of 1959, this set was listed in 1960 as being 'Temporary Unobtainable'.

722 Manual Lighted Home Semaphore Signal (1954 to 1962)

This Home Signal formed part of a new and well-proportioned range of lighted, but manually operated, semaphore signals. The post and base cover unit, as used on this and the similar Distant

1954 production models of the single semaphore Home and Distant Signals, the pivot pin for the semaphore was of larger diameter than used on later models. A slot was fitted in the operating lever on the signal which allowed rods and levers to be fitted for bell-crank control from a remote control point on the layout. In 1960 a full range of these signals was included in the Lineside Accessories Set but without baseplates and hence no lights.

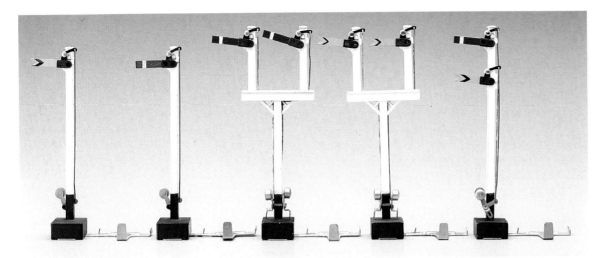

Above: the range of post-war manual signals with lights complete with track clips.

Below: plastic Colour Light signals on the left with the earlier diecast range on the right.

723 Manual Lighted Distant Semaphore Signal (1954 to 1962)

The comments regarding the above Home Signal also apply for this Distant Signal, except that the lenses in the spectacle plate were amber and green.

724 Manual Lighted Distant Bracket Signal

See catalogue number 727 below.

725 Manual Lighted Double Lighted Signal (1955 to 1962)

This signal comprised a Home and a Distant Semaphore Signal on a common post and served by a single perspex light rod. The post and base diecasting, of which almost 22,000 were produced, was different to that used on the separate Home and Distant Signals. Two manual operating levers were fitted. All other details were as the Home Signal.

726 Manual Lighted Bracket Signal, Home (1955 to 1962)

Once again this required a different diecasting for the integral base, post and bracket assembly. The bracket assembly contained two shorter posts, each with a Home semaphore. Each semaphore spectacle was illuminated by a common perspex light rod

Signal, were diecast by Fry's Diecastings, who initially produced a quantity of 25,000 with a repeat order by Dufay Ltd in 1961 for a further 1,700 units. The tinplate baseplate, apart from securing the signal to the side of the bakelite track, contained the single light unit, terminal post and an integral centre rail contact. Light from the bulb was carried by a perspex

rod to the semaphore spectacle plate which, for this Home signal, had red and green lenses. With the introduction of the fibre-based track, an instruction was given to remove the part of the baseplate forming the 'centre rail contact and rail location'. The movement of the semaphore was effected by means of a lever and wire push-pull rod. On early

hidden in the hollow of the post and bracket diecasting. Two manual operating levers were fitted. All other details are common to the range.

727 Manual Lighted Bracket Signal, Distant (1955 to 1962)

This was basically the same as the Home Bracket Signal described above except that the two semaphore signals were Distant Signals. In 1957 the catalogue number was changed from 727 to 724 remaining thus until 1962. However, there seems to have been a modicum of confusion in the Trix camp, as the catalogues and price lists for 1957 quote 724, the 1958 price lists quote 727 while from 1959 for the duration of the signal life it had reverted to 724!

754 Colour Light Signal (1961 to 1966)

This was the plastic replacement for the earlier diecast Colour Light Signals, catalogue numbers 752 and 756. The base, post and lamp head assembly were almost identical to the diecast version, but the connections in the base were more prominent and of the spring-loaded type which gripped the wire. The complete signal was finished in black with a white post. A set of interchangeable bulbs or bulb lenses were included so that the signal could be made Home or Distant. The catalogue number was changed from 754 to 1454 during 1963.

1477 Block Signalling Set (1963 to 1964)

Although there was no alteration in the operation of the Indicating Check Switch, (Cat. No. now changed to 1439) and its associated wiring (as mentioned earlier in the description of the Block Signalling Set Cat. No. 777), there was only one Colour Light Signal included in this set which was the plastic version, Cat. No. 1454 with its associated Yellow Switch Cat. No.1438. No centre rail connector was included.

1497 Colour Light Signal

Between 1964 and 1966 a Colour Light Signal was listed with the catalogue number of 1497. This was to have been a British Railways two, three or four-aspect signal based upon the construction of Trix Express signals of that era. It never got beyond the drawing board stage.

1498 Distant Colour Light Signal (1964 to 1972)

This was a Trix Express signal with the catalogue number of 6728 to which the British catalogue number was changed to in 1969. It had two lights, green and red. The design of the signal was based upon German railway practice. In the 1964 British Trix catalogue the catalogue numbers for this and the following signals were each allotted to the wrong signal.

1499 Home Colour Light Signal (1964 to 1972)

This also was a Trix Express signal with the catalogue number of 6729 to which the British catalogue number was changed to in 1969. It had four lights, two amber and two green.

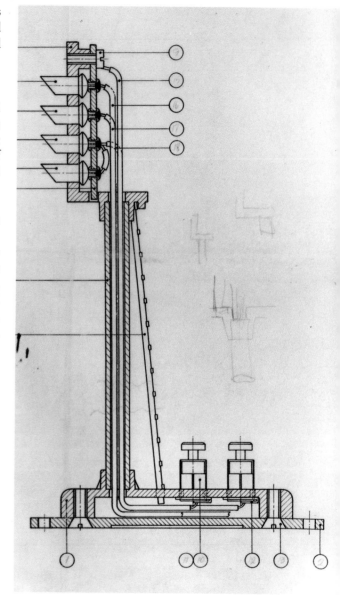

Unsuccessful proposal for a four-aspect colour light signal circa 1965.

POWER SUPPLIES
AND CONTROL EQUIPMENT

As with the majority of major toy railway manufacturers most of the control equipment was designed around the requirements of their own system, and Trix was no exception. With the introduction of the Trix Express, (or Twin Train), model railway in Britain during 1935 it was obvious that the power supply and control units suitable for the 14 volt AC system were not available in Britain. Thus, in 1935 Trix Express units were supplied. Power was supplied by either a Single Transformer, Cat. No. 21/41, which gave 14 watts (1 amp), enough to drive one locomotive plus accessories or a Double Transformer, Cat. No. 21/43, giving 40 watts of power (approximately 3 amps), ample to drive two locomotives and many accessories. The voltage output on these and all subsequent TTR transformers for the AC system was 4-10-14 arranged so that across terminals A - B gave 4 volts, B - C gave 10 volts and across A - C gave 14 volts. Input voltage was rated to cope with the British domestic supply of approximately 240 volts AC.

When these transformers were designed, plans must have been well ahead for the addition of accessories, especially the German version of the Trix Express Remote Control Points with Indicator Light, as the special bulb in these signals was rated at 10 volts. The version of this Trix Express Point for the British market did not have a light unit fitted, but the 10 volt outlet was used for the special bulb in the TTR Remote Control Signals with Light until 1953 when the rating was increased to 14 volts.

During the pre-war years all the controllers were supplied by the Nuremberg factory. These Trix Express controllers provided speed control for the locomotive, a safety cut-out feature and a button which operated the sequence reversing mechanism on the locomotive chassis, the latter two features being a function of the red button located at the centre of the speed control knob. The speed of the locomotive was governed by revolving the control knob which selected one of the 16 series-wound resistance stages. By depressing the button a break was made in the current feed to the locomotive, thus operating the sequence reverser relay. If a short-circuit on the layout occurred, a large current was passed through the coil of the safety solenoid which activated a mechanical break in the circuit which could be reset.

The tinplate sides of the early Trix Express controllers of 1935/36 vintage, Cat. No. 21/42, had a multitude of narrow slots which were replaced in 1936 by sides having a row of holes top and bottom. The graduations on the printed dial of this later version were more finely delineated. The British catalogue number given to this version was 470, although the base still retained 'Trix Express 20/42' usually accompanied by the word 'Foreign' stamped in yellow letters. By 1937 the catalogue number 20/42 was omitted from the bakelite base on controllers manufactured for the British market although retained on the German versions. Also at this time, the inscription TRIX EXPRESS in large black letters was added to the dial of controllers for the German and export markets, but never on the controllers manufactured for Britain.

In 1938 a Super Controller, Cat. No. 475, was introduced coinciding with the introduction of the British Pacific locomotives. It was designed to give greater flexibility in the control of the Pacific locomotives than earlier controllers being fitted with 24 resistance stages instead if 16. The basic design of the controller was no different to that of the ordinary one, except that the case was finished in blue-grey instead of black, and the added printed tinplate dial had a greater number of graduations. On versions made for the British market the dial

Early Trix Express Transformers. From left to right: 25/41 (French), 21/43 and 21/41.

bore the inscription '14 volt Foreign', while German versions were inscribed '14 volt Germany'. On a practical note, the bakelite Rail Clamps, Cat. No. 31/25, were used to clamp the base of the controllers to the train layout board.

By the middle of 1936, the Trix Express transformers had been replaced by versions manufactured in Britain. The 1 amp version, Cat. No. 481, was enclosed in a bakelite case with a base similar to the Trix Express Controllers that could be secured to a base-board by Rail Clamps. The 3 amp version, Cat. No. 485, was enclosed in a steel case 6½"x 4¼"x 2¾" high. A special mains plug assembly was attached to the input leads allowing the transformers to be connected to a two-pin 5 amp socket or a bayonet light fitting. During the 1930s many households still retained a 200 to 240 volt Direct Current (DC), mains supply and to operate the TTR locomotives it was necessary to convert this to 14 volts AC. For this conversion a TTR Rotary Converter, Cat. No. 498, was made available from 1937 of 'Foreign' (German) manufacture. This unit employed the incoming current to drive a motor which was coupled to a special generator delivering the current at the correct voltage for the TTR locomotives. The output was rated at 30 watts. With the issue of the 1939/40 TTR catalogue a new version was listed, Cat. No. 491/240, rated at 40 watts output. With later wartime issues of the same catalogue (no dates on the cover), it was no longer offered. The TTR Rotary Converter was not listed in TTR literature after the war, although the fact that the 1950, 1951 and 1952 Trix Express catalogues showed a similar version leads one to believe that certain areas of Germany were still on a DC domestic supply at this time!

Only two types of switch were used and

TTR pre-war Transformers Cat.Nos. 481 and 485.

A range of Trix Express pre-war Controllers with the Super Controllers Cat.No.475 on the outside and the 1935/36 version Cat.No.21/42 in the middle.

378

manufactured in Britain before the war, a Black Impulse Switch, Cat. No. 448, and a Red Permanent Switch (On/Off), Cat. No. 418. However, in 1935 the Black Impulse Switch provided with the Remote Control Points was the Trix Express version with the catalogue number of 20/20. The British versions of both the Red and Black Switches were first manufactured in 1936 and were no different from those of German manufacture except for the words 'Made in England' embossed in the casting of the rear mounting lug. Apart from their own domestic market, the German-made switches were issued for the joint German/British export ventures but were stamped 'Made in Germany' in red or black letters on the underside of the base. The Red Permanent Switch was used for track sectioning or lighting etc, and the Black Impulse Switch was used for remote points and semaphore signal control, or any circuit requiring an impulse of current. Any number of switches could be coupled together by means of the two screwed brass plugs securing the cover, and these plugs fitted into corresponding sockets on the casting of the next switch. The body of the switch was used as part of the circuit with the switched current fed to a single insulated output socket.

With the new British design of the Remote Points in 1948 with its twin operating solenoids came the necessity to redesign the Black Impulse Switch. The switch required two independent outputs for each Point solenoid and these were provided by a black moulded terminal block with screw fixing wire terminals. The slot in the body casting for the flat operating lever was modified so that it could be latched into a position to operate either one or the other of the Remote Control Points solenoids. The catalogue number given to this redesigned switch was 449. In 1950 the design of the switching mechanism was simplified and made more efficient by altering the lever assembly. The flat operating lever was now replaced with a round version secured and located to the base of the switch by a coil-spring. This new lever necessitated the widening of the keyed lever slot in the body casting. At about the same time the terminal moulding colour was changed to red.

Although the function of the post-war Red Permanent Switch did not alter from that of the pre-war version, the body casting and lever assembly followed the same modifications as that of the post-war Black Impulse Switch. The terminal block only contained one terminal, and in operation the lever

could be locked in the 'On' or 'Off' position. The catalogue number remained at 418. This post-war Red Switch was also available in a box of Accessories (without catalogue number), which also contained a Bottle of Shell Oil 31/78, a Coil of red Wire 31/85, and two plugs 96. The numbers quoted refer to those printed on the box label and are all TTR catalogue numbers, except 96 which is the Precision Models drawing number for the plug. No catalogue number exists for an individual plug and the only catalogue numbers relating to plugs are 31/50 for a box of six and later SP63 for a packet of six.

In 1953 a Yellow Two-Way Switch, Cat. No. 438, was introduced to control the lights in the Colour Light Signals. This was constructed in the same way as the black Impulse Switch except that a central notch was machined in the lever slot to give

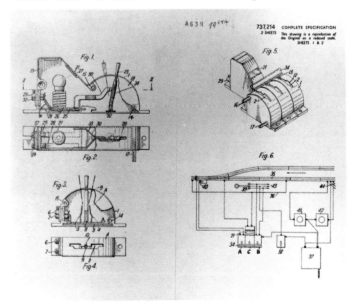

Extract from Patent No.737,214 showing the use of the Indicating Check Switch Cat.No.439.

A selection of TTR switches.

a central 'Off' position. Also the contacts inside the switch were arranged to give two independent 'On' positions. During the same year, a completely new type of switch was added to the range as part of the Block Signalling Set, Cat. No. 777, and this was the Indicating Check Switch with Link Bar, Cat. No. 439. The shape of the diecast body containing the lever and contacts matched that of the Yellow Switch with which it was designed to operate. However, the front portion of the body casting was extended to include a 13 volt 0.3 amp bulb, a red lense, a two-way terminal block and a piece of white card, the latter item only used for the operators' identification. The contacts were so arranged that when they were closed full power was fed to a sectioned length of track, but when the contacts were open current was taken by the bulb illuminating the red lense and slowing a locomotive to a stop on entering the section. The Link Bar, of which a short and long version were included with the switch, were used to link the levers of this switch to two or three other lever frame switches.

The Black Impulse Switch, the Red Permanent

Switch and the Yellow Two-Way Switch were listed until 1972, but the Indicating Check Switch was withdrawn from production in 1965. All four switches had a prefix number 1 added to the catalogue number in 1963.

Not surprisingly, at the end of the war, it was felt necessary to eliminate all public ties with Trix Express, and although Trix Express controllers were issued with a few early sets, from late 1947 a completely new TTR Controller, Cat. No. 472, was made available. It was almost the same size and shape as the Trix Express version, but the control layout differed by having the sequence reversing/automatic cut-out switch positioned in the bottom left-hand corner. The electrical function remained the same except that the various resistance stages were replaced by a continuously wired rheostat. This resistance wire, (2.82 yards of 0.0149" dia. Eureka or Constana wire with a resistance of 11 ohms), was wound on two formers separated by a brass rotor shaped in the form of a helix which altered the effective resistance, and thus output current, as it was rotated.

The colour of the nameplate containing the graticules, TTR logo, etc. was changed from green to straw in 1950, and at the same time the printed inscriptions were formed from larger letters. Incidentally, the earliest known 1948 date codes were applied to the inside bottom face of the baseplate on these controllers, i.e. F48 was June 1948. With the introduction of this item, which remained in the price lists up to 1958 inclusive, large quantities of the pre-war Trix Express controllers were destroyed in the Northampton factory.

Obviously one must have a suitable power supply for successful operation, and this was accomplished in 1948 by providing a redesigned and more efficient Transformer, Cat. No. 485/240, with a 3 amp output. (The 1950 TTR catalogue/leaflet listed it in error as 458/240.) The actual transformer was housed in a pressed-steel case with a shape that became identifiable with TTR during the 1950s. The case measured 3¾"x 4"x 4" high. The two-core mains lead was fitted with the special mains plug adaptor assembly as in pre-war models.

In the early 1950s, new safety regulations required that all domestic electrical appliances should be 'earthed', and to comply with these instructions an earth terminal was provided at the rear of the transformer case on production models from 1952, although the two-core cable and special mains plug adaptor remained. This 3 amp Transformer was given a new catalogue number of 494/240, and to distinguish it from earlier models a new label was provided quoting the catalogue number. By 1953 the earth terminal and special mains plug adaptor were dispensed with and the two-core cable replaced by a three-core one. This transformer was listed up to and including 1957.

Post-war TTR Controllers
Cat.No.472.

From 1950 until approximately 1953, a Trix Express version of the 3 amp 14 volt transformer complete with special mains plug adaptor assembly was available initially without, but later with, an earth terminal. Although this was exactly the same as used in Germany, the label giving technical details on the model for the British market bore no mention of Trix Express but only that the transformer was FOREIGN. The catalogue number of this transformer was 494F.

A 1 amp transformer was not provided in the post-war years as it had very limited use in view of the power available for the TTR system. As the TTR transformers were very heavy and bulky and the domestic electric supply voltage and connecting plugs varied from one country to another, it was obvious that a locally-manufactured transformer would be more cost effective than one being supplied from Britain and thus was not listed in the

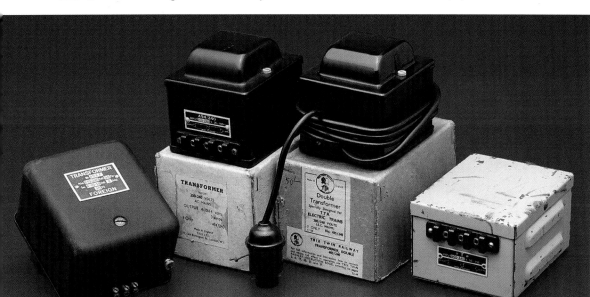

Power Supply Unit Cat.No.492/240.

Above left: a range of Transformers with a 3amp output. From the left: Cat.Nos. 494F (post-war Trix Express), 494/240 (post-war TTR), 485/240 (pre-war TTR) and a demonstration layout transformer.

Left: Master Switches and special Control Boxes for the Meteor and Whistling Coach. A Suppressor Set Cat.No.477 is shown in the middle.

general 1950 TTR export catalogues. One such locally-manufactured transformer, amongst others, to the standard 4-10-14 volt AC output was the Australian 'Amplion-Trix Twin Railway Transformer' Type TR1. This unit had three screw terminals on the top cover instead of the normal sockets.

A circuit protection factor that had been overlooked up to 1952 was that associated with the accessories. This was rectified with the introduction of the Master Switch, Cat. No. 464. This Master Switch plugged directly into the 'A' and 'C' sockets on the post-war TTR transformers and was fitted with an automatic cut-out similar to that fitted to the AC Controllers. It did not replace the cut-out on the Controllers, but brought the accessories under similar control enabling one to distinguish between locomotive circuit fault and accessory circuit fault. This was achieved by the design of the cut-out which was less sensitive than that on the Controller. For example, if the cut-out on the Master Switch had operated and not the one on the Controller, it was obvious that the fault lay in the accessories circuit or circuits. The base and cover were made from moulded black bakelite with a matt or gloss surface finish. This Master Switch was listed from the autumn of 1952 until the end of 1958.

The 1954 TTR price list catalogues a 4-way Switch, Cat. No. 476. Drawings for this switch were prepared but it never went into production. The title given to it by the draughtsman was Multi-Control and it was intended that it would be able to select any one of four circuits from a single source.

In 1953 a Power Supply Unit, Cat. No. 492/240, was introduced for the 14 volt AC TTR system. This incorporated a transformer, controller with cut-out and a separate accessory circuit cut-out switch in a steel black crackle-finish case. The outputs were a controlled 6 - 14 volts for a locomotive plus an uncontrolled 14 volt for the accessory circuits, and the mains input was via a three-core cable. The total output current was 1.5 amps which was deemed sufficient for most purposes. It was listed up to and including 1957.

The Meteor Diesel Express and the Whistle Coach introduced in 1955 required the use of a special switch for correct operation. Apart from the cases, the construction and electrical circuits were exactly the same. The idea of this switch was to superimpose a negative or positive DC current on the normal 14 volt AC operating supply to the Meteor or Whistle Coach to operate the special relay incorporated in these items. The DC current was provided by a ¼ amp 12 volt single plate metal rectifier fed to the terminals by a rotary switch. Terminals 1 and 5 had no function in the switch and were connected together internally. The case of the Meteor Positive Direction Control Switch was grey and incorporated a red lever-operated slide which reminded the operator of the direction of the train. The case of the Train Whistle Control Box for the Whistle Coach was black. Neither switch was given a catalogue number, and were only normally supplied with the Meteor or Whistle Coach.

One of the problems of operating Trix Twin Railway AC locomotives was the interference caused to television reception. To help reduce this problem, Trix brought out a TV Suppressor Set, Cat. No. 477, containing a suppressor unit to be wired into the external control circuitry, plus two

Transformer/Rectifiers. Left to right: Cat.Nos. 291/240, 293/240 and 291/240A respectively.

NOTES FROM OUR SERVICE DEPARTMENT

"IF YOU USE MORE THAN ONE TRANSFORMER . . ."

Special Notes on Twin Wiring.

To those of our friends who are about to augment their original installation of one TRIX TWIN by adding their second train—and to others wishing to expand their present set-up still further and who contemplate adding a second transformer—we offer the following notes as a guide on how to accomplish the wiring without getting into unnecessary difficulties. To an experienced electrician all this will appear elementary, but others not so well versed will find it of real service !

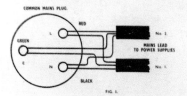

COMMON MAINS PLUG.

FIG. I.

MAINS PLUGS

If two or more Power Supply Units are used in one system, their mains leads must be wired in correct phase to the same common mains plug.

Standard mains plugs obtainable from electrical stores are now fitted with three pins marked, L. N. and E. The E is intended for the connection to earth and is larger than L and N. This is how to proceed :

The two earth leads (usually green and labelled " earth ") of the two transformers must both be connected to the pin E, the two red leads to pin L and the two black leads to pin N, as shown in Fig. I.

Pins of older two pin plugs are not so marked. When using a two pin mains plug the earth leads of both transformers should be cut short and their ends should be insulated. Then connect the two red leads to one of the two pins, and the two black leads to the other. **When in doubt ask your electrician.**

WIRING

(a) Where two Power Supply Units with an output of 1¼ amp. each are used, connect the terminals marked C of both to the red socket of the terminal rail—but never connect, either directly or indirectly, the other terminals (marked A or V).

Having carefully observed this caution, carry out the rest of the wiring as shown in the black part of Fig. 2. The grouping of switches may, of course, be varied to correspond to the sites of the accessories on the layout. If it should be more in line with your own plan, each block of switches could control some of the points and some of the lamps, as long as the switches served by the first Power Supply Unit are kept separate from the switches served by the second.

Thus, in our diagram the switches operating points, etc., are kept separate from the switch operating the yard lamps, which is wired to the second Power Supply Unit. This is done to distribute the load as evenly as possible between the two sources of power.

(b) If you have a transformer with an output of 3 amp. and two controllers, follow the black part of Fig. 3, using a master switch.

HOW TO LIGHT UP WITHOUT SHEDDING THE LOAD

With one 1¼ amp. supply, you can safely connect 10 to 12 TRIX bulbs besides operating one train. With one 3 amp. supply (or two 1¼ amp. supplies) you can connect 20 to 25 TRIX bulbs besides operating two trains. For this purpose colour light signals count as one lamp for each signal.

The operation of points, uncoupler rails and similar equipment uses current only momentarily and need not be considered.

Should you want to install more extensive lighting, add another transformer and master switch. One of 3 amp. used for lighting only will serve up to 50 additional TRIX lamps.

IMPORTANT

To install an additional transformer for lighting, follow those parts of the wiring diagrams below (Fig. 2 and Fig. 3), which are printed in red, using an additional master switch as indicated.

The wiring of the additional transformer (and the switches served by it) must never be connected, directly or indirectly, to the wiring (or switches) of the original Power Supply Units (Fig. 2), or transformer (Fig. 3) which feed the train circuits.

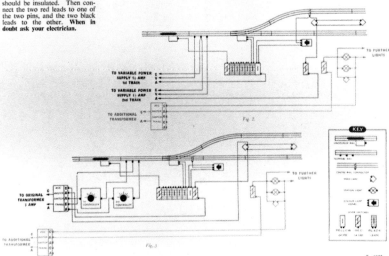

TO VARIABLE POWER SUPPLY 1¼ AMP 1st TRAIN
TO VARIABLE POWER SUPPLY 1½ AMP 2nd TRAIN
TO ADDITIONAL TRANSFORMER
TO FURTHER LIGHTS
Fig. 2.

TO ORIGINAL TRANSFORMER 3 AMP
TO ADDITIONAL TRANSFORMER
TO FURTHER LIGHTS
Fig. 3

KEY

'Notes from our Service Department' AC version.

NOTES FROM OUR SERVICE DEPARTMENT

"IF YOU USE MORE THAN ONE TRANSFORMER/RECTIFIER . . ."

SPECIAL NOTES ON TWIN WIRING

To those of our friends who are about to augment their original installation of one TRIX TWIN by adding their second train—and to others wishing to expand their present set-up still further and who contemplate adding a second transformer/rectifier—we offer the following notes as a guide on how to accomplish the wiring without getting into unnecessary difficulties. To an experienced electrician all this will appear elementary, but others not so well versed will find it of real service.

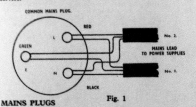

COMMON MAINS PLUG.

RED

GREEN

BLACK

Fig. 1.

MAINS PLUGS

If two or more transformer/rectifiers are used in one system, their mains leads must be wired in correct phase to the same common mains plug.

Standard mains plugs obtainable from electrical stores are now fitted with three pins marked L, N. and E. The E. is intended for the connection to earth and is of larger diameter than L. and N. See Fig. 1. This is how to proceed:

The two earth leads (usually green and labelled " earth ") of the two transformer/rectifiers must both be connected to the pin E., the two red leads to pin L. and the two black leads to pin N., as shown in Fig. 1.

Pins of older two-pin plugs are not so marked. When using a two-pin mains plug the earth leads of both transformer/rectificers should be cut short and their ends should be insulated. Then connect the two red leads to one of the two pins, and the two black leads to the other. When in doubt ask your electrician.

WIRING

The D.C. (=) output is used for operating each train separately. The A.C. (~) output operates the accessories.

When two transformer/rectifiers are used connect the LEFT-HAND A.C. (~) terminal of one unit and the LEFT-HAND A.C. (~) terminal of the second unit to the centre terminal of the terminal rail.

The other terminals (A.C.) are each connected to the switches controlling the accessories.

NOTE.—Each bank of switches controlling points, uncoupler rails, magnetic rails, etc., are separated into two groups and it is advisable not to wire or connect them together.

Having carefully observed this caution the rest of the wiring can be carried out in accordance with the example shown in Fig. 2. The grouping of switches may be varied to coincide with the sites of the accessories on the layout, e.g., each block of switches could control some of the points and some of the lamps, if that should be more in line with your own project.

HOW TO LIGHT UP WITHOUT SHEDDING THE LOAD

With one transformer/rectifier you can safely connect ten Trix bulbs besides operating one train on the D.C. circuit as well.

The operation of points, uncoupler rails and similar equipment uses current only momentarily and need not be considered.

Should you want to instal more extensive lighting (not counting coach lights) add another transformer. One of 3 amps used for lighting only will serve up to 50 additional 14-volt Trix lamps. For this purpose Colour Light Signals and lighted semaphore signals count as one lamp for each signal unit. These should all be kept on a separate circuit similar to the A.C. on the second transformer rectifier.

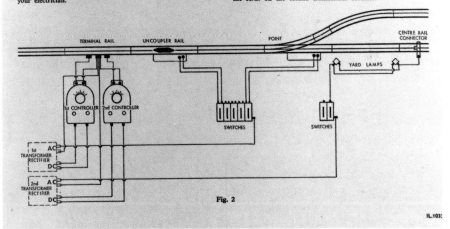

TERMINAL RAIL   UNCOUPLER RAIL   POINT   CENTRE RAIL CONNECTOR

YARD LAMPS

1st CONTROLLER   2nd CONTROLLER

SWITCHES   SWITCHES

1st TRANSFORMER RECTIFIER   AC   DC

2nd TRANSFORMER RECTIFIER   AC   DC

Fig. 2

IL.103

'Notes from our Service Department' DC version.

Left to right: DC Control Unit Cat.No.271,
Control Unit and box Cat.No.275: Cadet Speed
Controller with box and batteries.

0.01 micro farad condensers. Each condenser was for fitting across the field-coil winding of a 14 volt AC locomotive. This set was listed from 1955 to 1958 inclusive.

With the change from AC to DC current required to operate the Trix Twin locomotives came the need for new control systems. The first requirement came at the beginning of 1957 in the form of a Transformer/Rectifier, Cat. No. 293/240, delivering 14 volts AC at 1 amp and 10.5 volts DC at 0.75 amps. To compliment this transformer/rectifier a new train controller was introduced at the same time. This was the Train Controller with Whistle, Cat. No. 271, designed for use with the locomotives operating on 4.5 to 12 volts DC at no more than 0.5 amps. It was complete with variable forward/reverse speed control, automatic safety cut-out with re-set button and whistle simulator with operating button. The whistle simulator was the same unit as fitted to the Meteor and Whistle Coach with access to tuning on the rear face of the case. The case was dark grey

plastic. Connection to the track was made by using spring-loaded terminals, but the input to the controller was via a two-core cable which unfortunately could be mistaken for a 240 volt mains lead. Within six months the design was changed and the input lead was replaced with a block moulded into the now light grey case containing two spring-loaded terminals. The catalogue number was changed to 275, although basically all other details remained the same, except that the maximum current rating was raised to 0.8 amps and the granted British Patent 767059 relating to the Whistle Unit added to the mould of the case. Surprisingly, the Controller 271 was never officially withdrawn from sale and was even offered in the 1963 Trix Bargains Sale. The Transformer/Rectifier 293/240 remained in the price lists until 1959 and the Controller 275 until 1961, both dates inclusive.

To control the Cadet 6 volt locomotives, a Speed Controller with Reverse, Cat. No. 272, appeared in 1957. This contained a simple rheostat

and a current reversal switch. Output was via two spring-loaded terminals, but the input allowed the use of one or two large 4½ volt batteries with screw terminals onto which the switch was mounted. A mains Transformer/Rectifier Unit, Cat. No. 291/240, with an output of 4½ volts at 0.1 amp DC was provided at the same time for use in place of the batteries, the output being from two screw terminals at the same pitch as the battery terminals. In 1959 this unit was replaced by a mains Transformer/Rectifier, Cat. No. 291/240A, giving an increased output of 6 volts at 0.18 amps DC. The plastic case of model 291/240 was black and that of 291/240A was grey which continued to be listed up to and including 1961. In Australia a similar 6 volt DC transformer/rectifier was manufactured for use with the Cadet system by the Ironcore Transformers Pty Ltd. This unit was also given the catalogue number of 291/240 but designated Type T4/26. It was rather more bulky than the British version.

In 1959 it was decided by Dufay Ltd that a

more professional approach to the power supply and control unit facility was required. Dyke & Ward Ltd of London, who were already producing their own successful units, supplied Dufay Ltd with a printed circuit Transformer/Rectifier/Control Unit, Cat. No. 498/240, initially in the style and finish of their own unit with 14 volt AC and controlled 12 volt DC output sockets at the front. These outputs were each protected by an automatic re-set thermal overload switch. The catalogue number printed on the black front plate was 498/240A and across the top was the inscription 'Made by TRIX Birmingham 19'. In 1960 the unit was redesigned although the facilities and catalogue number remained the same. The front plate was now printed in red with the inscription 'Made in England by TRIX Ltd' below the control knob, and the output sockets were replaced by spring-loaded terminals with the addition of overload indicator bulbs above each outlet. In 1962 the nameplate inscription was changed to 'Made in England by TRIX PRODUCTS'. The units were discontinued when Courtaulds Ltd took over in 1963. Incidentally, the operating address of Dyke & Ward Ltd was 12 - 14 Berry Street, London, the same as Miniature Construction Ltd, although there was no connection between the two businesses.

The final power unit manufactured specifically for a British Trix company included the Trix TTR-1 single Power Control Unit and the Trix TTR-2 Twin Supply Power Unit with controlled 12 volt DC and uncontrolled 16 volt AC outputs. These units were available circa 1963/64 but were replaced during 1964 by the single Trix Control Power Unit, Cat. No.1805, giving the same outputs but protected by thermal cut-out. This latter unit was included with the complete train sets up to and including 1966. The above three units were

manufactured by Hammant & Morgan Ltd.

For many years a coil of Red Wire, Cat. No. 31/85, was available and listed in the spare parts section of the price list. From 1963/64 to 1971 coils of wire were shown in the catalogues and given the catalogue numbers of 1471 to 1476 inclusive for red, green, white, black, yellow and blue coloured wires respectively. Also from 1963 Trix Express control accessory items were offered, firstly listed with British Trix Ltd catalogue numbers and then from 1968 with the original Trix Express numbers. These items are listed below and were available until 1972 unless otherwise stated. Where two catalogue numbers are given, the first is the British Trix number and the second the Trix Express number:

5529 Trix Express Power Unit Type 529 Gives four switched speeds forward and reverse with a maximum output of 12 volts DC at 0.2 amp plus two other AC outputs. Bright red plastic case. Used in 1963 0-6-0 Goods Set, Cat. No. 1255, only.

1490, 6590 Relay – single pole double throw. (1963 and 1964 only).

1491, 6591 Relay – 4 x single pole double throw. (1963 and 1964 only).

1492, 6592 Relay – 2 x single pole double throw with safety cutout.

1495, 6582 Distribution terminal block. (From 1966)

6594 Yellow Switch – plastic - single pole On/Off type. (1971 and 1972 only)

6595 Green Switch – plastic - for points, semaphore signals etc. (1971 and 1972 only)

6627 Track Rectifier – for bridging block sections and reverse loops etc. (1971 and 1972 only)

1496, 6630 Variable Resistance for slow sections. (From 1966 to 1968)

Transformer/Rectifier/Control Units. The left-hand unit Cat.No. 1805 is by Hammant & Morgan Ltd and the other units, both Cat.No.498/240, are by Dyke & Ward Ltd.

TRACK AND ASSOCIATED ACCESSORIES

The Trix three-rail bakelite track was probably the most efficient and robust toy railway track system ever designed. Its initial prime role was to enable a young person to easily and quickly clip the track units together to form a layout to work equally well on a table or on the floor, carpeted or otherwise. The track units were also designed to allow the layout to be quickly and easily dismantled, by lifting the rails upwards or sideways but not by a straight pull, so that the toy train set could be stored away until the next time. The base of the rails was formed from a black bakelite moulding on to which were mounted three tinplate running rails connected at each end to the special electro-mechanical joints. The only disadvantage that became more apparent as the toy railway became more of a model railway, was the height of the bakelite base which was 10.5mm and the height of the rail section was 3.8mm, making a total height of 14.3mm

The 16mm gauge Trix track units were made in a geometrical formation based on a true circle of 685mm measured to the centre rail. This circle was made from joining 12 curved rails together, and thus each curved rail turns the track through an angle of 30 degrees. Curved Half rails were available so that when joined to a full curved rail a turn of 45 degrees was possible. Full straight rails were 182.5mm long and the make-up length called a Quarter Straight was 46mm long. When formations such as a 'passing loop' or 'run round' at a Station were constructed, due to the geometry of the track the Quarter Straight rail was required to bridge the gap between full length rails. Four of these Quarter Straight rails joined together were not intended to replace a full straight rail as 4 x 46mm = 184mm, and that is

2.5mm too long. The turnout section of the Points and the Diamond Crossing were designed to fit into the standard curved and straight sections of the track. The distance between the centre rails of parallel running tracks, based on the geometrical construction of the track units, was 92.5mm, which gave an inside measurement of approximately 73mm allowing for a platform to be fitted between tracks. Distance between the tracks could be decreased or increased by the use of two Curved Half rails joined together in the shape of an 'S' at the start and ending of the required section.

As a tribute to the track design, although the construction of the rails was altered over the years and other rail units of different but complementary radius and length were added to the basic system, including 2-rail track, the basic geometry of the track, remained unaltered throughout its life.

The Pre-War Period

In 1935 the track units supplied with the train sets and available separately were manufactured and

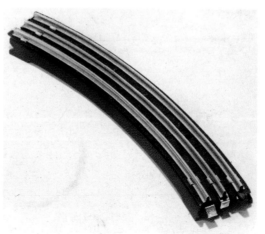

supplied by Trix Express. (The bakelite bases were moulded by Presswerk AG of Essen). They were exactly the same as used in Germany, but the catalogue prefix number was altered to '21' instead of the normal Trix Express '20'. They were as follows:

Cat. No.
21/1 Straight Rail – marked TRIX EXPRESS 20/1.
21/3 Straight Quarter-Rail – no markings.
21/4 Curved Rail – marked TRIX EXPRESS 20/1.
21/5 Curved Half-Rail – no markings.
21/7 Points (a pair) – Hand Operated.
21/8 Points (a pair) – Remote Control, complete with six plugs, wire and two Black impulse point switches.
21/9 Diamond Crossing
21/10 Terminal rail – straight or curved.
(Later given different catalogue numbers).

By the end of 1936 new catalogue numbers had been allocated (see over), plus the addition of Cat.No.865:

Interesting production trials showing the sides of the bakelite base with triangular male and female interlocking points. This idea was not adopted.

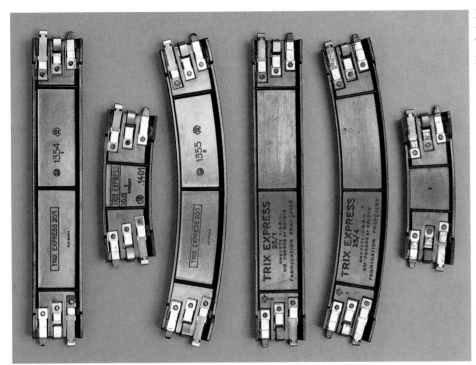

Markings on
the bases of
Trix Express
pre-war track.

410/1   Curved Rail
410/½   Curved Half-Rail
415/1   Curved Terminal Rail
420/1   Straight Rail
420/¼   Straight Quarter-Rail
425/1   Straight Terminal Rail
430   Diamond Crossing
440   Points (a pair) – Hand operated.
443   Points (a pair) – Remote Control,
complete with two Black 448 switches, plugs and
wire.
865   Buffer Stop with Straight Rail.
31/25   Packet of 25 Rail Clamps and screws.

These were formed from 0.02" thick mild steel and
were ribbed. Trix Express versions, Cat. No. 30/25,
were from heavier gauge steel, unribbed and a
slightly different shape at the base.

By the end of 1937 the bakelite bases for all the
straight and curved rails were being manufactured in
Britain by Ebonestos Industries Ltd of London who
supplied them to the Winteringham factory at
Northampton for assembly into complete track
units. The first of these bases were for the Straight
and Curved Rails which were embossed on the
underside:

TTR
TRIX TWIN RAILWAY
(relevant catalogue number)
Made in England
British Patent Pending
Patented Abroad.

On 11 June 1937 the British Patent No. 459744
was granted with respect to the design of the rails,
and with immediate effect the word 'Pending' on the
rail bases was crossed out using white paint and the
number 459744 substituted. It was not long before
the base moulds were similarly altered replacing the
word 'Pending' with 'No.459744' in its place. The
Curved Half-Rail and the Straight Quarter-Rail
bases were initially manufactured in Britain only
after the British Patent had been granted. The
markings on the Curved Half and Straight Quarter
rails are as shown below:

TTR
TRIX   TWIN
RAILWAY   TRIX TWIN RLY.   Pat.No.459744
410/½   420/¼ Made in   England
Made in England
British Patent
No.459744
Patented Abroad

Apart from the identification markings, the only
major difference between the TTR and Trix Express
rails was the pitch between each of the three sockets
on the Terminal Rails, which was 33mm on the
TTR rails and 18mm on the Trix Express rails. The
Points, Diamond Crossing and Buffer Stop buffer
beam assembly continued to be manufactured and
supplied from Germany up to the start of World
War 2, despite the break-up of the old German Trix

company and the formation of a new company by 'authorised personnel' in 1938. This was due to an enforced agreement between the new Trix company and the partners of the old German Trix company that certain items of track, along with other Trix items, had to be purchased to a minimum value. These items could not be manufactured in Britain, although the partners of the old German company had previously established Trix Ltd and a manufacturing base in Northampton.

The remote control versions of the Points were available from 1935 and were operated by means of an electro-magnet. When the electro-magnet received an electric pulse from the Black point switch, Cat. No. 448, the armature, through a system of levers, moved the frog, (or blades), to select one of the two turnouts. The armature automatically returned to its original position ready for the next pulse which would move the frog in the opposite direction. To enable the operator to observe which turnout had been selected, a point 'lamp' was mounted on the base which revolved through 90 degrees every time the frog moved, this being an essential visual aid as the mechanism was not always totally efficient in its operation. During 1935/36 a German pattern 'lamp' was fitted with a white rectangle, circle and diagonal arrow, the latter pointing to the left or right turnout depending upon the 'hand' of the point. This 'lamp' was keyed onto a brass square and held in place by a domed nut. By the end of 1936 the German lamp was replaced by one reflecting British railway practice which showed a yellow face for straight-ahead and a green circle for a right or left-turn, again depending on the 'hand' of the point.

Hand-Operated Points were also available from

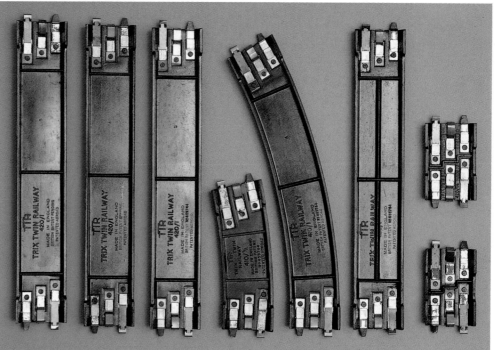

The various markings on the TTR track units.

1935 using the same basic bakelite base and operating mechanism except that the electro-magnet assembly was replaced by a hand-lever assembly. Up to 1938 the lever was 33mm long, and later 20mm long corresponding to an alteration in the lever-operated slide giving a smoother and more positive action. The remarks regarding the above Remote Control Point lamp also apply to the Hand-Operated Point lamp whose mounting assembly remaining unchanged.

In Germany during 1938, Trix Express Remote Control Points were introduced with an illuminated point lamp (Cat. No. 20/28). Although the Points

were never adapted for the British market, they influenced the design of the point lamp and mounting assembly on the Remote Control Points as supplied to Britain from this date. The lamp assembly was now much smaller with a slotted circular socket which could be fitted over a corresponding boss in one of two positions, thus eliminating the need for a left or right-hand lamp The only problem with this type of mounting was that it was a loose fit and the lamp tended to be misplaced. In 1939 a screwed terminal was added in place of the standard plug socket.

All the tinplate base covers of the Points for the

British market were stamped FOREIGN. The early designs of the Remote Control Points up to 1938 had recessed areas, whilst later versions, including all the Hand-Operated Points, were more or less flat. On the inside of many of the later base covers can be found extracts of colourful printed designs that had been used for discontinued toys or Trix Express rolling stock showing that maximum use of new or old materials at the Trix Express factory was important!

The design of the Diamond Crossing did not change throughout this pre-war period and for the British market the underside was stamped with the word FOREIGN. There were no other markings. The Buffer Stop with Rail was made up from a normal TTR Straight Rail with most of the electrical and mechanical connections removed at the buffer beam end. The Buffer Beam Assembly, also made in Nuremberg, comprised a grey tinplate frame onto which was mounted a red wooden beam held in place by two long turned buffers.

To help in the realistic operation of the Trix Twin Railway, an Uncoupler Set, Cat. No. 427, was introduced in 1938 enabling rolling stock to be remotely uncoupled. The set contained an Uncoupler Ramp Rail, Red Switch 418 and plugs and wire. A ramp formed from thin vulcanised fibre board and pivoted in a slot in the centre running rail of a TTR Straight Rail was raised by the action of an electro-magnetic assembly. This Uncoupler Rail was designed for use with special Uncoupler Parts, Cat. No. 31/90, which were fitted to the rolling stock couplings. These Uncoupling Parts consisted of striker stirrups and special curved wire links, the latter replacing the normal wire link. With the ramp of the Uncoupler Rail raised and the train travelling in a forward direction, the striker stirrup would lift the wire link as it passed over the ramp causing the wagon to uncouple. The electro-magnet assembly was manufactured in Nuremberg.

In 1939 it was the intention to produce an Impulse Rail, Cat. No. 428, for train controlled operation of lineside accessories such as the proposed Level Crossing Gates. The idea was that when a locomotive passed over this special rail it would cause an electrical pulse to be transmitted to an accessory. Once again the political problems of 1939 halted work on the project and it never saw production even though the idea was revived on the drawing board after the war.

Although not strictly 'Trix' it has been decided to include a description of the 'Lowko' Gradients for the Trix Twin Railway manufactured during 1939 by Bassett-Lowke Ltd. Similar gradients were first seen incorporated on the display layouts of Bassett-Lowke in their shop premises and on major Trix displays. The gradients appeared to be popular, so it was decided to standardize the units and make them available to the public. The following is a list of units available:

Pier A 1" high   **Pier B** 1½" high.
Pier C 2" high   **Pier D** 2½" high.
Pier E 3" high   **Pier F** 3½" high.

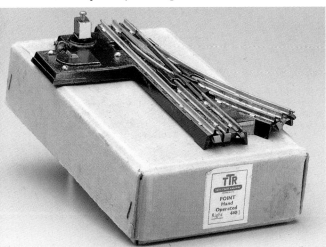

Late pre-war Hand Operated Point.

Late and early pre-war Remote Control Points.

Extracts from the pre-war TTR Automatic Uncoupling instruction book regarding the Uncoupling Set Cat.No.31/90.

TTR AUTOMATIC UNCOUPLING BY REMOTE CONTROL

WAGONS & CARRIAGES

FOR rolling stock the uncoupling problem has been solved in a different manner. Here it is desirable to effect the detachment of the individual vehicles while the trains are moving. With the new parts, attachable to any vehicle and fitted to any railway according to requirements, remote control un-coupling can be performed in a trailing direction at the command of the operator at his control switch board. The main principle of the wagon and carriage un-coupler is the use of an electrical remote-controlled ramp acting on a special lifting striker stirrup or trigger, fitted on the coupling and a new coupling link wire.

To allow the new device to be used on existing T.T.R. systems, the Uncoupler Set is supplied and listed, comprising :—

(a) Electrically operated rail ramp, in a special standard length of rail.
(b) Switch (" on " and " off " type Standard " Red " Switch No. 418).
(c) Plugs and wire.
(d) Instruction Leaflet.

Striker Stirrups for attachment to existing Couplings and new shape Coupling Links are supplied separately in Sets, No. 31/90.

The system as designed works only in a trailing direction. When a vehicle so fitted with the new uncoupler passes the special ramp rail in its raised position, see Fig. 4, the un-coupling device is operated and the coach and its following vehicles " slipped " i.e., detached.

Fig. 4

The uncoupler cannot be used for flying shunting. It is a " slip " un-coupler and works when the train is moving over the magnetic ramp.
The special " ramp rail " is fitted with a large number plate which both marks its position and identifies it with the switch which can be similarly numbered.

To alter existing vehicles, the parts involved are the coupling link, for which a special bent wire piece is supplied and the striker stirrup, also included. The wire link is fitted outside the striker as shewn in the sketch, Fig. 5. If the stirrup part of this striker is

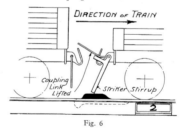

Fig. 5

moved, i.e., lifted, on meeting the raised up rail ramp it lifts the coupling link off the hook, as shewn in the next drawing, Fig. 6, by virtue of its projecting pieces at the upper part of the striker immediately under the sides of the coupling link.

DIRECTION OF TRAIN

Coupling Link Lifted

Striker Stirrup

2

Fig. 6

Level with Rail

Fig. 7
shows ramp at rest and level with rail.

The rail ramp is a magnetic device inserted in a special length of straight rail in the centre of the middle conductor rail. The actual ramp piece is of non-conducting material and does not interfere with the electric propulsion system.

The special ramp rail has plugs for wiring up, similar to a signal. An ordinary Red switch (No. 418) giving an " on " and " off " connection is interposed in the circuit. When moved to the " off " position the ramp piece returns to the concealed position by gravity, see Fig. 7.

Piers are marked with an identification letter.

Gradient 1 zero to ½" high, 14½" long x 2½" wide.

Gradient 2 ½" to 1" high, 14½" long x 2½" wide.

Straight Track Base 14½" long x 2½" wide, ½" thick.

Curved Track Base (to suit standard Trix track radius) 14½" long x 2½" wide, ½" thick. Three are used for a half-circle.

½-Length Straight and Curved track bases to suit one length of Trix rail for making ¼-circles. (Production uncertain).

One Straight and One Curved track base shaped for supporting right or left-hand points. (Production uncertain).

A Standard Gradient Set was available consisting of: two tapered Track Bases, six Piers lettered 'A' to 'F', five Straight Track Bases plus clips and screws.

Each unit was made from African white mahogany and finished in a matt colour representing concrete construction. When assembled in the shape of a 'U', the units gave a gradient of 1 in 30 rising to a height of 3½ inches to the underside of the curved bases over a length of 116½ inches, with a width of 26 inches between the centres of the legs of the 'U'.

The 3½ inch clearance was adequate for Trix locomotives and rolling stock running on Trix bakelite track.

From 1937 until 1939 a small amount of track was made in France but only Straight and Curved rail units. The markings moulded into the bakelite bases and the Straight Rail were:

TRIX EXPRESS
25/1
Brevete SGDG
Nos. 796303 et 801015
Fabrication Francaise

'Lowko' Gradient parts.

An extract from a special Bassett-Lowke leaflet.

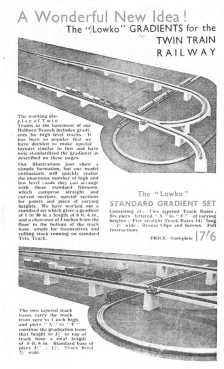

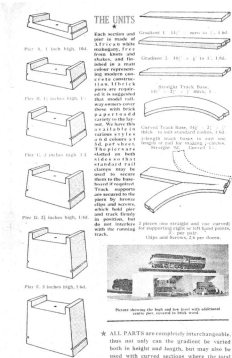

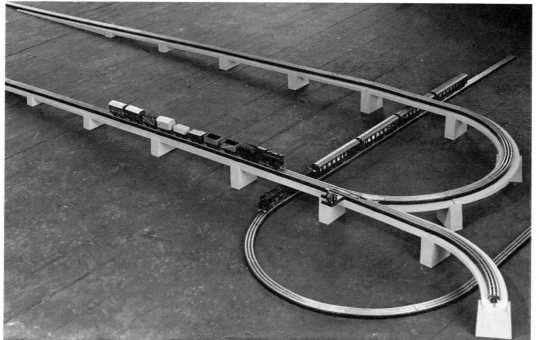

A Bassett-Lowke photograph taken at their premises at St Andrews Street, Northampton during August 1939 of the 'Lowko' Gradient set for the Trix Twin Railway. Note the rather precarious way that the point motor assembly hangs in mid-air at the rail junction.

French Trix Express rail boxes.

French Trix Express Track Set No.3 box lid.

Extract from
Patent Nos.
545,033 and
607,652 showing
the details of the
new bakelite
track.

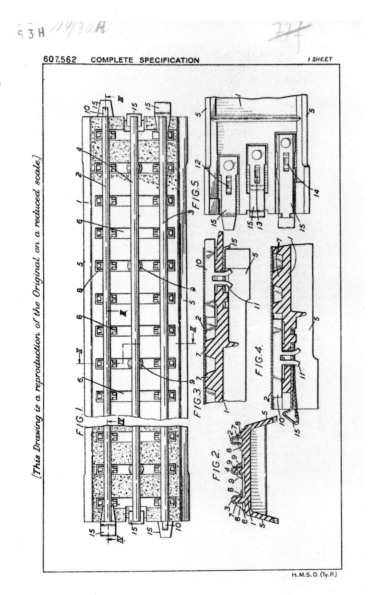

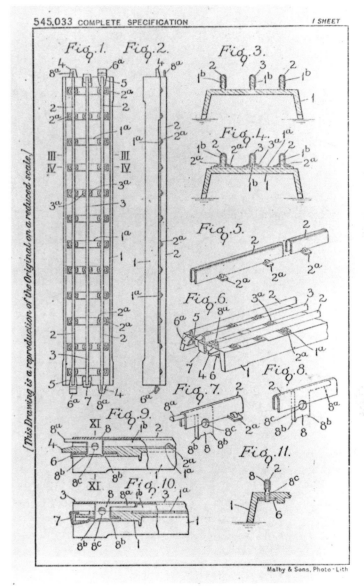

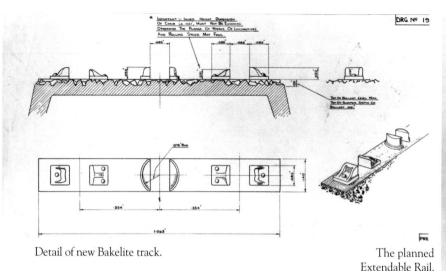

Detail of new Bakelite track.

The planned
Extendable Rail.

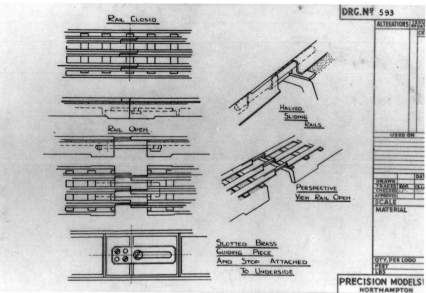

Listed below are the French catalogue numbers:

Cat. No.

25/1 Straight Rail

25/3 1/4-Straight Rail – (Trix Express Germany)

25/4 Curved Rail

25/7 Hand-operated Points – (Trix Express Germany)

25/8 Remote Control Points – (Trix Express Germany)

25/9 Diamond Crossing – (Trix Express Germany)

25/10 Curved Terminal Rail

Between 1937 and 1939 as part of the joint TE/TTR American catalogue, track units were listed, and for reference purposes are listed below. The first number relates to the 1937/38 catalogue and the second to the 1938/39 catalogue:

Cat. No.

——, **9/121** Uncoupler Rail Set (Uncoupler Parts Cat.No.30/16)

9/190, 9/11 Crossings.

9/207, 9/21 1/4-Straight Track.

9/209, 9/23 Straight Track.

9/233, 9/33 Hand-operated Switches (Points).

9/234, 9/34 Distant-controlled Switches.

——, **9/119** Distance-controlled Switches with Lights in the switch lamps.

9/235, 9/35 Connection Track – straight.

9/237, 9/37 Bumper with track (Buffer rail).

9/255, 9/45 1/2-Curved Track.

9/256, 9/46 Connection Track – curved.

9/284, 9/59 Curved Track.

These were all stamped on the bases with the name 'Germany' or 'Made in Germany' in red or yellow letters.

Post-war bakelite track

With uncertainty regarding trade relationships and the supply of certain track units and essential items from Germany, the immediate post-war period was a time when plans had to be swiftly made to manufacture them in Britain if the Trix Twin Railway was not to lose the popular appeal it had enjoyed in the late 1930s. It was obviously a time that if any major alteration in design was deemed necessary it had to be carried out. This was the case as regards the design of the rail section and bakelite bases which, although retaining the same outline and depth, were to be more realistic in appearance. The rail section was in the form of a plain inverted 'U', and the outside rails of each track unit were located on rail chairs moulded into the base, with the centre rail located on 'insulators' as seen on full-size electric track. This new rail section was to a Patent

'Specification No. 545033 granted to Trix Ltd in 1942! It was unfortunate that only the points and uncoupler rails were to receive this treatment.

Other ideas to receive consideration were a Large Radius Curved Rail, an Extendable Rail, a Diamond Crossing with 3/4-length straights and the pre-war design of an impulse rail, none of which ventured beyond the conception or drawing board/mock-up stage. The Extendable Rail would have been a useful addition to the system as with large layouts one usually found that two rails would not quite meet correctly due to accumulated inaccuracies in the manufacturers' construction of the track units. It would also have been useful in allowing non-standard Trix geometric track formations to be employed. The Diamond Crossing with 3/4-length straights, Cat. No. 432, must have been the closest to actual production as it was shown in 1948 catalogues and other TTR literature up to and including 1950.

As it happened, production in Germany of special Trix Express track units was more advanced than TTR production and a few pairs of normal Hand-Operated Points, intended for the American market and listed in the 1949 Polk's catalogue, found their way onto the British market at this time to supplement the domestic market which was restricted by the export drive. A label printed with the TTR catalogue number 440 was stuck over the special catalogue number on the 'Americanised' Trix Express Points box labels. These Hand-Operated Points were similar to the pre-war versions with the German pattern point 'lamp' except that contact blades were added under the movable point blades, the counterweight on the point lever was formed from two washers instead of lead and TRIX EXPRESS was moulded into the base near the pivots of the point blades with a TRIX MODELL - Germany transfer in the same area. It is unlikely that the Remote Control version with Lamp Light found its way officially onto the British market. The catalogue numbers listed for track items in the 1949 Polk's catalogue are listed below:

Cat. No.

Cat. No.	
29/1	Straight Track.
29/3	Quarter Straight.
29/4	Curve Track.
29/5	Half Curve.
29/7	Hand Switches – pair. (Points)
29/9	Crossover.
29/28	Illuminated Remote Control Switches – pair. (Points)
423	Hand Uncoupler Track.
425/1	Connection Track – straight.

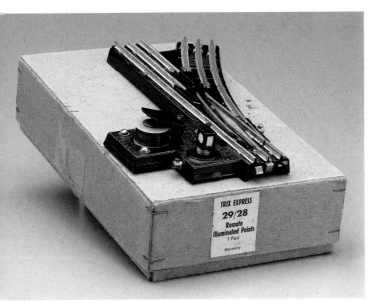

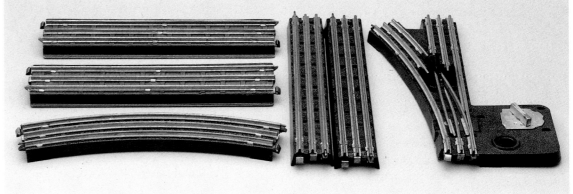

Post-war Trix Express Remote Control Point with point lamp for the American market.

Czechoslovakian copies of the bakelite track by Karel Gewiss with a longer TTR Straight next to a copy. A Trix Express fibre straight rail is at the rear.

429 Remote Uncoupler Track.
865 Track with Bumper.

After the war many small firms throughout Europe struggled to make a living by any means at their disposal, one being to almost copy or adapt the designs of successful pre-war products. One such company was Karel Gewiss of Gablonz in Czechoslovakia who produced Trix-like track units (including locomotives), between 1948 and 1950 with a brown or black bakelite base which interlocked perfectly with Trix track. The Straight Track units were 2.5mm shorter and the base moulding approximately 2mm narrower than the standard TE/TTR item, yet the Curved Track units were 2.5mm longer than the equivalent TE/TTR item. The Hand-Operated points were activated by a crude hand-operated rotating switch. There were no identification markings on the bases whatsoever.

By 1948 the following items of TTR track was available to the British public:

Cat. No.
410/1   Curved Rail.
410/1/2 Curved Half Rail.
420/1   Straight Rail.
420/1/4 Straight Quarter Rail.
423   Uncoupler Rail, hand operated.
425/1   Straight Terminal Rail. (No Curved
         Terminal Rails were produced post-war).
429   Uncoupler Set, remote control with switch
         and wire.
442   Pair of Points, Hand operated.
445   Pair of Points, remote control with
         switches and wire.
865   Buffer Stop.

Production of the the track units increased after 1947 and by October 1950 Trix Ltd were estimating that they would need the following quantities of bakelite track unit mouldings and other parts from Ebonestos Industries for the first six months of 1951. This included 225,000 Straight Rail bases, 200,000 Curved Rail bases, 15,000 of each of the new Left- and Right-Hand Point bases and 18,500 new Uncoupler Rail bases of which delivery was more or less met for all items in the time specified. Even during 1955 large amounts of track unit mouldings were still being supplied. For example in the second four months of that year a combined total of almost 230,000 Straight and Curved bases were supplied to Trix Ltd showing that projected sales were still strong. In fact, all the basic track units were listed up to and including 1958.

There was essentially no difference between pre- and post-war production on the basic track units except that in 1952 the rail joint tinned angle piece as used on all track units (the right-hand part of a rail joint when viewed from the underneath), received two strengthening ribs. Nine different moulds were continually used by Ebonestos Industries for producing the Straight Rail bases. These were numbered 1 to 9, and the individual mould for each rail base could be identified from the number moulded into the base. Distortion during the manufacturing process was a major problem, and in an attempt to lessen this effect a central strengthening rib was added in 1949 to the number 5 mould. The modification did not help the situation.

With the introduction of the new coupling fitted to locomotives and rolling stock in 1948 it became necessary to provide an Uncoupling Rail as part of the new system. In 1947 the idea was to convert the pre-war uncoupling rail to accept the

Post-war TTR Hand and Remote Control Points.

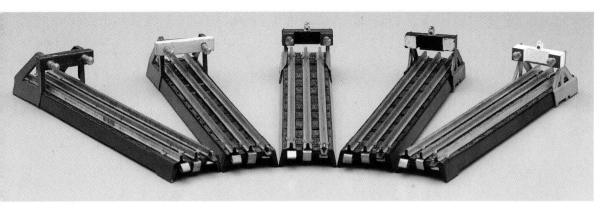

Buffer-Stop rails, pre-war on left through to post-war.

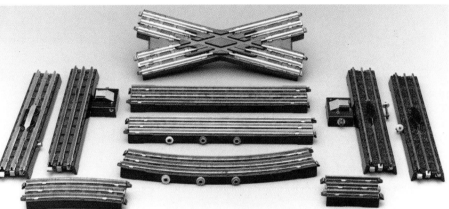

Bakelite track units with various Uncoupler rails and the Magnetic rail on the right.

the fixing tags, whilst the effective part of the cover plate used after 1950 was only 1.55" long with the manufacturing month/year code stamped into the metal. A small hand lever pivoted in the base of the rail to operate the ramp. On the Remote Control model, this hand lever remained, but a solenoid assembly was added of virtually the same construction and action as the pre-war Remote Control Uncoupler Rail. A Red Switch and wire was included with the Remote Control Uncoupler Rail with both versions being listed in the price lists up to and including 1958.

The design for the new Points was started in 1946, and when they appeared in 1948 they were well received by the TTR enthusiasts as they were far more realistic in appearance with the new rail section and a very positive change-over action from the new push-pull solenoid assembly on the Remote Control model. One other interesting modification was the reduction of the standard length of the straight rail to a 3/4-length which allowed for closer running tracks without the use of 1/2-Curved Rails. The left- and right-hand base mouldings were used for both Hand and Remote Control versions and with a similar hand lever assembly. The solenoid assembly, also used as part of the uncoupling mechanism in the 'Scotsman' 4-6-2 Pacific locomotive tender, was cleverly concealed in the base recess and was linked to the hand lever assembly. A new Black Impulse Switch, Cat. No. 449, had been designed to give two separate impulse feeds to the solenoid. During the production life of the points, various small modifications were incorporated, the most important being the change in 1952 from the two movable blades being mounted on a single pivot plate at the junction of

new coupling which was was taken to the pre-production stage as shown by the illustrations in the 1948, and later, catalogues and literature. However it was decided to make a new base mould with more realistic detail which also used the new design of running rails. This new base moulding was designed not only for assembly into an Uncoupling Rail, but also as a Terminal Rail, although the latter never materialised.

Two versions of the Uncoupler Rail were made, a Hand-Operated model, Cat. No. 423, and the Remote Control model, Cat. No. 429. The actual uncoupling ramp was moulded from bakelite and in the raised position was designed to spread two coupled rolling stock couplings apart as the striker arm of each coupling passed either side of the ramp. On the Hand-Operated model, the first base cover plate in use up to 1950 was 3.3" long, not counting

the two tracks, to the individual pivoting of each blade. A lighter counterweight on the hand lever was also fitted at this time. Various markings on the base covers were applied.

1) In 1948 mainly for export market. Printed in white letters.

TTR
Made in
England

2) 1948 to 1949, again mainly for export. Printed in white letters.

TTR
BRITISH PATENT
No. 545033
Patents Pending
Made in England

The Patent number related to the new rail section.

3) 1949 to 1950, stamped in the metal.

TTR
Made in England

4) 1951 onwards, stamped in the metal.

TTR
Made in England
British Pat. No. 644346

The Patent number related to the general concept of the new TTR Remote control Points and was granted in October 1951. The month/year production code was also stamped in the metal.

The Hand-Operated Points were offered as a pair, Cat. No. 442, as were the Remote Control Points, Cat. No. 445. However the Remote Control Points could also be purchased individually boxed as Cat. No. 445/½ RH or Cat. No. 445/½ LH. The Points were available up to and including 1958.

The Diamond Crossing, Cat. No. 430, was a Trix Express product imported into the TTR range

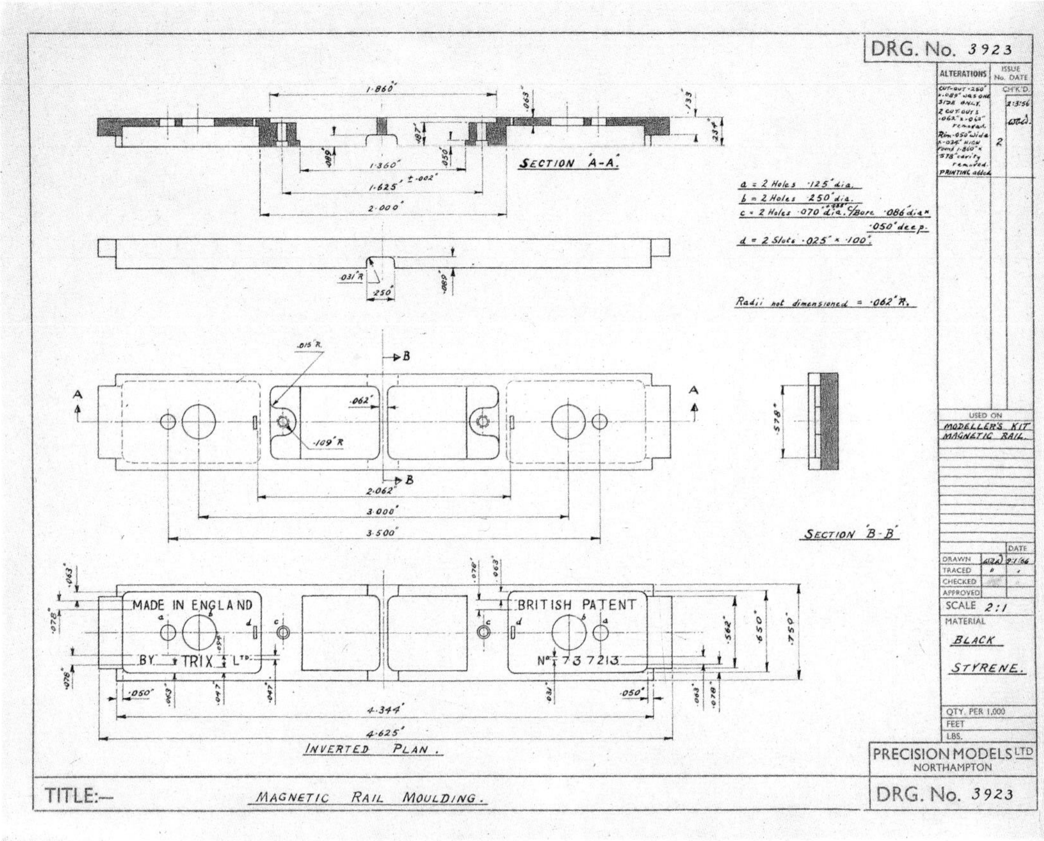

A proposed base for a Modellers Magnetic Rail Kit.

between 1950 and 1956. It had no markings and was no different from the pre-war production, except that the insulating sheet on the underside of the base passed under all three top connecting straps, whereas on the pre-war version only the outside two top straps passed over the insulator.

The beginning of 1947 saw the production of a new Buffer Stop tinplate stamping of typical British pattern, to which was fitted a white-metal buffer

beam. This buffer beam was not fitted with buffers until the end of 1950, at which point holes were added for turned buffers to be pressed into the white-metal. Up to 1951 the buffer beam was black with white or red buffer plates, after then being finished in white with red beam plates. The catalogue number of the complete Buffer Stop Rail was 865.

The final major development in the bakelite

398

track was the Magnetic Rail Set with fittings, Cat. No. 427, (the same number as the pre-war Uncoupler Rail Set), designed in conjunction with the Dump Wagon, Cat. No. 666, and the Elevator Conveyor. The special rail was fitted with an assembly containing two small electro-magnets located through holes in the bakelite base. The resultant gap in the centre rail was bridged by a nickel silver strip, or to give its correct name, residual, over which the locomotive collector shoes would pass unimpaired. With a Dump Wagon located over the electro-magnets, a pulse from the Black Impulse Switch, (included with the rail), would cause the Dump Wagon to discharge its load. When introduced at the beginning of 1953, the rail base used was the standard Straight Rail machined to accept the electro-magnet assembly with the two ensuing lengths of centre rail joined electrically by a wire link. By the end of 1953 the bakelite Straight Rail base mould was altered to accept the electro-magnet assembly and other essential fittings with the minimum of machining. In addition, the normal Trix Twin Railway moulded inscriptions had been removed and replaced with just 'TTR - Made in England'. Also at this time, the wire joining the two lengths of centre rail were replaced by a tinplate connecting strip. In 1954 the two electro-magnets were mounted in a special frame to enable an enthusiast to fit them to scale track. This unit was only available in the American 'Aristo Craft Miniatures' set containing the Trix Dump Wagon, or Car as the Americans preferred to call them, although a Modellers Magnetic Rail Kit was proposed unsuccessfully in 1956. The Magnetic Rail was listed up to and including 1960.

Trix bakelite Track Formations.

Track or Permanent Way Formations were available in boxed sets complete with Track Manual, Rail Clamps and screws, etc. They are listed below with contents and inclusive dates shown in Trix literature. To save space the following key letters are used, and the set dates denote whether the pre- or post-war bakelite rail patterns are included:

A – Curved rail, **B** – Curved Terminal rail, **C** – Straight rail, **D** – ¼-Straight, **E** –Hand-operated Point LH, **F** – Buffer Stop, **G** – Hand-operated Point RH, **H** – Pair of Hand-operated Points, **J** – Pair of Remote Control Points, **K** – Diamond Crossing. **L** – Remote Uncoupler set. **M** – Manual Uncoupler rail. **N** – Straight Terminal rail.

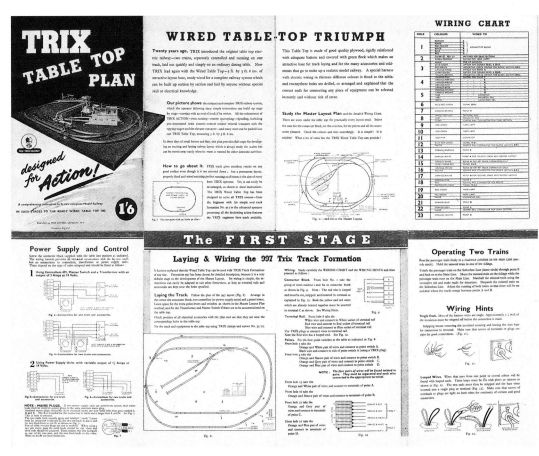

Left and overleaf: Trix Table Top Plan.

Cat. No.

914 Oval track – 11 x A, 1 x B, 4 x C. (1937-1941)

915 Oval track – 12 x A, 2 x C, 1 x M, 1 x N. (1948-1957)

924 Oval with siding – 12 x A, 1 x B, 6 x C, 1 x E, 1 x F. (1937-1941)

925 Oval with siding – 13 x A, 4 x C, 1 x D, 1 x M, 1 x E, 1 x N, 1 x F. (1948-1957)

932 Oval with passing loop – 13 x A, 1 x B, 9 x C, 1 x D, 1 x H. (1937-1941)

935 Oval with passing loop – 14 x A, 7 x C, 3 x D, 1 x M, 1 x H, 1 x N. (1948-1957)

937 Oval with passing loop – 13 x A, 1 x B, 9 x C, 1 x D, 1 x J. (1937-1941)

939 Oval with passing loop – 14 x A, 7 x C, 3 x D, 1 x L, 1 x J, 1 x N. (1948-1957)

945 Oval with relief line and siding – 19 x A, 7 x C, 3 x D, 1 x N, 1 x M, 1 x H, 1 x E, 1 x F. (1948-1957)

947 Oval with relief line and siding – 18 x A, 1 x B, 9 x C, 1 x E, 1 x J, 1 x F. (1937-1941)

949 Oval with relief line and siding – 19 x A, 7 x C, 3 x D, 1 x N, 1 x L, 1 x E, 1 x J, 1 x F. (1948-1957)

956 Oval with relief line and Uncoupler siding – 18 x A, 1 x B, 9 x C, 1 x G, 1 x J, 1 x L, 1 x F. (1938 - 1941)

965 Double oval with loop and crossovers 23 x A, 1 x B, 20 x C, 2 x D, 1 x H, 1 x J. (1937 - 1941)

969 Double oval with loop and crossovers 24 x A, 18 x C, 6 x D, 1 x N, 1 x L, 1 x H, 1 x J. (1948 - 1953)

991 Oval line with goods, locomotive and carriage sidings – 12 x A, 1 x B, 18 x C, 1 x E, 2 x G, 2 x J, 1 x K, 7 x F. (1937 - 1941)

997 Double oval with goods sidings - 22 x A, 14 x C, 8 x D, 1 x M, 1 x N, 2 x J, 2 x F. (1954-1957)

1159 Combination Set - 13 x A, 12 x C, 4 x D, 1 x M, 1 x N, 1 x H, 1 x J, 1 x F, 1 x Manyways Country Station 3007, 6 x Yard Lamps Cat. No. 761, 2 x Home Colour Light Signal Cat. No. 752, 1 x Distant Colour Light Signal Cat. No. 756. (1953 - 1954). This Combination Set was intended for use with the Table Tops but did not sell well.

The standard rails in the Track Formation Sets were normally packed in rail boxes containing six of that particular type of rail. obviously in most of the sets odd numbers of track units were required. This resulted in various boxed combinations of rails. For example, the Cat. No. 937 set included two non-standard boxes one of which contained three Straight rails only and the other 1 x Terminal rail

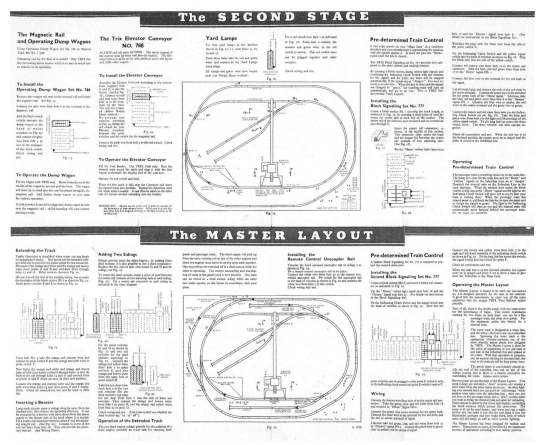

(curved), 1 x Curved rail and 1 x Quarter Straight rail. Each box carried a TTR label stating the contents but without any catalogue number. These special boxed combinations of rails were not available separately.

On a note of interest, Half-Curved rails were never included in the Track Formation Sets. TTR layout designs in the form of Blue Prints numbered 1001 to 1012 inclusive were listed in the 1939/40 Trix Twin Railway catalogue and continued to be available through the early war years. They were not re-introduced after the war. However, various items of pre- and poat-war literature showed suggested layout formations.

TTR Table Tops

The room sizes in the average domestic house in the mid-1950s did not usually provide space for a permanent model railway layout, and it was with this in mind that Trix Ltd introduced in 1953 the TTR Table Tops onto which a layout could be permanently fixed. This Table Top could be lifted off a surface such as a dining room table when it was otherwise required and stood upright against a wall. Two sizes were available – the Main Unit (5 feet x 3½ feet, Cat. No. 1053) and the Extension Unit 5 feet x 2 feet, Cat. No.1052. Each table top was substantially built of heavy calibre hardboard mounted on a strong hardwood frame. They were slotted on all four sides and by means of nuts and bolts could be joined to other units in any direction. In addition, they were strengthened with transverse bracing to prevent warping and were covered with flock which gave a green baize effect. These Table Tops were made for Trix Ltd by Vono Ltd, a famous bed-maker, and were listed up to and

The basic Fibre based track units.

including 1959.

From 1956 to 1958, inclusive, the Main Table Top Unit was available complete with detachable legs similar to those of a trestle table. This combination was given the catalogue number of 1205. Another extension to the idea of the basic Main Table Top Unit was the Ready-Wired Table Top (5 feet x 3½ feet, Cat. No.1085), first introduced in the shops during the autumn of 1954. The wired table had 23 small holes drilled in the surface, and to the underneath was fitted a harness with 13 different distinctively coloured wires plus a connecting block. These wires were fed through numbered holes as instructed in the Table Top Plan leaflet (available separately), depending upon the layout chosen, and then connected to the appropriate track unit, accessory, switch or control unit. This Wired Table Top was not available after 1956.

The Trix Twin Track with a Fibre Base

The Trix company in Germany realised very quickly that the Trix Express bakelite track was not

as realistic as some of their competitors and embarked on modernising the rail construction, yet maintaining the 3-rail configuration. In 1953 they presented to their model railway public 3-rail track units which still retained the original Trix geometry but was constructed upon realistic bases with open fret-sleeper detail stamped from 'fibre' sheet, or to be more correct, bitumen paper. The centre rail was now less obtrusive and formed from chemically blackened tinplate with a very narrow section, while the Point solenoid was based upon that used for the TTR bakelite Points. However the track running rails used exactly the same profile as before although fixed by a different method. One major rethink was the introduction of larger radius curved rail units which, when used in conjunction with the standard curved rail units, enabled a double curved track to be laid with a constant distance between the two tracks, something that could never be achieved with the bakelite curved rails. The only drawback to the new design was that the rail connections were of a conventional nature, in other words pin-and-socket arrangement as used by most other model rail manufacturers. With these modifications, Trix Express moved away once and for all from the concept of a toy railway into the realms of the model railway. Spring loaded electrical terminals were used throughout.

It took until 1956 for Trix Ltd to also realise that it was about time that they should also provide a rail system more in keeping with the general trend of model railways at that time. It was decided to copy the track with bitumen paper bases as used by Trix Express, and the necessary drawings were started in the summer of 1956 with the idea of manufacturing the basic track units in Britain. Due to the change in ownership of Trix Ltd at the beginning of 1957, it was not until the autumn of that year that the first of the new 'Fibre' track was on sale in the shops. Below is a full list of all available units in this system up to and including the end of the Trix Products Ltd era at the beginning of 1963. Unless otherwise stated, these were introduced in 1957 and manufactured in Britain. The catalogue numbers were exactly the same, initially, as those for the Trix Express track.

Note:
Radius 1 = 342.5mm, and radius 2 = 401.7mm.
Cat. No.
701 Straight rail – 183.5mm.
702 Curved rail – 24 degrees = 4/5 of full radius 1 rail.
703 Straight rail – 49mm.
704 Curved rail – 30 degrees = full radius 1 rail.
705 Hand Uncoupler rail – 183.5mm
706 Curved rail – 6 degrees = 1/5 of full radius 1 rail.
707 Diamond Crossing, for scale wheels – first listed in 1963 but never produced.

708 Straight rail – 88mm.
709 Diamond Crossing – rails 183.5mm long set at an angle equivalent to full radius 1 rail. Centre moulding Trix Express manufacture.
710 Curved Terminal rail – 30 degrees = full radius 1 rail.
711 Straight Terminal rail – 183.5mm.
712 Remote Control Uncoupler rail – 183.5mm, with fittings.
716 Buffer rail – 183.5mm.
717 Straight Contact rail – 88mm, Trix Express, 1963 only.
718 Track Isolating Straight rail – 88mm, Trix Express, from end of 1962.
719 Track Isolating Curved rail – 24 degrees = 4/5 of full radius 1 rail, Trix Express, from end of 1962.
720 Remote Control Double Slip – dimensions as for Diamond Crossing, Trix Express, from end of 1962.
727 Hand Operated Points – pair.
U727 Universal Hand Operated Points – from April 1959 to beginning of 1960.
U727LH Universal Hand Operated Point, Left hand – from beginning of 1960.
U727RH Universal Hand Operated Point, Right hand – from beginning of 1960.
728 Remote Control Points – pair with fittings, up to beginning of 1959 only.
728 Remote Control Points – pair without fittings, from spring to autumn of 1959.
U728 Universal Remote Control Points – with fittings, from April 1959 to beginning of 1960.
U728LH Universal Remote Control Point, Left hand – without fittings, from beginning of 1960.

U728RH Universal Remote Control Point, Right hand – without fittings, from beginning of 1960.
732 Straight Centre Isolating rail – 88mm, Trix Express, from end of 1962.
733 Curved Centre Isolating rail – 24 degrees = 4/5 of full radius 1 rail, Trix Express, from end of 1962.
735 Centre Rail Contact Strip – Trix Express, from end of 1962.
737 Curved Centre Isolating rail – 24 degrees = 4/5 of full radius 2 rail – Trix Express – from end of 1962.
802 Curved rail – 24 degrees = 4/5 of full radius 2 rail.
804 Curved rail – 30 degrees = full radius 2 rail.
806 Curved rail – 6 degrees = 1/5 of full radius 2 rail.
20/15 Transition rail – 183.5mm for joining bakelite track to the new 'Fibre' track.

One major factor in the design of the Trix Express Points was the short curve adopted which was equal to 4/5 of the length of a standard radius 1 curved rail. This enabled the use of close parallel tracks without any manipulation of other rails at the crossovers as in the case of the pre-war points. A 1/5 length radius 1 curve, Cat. No. 706, was included with each point to make up a full curve if desired. Initially the Remote Control Points were activated by a small push-pull solenoid assembly connected by a spring to the moving blade assembly. This enabled a train to be driven against the point as the weight of the locomotive and wagons would push the blade assembly over.

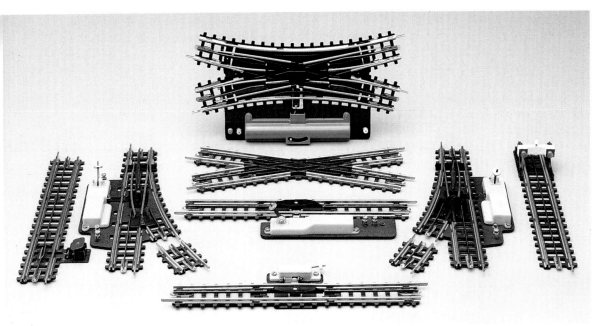

Various fibre-based type track units. The Universal Point is on the left with the earlier Point on the right. The Trix Express Double Slip has a plastic base.

The first British 'Fibre' Remote Control Points were more or less the same as the Trix Express versions, except that in place of the illuminated point lamp, a point lever was fitted to the light grey plastic cover of the point solenoid assembly, although the shape of the bitumen paper base still showed where the mechanical and electrical connections for the lamp would have been. Within a year these point lamp connection points were blanked out on the bitumen paper base. The British Hand-Operated Points were built on similar bitumen paper bases and were the same mechanically as the Remote versions.

The above rail system was designed primarily for use with Trix locomotives and rolling stock with the coarse wheel flanges, and, unfortunately, scale wheels could only be used on the basic track units and not on the points. To overcome this problem the frog moulding and movable blade assembly were redesigned to enable both standard Trix and scale wheels to be run over the points. These new points were given the name 'Universal'. At the same time the movable blade pivot plate was altered together with the solenoid linkage. This resulted in

the blades, once operated, being rigidly fixed in the position required. However derailments still occurred if a locomotive was operated 'against' the point. These Universal Points were on sale in the shops during the spring of 1959, but problems were initially experienced with the movable blade pivot plate which allowed the centre rail collector shoe to drop too low and snag on other parts. This was overcome at the end of 1959 by adding a ridge at the centre of the pivot-plate moulding. At approximately the same time, the large central frog rail was modified and received a ridge on the top face. Various other unimportant production method changes were also carried out. The Diamond Crossing and Trix Express Double Slip, the latter having a plastic base, were never modified for scale wheel running.

The British Remote Uncoupler Rail Ramp was operated by the same solenoid assembly as used for the Points except that the mechanical linkage was different. However unlike the Hand-Operated Points, the Hand-Operated Uncoupler Rail used a different and very much smaller assembly. The Buffer Rail buffer beam and support frame assembly were plastic mouldings held on to a standard straight rail by a keyed metal plate. Turned metal buffers were fitted to the buffer beam. The Transition Rail was initially constructed on a bitumen paper base, but in 1961, with large stocks of redundant bakelite Straight Rail Bases remaining, it was decided to convert them to Transition Rails. The Transition Rail was sometimes quoted with a catalogue number of 20/15P, which was an imported Trix Express rail. As a point of interest, during the mid-1950s full Straight Rails were constructed in Germany as an experiment using bitumen paper as the base and brass-plated centre rails were also used together with brass-plated rail retaining plates.

With the change in ownership to the Courtaulds Group in 1963 came a change in the catalogue numbering system. Basically most of the track units just received the prefix number 1 to the original catalogue number but a few were changed completely as listed below:

Old Cat. No.	New Cat. No.
20/15	1715
U727LH	1726
U727RH	1727
U728LH	1728
U728RH	1729
802	1721
804	1722
806	1723

With the addition of Trix Express locomotives and rolling stock into the British range in 1963, it was felt necessary to provide a Manual Uncoupling rail for use with the Trix Express couplings. This unit, Cat. No. 1738 was an imported Trix Express item.

By 1966 the following had been removed from the catalogues and price lists: Catalogue numbers 1709, 1715, 1718, 1719, 1720, 1732, 1733, 1737, 1738. All other items were gradually phased out up to and including 1969.

Fibre-Based Track Formation Sets

Available with the introduction of the Fibre-based track in Britain in 1957 were the following Track Formation Supplementary sets designed to add to the basic oval track, as supplied in many train sets, to enable more ambitious layouts to be constructed:

Cat. No. 768 Containing 7 x 701, 4 x 703, 4 x 708, 12 x 804 rails plus Hand Uncoupler and two pairs of Hand-Operated Points.

Cat. No. 769 Containing 7 x 701, 4 x 703, 4 x 708, 12 x 804 rails plus Remote Control Uncoupler and two pairs of Remote Control Points.

The following supplementary set was introduced in 1960:

Cat. No. 770 1 x 704, 1 x 701, 1 x 716, 1 x Hand-Operated Right-hand Point.

All sets were withdrawn from the price lists in 1963.

The Trix Overhead Catenary System

With the EM1 Bo-Bo locomotive came the Trix Catenary equipment. This in effect allowed three locomotives to be independantly controlled using the Trix Twin system of track and control. The catenary masts were simple black plastic mouldings which at the base fitted into special tinplate track clips (location plates being a better description), whose lugs located the clip between the 'fibre' rail sleepers. The arm of the mast was fitted with a tinplate catenary wire retainer which on the terminal mast was fed by a wire from a spring-loaded terminal. Extension girders enabled two tracks to be

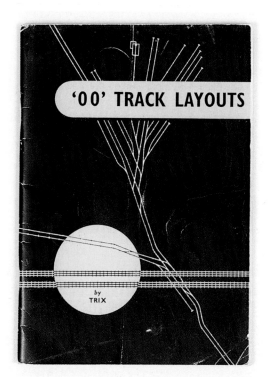

Layout plans for the Fibre track. The Trix book was published by Ewart Holdings Ltd but was more or less a direct copy of the Trix Express edition and thus subject to Copyright 1956 - Trix V.S.E.V.K.G. Nuremberg. The Beatibook No.1 was published in 1960 and incorporated similar layouts.

straddled, whilst wire joining clips enabled crossings and branches to be made at any point on the catenary wire, (0.04" diameter tinned iron wire 14" long). With the use of two-rail track in 1963 to a completely new design, it meant that the dimensions and lugs on the track clip had to be altered. Below is a list of the basic units with the first catalogue number corresponding to that given in the spring of 1959 or 1960, and the change in catalogue numbers in 1963 being given by the second number. The dates give inclusive years of official availability.

Cat. No.

B5, 1401   Standard Masts – initially 1 doz, later sold singly. (1959-1971)

B6, 1403   Set of Wires, 1 doz. (1959-1971)

B7, 1405   Extension Girders, 1 doz. (1959-1971)

B8, 1406   Wire Joining Clips, 1 doz. (1959-1971)

B7/B8   Extension Girders with Wire Joining Clips – 6 of each. (1960-1963)

B9, 1402   Terminal Mast. (1959-1971)

B10, 1404   Track Clips – 3-rail. Sold in packs of 1 doz. from 1961. (1960 – 1971)

—, 1408   Track Clips – 2-rail. 1 doz. (1964-1971)

Sets and contents below were listed in 1959 only:

Set O1 11 x Standard Masts, 1 x Terminal Mast, 1 x set of Wires, 12 x Track Clips (3-rail), 1 x 31/85 coil of wire.

Set O2 12 x Standard Masts, 9 x Extension Girders, 12 x Track Clips (3-rail), 1 x set of Wires.

Set O3 Sets O1 and O2 combined.

The British Trix 2-Rail Track

In 1964 designs were completed for a range of 2-rail scale track based on the Trix International track introduced in Germany at the same time. The nickel-silver rails used were of a section that would not accept the old Trix wheels with deep flanges. Unfortunately problems arose with production, and G. & R. Wrenn Ltd, who at this time were associated with the Courtaulds Group, were given the task of assembling most of the track units including the machining of certain parts used on the Points. Production only continued for about one year as one problem followed another resulting in commercial failure. Not all the track units advertised were produced, and below is a list of the British Trix track items that were actually manufactured and available from 1965.

Cat. No.

1501 Straight Rail, 7 ¼"

1502 ¾-Curve, radius 1 (radius as per Fibre track)

1503 ¼-Straight Rail, 2"

1504 Full Curve, radius 1

Catenary extension girders, terminal and standard masts.

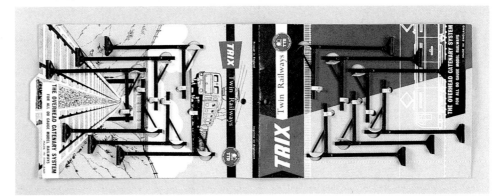

Opened pack of Catenary containing 11 standard masts and 1 terminal mast.

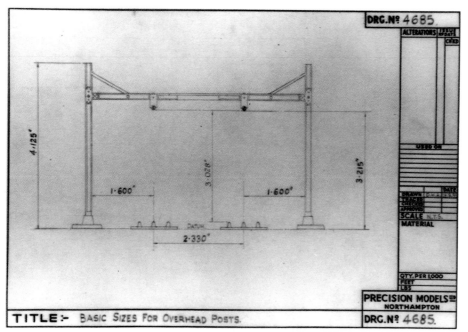

The geometry of the catenary system.

Showing use of the Catenary Extension Girders. Notice the Universal Hand Operated Points.

An exhibition layout circa 1959 in use with a style of Catenary Mast not adopted for production.

1505 Uncoupler Rail Hand Operated
1506 ¼-Curve, radius 1
1508 Straight Rail, 32"
1516 Buffer Rail, 74"
1521 ¾-Curve, radius 2 (radius as per Fibre track)
1522 Full Curve, radius 2
1523 ¼-Curve, radius 2
1526 Left-Hand Manual Point including 1506
1527 Right-Hand Manual Point including 1506
1528 Left-Hand Electric Point including 1506
1529 Right-Hand Electric Point including 1506
1531 Isolating Fish Plate

All other items, except the 14½" Straight Rail Cat. No.1500, shown in the catalogues and price lists were part of the Trix International range which, from 1968, were listed with their German

Trix catalogue number. To describe the Trix International range of track would clearly be beyond the scope of this book.

The geometry of the British Trix track remained as before. The units were built upon a brown plastic base moulded at the British Lego factory in Wrexham. Printed circuit boards were used in the Electric Points to mount the push-pull solenoid assembly, and the complete circuit board and solenoid assembly could be purchased separately to convert the Manual Points to electric – Cat. No. 1524 for a right-hand point and Cat. No. 1525 for a left-hand point, complete with printed instruction sheet. The points were constructed with a radius 1 curve but were supplied complete with a ¼-curve

to make up a full radius 1 curve. The Hand Uncoupler mechanism was virtually the same as used on the Fibre Rail Hand Uncoupler, and the Buffer Beam assembly although it had a brown frame was no different from that used previously except for minor fixing modifications. All rails used fish plates for joining two lengths together. All the British Trix track units were discontinued from 1968, except the Buffer Rail which continued until 1971.

The Trix Twin Super Track

The British Trix 1965 catalogue heralded the Trix Twin Super Track with a plastic base and solid nickel-silver rail section. This was actually imported Trix Express 3-rail track as first shown in the 1964 Trix Express catalogue and suitable for running

locomotives and rolling stock of all periods fitted with standard Trix wheels. The Points and Diamond Crossing would not accept scale wheels which were catered for with the Trix International range of track units. Despite being somewhat limited by being dedicated to the Trix Express system, this range had a comprehensive unit track system of excellent quality, which gave TTR enthusiasts a chance to provide a smooth and efficient track for their locomotives and rolling stock. In fact at the time of writing (1993), it is still produced at the factory of Trix Mangold GmbH in Nuremberg. Once again it is felt that a detailed description of this track and accessories is beyond the scope of this book. The track was offered in the British catalogues and price lists up to and including 1969.

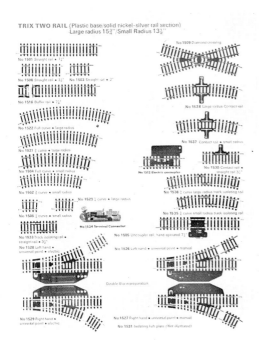

The 2-rail track as shown in the 1967/68 catalogue.

Trix Express Super Track and the British Trix 2-rail track.

GENERAL PACKAGING

Packaging has two main functions – to protect goods from damage and, where necessary, to attract the eye of a potential customer. Trix packaging definitely fulfilled both of these criteria. The main colour, used from the conception of the Trix toy/model railway system until the late 1950s, was red. The 1935/36 Twin Train sets were supplied in strong red cardboard boxes with metal corner reinforcements. The British Trix Twin sets came in long narrow boxes enabling a full length train to be displayed and yet allowing enough space to store a second train with coaches or wagons and a second controller. These boxes were not as strong as the German-made Twin Train boxes and were covered with a an enamelled paper called Celilynd, generally in red except for the special Southern Electric set which was in green. These long boxes continued in use until 1939 when there was a move to revert to square boxes, which were covered in normal red paper, as track was no longer included. The pre-war presentation sets were supplied in an attaché case style of box with a dark blue leather-cloth covering, these probably being the finest examples of packaging that any model railway set has ever received. A later version of this presentation case was finished in very dark green, but they were few in number.

Except for the scale-length coaches, the pre-war Trix Twin rolling stock, including most of the accessories, were supplied in thin plain cardboard boxes with shallow lids. Staples wrapped around the box corners were used to hold the butt-jointed box sides together in a similar fashion to the boxes used for the Trix Express rolling stock. The individual

Trix Twin 0-4-0 locomotives were similarly boxed but with full depth lids. A few of the accessories, including the Remote Control Signals, were contained in strong red boxes with full depth lids. Scale coaches received a conventionally constructed plain cardboard box with a full depth lid. When the German Trix company was involved with the manufacture of an item for the British range, it arrived in Britain already boxed with Trix Express labels advertising the contents, only to be covered over with Trix Twin Railway labels. The boxes containing the individual British Pacific and 4-4-0

A selection of box ends and styles.

locomotives with metal reinforcement corners were also manufactured in Germany. At the onset of war, purchase tax was imposed on a variety of goods and Trix items being subjected to this tax were over-stamped with a large 'X' on the box label.

After the war when sets were once again available, they were housed in the familiar red boxes which by 1948 had required hinged lids and were about 16" x 12", still giving space for a second train. The spacers for the partitions in these boxes were shaped pieces of blue-grey wood. By 1953 the box size was reduced to 13" x 12 ". In 1948 the boxes for the rolling stock and some accessories were maroon in colour and formed from folded thin cardboard with opening ends. They were affixed with a yellow TTR label with a representative picture of the particular item of rolling stock, although sometimes a pre-war model was shown. Individual locomotives were in plain cardboard boxes with the same type of descriptive label. By 1951 the rather flimsy rolling stock boxes were gradually replaced with a strong red box with a full depth lift-off lid and a small yellow TTR label applied to each end. This type of box was also used for the accessories. Individual 0-4-0 and 4-4-0 locomotives were packed into a normal buff coloured box, whilst the 'Scotsman' Pacific locomotive was packed into a red box with a resplendent specially designed label. The 2-4-2 Mixed Traffic locomotive (20/56) and the Diesel Flyer (20/58) were boxed (red) in Germany and applied with TTR labels in Britain.

The Meteor Diesel Unit received its own special box partitioned for each coach and the special controller (AC version only). A few were finished in red, but the majority in plain buff-coloured cardboard with an attractive label showing a picture

Pre-war Private Owner wagons and their boxes plus a red pre-1952 version.

Box for the SR Motor Coach showing label applied over original Trix Express labels.

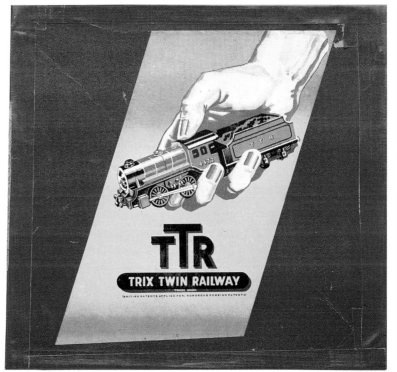

The colourful trademark applied to the red set boxes from 1938 until the post-war period.

409

of the pre-production model. As mentioned in an earlier chapter, the DC Meteor was also supplied with an oval of track in a shallow red box.

The basic bakelite track boxes in pre-war days were made from plain folded cardboard printed with the trademark, Patent information and other inscriptions advertising the virtues of the rails. Only the trademark and other minor printing details changed after the war.

Ewart Holdings Ltd, when they took over in 1957, reintroduced the long red set box made from good quality cardboard with yellow inserts for the new DC sets, plus the use of red boxes with an internal drop down flap (a legacy from the Whistling Coach set) for the locomotives. The rolling stock continued with the red boxes introduced in 1952. However, the boxes containing 'Fibre' track were a distinctive yellow printed with a repeated pattern made from a red TTR circular logo and black wavy track. The boxes containing the larger radius track, and occasionally other items of track, were coloured green with the same printed design.

Dufay Ltd redesigned the packaging in 1958 and provided a display-type box with a cellophane window for all the rolling stock and some of the locomotives. The black, green and red printed design on the box included a representation of a Britannia Class locomotive, the model of which Dufay Ltd were very proud. The sets also carried a similar design on the box lid, these boxes being made from rather flimsy printed cardboard in comparison to the very strong earlier 'red' boxes which had gained a good reputation for durability. The very early display boxes for the rolling stock, etc, were easy to open at the ends with the outside flap, fitted

with a small tongue, folding over the normal inside flat. On later versions, the outside flap, now fitted with a large tongue, was folded over two interlocking flaps, making access difficult without first opening the display part of the box.

With the formation of Trix Products Ltd came the beginning of a rather confusing design period. The boxes containing the track were now predominantly a light blue with design features picked out in red and white and with the name of Trix Products Ltd on the sides. The Dufay display type of boxes continued to be used for the locomotives and rolling stock, and when British Trix Ltd was formed the display boxes used for the rolling stock were gradually replaced by a basic folded box with a printed design similar to the Trix Products Ltd track boxes but with the name of British Trix on the sides. All three designs were used under British Trix with Dufay and Trix Products boxes receiving a British Trix over-stamp on the ends.

In 1965 a complete revision of the box designs took place. The basic colours were now a striking combination of yellow and black with many of the larger box lids receiving an appropriate black and white artistic impression. On the box lids of the train sets was an artist's impression of a family enjoying operating the train set.

The rolling stock boxes were initially of the plain folded type, but later the wagon boxes received a cellophane display panel and were made a little larger. When the name of the product was changed to Trix Trains in 1968, the coaches and locomotives were contained in long display-type yellow and black boxes which were not much different to the earlier British Trix boxes, except for the way that the

name TRIX TRAINS was printed using black lined yellow and white letters.

For a while Liliput Model Railways (UK) Ltd continued to utilise the remaining stocks of Trix Trains boxes until they were replaced with Liliput boxes from Austria. The boxes for the coaches and locomotives, usually a polystyrene base for the locomotive boxes, had a dark brown glazed wood-grain effect lid, whilst the wagons were boxed in light wood-grain effect display boxes which were eventually intermingled in circa 1980 by clear moulded plastic boxes. From 1988 plain white cardboard boxes were used for the locomotives.

A selection of Packing Slips.

SPARE PARTS

An important feature of a successful product is the availability of replacement parts should the need arise, and in the case of the Trix model railway, other small but essential ancillary items such as plugs, wire, special oil, etc. Trix dealers in Britain usually stocked a range of such parts neatly packaged in small matchbox-sized cardboard boxes or packets, with a few in the very early days of Trix Express packed in boxwood boxes with sliding covers. In the pre-war years nearly all the locomotive spares were Trix Express, and during 1935/36 the box labels on the lid were pink with a line drawing of the part, or parts, enclosed. The catalogue number on each box was the German version starting with the number 30/...

From 1937 the spares and other small parts were supplied in white cardboard packets of slightly smaller size to the early Trix Express boxes, and these carried a white Trix Twin Railway label stating their contents and catalogue numbers which started with 31/... After the war most of the spares were of British manufacture except those used used for the 'Scotsman' Pacific, 2-4-2 Mixed Traffic and Diesel Flyer locomotives which originated from Germany. Slightly larger white cardboard boxes were used with a yellow label displaying the round TTR logo and contents information, the latter mostly printed on the label but occasionally found rubber stamped with or without a label. With the introduction of the SP range of spares in the Dufay period, the cardboard packets were replaced with labelled clear plastic bags. By this time most retailers only obtained spares to special order, except for basic items such as collector shoes, etc., which were usually held as a stock item. After British Trix Ltd was formed, the

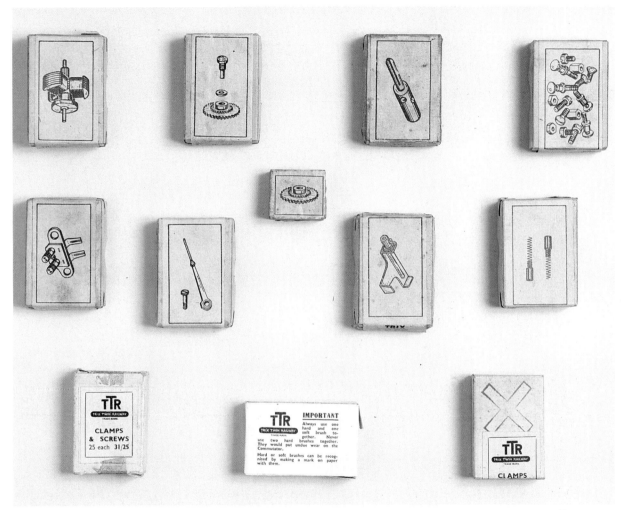

retailers were all given a large list of available spares, although these were not listed in the catalogues or spare parts lists available to the general public. Accordingly, it is felt that the British Trix range of spares does not come within the scope of this book. On the following pages is a list of the readily available Trix Twin spare parts listed in catalogues and other literature.

Pre-war Trix Express and TTR spares boxes.

411

Post-war TTR spares boxes.

Cat. No. Pre-war	
31/1	Armature with Commutator
31/2	Piston Rods and Arms
31/3	2 sets of Reduction Gears with Bolts and Washers
31/5	Reversing Control Shaft
31/10	Reversing Arm and Pawl with Pin
31/12	Assortment of Screws, Nuts and Engine Buffers
31/15	5 Coupling Hooks, 10 Links
31/20	25 Coupling Links
31/25	25 each Rail Clamps and Screws
31/27	Set of Carbon Brushes, 2 soft and 1 hard
31/30	Motor Side Frame
31/36	4 pairs of Bakelite Wheels
31/40	1 set of Collector Shoes (0-4-0)
31/50	6 Plugs
31/57/40	1 set of Collector Shoes for British 4-6-2 Pacific locos and German 20/57 and 20/59 Pacific locos
31/58/40	1 set of Collector Shoes for SR Motor Coach and 20/58 Diesel Flyer
31/75	2 Spare Electric Bulbs, 14 volt
31/78	1 Bottle of Shell Trix Oil
31/85	1 Coil of Wire
31/88	Bulb for Remote Control Electric Signal
31/90	Uncoupler Strikers and Links
31/94	Contact Shoes for Coach Lighting
31/99	TTR Instruction Book
31/200	Track Manual
31/212	Many-Ways Handbook

ACCESSORIES

Post-war, up to 1960

Cat. No.	Description
30/2/4	1 pair of Cylinders for Cat. No. 20/56 2-4-2
30/2/5	1 pair of Piston Rods with Crosshead and Connecting rods for 2-4-2
30/5/2	Reversing Contact Shaft for Diesel Flyer Cat. No. 20/58
30/5/3	Reversing Contact Shaft for Cat. No. 1/540 locomotive
30/5/4	Reversing Contact Shaft for Cat. No. 20/56 2-4-2
30/8L	Left Cylinder with Gearing for Cat. No. 1/540 Pacific
30/8R	Right Cylinder with Gearing for Cat. No. 1/540 loco
30/9/2h	Rear Bogie for 2-4-2
30/9/2v	Front Bogie for 2-4-2
30/12/2	3 Screws for Body and 2 long and 2 short Screws for Cranks, for 2-4-2
30/13	6 Screws for Wheel Bosses, 3 Screws for Body, for Cat. No. 1/540 Pacific
30/30/5	Motor Frame Assembly for 2-4-2
30/31/2	Right Hand Gear Plate for 2-4-2
30/40/2	Collector Shoes for Diesel Flyer20/58
30/40/4	Collector Shoes for 2-4-2 locomotive
30/41v	Lamp Holder, Front for 2-4-2
30/41h	Lamp Holder, Rear for 2-4-2

Oil plugs and wire.

Cat. No.	Description
30/57/1	Armature and Commutator for Cat. Nos. 1/540 and 20/56 locomotives
30/57/9	Trailing Bogie and Wheels for Cat. No. 1/540 Pacific
30/57/10	Reversing Arm and Pawl for Cat. No. 1/540 Pacific
30/57/27	Carbon Brushes and Springs for Cat. No. 1/540 Pacific
30/57/30	Motor Side Frame for Cat. No. 1/540 Pacific
30/57/31	Offside Gear Plate for Cat. No. 1/540 Pacific
30/72/1	Light Bulb for 2-4-2 locomotive
31/1	Armature with Commutator for 0-4-0s
31/2	1 pair of Piston Rods and Arms
31/3	Reduction Gear with Bolt
31/4	1 pair of American Piston Rods and Arms
31/5	Reversing Contact Shaft
31/10	Reversing Arm and Pawl.
31/12	Assortment of Screws and Buffers
31/15	5 Coupling Hooks (cast) and 10 Links
31/16	New Couplings for Locomotives
31/17	Uncoupler Couplings for 4-Wheel Wagons, Floating Axle
31/18	Couplings for Scale Model Coaches
31/19	Coupling Sets for Conversions
31/20	25 Coupling Links
31/25	25 each Rail Clamps and Screws
31/27	1 pair of Carbon Brushes and Springs
31/30	Motor Side Frame Assembly
31/36	4 pairs of Bakelite Wheels

Cat. No.	Description
31/40	1 set of Collector Shoes for 0-4-0 locomotive
31/45	Suppressor for Generator
31/50	6 Plugs
31/53	Collector Shoes for Lighted Goods Brake
31/60	Set of 2 Bogies for American Wagons
31/61	Set of 2 Bogies for American Coaches
31/72	Socket for 14 volt Bulbs Cat. No. 31/74
31/74	14 volt Bulb for Cat. Nos. 752, 756, etc., plus 9/520, etc.
31/77	Special Resistance Lamp for Indicating Check Switch
31/78	Bottle of Shell Trix Oil
31/85	Coil of Wire
31/88	14 volt Bulb for Cat. Nos. 732 + 736 Signals
31/94	3 Collector Shoes for Coach Lighting
31/99	TTR Instruction Book
31/200	Track Manual
31/285	Trix Table Top Plan
31/300	Track Layout Book
31/303	Year Book and Catalogue (1954, 1955, 1956)
57/40	1 set of Collector Shoes for 4-4-0 or 4-6-2 loco
57/42	Brushes for Brit./ Class V
57/54	3-Strand Cable and 3-Pin Plug for Cat. No. 1/540
57/55	Tyres for Diesel Shunter
57/57	Rubber tyres for Brit./ Class V
57/58	Shoes for Brit./ Class V
74/40	Collector Shoes for Whistle Coach
77/27	Brushes for Meteor
77/40	Collector Shoes for Meteor
77/70	Collector Shoes for Meteor

ACCESSORIES

From 1960 to 1962 inclusive

SP.2	Reversing Control Shaft, AC
SP.3	Reversing Arm and Pawl, AC
SP.4	Reversing Pawl Retaining Arm and Spring, AC
SP.5	Reversing Coil and Magnet, AC
SP.6	Motor Coil and Magnet, AC
SP.7	Reduction Gear and Screw, AC
SP.9	Motor Side Frame, 0-4-0 and 4-4-0, AC
SP.10	Brush Caps
SP.12	Set of 1 Carbon and 1 Gauze Brush and Spring
SP.13	Set of Brushes for 6 volt DC Cadet Motor
SP.14	Set of Brushes for 12 volt Main Line Motor
SP.15	Suppressor for AC locomotives
SP.16	Suppressor for 6 volt DC locomotives
SP.18	Suppressor for 12 volt DC locomotives
SP.19	Set of Collector Shoes for 0-4-0 AC locomotives
SP.20	Set of Collector Shoes for 4-4-0 AC & D.C. & 4-6-2 DC locomotives
SP.21	Set of Collector Shoes for Meteor
SP.22	Set of Collector Shoes for 6 volt Cadet
SP.23	Set of Collector Shoes for 12 volt 0-6-2 Tank loco.
SP.24	Set of Collector Shoes for 12 volt Britannia, Class V & Diesel Shunter
SP.25	Set of Collector Shoes for Bo-Bo and Warship Class
SP.26	Set of Collector Shoes for Lighted Goods Brake
SP.27	Set of Collector Shoes for Lighted Coaches
SP.28	Set of centre contacts for F106 Warship locomotive
SP.31	Piston and Connecting Rods and Screws for 0-4-0 AC
SP.32	Piston and Connecting Rods and Screws for 0-4-0 DC
SP.33	Piston and Connecting Rods and Screws for 0-4-0 Cadet
SP.34	Piston and Connecting Rods and Screws for 0-4-0 AC American type
SP.35	Piston and Connecting Rods and Screws for 4-4-0 AC or DC Pytchley and Schools locomotives.
SP.36	Piston and Connecting Rods and Screws for 4-4-0 or DC Midland Compound locomotive
SP.37	Connecting Rods and Screws for Diesel Shunter
SP.38	Connecting Rods and Screws for Class V and 0-6-2 Tank
SP.39	Connecting Rods and Screws for Britannia locomotive
SP.40	Assortment of Screws and Buffers for AC locomotives
SP.41	Assortment of Screws for DC locomotives
SP.42	25 Clamps and Screws for Bakelite Track
SP.43	Tyres for 0-4-0, 4-4-0 and 0-6-2 locomotives
SP.44	Tyres for Diesel Shunter
SP.45	Tyres for Bo-Bo and Warship locomotives
SP.46	Tyres for Britannia and Class V locomotives
SP.47	Gear Assembly kit for Cadet
SP.48	Gear Assembly for 12 volt 0-4-0 and 4-4-0 locomotives
SP.49	Gear Assembly for Britannia and Class V locomotives
SP.50	Gear Assembly for 0-6-2 Tank Engine
SP.51	Pantograph
SP.52	Coupling Hooks for locomotives, 1 hole
SP.53	Coupling Hooks for 4-Wheel Wagons, Old Type 2 holes
SP.54	Coupling Hooks with Boss for Scale Model Coaches
SP.55	Coupling Hooks for Cadet Wagons and Bogie Stock
SP.56	Coupling Hooks, New Type, for 0-6-2 Tank and New Plastic Rolling Stock
SP.57	Bulbs, 14 volt, packets of 50
SP.58	Bulbs, 14 volt, singles or less than 50. (This is a pricing reference)
SP.59	Resistance Bulb for Indicating Check Switch
SP.60	Special Bulb for Cat. Nos. 732,736 and 20/56
SP.61	Sockets for 14 volt Bulbs, packet of 50
SP.62	Sockets for 14 volt Bulbs, singles or less than 50. (This is a pricing reference)
SP.64	Bottle of Special Oil
SP.65	2-Rail Conversion Springs, Britannia and Class V
SP.66	2-Rail Conversion Springs, 0-6-2
SP.67	0-6-0 conversion springs
SP.68	Scale Wheels for Britannia and Class V
SP.69	Conversion Couplings
SP.70	4 Pairs of Bakelite Wheels on Axles, (ex 31/36)
SP.71	Coils of Wire, (ex 31/85)
SP.72	Coach scale wheels on axle point bearing
SP.73	Coach Trix wheels on axle point bearing
SP.74	Coupling hook for plastic coaches – 1 pair
SP.75	Commonwealth bogie
SP.76	12 volt DC motor
SP.77	4 pairs scale wheels for metal coaches and goods wagons

414

APPENDIX 1. TRADEMARKS

The registration of trademarks is an important step which must be taken by companies to protect their product name. Some of the Trix trademarks are listed here, (not diagrammatically), with the date that they were first registered. Certain of those mentioned below are still in use at the time of compilation.

Germany

A) The name TRIX was first registered on 1.9.1930.

B) TRIX-EXPRESS - 15.1.1935.

C) The picture of a hand holding a locomotive with the name TRIX EXPRESS below, (as used on train set lids), was registered 15.3.1937.

D) TTR and the name TRIX TWIN RAILWAY in one logo 22/11/1937.

E) MINITRIX - 6/12/1966.

Britain.

F) TRIX as used for the Construction system was registered 13.3.1933 but claimed from 12.1.1931.

G) TRICYTRIX as used for the Construction system on 7.6.1932.

H) SCIENTRIX on 6.11.1933.

I) TRIX as used for model railway items on 26.5.1938.

J) TRIX TWIN RAILWAY on 26.5.1938.

K) TRIX TWIN RAILWAY around the top part of a circle enclosing the fronts of two locomotives in silhouette above the letters TTR - 11.7.1939.

L) TRIX as used on bicycle parts on 21.3.1945.

M) TRIX as used for model aircraft, model watercraft and model road vehicles - 6.6.1945.

N) TRIX TWIN RAILWAY around the inside top of a circle also enclosing two locomotive fronts in silhouette above the letters TTR - 25.6.1945.

O) TRIX as used on locks and padlocks on 24.10.1945.

P) TRIX as used on toy models on 2.12.1952.

Q) TRIX METEOR - 12.1.1954.

R) TRIX TWIN CADET - 25.1.1957.

S) TRIX PICCADILLY CIRCUS as used for model signalling apparatus and mechanical advertising signs and similar - 26.4.1960.

T) TRIX, as used in 14) on 3.5.1960.

U) MINITRIX - 6.12.1966.

Trademark used by Andreas Förtner & Haffner which continued to be used by Trix in Germany on the Construction Sets and Boats in pre-war years.

F) First registered in Britain in 1931.

B) First registered in Germany in 1935

TRIX-EXPRESS

D) First registered in Germany in 1937.

K) First registered in Britain in 1939.

N) First registered in Britain in 1945.

L) First registered in Britain in 1945. Used on Bicycle parts.

1962–1963

APPENDIX 2.
RELEVANT BRITISH PATENT SPECIFICATIONS

Below are the known granted British Patents appertaining to the Trix model railway. The description following the Patent number relates to the relevant part of the Trix system but does not necessarily suggest the title. The dates given are the application date, (United Kingdom), and the accepted (granted) date respectively. The name(s) to whom the Patent was granted including inventor(s) where known, is given by key letters corresponding to the names given at the end of the list.

Patent Specification.

451,644 Original pre-war coupling with wire link. – 23/1/1936, 14.1.1937. (A)

459,744 Bakelite track.–23.1.1936,14.1.1937. (A)

465,168 Two trains running independently on one track with a centre rail– 31.10.1935, 30.4.1937. (A)

469,656 Addition to Patent 465,168 – Method of current collection on the 3-rail track. – 26.9.1936, 29.7.1937. (A, B)

471,304 Uncoupling device which dropped part of a rail to uncouple the wagons etc. – not used – 19.1.1937, 1.9.1937. (A)

485,170 Manyways Station System – 12.11.1936, 12.5.1938. (B, E)

488,357 Changing lights on 2-coach Diesel Unit, Cat. No. 20.58 – 4.1.1938, 5.7.1938. (A)

489,719 Remote control points – 2.2.1937, 2.8.1938. (A)

496,515 Scale time clock and locomotive speed control – not used – 12.8.1937, 1.12.1938. (A)

498,651 Pacific locomotive tender remote uncoupling device as fitted to 'Princess' etc. – 26.3.1838, 11.1.1939. (A)

499,554 Remote uncoupler rail – 26.3.1938, 25.1.1939. (A)

510,121 A device which does not allow a momentary break in the current supply to affect the locomotive reversing relay – not used – 27.9.1938, 27.7.1940. (C, T)

521,348 Construction of Pacific wheels – 14.11.1938, 20.5.1940. (C, T)

525,046 Locomotive uncoupling device – not used – 14.2.1939, 20.8.1940. (C, T)

525,308 Two aspect colour light – abortive British 1939 production – 16.2.1940, 26.8.1940. (B, D)

528,222 Extendable Bakelite rail – not made – 26.4.1940, 24.10.1940. (B)

545,033 New British Bakelite track with 'U' section rail as used on post-war Points – 7.4.1941, 7.5.1942. (E, F)

547,560 Modification the the reversing mechanism of the AC 0-4-0 locomotive chassis using a flywheel – not used – 8.9.1941, 2.9.1942. (G)

605,283 The post-war style of coupling adopted by Trix in Britain – 4.12.1946, 20.7.1948. (H)

607,562 Improvements for fixing rail sections to Bakelite base on new type British post-war track – 8.2.1946, 1.9.1948. (D, E)

619,481 Small electric motors as used in the Junior.Cadet locomotives – 12.12.1946, 9.3.1949. (J, K)

644,346 Post-war British point – 14.7.1948, 11.10.1950. (D, E, L)

644,540 Special terminal blocks – not used – 16.7.1948, 11.10.1950. (D, E, L)

A Machinery(Smith's Patents) Ltd. Patent reference drawing regarding the marking stamps.

646,770 Addition to Patent 644,540 Post-war British Points - 22.12.1948, 29.11.1950. (D, E, L, M, N, O)
646,975 Improvements to electrical terminals – not used – 14.7.1948, 29.11.1950. (D, E, L)
678,257 Post-war 'Scotsman' Pacific tender uncoupler – 12.3.1951, 27.8.1952. (E, L)
726,723 Elevator Conveyor – 22.4.1953, 23.3.1955. (B, E, L)
733,920 Remote stopping and starting of clockwork locomotive – not used – 16.3.1953, 20.7.1955. (B, E, P)
734,415 Electric.mechanical plug and socket locomotive to tender coupling – not used – 14.5.1952, 3.8.1955. (B, D, E)
737,213 Dump wagon and magnetic rail – 22.4.1953, 21.9.1955. (E, L)
737,214 Indicating check switch – 22.4.1953, 21.9.1955. (D, E, L)
757,222 Power supply unit with wiper on secondary winding of transformer – not used in Britain – 19.10.1953, 19.9.1956. (Q, R)
767,059 Sound generator for use in Meteor and Whistle Coach –18.11.1954, 30.1.1955.(B, D, E, L)
870,202 Cadet controller – 6.2.1957, 14.6.1961. (B, S)
877,102 Switch for superimposing AC on DC similar to that used for the Meteor – 26.6.1956, 13.9.1961. (L, S)
1,029,416 New design for transformer, rectifier control unit – not used in British units – 24.4.1964, 11.5.1966. (C, U, V, W, X)

Key to letters
A) Vereinigte Spielwarenfabriken Andreas Förtner & J. Haffner's Nachfolger GmbH
B) Siegfried Kahn
C) Ernst Voelk
D) Francis John Prior
E) Trix Ltd
F) Robert Bindon Blood
G) William Henry Norris
H) Sydney Charles Pritchard
J) Roy Cyril Vaughan
K) James Reginald Rotheroe
L) Werner Alton
M) Francis Wilson Gratton
N) Thomas Francis Shaw
O) Gilbert Ernest Twining
P) Sydney William Dumbleton
Q) Rudolf Insam
R) Trix Vereinigte Spielwarenfabriken GmbH
S) Dufay Ltd
T) Vereinigte Spielwarenfabriken Andreas Förtner & J. Haffner's Nachfolger
U) Walter Voelk
V) Gunther Kurz
W) Wilhelm Stein
X) Trix Vereinigte Spielwarenfabriken Ernst Voelk KG

The following British Patent Specification numbers, plus year of acceptance, are for the Trix Construction system:
363,547 (1931), **383,087** (1932), **383,240**(1932), **413,963** (1934), **421,924** (1935).

A large number of German Patents were applied for and granted over the years to the relevant German or British Trix company and their employees. The ideas represented in the Patent Specification were not always used for the Trix system, (including Trix Metallbaukasten), but for reference purposes a list of the known German Patent Specification numbers with acceptance dates up to 1962 are listed here:

592,063 (1934), 594,781 (1934), 630,570 (1936), 630,571 (1936),
631,542 (1936), 638,112 (1936), 641,862 (1937), 658,233 (1938),
659,063 (1938), 690,175 (1940), 690,176 (1940), 690,177 (1940),
691,677 (1940), 691,678 (1940), 692,886 (1940), 695,314 (1940),
699,702 (1941), 701,362 (1941), 708,708 (1941), 714,678 (1941),
715,714 (1942), 716,366 (1942), 718,737 (1942), 720,965 (1942),
730,220 (1943), 731,115 (1943), 731,287 (1943), 768,130 (1955),
812,293 (1951), 839,467 (1952), 839,619 (1952), 847,123 (1952),
847,874 (1952), 874,262 (1953), 890,028 (1953), 893,626 (1953),
909,556 (1954), 933,496 (1955), 938,476 (1956), 938,477 (1956),
938,654 (1956), 938,655 (1956), 938,714 (1956), 938,836 (1956),
940,454 (1956), 941,355 (1956), 941,536 (1956), 945,824 (1956),
960,978 (1957), 968,449 (1958), 968,989 (1958), 969,756 (1958),
970,861 (1958), 975,632 (1962).

Many other provisional Patent Specifications were issued. The Patents above represent many weird and wonderful ideas on which another whole book could be written! Patents appertaining to Trix were applied for and granted in many other European countries as well as the United States of America. Some of the above Patents are exactly the same as those granted in Britain.

APPENDIX 3.
ZINC ALLOY 'FATIGUE'

The predominant alloy used for the diecast parts of Trix model railway items was always zinc based. Zinc is a good general purpose alloy that has been used extensively in the toy industry due to its good flow properties when casting enabling small detail to be accurately reproduced. Unfortunately impact strength is not so good, and, more seriously, the stability of the alloy during pre-war and, to a lesser degree early post-war days, was unpredictable depending on the composition of the zinc alloy used and the storage conditions of the finished product. Many of the diecastings were soon to be found in an expanded and distorted condition which culminated in their crumbling apart. This effect was, and still is, commonly known as 'fatigue'.

Although this problem occurred throughout the diecast toy industry, the effect on Trix items was widespread in both Germany and Britain. Apart from the locomotive diecast wheels, motor side frames and other parts, the main problems arose with the 'Coronation' tender body, the 'Coronation/Princess' tender chassis, post-war German 2-4-2 tank engine chassis (20/56) and the chassis used for the Blue BR 'Scotsman' and early Green BR 'Scotsman'. It is heartbreaking when one has located one of these scarce models only to find that the working parts have seized and the diecast chassis is only held together by its associated parts, not to mention the distortion of sound components caused by expansion. This problem fortunately had been eliminated by about 1953.

It was discovered in the USA that failure of zinc diecast alloys was mainly due to tin, lead and cadmium impurities finding their way into the alloy. All zinc, aluminium and magnesium diecastings experience shrinkage over long periods of time which in the case of zinc alloys is enhanced by a larger than normal presence of copper.

The most probable cause of 'fatigue' in mazak is caused by stress corrosion. When the liquid zinc alloy, including the dissolved lead and other impurities, solidifies quickly as it is diecast the lead content remains in solution. Over a period of time this lead gradually begins to come out of solution as tiny particles of pure lead with perhaps a change in volume of the metal. (Mazak alloys normally shrink by 0.015 to 0.08%). This hardens the metal and produces microscopic stresses throughout the entire casting known as precipitation hardening. The rate at which the lead will come out of solution depends on temperature. The higher the temperature the faster the hardening will occur. Thus a situation arises where two dissimilar metals are present – lead and zinc. Contact between two dissimilar metals in damp or wet conditions leads to corrosion. The greater the dissimilarity of metals and the more conductive the water, the faster the corrosion. Zinc is highly reactive, while lead, probably the most damaging impurity, is fairly inert. Thus in damp condition with these two metals in close contact at the points of microscopic stress, corrosion will occur fairly rapidly with the most likely corrosion product being zinc oxide.

After a large amount of research, manufacturers in the USA in the 1940s developed a stable zinc alloy called zamak, (or mazak in the UK). There are two basic forms of this alloy but for Trix use in Britain in the post-war years Mazak 3 was chosen which is very similar to Zamak 3. The percentage of

additives to the basic zinc plus restrictions on impurities for Mazak 3 are listed below:

Additives

Aluminium	3.8 to 4.3%
Copper	up to 0.03%
Magnesium	0.03 to 0.06%

Allowed impurities

Iron	maximum 0.1%
Nickel	maximum 0.02%
Manganese	maximum 0.01%
Lead	maximum 0.005%
Cadmium	maximum 0.005%
Tin	maximum 0.003%

The addition of magnesium helps to reduce susceptibility to inter-crystalline corrosion, but above the accepted percentage mechanical properties suffer, whilst the aluminium helps as a grain refiner. Copper increases the tensile strength and hardness but introduces dimensional instability.

On an analysis of a typical 'fatigued' 1950s 'Scotsman' Pacific chassis the following results were obtained:

Aluminium	3.7%
Copper	0.71%
Magnesium	0.03%
Lead	0.084%

Most of the remaining percentage is made up by zinc.

It can be seen from the above analysis that the level of lead is almost 17 times that recommended for a stable zinc alloy. As stated in the main text on locomotives the diecasting of the various component parts was not restricted to one manufacturer, and thus it is safe to say that during pre-war days some manufactures were more careful than others in their preparation of the zinc alloy. In the post-war period, in both Britain and Germany, the diecasters generally adopted the chemical composition of the mazak or zamak alloys. Unfortunately in Germany up to the early 1950s due to many manufacturing restrictions imposed on materials used in non-essential goods, some German diecasters could not produce the zinc alloy to the required specifications. This resulted in many 21/56 2-4-2 tank engines falling to pieces in a few months !

As a footnote, it is recommended that any of the early models using a zinc diecasting should be stored in a dry even temperature and kept away from moisture and other corrosive elements. Do not put them in an environment similar to an airing cupboard which has a greatly varying temperature coupled with humidity, the breeding ground for corrosion.

The effects of 'fatigue' can be clearly seen on the body taken from a pre-war German-outline Electric 0-4-0 locomotive, Cat. No. 20/55, and a wheel from an 0-4-0 AC chassis of the same period. (C)

The TRIX family tree

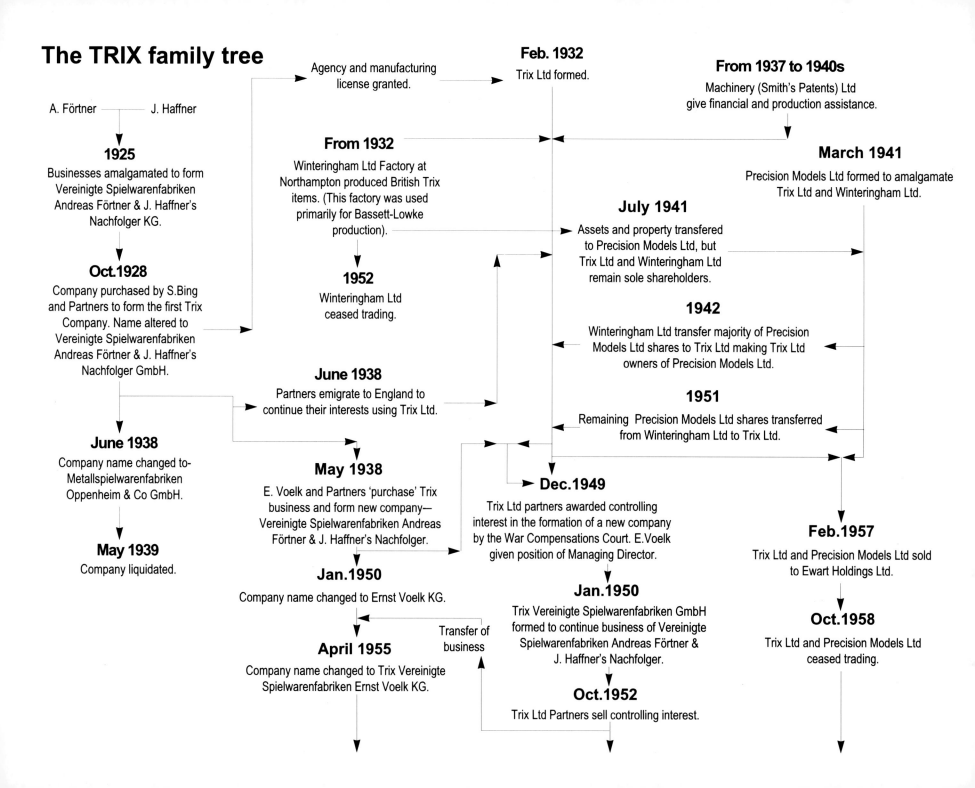

A. Förtner ——— J. Haffner

1925
Businesses amalgamated to form Vereinigte Spielwarenfabriken Andreas Förtner & J. Haffner's Nachfolger KG.

Oct.1928
Company purchased by S.Bing and Partners to form the first Trix Company. Name altered to Vereinigte Spielwarenfabriken Andreas Förtner & J. Haffner's Nachfolger GmbH.

June 1938
Company name changed to Metallspielwarenfabriken Oppenheim & Co GmbH.

May 1939
Company liquidated.

Agency and manufacturing license granted.

From 1932
Winteringham Ltd Factory at Northampton produced British Trix items. (This factory was used primarily for Bassett-Lowke production).

1952
Winteringham Ltd ceased trading.

June 1938
Partners emigrate to England to continue their interests using Trix Ltd.

May 1938
E. Voelk and Partners 'purchase' Trix business and form new company— Vereinigte Spielwarenfabriken Andreas Förtner & J. Haffner's Nachfolger.

Jan.1950
Company name changed to Ernst Voelk KG.

April 1955
Company name changed to Trix Vereinigte Spielwarenfabriken Ernst Voelk KG.

Transfer of business

Feb. 1932
Trix Ltd formed.

Dec.1949
Trix Ltd partners awarded controlling interest in the formation of a new company by the War Compensations Court. E.Voelk given position of Managing Director.

Jan.1950
Trix Vereinigte Spielwarenfabriken GmbH formed to continue business of Vereinigte Spielwarenfabriken Andreas Förtner & J. Haffner's Nachfolger.

Oct.1952
Trix Ltd Partners sell controlling interest.

From 1937 to 1940s
Machinery (Smith's Patents) Ltd give financial and production assistance.

March 1941
Precision Models Ltd formed to amalgamate Trix Ltd and Winteringham Ltd.

July 1941
Assets and property transfered to Precision Models Ltd, but Trix Ltd and Winteringham Ltd remain sole shareholders.

1942
Winteringham Ltd transfer majority of Precision Models Ltd shares to Trix Ltd making Trix Ltd owners of Precision Models Ltd.

1951
Remaining Precision Models Ltd shares transferred from Winteringham Ltd to Trix Ltd.

Feb.1957
Trix Ltd and Precision Models Ltd sold to Ewart Holdings Ltd.

Oct.1958
Trix Ltd and Precision Models Ltd ceased trading.

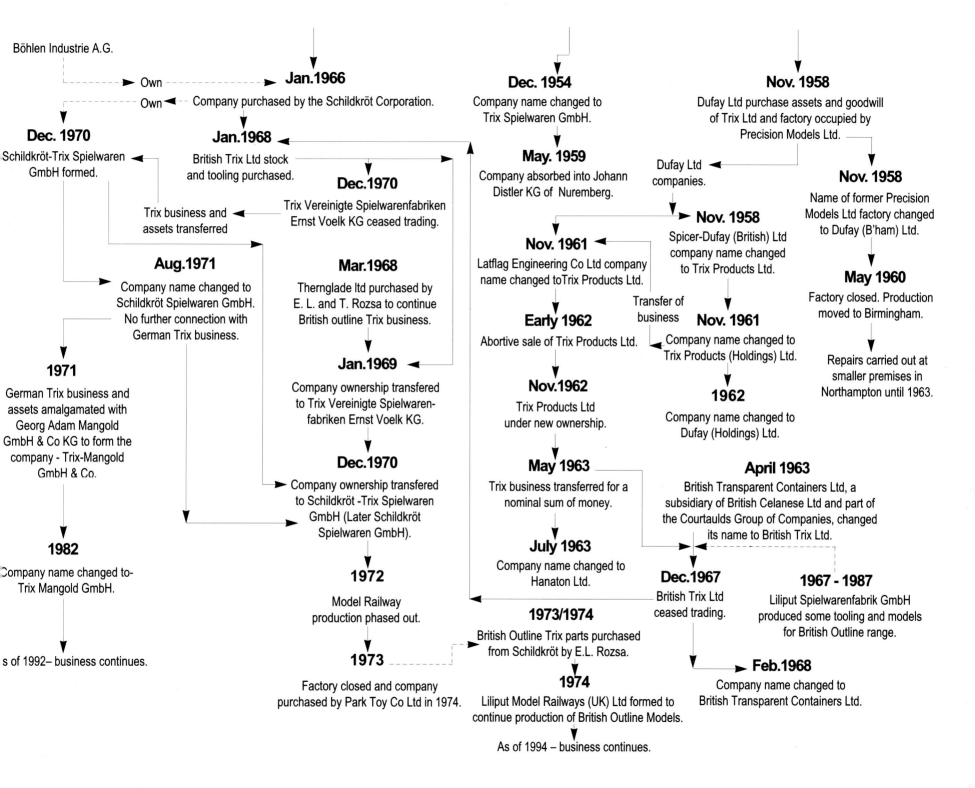

Böhlen Industrie A.G.

Own →

Own ←

Jan.1966
Company purchased by the Schildkröt Corporation.

Dec. 1970
Schildkröt-Trix Spielwaren GmbH formed.

Jan.1968
British Trix Ltd stock and tooling purchased.

Trix business and assets transferred

Dec.1970
Trix Vereinigte Spielwarenfabriken Ernst Voelk KG ceased trading.

Aug.1971
Company name changed to Schildkröt Spielwaren GmbH. No further connection with German Trix business.

Mar.1968
Thernglade ltd purchased by E. L. and T. Rozsa to continue British outline Trix business.

1971
German Trix business and assets amalgamated with Georg Adam Mangold GmbH & Co KG to form the company - Trix-Mangold GmbH & Co.

Jan.1969
Company ownership transferred to Trix Vereinigte Spielwaren-fabriken Ernst Voelk KG.

1982
Company name changed to- Trix Mangold GmbH.

Dec.1970
Company ownership transferred to Schildkröt -Trix Spielwaren GmbH (Later Schildkröt Spielwaren GmbH).

s of 1992– business continues.

1972
Model Railway production phased out.

1973
Factory closed and company purchased by Park Toy Co Ltd in 1974.

Dec. 1954
Company name changed to Trix Spielwaren GmbH.

May. 1959
Company absorbed into Johann Distler KG of Nuremberg.

Nov. 1961
Latflag Engineering Co Ltd company name changed toTrix Products Ltd.

Early 1962
Abortive sale of Trix Products Ltd.

Nov.1962
Trix Products Ltd under new ownership.

May 1963
Trix business transferred for a nominal sum of money.

July 1963
Company name changed to Hanaton Ltd.

1973/1974
British Outline Trix parts purchased from Schildkröt by E.L. Rozsa.

1974
Liliput Model Railways (UK) Ltd formed to continue production of British Outline Models.

As of 1994 – business continues.

Nov. 1958
Dufay Ltd purchase assets and goodwill of Trix Ltd and factory occupied by Precision Models Ltd.

Dufay Ltd companies.

Nov. 1958
Spicer-Dufay (British) Ltd company name changed to Trix Products Ltd.

Transfer of business

Nov. 1961
Company name changed to Trix Products (Holdings) Ltd.

1962
Company name changed to Dufay (Holdings) Ltd.

Nov. 1958
Name of former Precision Models Ltd factory changed to Dufay (B'ham) Ltd.

May 1960
Factory closed. Production moved to Birmingham.

Repairs carried out at smaller premises in Northampton until 1963.

April 1963
British Transparent Containers Ltd, a subsidiary of British Celanese Ltd and part of the Courtaulds Group of Companies, changed its name to British Trix Ltd.

Dec.1967
British Trix Ltd ceased trading.

1967 - 1987
Liliput Spielwarenfabrik GmbH produced some tooling and models for British Outline range.

Feb.1968
Company name changed to British Transparent Containers Ltd.

INDEX

Bold figures refer to illustrations